# Allegory in Dickens

# Allegory in Dickens

## Jane Vogel

Studies in the Humanities No. 17
*Literature*

The University of Alabama Press
*University, Alabama*

Library of Congress Cataloging in Publication Data

Vogel, Jane.
    Allegory in Dickens

    1. Dickens, Charles, 1812-1870—Allegory and sym-
bolism. 2. Dickens, Charles, 1812-1870. David Copperfield. I. Title.
PR4592.A4V6                823'.8                75-34485
ISBN 0-8173-7325-X

# Contents

FOR MY SON DAVID

# Preface

Herein we bring to light the Dickens of 'the little lower layer': author of the little known *The Life of Our Lord*, and devout Christian novelist and allegorist.

Chapter I, *David, Uriah, and Joram,* would found the thesis of religious allegory in *Copperfield* on a rock so strong that not all the winds and seas of disbelief can afterwards prevail against it. For far from veiling his great aim, Dickens in bold symbolic ways *declares* his David a spiritual son and heir of the Old Testament David. If the Biblical David had memorable dealings with both Uriah the Hittite and Joram (*2 Sam.* chaps. 8 and 11), Dicken's David is also involved with a Uriah—Uriah H. at that—and with a Joram. Astonishing surface correspondence between the Bible and Dickens! So do we first intuit that the Dickens history of the Copperfields, or Chuzzlewits, Cratchits, Dorrits, et al., is part of a continually unfolding Mystery drama that for Dickens debuts on the world stage in Old and New Testament times; and that the whole Dickens canon, obedient to the law of eternal recurrence and relevance of Heaven's truth, and of the conservation and undiminishing vitality of spiritual energy in a Christian universe, steadily sights the one far-off divine event from and to which the whole creation moves.

Thus, while David Copperfield is a living, breathing child of his time—in a general symbolic sense, of all time too, in the ever thriving contemporaneity of the work—he is also magically endowed with a pilgrim *David* life that takes the long way the spiritual consciousness of Western man itself took from (to Dickens) darkest 'In the Beginning' to Christian time, and thence to Eternity.

Chapter II, *The Christian Dickens,* gathers evidence from the fiction, essays, letters, and speeches of Dickens to do battle with the dragonish myth that Dickens was no serious Christian. On the contrary, as his own words attest, his vision is always and often explicitly Christian. Every work, we show, sets out to replace Old with New Testament precepts: to draw mankind still stuck in the selfish, ritual-bound 'Jonas Mudge' (*Pick-wick*) mud(ge) state of mind of B.C. from reliance on harsh (Hebraic-Roman) Law to renewed reliance on (Christian) forgiveness and mercy, as on faith, hope, and charity.

Few Dickens works are without a meek, mild Little Dorrit to recall to an unhappy old woman, a devotee of a God of wrath grimly exulting in her years of bitter self-inflicted suffering, taken as 'the just dispensation of Jehovah' (777), and in herself as His harshly retributive 'instrument of severity against sin' (792), the so-different example of Christ:

> 'O, Mrs. Clennam, Mrs. Clennam,' said Little Dorrit, 'angry feelings and unforgiving deeds are no comfort and no guide to you and me. My life has been passed in this poor prison, and my teaching has been very defective; but let me implore you to remember later and better days. Be guided only by the healer of the sick, the raiser of the dead, the friend of all who were afflicted and forlorn, the patient Master who shed tears of compassion for our infirmities. We cannot but be right if we put all the rest away, and do everything in remembrance of Him. There is no vengeance and no infliction of suffering in His life, I am sure. There can be no confusion in following Him, and seeking for no other footsteps, I am certain!' (LD, 792)

So rarely does timid, retiring Little Dorrit speak at such length that her words here have redoubled force. 'Later and better days' can only be the times of Christ and the New Dispensation which a world only nominally of A.D., its gaze still transfixed by Jehovah and mandates of severity against sin, has yet to enter. Christ says: 'I am the door' (*John* 10:9), and light, ethereal Little Dorrit, the portal of such pure Christian idealism, ever in and out of debtors' prison on errands of compassion, now comforting her father, now turning at the door to speak a soft 'God bless you!' (173), is in these and a hundred ways Christ's word and spirit made flesh: truly a little 'Dorrit,' or Do(o)r(it), opening upon His truth. To ignore the Christian Dickens, to blunt the force of his both explicit and symbolic religious message in such blurring epithets as 'ethical humanist' or 'sentimentalist,' is to falsify and risk seriously misreading him.

Dickens's unswerving Christian purposes in his art have gone unseen or, if noted, been little dealt with partly because Dickens himself, courting inattention, did not publicize them. As is shown the chapter *The Christian Dickens,* Dickens could not bear didacticism and rant, and strongly deplored the disservice he felt conventional Christian teaching did its professed aims. He came to distrust clamorous religious profession, see only futility in churchmen's sectarian squabbles and stress on dogma and doctrine, and disbelieve that the frowning, worldly brand of Christianity often preached from pulpits—a sinner-exhorting, anathematising kind—could ever make Christians of men, i.e., soften and change hearts and issue in new outlooks and acts of charity among the afflicted and fallen, 'in remembrance of Him.'

So Dickens himself takes another way. Avoiding noisy commercial routes, the 'Uncommercial Traveller' with 'a large connection in the fancy goods way' (UT,1)—'fancy' transparently a blithe pun meaning of the fancy or imagination; and 'goods,' it may be, moral objects of desire, the highest 'goods' of the spirit—displays his Christmas line of shining image, symbol, parable, holy ghost (Scrooge's Three Spirits), Heavenly mystery, all the year round, in allegory finding out forgotten skyways to the Above, and, like Little Dorrit's tender young knight, John Chivery, ever about his Father's business. Satirizing many a priestly Melchisedech Howler (*Dombey and Son*), Reverend Chadband (*Bleak House*), and Luke Honey-thunder (*Drood*) Howling and Thundering unchristian Christianity at men, Dickens implies what his self-effacing, Heaven-magnifying 'little' Nells, Dorrits, Tims, and, tinier still, crickets on the hearth, confirm: a love of the poor in spirit, a devotion to highest truth beheld and served in fit humility and quietude of spirit.

Once, reacting to criticism—a reader finds an allusion in Chapter X of *Drood* irreverent—Dickens is stung into making a rare public statement about the matter of his faith, as follows:

> I have always striven in my writings to express veneration for the life and lessons of our Saviour.... But I have never made proclamation of this from the housetops. (LLS,II,411)

And in an earlier era, remarking in a Second Preface on the brevity of the original Preface to *David Copperfield,* which he attributes to the hold upon him at the time of strong 'private emotions' about the work, Dickens adds the line:

> Besides which, all that I could have said of the Story to any purpose, I had endeavoured to say in it.

None of which bears directly on the question of whether Dickens wrote Christian allegory. But if in *Copperfield* David's ties to a Uriah and a Joram and youthful hymns of praise to 'Miss Shepherd' *should* prove buds of allegory, expect no authorial 'proclamation...from the housetops.'

Readers shocked at the mere idea of Dickens as allegorist and allegory in Dickens may wonder if all this means or implies that the familiar wide, spacious, and gently rolling domain of Dickens, one of the last great open greenswards of English letters, is now to fall to some denaturing, ruthlessly programmatic-minded critic Hell-bent on Enclosure. Is Dickens, realm of simple story long blessedly innocent of types of ambiguity, chains of being, dark conceits, the subtler language, and the rest; this other Eden, demi-Paradise, to suffer major ecological disaster in our time, even as in *Dombey and Son* Staggs's Gardens is destroyed by that most uncelestial railroad which Mr. Dombey of *anno Dombei* rides, the roaring, fiery black engine termed, in language boldly symbolical/allegorical, 'a type of the triumphant monster, Death' (280)? Everything possible is done to allay such fears—everything, that is, short of recanting the thesis of allegory.

But there is really no cause for alarm. Like all else in Dickens, allegory smiles. Even as young David Copperfield in church looks upon Miss Shepherd and, carried away by idealising emotion, inserts her name in the divine service and in Royal Family annals (!), no textual strain is felt. Yet surely this is allegory. Surely in a David with 'Royal' power thus to command and in a poetic David-Shepherd idyll with marked religious overtone the spirit of the immortal 'love' story of Psalms which flowered in 'The Lord is my shepherd' in some wise lives again—on what unique terms we must see. And so throughout Dickens.

Indeed, *Martin Chuzzlewit* can open one evening in late fall as a wrathful 'dispensation of Jehovah'-ish wind scourges trembling hosts of fallen leaves, and the bogus holy man Seth Pecksniff—a latter-day son of Adam, who (in case we missed *Seth*) anon boasts of 'do (ing) a little bit of Adam still' (384—fall down a flight of stairs in the serio-merriest tableau of the Fall since *Genesis* (and before Joyce in 'Grace'), and no trace of heavy, old-style 'Allegorical' formalism be found. The Dickens touch is ever light, a deft *fall* pun or two doing prodigious hidden work.

A Dickens Biblical adaptation is unique: recalling Jonah, a guilty and fugitive Jonas Chuzzlewit attempts flight on a ship; then in a closed dark conveyance, passing fishes slumbering in cold streams, hurtles Jonah-in-the-whale-like through the night; in the same work, recalling still another Hebrew prophet, Elijah fed by ravens, Dicken's Elijah Pogram, fierce prophet of America, pounces on his food (the motif given a sly ironic twist) 'like a raven' (MC,536). Such adaptation seems so natural, unstrained, contemporary, and in the reworking so much Dickens's own that, except in rare instances of our coming upon a wilderness *called* 'Eden' (*Chuzzlewit*), or on a 'ruined garden' (*Great Expectations*) unmistakably the lost Eden, and so recognized by Edgar Johnson and others, we have not dreamed what a Dickens text owes to extra-Dickensian sources. In short, allegory emerges as a wholly new form in Dickens.

Moreover, belated recognition of allegorical intent cancels nothing, only reveals the known more fully. What before was unaccountable if delightful oddity turns out to make brilliant sense, and be no less marvelous for that. In allegory a whole eclipsed world of invention—networks of metaphor; mysterious smiles, winks, nods, and Noddys dotting texts; bridegrooms who set out for their weddings shouldering fishing-rods (John Wemmick in *Great Expectations*); names like 'Hexam' and 'Magwitch' that, while they hint at hex-witch meaning, yet seemingly point nowhere—now angelically (and demonically) rushes in, in allegory restored to high visibility; in the famous words of *A Tale of Two Cities,* 'Recalled to Life.'

Young David at the homely, slighted 'Shepherd' trade quietly makes *Copperfield* a new work; and 'Mr. Venus' of *Our Mutual Friend,* when he 'brightens up,' like the morning star whose name he bears, does not shine in vain. And why *should* Dickens have advertised further when 'all that [he] could have said of the Story to any purpose, [he] had endeavoured to say in it'?

Aside from one very helpful article by Samuel F. Pickering, Jr. on Dicken's religious beliefs, our study makes virtually no use of secondary sources: there were few or none to consult. Bert Hornback's recent *Noah's Arkitecture: A Genesis Mythology in Dickens* is, I believe, the first study of its kind. (Note '*Ark*-itecture,' a borrowing from Dickens and typical Dickensian pun and ploy.) Yet even so, a 'Genesis Mythology' concerned with Beginnings is only a beginning. Dickens ranges far beyond Genesis and all Old Testament time, his purpose being to chart mankind's spiritual ascent from Old to New Testament time. We therefore focus almost entirely on the works of Dickens themselves.

With the awakening of belief in the meaningfulness of all design in Dickens, a new curiosity grows. Why indeed *such* outlandish names as 'Elijah *Pogram,*' 'Jeremiah *Flintwinch,*' or 'Mr. *Morfin*'? And why, early in the writing of *Great Expectations,* does Dickens suddenly decide to change the name of Pip's first protector the blacksmith from George Thunder to Joe Gargery? We may now hope to know why.

Whether or not readers find themselves in full sympathy with interpretations offered, we hope at least to win recognition that what is thus dealt with does in fact exist *to be* interpreted:--that in a figurative 'casting overboard of Jonas' (386) in *Chuzzlewit,* in midsts of sea imagery galore, while Sarah Gamp glooms on in her way about life as a dark 'wale' (MC,404,413) and curses a ship sunk in 'Jonadge's belly' (624) (she of course means the whale's belly) until the mighty *wale*-whale pun long straining at disclosure finally breaches and—thar she blows!; or in a ranting, raving Jeremiah Flintwinch who visits 'the Jerusalem Coffee House' (340) and co-rules an ancient, decaying citadel with charred look to its final fiery destruction ('Fire-making *Flint*winch'!) in *Little Dorrit,* something astoundingly like Biblical history reappears. Call it what we may, surely a 'Jonas-casting overboard' (*cast* an idom straight from the Book of Jonah) and a 'Jeremiah-Jerusalem-holocaust' motif, Hebrew to the core, must be raised as an issue, reckoned with.

Whole books could be written on the religious allegory in Dickens's works. The aim of a first study of this kind, however, was to establish the widest possible general base of argument; and the strategy, to touch numbers of familiar works in passing, delving most deeply into two. Gazing on so vast an uncharted Pacific as Dickensian allegory for the first time, one is dazed by its visionary riches, obviously more than any one maiden-voyaging book could hope to traverse in a first crossing, much less hold.

Why should a Dickens with inventive genius, creative energies, and originality enough to populate whole fictional worlds on his own ever have thought to look beyond himself to the Bible or anywhere else for inspiration, and, as we allege, do so in work after work?

Whatever the ultimate reason, Dickens did in fact look beyond himself— the texts are their own best witness of this.  Furthermore, what sustained Dickens in the monumental, undisclosed labors of allegory over a lifetime was a profound, humbly grateful love of God and the Saviour, the origins and nurture of which John Forster's *Life of Dickens* helps uncover.  One motivation, familiar to all, underlies both story and allegory.  The works of Dickens, so faithfully calling to the world's sleeping conscience in dramatizing the plight of orphans, debtors, factory hands, and of 'all the weary and the heavy-laden...the wretched, fallen, and neglected of this earth...the blind lame palsied beggar, the criminal, the woman stained with shame, the shunned of all our dainty clay' (DS,826), as Dickens in New Testament idiom words it, testify as one to his unconquerable hope of a spiritual, a Christian renewal of English society; of an England at last free from reliance on harsh law and strong with the strength of the Strongs' love in *Copperfield,* one perfect in constant faith and abiding love and (the Dickens metaphor taken from *Matthew* 7:25) 'founded on a rock' (DC,663):  like the word of Christ, STRONG to endure.

Whether the following work can prove its thesis; whether it can explain the knotty matter of why Dickens kept the secret of his allegory, while asserting that it was, first and last, his chief and abiding love, interest, and aim, these pages must show.

# Acknowledgments

I am deeply grateful to my dear father, Alfred T. Vogel, who long ago first explained to me what 'Dotheboys' meant, and whose interest in this project has never failed; and to Professor Robert M. Durling of the University of California at Santa Cruz, whose comments on the manuscript led to important changes and to whose great generosity of spirit and knowledge I owe so much.

I am also greatly and forever indebted to James Travis, whose magical recognition years ago of possibilities in an early draft and letters full of wisest counsel, friendship, and ideas flowing northward ever since have made possible the completion of the book in its present form. I can never thank him enough.

I want to thank Professors Isaac Rabinowitz, John Freccero, and Reeve Parker, in whose classes at Cornell I picked up ideas that in time helped shape the book. Also Professors Robert Martin Adams, Helen Vendler, and Ephim Fogel for their kindness; and the Late Professor Lionel Trilling of Columbia University, who was good enough to read and comment on parts of the manuscript.

My grateful thanks goes to family and friends: my dear mother and sisters Lynn and Anne; nieces Patricia and Alicia; Signe; Richard and Syd Vogel; the Jaffes and Broads; and to Florence Atkin, Jean Harris Lana, Cynthia Richardson, Ruth Hurwitz, William Thomas, Jed Niles, Gerard F. Endres, Nancy Cohen, Dewey Kailburn, Marguerite Rub, Rolfe Sokol, Kevin Miller, Harold Zlotnik, the David Jaffes and Julie and Michael Jaffe, the Frank Hanshaws, Paul Van Ripers, Thomas Willetts and Carter and Terence Willett, Kenneth Morustys, Irma Spielberg, Thomas Michalak, and Agnes Vadas-Meyers.

The writing of this book was advanced through the generous support during graduate school years and after of Cornell University, Ithaca College, the National Endowment for the Humanities, and the Mellon Foundation. I am glad for the chance to thank friends at Ithaca College for their interest and help, especially E. William Terwilliger, John Ogden, Daniel Hanavan, Charles Grace, Sanford Schwartz, Anne Blodgett, Joel Kaplan, Michael Bell, Robert Cosgrove, John Harcourt, Michael O'Brien, Donna Freedline, Ferris Cronkhite, Rosalind Grippi, Anthony Zahorik, Martin Sternstein, Jean Spitzer, John Maceli, Sheila Mitchell, Jane Crawford, Iris Carnell, Heinz Koch, Vivian Laube, Kevin Schmelter, Jane Ogden, Vergiu Cornea, Terry May, Ethelyn Maxwell, Jane Kaplan, Robert Ryan, Tom Longin, Shirley Hockett, Gus Hughes, Jim Conlon, Marjehne Hoefer, Marilyn Sgrecci, Arnold Gibbons, Elise Levy, Linda Struble, Stephen Zabriskie, Dotty Owens, James Porterfield, Einar Holm, Pat Pesoli-Bishop, LeMoyne Farrell.

Above all I thank David for his patience and help.

The publication of this book was made possible through a grant from the National Council of Learned Societies of the Andrew W. Mellon Foundation.

JANE VOGEL

# Abbreviations

I. The works of Dickens listed below are from 'The New Oxford Illustrated Dickens' published by the Oxford University Press.

| | | | | |
|---|---|---|---|---|
| BR | *Barnaby Rudge* | | MC | *Martin Chuzzlewit* |
| BL | *Battle of Life, The* | | MHC | *Master Humphrey's Clock* |
| BH | *Bleak House* | | MD | *Mystery of Edwin Drood, The* |
| CHE | *Child's History of England, A* | | NN | *Nicholas Nickleby* |
| TC | *Chimes, The* | | OCS | *Old Curiosity Shop, The* |
| CC | *Christmas Carol, A* | | OT | *Oliver Twist* |
| CH | *Cricket on the Hearth, The* | | OMF | *Our Mutual Friend* |
| CS | *Christmas Stories* | | PP | *Pickwick Papers, The* |
| DC | *David Copperfield* | | PI | *Pictures from Italy* |
| DS | *Dombey and Son* | | TTC | *Tale of Two Cities, A* |
| GE | *Great Expectations* | | SB | *Sketches by Boz* |
| HT | *Hard Times* | | UT | *Uncommercial Traveller, The* |
| HM | *Haunted Man, The* | | RP | *Reprinted Pieces* |
| LD | *Little Dorrit* | | | * * * * |

II. Works in other editions:

1) Dickens, Charles. *The Works of Charles Dickens*. Standard Edition. 20 volumes. London: The Gresham Publishing Company Limited, 1850.
   - MP  Volume XVIII: *American Notes, Pictures from Italy, and Miscellaneous Papers.*
   - HW  Volume XIX: *Papers from 'Household Words,' Contributions to 'All The Year Round,' and Miscellaneous Papers.*
2) SL  *The Selected Letters of Charles Dickens*. ed. F. W. Dupee. New York: Farrar, Straus, and Cudahy, Inc., 1960.
3) Dickens, Charles. *The Writings of Charles Dickens*. 32 volumes. Boston and New York: Houghton Mifflin Co., The Riverside Press, Cambridge, 1894.
   - PPM  Volume XXVIII: *Plays, Poems, and Miscellanies.*
   - LLS  Volume XXXI: *Life, Letters, and Speeches.*
4) LL  *The Life of Our Lord*. New York: Simon and Schuster, 1934.
5) OL  *Old Lamps for New Ones and Other Sketches and Essays*. ed. Frederick G. Kitton. New York: New Amsterdam Book Company, 1897.
6) CL  *Catalogues of the Libraries of Charles Dickens and William Makepeace Thackeray*. ed. J. H. Stonehouse. London: Picadilly Fountain Press, 1935.

7) FD   Forster, John. *The Life of Charles Dickens.* 3 volumes. London: Chapman and Hall, 193, Picadilly, 1873.

8) MI   Mackay, Robert W. *The Progress of the Intellect, as Exemplified in the Religious Development of the Greeks and Hebrews.* 2 vols. London: John Chapman, 142, Strand, 1850.

III. Articles on the works of Dickens:

TD   *The Dickensian.* ed. Leslie C. Staples. The Dickens Fellowship. The Dickens House, 48 Doughty Street, London, 1947.

PD   Pickering, Samuel J. Jr. *'Dombey and Son' and Dickens's Unitarian Period. The Georgia Review,* Winter, 1972, pp. 438-454.

# Allegory in Dickens

# ONE

# David, Uriah, Joram

But who is this that
breaks upon me? This is Miss
Shepherd, whom I love. (DC,265)

I propose a novel thesis: as well as we know Dickens and *David Copperfield*, we as yet hardly know them at all. A presumptuous thesis, but with apologies....

It is that *Copperfield* is allegory: that David its hero, pilgrim from Blunderstone Rookery to Canterbury time, is a spiritual kinsman of the Old Testament David. (Hereafter, Old Testament and New Testament are represented by 'OT' and 'NT.') He interacts with a Uriah and a Joram, two figures a David first met in Hebrew Scripture time. *Uriah* and *Joram*, decidedly odd, un-English names, one thinks, names hardly come across by chance. 'Hebrew' too, on the face of it, is a visit to Dan'l Peggotty's *ark*, as young David fancies it, the Yarmouth home of little Em'ly and Ham. In such early ages, a *Ham* aboard an 'ark' surely rings old bells, Ham being one of the sons of Noah. Further, David's love, 'Miss Shepherd,' amazes, David's rapt hymning of his 'Shepherd' vision in the tabernacle in a rosy dawn of praise, wondering eyes raised from his prayer book to gaze worshipfully upon her, Dickens's gossamer fantasy on that venerable Davidic theme of themes: 'The Lord is my shepherd,' from *Psalms*. '*David* loves Miss *Shepherd*,' a spiritual arabesque, symbolic grace note, starry reunion bright enough in Dickensian heavens to make Wise Men of all beholders at a glance.

Astonishing ideas, at this late date? But Uriah and Joram are not interpretation, but hard fact. Both appear in the Biblical David's life; both appear in David Copperfield's. And the order of appearance in Dickens is the very one in *2 Samuel:* Joram before Uriah.

Still, David Copperfield is and remains a unique, living David of our time. Ah, but who finally is that? Symbolic other selves regularly come and go in him like clues: Robinson Crusoe, Aladdin, Peregrine Pickle, Roderick Random. Moments from a goodly assortment of mythic lives enter in companionably and often at apt spots along the way, invisibilities all, fictions afoot in David's always hospitable fancy as livest kindred reality, their literary moorings lightly drifting away. Briefly becoming _ach in turn, David luxuriates in manifold extra life subtly extending his own. Finally, his triumphant homecoming to Agnes Wickfield in Canterbury near the end of *Copperfield*—Canterbury tolling loud and clear, and David, or Trotwood, on horseback—lightly dubs him a modern Canterbury pilgrim, in every sober and serio-comic sense of the venerable words. In short, David is not and never was a simple, one-dimensional character, but always a candidate for widely significant symbolic adventure, and allegory. Wild as it all may sound, especially in the shock of simplified statement, this is what I summon up the temerity to say, and hope to show.

Dickens himself invites to such special awareness, hinting now and then of truths unfound and revelation still to come. In *Copperfield*, how soon we move, in David's prophetic words, 'among the possibilities of hidden things' (36). Attuned to long-vanished, 'hidden' reality, his whole drift of consciousness towards the past, realm of shadow, of memories in part mythified through hazes of time and mind, David himself knows that in retracing time past he treads no solid ground:

> When my thoughts go back now, to that slow agony of my youth, I wonder how much of the histories I invented for such people hangs like a mist of fancy over well-remembered facts! When I tread the old ground, I do not wonder that I seem to see and pity, going on before me, an innocent romantic boy, making his imaginative world out of such strange experiences and sordid things. (169)

So the fine line between fact and fancy is soon well lost, as Dickens perhaps not idly suggests. Indeed, in his setting David's whole story within the vaporous world of memory; in incessant simile and metaphor always restlessly casting beyond the here and now, as if the narrative mind chafed at confinement in solely literal realms of truth; and especially in the tireless spectral energies of a Dickens text—visionary Christmases; marvelous apparitions; Chimes (*The Chimes*) intoning high truth in castled regions of air; ghostly Spirit messengers, stern yet gracious, granting the wayward tenant of Time, forgetful of where all mortal life inexorably tends, a solemn preview of Eternity—in all sprites angelic and demonic, all 'incessant labour by immortal creatures for this earth' (CB,20), all ardent fancy and breath of faerie in its multiform magic-wishbone life, Dickens, we say, reaching past one world to another, behind mundane to fairy housekeeping, draws on to allegory.

His reason for focusing on a living David in insistently 'David' terms slowly becomes clear. In the fullness of time, David of Israel gives rise to the Son of David, Christ (*Matt.* 12:23; 21:9 and on), of the royal House and seed of David. Seen in NT terms, the shepherd boy of Bethlehem and psalmist of the Lord as Shepherd points to the Good Shepherd.  Hence the germ of Dickens's lofty theme.  In Dickens, as once before in Judaeo-Christian history, a David journeys from darkness to light, after soul-transfiguring trials and sorrows attaining to the inner moment of highest hope, truth, and creativity in the love of the peerless Agnes:  *Agnes*, type of the *Agnus* Dei, the Lamb of God.  From OT to NT, Copper-field to Wick-field time of mind David journeys:  from old vision of treasure laid up on earth, 'copper,' to that of treasure in Heaven.  The candle *wick* bears the flame, symbol of spiritual illumination.  Thus *'Wick*field' completes Agnes, proclaiming the 'field' of endless light which is Christ, the light of the world (*John* 8:12).  Past the 'Shepherd' idyll, David's (and Western man's) awakening past a God of Law to one of love, the radiant Agnes awaits, she in whom David glimpses a hope which both blesses and out-lasts this life:  Agnes, in David's mind one with the idea of her abode, Canterbury, pilgrim's guerdon, journey's happy end, ultimate point of spiritual arrival.  In time the 'Hebrew' David, his soul long mired in pain, punishment (Law), error, mortal blindness and sense of loss, fades, and a self emerges which finally sees and embraces its destined futurity and highest flowering in the 'Agnes' era of the Son of David.

David Copperfield shows a rare spiritual promise from the start.  Early in the journey of his tale ('journey' his own metaphor, intended in the Christian sense:), he is clearly of the intuitive, idealising, quickly kindled, god-seeking stuff that implies his origins and destiny.  If the son of *Blun-derstone* ages long blunders in worship of false gods, so did Blundering, Blunder-(on)-stone-law Judaeo-Christian man struggling forward from dim *In the Beginnings*.  His way beset for ages, David finally discerns his long-elusive all in Agnes, revealed to him as the source of his every aspiration and inspiration to write, his as Dickens's noblest self-expression.  Agnes shines as a mirror of Christ; she is the soul in its perfect bridal with the ideals of Christ reflected in a life lived wholly for others, and in its unquestioning self-sacrifice and submission in all to her (the) Father.  Agnes is the perfect confidante, guide, example, reliance, balm for a troubled heart, this from the first moment David enters the Wickfield manse with its snow-white steps and windows (fancy!), and door knocker that 'twinkled like a star' (218).  How transparently emblematic are gleaming façade and starry portal, as if to recall:  'I am the door; by me if any man enter in, he shall be saved' (*John* 10:9).

Thus the tired old complaint that the angelic Agnes is 'not natural' or 'too good' is marvelously vindicated before melting at a glance.  True, not natural:  supernatural.  But true to life, after all, when we grasp that Dickens has in mind the first and higher truth to Life Eternal.

The least skeptical reader, not quite wincing, surely turns a shade pale.  Christian allegory??  And in *Copperfield*, of all works, long such an open book of a book, as it were?  Dickens having owned David as his favorite child, general recognition of the novel as a fantasy on themes from his own emotionally orphaned early childhood, and the many critical studies would seem to have put us in comfortably full possession of it by now, one would think.  Yes, but, we say, of the literal work only:  of *David Copperfield* as it depicts its hero's slow, painful discovery of the true and abiding norms of the moral life, a single life.  Hence, of a Victorian treatise enlivened by the Dickens comic genius on the ruin spread by selfishness, hardness of heart, harsh judgment, and indulgence of the wayward, or, as David calls it, the 'undisciplined heart' (698).

To sum up briefly, the novel as known is about spiritual growth and re-covery; about the eventual triumph in most of 'generous feeling' (638) over ungenerous, better purposes over worse; the *Agnes* component of the soul over the *Heep*.  *Copperfield* tirelessly asserts the *ne plus ultra* of the Dickens creed:  the virture of outgrowing the reclusive 'lone lorn' state, as even Mrs. Gummidge does at last, and entering sympathetically and with a will into the life of straining, striving humanity.  And in Dickens what droves of misanthropic, isolated Scrooge, Miss Havisham, Haunted Man, Mopes the Hermit, Mrs. Clennam figures who must learn, or who in self-ruination reject, the lesson of 'entering in.'  Further, the novel as presently understood is eminently Victorian in its steady exposition, mainly through its heroine, Agnes Wickfield, of all that is won for mankind through the gift of the constant, tirelessly serving, selfless life.  Here, in short, is 'our Dickens,' opponent of social injustice in the name of all victims, especially children, the orphaned, magistrate-hounded, mistaught, neglected, half-starved Olivers, little Dicks, Nells, Smikes, Dorrits, Davids, Jos, Pips wandering in the wilderness (Dickens's figure) of an uncaring because still un-Christian world:  children sunk back into 'the brutish state, with all the gifts of God perverted in their breasts or trampled out' (OL,255), as Dick-ens puts it in *A December Vision*.  The Dickens of unwavering belief that through man's earnest efforts and faith—faith above all:  the youthful Her-bert Pocket's confidence in the Opening just ahead; the 'Wait and hope!' hearth-cricket optimism of a Tommy Traddles, or a Scrooge's nephew, or Cheeryble brother of indomitably cheery mien[2]—all comes round to good, and God, in the end.

With all this well in mind, I now suggest that the deepest of Dickens's intentions is still undisclosed, as a shining 'David-Miss Shepherd' pastoral points the way.  The foregoing picture of Dickens as ethical humanist is in no sense its adversary, nor is it diminished along the way.  Rather, all views stand as appointed guides, the Ghosts of Dickens Yet To Come.  As David more than once hints, *Copperfield* is a deep mine of precious 'hidden things,' its bedrock symbolic/allegorical life a radiant concealed moral source, a slow-emitting ore deep within, a layer of sacred history present from its In the Beginnings which invisibly charges the whole, all plot, char-acters, theme.  Once seen into, allegory looses new meaning everywhere, Dickens, as might be supposed, proving as genial and candid an allegorist as (for want of a better term, long sought) a 'romantic realist' or 'symbolic poet,' allegory becoming a spritely new form in his hands.  Nothing is lost, and much is gained.  Suddenly all kinds of detail, from expressions like 'Barkis is willin',' long a household word, to names like Joram, Flintwinch, and Pogram, which always *were* more than a bit odd, shake off the soporific of over-familiarity, and, seen into anew, must astonish.  Two genuine OT spectres (if it can be shown) like Uriah and Joram renewing ancient relations with David must start spirits everywhere, transforming the novel as known.

If amazed, we should still not be too surprised.  For in Dickens the unexpected is always bursting in.  Overturning an old order, it dismays only those reactionary and benighted 'lords of the State preserves of loaves and fishes,' blind mouths who, in their arrogance and pride of place, suppose that 'things in general were settled forever' (TTC,1).  Far from it.  In Dickens, the wondrous New always arrives, a godsend, a 'Lucie' or Light suddenly appears in darkness, and welcome.  The time comes in *Copperfield* when even Dan'l Peggotty breaks out in rhyme:  "'Which is verse,' said Mr. Peggotty, surprised to find it out, 'though I hadn't such intentions'" (66l); as in *Great Expectations* Pip will recall 'what I hardly knew I knew' (17).  But there it is.  Some bounty unforseen or far greater Expectation emerges at last.  In Dickens, growth and revelation come hand in hand.

To begin, then, the David of *Copperfield* is first born, not in Dickens, where he is so memorably recalled to life, but in OT time, and in spirit looks homeward, Biblewards, all his life.  For example, in the novel a muted enmity exists between David and Uriah Heep, David long agonizing slow-motion in its toils; its focus, Agnes.  Not to delay, a muted David-Uriah antagonism brewing beneath outwardly calm surfaces and centering on a woman is the boldest of cribs from the OT.  Where before in the spiritual annals of Western man are a David and Uriah locked in dire, secret rivalry to which Uriah is oblivious, David always tensely watchful of this Uriah and inwardly set against him, while Uriah the underling, baffling riddance by his devotion and virtue, declaiming high aims and apparently unaware of David's mounting ire and passion, waxes confident in possession of the woman, the mutual object of desire?  Where?  Before Dickens, nowhere but in *2 Samuel* in which, in stark woodcut-like outline, is found the tale of hidden warfare between a David and Uriah upon which Dickens builds with creative additions and aims of his own.

In the Bible and Dickens, the David-Iriah enmity has one cause: Uriah's secure (as he supposes) claim upon the woman, and David's undisclosed (in Dickens, long un-self-disclosed, too) counter-claim.  In Scripture, the woman is Uriah's wife; in Dickens, Uriah's wife-to-be, Uriah Heep loudly and often claiming her as his own.  As once before the Hebrew David vs. Uriah the Hittite, so in Dickens it is David vs. Uriah Heep.  *Hittite-Heep:* even the 'H' corresponds.  Long before Dickens sends David into dubious battle with a tenacious, not-to-be-evaded Uriah Heep who rouses David to

uncharacteristic violence of mind and hand, Yahwist or Elohist records how
the Biblical David and Uriah clash and sunder.  The echo of Biblical names
alone, not to mention the 'H' initial, is impressive.  But more impressive
still is a strong situational likeness, namely the old concealed enmity in
David's heart and the love triangle.  For all Dickens's changes, his modern
David-Uriah story shouts its orgins, Scriptural echoes reverberating like
Jehovah thunder down the long sounding Dickensian corridors of Judaeo-
Christian time.

   Differences momentarily aside, we first note points of likeness, polished
to high lustre.  In *2 Samuel,* King David, desiring Uriah's wife, maneuvers
to be rid of Uriah.  Dickens can afford no such murderous hero, nor is he
bound to reproduce each fact of the Biblical David's life.  Considering
Davidic within the larger governing context of Christian history, he bypasses and interprets at will.  Yet, while muting David's crime, Dickens
recreates the Biblical atmosphere in an adaptation hot upon the original.
For germs of murder also lurk in David Copperfield's soul.  Smouldering
under the burdensome presence of Uriah Heep, even as David under that
of Uriah the Hittite, David chafes at the necessity of tolerating Uriah's
loudly-voiced, galling claims to Agnes.  The Biblical David dispatches
Uriah to death in battle.  Obviously Dickens's David does not.  BUT, while
David is driven to no such *literal* extremity, nevertheless vivid ideas of
murder darken his mind as though the OT spirit of David, like some rank
vestigial force, unworthy pioner, were mining deep within.

   It is in fact *as if* David slays Heep, doing so in mind more than once.  Recalling Uriah gloating over Agnes, David states: 'I believe I had a delirious
idea of seizing the red-hot poker out of the fire and running him through
with it' (381).  Bold image!  The murder wish again haunts David that very
night: 'I thought, between sleeping and waking, that it [the poker] was
still red-hot, and I had snatched it out of the fire, and run him through the
body' (383).  As this second 'murder' occurs not quite in sleep, note, but in
dreaming limbo, 'between sleeping and waking,' it subtly gains status as
action in reality, Dickens in that one phrase deftly moving it closer to an
event in waking life.  Furthermore, in the first red-hot poker scene, David
grows so furious at Uriah that he 'could joyfully have scalded him' (377),
more proto-action or fantasy laced with lethal violence.  At a later date
(Dickens adroitly staggering occasions lest together they loom too large),
Uriah, David says, 'looked at Agnes so, that I would have given all I had,
for leave to knock him down' (576).  At still another time, in 'a towering
rage,' David actually strikes Uriah's lank cheek, and 'with that force that
my fingers tingled as if I had burnt them' (620).  'Burnt' reinforces the
earlier red-hot poker motifs.  This is all pretty heavy stuff, as heroes',
especially Victorian ones, fantasies and acts go.

   I think Dickens harps so on this startling, most uncharacteristic death-
wishing in David to set his temper momentarily in closest possible moral

parallel with that of the Hebrew David who in effect sent Uriah to his death. (We note, parenthetically, that neither David actually slays Uriah; it forges another link between the two that in both hostility towards Uriah operates covertly and at a distance.) The ancient *slay Uriah* theme is preserved in a modern David's morally primitive racial-throwback fantasies, that one actual blow aside, of impaling Uriah on a fiery poker, a vivid symbolic equivalent. In short, the spirit of King David's ancient sin lives again in a David of later time, but is transmuted to a restless atavism, a criminal 'Hebrew' temptation to punish foes entertained in the unregenerate B.C. self in David as in all men, a self wishfully indulged then outdistanced in Christian time of the evolving Davidic spirit, transcended as the old (OT) 'slay thine enemy' inheritance of man is left behind by a pilgrim of the absolute journeying to a rendez-vous with the high moment of Israel To Be, its Messiah, the Son of David.

Not all points in the Biblical-Dickensian stories match, or have to. Dickens's symbolic-impressionistic account of the unfolding fortunes of the House of David does not *copy* the Bible, it distils an essence; its aim, to cast some faithful 'David' light and shadow. Clearly, Agnes is not the Hittite's wife, Bathsheba. *Copperfield* enfolds a free-hand poetic reworking of certain key Bible episodes, one even so entirely recognizable as a set of ingenious variations on a theme.

At least one Biblical moment survives intact in Dickens, startling in its fidelity to the source. In chapter eleven of *2 Samuel*, a self-invited Uriah the Hittite spends the night in David's house. David wishes him gone. 'But Uriah slept at the door of the king's house with all the servants of his lord, and went not down to his house' (11:10). In Dickens something remarkably like happens. Inflicting himself on David one night, Uriah Heep beds down before David's sitting-room fire; this night he thus 'goes not down to his house,' even as the clinging Uriah of old. Humbly, or rather, 'humbly' declining the offer of a bed, his habitual, oppressively self abasing manner forcing the role of overlord on a reluctant David, the master David literally was to Uriah in olden time, Uriah snores outrageously before the fire while an imposed-upon David helplessly tosses and turns in an inner room. Like the OT David, this David cannot vent his feelings or work free of Uriah; despite advantages of position, family, education, he is and remains baffled and mute. On this as on other occasions, he must endure the ironic defeat of Uriah's elaborate deference and shrill acclaim while a thousand muzzled demons churn within.

Behold a close copy of the Bible episode in modern dress. Two leech-like, highly virtuous (in Heep's case, 'virtuous') Uriahs contrive to spend the night in the dwelling of a David upon whom the office of hospitality is imposed. Even the 'slept *at the door*' detail returns. Far too 'umble to accept the bedroom, a self-nullifying (actually, encroaching) Heep insists on sleeping in the outer chamber, and on the floor. Both Uriahs have the

marked underling manner; of course Heep's egregious civility and relentlessly worshipful mien are feigned. Incidentally, this 'biblical' night when
Uriah billets himself on David is the very night of David's (again, 'biblical')
murderous seizures in sleep, the night when, once more, 'the poker got
into my dozing thoughts' (383).

Two ancient *David* motifs—willing death to Uriah and having to suffer in
silence Uriah's unwanted presence overnight—fuse in Dickens, redoubling
Biblical force. The *sleep* scene shows that Dickens was not blowing a
merely random David-Uriah Sunday School-ish memory about in mind like
milkweed in some vague, intentionless way. Rather, the design is finely
crafted, hard worked, as we have seen.

And Dickens labors to keep it alive. Some time after, Heep ferrets out
occasion to revisit the old and galling imposition on David by slyly recalling
to one who would gladly forget it, on pretext of undying gratitude, 'the
night I put you so much out of the way by sleeping before your sitting-
room fire' (574). *'Put you...out of the way.'* A pun heavy with murder
stalks these words. Beyond 'put you out' in the ordinary sense of, in-
convenienced you, lies the cunning, darkly insolent hint of 'put you to
death.' In reworking the murder theme, this time from the Uriah side,
Dickens again contrives to link David and Uriah by a hidden verbal cause-
way of death, as if to show that just as David implies death for Uriah, so
Uriah does for David in the sense that, embodying the temptation to do
murder, Uriah, now as then, is the way of undoing of a royal David's immortal soul. We note the double-flowering meaning in a pun, the pun one
foundation stone of allegory in Dickens, we will see, the astonishingly open
way-in-hiding by which the second story is in part told.

What of differences between the Bible and Dickens? For one, the
Hebrew David covets a Uriah's *wife,* and Agnes is not Heep's wife. No,
but, anticipating matrimony, Heep smugly and often calls her his own. To
wit.: 'Oh, Master Copperfield, with what a pure affection do I love the
ground my Agnes walks on!' (381); and: 'My Agnes is very young still'
(382); and: 'My Agnes! Would you be so good as to call her Agnes,
Master Copperfield!' (573) Heep's presumptuous 'my,' the assuming of
proprietary rights in advance as he magnanimously extends the privilege of
addressing Agnes by her Christian name, is Dickens's masterful way
around it. As blind as Uriah the Hittite once was to David's outraged feelings, Uriah Heep in classic 'Uriah' style sees, or pretends to see, nothing of
David's frigidity of response. So again it is Uriah's possession of a woman
whom David prizes and will one day make his own that feeds the latter's
unholy hate and rage. As we said, both Davids hide a mounting black
passion which smoulders beneath tensely calm surfaces, for what pretext is
there to strike out at so humble, virtuous, modest, pious, devoted, so
scrupulously deferential a pair of Uriahs? King David wills, David Copperfield wills but bypasses the ambition to dispatch Uriah. But a like

killing fury works mightily in both.

Dickens's David 'kills' Uriah without killing him; is guiltless of his fall. He has the advantage of the OT David in belonging spiritually to A.D., and, obedient to the Son of David destiny ever stirring mystically within, passes unharming and unharmed through the valley of the shadow of B.C. man's moral heritage of too-ready recourse to retributive violence, that of 'slay thine enemy.' In work after work Dickens identifies eruptions of the eye-for-an-eye passion—stoning of sinners, harsh judgment, the merciless punishment under Law which a Mrs. Joe strongly approves and a Miss Havisham in the private sphere practises in her merciless heart-for-a-heart creed (*Great Expectations*)—with the still-virulent, pre-Sermon on the Mount time of the wrathful Yahweh-forged, Christ-unfound soul. In Dickens, where legalized or other violence is, a superannuated B.C. ethic reigns, to be undone once more only by men's rededication to Christian precepts and to the struggle in defense of good that first brought A.D. into the world: to pity like a naked new-born babe striding the blast, mirror of divine love, which was and evermore is the Babe of Christmas.

There remains the thorny fact that the Biblical Uriah was wholly good, while Uriah Heep is a heap of infamy. One could beg the question by arguing that such perfection of virtue and of vice are related in the sense that perfect oppositeness argues likeness. But, casuistry aside, things are simpler still. Uriah the Hittite addressing his lord is humility and self-abnegating goodness itself. Ah, but so is Uriah Heep 'humility' and 'goodness,' i.e., the masterful impersonation thereof, his lowliness before 'Mister' and 'Master' Copperfield so well counterfeited it long battles unmasking. (The Scriptural fiat: 'Neither be ye called masters: for one is your Master, even Christ' (*Matt.* 23:10), if Dickens had it in mind, would make Heep's unrelenting use of the title 'Master' to disarm David the more insidious.) In Heep's manipulative meekness and mock fealty that so discomfits and disempowers David before he sees through it, then, one may find a parody of the true meekness and fealty which Uriah the Hittite preferred to David. So viewed, the two Uriahs are not opposites. Exemplary goodness, real in one, brilliantly feigned in the other, is the key to each.

Perhaps we may even hope to guess what inspired Dickens's conversion of a good Uriah into a 'good,' or evil one. Consider Uriah's response when David tries to send him away:

> And Uriah said unto David, The ark, and Israel, and Judah, abide in tents: and my lord Joab and the servants of my lord, are encamped in the open fields; shall I then go into my house, to eat and to drink, and to lie with my wife? as thou livest, I will not do this thing. (*2 Sam.* 11:11)

Well, for all his fluent 'my lord,' Uriah stands firm. *His* will, not David's, be done. His speech is terribly high-minded, of course. Yet what a prating Uriah it is. Surpassing good, no doubt, but goodness so unaware seems flawed, and Uriah more than a little verbose, tiresome, blind. As the Bible records no word of David's at this point, Uriah comes off sounding almost strident, a narrative fluke, the silence of David, in a curious way working against Uriah. Uriah's apparently intuiting nothing of the feelings of his listener, walled in by this outburst, makes Uriah seem all the more clumsy and queer. Uriah Heep will make a career of such speech-making and moral obtuseness, of marvelous non-recognition of how his piety and cant, served up in equal portions, choke David. The two *Uriah* portraits coincide in this respect too.

As to that ill-advised speech (what dainty moralising to set before a love-maddened king!), we note that no Dickens hero or heroine ever declaims so, though many a fatuous, detestable, falsely virtuous Pecksniff (*Chuzzlewit*); Reverend Chadband, Mrs. Pardiggle, Turveydrop (*Bleak House*); Bounderby (*Hard Times*), and Honeythunder (*Drood*) regularly does. By marked contrast, Dickensian virtue whispers, its crowning glory that it would neither ever a vainglorious orator or a Bounder-by. No one Dickens likes ever, ever catalogues his own virtues so. Indeed, David once trounces Heep with: 'I am not fond of professions of humility, or professions of anything else' (574), in which sentiment there can be no doubt he speaks for Dickens.

To conjecture further, possibly it is Uriah's loud, claimful disclaimers that inspire the translation of the self-congratulatory Hittite into the self-glorifying Heep. Perhaps the first Uriah struck a Dickens sensitive on the subject (see Preface and Chapter II) as too unabashedly self-presentational, his humility itself suspect in being facile and glib. Goodness swollen with 'I' and wordy on its own behalf contradicts itself. Perhaps Uriah Heep, who trills on in that maddeningly oblivious way of his, too full of sweetness and light to know (*he* knows!) that David must choke on every word, springs from the Uriah who also served up generous helpings of a noble soul to David. A walking copy-book of virtuous maxims, Heep seems the Hittite caricatured. Uriah I commends his own virtue to David, but his refusal to obey belies his obeisance. Just so Uriah II commends his virtue *ad nauseam* to David, just as stubbornly serving his own needs upon David the while. The Heep, malevolent perfection of Tartuffean, unruffleably serene, seraphic (demonic) strength of the pure in heart and armed in righteousness, is the Hittite seen in the distorting concavities of a Fun House mirror. In the virtue of the one and mock-virtue of the other, opposites meet, becoming one.

The Biblical David fell before the temptation to undo Uriah, destroying him. Fated to touch down at old bases, Dickens's David symbolically revisits the ancient 'Uriah' experience still aswirl in clouds of sexual jealousy, hidden tension, temptation to kill, and the unassailable virtue, and Virtue, of Uriah. What a foe a good, or 'good' man makes, two Davids to their sorrow find. David Copperfield succumbs to Uriah in another

disastrous way too as he comes to believe Uriah's false insinuations about
Annie Strong, thus lending support to the foes of the 'Strong' union, identified by Dickens with the Christian metaphor of the love founded on a rock.
To undermine faith, hope, and charity so *Strong* in constancy and abiding
love is to undo a human form of love divine. Clearly, then, two Uriahs represent the way of Fall for two Davids in drawing them onto ground where
hatred, death, and dissolution of character lie. Now as then, past the rocks
of *Uriah* lies the destiny of the House of David, 'Agnes.'

To sum up, Dickens works vigorously in both the letter and spirit of the
Bible story of David and Uriah. In each case David tries to evade Uriah,
and Uriah *will not* know it. What in the original Uriah is genuine selflessness and humility becomes in the other a diabolical imposture of the same;
unfeigned ignorance of David's hostility towards him in the first Uriah is in
the second a hypocritical version of the same. The raw, unmanageable fact
of King David's outright wickedness—his sending Uriah into battle to
die—Dickens must perforce juggle, and as he is not writing a factual biography of David's life, may. Yet the recurrent murder fantasies in
Dickens's David surely incur comparable spiritual guilt, *sub specie aeternitatis.*

Meanwhile, Dickens is actively urging recognition of the David-Uriah
allegory in another way. In the 'slept at the door' scene, as David is being
lashed to impotent fury by Uriah's sweetly confidential disclosures of his
designs on Agnes (friendship and confidentiality, like all virtues become
weaponry in Heep's hands), suddenly David's very perception of Uriah undergoes a startling change, one with deepest implications for allegory:

> He seemed to swell and grow before my eyes; the room seemed full of the
> echoes of his voice; and the strange feeling (to which, perhaps, no one is quite
> a stranger) that all this had occurred before, at some indefinite time, and that
> I knew what he was going to say next, took possession of me. (381)

A dead giveaway. How fantastically bold of Dickens! It all *has,* of course,
in the most intensely literal sense of the words, 'occurred before,' although
here the phrase slips by innocently enough, passing, if noted at all, as a
moment of *déja vu* disclosing David's feverish, momentarily rage-dis-
ordered mind. Dickens can *be* thus bold and even bolder, running little
risk of being taken at his word. Brilliant ironic strategy. Further, the par-
enthetic remark, 'to which, perhaps, no one is quite a stranger' would
seem to serve both to soften what is being said, to muffle symbolic resonance, and to universalize David's experience, gathering all men to allegory and 'the journey,' the morally significant life in which all move and
have their being. Dickensian man lives simultaneously in realms temporal
and eternal. *Homo viator* from B.C. to A.D. and beyond, he is both surface
and symbol: his life unique and of its own time and place, yet profoundly
inwoven with timeless meaning and purpose, 'echoing' as the room in
which he and Uriah stand acting out the old roles echoes in that uncanny

instant for David, within the larger providential scheme, every man's life related to the definitive events of the Bible, in Dickens the loadstone rock to which all temporal adventuring was, is and forever shall be drawn to the end of time.

Dickens would not see himself as imposing allegory. Rather, allegory, witness to the attraction of all reality to an overmastering divine fund of mystery and ongoing revelation, reveals the immanent Christian soul of history. Like all men, David lives out a God-ordained destiny of which he is largely unconscious; it would hardly do for him to realize he is among the sons of the Son of David. But now and then, as here, otherness brushes him in passing. The immortal religio-poetical visionary 'David' soul within stirs, he senses inclusion in something more. Looking at Uriah, he intuits the mythic, ancient David-Uriah relationship, a reality normally out of reach; is sprinkled with the dust of stars long extinct in history, but from which spiritual light still travels; senses life as mystery, a mystic fellowship of souls in and out of bounds, the 'possibilities of hidden things,' a lasting order underlying and overlying the flux of things: the abiding, the eternal. In its quiet way, no theme recurs more often in Dickens. [3]

Thus recast and enlarged, the *Uriah* figure in Dickens comes to symbolize the hopeless impasse in man's relations to word and world before Christ. Uriah, quicksand for David's pilgrim foot, is, I think, Dickens's impression of what virtue amounted to B.C., before Christ revealed the true nature of God to man. That is, Uriah is the letter of such holy ideals as humility, worship, friendship, gratitude, barren of the spirit, all that, in Dickens' view, Judaism ever found its tortured, self-lacerating, Law-bound way to under its fealty to Jehovah. Uriah symbolizes the recourse to violence that overcomes before the advent of the Prince of Peace. He is also the triumphant way of Law, Hebrew invention of inventions, Heep coming to rule many destinies with an iron fist through power doggedly acquired via mastery of his, and B.C.'s, sharpest weapon, the Law. The *Uriah* element eventually knows its most infamous hour of triumph in the high priesthood that, while mouthing virtuous words and exhibiting a faultless, fluent piety, proceeds to condemn Christ to death in the name of the Law. 'Heep' also has dark burial mound or 'heap' connotations, we will see.

There is that in David Copperfield, and in mankind, which is long susceptible to Uriah Heep and seducible by his guile. David stands helplessly by while Uriah forges inroads into the lives of many dear to him, including the Wickfields, Micawbers, Betsey Trotwood, and the Strongs. Though instinctively distrusting Uriah from the start, David nevertheless suffers Uriah to link arms with him as they walk by moonlight on the Ramsgate road. Whither Israel: with *Uriah,* way of malice, 'the word,' law; or with the sons of David, chief of whom is Christ? Then at long last David is roused to resist. The latent, Christ-forthcoming self awakens, the spirit of his ancestor, the David of *Psalms,* which, transcending the mere mortal man of lust and lapses into sin, lifted its eyes unto the hills, the spiritual heights of a God of mercies, enthroning Him far above the Deity imagined as preoccupied with man's first, and next and next, disobedience to the Law of Moses. David triumphs. In time, all that Uriah in Bible time was and in Dickens by extension comes to be, an epitome of the worst tendencies of the Judaic code, is left behind on his accelerating forward way. But the *Uriah* lure is strong, and long threatens to be the grand lapse it proved for another David in a bygone, or, rather, not-so-bygone time.

That Dickens did consciously, purposefully devise just such a David-Uriah design the novel elsewhere dramatically affirms. Behold the arrival of another OT figure in David Copperfield's life, 'Joram.' Not 'Mr. Joram' or____Joram, with proper first name, but only and always *Joram*. Odd name for a true-born Englishman! Where did it come from? Strikingly un-English, in point of fact Hebrew, its oddity, increased by the fact that Joram has no Christian name, is masked only by a text so crowded that much detail inevitably slips by, and by the disarming naturalism, informality and charm of the Dickens style.

In *Copperfield* Joram works in Mr. Omer's drapery and funeral furnishing shop in Yarmouth, a thriving business one day to become *Omer and Joram's* as Joram rises in life. The spectacular thing about Joram, insignificant enough in *Copperfield,* is that he once appeared just as insignificantly in the life of the Hebrew David. And as Joram precedes Uriah Heep into the pages of *Copperfield,* so in *2 Samuel* a Joram—just so—arrives before Uriah the Hittite, as follows:

> Then Toi sent Joram his son unto king David, to salute him, and to bless him, because he had fought against Hadadezer, and smitten him: for Hadadezer had wars with Toi. And *Joram* brought with him vessels of silver, and vessels of gold, and vessels of brass:
> Which also king David did dedicate unto the LORD, with the silver and gold that he had dedicated of all nations which he subdued; (*2 Sam.* 8:10-11)

With mounting awe and a dizzy sense of expanding universes we behold *Joram,* living, breathing proof that Dickens closely sifted the Biblical life of David in shaping his hero's life. With the coming of Joram, the *Copperfield*—OT link we have alleged immeasurably tightens. First, dealings with Joram, then the old compromising ones with an encumbering Uriah (the) H. If *David* and *Uriah* are names little likely to recombine by chance in the work of a Victorian Christian author, how much less likely the conjunction of *three* figures from the Bible, David, Uriah, *and* Joram.

And Dickens's Joram bears a likeness to the Joram of old, a remarkable one. The Biblical Joram, we saw, brought David vessels of silver, gold, and brass which David dedicated to the Lord. In *Copperfield,* Joram executes a figurative, or figuro-literal version of the same. On David's first visit to the Funeral Furnishing shop in Yarmouth where he is to be measured for mourning clothes, an unseen Joram is somewhere out back, the steady, unending 'RAT-tat-tat' (125) of his hammer reporting him hard at work on—something. What? A coffin, we shortly learn. Significantly, the object unnamed and unseen is one in which David's poor young murdstoned-to-death mother, her dead infant in her arms, will be lowered into the ground as the clergyman intones: 'I am the Resurrection and the Life, saith the Lord!' (131) Thus is the Bible fulfilled in our time. For the coffin Joram makes ready (both it and Joram the more symbolic, perhaps, in being for a time invisible and nameless) is truly a 'vessel,' and in the most solemn sense destined for 'dedication unto the Lord,' as Dickens's stress upon the religious aspects of the burial service shows. Thus the Biblical *Joram-vessel* theme is rendered anew in both a traditional and reverently poetical, original way.

We marvel at the artistic depth and finesse of the design. No mention is made, on that first occasion or ever after, of what it is Joram makes year in and out. Disclosure is solely by inference. This allows the nameless objects of his dutiful crafting and presentation to be anything—or at least not just one hard and fast, single thing. On David's first visit Joram is hammering out back (far, far 'back' in time, too, as it were), and from site unseen issues the relentless 'RAT-tat-tat, RAT-tat-tat, RAT-tat-tat, without any variation' (125) of nails being driven into coffin wood—ominous embryonic motif of crucifixion, dare we imagine, deep in the bowels of B.C. as from always. In thrice-clamorous letters, 'RAT' is surely a grim 'rat' or rodent-of-graves pun making Joram's hammer tap an even more awful, insistent summons of sad Mortality. The sound fills the parlour of Omer's little shop in which a lonely, grieving child waits to be draped in black mourning. In years to come, whenever he returns to the place, David will continue to hear the 'old tune,' as he calls it, *RAT-tat-tat.* [4]

Joram and 'old tune' go together, symbolizing for Dickens what overcomes in human destiny as man loses touch with a Christian faith however much he continues to parade in Christian forms. In Dickens, Joram is the same recessive intermediary of the 'vessel' he was in *2 Samuel,* a flat figure. In Scripture he does not speak; in Dickens, he hardly says a word. Once again he is a little-seen functionary under orders, his 'vessels' or coffins seemingly his whole excuse for being. A one-name, one-dimensional character, he and the changeless little domain of Funeral Furnishing stand still to the end of the story, and as if of time.

Joram delivered vessels to King David. Although in the novel Joram must make many coffins, he appears to make 'them' only for David. First there is Mrs. Copperfield's, little David riding with it in a van. Then, late in the story when Steerforth dies and David and some others bear him, townsman of a stiller town, to his first resting place, we read:

> We went into the town, and took our burden to the inn. So soon as I could at all collect my thoughts, I sent for Joram, and begged him to provide me a

conveyance in which it could be got to London in the night.(796)

Note the heightened, dramatic language: not 'body' but 'burden;' not 'asked' but 'begged;' not 'coffin' but, more shadowily, 'conveyance;' not 'provide a' but, in idiom more archaic and rare, 'provide me a': Aweful diction, shadowed with Eternity. *Burden* is soon more etherealised, become 'it.' Like figures in profile on an ancient frieze, David and the nameless, faceless others move in obedience to Death's strict arrest, bearing shoulder-high the vessel made ready and delivered by Joram. The moment in time fades; all exists in the perspective of Eternity. Once again, as to David alone, Joram brings a vessel for dedication unto the Lord.

We do not witness the funeral. No need. The religious service has already been held in David's heart at the time the news of Steerforth's betrayal, his elopement with little Em'ly, first broke, and David, his anger so soon passing, thought beyond time to Eternity:

> Yes, Steerforth, long removed from the scenes of this poor history! My sorrow may bear involuntary witness against you at the Judgment Throne; but my angry thoughts or my reproaches never will, I know! (455)

So David of the inherently God-turned mind, like a David of long ago, dedicates a beloved fallen friend unto the Lord.

Detail of great significance for allegory is superbly handled. On David's first visit to Mr. Omer's shop, the genial old timer says to him: 'My dear, would you like to see your—' (127), then stops short. Though only a child, David knows he means 'mother's coffin;' knows intuitively, the Davidic in Dickens ever the finely instinctual, supra-rational way of knowing. The blank ('your—') is Dickens's well-wrought opportunity through which, as it keeps the issue of *what* open, ambiguity subtly gains. On David's next visit, Joram is again at work on something Mr. Omer refers to only as 'a grey one with silver nails' (304). A grey *what*?? Coffin, to be sure. But again the blur, the artful leaving to inference. The twice-missing noun shimmers, greatly enlarges, attracting mystery and 'the possibility of hidden things.'

Microscopic detail of the kind easily, in fact inevitably escapes detection in story. But in allegory, like long-buried treasure, it in patience abides, emerging untarnished. Joram, recall, works on 'a grey one with silver nails.' Perhaps *silver,* finest symbolic scrollwork, hails the Biblical Joram who bore vessels of *silver,* gold, and brass. Ever the exquisite miniaturist, Dickens works designs in large and small too until the tiniest speck in the Creation mirrors his Heaven-reverencing themes. (See Chapter III.)

Old Time, or the early ages in *Copperfield,* hears a good deal of the 'old tune,' Death. Em'ly, Ham, and soon David, fatherless from the start, are orphans; Steerforth has no father. Fatherless too is the deathly pale,

cadaverous, bony, skeleton-like (Dickens images all) Uriah Heep, grinning
type of Death Triumphant.  More benignly yet no less surely, Joram too
implies the Old Mortality in its shocking impersonalness.  Day in and out
laboring impassively amid black veils and coffins, stolid Joram remains unmoved by the solemn spectacle of the relentless moving on of human life into
death.  As such he symbolizes for Dickens the OT mind in its small, overheated, bustling incuriosity shop of funeral furnishing (B.C. time 'furnished'
many a funeral, too) far to the rear of the clarion call of New or NT time, the
*new* tune, Sleepers, awake!  Without spiritual roots deep in the Gospel of
Christ, man has only Joram's hollow box and RAT-tat-tat in the end.

Behold, then, David, Uriah, and Joram, three mutually illuminating and
reinforcing portraits.  Dickens's recreations are done with a free hand, we
have seen, yet each is entirely recognizable as his former self.  How far
does this mining of the OT go?  A symbolic likeness of the first David
falling like Elijah's mantle onto the shoulders of a young David of Christian
time must radically alter our sense of the meaning of the latter's life, must
it not?  Suddenly hosts of figures and names, from *Blunderstone* Rookery,
*Murdstone, Steerforth, Strong* to Barkis's fatal fiction, Mr. *Blackboy,* fairy-
tale or *Pilgrim's Progress* names all, look up and wink at allegory.  As to
*Joram,* how interesting to find the common noun derived from the name,
*jorum,* appearing in old morality and mortality circumstances in a telling
way in no fewer than four major Dickens works, at last count. [5]  Can this be
only coincidence?  As the shade of an immortal David erupts in David Copperfield's life, familiar things grow portentous, magical, strange; curiosity
grows about what seemed settled forever.  Exciting possibilities of
meaning, copperfields full, are everywhere, perhaps even as early as the
famous opening line of the novel:

> Whether I shall turn out to be the hero of my own life, or whether that
> station will be held by anybody else, these pages will show. (1)

If there lives in this David a greater David and Son of David, who then *is*
the hero of his multifold life?  How mysterious and ambiguous the familiar
words suddenly seem.

May we not now experience anew other things in the story, such as
David's dateless, yearless, century-less, always vague time sense.  He records a life looked back on, remembered, but from precisely what futurity?
One never learns.  Recalling a youthful 'fairy marriage' (631) with Dora,
the bride (by then dust how long?) invoked from out 'the mists and shadows of the past' (644), David skirts the whole issue of when.  His father's
funeral was 'I don't know when, but apparently ages ago' (14).  *Ages ago*
passes as a figure of speech, as it should and in one facet of its life indeed
is.  But what if, having the Bible somewhere in mind, a writer for once
really *meant* 'ages'?  The old Blunderstone life, once past, seems to David

'to lie in the haze of immeasurable distance' (215), and Uriah to have faced him and infuriated him, we saw, 'at some indefinite time' before. How hazy all such passage of time; what infinite leeway herein for aeons to slip quietly away, or for generations to expire in a refrain like: 'Oh, long, long afterwards' (580), or in an impression of having bitten Mr. Murdstone 'in such a remote antiquity' (70). *Antiquity,* like *ages,* soaks up mighty literal force, coming to seem less and less merely figurative as in his childhood David, exiled from home, wanders in a city twice termed 'the Modern Babylon'—*Babylon* in truth, for him a place of enslavement, unrelieved agony of body and spirit, and near starvation; *antiquity* indeed, as David haunts the arches of 'the Adelphi' (160) or takes many a cold plunge in a Roman bath.

That is nothing, the reader protests. London styled as sinful 'Babylon' is in the Dickens-Carlyle era a cliche, and one allows for Greek and Roman place names in modern times. Nothing strange about the mention of Roman ruins. Normally, all such would go unnoticed; in fact, it would border on perversity to notice it. But as a Biblical design of some scope amazingly unfolds, as Uriah imports the old trials and Joram his 'vessels,' detail of all kinds takes on visibility. David *himself* senses he but repeats what was said and done (it echoes again) 'in a remote time—of having been surrounded, dim ages ago, by the same faces, objects, circumstances' (566). This is the second time he voices the feeling. Was ever hint more plain?

David's persistent evasiveness about time takes on an electrifying new force. This evasiveness runs through Dickens, from the airy 'Once upon a time, it matters little when' opening of *The Battle of Life* to a 'They were old Chimes, trust me!' approach in *The Chimes,* which insists on faith ('trust me') while neatly sidestepping the whole matter of just how old. In the same spirit *Our Mutual Friend* opens with the words: 'In these times of ours, though concerning the exact year there is no need to be precise....' Imagine, for once, letting 'dim ages ago' or 'old' out to their utmost length; that is, simply taking Dickens at his word. One is back In the Beginning in a flash, or could be. If Christian, 'these times of ours' do not exclude certain happenings in a Garden. Early in *Great Expectations* Pip recounts that he never saw a likeness of his dead parents, '(for their days were long before the days of photographs)' (1). *How* long, exactly, when as the story opens there springs up from among gravestones, as from his ancient unquiet grave in *Genesis* time, an *Abel* innocent and doomed who wanders the misty primordial wilderness marshes like the ghost of Abel, and is again slain by a murderous, remorseless 'C' figure (Compeyson, Cain!) with an identifying mark on him. As Abel is stowed aboard a 'wicked Noah's ark' (36), what *is* the true date of this markedly unchristian era of Judaeo-Christian time? As such imagery suggests, layers of ancientness, Bible-haunted, texture contemporary reality in Dickens. One sees the point. Until Christ comes again to men's hearts, *Genesis* of Flood and Mosaic bedrock of stony law, Murd-stone heartlessness, fanatical fixation upon rule, and passion for punishment for any infraction thereof, are all.

Returning to *Copperfield,* we note that one one occasion David wears his aversion to being pinned down to dates and times with an oddly showy air:

> Whether it was the following Sunday when I saw the gentleman again, or whether there was any greater lapse of time before he reappeared, I cannot recall. I don't profess to be clear about dates. (24)

David's professing not to profess is more than a little out of character, as his anti-profession speech to Uriah cited before shows. Anyhow, why bring up the subject at all? Of course, for readers not on the lookout for oddity, the forward surge of story sweeps a hundred such moments swiftly along and no strain is felt, the great Dickens momentum, the teeming, crowded Hogarth-Breugelesque life on all sides competing for even a glance ever impelling us on. Yet, if the foregoing David-Uriah-Joram discussion has any validity, surely we now register the insistently sliding quality of time in Dickens, *déja vu* and the rest, with a difference. 'Long, long ago,' so radiantly simple, bids fair to be easily as 'long' as Bible time; the phrase is elastic enough, if that were wanted. We think it is. Not that every Victorian author must begin a work as Thackeray does *'Vanity Fair:* 'While the present century was in its teens, and on one sunshiny morning in June....' Or, to be fair, as Dickens begins *Pickwick,* with a flourish of May 12, 1827 on page one. But that is not typical. When a writer most often seems bent on avoiding just such specificity, one may reasonably wonder why.

All such easing of time lines, we suggest, sets the stage for timeless allegory, for the symbolic passage of epochs in the wink of an eye. A semi-timeless setting further serves to dismiss the whole idea of both the solidity and importance of time, along with men's chronicles so fussy about and jealous of the exact 'when' of events, and their myopic infatuation with the years of their days. A gentle slighting of Time implies the relative insignificance and oneness of all time from the perspective of Eternity. How often Dickens records human life from this very height, Heaven's vantage point. In *The Old Curiosity Shop* the heroine, little Nell, in everything attuned to the Above and pointing to the world to come as if the chart were given, sees in crumbling ruins come upon on her journey from an old to a new life 'the work of ages that have become but drops of water in the great ocean of Eternity' (386). (How *Nell Trent,* knell of coming Day, embodies the spirit of NT ideals, flowing even as the river Trent, even as mortal life to meet Eternity; and how after her holy passing her faithful friend *Christopher* keeps her memory alive, awaits telling at some future time.) The theme also runs in *Barnaby Rudge,* notably when Mary and her son—rare, prophetic, crucified sons of Mary!—learn he is condemned to

death under Law.  Dickens intones: 'With them who stood upon the brink
of the great gulph which none can see beyond, Time, so soon to lose itself
in vast Eternity, rolled on like a mighty river, swoln and rapid as it nears
the sea' (584).  Dickens loves to mount such visions in figures of the life to
come.  In *Our Mutual Friend,* the narrator, yet once more, sights 'the
solemn river, stealing away by night, as all things steal away, by night and
day, so quietly yielding to the attraction of the loadstone rock of Eternity'
(751).  Therefore, when in *A Tale of Two Cities* Charles Darnay is 'Drawn
to the Loadstone Rock,' shall we understand it as a journey undertaken
only in Time?  No, as the 'crucifixion' and resurrection of a 'C' figure,
Carton, which follows, affirms, history bound to retell the old, old tale.
(See Chapter III.)

Released from strict accountability to time, David moves closer to the
state of pure metaphor wherein the spirit of David lives unto the generations; and through him the Son of David is born again to gladden the
greatly expectant souls of men.

To conclude, the interaction in Dickens of one David and Shepherd, or
David and Uriah, or David and Joram, while interesting, might soon be
forgotten or seen as but one thread among many, one isolated dab of
figural coloration with local, not global interest.  But such Scriptural plenty
as we have glimpsed cannot be lightly dismissed.  To what shining spiritual treasure these first unearthings lead we now set out to see.

# TWO

# The Christian Dickens

"So, says Edwin:
    'I don't know, Mr. Neville' (adopting that mode of address from Mr. Crisparkle), 'that what people are proudest of, they usually talk most about; I don't know, either, that what they are proudest of, they most like other people to talk about....'"

*The Mystery of Edwin Drood,* 71.

I have always striven in my writings to express veneration for the life and lessons of Our Saviour....But I have never made proclamation of this from the housetops.

letter to John Makeham, LLS,II,411.

As the above reminds us, how Dickens intrigues with the ideals of silence and containment! And how wise of young Edwin Drood to adopt the Christian name mode of address of Mr. Crisparkle: *Crisparkle,* here as always a gleam, ray, reflection of the light (*sparkle*) of Christ (*Cris.*)

In a consideration of Dickens's use of Biblical and other myth and its transfiguring force in his works, questions crowd the mind. For one, what would impel a Dickens with such grand creative powers of his own to shoulder the burden of religious allegory? For another, how could he possibly have designed complex mythic-within-realistic plots when, as often, publishing in instalments and so both pressed for time and kept from revising back? A great puzzle, admittedly. But then, how is the colossal imaginative genius of Dickens to be accounted for anyway?

Dickens's apparent ease in overlaying 'real' upon mythic figures like David, his spinning allegory so unlike Allegory and like Nature, or nature, it has gone unseen, surely owes much to what his fiction, essays, speeches, letters, and philanthropic activity in public life all affirm: a profound life-long devotion to 'the life and lessons of Our Saviour.' This, the Christian aspect of Dickens, has been too little taken into account; explicit Christian utterance, when not wholly overlooked, dismissed as an embarrassing, intrusive lapse into sentimentality. Thus we are the more unready to uncover the radiant secret of 'Agnes Wickfield.'

A man of unwavering personal faith, as Forster's official biography *The Life of Charles Dickens* and as his works themselves show, Dickens also lived in the Victorian Christian age—more formally than actually Christian, he would charge—in which the Bible held the oratorical and literary foreground, its lofty tone aspired to on platforms and in pulpits: an evangelical, sermon-prizing, morally earnest age in search of revelation. Dickens strongly disliked the dominant prophetic, fiery, doctrinal, i.e., OT tone of many Christian divines of his day, like that of the 'Boanerges Boiler' or industrial-age Son of Thunder satirized in the essay 'City of London Churches,' a preacher in whose scalding rant Dickens as a boy was, he relates, 'steamed like a potato.' [1] (Calling him *Boanerges,* Dickens borrows Christ's nickname for his two loud-voiced disciples, the brothers James and John.) As religion was a great public issue in Dickens's day, the Bible as moralised lore, theme, ornament fell into the literate and illiterate man's possession as it never would again, enjoying widest social currency. Thus, whatever problems the allegorical venture doubtless entailed for Dickens (*Uriah* and *Joram* first evidence he lived them down, by wizardry unknown), the task, staggering and unimaginable as it seems, was hardly what it would be in, for example, our time, when Scripture is little and ever less well known, Elijah's ravens, Jeremiah's yoke, the voice of the turtle gone from the common cultural treasury; not, as once, breathed in with the conversational air, imbibed with our mothers' milk, or in Bible-reading at school assemblies, much less lived conviction. (Today I find few college students who have ever heard of David and Jonathon or 'Vanity of vanities;' and Lazarus and Pilate in the NT fare no better.) Undeniably, since the last century the Bible has lost ground. But Dickens's is another world. As a Christian with a strong social religious heritage and strong (also strongly private) personal faith, Dickens is seized by a 'David' or other Biblical inspiration, not in a vacuum, but as deepest resources of mind and spirit, culture, and personal genius point the way.

Our theme is Dickens as anti-formalist Christian bent on dramatizing those lost saving truths and spiritual directions that in his view Christianity alone reveals. The notion that Dickens was a lukewarm or even no believer because no steady churchgoer is simply false. His own words constantly and firmly refute it, we show, even as such brilliant symbolic witness as 'Agnes Wickfield' wordlessly dispels it forever.

In a recent article titled '*Dombey and Son* and Dickens's Unitarian Period,' Samuel F. Pickering, Jr. reviews the history of Dickens's long religious quest, his lasting dissatisfaction with sects, and search for a form of public worship compatible with his own ideals. The confessional issue is much in mind, as his fiction reflects.  One recalls his false preachers, the howling Melchisedech Howler in *Dombey and Son* (the words: 'Thou art a priest for ever after the order of Melchisedec,' *Heb*. 7:17, come to grief in him) and the Reverend Chadband in *Bleak House,* his sermons, overrun with Hebrew imagery of flocks, tents, herds and prophetic doom-saying, wholly devoid of compassion for the lone, lorn child, Jo.  No comfort or Christianity there.  Pickering states:

> Although the landscape of his novels was filled with churches and his world peopled with divines of all theological hues, Charles Dickens, with the exception of a short period of his life, rejected formal Christianity after his childhood.  In his view, Anglicanism, closely identified with Tory politics, had become spiritually moribund.  Likewise Catholicism, emphasizing dogma to the detriment of good deeds, abstracted man's thoughts from his feelings and undermined Christian action.  Evangelicalism, stressing the Old Testament and the individual's sense of sin, seemed to fragment the Christian community and to neglect the New Testament's moral code. (438)

In the search for formal church ties, Pickering relates, Dickens briefly found in Unitarianism a congenial 'moral code of Christian action, based on the New Testament in general and the Sermon on the Mount in particular;' also 'an escape from binding dogma and a commitment to personal benevolism' (439).  Soon, however, the ties with Unitarianism and all 'isms' dissolve, and Dickens, we think, slips into the 'Mr. Crisparkle' life-in-allegory of Christian devotions of a unique kind.

The Christian character of Dickens is reflected in a letter to a son, Edward Bulwer-Lytton Dickens, which reveals both the depth and strongly private nature of Dicken's faith, one founded on a solemn reverence for Christ and the NT: for 'the life and lessons of Our Saviour.'  Following some general fatherly counsel to a son leaving home, Dickens turns to his chief subject, living the Christian life:

> Never take a mean advantage of any one in any transaction, and never be hard upon people who are in your power.  Try to do to others as you would have them do to you, and do not be discouraged if they fail sometimes.  It is much better for you that they should fail in obeying the greatest rule laid down by our Saviour than that you should.
>
> I put a New Testament among your books, for the very same reasons, and with the very same hopes, that made me write an easy account of it for you, when you were a little child; because it is the best book that ever was or will be known in the world, and because it teaches you the best lessons by which any human creature who tries to be truthful and faithful to duty can possibly be guided.  As your brothers have gone away, one by one, I have written to each such words as I am writing to you, and have entreated them all to guide themselves by this book, putting aside the interpretations and inventions of men.
>
> You will remember that you have never at home been wearied about religious observances or mere formalities.  I have always been anxious not to

weary my children with such things before they are old enough to form opinions respecting them. You will therefore understand the better that I now
solemnly impress upon you the truth and beauty of the Christian religion, as
it came from Christ Himself, and the impossibility of your going far wrong if
you humbly but heartily respect it.

Only one thing more on this head. The more we are in earnest as to feeling
it, the less we are disposed to hold forth about it. Never abandon the wholesome practise of saying your own private prayers, night and morning. I have
never abandoned it myself, and I know the comfort of it. (LLS,II,370)

For Dickens, religious integrity and privacy, an avoidance of public shows
of faith, go together, a disclosure richly significant for this study. The
'easy account' of the NT Dickens wrote for his children and briefly cites
here is *The Life of Our Lord*. How deeply sincere Dickens was in avowing:
'The more we are in earnest as to feeling it, the less we are disposed to hold
forth about it,' the history of this little book shows. Dickens insisted it was
not to circulate outside the immediate family circle, and forbade its publication. His wishes in the matter long prevailed with his heirs, and it was
not published until 1934. Although in print, today it is all but forgotten
(luckily, not entirely), quite as Dickens wished, time and history, if not his
heirs, keeping faith with his design.

Perhaps the sacred nature of its subject and the reverence he held it in,
perhaps a reluctance to turn a Life of Christ to personal profit, perhaps
some other motive altogether, led Dickens to deny *The Life of Our Lord* to
fame. Note in his letter he does not refer to it by name. In Christian
matters Dickens is often curiously shy. Alluding for one instant only to 'an
easy account' of the NT, he thereby graciously puts not his own work or
title, but the great Original forward, a gesture that quietly says much.

The *The Life of Our Lord* editor interprets a firm refusal to publish it as
follows:

> During his lifetime Charles Dickens refused to permit the publication of
> *The Life of Our Lord* because he doubtless felt that it was a personal letter to
> his own children, and feared that a public disclosure of so intimate a document
> might involve the possibility of attack and defense of his deepest religious
> convictions. In a letter to a clergyman he said:
> "There cannot be many men, I believe, who have a more humble veneration
> for the New Testament, or a more profound conviction of its all-sufficiency
> than I have....My observation of life induces me to hold in unspeakable dread
> and horror these unseemly squabbles about 'the letter' which drive 'the spirit'
> out of hundreds of thousands." (LL,4)

In such glimpses now and then we discover, with some surprise, that the
famous public Dickens, tireless performer on platforms, enthusiastic
sponsor of private theatricals, a very Pickwick of conviviality among
friends, is not the only Dickens. Another exists averse to 'holding forth,'

given to saying '*private* prayers, night and morning,' as if watchful to guard from compromise of publicity or vulgar praise, as from the insidious note of self he deplores in his fiction, the integrity of a 'humble veneration for the New Testament.'

*The Life of Our Lord* is a tender, devout Child's history of the NT that brings key moments in the ministry of Christ to within both reach and grasp of a child's understanding, as if in token of what a Heaven's for. Dickens clearly values Christian truth highly enough to want it communicated to young minds in just the right way—lightly, simply, in easy language free from the clang and twang of the conventicle, from all *Boanerges* self-puffing 'fifthlys' and 'sixthlys,' all dry drills in 'the letter.' Mainly following *Luke* but close to all four Gospels, the text carefully steers clear of what in the Edward Bulwer-Lytton letter Dickens calls 'the interpretations and inventions of men.'

In this Life of Christ many NT figures— a centurion; Christ walking in the fields with the disciples on a Sunday; the devil-ridden, tormented man who suddenly springs up among tombs (like which memorable character in Dickens?); the sinful woman whose tears wet His feet, which she dries with her hair; the many an ever-compassionate Christ heals; the farmer and his servants of the parable; high priests and Pharisees, and many more—come warmly, humanly to life. Like David in *Copperfield* they seem living contemporaries: seem and are. *The Life of Our Lord* shows how intimately well Dickens knew the NT. One imagines him year in and out, making no point of it to anyone, poring over 'the best book that ever was or will be known in the world,' steeping heart, mind, and imagination in it; imagines its episodes, drama, its very linguistic cadences in time becoming second nature to him, its mysteries, figured forth in metaphor wonderfully congenial to his own highly figural imagination, exciting both the Christian and artist in him.

*If,* therefore, Dickens wrote religious allegory, his would have been no last-minute regimen of Bible-cramming, no shallow, artificial mental athleticism or merely intellectual tie to his theme. Moreover, Dickens was interested in Bible times and cultures, as certain books in his Gadshill library at the time of his death show, one in particular tracing in great detail what its author calls 'the progress of the intellect' from Greek-Roman and Hebrew to Christian times. [2] Thus, in approaching the subject of the rigors of allegorical composition, we should avoid projecting onto Dickens ideas of what attempts in that direction would entail in our own time. How Dickens, Christian, devoté of prayer and the New Testament, also genius, confronted the superhuman labors involved is quite another matter, whatever matter it may be.

The celebrated Dickens humanism, we suggest, is first and foremost Christian. Caring little for churches but much about men's need to know God, put off by institutional and factional squabbles among clergy given to

confusing true Christianity—Christ-imitating service to God and man—
with a proliferation of forms, dogmas, diocesan conferences, self-noising
Temperance societies (like the *Ebenezer Temperance Association* in *Pickwick*) and sabbatarian crusades and crusaders, whom Dickens once bitterly
hails 'in the name of all the Pharisees of Jerusalem' (OL,230),[3] Dickens,
shunning these, is the more, and more quietly, devoted to the unadorned
word of the NT. Bypassing the special tonality and chilling solemnity that
customarily sets religion apart from life, an outcome he deplores, he cuts
straight through to the lessons of Christ, Dickens's way—like that of Christ
and the disciples through the field, that Sunday—ever through Nature and
the homely scenes of everyday life.

Dickens scenarios, like the NT parables, are filled with widows, widows'
houses, prodigals, rich men, camels and needles' eyes. Typical of the informal yet reverent Dickens approach to the sacred is this passage in *The
Seven Poor Travellers* in which profound Christian sentiment arises by
natural association in a wanderer's mind:

> Going through the woods, the softness of my tread upon the mossy ground
> and among the brown leaves enhanced the Christmas sacredness by which I
> felt surrounded. As the whitened stems environed me, I thought how the
> Founder of the time had never raised his benignant hand, save to bless and
> heal, except in the case of one unconscious tree.
> By Cobham Hall, I came to the village, and the churchyard where the dead
> had been quietly buried, "in the sure and certain hope" which Christmas-
> time inspired. What children could I see at play, and not be loving of, recall-
> ing who had loved them! No garden that I passed was out of unison with the
> day, for I remembered that the tomb was in a garden, and that "she, sup-
> posing him to be the gardener," had said, "Sir, if thou hast borne him hence,
> tell me where thou hast laid Him, and I will take Him away." In time, the
> distant river with the ships came full in view, and with it pictures of the poor
> fishermen, mending their nets, who arose and followed Him,—of the teaching
> of the people from a ship pushed off a little from shore, by reason of the
> multitude,—of a majestic figure walking on the water, in the loneliness of
> night. My very shadow on the ground was eloquent of Christmas; for did not
> the people lay their sick where the mere shadow of the men who had heard
> and seen him might fall as they passed along? (CS,93)

Here in all freshness of immediacy and simplicity is Christmas fervor which
blends intensity with perfect quietude of expression. No vain clamor of
'Christ.' Rather, a studied avoidance of 'sacred' tone and diction, a keeping lowly among common nouns, as it were, as befits a friend of 'Poor
Travellers,' *poor* taken in the Biblical sense, too. The vast distance normally imagined to exist between Scriptural then and living now, as between
man and God, seems none at all. A verse from *John* blends in; the text
easily receives it. The narrator just as easily moves from the living reality
of woods, garden, children, shore, to the NT scene each recalls to an

attuned mind, the Christian drama vitally present to the fancy as kindred, eternally apposite reality, natural and supernatural landscaped merging in confluence free from strain. In the same way, in *Our Mutual Friend:*

> She placed her orderly little basket at her side, and sank upon the ground, supporting herself against the tree. It brought to her mind the foot of the Cross, and she committed herself to Him who died upon it. (511)

Here epitomised is the genius of Dickensian allegory: the Christian moment is one with the living scene, nothing of it awesomely apart, but, released from conventional pallor of abstraction, near, accessible, ever-presently alive. For Dickens, 'the Christmas sacredness' and Christianity exact no stiff price of discomfort of body or mind, no Sunday clothes or 'best parlour' demeanour, or ungodly pharisaical cleanliness of the sort Mrs. Joe inflicts on Joe and Pip, martyrs in stiff collars for religion's sake (*Great Expectations*). It is this widespread captivity of things divine to such formalism, a hangover from Old Law or OT time, that Dickensian story and allegory come to end.

A like informality marks religious allusion in the chapter 'England Under Elizabeth' in *A Child's History of England,* in which Dickens tells how the new monarch learned of the realm's crying need for a Church Service in plain English:

> The coronation was a great success; and, on the next day, one of the courtiers presented a petition to the new Queen, praying that as it was the custom to release some prisoners on such occasions, she would have the goodness to release the four evangelists, Matthew, Mark, Luke, and John, and also the Apostle Saint Paul, who had for some time been shut up in a strange language so that the people could not get at them. (CHE,413)

Again, note Dickens's amazingly informal way of citing Scripture. Thus personified, Matthew, Mark, Luke, and John sound for all the world like living men. It only belatedly strikes the reader that Dickens is 'really' referring to the four Gospels printed—in his prison metaphor, incarcerated—in Greek or Latin. (It goes on into modern times; in *Dombey and Son,* an unlucky lad, Johnson, is punished at school by having to learn by heart an Epistle of St. Paul's in Greek.) The point is that to Dickens, as in Dickens, the evangelists and Saint Paul *are* alive, in the sense that the divine energies they embodied still circulate in the world, or gladly would. All the more reason to suspect earth-shaking symbolism at work as the novel *Little Dorrit* opens upon the scene of a John Baptist Cavalletto in prison, so casually may some living John (the) Baptist figure slip in, and, once set free, resume the work of the Lord.

Again on the stage of history, John the Baptist lives in his spiritual son and heir. Seeing the prisoners, the jailer's little daughter timidly approaches the bars:

> 'Poor birds!' said the child.

> The fair little face, touched with divine compassion, as it peeped shrink-
> ingly through the gate, was like an angel's in the prison.  John Baptist rose
> and moved towards it, as if it had a good attraction for him. (5)

The words 'divine compassion' and 'angel' lead the way.  Here is one more
Child's history and child like Tiny Tim, David, or little Nell, she who is 'so
fresh from God' (OCS,4), to pity the caged 'birds,' men's souls.  As will be
seen, Dickens's is invariably a Christian sense of 'little children, like the
Angels, who behold the Father's face!' (CS,514), as he says in *Mugby
Junction*.  Dickensian children are set in our midst as a child once in the
midst of the Disciples.

In Dickens the NT speaks in the voices of living men.  Bursting bonds of
time, language, custom, the four evangelists leap barriers of usage and
plunge back into living fellowship with men.  Or would, if allowed.  Sadly
enough, religious instruction itself too often blocks the way.  In *Copperfield*, one Sunday evening, David as a small child is read the story of how
Lazarus was raised from the dead; thanks to the austerity of the setting, the
best parlour, in David's mind associated with stories of black-garbed
mourners of his father who once gathered there, and thanks to the late
hour, David takes the story greatly amiss.  He recalls:

> And I am so frightened that they are afterwards obliged to take me out of bed,
> and show me the quiet churchyard out of the bedroom window, with the dead
> all lying in their graves at rest, below the solemn moon. (14)

With the best intentions in the world, David's mother and nurse blunder.
Ironically, the son of a David who named his home the *Rookery* for birds he
never saw, because the nests were there—a David of faith in wonders of
air unseen—shrinks from the Mystery of faith, and is unable to sleep until
reassured that the dead are *really* dead and unrisen, and no death-
subverting Lazarus activity in sight  No one explains 'risen' to the child, as
good Polly Toodle will explain it to little Florence in *Dombey and Son*.  Sad
demystification of Mystery for a son of David!  Well may the eye of Heaven
beholding such a sad scene be a '*solemn* moon.'

We imagine that Dickens wrote *The Life of Our Lord* to save his own
children from just such confusion and fright, from such nights and sinkings
into Sleep.

In *Great Expectations* too, little Pip's 'religious' training delivers him to
the same narrow literalism of mind:  to fixation in 'the letter' which,
Dickens held, 'drives 'the spirit' out of thousands' (LL,4).  Pip recalls:

> Neither were my notions of the theological positions to which my Cate-
> chism bound me at all accurate; for I have a lively remembrance that I sup-
> posed my declaration that I was to 'walk in the same all the days of my life,'
> laid me under an obligation always to go through the village from our house
> in one particular direction, and never to vary it by turning down by the wheel-
> wright's or up by the mill. (39)

Funny-sad blunder.  So much for Roman-nosed (and souled) Mr. Wopsle's great aunt's myopic instruction, and the local clergyman's.  Ah, but, left to his own devices, Pip does better, his child's fertile fancy outsoaring such nights of constraint and law and instantly grasping the words 'wife of the Above' carved on his parents' tombstone 'as a complimentary reference to my father's exaltation to a better world' (39).  Happy 'inaccuracy,' as Pip's training leads him to suppose it.  The same soul-fettering education or mis-education is temporarily or permanently the undoing of young Robin Toodle (*Dombey*), Sissy Jupe and Tom and Louisa Gradgrind (*Hard Times*), and Charley Hexam (*Our Mutual Friend*).  Dickens is haunted by the faces of Christendom's children reared shortsighted, the wings of figurative imagination on which men may mount to Heaven, transcending at last all earthly 'walk in the same,' clipped early and forever.

To read the NT with understanding, as such children do not, is to find strength to bear life's otherwise felling blows.  This is seen in, again, *The Seven Poor Travellers* in which brave Major Taunton's mother has learned he was killed in war.  A comrade, Richard Doubledick, comes to visit her:

> It was a Sunday evening, and the lady sat at her quiet garden-window, read-ing the Bible; reading to herself, in a trembling voice, that very passage in it, as I have heard him tell.  He [Ensign Doubledick] heard the words: "Young man, I say unto thee, arise!"
>
> He had to pass the window; and the bright, dark eyes of his debased time seemed to look at him.  Her heart told her who he was; she came to the door quickly, and fell upon his neck.
>
> "He saved me from ruin, made me a human creature, won me from infamy and shame.  O, God for ever bless him!  And He will, He will!"

Hope in resurrection born of the raising of Lazarus ('I say unto thee, arise!'), together with Doubledick's devotion to the mother of his dead reclaimer (the unnamed 'He' and 'him' a type of the Redeemer, even Christ), sustain the grieving woman.  Such consolation stands forever in Dickens, with always a grateful Doubledick, or Dickens, to recall it.

The invaluable gift of the NT to the bereaved, fallen, and dying is a theme in Dickens's 'Book of Paul,' *Dombey and Son*.  (See Chapter III.)  In it, Alice Marwood, née Brown, lies dying.  Hers has been a life of cruel betrayal by both her mother and lover, James Carker.  Long embittered in the Miss Havisham way, Alice before she dies undergoes a dramatic change of heart which, although not labelled Christian, is very much so, as this scene between her friend, Harriet Carker, and the dying Alice shows:

> Harriet was withdrawing her hand to open the book when Alice detained it for a moment.
>
> 'You will not forget my mother?  I forgive her, if I have any cause.  I know that she forgives me, and is sorry in her heart.  You will not forget her?'
>
> 'Never, Alice!'

'A moment yet. Lay me head so, dear, that as you read I may see the words in your kind face.'

Harriet complied and read—read the eternal book for all the weary and the heavy-laden, for all the wretched, fallen, and neglected of this earth—read the blessed history, in which the blind lame palsied beggar, the criminal, the woman stained with shame, the shunned of all our dainty clay, has each a portion that no human pride, indifference, or sophistry, through all the ages, can take away, or by the thousandth atom of a grain reduce—read the minis- try of Him who, through the round of human life and all its hopes and griefs, from birth to death, from infancy to age, had sweet compassion for, and inter- est in, its every scene and stage, its every suffering and sorrow. (826)

Mounting like a great three-in-one trinitarian wave, 'read the eternal book,' 'read the blessed history,' to 'read the ministry of Him,' *Him* the shining crest of Christ, the long final sentence, slowly gathering force, ascends, subsiding at last, its incremental riches spent, into the spiritual quietude and finely balanced, alliterative poetry of the close: 'its every *s*cene and *s*tage, its every *s*uffering and *s*orrow.' The very rhythms of the final cadence seem Biblical, as in: 'For unto us a child is born, unto us a son is given.' Here Dickens highlights Christ's unfailing compassion, mercy, and love for all humanity, especially the last and least. Significant- ly, Alice not only hears, she longs to read the words of the NT in a kind face. So in *A Christmas Carol* Tiny Tim, attending church, is glad the people not only hear a sermon, but see him, a cripple, a living symbolic sermon, as it were, and so 'remember upon Christmas Day, who made lame beggars walk, and blind men see' (CB,45). Harriet Carker's model is clearly Christ's concern for (recalling Alice) 'the woman stained with shame.' Pickering tightens the connection, stating: 'Harriet Carker, as an emblematic human savior, bathe[s] Alice Marwood's cut foot' (PD,453). Her ministering kindness at the bedside further commemorates what in *Mugby Junction* Dickens calls 'the Redeemer's presence beside the bed- ridden' (CS,494).

In his article, Pickering also points out that in *The Life of Our Lord* the miracles Dickens chooses to recount are 'primarily those showing Jesus as a personal benevolist, helping individuals by curing their illnesses or for- giving their sins' (PD,441). In Dickens, the sea of faith is still at the full and brightly girdles the world. The great human adventure is to rejoin it, be reclaimed, as Doubledick and Alice and many another are, uplifted, and in sweet expectancy, borne forward in the Mystery and the Hope, sur- rendering old hatred, sin, schemes of vindictive triumph and revenge, and fixation in sorrow or in sense of sin unforgiven under Heaven—an Hebraic, sackcloth-and-ashes conviction of sin—such frozen deeps and states of mind being at odds with the ideal of Christian clemency of the NT. Clem- ency triumphs in Alice's: 'I forgive her, if I have any cause.' She has cause enough, God knows. But the point is, hatred has relaxed its once deadly grip on Alice.  Forgiving in her final hour, (one may hear the faint echo of, 'Forgive them Father'), she may hope to be forgiven.  Dickens does not have to use a highly colored religious vocabulary here, any more than he has to name Lazarus or Christ in the Doubledick passage cited before.  It would be superfluous.  Clearly, Alice Marwood, mar(red) wood of the Tree of the Kingdom, dies a Christian.

Society as a whole, however, lags behind.  *Great Expectations* opens in a Scrooge-ish, unchristian Christmas season of Christendom which harshly, blindly rejects 'the criminal,' the man of sorrows wandering in pain in bone-chilling cold, and in the still colder, more bleak wilderness marshes of men's uncharitable minds.  Dickens's social blueprint is, first and last, the NT, which teaches the forsaken and fatherless of a Father in Heaven as loving and forgiving towards them, every one, as the father in the parable of the prodigal son.  Dickens means that, following Christ to the Father, men could not as they now do abandon 'the wretched, fallen, and neglected of this earth' like Little Dorrit's poor deformed 'child' Maggy, who is the 'blind lame palsied' beggar all in one; or scorn 'the woman stained with shame' of many Dickens stories:  Alice; Martha Endell (*Copperfield*); Nancy (*Oliver Twist*); Lilian (*The Chimes*); and Lady Dedlock (*Bleak House*).  The Dombey passage covers them all, as did Christ's love.  A love Harriet not only recommends in 'the letter' but exemplifies in the spirit in the personal, Christ-reflecting comfort she offers Alice.

The great Dickens purpose is just this:  to make the saving force in Christianity not only known but felt in the blood and along the heart.  Dickens would see mankind wake from a crabbed or unconscious life and, like Scrooge, find Christmas morning not past and lost but, by God's grace, *now;* find an Alice, Tiny Tim, Abel Magwitch the convict to be helped and saved *now.*

The Dickens Christ, all texts show, is a Christ of mercies.  In *Pictures from Italy,* his chronicle of a journey, Dickens at one point describes relicts of the inquisitors' deadly art seen in the Palace of the Popes in Avignon, and expresses outrage at the idea that torturers could actually have supposed themselves 'His chosen servants, true believers in the Son of Man, elect disciples of Him who never did a miracle but to heal; who never struck a man with palsy, blindness, deafness, dumbness, madness, any one affliction of mankind; and never stretched His blessed hand out but to give relief and ease' (PI,276).  Again we note that Dickens's Saviour carries the Father's blessing to all mankind.  No doubt Dickens's special sympathy for the lower classes, simple fisherfolk like the Peggottys of Yarmouth in *Copperfield,* for example, is founded on the example of Christ.  In this regard Pickering notes:

> Like Carlyle in *Past and Present,* Dickens stressed the unity of society.  Arguing that the parable of the Good Samaritan illustrated the brotherhood of

all men and re-telling the story of Dives and Lazarus, Dickens emphasized that barriers between men were both artificial and unnatural. Heavy stress was laid on this, perhaps in response to the evangelical doctrine of Special Providence which viewed the divisions of society as ordained by God. To counteract this doctrine, Dickens repeated that heaven was made for both the rich and the poor and that the disciples were chosed from the poor. (PD,441)

Such values Dickens folds into a pervasively Christian fiction, his works, we think, a string of shining matched pearls of great price. He looks, not to doctrine but to poetry to save us; it is the last hope. For institutional official Christendom leads men the wrong way. Writing to his friend Cerjat, Dickens states:

> As to the Church, my friend, I am sick of it. The spectacle presented by the indecent squabbles of priests of most denominations, and the exemplary unfairness and rancour with which they conduct their differences, utterly repels me. And the idea of the Protestant establishment, in the face of its own history, seeking to trample out discussion and private judgment, is an enormity so cool, that I wonder the Right Reverends, Very Reverends, and all other Reverends, who commit it, can look in one another's faces without laughing, as the old soothsayers did. Perhaps they can't and don't. How our sublime and so-different Christian religion is to be administered in the future I cannot pretend to say, but that the Church's hand is at its own throat I am fully convinced. Here, more Popery, there, more Methodism—as many forms of consignment to eternal damnation as there are articles, and all in one forever quarreling body—the Master of the New Testament put out of sight, and the rage and fury almost always turning on the letter of obscure parts of the Old Testament, which itself has been the subject of accommodation, varying interpretation without end—these things cannot last. The Church that is to have its part in the coming time must be a more Christian one, with less arbitrary pretensions and a stronger hold upon the mantle of our Saviour as He walked and talked upon this earth. (LLS,II,204)

Strong words, these, evincing strong emotion on the subject. Note the rather drab cast of the prose, blank abstraction greying all, until the image of the mantled Christ arrives at the end and a B.C. of 'the letter' cedes to an A.D. of 'the spirit,' as though to say, Behold, thy King cometh unto thee. The pressing need for a Christian renewal of society is again Dickens's theme in the essay 'Ignorance and Crime':

> The comfortable conviction that a parrot acquaintance with the Church Catechism and the Commandments is enough shoe leather for poor pilgrims by the Slough of Despond, sufficient armour against the Giants Slay-Good and Despair, and a sort of Parliamentary train for third-class passengers to the beautiful Gate of the City, must be pulled up by the roots, as its growth will overshadow this land. Side by side with Crime, Disease, and Misery in England, Ignorance is always brooding, and is always certain to be found. The

union of Night with Darkness is not more certain.  Schools of industry, schools
where the simple knowledge learned from books is made pointedly *useful*,
and immediately applicable to the duties and business of life, directly con-
ducive to order, cleanliness, punctuality, and economy—schools where the
sublime lessons of the New Testament are made the superstructure to be
reared, enduringly, on such foundations; not frittered away piecemeal into
harassing unintelligibilities, and associated with weariness, languour, and
distaste, by the use of the Gospel as a dog's-eared spelling book, than which
nothing in what is called instruction is more common, and nothing more to be
condemned—schools in such principles, deep as the lowest depth of Society,
and leaving none of its dregs untouched, are the only means of removing the
scandal and the danger that beset us in the nineteenth century of our Lord.
(MP,446)

A farewell letter to another son leaving the Paradise Hall of home, Henry
Fielding Dickens, strengthens our sense of the deeply Christian core of
Dickens's most cherished convictions, and, again, of his determined
reticence in matters of belief:

As your brothers have gone away one by one, I have written to each of them
what I am going to write to you.  You know that you have never been hamper-
ed with religious forms of restraint, and that with mere unmeaning forms I
have no sympathy.  But I strongly and affectionately impress upon you the
priceless value of the New Testament, and the study of that book as the one
unfailing guide in life.  Deeply respecting it, and bowing down before the
character of our Saviour, as separated from the vain constructions of men, you
cannot go very wrong, and will always preserve at heart a true spirit of veneration and humility.  Similarly I impress upon you the habit of saying a Christian prayer every night and morning.  These things have stood by me all
through my life, and remember that I tried to render the New Testament
intelligible to you and lovable by you when you were a mere baby.
     And so God bless you.  (LLS,II,360)

The lofty, sustained Christian tone of both letters to his sons is impressive.
Here is no hollow, stereotyped, pontificating Pontifex sort of religious cant
the Victorian patriarch ladles out by the quart in Butler's *The Way of All
Flesh*.  In Dickens, all rings true, proving consistent with religious utterance elsewhere.  Note again the avoidance of any direct reference to *The
Life of Our Lord*, almost as if to say, Not *my* title, Lord, but Thine.
     The letter touches upon a wish close to Dickens's heart:  to render the
NT 'intelligible' and 'lovable' to his children.  In this context, how newly
forceful *God* is in the closing line:  'And so God bless you.'  Like many
another common phrase grown invisible through indifferent usage, it is
here wonderfully Recalled to Life.
     Much explicit NT reference in Dickens is one support of the thesis of the
existence of the implicit, or allegorical.  For example, in *Little Dorrit,* the

portrait of a figure known only as 'Physician' joins Little Dorrit in pointing to the NT. We read:

> Many wonderful things did he see and hear, and much irreconcilable moral contradiction did he pass his life among; yet his equality of compassion was no more disturbed than the Divine Master's of all healing was. He went, like the rain, among the just and unjust, doing all the good he could, and neither proclaiming it in the synagogues nor at the corner of streets. (702)

Without mentioning *Matthew,* the passage smoothly conflates two neighboring verses in that Gospel: one on how the Father 'sendeth rain on the just and on the unjust' (5:45), and one on how hypocritical alms-givers, courting men's eyes and praise, 'love to pray standing in the synagogue and in the corners of the streets' (6:5). The nobility of Physician, a Christ figure, is enhanced by his carefully cultivated anonymity in the doing of good works. One is again struck by the hold this particular ideal has on Dickens, who, we think, also would make no show in a greatly Christian life's work. Dickens clearly knows his *Matthew* verbatim. When elsewhere he speaks of the NT as 'the one unfailing guide in my life,' with such evidence at hand, we are fully prepared to believe him.

Often involved in Christian matters, Dickens nevertheless avoids much 'Powerful Preacher'-style naming of Jesus Christ. He prefers, as with lowered glance, 'the Founder,' 'the Divine Master;' 'our Saviour' or 'the Saviour' (PI,360); 'the Founder of the time' and 'the Divine Forgiver of injuries' (CS,71); 'the patient Master' (LD,792); 'the Searcher of all hearts' (MD,105); and 'that divine and blessed Teacher' (LLS,II,440). In *A Christmas Carol* he refers, not to the manger in Bethlehem, but only to 'a poor abode' (CB,21), which gives it more human content and ongoing relevance. Such muted Christian reference is a Dickens hallmark. Earlier we cited. 'What children could I see at play, and not be loving of, *recalling who had loved them!'* After the quiet 'who' (not even 'Who') comes, not 'the Tomb,' but 'the tomb;' not 'Christ,' but simply 'a majestic figure.' Dickens likes indirect allusion and understatement. The NT itself is a 'book,' by no sounding title of awe or capital letters or syntactic flourish removed from the common life of men. Dickens shuns prescriptive reverence as he does 'unmeaning forms,' to him the beginning of the end of a truly Christian Christian faith.

If in Dickens faith runs silent, it runs deep. So precious is it to Dickens that he writes a Life of Christ for his children and would plant it in newest, freshest minds, there root it so deep that the budding young affections in their first purity and strength would twine round it, their prime supportive frame. In Dickensian childhood, that fairest seedtime of souls, the clear spirit first raises bright shoots of everlastingness. Dickens well knows 'the harvests of tenderness and humility that lie hidden in early-fostered seeds of the imagination,' and 'the oaks of retreat from blighting winds, that have the germs of their strong roots in nursery acorns' (LD,815). From seed sown in good ground, as in the parable, grows not just charming flights of fancy, but Christian virtue: 'harvests of tenderness and humility.' In Dickens, note, it is not imagination for its own sake, but above all else for God's.

Near the end of his life, Dickens once speaks with unaccustomed directness about his faith. Forced into disclosure, he makes clear he would prefer to remain silent on the subject. The situation is this. A reader, John Makeham, writes to Dickens about a moment in Chapter X of *The Mystery of Edwin Drood,* suggesting that, as the editor of one collection of Dickens letters puts it, 'Dickens might have forgotten that a certain figure of speech alluded to by him was drawn from Scripture, and was a prophetic description of the sufferings of the Saviour' (LLS*II,411). Little does Mr. Makeham know that he is on his way to uncovering allegory in Dickens! Dickens's reply is uncommonly brusque in tone, as if to rebuke the writer both for his error ('might have forgotten,' indeed!) and for forcing him to make public pronouncement on a subject he would otherwise never dream of holding forth on. His reply is as follows:

Wednesday, June 8, 1870.

DEAR SIR,—It would be quite inconveivable to me—but for your letter—that any reasonable reader could possibly attach a scriptural reference to a passage in a book of mine, reproducing a much-abused social figure of speech, impressed into all sorts of service, on all sorts of inappropriate occasions, without the faintest connection of it with its original source. I am truly shocked to find any reader can make the mistake.

I have always striven in my writings to express veneration for the life and lessons of our Saviour, because I feel it, and because I re-wrote that history for my children, every one of whom knew it from having it repeated to them, long before they could read, and almost as soon as they could speak.

But I have never made proclamation of this from the housetops.

Faithfully yours, (LLS,II,411)

The point at issue in *Drood,* I think, is a comparison of the Reverend Crisparkle to 'the highly popular lamb who has so long and unresistingly been led to the slaughter, and there would he, unlike that lamb, bore nobody but himself' (MD,101). A most puzzling image. Perhaps the Crisparkle-lamb simile protests the overuse and trivialization of sacred imagery; 'submissively...led,' Mr. *Crisparkle* is the more like Christ. But then comes 'bore,' and the purpose grows cloudy. In any case, apparently stung by a charge of irreverence, Dickens lashes out. After a lifetime in which his secret was not suspected, Dickens was perhaps prepared to be understood (although the words, 'I don't know, either, that what they are proudest of, they most like other people to talk about...' casts some doubt), but not so ironically misunderstood.

'The more we are in earnest, the less we...hold forth' remains his ideal. Twenty-five years earlier, in *The Life of Our Lord,* Dickens holds up the same ideal of quiet Christian witness:

> Remember!—It is Christianity TO DO GOOD, always—even to those who do evil to us. It is Christianity to love our neighbours as ourself, and to do to all men as we would have them do to us. It is Christianity to be gentle, merciful, and forgiving, and to keep those qualities quiet in our hearts, and never make a boast of them, or of our prayers or of our love of God, but always to do right in everything. If we do this, and remember the life and lessons of Our Lord Jesus Christ, and try to act up to them, we may confidently hope that God will forgive us our sins and mistakes, and enable us to live and die in peace. (134)

*And never make boast.* Love of God free from clamor of self remains the Dickens ideal from *Pickwick* to *Drood.* Bravura performances in the Dickens theatre—Pecksniff and zany Sarah Gamp soliloquies; boastful Pardiggle, Turveydrop, or Bounderby recitatives before the footlights—betray deformity of mind and heart. True religious sentiment avoids display. Mourning Dora, David Copperfield says: 'I have remembered Who wept for a parting between the living and the dead. I have bethought me of all that gracious and compassionate history' (766). In the subdued poetry of the lines, a shadowy Christ ('Who') is the more sublime; nor is there less divine *grace* in 'gracious,' a pun, for its keeping small. To interpret such habitual quietude of utterance as a sign of how *little* Dickens felt on the subject is to misunderstand all. Far from reductive, smallness in Dickens—of a *little* Nell, *little* Dick, *Tiny* Tim, a meek little Mr. Chillip, a *Minor* Canon like Mr. Crisparkle, a *little* Dorrit, et al.—holds spiritual worlds and otherworlds in reserve, the poor in spirit in their humility rebuking swollen human pride and 'Self—grasping, eager, narrow-ranging, overreaching self' (MC,796). Such as these cannot see, in little Paul Dombey's ecstatic words of vision, 'farther away—farther away!' In Dickens, only the underreacher truly kneels to the ideal of a selfless Christ Who came not full of self, but of the Father.

The muted NT reference, set in the shade of a parenthesis, is a favorite Dickens veiling device. It avoids symbolic glare, like some Nell or Dorrit softly slipping by. We slowly grasp that, in Dickens, things not of least but of great—greatest—moment shy away from a too direct regard, their very lightness of footfall and quickness to vanish signs of heavenly origin. By contrast with Uriah Heep Humility, true humility whispers. In *The Chimes,* for instance, Dickens plays down a NT allusion in his typical way, though it is clearly the Star the narrative mind steers by:

> She mingled with an abject crowd, who tarried in the snow, until it pleased
> some officer appointed to dispense the public charity (the lawful charity; not
> that once preached upon a Mount), to call them in, and question them, and
> say to this one, "Go to such a place," to that one, "Come next week;" to
> make a football of another wretch, and pass him here and there, from hand to
> hand, from house to house, until he wearied and lay down to die....(148)

The key to value—'the lawful charity; not *that once preached upon a
Mount'*—shines in that sudden blaze of parenthesis, which, like an allegory in small, begins in old Law times ('the lawful charity') and ends aloft
in New ('upon a Mount.') Its sentinel meaning is clear. Only in a Christendom grown deaf to the Sermon on the Mount could the Law, the
stinting, strictly to-the-letter dole or lawful charity (the ironic clash of
*lawful* and *charity,* a contradiction in terms, strong) reduce, beggar, and
finally kill the very poor to whom Christ ministered with such special love.
Here Dickens's own words confirm Pickering's impression that Dickens
subscribed to 'a moral code of Christian action based on the New
Testament in general *and the Sermon on the Mount in particular*' (PD,439).

Always Dickens insists that Christ's was no merely lawful relation to
men, nor should men bear a merely contractual relation to one another.
If two Murdstones as pitiless as the two stone tablets of Law graved in
stone suffer not little children to come unto them, but make them suffer; if
Yarmouth casts out the fallen woman, Martha Endell; if in many works the
Law towers remote and pitiless above an abject mankind, as in B.C.,
Dickens will recall that Christ walking the earth taught a better way. In
*The Chimes* the fantasy scene of a reunion between Margaret and Lilian, a
fallen woman, makes this clear:

> 'Forgive me, Meg! So dear, so dear! Forgive me! I know you do, I see you
> do, but say so, Meg!'
>     She said so, with her lips on Lilian's cheek. And with her arms twined
> round—she knew it now—a broken heart.
>     'His blessing on you, dearest love. Kiss me once more! He suffered her
> to sit beside his feet, and dry them with her hair. O Meg, what Mercy and
> Compassion!'
>     As she died, the Spirit of the child returning, omniscient and radiant,
> touched the old man with its hand, and beckoned him away. (CB,137)

In Dickens, Law in its icy incursions into the administration of Christian
charity negates it; beyond Law, such a passage recalls, is Christ's fulfillment of it in Mercy and Compassion. Christ's mercy is again the theme in
this stanza of the 'Child's Hymn':

> My sins are heavy, but thy mercy
>     Far outweighs them every one;
> Down before thy Cross I cast them,

> Trusting in thy help alone. (PPM,114)

So in 'Frauds on the Fairies,' an essay written in praise of faerie, or the beneficent invisible in the Creation, Dickens states: 'It would be hard to estimate the amount of gentleness and mercy that has made its way among us through these slight channels' (PPM,488).

Dickens invariably stands all serious moral argument on Christian ground. In 'Capital Punishment' he states:

> It is enough for me to be satisfied, on calm inquiry and with reason, that an Institution or Custom is wrong or bad; and thence to be assured that IT CAN-NOT BE a part of the law laid down by the Divinity who walked the earth. Though every other man who wields a pen should turn himself into a commentator on the Scriptures—not all their united lives, could ever persuade me that Slavery is a Christian law; nor, with one of these objections to an execution; in my certain knowledge that Executions are not a Christian law, my will is not concerned. I could not, in my veneration for the life and lessons of Our Lord, believe it. If any text appeared to justify the claim, I would reject that limited appeal and rest upon the character of the Redeemer, and the great scheme of His religion, where, in its broad spirit made so plain—and not in this or that disputed letter—we all put our trust. (PPM,488)

O, the letter of the Law: the 'post-office' (GE,198) mouth of Wemmick, functionary of Law in *Great Expectations,* a slot for (pun) the 'letter.' Far above the mighty Lawyer, servant of Mosaic Law, is the spirit reborn in the mercy and compassion of Christ that leaves all dry legalism of Old ways of knowing and serving the Deity behind. Again in 'A Nightly Scene in London,' it is as a Christian that Dickens refutes the voices of Malthusian determinism which call wasting poverty inevitable, stating:

> I know that the unreasonable disciples of a reasonable school, demented disciples who push arithmetic and political economy beyond all bounds of sense (not to speak of such a weakness as humanity), and hold them to be all-sufficient for every case, can easily prove that such things ought to be, and that no man has any business to mind them. Without disparaging those indispensable sciences in their sanity, I utterly renounce and abominate them in their insanity; and I address people with a respect for the spirit of the New Testament, who do mind such things, and who think them infamous in our streets. (PPM,488)

Everything ought *not* to be. And in Dickens the season for reconsideration of our lives arrives, 'the great forgiving Christmas time' (SL,203), when, Heaven leaving no stone or Ebenezer unturned, Scrooge and all are given one chance more, or Three.

Explicit and implicit (allegorical) Christian meaning combine in texts. In *Dombey,* after little Paul dies and the world of those who loved him

plunges into darkness, divine intercession alone recovers a distraught
Florence Dombey.  Noting her grief, Dickens states:

> But it is not in the nature of pure love to burn so fiercely and unkindly long.
> The flame that in its grosser composition has the taint of earth may prey upon
> the breast that gives it shelter; but the sacred fire from heaven is as gentle in
> the heart, as when it rested on the heads of the assembled twelve, and showed
> each man his brother, brightened and unhurt. (246)

Using low-case letters, in 'the assembled twelve' avoiding the sonority
that, say, 'the twelve Disciples' would have, Dickens sets the miracle of
Pentecost in place, foretelling the return to a dark world of *anno Domini*.
How such moments work into the allegory of *Dombey and Son* will be seen
in Chapter III.

The Christian Dickens dominates the essay 'The Shipwreck' in *The
Uncommercial Traveller,* telling of an obscure Welsh clergyman who
without warning finds himself charged with giving Christian burial to
scores of victims of shipwreck on a nearby coast.  Hearing of him, Dickens
recalls thinking:  'In the Christmas season of the year, I should like to see
that man!' (UT,6)  Setting out for Wales, Dickens is rather like the narrator
in his own *The Seven Poor Travellers,* one who toasts: "CHRISTMAS,
CHRISTMAS-EVE, my friends, when the shepherds, who were Poor
Travellers too, in their way, heard the Angels sing, 'On earth, peace.
Good-will towards men!'" (CS,77)  What the latest 'poor traveller' finds in
Wales does not disappoint a pilgrim of the holy Season:

> So cheerful of spirit and guiltless of affectation, as true practical Christi-
> anity ever is!  I read more of the New Testament in the fresh frank face going
> up the village beside me, in five minutes, than I have ever read in anathema-
> tising discourse (albeit put to press with enormous flourishing of trumpets),
> in all my life.  I heard more of the Sacred Book in the cordial voice that had
> nothing to say about the owner, than in all the would-be celestial pairs of
> bellows that have ever blown conceit at me. (UT, 6)

Allegory too, we note, transmits 'the Sacred Book' in a voice 'that ha[s]
nothing to say about the owner.'  So strong a burst of Christian emotion
again records that behind the public is the unpublic Dickens; behind the
commercial, the Uncommercial Traveller going about his Father's
business.  Knowing well what he is up to in Chapter X of *Drood* and everywhere else, Dickens keeps his peace, saying with Mr. Crisparkle: 'I don't
preach any more than I can help, and will not repay your confidence with a
sermon' (MD,63).  He celebrates the unsung Welshman in his tiny hamlet
off the beaten paths of world and fame because his ministry does not
declaim, it embodies the word.  In such a good and faithful servant the
hope of Christianity lies.  Dickens continues his tribute:

> In this noble modesty, in this beautiful simplicity, in this serene avoidance of
> the least attempt to "improve" an occasion which might be supposed to have
> sunk of its own weight into my heart, I seemed to have come happily, in a
> few steps, from the churchyard with its open grave, which was the type of
> Death, to the Christian dwelling side by side with it, which was the type of
> Resurrection. I shall never think of the former without the latter. (UT,10)

'The type of Death,' 'the type of Resurrection.' The Dickens mode of perception is ever Christian and emblematic, the smallest speck in the
Creation pretext to the discovery in Nature and history of the symbolic
tracery of Christian truth. With his Welsh hero Dickens walks 'up the
village,' *up* in this praiseful context a tiny added grace note pointing to the
raising power in the true man of God.

Then he fades, as dwelling and churchyard do. The Dickens + -ray
vision sees beyond Death to Immortality. As Dickens gazes, the eternal
lineaments waiting beneath ephemeral form, Lazarus-like, come forth;
transfiguring insight discloses the immaterial base of material reality. In a
'few steps,' as the soul journeys, one passes from the grim terms of the Old
dispensation, Death, to the hope found only in the New, Resurrection.

Because man is not, like the mysterious traveller in *Mugby Junction*,
'the gentleman for Nowhere' (CS,491), but for Heaven, how he is guided to
truth and led to discern 'the beneficent design of Heaven' (CB,379) and
'the appointed order of the Creator' (TTC,353), matters intensely. Hence
Dickens's great concern about the quality of all guardians of the public
trust: lawmakers, preachers, teachers, masters of the workhouse,
hospital, prison, officers of the lawful charity, et al. Among Dickens's
worst villains are betrayers of this trust, teachers like Pecksniff (*Chuzzlewit*) who mislead and dishearten young men starting out; and Mr.
Murdstone (*Copperfield*) or Headstone (*Our Mutual Friend*), destructive
guardians of the young. Following them, man and child hear no voices
impelling them upwards and so are lost to the greatest of man's Expectations, Heaven. If such partisans of the Old (OT) order, imaging *its* stern
Father in Heaven, were to be replaced by men of the New, then, in
Dickens's words, 'many low roofs would point more truly to the sky, than
the loftiest steeple that now rears proudly up in the midst of guilt, and
crime, and horrible disease, to mock them by its contrast' (OCS,282).
There is nothing lofty about steeple or Church that, serpent-like, Satan-
like, 'rears up' so, in disdaining 'low roofs' and lives mocking the great
charge laid upon it by Christ.

Closing his tribute to the Welsh clergyman, Dickens voices the doubt
that 'Convocations, Conferences, Diocesan Epistles, and the like...will
ever do their Master's service half so well...as the Heavens have seen it
done in this bleak spot upon the rugged coast of Wales' (UT,16). Note: as
was noted in Chapter I, it is not what men see, but what the Heavens see

done, as the swift seasons roll.

Our point is the always *religious* coloration of Dickensian art.  For example, satire on the high priests and scribes of the day, banker, bishop, baronet, beadle, mighty lawyer at the bar, Lords of the state preserves of loaves and fishes who hold the keys to the lower kingdom, and in hoarding its riches destroy for the multitudes all hope of 'on earth as it is in Heaven.' Mankind is misled by the diabolical Jingle (*Pickwick*), as by 'the incessant jingle of little worldly things' (LD, 546).  Rebuking pharisaical lawmakers in Parliament, dour sabbatarians bent on turning the seventh day into a day of gloom, Dickens's model, once more, is the example of Christ.  'The Sunday Screw' closes with the words:

> Lord Ashley had better merge his Pariahs into the body politic; and the Honourable Member for Whitened Sepulchres had better accustom his jaundiced eyes to the Sunday sight of dwellers in towns, roaming in green fields, and gazing upon country prospects.  If he will look a little beyond them, and lift up the eyes of his mind, perhaps he may observe a mild, majestic figure in the distance, going through a field of corn, attended by some common men who pluck the grain as they pass along, and whom their Divine Master teaches that he is the Lord, even of the Sabbath-Day. (OL,236)

Again in the essay 'Sunday Under Three Heads,' Dickens sets Christ above the Law, saying:

> Let divines set the example of true morality; preach it to their flocks in the morning, and dismiss them to enjoy true rest in the afternoon; and let them select for their text, and let Sunday legislators take for their motto, the words which fell from the lips of the Master, whose precepts they misconstrue, and whose lessons they pervert—"The Sabbath was made for man, and not man to serve the Sabbath." (RP,663)

And again, in *Chuzzlewit*, Dickens in Christian accents sternly calls modern lawmakers to account:

> And, oh! ye Pharisees of the nineteen-hundredth year of Christian Knowledge, who soundingly appeal to human nature, see first that it be human. Take heed it has not been transformed, during your slumber and the sleep of generations, into the nature of the beasts.

To sum up, Dickens's Christian faith is the bedrock of story and allegory. His allegorical labors, thus far merely glimpsed in *Copperfield,* are labors of love of Christ.  Why did Dickens bother?  The answer would seem to be, to glorify 'the life and lessons of Our Saviour;' to retell The Life of Our Lord in a way free from all clamor of self.  To a Christendom that has lost hold of the mantle of Christ, Dickens shows forth a God, not of jealousy and wrath, but of mercy and salvation, refuting the wasting unchristian class mentality of England in the pure, bell-like tones of a little child: 'God bless Us, *Every One!* ' (Italics mine.)

His parables tell how the House of David still puts forth spiritually gifted sons of David, and how Paul's missionary journeys and Stephen's martyr-dom have not ended in a world not yet won for Christ. (See Chapter III.) In the story of the return of John Harmon from the 'dead,' *Our Mutual Friend,* a nodding Noddy, or Nicodemus, finally wakes up and asks the right questions, as did another Nicodemus in another Book of *John.* In Dickens, the enormous spiritual energies that first made human history purposeful and set man's soul on a course straight for Heaven still exist and work for man's salvation, inspiring him to believe in and await the Kingdom of Heaven.

But as the proof of even the most exalted pudding is still in the eating, we briefly turn from the study of *David Copperfield* to survey the range of allegory in a goodly number of popular Dickens works.

# THREE

# An Overview of
# Allegory in Dickens

'Ah!' said my aunt, rubbing her nose as if she were a little vexed. 'That's
his allegorical way of expressing it. . . .' (DC, 205)

At moments any Dickens reader will recognize that he has left the realms of
realism behind and entered a *Pilgrim's Progress*-like world of giant
symbols. As early as *The Pickwick Papers* many a 'Samuel Slumkey,'
'Count Smorltork,' and 'Bob Sawyer' thrusts symbolic interest blatant or
subtle upon us: *Slumkey,* KEY to the SLUM; Smorltork, SMALL TALK.
Bob Sawyer, whose sign reads 'Sawyer, late Nockemorf' (532), exhibits a
Dickens both nimble and highly serious at such play. In medical student
'Sawyer' the 'Sawbones' (406), as Sam Weller irreverently calls him, 'Saw'
proves a swipe at the breed whose indifference to life and limb of patients,
to *Sawyer* & Co. mere machines for 'saw off' operations and fat fees, is
tantamount to a policy of 'Nockemorf': *Knock 'Em Off.* Thus 'Sawyer,
late Nockemorf' (many besides old Nockemorf will be 'late' before Sawyer
is through, we fear) chides a flourishing *Nockemorf* trade and veils a serio-
comic moral treatise in minature.

Dickens constantly, and seemingly effortlessly, invents in this vein. In
*Nicholas Nickleby,* to cite a famous example, Squeers, vicious master of the
infamous *Dotheboys* Hall, lives to 'Do the boys,' i.e., Do them in, DO for
'em, so to speak, *nockemorf,* in the spirit of Jonas Chuzzlewit's rule for
bargains: 'Do other men, for they would do you' (MC,181), an open sneer
at the Golden Rule. Once 'Do-the-boys' is seen, 'Doth-boys' or other unmeaning pronunciation is gone for good.

Everywhere Dickens hints broadly to catch the eye. Sallies of light puns
in *Pickwick* and all works prompt a looking alive to double meaning, as in
Sam Weller's snappy: 'Don't call me Valker; my name's Veller; you know
that vell enough' (318); or in 'Your worship' become 'Your wash-up' (347).
Such sport might seem idle if it were not clear that even miniscule puns
often take careful aim. For example, in a town where villains 'hocus the
brandy' (166) to fuddle rival party voters, Sam Weller terms a dire
coincidence—two coaches overturning at the same spot—'hex-traordinary'
(168), the screaming *hex* pun reinforcing *hocus*. Amid such signs that the

Devil is at large in Eatanswill, Pickwick himself, but newly arrived, swells the mindless election cry, 'Slumkey forever!' and to his friend Tupman's puzzled query returns: 'Hush. Don't ask any questions. It's always best on these occasions to do what the mob do.' And if there are two mobs? 'Shout with the largest' (159), our hero replies. Recalling the scene of a loutish mob of boys led by Steerforth reviling and persecuting the good Master (*David Copperfield*), or of savage mobs storming the Bastille and hooting for Carton's death (*A Tale of Two Cities*), one knows very well Dickens's own view of the dark motto: 'do what the mob do.'

In a curious way 'Sam' and 'hex' touch again in a work of four years after, *Master Humphrey's Clock,* as Sam Weller revives an ancient title 'nearly hex-tinct' (6). A trifle, perhaps only a verbal twitch. Yet how many patterned oddities of the kind recur. And in *Pickwick,* note the hex-ceptional quantity of *Samuel* always on tap: Samuel Pickwick, Sam Weller, Samuel Slumkey, and Samkin and Green: *Samkin,* or *kin* of *Sam*(uel) galore. *Pickwick Papers,* a 'Book of Samuel,' it would seem. But why?

If Bunyan comes to mind as a likely model in symbolic portraiture of the kind (the 'Giant Despair' in *Chuzzlewit* and 'Giants Slay-good and Despair' in the essay 'Ignorance and Crime' two open Dickensian tributes to Bunyan), so might Shakespeare, Fielding, and others. The Dickens who, Forster relates, plays Justice Shallow in *The Merry Wives of Windsor* and Sir Epicure Mammon in Jonson's *The Alchemist* (FD,II,364); who names a son Henry Fielding Dickens after the creator of that most symbolic-sounding personage, Squire Allworthy of Paradise Hall; who in *Copper-field* tips his hat to Smollett's Roderick Random, and in an 'In Memoriam' lauds Thackeray from whose pen symbolic worlds of 'Sharp,' 'Crawley,' and 'Sheepshanks' flow:-this Dickens carries forward and extends a noble English comic tradition both 'Shallow' and Deep, 'Random' and Purposed, of 'Mammon' and God, half way and more to allegory: of easeful moral-istic genius that instructs the better in avoiding too serious an air.

Signposts to allegory in Dickens stand high and are writ in letters so bold that he who runs may read. Typical ones are *McChoakumchild* (HT), child's spirit-'choaker,' and that other child-queller, Pip's nemesis, *Pum-blechook* (GE): more *chook*-choke, also Uriah Heep-ish '(P)*umble*' fawn-ing fraud there too, one suspects. In *Copperfield* and *Our Mutual Friend* the Messrs. Murdstone and Headstone are grave and 'headstone' to mark the *Murd*-er or unnatural, untimely decease of wonder, reflection, and hope in young minds entrusted to their care. We *know* that MURDstone is fully intentional when Betsey Trotwood puns Murdstone into 'Murderer' (197), capital 'M' and all.

Note: such drear guardians of youth in Dickens are not weighed and found wanting only by general ethical, humane standards, *but first and foremost by Christian ones.* Mr. Murdstone deeply distrusts children, '(though there *was* a child once set in the midst of the Disciples)' (55),

David quietly adds.  (One does well to keep an eye on Dickensian paren-
theses.)  Murdstone regards children as 'a swarm of little vipers' (55), or
spawn of Satan, a further outrage to Christ's teaching.  Then late in the
story Mr. Chillip, David's old friend, delivers himself of words the more
memorable for his customary timidity and forbearance:

> 'And do you know I must say, sir,' he continued, mildly laying his head on
> one side, 'that I *don't* find authority for Mr. and Miss Murdstone in the New
> Testament?'
>    'I never found it either!' said I. (834)

Equally unauthorized, in Dickens's view, is schoolmaster Headstone's use
of the New Testament for reading drills, which effectually kills all sense of
it as 'the sublime history' (OMF,215) in pupils stumbling over syllables in
turn.  Set thus firmly in an anti-Christ context, the two are being indicted
not only for a general 'stony' hardness of heart; but as potential slayers of
the fledgling spirit, in cutting charges off from knowledge of a benign
Father in Heaven and of the Resurrection and the Life—while gloomily professing religion, yet mocking the every meaning of the word—they seem
allied to the stone (Murd*stone*, Head*stone*) used to stone sinners and
saintly Stephens under Old Law, the Law graved in *stone;* also, perhaps, to
the stone set before the sepulchre that seals the soul, as it once sealed
Him, in the tomb.

Dickens presses *stone.*  Another schoolmaster, Mr. Gradgrind of *Hard
Times, grad*ually *grind*s childish fancy, curiosity about wonders seen and
unseen, and sympathy outflowing towards all Creation—which ways faith,
hope, and charity lie, and, implied in all expectant seeking, God—on the
remorseless grindstone of fact, rule, law.  The grindstone in the courtyard
of La Force prison in *A Tale of Two Cities* which sharpens bloody weapons
does not turn to more cruel ends.  Confining young minds in 'the letter'—
in 'Quadruped.  Gramnivorous' (HT,5) when every circus-spun leap of
little Sissy Jupe's heart says 'horse'—Gradgrindism not only dims present
prospects but grinds eternal ones, the immortal spirit itself, to dust.  No
riding old *Quadruped.  Gramnivorous* (note:  dead halt between) to Canterbury.

New Testament allusions such as 'child in the midst of the Disciples'
create a Christian force-field the length and breadth of Dickens.  Similarly,
where narrow legalism and lack of charity dominate, an allegorical B.C.
thrives too.  For example, in the *Pickwick* episode of hex-hocus, mob rule,
and Slumkey dirty election tricks cited before, the appearance of a Mr. and
Mrs. Leo Hunter of 'the Den.  Eatanswill' (193), a lions' ('Leo') Den
complete with starving human 'lions' (201) in which 'Hunter' and hunted
go their savage, élite-society ways, further indicates that the *eat-and-swill*
trough of Eatanswill and the ancient Babylons and Romes with their lions'
dens and Colosseums in which the faithful perished, are one.  Call it

Christendom, but Eatanswill unmasked is one more infernal realm of treachery, ill will towards men, and violence ruled by (the pun at the allegorical heart of all) (S)*eatan's will:* Satan's will. 'Do as the mob do'? A mob not unlike attended the crucifixion.

Indeed, ancient Hebrew time casts a long shadow over present *Pickwick* time. Behold a weepy Job Trotter (the woes of *Job* wear on); and an impassive gentleman sporting 'Mosaic studs' (277), the oft-cited 'Mosaic jewellery' (277) and 'Mosaic decorations' (283), capital 'M' each time, fairly shouting a likeness to the original 'Mosaic' gentleman, Moses. When Samuel Pickwick is called 'Moses Pickwick' (493), the motif trills again. Boldly piling pun atop pun, Mosaic *jew*ellery to boot, Dickens in artful comedic style throws a handful of 'Hebrew' glitter to the wind, then flashes off to fresh pointillist/allegorical feats of derring-do.

Wherever one looks, the Dickens world of Mr. *Mould* the undertaker, Mr. *Gallanbile, Hex*am and Mag*witch, Fang* and *Wolf, Feenix* (Phoenix) et al., is clamorously symbolic; and like the voices in waves, bells, gongs, or white arms 'beckoning in the moonlight, to the invisible country far away' (587) in *Dombey and Son,* points afar. Always it points by Christian lights. To wit., late in *Great Expectations* as Pip, Herbert Pocket and Provis make for the open sea and, they hope, freedom for Pip's convict, their little boat, passing other river craft, moves momentarily 'under the figure-head of the John of Sunderland making a speech to the winds (as is done by many Johns)' (414). The image of John the Baptist crying in the wilderness is unmistakable. Though in the shade of a parenthesis, veiled like 'child among the Disciples' in *Copperfield,* it is somehow not less visible, but more.

Note: it is not 'the *John* of Sunderland,' but the John. Thus unbound by punctuation, John is all the more free for double duty as ship *and* ghost of Baptist too; also, in that line, to play forerunner or John to the 'many Johns' coming after. A small touch, but like many of the kind in Dickens, greatly significant.

But why invoke John the Baptist at all? In Chapters IV and V which follow, we show that even so minute a Scriptural motif, bobbing only briefly in the swift-running waters of the novel and soon swept by, urges recognition of divine meaning in the fateful journey of Abel from a starting point at the 'Temple stairs' (412) to a new life; as Judaeo-Christian man from earliest Hebrew ('Abel,' 'Temple') to Christian ('John'-signalled) time; and more widely still, of the whole of *Great Expectations* as religious parable.

The 'John' moment is long in the making. Some time before, Pip and Herbert visit the Pocket home in Hammersmith where, in a garden, Mrs. Pocket sits in state amid servants and children and gazes absently about while her offspring endlessly trip, tip, and tumble at her feet. She herself constitutes no small danger to them; straying near, they promptly stumble

over a footstool concealed beneath her skirts.  Scissors, nutcrackers, and
knives also menace the hapless, harmed and self-harming children, the 'six
little Pockets present, in various stages of tumbling up,' and 'a seventh...
heard, as in the region of air, wailing dolefully' (176).  Six plus the aerial
one makes seven, as 'seventh' firmly hammers home.

*Seven* has stronger play still.  When Mrs. Pocket drops her pocket handkerchief, Flopson the nurse speaks up:

> 'Well!' she cried, picking up the pocket handkerchief, 'if that don't make
> seven times!  What ARE you a-doing of this afternoon, Mum!' (176)

What doing?  Why, rehearsing the Fall in the Garden, of course.  *Seven*
little *Pockets* fall, Fall; a *pocket* handkerchief falls (odd to note it!) *seven*
times.  Strange symmetry, if for nothing.  But no, decidedly for something.
Seven, holy cypher of the Creation, the sabbath, and myriad Old and New
Testament mystery, falls.  The unhappy 'children' of Israel of our time,
tended (hardly:  though policed, neglected) to their harm and as deep in
'lamentation' (177) as any ancient Hebrew in *Lamentations,* Fall on; and
Matthew Pocket, their father, can only look on in deep distress of spirit and
tear his hair.  Correction:  try vainly several times to 'lift himself by the
hair' (182).

Now upon the scene, shifted indoors, comes the Pockets' 'toady
neighbour' (180), a Mrs. Coiler.  Pouring suave flattery into Mrs. Pocket's
inclined ear, Mrs. Coiler, Coiling round her victim, plays the Serpent of
Eden in no indifferent way.  Beyond 'toady' to get her down in the dust,
there is her marked 'serpentine way of coming close' and feigned interest
in him which Pip finds (who dares accuse Dickens of concealment?)
'altogether snaky and fork-tongued' (181).  To hear Mrs. Coiler, one would
think there was nothing so divinely ordained to command universal
worship as high station:  ancient name, noble origin, blood.  And so the
mother of seven falling children in a garden, a dewy-eyed seven fresh as in
the Creation, proves as sadly permeable to the word of Satan, the original
'Coiler,' as ever Eve, the mother of all and of Adam's Fall.

The Fall in modern dress.  Not quite *the* Fall, perhaps, what with the
woman so far gone in vanity even before the intruder arrives; but even so.
We marvel at the boldness and finesse of an art which spins the serious and
farcical together so smoothly on one loom.  Detail especially delights.  Lo,
*Flopson,* who retrieves falling objects seven times, surely named for her
part in the great ongoing 'Flop,' or Fall.  Funny as this is, Dickens in no
way intends her ineffectual care of 'the children,'—Christendom's
woefully inadequate stewardship of mankind's spiritual destiny temporal
and eternal—as a joke.  Far from it.  Christ's coming cancels the moral law
of gravity operant after the Fall.  Nor is this B.C., with no help for it, but
A.D.  Yet, Dickens shows, Christians everywhere, as if the hapless,

unchampioned Hebrews of old, Fall on.  Child-rearing is a perilous 'tumbling up' (175), *up* itself made an ironic adjunct to *down*.

Here is the point Dickens is always making in non-symbolic ways too: that in its neglect, abuse, murdstoning punishment or (same thing) super-vision under law of orphan, convict, factory hand, debtor, inmate of work-house or treadmill, Dotheboy'd child, modern English Christian society, though rife with preachers, churches, Chief Composite Committees of Philanthropy (*Drood*), shibboleths of spiritual progress, and the lawful charity, that model of service only in 'the letter,' is in fact not Christian at all.

It soon becomes clear that Dickens founds moral sentiment of the kind on the rock of religious authority, showing social idealism and the will for reform to be not only the highest wisdom of man, but also, and first, of God.  One beauty of Dickensian doctrine is that it is not preached.  For while conventional moralising exhorts, as Dickens on rare occasions will, implicit or allegorical quietly releases meaning.  Further, allegory intensi-fies, extends, raises the unique but limited (because temporal, transient) drama of human lives to new poetic heights in unveiling its relevance to the abiding and eternal.  In Dickens, the original saving force in Biblical truth is never spent.  How Timeless the timeless pages of Dickens are, how Hopeful tales of seasons of Darkness turned to Light, we have only begun to dream.

A sense of authorial purpose grows as the 'Fall' scene in *Great Expecta-tions* proves no lone mythic divertissement but part of a larger design. Flopson and Millers, two nurses, tend the Pocket children.  'MILLERS' also signifies.  Soon after her arrival in the story, Jaggers the lawyer reappears, the cold, impersonal steward of the fate of multitudes doomed under Law, who, like Pontius Pilate, ritualistically washes his hands (if one could!) of the deadly work of the law:  Jaggers, 'defending' felons in a defense not so much a championing of the accused as a dire 'grinding the whole place in a mill' (191).  Grinding: shades of Grad*grind*.  Law in 'mill' and 'Millers,' one of two 'non-commissioned officers' (182) policing the young and symbol of the law which grinds the fallen in the inexorable mills of the Law—between the two stone tablets of Mosaic Law, as it were, as Israel was perpetually ground in ancient mills of its God, mills like Babylon—this is hardly what is needed, hardly the cure.  Rather, the distressful situation calls for Christ's own compassion for sinners, the for-giveness full and free that raised up the fallen with the words, 'Go, and sin no more.'

What law is it in *Great Expectations* before which terrified droves of the accused cringe, and which Pilate's guilt still haunts?  The old Hebraeo-Roman Law that condemns Christ again in every *Abel* Magwitch, archtypal slain innocent and OT type of Christ, undone by Law.  At one point Jaggers, the blank, pitiless face of Old Law itself, is pursued in the street by a desperate client, a Jew who begs his favor in the name of a kinsman, 'Habraham Latharuth' (158), or Abraham Lazarus.  Wholly unmoved by mention of a name obviously sacred to the Jew (his speech defect scattering 'H' and 'h,' as for *H*ebrew, and coaxing a hidden 'ruth' out of '*Latharuth,*' Naomi's Ruth as well as rue, perhaps), Jaggers in effect rejects Abraham Lazarus.  Was Dickens thinking of the NT parable of Dives, Abraham and Lazarus, recounted in full in his child's Life of Christ, *The Life of Our Lord?*  Certainly the Jew thus cast off and left 'dancing on the pavement as if it were red-hot' (158) sounds like the one in the parable who pleads and parches in Hell's flames.  One thing is sure.  Dickens's Law v. Jew episode dramatizes that in A.D. the Law still comes down on sinners without mercy, as if, in Dickens's words, the Saviour had never walked the earth teaching a better way.

Returning to the garden, the figure at the center of the Fall is Belinda Pocket.  BELINDA!  Now we better understand that impassivity and statuary calm in frantic midsts of Fall.  There exists in a woman of modern times the BEL-inda taint as old as BEL, heathen deity of Babylon:  BEL of 'Bel and the Dragon' in the *Apocrypha;* of Belshazzar.  Her footstool gives her away.  Yahweh promises Israel to 'make thine enemies thy footstool' (*Mark* 12:36); He claims earth as His footstool (*Matt.* 5:35).  We *know* Dickens is mindful of the Biblical symbolism when in *Little Dorrit* the figure who welcomes suffering ages as 'the just dispensation of Jehovah' and is served by a fierce Jeremiah speaks in OT idiom of 'my enemy that became my footstool' (LD,776).  In Dickens, 'the children' trip over the footstool concealed beneath Belinda's skirts as once Israel over the Assyro-Babylonian Empire, a perpetual stumbling block with its lure of forbidden idols.

Now as then BEL usurps the central place, displacing the one God.  Her worship of her ancient glory is idolatry; like an Idol she is enthroned in the children's midst.  Whipped on by the 'Coiler,' Satan, Belinda Pocket exults in her ancestry and apartness from the herd, 'election' ever Dickens's *eatanswill-Satan's will* theme of themes.  One recalls how the passion to make a lady and a gentleman is long the undoing of Estella and Pip in another part of the garden.

Wherever social snobbery rules in Dickens, we are swiftly back in a condition of Fall, and B.C. glares.  In *Our Mutual Friend,* a Chosen Few soiree featuring the ancient relict named Lady Tippins ('TIP-pins,' like Flopson, for Fall[1]) and a Mr. Akershem (*shem* like a speck of the age of the sons of Noah) shows that in Podsnap-Veneering England A.D., the moral leftovers of B.C. are all too many.  In the ruined garden a *Podsnap, snap*(ped) *pod,* is all that grows.  Christian civilization is mere *Veneering,* the spiritual reality beneath, Dickens shows, rooted in concepts predating the Christian by far.  For Dickens, any nation basking in outworn myths of racial superiority (shades of the Chosen People myth), Mr. Podsnap's withering, imperious 'Not English!' sweeping all peoples else into outer darkness; a nation maintaining a rigid hierarchic class structure that consigns the masses, like the Jews the gentiles of old, to ignorance, oblivion, death, builds not the new but the old Jerusalem in England's green and pleasant land.

Woe unto the idolaters of Belinda Pocket, so smooth, plausible, fair-seeming, so mined with disaster below. And woe to you, ye lawyers! Oblivious of the ruin around her, leaving governance to Flopson and Millers, Fall and Law, *Belinda* is the self-absorbed Idol of class privilege anciently/modernly lord-and-ladying it in the Garden, an otherwise Eden: is self-infatuated aristocracy in its fatal innocence and detachment, its hollow pretention to rights of unending rule and exemption from knowledge of conditions of life for the masses going to rack and ruin around it, that must bring all England Falling down in the end.

Poor *seven* in the garden, and, high in a 'region of air' striding the blast, as if the immaterial essence of *seven* itself in the empyrean, the weeping babe. NOW the John the Baptist image coming after makes clearer sense. A world still in the grip of idolatry and Fall, and, Law and Pilate looming, still unfound to Christ despite the passing of nineteen hundred Christian centuries, cries out for a John to (re)appear and in the time-honored way help prepare the way of the Lord, a labor for each generation to accomplish anew, in renewed faith that 'The Kingdom of God is at hand.'

In Dickens, though, Christian hope springs Eternal. Happily, the children of Belinda are also the children of Matthew, the same one driven from Satis House for daring bid Miss Havisham open her tomb-like house and nighted soul to Heaven's light, sunlight in Dickens a symbol of the healing powers of forgiveness won through the Son. Conciliatory voice of *Matthew* piercing the ancient retributive darkness! Though long unheeded, and though not even the best of mortal men can lift themselves by the hair, i.e., rise without a Saviour, reverse the effects of Fall on their own, still Matthew Pocket, becoming Pip's tutor, *is* heard in the fullness of time; and the long dying of Abel, an ancient death whose meaning is not fully revealed until NT time, ends. In Dickensian allegory *John* and *Matthew*, spiritual heirs of the Baptist and the Evangelist who writes the first Gospel of the NT, again pioneer the advent of Christian time.

*John* lives! As dry, wooden, unfeeling Wemmick he serves Jaggers and Law. But in his *John,* or profoundly Christian Christian-name life, he aids Pip's efforts to save Provis, Providential agent through whom Pip, like Sydney Carton after meeting Lucie Manette, reawakens to a morally purposeful life. (In *David Copperfield* we learn that the word 'wimmick,' in Dan'l Peggotty's explanation, is 'our old county word for crying' (731). Maybe *wemmick,* which looks so much like it, is the name Dickens invents for someone seemingly incapable of feeling, tears, compassionate concern: an ironic name. Or, like *Twist* or *Pinch,* it looks to sad OT time.)

Stage Three of Pip's Expectations, *three* in Christ, arrives. Then one fine day John Wemmick takes up a fishing-rod, puts it over his shoulder, and, smiling, heads for a wedding. Pip is wholly baffled:

> 'Why, we are not going fishing,' said I. 'No,' returned Wemmick, 'but I like to walk with one.' (429)

Eh?? The wedding takes place, the groom's father, the dear old Aged P., having been wrestled into his gloves by Pip and his son, 'most amiably beaming at the ten commandments' (430) the while. The ceremony ends. Before leaving the church, John 'took the cover off the font, and put his white gloves in it, and put the cover on again' (431). Curiouser and curiouser. All ends as it began:

> 'Now, Mr. Pip,' said Wemmick, triumphantly shouldering his fishing-rod as we came out, 'let me ask you whether anybody would suppose this to be a wedding-party!' (431)

Amid such oddity and twinkling hints of more than meets the eye, John treating the 'fishing' expedition as if in one some immense secret about it, as indeed he is, we look closer.

What are fishing-rod, the Aged's mighty resistance to being gloved for the wedding, his beaming up at the commandments, and the very deliberate placing of white gloves in the baptismal font, all about? '"Twere to consider too curiously, to consider so,' some will say. Nevertheless, on the strength of seven-times-falling pocket handkerchiefs, Coilers, Flopsons et al., we respectfully press on.

Even as 'Wemmick' lightly veils 'John,' and 'font,' baptismal font, the Biblical wedding metaphor grows luminous in allegory. Before our eyes a living John, one foretold in '(as is done by many Johns),' resumes the Baptist's work symbolized in white gloves, the purifying work of hands. His filial and gardening work done, the ears of the deaf unstopped (setting off Stinger, a miniature cannon, he gets his father, like ancient Israel set in old ways and 'deaf' to New truth, to hear!), the bride brought to the Bridegroom, our John replaces his gloves in the font in sign that he relinquishes the power of baptism to One greater Who comes after. It was hard work bringing Aged P. around and winning his: 'All right, John, all right!' (283), and Heaven knows what the old Mosaic loyalist was thinking during the ceremony, gazing at the commandments. But it is done. Then John triumphantly resumes his fishing-rod, for although one great Christian role is laid aside, he remains forever a Christian disciple, a 'fisher' of men.

What other possible explanation is there for all the air of mystery, fishing-rod at a wedding, and gloves and font? Christian allegory alone holds the key.

When during the ceremony the Aged fails to hear the question 'WHO giveth?' Pip, noticing the clergyman's impatience, privately wonders 'whether we should get completely married that day' (431). In one sense 'we' is just fun, the editorial 'we,' or a bit of whimsical fraternal irony. But in another, yes, 'we,' all mankind, are implicated in what happens here as once again a John brings 'the bride,' Israel and the soul still unwed, to Christ. One imagines that ancient Israel was hardly more stiff-necked than the latest John's bride, Miss Skiffins. True, all weddings are in a general way symbolic. But this one, so pointedly signed with John, 'fishing' (one wants a *skiff* or Skiffins, a light sailing vessel, to preach and fish from), white gloves, is symbolic in vividly Christian ways. If in addition all is perfectly pleasant and natural, so much the better. In Dickens as in Scripture, what is planted a natural body is, in the joyful mystery of allegory, as of man in a Christian destiny, raised a spiritual one.

Such brisk Christian currents flow not only intermittently through Dickens but, bubbling everywhere, merge into one continuous, sparkling watercourse. All of *Great Expectations* is allegory, as can only be glimpsed here. A Pip, or tiny seedling of the spiritual life of Western man *in potentia,* its mystery unfolding in three providential stages, is first sown in a dark, wet, sunless and Son-of-God-less in the beginning time of an oft-slain Abel, a Ruined Garden, type of the lost Eden barred to man after the Fall, and harsh law. A neo-*Genesis* time, the novel's In the Beginnings affirm, with Abel no sooner seized by pitiless captors than stowed aboard 'a wicked Noah's ark' (36). The ark, OT symbol of salvation both as vessel and stone tablets of the Law, clearly saves no more. Soon trapped in the pursuit of a remorseless retributive scheme aimed against all men, the heart-for-a-heart creed of vengeance that blights the unwed bride as it does her House in which a jealous Sarah Pocket dwells—Sarah, one more exhumed spectre of *Genesis* time of mind—Pip also faces a deadly foe, Orlick, who prowls the ancient marshes 'like Cain or the Wandering Jew' (105). How Pip contracts the 'election' sickness of soul and falls into a law-shadowed pseudo-life of vain worldly expectations; how, with the return of the man of sorrows whose loyalty and suffering are so deeply interwoven with Pip's first and last impressions of the identity of things, Pip is recalled to life; and, finally, how profoundly Christian this journey of Expectations is, awaits further telling in Chapters IV and V.

Once one pattern is glimpsed, as if all texts had been dipped in a magic solution, suddenly the hidden tracery of allegory appears everywhere at once. For example, in *Oliver Twist* young Oliver is apprenticed to a Mr. Sowerberry, the undertaker. Man and calling are well matched. An undertaker is indeed a *Sowerberry,* or *sower* of the *berry,* man, the immortal seed which, in the solemn berry-bury of Christian death, grows upward to life eternal; man 'sown a natural body...raised a spiritual body' (*1 Cor.* 15:44). So it *should* be, but many a sweet young Berry Pipchin (*Dombey and Son*) and fond, clinging, tender Miss Peecher (*Our Mutual Friend*), berry and peach of the world's garden, bloom only to wither. So in the bleak, nockemorf A.D. of *Twist,* Mr. Sowerberry runs a brisk, soul-less *shovel 'em under* grave-filling business, dispatching bodies with nary a thought to immortal destinations.  Such, Dickens shows, is the 'sour bury'-Sowerberry way of the Old Mortality, the blank that death was and is Before Christ:  the dust-to-dust end in what poor Toots in *Dombey* despondently calls 'the silent tomb':  Death less the saving hope of resurrection, the residue of B.C. with us yet, lest we forget.

Again Dickens's point is a creeping spiritual retrogression that changes A.D. back into something ominously like B.C.  Laboring among Sowerberry coffins, young Oliver languishes.  In this early era of the book, not surprisingly, law looms; law dominates most early Dickensian as it did early Judaeo-Christian history.  Its servant in *Twist* is Mr. Bumble the Beadle, a dim-souled officer of the bankrupt lawful charity:  a *Bumble Bee*-dle or drone of the ruined garden, symbol of a Christendom unsown in the seed which is the word of God, the word of Christ.  How Bumble fancies his wee drop from green bottles; and *how* he buzzes around Mrs. Corney in metaphoric midsts of alien 'CORNey,' 'farming' (4) of orphans in a branch-workhouse, and the like.  Though there *was* a child set in the midst of the Disciples, Mr. Bumble names two foundling infants 'Twist' and 'Unwin,' as if to insure that the crooked shall NOT be made straight, but the straight crooked ('Twist'); and none win ('UNwin') the Kingdom of Heaven!  In like mood, Pecksniff in *Martin Chuzzlewit* with gloomy satisfaction proclaims life a journey from 'The Mothers Arms' to 'The Dust Shovel' (MC,117).

A Dickens story seems to ask, why such lingering of man in lost Edens and fatalism of death when man has but to go forth and seek the higher, the heavenly Paradise?  In Heaven's name, why such OT sowing, sower-berrying and reaping in the times of Christ?

We know beyond any doubt that Sowerberry & Co. exists in an OT-NT connection for Dickens when in Sowerberry time Oliver Twist falls victim to another apprentice, Noah Claypole:  Noah, an arrogant, mean-minded bully and all proof in one that B.C. is back in style.  Perching high on a post, then 'descending from the top of the post' (30), boorish Noah enacts his soul's chief feature:  a smug delight in looking down on supposed inferiors like Oliver, whom he calls 'Work'us,' a sneer at fancied low origins. (Noah being only a charity boy himself, his snobbery is the more farcical.) When Oliver can bear no more jeers at his dead mother and strikes back, in the ensuing melee the blubbering, cowardly Noah drenches Mrs. Sower-berry in 'a sufficiency of cold water' (42), which act, amid cries of murder, cries for help, metaphoric 'plunges' (43) against furniture, and an unavailing universal struggle to escape, leads to a 'flood of tears' (47).  Dickens cannot resist a curtain-call:  once more, on the very next line, 'flood of tears' (47).

Well!  It is *Noah* and *flood* time of *Oliver Twist* and as if of sacred history once again, it seems.  In yet another symbolic *Genesis* era in Dickens a primitive Noah manages in the good old (OT) way to stay high and dry while mankind, or a representative morsel thereof, is redelivered to the Flood.  As well a well-wrought miniature becomes the greatest ashes as half-acre tomes, or so it is in Dickens.  Noah Claypole cartoons the Chosen People mentality fixated on the principle of selective salvation, solely its own.  Despising the unelect (Oliver is actually high born, if the truth were known), Noah Claypole is all that Dickens deplores in social attitudes, and all that the new Noah, Christ, comes to change.

   *Sowerberry* and *Noah* epitomise early prospects in *Oliver Twist*.  Their triumphant return to the world stage suggests that, like Scrooge before the advent of Three Spirits, mankind has lost the forward, true way.  Suffering a Christianity of mere forms, one devoid of faith, hope, and charity as sounding brass, man reinherits 'Sowerberry' ways of life and death; or rather, *Sowerberry* inherits man:-the deep, dark, sealed pocket of the grave; the B.C. decree that, dying, man must die.  Always in Dickens, whenever one race, class, or nation arrogates to itself sole rights to the first fruits of earth or Heaven—for example, the Old Regime lords in *A Tale of Two Cities,* or the Podsnap-Veneering social set in England—there Fall, Noah, and such rear-regarding sons of Adam as *Seth* Pecksniff are, Christendom drowning in the injustice thereby done millions, as in their unheeded cries for deliverance, martyrdoms under law, and 'flood[s] of tears.'

   The *Noah Claypole* cameo of a squint-eyed B.C. again on the march is a typical Dickensian sermon in small.  Its moral: there is no way of ascent in Noah, no height in him but that of the post (ominous preview of the Cross!).  Symbolism shouts that there is no climbing a *Claypole,* a *pole* made of the mortal element itself, *clay.*  Losing touch with a living Christian faith, man sinks back down into B.C. night, cut off from what Dickens elsewhere in *Twist* calls 'the beaming of the soul through its mask of clay,' and deaf to the divine voice within 'whispering of beauty beyond the tomb' (70).  In the No*ah* parody, behold salvation Old Style: cold water, the universal dunking of the Flood.  The hole in the OT Providential scheme gapes; injustice triumphs as Noah and his friend escape the day of wrath in which humanity else, the guilty (Mrs. Sowerberry) and innocent (Oliver) alike, sink ten thousand fathoms deep.  Clearly, Dickens takes a dim view of Hebrew 'Ark-itecture' with its devotion to a God imaged as abandoning His people to Flood, famine, the sword, lions dens, fiery furnaces, and strange gods of Babylon, forms of which reappear in Noah, Leo-Den, and like symbolism throughout Dickens.

   In Dickens Biblical truth lives on, the great lodestone rock drawing all subsequent moral adventuring down through time.  No sacred 'then' and profane 'now' exist, but one continuous intercommunicating time of Christ.  Deity and the 'Coiler' perpetually contend.  Pre and anti-Christian forces regrouping would traduce Time backwards into ancient B.C. fog, murk, mudge: would snuff out NT light and waylay young heroes like Oliver Twist, Tom Pinch (MC), Stephen Blackpool (HT), Pip and John Wemmick (GE) in the dark *twist, pinch, blackpool, wemmick*-wimmick fates of old.

Yet even in seasons of Darkness and in the worst of times, times recalling the long ago before man's age-old hope of a Messiah was requited in a Star, NT time once again begins the hard, hopeful journey to Bethlehem to be born a babe. In blackest Dickensian hours, carriers of the light of the world one by one appear, dispelling darkness: little Nell's faithful friend, *Christopher,* carrying his little brother, Jacob, or Israel, on his back in true Christopher style (OCS); angelic Ada *Clare* (BH); and in Dickens's last work and as if literary will and testament, the good clergyman, Mr. *Crisparkle* (MD), the light (*sparkle*) of Christ (*Cris*) shining in a darkling world.

'Christopher,' 'Clare,' 'Crisparkle' and many another have life abundant in allegory, the texts showing they are just what they seem, Christian and allegorical. In *Bleak House,* for example, heights of the true, lost A.D. shine in ADa Clare. Visiting a worker's hovel in which an infant has died of want, Ada and Esther Summerson to comfort the distraught mother 'whisper[ed] to her what Our Saviour said of children' (109). Her exquisite outward and visible blue-eyed, golden-haired beauty reflecting an inward and spiritual grace, Ada Clare shines as azure and gold as the blue sky and golden sun of Heaven, abode of the Son and light of the world.

*Dickens himself* makes the sun-Son connection! It is in *A Tale of Two Cities* when, on the fateful night on which Sydney Carton reaches the decision to die in place of Charles Darnay, the long-forgotten words last heard at his father's graveside: 'I am the resurrection and the life, saith the Lord: he that believeth in me, though he were dead, yet shall he live: and whosoever liveth and believeth in me, shall never die' (298), echo twice, in full text, in Carton's slowly reviving will for good and consciousness of higher things.

The golden trump of Christian allegory now sounds its fullest note. As if heeding one divine summons, Nature and the soul of man tremble together on the brink of a 'recall to life':

> The night wore out, and, as he stood upon the bridge listening to the water as it splashed the river-walls of the Island of Paris, where the picturesque confusion of houses and cathedral shone bright in the light of the moon, the day came coldly, looking like a dead face out of the sky. Then, the night, with the moon and stars, turned pale and died, and for a little while it seemed as if Creation were delivered over to Death's dominion.
>
> But the glorious sun, rising, seemed to strike those words, that burden of the night, straight and warm to his heart in its long bright rays. And looking along them, with reverently shaded eyes, a bridge of light appeared to span the air between him and the sun, while the river sparkled under it. (299)

There is no mistaking the sacramental character of this sunrise: a radiant, world-redeeming Son-of-God-rise. The sun's 'glorious' rays (literally so: born afar in Glory) triumphant over night, or Death, strike 'those words,' 'I am the resurrection...,' that 'burden of the night,' *burden* both as theme and Cross, to Carton's inmost being. It briefly seems *'as if* Creation were delivered over to Death's dominion.' But Death shall have no dominion. The long dark night in the City and soul of man ends in symbolic promise of resurrection to Life Eternal. With 'reverently' shaded eyes—Heaven's tides too dazzling to the naked gaze in this life—Sydney Carton standing on a bridge of earth sees a mystic one of light spanning the air and linking the here and hereafter, the Two Cities of God; beholds an opening pilgrim way of ascent: the way, the truth, and the life.

'I am like one who died young' (143), Carton once told Lucie Manette. 'Dead' no more; through love of *Lucie,* the ideals and light of Christian truth mirrored in an exquisite soul, reborn from indolence and dissipation to vision and purpose, the glory of the Lord risen upon him, Carton with atoning speed now moves unswervingly towards the sublime act of 'dying for him' (337), *him,* whispered, thrilling in its ambiguity; towards the death that will ransom those trapped in the valley of the shadow and the yet unborn; the self-sacrifice on the cross-like guillotine ('It superceded the Cross' (260) identifies them) of a 'C' figure, unnamed in that final hour, *in imitatio Christi.*

In such breathtaking allegorical moments we first intuit that in Dickens, as in both Old and New scripture, an interwoven imagery of sower, seed, dark, light (such wealths of 'Clara' on Clara in *Copperfield* and *Great Expectations,* as elsewhere of 'Lucie,' 'Lightwood,' 'Clare'), garden, serpent, tree, branch, fruit, pearl, etc. employs objects in Nature to supernatural ends, Dickensian naturalism and Christian idealism fused in natural piety.

Patterns of allegory in Dickens prove highly coherent, a fact promoting belief in the existence of allegory. Even as *Oliver Twist* and *Great Expectations,* the book of Esther Summerson and Ada Clare, *Bleak House,* opens in dark, primordial ('Megalosaurus' (1)) sunless, Christless weather and time in world and soul. Law as hard and comfortless as Mosaic Law was, and in lingering influence is, looms over stricken multitudes, and as if all mankind. Those great, gloomy, crashing cathedral-organ dissonances of Law resounding through the novel, Law that thrills those with expectations of it to foredoomed ecstasies of hope while leading unkindly on only to despair, madness, and death, sound, one senses, in no merely local, limited human drama, but in one as ancient as the time of the first Esther, and older still. Over a grey, then-now symbolic landscape Law lowers, its symbol heavy, unlifting fog which blankets and hides from view the beneficent face of heaven and the sun, also Heaven and the Son. *Bleak House* captives to futile hope in an unending law suit who look aloft for divine solace see only what the Jews of old in *their* endless, futile 'suit' to

Heaven, the contractual arrangement instituted under Mosaic Law, saw: dimly through Fogs of legalism, in Captivity after Captivity suffered for infractions of the Law, a stern Lord of Law remote above the world Who never freely forgave, nor willingly released Israel to a better fate, the Good News Christ brings of divine love not limited by law.

*Bleak House,* we think, retells still another chapter of the old (OT) story of man's fate under the law-centered bargain B.C. man strikes with Heaven. Misconceived as a stern Law-giver, the God of the Hebrews towers menacingly over His people. Disobedience to this complex, demanding Law is inevitable; in vain the prophets over the centuries rail against backsliding Israel. The minutiae of ritual and statute blind men fixated on law to the simple meaning of faith, hope, and charity; the gainless centuries of divine jealousy, wrath, fall and punishment wear on. Then, into the foggy, unlifting winter of Western man's profound spiritual discontent and fruitless waiting upon Law comes grace: as in the first B.C. an *Esther* and hope of deliverance from bondage are born, so in Dickens an Esther *Summerson* and shining Ada *Clare* appear, first *summer* rays and *clare* of the *son* to illumine and warm a frozen world with words of comfort of 'Our Saviour.' So the message first came by night to woeful shepherds abiding in the fields, Weep no more; Lazarus your sorrow is not dead.

As Christian mythologist, Dickens gives immortal A.D. themes a home in his time, a local habitation and a name. In what remain perfectly modern, perfectly English dramas, Biblical and post-Biblical Christian essences dwell, shaping fresh historical events from within. No clash of 'levels' mars Dickens. Rather, the easeful blendings of then and now, natural and supernatural, and word and flesh in texts arise from the author's evident persuasion of its being just so in the world. A Fall of seven in a garden; Old (Esther) and New (Ada) ideals of grace meeting in harmony in the Gospel of Christ....

...a young *Oliver* as 'green' (OT,53) or innocent as a green olive tree in the house of God (*Psalm* 52), or an Oliver growing in grace to the height of the Mount of Olives, or as an olive-branch of the Prince of Peace: all point upwards. Oliver buds out past 'O.T.'-Oliver *Twist* origins in Sowerberry-Noah Claypole times of flood, law, and death: past Jew (Fagin) and crazed Monks (mediaeval Catholicism) which would confine the evolving spirit, arriving at last in fairest seed-time of the soul, its symbol *Rose Maylie,* in her compassion, charity, and faith the perfect beauty of a May rose, her soul mirroring the perfection of One Who 'rose' from the dead:-such in outline is Dickens's praiseful tale with its striking surface symbolism that bids us scan all texts with new, searching care.

Such symbolic signposts have always stood. But like the mist-hung finger-post pointing to Pip's remote village, they have in effect pointed nowhere; for, as Pip records, nobody ever came there. None saw the pointing finger; none took up a sturdy pilgrim's staff and actually set out on the long, untravelled way.

Seen into as a religious parable, *Bleak House* is fulfilled.  Its theme: how Biblical heroes and heroines and their spiritual heirs in all times bring NT time out of Old.  In her devotion to Ada Clare, her carrying Christian hope ('Our Saviour') where none is, receiving little children (Peepy Jellyby; Charley and her brood), sweeping cobwebs of Law out of the sky, and bringing 'sunshine and summer air' (426) wherever she goes, Esther Summerson is truly a *Summerson:* a season hospitable to the seed which is the word of God, a harvest-readying, ripening *summer* in the *son.*  As sun and Sonrise in *A Tale,* so Summerson-Summer sun.  In Dickens the Books of Nature and God, of physics and metaphysics, are but a breath apart.

Esther Summerson is explicitly tied to NT revelation early in the novel as she narrates events of one fateful evening in her childhood:

> I was reading aloud, and she [Esther's godmother] was listening.  I had come down at nine o'clock, as I always did, to read the Bible to her; and was reading, from St. John, how our Saviour stooped down, writing with his finger in the dust, when they brought the sinful woman to him.
>
> '"So when they continued asking him, he lifted up himself and said unto them, He that is without sin among you, let him first cast a stone at her!"'
>
> I was stopped by my godmother's rising, putting her hand to her head, and crying out, in an awful voice, from quite another part of the book:
>
> '"Watch ye therefore! lest coming suddenly he find you sleeping.  And what I say unto you I say unto all, Watch!"' (19)

This passage from the Gospel of *John* stands like a spiritual sentinel or angel of NT law, a law of forgiveness and love, at the portal to *Bleak House;* all human adventure within hearkens to it.  Old (OT) Law offers no help, comfort, certainty, or expectation of a favorable judgment in the end; just so with respect to final things.  One half suspects that poor mad Miss Flite's fancy that the awaited judgment in Jarndyce v. Jarndyce fore-shadows the Day of Judgment is sound, and neither will favor man.  With only the law and a stern Lord of the Law to trust in, all bound to the suit are lost.  Before Christ, they are unchampioned before the Judgment Throne.

Philosophically speaking, *Bleak House* proceeds from the *St. John* moment in which Christ confronts the fanatics of Law, the Pharisees.  For none more than Esther's godmother (ironic title!) merits Christ's rebuke to the bigots of Old Law set to stone the sinful woman.  The godmother, who condemned Esther's unhappy mother for her sin, never relented, took her child from her and, compounding the evil, reared it to believe itself the fruit of shame, is surely foremost among 'them' in the NT tale.  Her of-fenses against mother and child, types of the Mother and Child, cry to Heaven; and in a sudden access of insight she knows it.  An earlier Miss Havisham, the hard-bitten woman finally sees Whom she has offended in visiting the sins of the fathers on the innocent children, a passion deeply

Hebraic at the core.  It is nine o'clock, Esther relates, *nine*, perhaps,  for the ninth hour at which Christ crucified gives up the ghost.  Fit hour for a fanatic of Old Law with its zeal for retribution and judgment to be forced to recall the infamy it led to, once, upon a Cross, and leads to still.  She who 'first cast a stone,' who did not 'watch' but lived blindly, vindictively on, suddenly appears to see into her unholy cause, and uttering an unearthly cry, falls, never to rise again.

The godmother soon after dies.  Then a second pitiless, self-appointed and unholy hound of Heaven, lawyer Tulkinghorn, pursues retribution against Esther's mother, Lady Dedlock, until he too is struck down by a vengeful hand.  Such, we see, is the ultimate futility of the eye-for-an-eye justice mandated by OT law, and such the fate of all self-elect, unchristian 'instrument[s] of severity against sin.'

In *Bleak House,* the undoing of the old fatality imposed by Law begins when a certain attractive if eccentric gentleman, one John Jarndyce, another of Dickens's 'many Johns' making speeches to the winds (and how he does roar up in his Growlery!), rescues three wards of the Court of Chancery:  Ada, Esther, and Richard Carstone.  Cutting the three loose from the Law, John starts them on the road to a new life.  *'In the beginning was the ward,'* man in a helpless state of dependency on a Lord of Mosaic Law in a universe of Fall, defeated expectations, flux and chance, for which *Chancery* is Dickens's deft punning symbol.  Opposing the Law, John turns the tide.  Shepherding the protectorless wards, he keeps them from the foggy foggy dew of legal Fog as best he can, in so doing forecasting the day of the return of the Son Who alone turns Bleak Houses bright.

It may not be stretching things to glimpse the Biblical Esther theme in this 'Story of Esther.'  For as once before in history an Esther tried to save a People captive to a long, wearing punishment under Law, so in Dickens an Esther does what she can to rescue the helpless victims of life and law around her in a social arrangement in which charity is a hollow enterprise and law an impenetrable barrier between man and Heaven, not, as Christ proves, a portal to the Above.  Might not the weary waiters for a judgment in the *Bleak House* suit wearing on as from time immemorial to the crack of doom, a suit neither won nor yet ever wholly lost, its penalties cruel and benefits not forthcoming but in waning hope ever longingly awaited, be those very 'waiters' for redemption of old who manned the watchtowers in ancient deserts of one and then another Captivity?  The prayerful hopes of generations captive to futile hope waiting upon the resolution of *Jarndyce v. Jarndyce* waft upwards through dense legal Fog to an unreachably high Lord as removed from souls yearning below as ever the Lord God of Law from the Hebrew nation weeping in exile by the waters of Babylon in OT time.  Two uncommunicating empyreans; two Peoples, of B.C. and A.D., become ironically one in tranced fixation upon Law, even as in *Great Expectations* the pleading, doomed Jew upon the unwinable favor of a high priest of the Law.

Clearly the Ghost of Time Past casts a long shadow over Dickensian Christian time as men blighted in yet still curiously zealous for the law languish lives away, 'Tip' or fall time and again, lose hope, go mad, commit suicide, and finally die in despair. Dickens's point, we think, is that without faith in what lies *beyond* Law, namely a personal Saviour with compassion for the fallen, A.D. and B.C., in essence so different, are ironically and terribly one.

Dickens an anti-semite? Hardly, as the Books of Samuel (*Pickwick Papers*), of David (*Copperfield*), and Esther show, books which celebrate the spirit of those heroes of OT time who somehow saw past a God of stern law to one of tender concern for man, a concern and love which would be most perfectly exemplified in the teachings of Christ. As we saw in the *St. John* passage, Dickens is at pains to stress Christ's strong sense of men above law. Elsewhere too he pointedly quotes: ' "The Sabbath was made for man, and not man for the Sabbath" ' (OL,227), to refer again to words cited in Chapter II. Rightly or wrongly, Dickens firmly associates Judaism with law, a depersonalized, narrow-constructionist law, and stresses that a Christianity which fails to befriend the poor and administer justice by NT lights—which uses Old Lamps for New Ones, to borrow Dickens's words— is not really Christianity at all, but Judaism thinly disguised. Lo, the Ghost of Christianity Past, worship still heavy with B.C. and later pre-Protestant forms, like some still unrepentant ghost of Marley rattling its chains stalks the land. O when may it suffice? When will *Jacob*, Israel, look up, as Jacob Marley in life never did, and see a great Light?

Dickensian allegory, though always absorbed in its lofty theme, does not point or shout; it does not have to. Like Ada Clare it prefers to 'whisper' the Saviour's words of comfort, 'whisper' of beauty beyond the tomb. Housetop sermons and loud anathemas it gladly leaves to others. By contrast, its forte is the very small symbolic moment, such as the one in which mild Esther Summerson, tending little Peepy Jellyby at breakfast, reports:

> He was very good, except that he brought down Noah with him (out of an ark
> I had given him before we went to church), and *would* dip him head first into
> the wine-glasses, and then put him into his mouth. (BH,423)

Into the mouths of babes! If Peepy, wise innocent, 'brought Noah down,' Noah, Lord knows, needs (pun) 'bringing down.' A royal wetting for *Noah* at last. Take *that,* Noah Claypole! Esther's modest little gift of a Noah's ark is an allegorical nosegay. And Peepy puts the ark to excellent new use. One might say that Queen Esther herself was not a much more adept mover in her unhappy nation's destiny than is this latter-day Esther who, finally outdistancing a cruel 'Hebrew' past darkened by notions of sin and guilt, inexorable guilt, emerges from fog into a rosy Summer Sonrise to say:

> I knew I was as innocent of my birth as a queen of hers; and that before my
> Heavenly Father I should not be punished for birth, nor a queen rewarded
> for it. (516)

As the above shows, in Dickensian allegory it is often a matter of grasping the vast symbolic implications of something surpassing small, such as
one toy Noah going headlong into the drink.  Hail little Peepy, who peeps
at life with new eyes.  Once again, 'And a little child shall lead them,' in
the Scripture-mirroring work of Dickens, Christian naturalist *par
excellence*.  In the *Peepy* miniature, water in wine-glasses is an inspired
touch.  Though in water, Noah is yet in 'wine,' as if the NT day of such
miracles as the water turned to wine were once more at hand.
    In a speech he makes in 1842 Dickens praises, as he terms him, the
inspired man who celebrated:

> "Tongues in the trees, books in the running brooks,
> Sermons in stones, and good in everything." (LLS,II,421)

These are the kinds of sermons he would have us read.  In Dickens, many a
'sermon in stone' is inscribed in a Murdstone, Headstone, or Richard
Carstone who foolishly turns from his beloved Ada Clare to hang madly on
the grinding, destroying machinery of Law.  As to 'books in the running
brooks,' the essence of A.D. shines in a droplet of the fountain of Eternal
Day, the wholly selfless, all-forgiving, loving Ada Clare.
    Visibly, vast symbolic effects dance angelically on a pin head.  Nothing
less than the Fall itself operates full blast in that worldly creature of vanity,
Mr. Turveydrop, the Model of Deportment in *Bleak House*.  Alas,
TURVEYDROP, whom the X-ray vision of allegory reveals as named for the
topsy-*TURVEY* state of man still plummeting dizzily downward in that ongoing inglorious plunge or *DROP* of old, the Fall.  Bravo, Dickens!
    And Turveydrop, the aging dandy and parasite, lives up (down) to his
name.  Comic old villain.  In him behold unregenerate man, the unapol-
ogetic immoralist who, under the guise of giving all, a rank imposture,
coolly expects and snatches up all.  Turveydrop, with moral taste to match,
names his only son 'Prince' in honor of that other bloated model of vanity,
the Prince Regent.  Yet, wonderful to tell, young Prince turns out to be as
sweet, high-souled, generous, and selfless a young man as ever lived,
living up to the lofty ideal embodied in his Christian name and proving a
'Prince' in ways his fatuous father, idolater of debased royalty, never
dreamed.  All sham elegance, showy form, the letter of high utterance
entirely barren of the spirit, the father shamelessly exploits his only-
begotten son who, serving his father at his own expense, but always gladly,
uncomplainingly, and with all his heart, mirrors the Son of sons, even

Christ.

Happy, unconscious *imitatio*: happiest *because* unconscious. Once more, unto us a Son is born, a Prince given. As in Bible times, the gross *Turveydrop* world of selfishness and sin of the Father rests upon the shoulders and self-sacrifice of the (S)on, without whom all would collapse. Here is one sign more that except for the light of Christ still shining in hearts and in lives lived far from the pomps and parades of worldliness—in people like Esther, Ada, John, Prince, and others—Time would belong to the Fall.

Allegory in Dickens discovers one more way to dramatize ideas about the superiority of Christian to Hebrew law that we know greatly interested Dickens. In evidence whereof consider his own words. In 'Capital Punishment,' an essay in *Old Lamps for New Ones,* Dickens deals head on with the OT-NT issue, at one point stating:

> We know that the law of Moses was delivered to certain wandering tribes, in a peculiar and perfectly different social condition from the one that prevails among us at this time. We know that the Christian Dispensation did distinctly repeal and annul certain portions of that law. We know that the doctrine of retributive justice or vengeance was plainly disavowed by the Saviour. (OL,151)

In the name of 'the Christian Dispensation' Dickens opposes capital punishment. Yet, as a Miss Havisham or Tulkinghorn who grimly embrace it and an Abel Magwitch who suffers under it show, the 'doctrine of retributive justice or vengeance' of OT time continues to exact the old price in pain, captivity, and death; and it is Dickens's agonized sense that this is so that animates his powerful social statements and allegorical visions.

Granted, one *Coiler, Flopson, Tippins,* John with fishing-rod or Esther with Noah's ark, or *Turveydrop,* does not an allegorical summer make. In this study we try to show that here is no Biblical confetti, no loose, random, systemless mythic filigree occasionally crisparkling on surfaces here and there. Rather, motifs are firmly anchored in fiction-wide themes. *Bleak House* furnishes a fine example. In its 'in the beginnings,' ages before Peepy's Noah meets his waterloo, we enter an enclave of Old Time, the Dedlock ancestral manse, by name Chesney Wold, a domain of ancient name, power, and ancestral pride. Not a soul is by; all is silence and 'Rain, rain, rain! nothing but rain—and no family here!' A deserted world in which it 'rained so hard and rained so long' (82) that rain seems the one existing reality; and in which someone unseen, the only living soul left on earth, it might be, says to a horse in the stable: 'Woa, grey, then, steady! Noabody wants you to-day!' (81)

Amid signs of a deluge ('Rain, rain, rain!') in an as if unpeopled, intensely wet and ever wetter world inhabited only by animals—horses, hounds, rabbits, turkeys, geese—'NOAbody,' a stunning pun, silently shouts of NOAh, and the abundant creature life of Noah's ark. All fits snugly. In a *Dedlock* or deadlocked world at a standstill, a pocket or backwater of Christendom, Time is trapped back in the Noa or Flood age; elsewhere law and lawyer in hebraeo-roman style defeat tremulous expectations in a Turveydrop-Fall world, and children like Jo wander in the wilderness of the city, and workers' infants die of want. Thus in another work Dickens shows the backward drift of human society. His purpose, to appeal for a return to A.D. and the spirit of the Gospels, never again 'the Master of the New Testament put out of sight' (LLS,II,204); and for a Church which, in his words, is 'a more Christian one, with less arbitrary pretensions and a stronger hold upon the mantle of our Saviour, as He walked and talked upon this earth.' (letter to Cerjat, LLS,II,203)

Flood time returns. And yet, as surely as it arrived once before, NT time reappears. Be it ever so cold out and wet, a cricket on the hearth chirps and chirrups 'he's coming, coming, coming!—' (CB,161), in trinity of 'c' and 'ch' in Christ, inviting us to 'Chirrup,' or Cheer up, for He *is* coming soon. From *Pickwick* to Eternity the Good News flies, nor does it fail to find out the quiet, shady nook of Mr. Crisparkle in *The Mystery of Edwin Drood*.

Is 'Crisparkle,' the name alone, not all proof of Christian allegory in one shining symbol? Crisparkle, a modest Minor Canon of the Church who stands with bent head to hear the Lord's Prayer recited in his home; who loves best the music of Handel, and in the quiet watches of the night when all are asleep, softly plays his favorite choral airs on the piano; who, while the professional Philanthropist Luke Honeythunder thunders pious cant, but quietly reverses the crossing of his legs and abides in patience. Who, when Honeythunder rejects them, receives into his care two strangers named Landless, symbolizing the *landless* or spiritually disinherited, outsiders, gentiles, and civilizes, teaches, and guides them into paths of hope and peace:-here is a *Crisparkle,* a light lit at the light of the world, worthy of the name. No 'Right Reverend, Very Reverend,' or any other Reverend here. Unassuming, boyish, musical Mr. Crisparkle, free from worldly ambition and vanity, hope of the Landless, is Chaucer's good, poor parish priest come back to life; and in every shapely thought or word, every sip of home-made Constantia wine taken with 'an excellent grace' (101), symbolizes the grace of a Christian ministry in rare attunement to the life and lessons of Christ.

*Crisparkle* is only the tip of the Star. Dickens lavishes exquisitely fine sacred detail on Crisparkle passages. His 'crossing' his legs before the claps of Honeythunder, making a sign of the cross while riding out the storm, is typical. As the devoted son of a 'china shepherdess' (65) lady mother, Mr. Crisparkle is the more in the 'son,' and the more a 'shepherd' who with Handel keeps watch over His flocks by night. ('Watch ye therefore!') Not in loud, disputatious Christian officialdom and diocesan epistle-dom does Dickens rest his hopes for the survival of 'the Christian religion, as it came from Christ Himself' (LLS,II,370); but in the 'Crisparkle,' the good and faithful servant of the absent Master, a 'fresh and bright' (277) not Major but *Minor* Canon (canon: in view of an affinity for Handel, very likely a blithe sacred/musical pun) steadily about his Father's business of rescuing the lost and raising the fallen, *in imitatio Christi*. Here is the true, the blushful Hippocrene, the Constantia or communion wine of Constancy to the Ideal object.

The china shepherdess's Constantia wine is the more celestial, one thinks, for being kept in a closet filled to the brim with fruit preserves 'for ages hummed through by the Cathedral bell and organ,' a wonderful closet in which the very dippers plunged into sweet stores undergo 'a saccharine transfiguration' (100), and crowned by a portrait of Handel. Thus naturally and deliciously do Heaven and high earth meet in Dickens, and is man, not by batterings under Law but by ways of delight entrancing to his soul, gathered into the artifice of Eternity.

Our hero's name, Septimus Crisparkle, first and last speaks NT volumes. 'Sept,' as his fond mother calls her seventh child, points as the Septuagint read aright, and as his exemplary pastoral care and beloved Handel (the 'Creation;' 'the Messiah') point, to God, the Creation, and the Messiah! In speaking of Mr. Crisparkle, Helena Landless adjures her wayward brother: 'Follow your guide now, Neville, and follow him to Heaven!' (106) As never before we believe her.

In *Drood*, one senses the immediacy to the present of major religious events of early NT times. In Cloisterham, termed 'a city of another and a bygone time' (19), 'bygone' horrors return as 'Christians are stoned on all sides as if the days as Saint Stephen were revived' (48). The stoning of Stephen is much on Dickens's mind, the motif making its debut even earlier in crypto-symbolic form when Stony Durdles, stonemason of graves, is asked point-blank, concerning his odd name, 'whether Stony stood for Stephen' (40). *Stony-Stephen:* ominous words to come within striking distance of one another! Was Dickens unconscious of what such nearness implied? Hardly, what with the explicit 'days of Saint Stephen' reference hard by.

Hardly, too, after *Hard Times* in which Stephen, its hero, is martyred in the Stone Lodge world of 'store' figures like Gradgrind, a world in which strict adherence to the letter of adamantine Law killeth the spirit, even as the Old the budding New consciousness of man. *Stephen-Stone* Lodge: death by stoning nears Stephen again in a Christian drama and parable.

*Hard Times* in its turn is set in what Dickens calls 'Old Time,' the initials OT aglare, in an English factory town in which eatanswill-ish 'Smoke-serpents' (69) coil overhead, shutting out the sun, and chimneys like 'Towers of Babel' (80) (Old Time indeed) loom. Hebrew and Roman spirits command here. One is *Josiah* Bounderby; another is a dour matron of the

'Coriolanian style of nose' (43) (anticipating Wopsle's like-aggravating Roman nose in *Great Expectations,* perhaps), pagan to the root in her obsessive visions of stairs that lead down, down, as into an underworld or abyss. Again, it might be B.C. as an Elect flourishes while the abject masses toil in despair, fade, and die. Rising up against intolerable conditions, Stephen, a factory hand, confronts forces that crush him. One adversary is the demagogue, Slackbridge: *Slackbridge,* symbolically a *slack bridge,* a spiritual No Thoroughfare, sign of treacherous footing over the void. No Two Cities, Christ-celebrating sunrise is seen from the vantage point of a Slackbridge. Following him, men follow a false saviour and reject the Stephen-revealed, true way.

Stephen Blackpool suffers further in loving a high-souled, spiritual Rachael, kept from him by an archaic marriage law. As in first OT time her hard-bargaining father kept Rachael from Jacob, so in Dickens Rachael symbolizes the joy of man's desiring unattainable, or won only at soul-wearing cost, under the old covenant. The motif first appears in *Pickwick;* in the household of her old curmudgeon of a father, Mr. Wardle, Rachael is an old maid, a wretched 'ward(le).' As Stephen was stoned to death under Law in OT time, so in *Hard Times* a Stephen defeated by Law is 'Stone Lodge'd' to death, as it were; in the end he falls down a mine shaft, called the Old Hell shaft, as man without a Redeemer into Hell. Yet man in A.D. was not meant for the Old Hell, but the New Heaven. Hard, stoning-*Hard* Times, indeed.

In *The Mystery of Edwin Drood,* Dickens's last work, the query 'whether Stony stood for Stephen' invokes the issue again. Is 'Stony,' death by stoning, still man's way? Signs are dark. Stones fly; primitive Stony carves headstones in the Cathedral Close; while in the gloomy, sunless stone tabernacle highly ritualized worship and priestly influence overcome. Heaven darkens; Luke Honeythunder turns the honey of Luke to rant; a High Protestantism grows too high, as the names *Cloister*ham and *Nuns'* House show. Whither Christianity when the religious institution, moribund and drear, has such power, and simple faith, hope, and charity so few witnesses?

Against this setting our hero, young Edwin Drood, disappears amid signs of murder most foul. No one knows, but perhaps Drood's uncle, John Jasper, or Neville Landless, his rival, has slain him. Mystery gathers. Is Drood gone forever, or does he still live and will he return? In the Mystery of a death not surely a death—feared forever lost, Drood may not be, though at present he no longer revisits the light of the sun— Dickens, we suggest, meditates on a pattern of mystery which typifies or enfolds the Mystery, in the divine sense as well, of Christ, the death not a death: the Mystery of the (D)*rood* or Cross, and its troubled progress through world and time.

Christendom darkens. John Jasper, the Cathedral choirmaster, daily sinks deeper into opium addiction and crazed fantasy, so far forgetting himself as to covet the treasure he holds in trust for the missing bridegroom, Drood's fair fiancee, Rosa Bud: 'Rosa,' like Rose Maylie, symbol of the fair garden of the Lord, the world and soul awaiting the summer son to bud in glory.

An allegorical masterpiece unfolds. Which of the 'many Johns' is this gifted, tormented, lost John who would come between the Bridegroom and the bride; who, obsessed in his mania by 'Paradises and Hells of vision' (220), wanders in wild imaginings through unearthly landscapes traversed by glittering phantom processions? *John, Jasper, Paradises* and *Hells* all point as one to St. John and the lurid fantasy-theology of the Book of *Revelation*. Its description of the City of God may hold a clue: 'And the building of the wall of it was of jasper' (21:18), and: 'The first foundation was jasper' (21:19). Like all Christian Johns, *Jasper* is intended as a support and pillar of the City, a trustee of the treasure Drood left behind when cruelly torn from the world, in the sense that all churchmen are trustees of His estate on earth and keepers of the keys of the Kingdom. But with John Jasper fallen and only Mr. Crisparkle on watch, what hope is there for Drood?

In the John Jasper plot of *Drood* Dickens, we believe, explores the great danger to Christendom of the 'addict,' the overzealous ecclesiastical servant of the absent Master lost in the fanaticism of private vision, intense subjectivity, evangelical excess, 'revelation.' In Chapter II, *Dickens the Christian,* we saw how wary Dickens was of self-serving clergymen and their loud battles over Scripture, and wary of the encrustations and barnacles men had attempted to fix to the Gospels. One recalls Dickens's counsel to one of his sons to read the New Testament and that alone, 'putting aside the interpretations and inventions of men' (LLS,II,370).

In the closing scene of the unfinished novel, members of the Choir, late to the service and as they struggle into 'nightgowns,' or choir-gowns, looking 'like children shirking bed' (277), hurry in disorder after John Jasper. Does he lead 'the children' the way of Life Eternal, or but from 'sleep' to Sleep? The signs are dark. In Jasper, Christendom has clearly chosen the wrong singing-master of its soul. In Dickens's view, as we understand it, no wild, heated visionary zeal and Gospels-overshadowing passion for spiritual invention in the *Revelation* vein will help build the City of God on earth. Instead, if it is ever to rise, a Mr. Crisparkle will found it in fleshly tables of the heart, as he labors to do in the heart of young Neville Landless: NEVILLE, hope of the *NE*(w) *Ville*, built in men's souls as a Scrooge, Dombey, or Landless is by quiet ways of love, peace, and understanding led into Christian paths.

Still we feel for Jasper, too. His situation is tragic; he does evil he would not do. Far from where illicit longing after the rose of the world and feverish vision rage, Jasper truly loves the missing Drood. As in NT time, one who would not betray Drood betrays (H)im.

Sometimes called Dickens's most pessimistic vision, *Drood* instead proves much like all others, one of Christian civilization, now as in its first hours, precariously balanced between Darkness and Light. Drood may yet live, and, returning, claim his bride. Not completing the book, it is as if Dickens with rich symbolic intent left it all up to mankind and history. Meanwhile, Dickensian Providence mercifully blows one bright, steady *Crisparkle* into being as cause for rejoicing still.

Moving from book to book, we find new reason to suppose Christian allegory the key to all of Dickens. In *Dombey and Son* too the religious issue is immediately joined. The novel opens with an Opening event, a Creation, and with the arrival in a great House of a son and heir; thus are fused two spiritual dawns, of Old and New Testament time. 'Dom-bey and Son' (1), exults the proud father:

> And again he said 'Dom-bey and Son,' in exactly the same tone as before.
> Those three words conveyed the one idea of Mr. Dombey's life. The earth was made for Dombey and Son to trade in, and the sun and moon were made to give them light. Rivers and seas were formed to float their ships; rainbows gave them promise of fair weather; winds blew for or against their enterprises; stars and planets circled in their orbits, to preserve inviolate a system of which they were the centre. Common abbreviations took new meaning in his eyes, and had sole reference to them: A.D. had no concern with anno Domini, but stood for anno Dombei—and Son. (2)

With the hyphen in 'Dom-bey' highlighting DOM the more, 'anno *Dom*bei' is even more clearly the anti-type of anno *Dom*ini; and ruthless Dombey is revealed as the impious Dom-inus/Dom-beyus of a counter-Creation, the luciferean Dombey omnipotent who reigneth over an usurped world, the fullness thereof not, as rightfully it should be, Heaven's, but his own. Dombey's 'three words...one idea' rivals and mocks the sacred three-in-one of the Trinity. As Dominus the Father presided over the canonical *In the Beginning,* the miraculous issue of which is commandeered in the passage above, so Dombey the Father presides over his own. Dickens in this poses a question: which A.D., anno Domini or anno Dombei, will prevail in our time?

Then 'Son' is born, like another Son of man, fated to change all. Little Paul is christened in a cold, dank church in which the Beadle (shades of Bumble) wears a 'Babylonian collar' (55); and at the drab feast that follows, a Dombey retainer starts still other Hebrew spirits by humming 'a fragment of the Dead March in Saul' (60). *Saul!* How dark a shadow to fall athwart 'Paul.' The *Paul-Saul* connection, like the *Stony-Stephen* ones of *Hard Times* and *Drood,* fairly astounds. Dead March and Saul, being unpunctuated, start forth boldly from the page like the John of Sunderland in *Great Expectations* cited before. Thus unbound, they are less involved with an opera than with religious history, *Saul* being, of course, the Hebrew fanatic of the law St. Paul was in his Stephen-stoning days before his conversion on the road to Damascus. Dickens is in earnest. It *is* Saul or spiritual time B.C., is it not, with Babylonian yokes in view worn by stern figures of church law, and when the best anyone at a christening can come up with is a dirge of the Old Mortality, 'the *Dead* March in Saul.'

Allegory thickens apace. Humming Saul is Mr. Dombey's right-hand-of-the-Father man, John Chick. Ah! As the true Dominus and Father has His J.B., John the Baptist, and J.C., Jesus Christ, so the false Dombey has *his* J.B., the devilish *Josh (Joe) Bagstock* and J.C., John Chick, a J.C. whose counterChrist theme is the old tune, Death Eternal, the Dead March in Saul.

Still, unto us a child is born, a Son given. As in bleakest Turveydrop time of *Bleak House* a 'Prince' magically appears, so 'Son,' Paul, a little Pauline, lives and breathes to mirror and magnify the forgotten truth of Heaven. Soulful Paul, shining in his angel infancy of sky-blue fancy and wonder, yearns ever past solid world and time to an invisible shore he can only describe as 'farther away—farther away!' (109) At school, Paul thinks of a picture, 'where, in the centre of a wondering group, one figure that he knew, a figure with a light about its head—benignant, mild, and merciful—stood pointing upward' (194). (*Copperfield,* a work of two years later, ends on the very same words, and with the divine Agnes 'pointing upward!') Set in a trinity of high attributes, 'benignant, mild, and merciful,' the figure the more ethereal for being unnamed, in the reverent Dickens way, can only be Christ.

At school, a sorry place, they call Paul old-fashioned, and . . .

> What old fashion could that be, Paul wondered with a palpitating heart, that was so visibly expressed in him; so plainly seen by so many people. (191)

'So visibly expressed in him' sounds like the symbolic language of the Catechism. When Paul lies dying and the great Mystery begins, this mystery is solved:

> The golden ripple on the wall came back again, and nothing else stirred in the room. The old, old fashion! The fashion that came in with our first garments....The old, old fashion, Death!
> Oh, thank GOD, all who see it, for that older fashion yet, of Immortality! And look upon us, angels of young children, with regards not quite estranged, when the swift river bears us to the ocean! (226)

Paul's last words to his sister Florence are: 'But tell them that the print upon the stairs at school is not divine enough. The light about the head is shining on me as I go!' (226) *Tell them!* To the end Paul teaches of Christ.

Like St. Paul, Dickens's Paul points past the old fashion and B.C.

garment of the soul, Death, to hope of resurrection. St. Paul poetically reveals death as a being born into Life Eternal. So does little Paul, for 'all who see it,' words which remind us that even greatest marvels can go unperceived by those who, in the words of Christ, 'seeing see not,' and neither hear nor understand. (*Matt.* 13:13)

*Dombey and Son* is first to last a devout Book of Paul. In the school to which Paul is sent by his father, Greek and Latin dominate the curriculum. Pupils are constantly drilled in 'principles of classicality and high breeding' (188), that is, social snobbery; and the Masters, hot for the ancient glories of Rome, chant the praises of (the bloodier the better) 'a Nero, a Caligula, a Heliogabalus, and many a more' (158). Never, we venture to say, were Corinthians, Ephesians, Colossians, Thessalonians, and Philippians of old more caught up in gruelling olympics of Cicero, Plautus, Ovid, and Virgil, to name but a few, than are the wretched young inmates of Dr. Blimber's academy. On one memorable occasion when the students are being regaled with tales of Roman conquests and costly entertainments (costly indeed, especially in one remote province of the Empire), at each fresh proof of Roman rapacity a lad named Johnson chokes and splutters more violently. Doctor Blimber promptly retaliates in Roman style, with punishment:

> 'Johnson will repeat to me to-morrow morning before breakfast, without book, and from the Greek Testament, the first chapter from the Epistle of Saint Paul to the Ephesians.' (158)

Such is the use modern Christian schoolmasters put the New Testament to. We smile, struck by the irony of forcing St. Paul in Greek on a boy, with a living Paul so near by.

Allegory thrills in the design of the little scene. As in early NT time St. Paul journeyed through the Greek and Roman world carrying the word of Christ, so in later Dickensian NT time a Paul, also far from home, sojourns among 'Greeks' and 'Romans' in a stronghold of Old Time. And rabid pagans these Christians might be, down in (Dickens's metaphor) the grave of dead languages day and night, and laying on the NT instead of the strap. But three cheers for young *Johnson,* a true *son* of *John,* who obviously can swallow none of the passion for ancient barbarism that the Doctor and his sidekick, Mr. Feeder, B.A. (B.C., more like), force-Feed(er) him. Johnson's punishment, or rather reward, is the Epistle of Paul, which, though doubtless unreadable by him in the original Greek, has been the consolation of many a martyred Johnson down through time. And would be his, but for the pedantry of the time.

The Greek-Roman school to which the Father sends his only-begotten son is an extant outpost of the heathen world in which St. Paul and the disciples like Timothy were also 'schooled' long ago—hard schooling it proved, too. Yet nothing daunted, Paul by his sweet, gentle goodness wins over many a pagan in the place such as Toots, the devoté of Apollo. He even converts the xenophobic dog named Diogenes who, knowing a wise man when he sees one, stops barking and becomes a tail-wagging apostle of sweetness and light.

In a world that received Him and His not, one no better now than then, little Paul soon dies. Yet lives on in hearts that loved him, as in the ship which bears his (and His) name, the *Son and Heir*. The allegory widens. St. Paul, in NT metaphor termed the 'chosen vessel' of Christ (*Acts* 9:15), 'sails' again, it would seem, in the Chris-craft named for Paul. How after Paul's passing a certain hearty Captain Cuttle restores Paul's grieving sister's hope and faith, bidding her keep a bright lookout forward for the *Son and Heir;* how, in the Captain's allegorical vision, life is a journey by sea, with man, the celestial seafarer, ever 'a-driving, head on, to the world without end, evermore, amen' (689); how, in praising his pal, old Solomon Gills, ships' instrument-maker, Captain Cuttle reweaves those very poetic garlands first woven in another 'song of Solomon,' the *Song of Songs;* and how, speaking for Dickens, who can doubt, he bids us 'overhaul the Catechism' (331), the chart by which man sets a course for Eternity:-these wonders and more must await fuller telling at some future time.

Finally, *Dead March, Saul,* and Greek-Roman ages are again left behind as the time of the Dominus and Son comes round. The winter of *anno Dombei* past, the flowering season of 'Florence,' Paul's faithful sister, arrives, and the voices of *anno Domini* are heard in the land. Again we see that in embracing the vision of allegory in Dickens, the world does not lose a Dickens, it gains the Son. Can so Christian a tale of Paul, only sketched here, be aught but allegory? No Dickensian John with fishing-rod and bride named Miss Skiffins—a 'skiff(ins)' to make 'the journey' in the wake of the *Son and Heir* as 'the swift river bears us to the ocean'—no *Gabriel* 'blessing his stars' (BR, 144) and watchful of a *Mary* and her most rare, martyred son (*Barnaby Rudge*); no nigh-invisible cricket joyfully insisting 'he's coming, coming, coming!—': in Dickens, none but helps celebrate the mystery of Mary, the Son ('he's coming!'), and Christmas.

In a Crisparkle Canon melodic with Handel and his sacred works, Dickens himself composes a sustaining Pilgrims' Chorus and Christmas Carol. Lo, souls in Dickens are musical instruments. In *Dombey,* for example, the Toodles clan and Mr. Toots, all devoted to Paul, are nothing less than 'toots' and 'toodles' of an orchestra warming up for the 'Alleluia Chorus.' In teaching little Florence to hope in the rising up of the dead to eternal life, kindly Polly Toodle makes a joyful noise unto the Lord. And playing Handel on his violoncello at the close of *Dombey,* as Mr. Crisparkle will on his piano in time to come, Mr. *Morfin* symbolizes the spirit of celebration of the end (*fin*) of Death (*Mor*): Christ's victory over 'Dead March,' Satan, and Saul. So too in *Our Mutual Friend* the return as from the dead of John Harmon, another of Dickens's 'many Johns' with a heavenly mission to perform, restores a long-lost Harmon-y.  In *David Copperfield* David's good friend, the Master, Mr. Mell, plays his three-pieces-in-one flute, as if in symbolic tribute to *the* Master, even Christ, with all the Mel(1)odious strength of his soul.  And in *Great Expectations* Pip is rechristened 'Handel' by the son of Matthew, a son worthy of his Father.  As this mighty chorus swells, the old Sowerberry universe finally puts off its tragic mask to reveal the return by popular demand of the Comedian as the letter 'C,' Christ.

Come Christmas, and Dickensian allegory wears a holiday face wreathed in smiles like a holly-and-berry door knocker, a veritable Scrooge's nephew of a face aglow with brisk walking out of doors (man ever the *homo viator* of City pavements) and with the incurable hope of converting an avuncular world of 'Bah!  Humbug!' to 'A merry Christmas, God save you!'  Dickens, it seems, will settle for nothing less than the conversion of the Jews—and Christians too.

*A Christmas Carol* too imparts its holiest Christian message in allegory.  Tiny Tim, we know, points to Christ; no secret here.  As Bob Cratchit his father tells his wife: 'He told me, coming home, that he hoped the people saw him in the church because he was a cripple and it might be pleasant to them to remember upon Christmas Day who made lame beggars walk, and blind men see' (CB,45).  The child is a divine transparency:  'Spirit of Tiny Tim, thy childish essence was from God!' (69)  It only remains, then, to recognize Tim as a spiritual sprite or sprig of Timothy, the youthful disciple of St. Paul, the frail and unwell follower whom Paul calls his child and son in Christ. (*1 Tim*. 1:2)  Thus seen into, Tiny Tim is like the shining star set atop the Christmas tree last of all amid a universal chorus of 'Ah!'

If Tiny Tim points to Christ, Jacob Marley and Ebenezer Scrooge point to Hebrew time and values past.  Wandering in chains for eternity, Marley's wan ghost laments a selfish earthly life in which he never raised his eyes to (in his words) 'that blessed Star which led the Wise Men to a poor abode' (CB,21).  *Jacob,* Israel, rejected Christ and does so still.  To see him, picturing what he was in life, or see Scrooge in his dismal room staring at fireplace tiles that depict motifs of ancient Judaeo-Christian history, scenes of Cain and Abel, Pharoah's daughter, Belshazzar, and Aaron's rod, etc., is to grasp the deep-dyed Hebrew components of their souls.  To be 'Christians' in such wise, Dickens shows, is in effect to be Jews.  Indeed, *Ebenezer* is the name of the stone set by Samuel, Judge of Israel, to commemorate a Hebrew victory over foes.  Ebenezer means:  'Hitherto hath the Lord helped us' (*1 Sam*. 7:12)  Ebenezer is a stone, and stony-hearted Ebenezer Scrooge lives up to his name.

Thus in allegory the question is no longer only, Will Scrooge, coming to honor Christmas, save a crippled child, but:  Will an Ebenezer turn in time FROM Ebenezer or B.C. spiritual ways of vindictive triumph over foes and misanthropic, embattled separatism ('...hath the Lord helped US') reminiscent of Israel's pride in exclusive election and disdain for gentiles, TO the ways of Christ mirrored in 'Tiny Tim,' the child poor in spirit and of lowly origin, the 'Tiny' or fragile Christian enterprise debuting then as now and evermore in a cold world. In Scrooge's fanatical resistance to Christmas (Marley, who now sees all, resists no more) is symbolized Israel's blind refusal of its awaited Messiah, and entrenched, age-old enmity towards Christmas. It is all over with Scrooge's seven-years' dead partner, Marley (sad, ironic *seven*.) But in this hopeful seventh anniversary time, will Scrooge finally turn from his and the Hebrew past and, in the spirit of sabbath and seven, looking up at last, see the Star?

Yes! Divine opportunity knocks thrice. Three Spirits guide Scrooge on a journey through time; one misguided earth-traveller is granted a privileged vision of the whole, *sub specie aeternitatis*. Changed wholly by what he sees, the worldling's 'wicked old screw' (6) Screw-*Scroo*-ge *thy neighbor* policy blown clean away (as if one *could* hold fast to the things of this world!), Scrooge awakens on Christmas morning—wakes as for the very first time, born again. The holy Ghosts are with him yet. 'The Spirits of all Three shall strive within me' (70), he vows. *Three-me:* he rhymes, suddenly all rhymes.

Wild with all happiness, frisky as a new-born colt (or soul), Scrooge scrambles madly out of bed this Christmas Day in the morning as from the grave of a long buried life, or waiting death, Marley's inconsolable ghost its symbol, of his soul. Rushing over, he flings wide the sash. The window open: another coffin-casement sprung wide. Ah! Never before such 'golden sunlight; Heavenly sky; sweet fresh air; merry bells. Oh, glorious! Glorious!' (72) Ring out, wild bells! And Heaven and Nature sing. In such descent of radiance from above and rising up in exultation to behold it is previewed the hoped-for resurrection of man to Glory. Scrooge's irrepressible, endless capers, chortles, exclaimings may well recall a child's boundless delight in opening colorfully-wrapped gifts on Christmas morn, which, figuratively speaking, is just what is happening here. How surpassing good to be born again, *and,* of all happy coincidences, born a child 'at Christmas, when its mighty Founder was a child himself' (53).

Why *such* thanksgiving? Because, the long transfigured night of vision past, it dawns on Scrooge that golden sunlight below ('Oh, glorious!') prefigures ('Glorious!') Glory; that, hark, the whole caroling Creation—sun, air, sky, bells—like the lark at Heaven's gate sings. In Joe Gargery's words, What larks! This is surely no common joy, but tidings of comfort and joy born of revelation of the Joy of joys, Jesu, joy of man's desiring. Of remembering Christ our Saviour was born on Christmas Day. The Eternal bursts in, finally revealed as the wondrous secret of all. The glory of the Lord *shall* be revealed! A 'Heavenly sky,' capital 'H' lofty, intentful, prefigures, promises—Heaven. In such dazzling sunrise, Sonrise; on earth as it is in Heaven. One gust of truly 'fresh air' blows a masking

earthly usage from common sights, words, world.  In short, Scrooge mi-
raculously reborn intuits the world as allegory, a running figure of the life
to come.

   How clever the boy is whom he dispatches for the Cratchit turkey (a child
ever the angel messenger in Dickens) Scrooge wont, can't, can not, *never
can or will* get over.  This is because suddenly the whole intelligent, intelligible, intellectually thrilling order the Creator built into Nature and
world dawns upon his waking soul.  Good Morrow!  Dizzy and all but helpless with the wonder of it all, Scrooge grasps the simple secret of Christmas
and the uncommon meaning of its dear, common sights.  Once, Christmas
for Scrooge was a time of feeling imposed upon, of a holiday for his clerk
and alms for the poor extorted by foes.  Now the reborn Scrooge knows it as
a time when the soul of man in outpouring of gratitude inexpressible for the
gift of a Saviour must give, and unrelieved of its burden of thanks, give still
more.  Never enough!  In, as Dickens calls it elsewhere, 'the great forgiving Christmas time' (SL,203), dare we imagine Scrooge dares hope
himself forgiven.

   The old, crabbed, sunderland 'B.C.' self is no more.  The self that stood
on the Law, dismissing two gentlemen come seeking Christmas donations
for the poor with: 'Are there no prisons?  And the Union workhouses?'
(12); that in Hebrew fashion upheld the lawful charity, which in Dickens, is
synonymous with service only in the letter, not the spirit of heavenly
charity.  Now, though, Scrooge realizes that Christmas marks the birth of a
spirit of compassion and spiritual largeness not to be so confined.  Coming
to care tenderly for a crippled child, undertaking to relieve a humble
family's sore poverty and to raise its hopes, Scrooge at last enters into full
harmony with a Season in which, in Dickens's words, 'we celebrate the
birth of that divine and blessed Teacher, who took the highest knowledge
into the humblest places, and whose great system comprehended all mankind' (LLS,II,400).  Note, not a Chosen Few, but '*all* mankind,' which
sublime ideal shines no less bright in Tiny Tim's message to the world, one
so familiar, it may be, we have ceased to see or grasp it any more:  'God
bless Us, *Every One!*'  (Italics mine.)

   In every nook and cranny of this magic time allegory gleams.  Consider
Scrooge's spectacular, prolonged fit of chuckling: 'The chuckle with which
he said this, and the chuckle with which he paid for the Turkey, and the
chuckle...and the chuckle...only to be exceeded by the chuckle...and
chuckled till he cried' (73).  Echoing still the joyous strain, never before
such *ch*uckling, *C*ratchit-cherishing, and *c*abs to *C*amden town for the lad
(Scrooge insists) upon a Christmas Day.  In flurries of snowy 'c,' 'ch,' and
'C,' Christ particles loosed and scattering all over Creation, the boy is off
like a shot after the gift intended for secret giving, the gift which, as in
allegory itself, the giver remains invisible, the most selfless and so surely
the best, truest Christmas gift of all.  'Chirrup, Ebenezer!' (13), words

which in Scrooge's youth signaled an end to business and the start of Christmas, the Season to be jolly, are heard again. 'Chirrup': *Cheer up, merry gentlemen, let nothing you dismay!* All is as it was. In one little child found in a poor abode, in Tiny Tims evermore, behold the emblem of the Christ child. 'O, come let us adore Him;' carols the *Carol.*

It is interesting, in the light of the above, to discover a 'Tim-child' motif in a work of four years earlier, *Nicholas Nickleby.* In it, an employee of the Cheeryble Brothers, Tim Linkinwater, a kindly, grey-haired eternal child of the Mr. Dick (*Copperfield*) sort who is 'younger every birthday than he was the year before' (473), is sympathetically drawn to an ailing young boy. In *Nickleby* the 'Tim' child dies; in the *Carol,* thanks to an influx of spirit in a human heart, it lives. Two 'Tim' figures pointing to the needy child, two appeals for a rebirth of charity, two glimpses of what it means to become as a little child and enter the Kingdom, suggest that a NT-inspired 'Tim' symbolic cluster, *Timothy* a young disciple of St. Paul's, was lodged in Dickens's emblematic imagination and predated its embodiment in the two works. And a Tim-*Cheeryble* link is likewise Christful to the soul.

The yoke of Dickensian allegory is easy and its burden light. Tiny Tim, recall, hopes it is 'pleasant' for people in church to see him, a cripple, and so be led to remember Christ's kindness to the halt and blind. Note: in Dickens the living symbol more than the preached sermon strikes the Christian lesson warm to the heart. Likewise, in the Crisparkle home:

> It was pleasant to see (or would have been, if there had been anyone to see it, which there never was), the old lady standing to say the Lord's Prayer aloud, and her son, Minor Canon nevertheless, standing with bent head to hear it. (52)

Again, not instructive or improving, but 'pleasant.' In his new self and life, Scrooge too looks 'irresistibly pleasant' (73). Mr. Crisparkle's 'please God, ma dear' (52) perhaps indicates in what special sense 'pleasant' is to be understood in such markedly Christian circumstance: that of pleasing to God. But Dickens would not insist.

Unseen at the devotions of religious allegory, like the Crisparkles at prayer, Dickens both veils and reveals the mysteries of the Kingdom he reinterprets, hinting in quiet ways of secrets to be revealed in the fullness of time and the design. For example, in *Great Expectations,* just when the long concealment seems at an end and the author of Expectations revealed, an all-overturning truth comes to light. In a curious way his allegories go unsuspected and unseen in Dickens's lifetime, thus coming to share the fate of the NT parables inherited by those who 'seeing see not; and hearing [they] hear not, neither do they understand' (*Matt.* 13:13). Dickens is not believed, and neither is Scrooge. But the changed Scrooge ignores the skeptics and scoffers, 'knowing that such as these would be blind anyway' (76). How very tempting to fancy that in Scrooge's moral victory and secret triumph, as in the Crisparkles' worship unseen by a living soul, and perhaps all the worthier for that, Dickens records the essence of his own story. If so, what incomparably rich resonance in the line describing Scrooge: 'His own heart laughed; and that was quite enough for him' (76).

Through all this and more Dickens remains Dickens. Drawn to the traditional moralist's form, allegory, but finding it too formal (the satire on Roman Allegory in *Bleak House* shows why), Dickens reworks it: softens, naturalizes, small 'a's,' and in effect reinvents it for his own purposes.[1] We have greatly enjoyed an unallegorical Dickens for well over a hundred years now and felt no lack. So doubtless could we go on doing for hundreds more. But once the secret is out; once, as in *The Battle of Life,* we begin to hope that sour, cynical, Scrooge-ish Benjamin Britain will stop moping and wed dear, good, plain, serviceable Clemency Newcome: i.e., that 'BRITAIN,' or England, will finally see the light and embrace 'CLEMENCY,' forgiveness, mercy mild, the God-and-sinner-reconciling spirit of her most eloquently Christian Christian name, things are never quite the same again.

Naive allegory beams afar. Symbolic detail is especially telling, in the Dickens way. With her thimble that reads 'For-get and for-give' (CB,255) and nutmeg-grater inscribed 'Do as you-wold-be-done by' (256), Clemency *Newcome* is the Golden Rule of the Gospels in a nut(meg) shell: is New Testament law *New come.* 'Do as you wold be done by,' its wold-wood or would pun sowing woodsy groves in Heavenly willing, implies nutmeg enough for all the Christmas eggnogs in Christendom. No nutmeg-greater. Hyphenated so, 'for-give' stresses *give,* releasing more Seasonal sentiment still. If '"By their fruits ye shall know them," said OUR SAVIOUR' (411), as Dickens quotes in *A Child's History of England,* then Sowerberry is sour enough, and Clemency Newcome, first seen (rather, unseen) in thick foliage, is a whole aromatic 'wold' of NT truth.

'Britain loves Clemency.' Happiest of wishful fancies. Yes, only let the tribe of Benjamin (*Benjamin* Britain) renounce old ways; let *Britain,* clasping *Clemency* to that manly heart, own her before men and nations, and there is an end to all in-Clement laws: to the policed wilderness wanderings of orphans like Oliver Twist and Jo, and martyrdoms under law of many a slain Stephen and Abel.

Wrestling with her pocket for its treasures, Clemency spies the thimble gleaming in the dark depths 'like a pearl of great price' (255). Shining emblem! So does *Clemency* harrow the deep dark 'pocket' of the grave and hell, plucking from its jealous maw 'the pearl,' symbol of the priceless hope of Heaven. In Dickens, no need for dusty law tomes. Thimble and grater, the whole of 'the pocket library of Clemency Newcome' (255), is all man needs. Let droppers and flourishers of *pocket*-handkerchiefs like Belinda and Jaggers, and all dark-souled *Pockets* else let in *that* light! Thus does Dickens show that only as *Clemency* ceases to be a remote abstraction and comes to dwell familiarly—indeed, familial-y—among men in ties of love, is Heaven truly served.

Without Clemency Newcome, Britain's prospects dim. In *Great Expectations,* in the deep, dark house of Pockets that scorned the 'forgive and forget' counsel of Matthew, a ghostly bride wanders and fancies the song 'Old Clem' with its terrible refrain: 'Blow the fire, blow the fire—Old Clem! Roaring dryer, soaring higher—Old Clem!' (89) Such is the old or OT idea of 'Clem,' or Clemency; such Yahweh's ironic 'forgiveness' gained only at the stiff price of the fiery furnaces of Babylon. Whereas the *New* Clem, Clemency Newcome, wrests Heaven for man in Hell's despite. Hopeful as a smiling Spirit of Christmas Yet To Be, Dickensian allegory foretells that, God willing, *Clemency* will save *Britain* yet.

Never was allegory more accessible and plain in work after work. Clues proliferate and abound. A fiction that piles Samuel on Sam and Clara on Clare; that piles Dick the blackbird (*Nickleby*) on Dick Swiveller (*The Old Curiosity Shop*) on Mr. Dick (*Copperfield*) on Dick Datchery (*Drood*) on Richard Doubledick ('The Seven Poor Travellers') shouts in *Doubledick* style of *double Dick*ens, the Dickens of allegory. (Dickens even calls himself 'Dick,' we will see.) He must half want his great scheme discovered. Why else does he labor so at allegory, as when he portrays a learned Doctor hard at work on a great Dictionary, capital 'D' and all, in *Copperfield*, with a worshipful admirer, a modest scribbler, trailing devotedly behind? It is Doctor Johnson, the immortal Dictionary, and Boswell to the life. And in *Great Expectations,* again mining English literary history, Dickens in relating Pip's or Philip's story of a deep, tormented, poetic love for Estella surely echoes the love story of the sonnet cycle of yet another Philip, Sir Philip Sidney, 'Astrophel and Stella.' Why look thus to Biblical and other monumental spiritual myth? Remounting such lofty adventures of the human spirit in all ages, playing Host to pilgrims of the absolute from every shire's end of Judaeo-Christian time colorfully assorting for the ride, 'the journey,' Dickens shows all of history read aright to be in truth a Christian, a Canterbury Tale.

Nearing the end of what he calls 'the journey of my story,' David Copperfield, returned home from abroad, sets out on horseback for Canterbury where awaits him his soul's love, the peerless Agnes Wickfield: Agnes, mirror of the Agnus Dei, Christ. A David or *Trot*wood *trot*ting and cantering to Canterbury is a living, breathing Canterbury pilgrim for our time. And as David's is well known to be Dickens's own story—the life of 'D.C.,' David Copperfield, a symbolic version of that of 'C.D.,' Charles Dickens—there is added intrigue in the search for the allegorical meaning of that life. The visible heights of story long since scaled, those untold, unscaled await us.

The Dickens message was, is, and will always be, love thy neighbor as thyself. Or, to borrow the symbolic language of Fielding, so admired by

Dickens:  Be like Squire Allworthy, 'a human being replete with benev-olence, meditating in what manner he might render himself acceptable to his Creator by doing most good to His creatures.' (Henry Fielding, *Tom Jones,* Chapter XV.  The remarks on allegory in the novel derive from a talk given by Earl Wasserman at the University of Rochester several years ago.)  As after long trials and wanderings Tom Jones returns to his true love, Sophia—and *Sophia* or Wisdom she proves to be in prizing above all other music the works of Handel—and inherits Paradise Hall, so that other foundling and wanderer on the face of the earth, man, proving worthy of the 'Allworthy,' the Father, may one day hope to enter into the Paradise Hall of Halls, Heaven.  As to familiar Dickens lessons in brotherly love, we are now only to discover how entirely and religiously, in Christian wise, Dickens meant them.

Mystery opens into mystery.  It seems incredible that Dickens could have struck out for Biblical present and past, surface and symbol, Time and Eternity, and been one traveller.  But he did and was.  Following in NT footsteps, he spins new garments of the soul on the pattern of 'that older fashion yet, of Immortality!'  The coming of Christ into history present and past is his seminal theme.  His heroes love 'Christiana,' 'Lucie,' 'Estella,' 'Magdalen,' 'Clara,' 'Ada Clare,' all shining with Heaven's light.  And, in *A Tale of Two Cities,* as one worthy Charles D., Charles Dickens, relates how another worthy Charles D., Charles Darnay, is delivered from death by the sublime self-sacrifice of a 'C' or Christ figure upon the 'Cross,' an act inspired by the love of Lucie, Light, and the recovery of a faith that looks past death ('I am the resurrection...'), and sealed in a world-redeeming sunrise in the Son of God, one begins to see with new eyes into the spirit, purpose, and art of 'C.D.'  Could someone named *Charles D.* name a character in one of his works *Charles D.* and do so unawares, and for no reason?  We think not.

Rather, we suggest, in the privacy of the realm of allegory with its veiled disclosure, far from flare and blare of public testimonial, 'Charles D.,' Dickens, reveals a deep sense of indebtedness to his Saviour.  Consider this.  In *A Tale of Two Cities* a Charles D., a good man but even so far from meriting or even fully realizing it, is through the death of 'C' recalled to life.  In triumphal glory of a death on the 'Cross' mounted in *three*—Darnay apprised 'that the final hour was Three' (332); the mob looking eagerly 'towards the third cart' to discover 'which is he' (354); Barsad in agony, fearing betrayal, searching the faces of the condemned, his face clearing 'as he looks into the third' (354); the City clocks chiming 'on the stroke of three' (355); Jerry Cruncher and Miss Pross, two among many ransomed by this death, fleeing the City exactly 'at three o'clock' (345); the words:  'I am the resurrection and the life' sounding in full text a third and final time as an unnamed 'he,' number Twenty-*Three,* dies and is born into Life Everlasting, as his prophetic words uttered from a Beyond at the end make clear—Dickens in full, fervent, soaring power of his Christian faith and art celebrates Christ:  crucified at the third hour (*Mark* 15:25), risen on the third day, in the Trinity one with the Father.  'RECALLED TO LIFE,' the hopeful message long before carried in darkness, symbol of man's age-old, long-cherished hope of deliverance from death, is realized at last in Christ.

In other stories too, of half-dead, lost, abandoned or morally adrift *Dick* figures, from Dick the blackbird to Doubledick, Dickens time and again memorializes the central spiritual adventure of his youth:  his rescue by the grace of God from the life of despair and slavery in a blacking warehouse, his leaving the 'Dick Swiveller' '*Swivel*(ler)' life of spiritual vacillation behind, and his becoming a serious, committed Christian.  In what follows part of that amazing story is told.

Can the case for allegory be proved?  The piling of Christianas in Castles in air on Crisparkles reciting the Lord's Prayer on Clares whispering of Our Saviour as high as Heaven may not be enough.  Yet perfect proof may be beside the point; it instead may or perhaps must come down (or up) to the sudden moment of private conviction, the instant all falls into place, the leap of faith that brings the astounded soul to its celestial feet with a shout of 'Credo!'  But what should the question of Christian allegory in the final analysis be if not a matter of faith?

Having surveyed parts of the kingdom of allegory in Dickens in this chapter, we now set out again to overtake the Dickens of allegory in the pages of *Great Expectations*.

# FOUR

## Star of David, Star of Pip

'Did you give your son the name of Ham, because you lived in a sort of ark?' (DC,32)

David Copperfield's childish question points the way. Why *Ham* indeed, if not for *ark* reasons? And what essence of the Biblical David dwells in a young David of, as it seems and is, the nineteen hundredth year of Christian time?

One might also ask, why *Abel* wandering in a foggy, drenched, primordial wilderness at the dawn of *Great Expectations,* and as if of Judaeo-Christian time itself; surely the ghost of the Hebrew Abel in dying at the hands of the eternal 'C' foe of his life and slayer of its youthful hopes: a 'C,' Compeyson, with an identifying mark on him, no less, even as Cain.[1] Springing up among tombstones in the little churchyard, this might be Abel risen from his uneasy grave in *Genesis* time, his blood still crying from the ground. He stumbles, and it seems to Pip that the hands of dead people are reaching up 'out of their graves, to get a twist upon his ankle and pull him in' (14). The ancient *Abel* fate, the evil unredressed, dogs modern time as man stumbles darkly onward, unchampioned against the Fall.

Like David before him, Pip Pirrip inherits a most bleak In the Beginning consciousness of 'the identity of things' (1) in the Christmas season in which his story begins. Truly a poor, cheerless Christmas, none at all, as nominal Christians of the Mrs. Joe, Wopsle, and Pumblechook sort keep the Day shut up indoors in formally festive, snappish, self-meritorious, child-harassing mood while outside in bitter cold a man of sorrows, in forlorn innocence and suffering a type of Christ (Abel is traditionally seen as an OT type of Christ), shivers and starves, despised and rejected of men. Time B.C. returns, literally with a vengeance, belieing Christendom's proud shows and forms.

Pip's tale begins at sunset as all sinks down into darkness. Bleak sign!

If the Creation has taken place and the waters have been divided from the land, in Pip's country the good news has not been heard, any more than the Good News. In a watery world stones are the only footing 'when the rains were heavy, or the tide in' (4). Pip sets out for the marshes on 'a rimy morning, and very damp' (14). Wetness is everywhere, goblins' tears on windowsills, and 'damp lying on the bare hedges and spare grass' (14) and on the dripping finger-post. It is wet near home, but 'the mist was heavier yet' on the marshes where the awful man waits, a man 'soaked in water' (2) and the more unreal, ghostly, symbolic in heavy mist. Has the Flood really receded from the earth when soon after the man is hunted down, captured, and shipped back to the old captive existence of *Genesis* time, it might be, on a prison ship termed 'a wicked Noah's ark' (36)? After the chase, and much black mud and 'splashing into dykes' (32), comes the battle with the cruel, remorseless 'C.' If Abel does not actually die, he in effect or symbolically does, for, the search over, the torches are flung hissing into the water, 'as if it were all over with him' (36). Hissing. As in Eden, Satan and darkness win the Day.

The *ark* impression haunts Pip. Years later, as he broods over the memory of the stranger he would at that point so gladly forget and whose coming so profoundly and forever changes all, it comes back:

> In my fancy, I saw the boat with its convict crew waiting for them at the slime-washed stairs,—again heard the gruff 'Give way, you!' like an order to dogs—again saw the wicked Noah's Ark lying out on the black waters. (217)

The Law of the ark of the covenant, of Mosaic law, is the spirit behind this merciless instrumentality of 'corrective' punishment, the ark. Dickens thus shows that OT Law and ark, still dominating the social scene, carry no man to salvation. Call it Christendom, but in an age so scant of charity and heavy with Law, so rife with Joseph and child-quelling spirits like Mrs. Joe & Co. who keep Christmas only in the letter—*keep,* quite literally, rather than share it—man still belongs to the Fall, the rampaging spectre of Old Time with us yet, lest we forget.

'Rome' also looms, as of old. At the Christmas dinner, Pip's peculiar torment is 'Mr. Wopsle's Roman nose' (24). Behold 'Mr. Wopsle, united to a Roman nose' (21). Wopsle, who in church 'punished the Amens tremendously' (21), plays Rome ('punished'!) in no merely comic way. Rather, his overbearing 'Swine were the companions of the prodigal' (23), delivered with flourish of fork, is aimed at Pip in rancorous and accusatorial, not to say stabbing fashion. Fierce-souled, unchristian Wopsle is subsequently more symbolic serio-comic 'Rome' and other assorted pagan antiquity as he renders 'Mark Antony's oration over the body of Caesar' (40); and, gleefully 'imbrued in blood to the eyebrows' in Roman style, reports a local murder with relish for gory detail: 'The coroner in

Mr. Wopsle's hands became Timon of Athens; the beadle, Coriolanus'
(127). Wopsle even plays the Roman Colosseum to Pip's early Christian
martyr, symbolically speaking, as follows:

> In my hunger for information, I made proposals to Mr. Wopsle to bestow
> some intellectual crumbs upon me; with which he kindly complied. As it
> turned out, however, that he only wanted me for a dramatic lay-figure, to be
> contradicted and embraced and wept over and bullied and clutched and
> stabbed and knocked about in a variety of ways, I soon declined that course of
> instruction; though not until Mr. Wopsle in his poetic fury had severely
> mauled me. (102)

Ancient Rome, a fragment of which lodges in the soul of this petty church
official of later time, 'mauls' like a lion. Rome too may be said to have
'punished the Amens tremendously' in its day. And how avidly Mr.
Wopsle, fresh from baiting Pip yet still hot for punishment, joins the
soldiers in pursuit of the victims of an inhuman Hebraeo-Roman kind of law
of retributive justice untempered by mercy, and with satisfaction watches
the prisoner remanded to custody on that sad Christmas Day.

One thinks of 'him,' still nameless, the stranger so deeply interwoven
with Pip's awakening in his seventh year (*seven:* apt time to awaken to the
holy), and with all moral adventure, all events terrible and wonderful that
befall him ever after. With a load of bread-and-butter down his trouser
leg, which he is saving for the convict, Pip finds himself remembering 'the
man with the load on *his* leg' (11), 'his' enriching ambiguity. Imagining
'his' burden and pain, Pip, *anima naturaliter Christiana,* the promising
child imprisoned in a narrow world of forms, of pharisaic fanaticism for law
and 'the letter,' first intuits the mystery of Him Who bears the burden of
the sins of mankind; personally, pityingly is put in touch with one that
society, with stony Hebrew-Roman conscience, would and will not see. Despising 'him,' whose condition cries out for relief, the world still rejects,
abjures, and crucifies Him. Like a floating Captivity still awash on the
Flood, the prison ship 'ironed like the prisoners' (36), the 'ark' impressed
into such infamy, bespeaks a resurgent B.C. In an all-but-effaced A.D.,
only Joe and Pip—Joe a *Joseph* figure, we will see, and Pip a tiny seedling of
the moral life, one of Time's 'pips' or seeds destined to grow—in pitying and
in small ways relieving him, keep the spirit of Christmas alive.

The stranger who first appears to Pip in the lonely churchyard, and who,
turning Pip upside down, makes the church leap over its own steeple, as if
Christendom itself felt the shock of His coming in its institutional soul,
wears the mantle of Christ and the NT in multiple dramatic ways. First,
'he' comes *exactly as Christ tells the disciples He will come again.* To wit.:

> Then shall the King say unto them on his right hand, Come, ye blessed of
> my Father, inherit the kingdom prepared for you from the foundation of the

world:

For I was ahungered, and ye gave me meat: I was thirsty, and ye gave me
drink: I was a stranger, and ye took me in:

Naked, and ye clothed me: I was sick, and ye visited me: I was in prison,
and ye came unto me.

Baffled, the disciples ask: 'When saw we thee a stranger, and took thee
in? or naked, and clothed thee? Or when saw we thee sick, or in prison,
and came unto thee?' Christ answers:

And the King shall answer and say unto them, Verily I say unto you, In-
asmuch as ye have done it unto one of the least of these my brethren, ye have
done it unto me. (*Matt.* 25: 31--46)

Lo, Pip's convict comes exactly as Christ, self-identified with 'the least of
these my brethren,' says He will come: 'ahungered,' 'thirsty,' 'a
stranger,' 'naked,' 'sick,' 'in prison,' *and in that exact order.* He comes
starving and thirsty, and Pip brings him pork pie and brandy. Long after,
in a momentous (S)second (C)coming, he is a 'stranger' in the sense that
Pip fails to recognize the yet-unrevealed author of his Expectations. He is
'naked' too, requiring all new clothes for a disguise, which Pip furnishes
him. In time, Pip visits the mortally wounded man in the prison hospital ('I
was sick;' 'I was in prison, and ye came unto me'), and there reads the New
Testament with him.[2] Thus as Abel; as Provis, Providential comer who
fulfills NT prophecy, and as 'him,' Pip's convict is a page torn from related
OT-NT revelation.

His mystery is deeper still. If *Abel* is an OT type of Christ, what of *Magwitch?* MAG, we submit, looks to the Magus, the ancient Magian or priest
of the Zoroastrian religion, a master of the occult, of *magic* and dark
mysteries. As *Mag*witch, the fearful stranger takes still another route
from man's primitive moral-religious beginnings to NT time. As the
Magian priest kept the uninitiated in cowed, terrified subservience to
priestly rule, so in early time of the story Magwitch terrifies Pip. The *witch*
in 'Magwitch' redoubles primitive *Mag* force. Dickens is mindful of
'witch' in the Magwitch connection, as we know when Magwitch's wife,
Estella's mother, reminds Pip of the witches in *Macbeth.* Dark are
Western man's hex-traordinary religious origins, as a fearsome Jesse
Hexam (*Hex 'em!*) (*Our Mutual Friend*) and Magwitch show. The mystery
deepens. *Abel Magwitch—Abel* pointing forward across martyrdom to
Christ; *Magwitch,* to non-Judaic B.C. which in the Magi would cross over
into Christian time—epitomises early moral directions within and without
the Judaeo-Christian pale, in Dickens the more primitive, unevolved 'Magwitch' element slowly fading as the 'Abel' grows. Yet even as Magwitch,
born of B.C. man's traffic in superstition and the supernatural conceived
under its darker aspects, the stranger, like all else in Dickensian history,

ultimately leads to Him.

It is largely as Magwitch that the man starts up from among graves in the memorable opening scene of *Great Expectations*. Making at Pip, invoking a familiar spirit he claims can get at a boy's heart and liver, he spouts oaths: 'Keep still, you little devil, or I'll cut your throat!' (2) and asks: 'You're not a deceiving imp?' (16) *Devil, imp*. Under his influence Nature assumes a fearful animism in Pip's credulous young eyes. Goblins appear in dew; a snorting black ox with 'something of a clerical air' (14) (like many a human clerical ox in Dickens) blows smoke out of its nose, then satanically vanishes with a parting flourish of its tail. No great surprise here. As the Wopsle portrait shows, the clerical and satanic are old bedfellows in Dickens.

The menacing, spell-casting Magian element in Magwitch does not soon or easily die; nor did it in man. Even as the Christ-forthcoming self moves to the fore, on his return the convict can still pull a 'greasy little clasped black Testament out of his pocket' (315) and force Herbert Pocket to swear a self-anathematising oath on it: 'Lord strike you dead on the spot if you ever split in any way sumever' (321). A *black* Testament, indeed. Surely no *New* Testament or usage, that. Yet at heart, in his Abel or Christian name self, Pip's convict is always noble and generous. Pip proves ungrateful to his early benefactor, Joe; but the convict's gratitude to the child who fed and timidly pitied him becomes his life's ennobling theme. Facing all he must face on the night of his capture, the convict nevertheless remembers to speak up and exonerate Pip of the theft of the pork pie; taking the guilt on himself, he again mirrors Christ Who bore the burden of the sins of mankind. All points to Pip's having led the soldiers to him, but somehow the convict knows Pip did not betray him. Shut off from all human and Christian influence, save for Joe, Pip in his seventh year, through 'him,' confronts the mystery of *seven*, that of the generous love that inspired the Creation and forged the link between erring man and a loving God, a mystery shadowed and embodied in 'Him.'

The man deeply torn in body and soul who springs up stark and terrible among tombstones leaps from the pages of the NT in yet another memorable way. In the Gospel of *Mark* we read:

> And they came over unto the other side of the sea, into the country of the Gadarenes.
>
> And when he was there come out of the ship, immediately there met him out of the tombs a man with an unclean spirit,
>
> Who had *his* dwelling among the tombs; and no man could bind him, no, not with chains;
>
> Because that he had been often bound with fetters and chains, and the chains had been plucked asunder by him, and the fetters broken in pieces; neither could any man tame him.
>
> And always, night and day, he was in the mountains, and in the tombs,

crying, and cutting himself with stones.

But when he saw Jesus afar off, he ran and worshipped him,

And cried with a loud voice, and said, What have I to do with thee, Jesus, *thou* Son of the most high God? I adjure thee by God, that thou torment me not.

For he said unto him, Come out of the man, *thou* unclean spirit.

And he asked him, What *is* thy name? And he answered, saying, My name is Legion: for we are many. (*Mark* 5:1-9)

In *Luke* the story reads as follows:

And they arrived at the country of the Gad-a-renes, which is over against Galilee.

And when he went forth to land, there met him out of the city a certain man, which had devils a long time, and ware no clothes, neither abode in any house, but in the tombs.

When he saw Jesus, he cried out, and fell down before him, and with a loud voice said, What have I to do with thee, Jesus, *thou* Son of God most high? I beseech thee, torment me not.

(For he had commanded the unclean spirit to come out of the man. For oftentimes it had caught him: and he was kept bound with chains and in fetters; and he brake the bands, and was driven of the devil into the wilderness.)

And Jesus asked him, saying, what is thy name? And he said, Legion: because many devils were entered into him. (*Luke* 8:26-30)

Dickens knew the story well, as Chapter the Fourth of his Life of Christ, *The Life of Our Lord*, shows. In Dickens we read:

When they [Christ and the disciples] came to the other side of the waters they had to pass a wild and lonely burying-ground that was outside the city to which they were going. All burying-grounds were outside cities in those times. In this place there was a dreadful madman who lived among the tombs, and howled all day and night, so that it made travellers afraid, to hear him. They had tried to chain him, but he broke his chains, he was so strong; and he would throw himself on the sharp stones, and cut himself in the most dreadful manner: crying and howling all the while. When this wretched man saw Jesus Christ a long way off, he cried out, "It is the Son of God! Oh, Son of God, do not torment me!" Jesus, coming near him, perceived that he was torn by an evil spirit, and cast the madness out of him, and into a herd of swine (or pigs) who were feeding close by, and who directly ran headlong into the sea, and were dashed to pieces. (LL,40)

Is not the sore-afflicted man in *Mark* and *Luke* who becomes the 'wretched man' in *The Life of Our Lord* strikingly like the man found among tombstones in scene one of *Great Expectations?* Surely it is the same 'wild and lonely burying-ground' (*The Life*) of the Bible story, or a close symbolic facsimile thereof, in which Pip and the man meet. In Dickens's version, the man possessed by devils is a 'dreadful madman' who has broken the chains 'they' put on him, and who in his anguish throws himself on sharp stones, a detail picked up from *Mark* in which he cuts himself with stones. In all three versions, the man found in the place of tombs mutilates himself and suffers terribly in his devil-made pain. In *Great Expectations* all major particulars—dreadful man, chains broken, stones, suffering—reappear. Dickens even contrives to reproduce the fact of madness. Cursing himself and his lot, Pip's convict is seen 'down on the rank wet grass, filing at his iron like a madman, and not minding me or minding his own leg, which had an old chafe on it, and was bloody, but which he handled as roughly as if it had no more feeling in it than the file' (18). *'Like a madman.'* Also, if the stranger does not *throw* himself on stones, as in *Mark,* he has been cruelly 'lamed by stones' (2).

The Dickens novel also captures the dramatic quality of the man's appearance to Christ. In *Mark:* 'immediately there met him out of the tombs a man.' The convict confronts Pip with the same stark, sudden immediacy:

> 'Hold your noise!' cried a terrible voice, as a man started up from among the graves at the side of the church porch. (1)

Thus the 'man possessed by devils' appearing in the NT and in Dickens's version, *The Life of Our Lord,* lives again in the 'devil-imp'-torn man who launches Pip's complex Christian journey of Expectations.

Magwitch is also Abel, looking backward as well as forward in sacred time. In the OT Abel is a 'keeper of sheep' (*Gen.* 4:2); in Dickens, the transported convict becomes 'a sheep-farmer, stock-breeder' (302). Thus as a shade of the OT Abel, and as Abel seen as an early type of Christ; as 'one of the least of these my brethren' in whom Christ by His own pronouncement evermore is; and as the witched, devil-cumbered wretch among the tombs abandoned by all save a Christian Providence working through Pip and Joe, the stranger and author of Expectations who first appears in the Christmas season in multiple ways points directly to 'the life and lessons of Christ.'

He springs up among tombs as if risen from the dead. Wondrous duality, as in the very midst of Death man cherishes hope of resurrection to Life Eternal. Ironic 'rising up' that is no true one, yet dimly foretells it! Much in that first appearance is suggestive, emblematic. The man grabs Pip and turns him upside down, making the church go head over heels (such is Pip's illusion) til Pip sees the steeple under his feet. As the church leaps over its own steeple, it is as if Christendom itself in its institutional soul knew His overturning might. When the Church comes to itself, Pip finds himself seated 'on a high tombstone' (2). So through 'Him,' by 'him' recalled as foreshadowed, is man raised high above death and the grave.

In Dickens, the seed of hope of a Saviour and Redeemer, a champion against Death, is deep in the germinal layers of the world soul from darkest, coldest and earliest OT time. Many spiritual ages after, Pip will initiate another little Pip, Joe's and Biddy's son, into the mystery:

> And I took him down to the churchyard, and set him on a certain tombstone there, and he showed me from that elevation which stone was sacred to the memory of Philip Pirrip, late of this Parish, and Also Georgiana, Wife of the Above. (457)[3]

In the Christian mystery of death, the tombstone *is* an 'elevation,' Death the height from which man rises to Life. And, recalling one who first removed the sting of death, 'he' places mankind-in-germ upon it.

Coming multiply as Abel, Magian, and Promethean Provis, giver of gifts to mankind, the stranger symbolizes all within Providence from earliest time, and is the composite of all earlier champions of mankind, all heroes and gods, religious stirrings and powers which would be summed up, perfected, fulfilled in Christ in the pilgrim unfolding of Time. The world sorely needs to remember Him. The child is sacred to Christmas, yet Mrs. Joe and her guests—hers, not Joe's—bait and badger Pip, also Joe, who is but 'a larger species of child' (7). (Dickens adores child-men like Joe, Tim Linkinwater (*Nickleby*), and Mr. Dick (*Copperfield*). Of course, Pip and Joe suffer under Mrs. Joe in all seasons, Joe's crossed forefingers a perennial warning to Pip that his wife, Tickler in hand, 'was in a cross temper' (19). Hers is a crucifying 'crossness;' whereas Pip and Joe, fingers crossed in their shared martyrdom, and legs too, often 'like monumental crusaders as to their legs' (19), in a very different sense carry the Cross.

*Great Expectations* opens in a world all but emptied of the spirit of A.D. Flanked by stern 'Rome,' Mrs. Joe, ruler of the Forge, is all ancient moral time in one great warlike swatch. Dark of eye, hair and heart, jealous, wrathful, harsh, she is dead set against Pip's knowing the smallest kindness from anyone against his being, in Pip's words, ' 'Pompeyed or (as I render it) pampered' (39). That 'as I render it' invites rendering in at least one other way; as for example, quite literally as '*Pompey*-ed,' as in Rome and Caesar. A classic Dickens pun triumphantly springs all antiquity underfoot in a trice. That is not all. Mrs. Joe habitually parades her finery 'much as Cleopatra or any other sovereign lady on the Rampage might exhibit her wealth in a pageant or procession' (93). *Cleopatra* adds another touch of Egypt. For that matter, is Mrs. Joe with her whip and overseer's mentality, and bitter hatred of fleeing prisoners in the wilderness of the marshes, not the whole vindictive spirit behind the Captivity of Israel in Egypt? Consider her martial way of dealing with her own two convicts, Pip and Joe, who, cleaned out of house and home, 'had our slices out, as if we were two thousand troops on a forced march' (19). Shades of the Exodus, and, as soldiers pursue fleeing prisoners, sons of

Abel and 'C,' of Pharoah's troops in pursuit of the escaping Hebrews of old.

Mrs. Joe sneers down Pip and Joe as 'mere Mooncalfs' (47). *Mooncalf,* capital 'M' urging it the more, is an ancient superstition,[4] and not found by accident on her lips. Perhaps too she goes on the 'Ram-page' (44) the way the Medo-Persian Empire, whose symbol was the two-horned ram, did; one may also recall how Abraham caught a ram in a thicket and offered it up as a burnt offering in place of Isaac. With RAM-page made much of, it would seem Dickens wants it seen. Then there is Mrs. Joe's ungodly cleanliness while all is ravening within in a life barren of faith, hope, or charity, a fanaticism which also smacks of the Pharisees.[5] Running over at the mouth with 'where the deuce' (19), Mrs. Joe scrubs Pip to within an inch of his life just the way a harsh female hand washed the young Charles Dickens 'as a purification for the Temple.'[6] Mrs. Joe's very language gives her away. When Pip returns home after the chase on the marshes, she thumps the half-asleep boy on the back, exclaiming: 'Yah! Was there ever such a boy as this!' (38) YAH, or Yahweh, it is; her God is the ancient Hebrew one of jealousy and wrath. And: 'Lor-a-mussy me!' (47) she cries before pouncing on Pip. The words prove chillingly prophetic. Her 'Lor,' or Lord of Law, does indeed 'mussy' her; not long after she is struck down. In OT time, man's allegiance was to a Lord Whose mercy was all too often 'mussy.'

Thus Mrs. Joe has stored within those components of B.C., the hard-heartedness bred by a harsh Law, punitive zeal, and want of the spirit of mercy, that would lead to the Crucifixion. By contrast, the man of sorrows excluded from her christless Christmas so full of hard thoughts of convicts and grim satisfaction at their capture and return to captivity, is the way of the Cross. Dickens cannot but pun many times on *cross*. For example, as Pip's convict lies dying:

> A smile crossed his face then, and he turned his eyes upon me with a trustful look, as if he were conficent that I had seen some redeeming touch in him, even so long ago as when I was a little child. (433)

'Crossed,' 'trustful,' and 'redeeming,' *redeem* too a pun, all look to Christ.

In such sad 'B.C.' In the Beginnings of his life, Pip might well be wholly lost to the knowledge of a beneficent Father in Heaven. But happily he has Joe, a very NT Joseph figure in his simple artisan's life and tenderness to the boy child not of his own flesh. Joe is a Christian:

> 'But I did mind you,' he returned, with tender simplicity. 'When I offered to your sister to keep company, and to be asked in church, at such times as she was willing and ready to come to the forge, I said to her, "And bring the poor little child. God bless the poor little child," I said to your sister, "there's room for *him* at the forge!"' (44)

'Room for him,' *him* familiarly alight with ambiguity, may recall:

> Joseph came seeking a resting place
> Where Jesus might be born,
> No room at the Inn for Mary's sweet grace,
> Only a stable forlorn.

In darkest B.C., 'no room at the Inn;' but thanks to Joe there *is* 'room at the forge' for the child which, outliving a symbolic (and not-so-symbolic) neo-Hebrew-Egyptian-Roman, law-shadowed time of mankind's spiritual infancy, finally sees past vain worldly goods and pleasures to Him. In Dickens, Christendom survives so long as one Joseph receives a little child; for 'whoso shall receive one such little child in my name receiveth me' (*Matt.* 18:5), words which echo in Dickens's 'The Long Voyage' (RP, 377).

Dickens intended *Joseph* in no casual way. In a *Dickensian* article we learn that Pip's first protector originally bore the name 'George Thunder.'[7] But almost immediately Dickens changed George Thunder to Joe Gargery (GARgery for its Joseph-supporting *guar*dian or God sound?), as if to house some conception newly come to mind. Exit George Thunder. Yet vestiges of the early *Thunder* intention, fossil-like, lie buried in oldest layers of the text. In witness whereof, consider Joe's comic speech to Pip on the perils of gulping or 'bolting' down bread-and-butter, as Joe imagines Pip has done:

> 'You know, old chap,' said Joe, looking at me, and not at Mrs. Joe, with his bite still in his cheek, 'I Bolted, myself, when I was your age—frequent— and as a boy I've been among a many Bolters; but I never see your bolting equal yet, Pip, and it's a mercy you ain't Bolted dead.' (10)

A giant of a powerful fellow named Thunder goes on and on about Bolting. With capital 'B' hurling it at us the harder, the Thunder-*Bolt* pun delights. Pip's simple-souled champion, termed 'a sort of Hercules in strength, and also in weakness' (6), would seem to have first been conceived as a Greek nature god of sorts, Hercules plus, as he is a blacksmith, Hephaistos, the composite portrait garnished with many a 'Greek' motif.[8] Then apparently Dickens shifted his focus, and while the Nature (Thunder, fire-tending) god intention held, it was subsumed in a complementary and higher Christian one. In Dickens as in early NT times, the Greek and Christian are mutual friends.

The Dickens myth is widely inclusive. Pip is not only the Prodigal son (what Wopsle cites fatuously Dickens means seriously), but also 'a young Telemachus' (218). Throughout Western history man seeks the Father, launching many a quest and journey of Expectations, all ending with the coming of Christ.

The 'Thunder' stilled, Joe Gargery crosses over. What depths of meaning lie in Pip's tribute to him: 'O God bless him! O God bless this gentle Christian man!' (439) No idle, vain 'gentleman' compares with the handiwork of heaven, the *'gentle* Christian *man.'* Joe quietly points upward: 'And so GOD bless you, dear old Pip, old chap, GOD bless you!' Noting Joe's simple dignity, Pip thinks: 'The fashion of his dress could no more come in its way when he spoke these words, than it could come in its way in Heaven' (212). In allegory, such sentiment finds its home of homes.

As once over young David Copperfield's, Hebrew-Roman shadows lengthen across Pip's young life. Not long after the Christmas that sees the end of 'him,' as we suppose, Pip is delivered to Satis House by the opportunitists, Mrs. Joe and Pumblechook, on fire with mercenary expectations. (The unctuous ''umble' postures of Heep and Pumblechook, those whited sepulchres, tell what a screwing, cadging, Pip-pummeling *Pumblechook,* half bogus-*'humble,'* half *'choke,'* is all about.) In the allegory, a little 'pip' or seedling of the spiritual life—in Scriptural metaphor, the seed which is the word of God—is transplanted to the dark, weed-choked, son-and-Sonless ruined garden of Old Time, the wasted Eden lost through the Fall but inhabited still, in perversity of mind and impious prolongation of man's First Disobedience, to his ruination.

That the great House in decay symbolizes the B.C. value system, seen especially in its enmity to Christ, is first grasped on that never-to-be-forgotten first visit through words Estella speaks to Pip:

> She [Estella] saw me looking at it [the brewery] and she said, 'You could drink without hurt all the strong beer that's brewed there now, boy.'
> 'I should think I could, miss,' said I, in a shy way.
> 'Better not try to brew beer now, or it would turn out sour, boy; don't you think so?'
> 'It looks like it, miss.'
> 'Not that anybody means to try,' she added, 'for that's all done with, and the place will stand idle as it is, till it falls. As to strong beer, there's enough of it in the cellars already, to drown the Manor House.'
> 'Is that the name of this house, miss?'
> 'One of its names, boy.'
> 'It has more than one, then, miss?'
> 'One more. Its other name was Satis; which is Greek, or Latin, or Hebrew, or all three—or all one to me—for enough.'
> 'Enough House!' said I; 'that's a curious name, miss.'
> 'Yes,' she replied;' but it meant more than it said. It meant, when it was given, that whoever had this house, could want nothing else. They must have been easily satisfied in those days, I should think. But don't loiter, boy.' (51)

One is mildly thunderstruck at that precise order: 'Greek, or Latin, or Hebrew.' For there hangs over the crucified Christ a sign...

> in letters of Greek, and Latin, and Hebrew, THIS IS THE KING OF THE JEWS. (*LUKE* 23:38)

Add to this implied link between Satis House and the crucifixion the creed of retribution that rules within, and Estella's indifferent slur of the Trinity, 'all three—or all one to me' (so has she been reared in this dark place), and the unchristian, indeed, anti-Christ soul of the place is laid bare. Once, Satis, Satyr, Satan, like Latin, Greek, Hebrew, were enough; but the House founded on the flood, not on a rock, is clearly no longer that. In its cellars is strong beer or 'spirits' enough to loose a second Flood. Abandon hope of A.D., all ye who enter here.

B.C. reigns within. The mistress of Satis House inhabits no living Christian present. In a timeless world of stopped clocks a 'skeleton' (53) in the ashes of a bridal dress, one 'corpse-like' (55) in a garment 'like grave-clothes' (55), is as if exhumed from the grave of time long past. Hence the extravagant symbolism of inner and outer ancientness, rot, decay everywhere. Ensnaring and breaking hearts without mercy; not loving but beggaring her neighbor (the card game she makes Pip play); converting the OT creed of an eye-for-an-eye into a heart-for-a-heart, the 'bride' holds fast to B.C. Through Estella, reared to break hearts without pity, she exacts over and over payment for ancient suffering, refusing to forgive and forget. So did Judaism, fanatic for retribution, the ultimate victim of its infamy Christ, pave the way to Calvary.

Dickens borrows traditional OT symbolism in creating 'the bride,' the prophets' metaphor for Israel. And he strongly and explicitly associates a passion for retribution with Judaism. In 'Capital Punishment' he contrasts the Hebrew and Christian codes as follows:

> The Rev. Henry Christmas, in a recent pamphlet on this subject, shows clearly that in five important versions of the Old Testament (to say nothing of versions of less note) the words, "by man," in the oft-quoted text, "Whoso sheddeth man's blood, by man shall his blood be shed," do not appear at all. We know that the law of Moses was delivered to certain wandering tribes in a peculiar and perfectly different social condition from that which prevails among us at this time. We know that the Christian Dispensation did distinctly repeal and annul certain portions of that law. We know that the doctrine of retributive justice or vengeance was plainly disavowed by the Saviour. (OL,151)

Again in 'The Sunday Screw,' cited in Chapter II, Dickens insists on the supremacy of Christ over the Law:

> One Christian sentence is all-sufficient with us, on the theological part of the subject. "The Sabbath was made for man, and not man for the Sabbath." No amount of signatures to petitions can ever sign away the meaning of those words; no end of volumes of Hansard's Parliamentary Debates can ever affect them in the least. Move and carry resolutions, bring in bills, have committees, upstairs, downstairs, and in my lady's chamber; read a first time, read a second time, read a third time, read thirty thousand times; the declared authority of the Christian dispensation over the letter of the Jewish Law,

particularly in this especial instance, cannot be petitioned, resolved, read, or committee'd away.  (OL,227)

It is clearly much on Dickens's mind that 'the doctrine of retributive justice or vengeance' which rules England and Satis House alike, macrocosm and microcosm, tramples 'the Christian Dispensation' in the dust.  We think Dickens would exorcise the Hebrew Ghost haunting Christianity, and so render the latter truly Christian at last.  Twelve months before his death, Dickens writes a will which closes with these words:

> I commit my soul to the mercy of God, through our Lord and Saviour Jesus Christ; and I exhort my dear children humbly to try to guide themselves by the teaching of the New Testament in its broad spirit, and to put no faith in any man's narrow construction of its letter here or there.  (FD,II,38)

Hebrew Law eyes 'the letter.'  By contrast, Christian law is written, not with ink, but with the Spirit of the living God; not in tables of stone, but in fleshly tables of the heart' (*2 Cor.* 3:3).

Retribution and Law rule in Satis House.  In its dark chambers a great Lawyer who casts off pleading Jews and like Pilate washes his guilty hands freely comes and goes.  So does jealous, wizened Sarah Pocket: *Sarah,* one more decayed remnant of *Genesis* time.  A Ruined Garden, sad memorial to the lost Eden, is outside; an identical figurative likeness exists within. Sarah Pocket's off-noted green and yellow complexion is the exact color of the weeds in the Garden, a 'wilderness' (83), in Dickens's telling word, in which humanity still wanders.[9]  The bride herself is as withered as the bridal flowers she wears.  Pointing up her life as in a garden is the trimming of her dress 'like earthy paper' (59), and the fact that Pip pushes her from room to room in a garden chair.  The face of Sarah Pocket, brown and shriveled, 'might have been made of walnut shells' (80).  No kernel within. ('"By their fruits shall ye know them," said OUR SAVIOUR.')  The 'Pocket' way symbolizes the deep, dark 'pocket' of the grave.  And no one in Satis House heeds the voice of *Matthew* Pocket, who alone points the way from Death to Resurrection, as did the *Matthew* Gospel.

Hebrew history and the history of Satis House run parallel.  The 'bride,' Hebrew symbol of the People beloved of Jehovah or Yahweh, was not always withered; she too once had Great Expectations.  But her lord, the Bridegroom, betrayed 'her,' as the Lord abandoned Israel to exile in Assyro-Babylonian deserts, the merciless just 'deserts,' as it were, mandated by His punitive Law.  In Dickens, the bride relives that ancient fate, adopting the old retributive formula that permits no healing.  Thus, like Israel, she is lost to the true bridal and the waiting Bridegroom, Christ.

The hypocritical Pockets, Miss Havisham's relations, soon reveal which Testament rules the House.  On one occasion Sarah, Camilla, and Raymond Pocket are discussing the banished Matthew's lamentably weak character:

> 'Poor dear soul!' said this lady [Camilla] with an abruptness of manner
> quite my sister's. 'Nobody's enemy but his own!'
> 'It would be much more commendable to be somebody else's enemy,' said
> the gentleman; 'far more natural.'
> 'Cousin Raymond,' observed another lady, 'we are to love our neighbour.'
> 'Sarah Pocket,' returned Cousin Raymond, 'if a man is not his own neigh-
> bour, who is?' (75)

Such, to paraphrase a sardonic remark in *Little Dorrit,* is 'the latest polite
reading' of the Sermon on the Mount in Pocket circles. The hollow and
corrupt Raymond, perversely rendering the verse from *Matthew* about
loving one's neighbor, is the light (*Ray*) of this world (*mond*) and voice of
*its* creed; such light is dark enough. 'Natural' feeling, enmity, is all he
recognizes. As to Camilla Pocket, who reminds Pip of his 'Egyptian'-
souled sister, a *Camilla-camel* pun neatly plants her back in barren deserts
of B.C. [10]

In allegory great symbolic wonders first come to light. Herbert Pocket
tells Pip how Satis House rose on the crest of a great brewing fortune. The
once-prosperous brewery now lies in ruins, Dickens making poetic much of
it, as follows:

> To be sure, it was a deserted place, down to the pigeon-house in the brew-
> ery-yard, which had been blown crooked on its pole by some high wind, and
> sould have made the pigeons think themselves at sea, if there had been any
> pigeons there to be rocked by it. But, there were no pigeons in the dove-cot,
> no horses in the stable, no pigs in the sty, no malt in the storehouse, no
> smells of grains and beer in the copper or the vat. All the uses and scents of
> the brewery might have evaporated with the last reek of smoke. In a by-yard,
> there was a wilderness of empty casks, which had a certain sour remembrance
> of better days lingering about them; but it was too sour to be accepted as a
> sample of the beer that was gone—and in this respect I remember those re-
> cluses as being like most others. (58)

The brewing which founded a small empire is no more. The dove-cot is
vacant; the Holy Spirit flown. No more melodious isle where 'spirits,' or
spiritual ferment, gat them home. In the vision of the brewery, the 'large
paved lofty place in which they used to make the beer' (58), Dickens in the
choice of 'lofty' (he might have said 'raised') pays tribute to the exalted
ideals of the Hebrew founders of monotheism, a vision now in ruins. No
malt or grains: if the seed is the word of God, the spiritual granaries are
empty. The 'wilderness' of empty casks-recluses comparison at the end,
implicating Miss Havisham and all her tribe, stresses a 'spirits'-people
connection; again Israel wanders in the 'wilderness.' Suddenly one discerns the masterful *brewi*ng-(He)*brew*-ing pun underlying all.

The great brewers of old were the *He*brew-ers! Now, though, in the time of 'the extinct brewery' (74), all is vacancy and void. The once-plentiful malt, symbolic of spiritual harvests gleaned from seed sown in Old Scripture, is no more. Judaism, it seems, brewed too-fierce spirits; the House floats upon them as upon the flood. Not that He-brewing ever produced the higher spiritual ferment, the wine.

Painting a tableau of B.C., Dickens recreates the ancient Wilderness Wandering in an ingenious way. In a 'wilderness' (58) of empty casks, become ghostly recluses, souls gone sour, Pip and Estella drift ever farther backward into 'Hebrew' time:

> For when I yielded to the temptation presented by the casks, and began to walk on them, I saw *her* walking on them at the end of the yard of casks. (58)

The Brewery world-in-ruins exerts the old, destructive fascination, and, succumbing to the 'temptation,' two children, types of the 'children' of Israel, together with other human 'spirits' (in the ongoing spiritous-spiritual pun), resume the old 'wilderness' wandering. Dickens keeps it alive. Returning as a young man, Pip again disconsolately surveys 'the wilderness of casks that I had walked on long ago' (379). Other symbolism also sends Time reeling backwards. When as young adults Pip and Estella stop at an inn for tea, they are served a lone lorn muffin in Captivity under an iron cover, and 'Moses in the bulrushes typified by a soft bit of butter in a quantity of parsley' (254). Dickens is only half joking. Pip has just come from a tour of Newgate Prison where he looked over long rows of doomed men, looked and then left without batting an eye. In his soul too it is B.C.

B.C. returns wherever the sins of the fathers are visited on the innocent children, as in the case of Pip and Estella. Satis House annexes young Pip to its creed; it also unheavens Estella, the Star. Coming to stress only an adamantine Law, Judaism stopped looking up and did not see the Star, the hopeful candle of Heaven meant to light men on their way. We are re-minded of Estella's lost destiny, her affinity with the Above. When she is summoned, 'her light came along the dark passage like a star' (54); in the brewery yard, see her 'pass among the extinguished fires, and ascend some light iron stairs, and go out by a gallery high overhead, as if she were going out into the sky' (59). *Light,* a pun, advances the design. The point is, 'Estella' belongs in the sky, not in the 'old and grave' (78) (*grave* a frequent pun) House. In Dickens, the Estellas of the Creation, like the Lucies, Agneses, Ada Clares, Christianas, are born to lift hopes; to exer-cise men's hearts in celestial ways of love, wonderment, and praise; as Beatrice did for Dante, to illumine the symbolic text written in the starry firmament, which declares the glory of God, of Heaven's compassion for man. But imprisoned in old creeds and ways, a denatured *Estella,* earth-bound, points downward, as when she scornfully sets Pip's dole of food and beer down on the stones of the yard, just as time and again she dashes his tremulous hopes in the dust.

In Satis House, the clock in Miss Havisham's room, her watch, and the clock on the outer wall of the brewery, long still, have all stopped at twenty minutes to nine. Christ is crucified at the ninth hour, the climactic Christian hour the bride holds at a distance. In Satis House, it does not arrive. Miss Havisham, with no first or Christian name, significantly enough, *will not* enter A.D. Instead, refusing to surrender the ambition for vindictive triumph, she impresses two children into the service of that old hate. As the three wander through the old house, Pip pushing her in her garden chair from behind, Miss Havisham croons the hymn to fiery vengeance, 'Old Clem.' Pip no sooner arrives at Satis House than he is caught up in the ancient cycle of fall, penitence, and expiation without end, the lot of the ancient followers of Yah. Punished by Estella, as B.C. man by Heaven— but Heaven misconceived by him, misread—Pip performs an old symbolic rite:

> I got rid of my injured feelings for the time, by kicking them into the brewery-wall, and twisting them out of my hair, and then I smoothed my face with my sleeve, and came from behind the gate. (58)

Poor Pip, poor mankind, in B.C.s ancient and extant so endlessly punished from above, and, in penetential performance, endlessly self-punishing. (One recalls Mrs. Clennam in *Little Dorrit*, exulting in her pain, 'the just dispensation of Jehovah,' its 'justice' clearly 'the doctrine of retributive justice or vengeance...plainly disavowed by the Saviour.') Like a latter-day wailing-wall, the brewery-wall is punished as its punisher was punished, in the credo of a blow-for-a-blow. Miss Havisham's bitter creed, 'Do unto others *as they have done unto you*,' perverts the Golden Rule. Unavailing pain and grief! Dickens deplores such self-'twisting' as Pip inflicts on himself in this poisonous place.

Such were, and, regrettably, are the early stages of man's journey of Expectations. Pip's fantasy of sitting with Estella and Miss Havisham in a coach without horses strikes truth. In B.C., man goes nowhere. Pushing the garden chair between rooms, in the bride-cake chamber cold smoky air hanging 'like our own marsh mist' (78), and shuttling back and forth between the marshes and Satis House, Pip, spiritually speaking, moves between identical symbolic pockets of ancient Time far to the rear of A.D.

To return to Pip's convict, in the NT story of the man among the tombs who confronts Christ, Christ to relieve him drives his devils out of him and into a herd of swine feeding nearby, which run headlong off a cliff and are drowned. What would the story be without the famous Gadarene swine? In Dickens, sure enough, they return. Indeed, Mrs. Joe and her unchristian cohorts feed on and pompously moralise about nothing but—pig! The sheer quantity of pickled pork, sermons on swine, hints about porkers, gifts of savoury pork pie, and references to stuck pigs on the Wopsle, Mrs. Joe, and Pumblechookian tongues, one way or another, is truly remarkable. Pig in all shapes and forms dominates the feast. A dinner featuring 'a leg of pickled pork and greens' (19), readied amid such holiday greetings as: 'And where the deuce ha' *you* been?' (19), is only the beginning. *Deuce:* see the devils fly. Mr. Wopsle, punisher of the Amens, impales a NT text with: 'Swine were the companions of the prodigal. The gluttony of Swine is put before us, as an example to the young.' Pip's wry comment: 'I thought this pretty well in him who had been praising up the pork for being so plump and juicy' (23). The Pumblechook contribution to Christian fellowship this Christmas Day also takes the form of pig: 'Pork—regarded as biled—is rich, too; ain't it?' (25) He it is who makes Mrs. Joe the present of the fatal pork pie she so prizes, and which Pip steals for the convict. *'Biled'* indeed; moralising to make one bilious.

Pig is the theme of a Pumblechook oration at dinner: 'Look at Pork alone. There's a subject! If you want a subject look at Pork!' (23) (Cool hint. Yes, *let* everybody look into Pork, really look, and it is only a stone's throw to the story of Christ's compassion for the man among the tombs.) Hot for 'subjects,' Pumblechook now turns on Pip, a perennial favorite subject for torture, inquisitorial interviews, and lessons in sums, with: 'If you'd been born a Squeaker—'(24). He proceeds to inform Pip that, under those interesting circumstances, he would have been raised only to be slaughtered under the butcher's sharp knife. Pumblechook visibly warms to the old theme of child-sacrifice, one which echoes in the Orlick adventures to come. In her turn, Mrs. Joe sneeringly calls Joe a 'staring great stuck pig' (9), which neatly spits him for the fire.

In short, Dickens plays a superb theological joke on this infernal set of Scripture-quoting Devil's disciples who stuff themselves and run over at the mouth with what might well be those devil-stuffed Gadarene swine. If ever company were possessed by evil spirits, Lord knows this one is. A herd of pigs flies in and out of the whole set of prating mouths as one after the other reviles what is sacred above all else to Christmas: Joseph, and the little child whose mother, recall, is 'wife of the Above' (39)! 'Misunderstanding' what those words carved on the tombstone mean, Pip in his wise innocence intuits more concerning 'the Above' than a Christendom full of clerks at church like Wopsle. Not harangues on the Prodigal, but the simple goodness of a child man and winged fancy of the child 'so fresh from God' (OCS,4) will save us, if anything can.

Will Wonders never cease? In Dickensian allegory, never. Abel Magwitch, 'A.M.' or Dawn-of-Christianity man [11] appearing in earliest Judaeo-Christian, neo-*Genesis* time of the novel, looks not only to but past dark Magian arts to the Magi, the Wise Men who journeyed far following the Star. Magwitch is the father of Estella. World-overturning revelation! Many are the divine mysteries long-concealed which Time brings to light. As Magwitch to Estella, so the Magi to the Star. As the gentiles, the Magi, crossed over into NT time, so the father of Estella completes the long journey that Abel, earliest glimmer of the profound Christian mystery of suffering unmerited, death, and resurrection, began.

Thus in way after way Pip's convict embodies the Christ-anticipating predispositions, glints, and testaments of the human soul in its history of yearning upwards to light. Pointing to NT mystery, he is the essence of the terrible and wonderful in the spiritual plasm of Western man, no originally terrible left unraised, untransmuted by the end of man's long night's journey into day, the Day of Christ. Reliving much Scripture Old and New, he is Dickens's living gospel of the life and lessons of Christ, a son of man whose passion stirs subliminal memories of the Passion of the Son of Man and His gift to a weary world (O thrill of hope!), *Estella,* the Star.

But the creed of vengeance dims her Light. Miss Havisham fashions of her an Idol. Then, perceiving that Estella feels nothing, not even for her benefactress, 'the bride' lashes out: 'You stock and stone! You cold, cold heart!' (289) This is Hebrew idiom. In the *Book of Jeremiah,* the prophet accuses the bride, Israel, of: 'Saying to a stock, Thou art my father; and to a stone, Thou hast brought me forth' (2:27); and, still in 'wedding' metaphor, of 'defil[ing] the land, and committ[ing] adultery with stones and stocks' (3:9). With calm, impassive face 'like a statue's' (254), Estella even looks like a graven image or idol, not a living girl. She speaks to Pip as one who has no will of her own, and as if wheeled in and out on casters, 'glides' away at a touch. Like ancient Israel lost to worship of the true God and caught up in the madness of Astarte or star-worship, 'the bride,' all 'witch-like eagerness' (288) as she probes Pip's wounds at Estella's hands, betrays the old '*magwitch*' fatality of soul as, decking her Idol in glittering jewels and chanting a litany of vengeance, she worships the abomination she has made, triumphant in having turned Heaven's light into heathen stock-and-stone darkness.

Dickens *means* stock and stone, sick love of which infests mankind still. Looking far to the rear of 'Macbeth,' he locates the source of demonism and of the witching evil behind the downfall of kings and commoners alike throughout the ages, in the *magwitch* dawn of time. The dire warnings of the Hebrew prophets could not cure an apostate People of a passion for idols like Moloch and Baal. In Satis House, *Matthew* Pocket, recalling to 'the bride' a loving, forgiving God Who exacts no bloody sacrifice, has the answer, but he is rejected. 'Pocketed' away in counterchrist darkness, Miss Havisham never knows that the true Bridegroom has come, One who never deserts or betrays. Thus Old Time wears on in the House with its monuments to religious time past—its branched candlesticks and yearly covenant-renewal ceremony. Behold 'certain wintry branches of candles' which do not shed light so much as they 'faintly troubl[e] the darkness' (78). Why 'certain' branches? I suspect Dickens is lightly hinting at the seven-branched candlestick of Temple worship. Even the bride-cake ceremony in the room used only on this occasion, a kind of Holy of Holies, has a religious air.  In time, the House with the Greek-Latin-Hebrew super-scription which 'brewed' the retributive spirit that killed Christ, comes down, and the bride, like the tree that brings not forth good fruit and is hewn down and cast into the fire (*Matt.* 7:19), is no more.

Magwitch too becomes an idolater.  As Miss Havisham to Estella, so Magwitch to Pip.  Returning from abroad, he seeks out the object of his idolatrous love in Pip's lodgings in the Temple.  (Dickens highlights 'Temple,'[12] a most useful pun.)  He discloses himself to the little idol of vanity his fortune has made.  Gloating over the gold watch, diamond-and-ruby ring, and fine linen Pip is wearing, he exults: 'Yes, Pip, dear boy, I've made a gentleman on you!' (304) (True, 'on,' not *of;* happily, a better Pip waits within.)  As the bride bedecks and worships Estella, so Magwitch in posture of worship kneels to the little idol of vanity, his 'gentlemen.'  Her '*witch*-like eagerness' and his greedy, hotly devouring 'Mag*witch*' adoration, perhaps a parody of the worship of the Christ child by the Magi, are one.  Dark Satis House, Hebrewing fierce spirits still; dark 'Temple' of such worship of idols.  In Christian time, Estella and Pip, twin objects of hideously misconceived expectations, are victims of a terrible retroversion of soul that gripped ancient man and grips him still.

Yet all the while A.D. is recruiting its loyal forces.  Matthew Pocket stops tearing his hair and becomes Pip's tutor; Pip reads with *Matthew,* i.e., studies the Gospel.  Cheerful, hopeful, generous Herbert, Matthew's son, befriends Pip and rechristens him Handel.  Happy opening strain of the 'Messiah'!  Coming to know John Wemmick in his 'John' life, John of the fishing-rod, Pip, always moving closer to Provis, comes out from under the shadow of Law, as this short but telling symbolic exchange between Pip and Jaggers late in the novel shows:

> 'As we are going in the same direction, Pip, we may walk together.  Where are you bound for?'
> 'For the Temple, I think,' said I.
> 'Don't you know?' said Mr. Jaggers.
> 'Well,' I returned, glad for once to get the better of him in cross-examination, 'I do *not* know, for I have not made up my mind.' (367)

The *double entendre* is heavy.  Law speaks in typical Captivity idiom: 'bound for,' a pun, as 'cross-examination' hints of the dire old searching out of victims on the cross.  However, for once Pip holds his own; he avoids being nailed down or committing himself to Jaggers's direction.  The question is significant.  *Is* Pip, once taken for one of Jaggers's apprentices by the turnkey of Newgate, bound for 'Temple' and 'Hebrew' life of law?  The Temple soon after becomes a place of danger.  Wemmick's note left for him 'at the Temple gate' (347) warns Pip away.  In time, Pip leaves the elitist gentleman life and the Temple for good.

Stage Three of Pip's unfolding Expectatiions, *three* in Christ, arrives. Pip is increasingly absorbed in protecting, caring for, watching ('Watch ye therefore!') and 'waiting for—Him' (311). 'He' becomes the theme of Pip's changed life. In putting the man of sorrows before himself; in no longer shrinking from one of 'the least of these,' but accepting all the stranger implies of love and sacrifice asked as given; and especially in coming to value him in his heart, realizing what the man endured for his own sake, what gifts he risked all to give, Pip at last regains his own soul. The profound, ever-deepening experience of 'Him' mystically blends into experience of Him, even Christ; the figure so long and well acquainted with grief, in chains of man's inhumanity and merciless Law, is more and more Christful a Christ figure.

Like the first in the little churchyard, his second coming changes all. And Second Coming it is. On the night of his return as from the dead ('as if it was all over with him'), all Christendom registers the shock. A storm of colossal magnitude drives over London from the East, just as Scripture foretells.[13] In his upper-storey lodging in the Temple, which is shaken by raging winds and rain, Pip is alone:

> I read with my watch upon the table, purposing to close my book at eleven o'clock. As I shut it, Saint Paul's, and all the many church-clocks in the City—some leading, some accompanying, some following—struck that hour. The sound was curiously flawed by the wind; and I was listening, and thinking how the wind assailed and tore it, when I heard a footstep on the stair. (299)

Eleven o'clock, the auspicious eleventh hour of the parable.[14] As the church turned upside down with (H)his first coming, now the churches hail him. A multitude of church-clocks, a sky-borne pilgrims' chorus in the company of Saint Paul, welcome him on high. Hosanna in the highest! The cadence of welcome echoes the Trinity in: 'some leading, some accompanying, some following.' In so rich a gathering to 'c' and 'ch,' '*ch*urch-*c*locks in the *C*ity,' capital 'C' another hint, might be striking the hour in the City of God.

Some short time after, Pip and Herbert plan a journey to save Pip's convict from the long arm of the Law. In a little boat they wait for him (how many 'waiters' there are in Dickens; men watch and wait, and the Waits play[15]), who comes in seafarer's garb. The river journey begins in a fit place for Beginnings, the Temple stairs. Again, through an unnamed 'him,' one glimpses the soul of Him:

> 'Is he there?' said Herbert.
> 'Not yet.'
> 'Right! He was not to come down till he saw us. Can you see his signal?'
> 'Not well from here; but I think I see it.—Now I see him! Pull both. Easy, Herbert. Oars.'

> We touched the stairs lightly for a single moment, and he was on board and
> we were off again. He had a boat-cloak with him, and a black canvas bag, and
> he looked as like a river-pilot as my heart could have wished.
>     'Dear boy!' he said, putting his arm on my shoulder, as he took his seat.
> 'Faithful dear boy, well done. Thankye, thankye!' (413)

Through his 'Faithful...well done' one hears a faint but clear chime of the
Gospel:

> His lord said unto him, Well done, *thou* good and faithful servant: thou
> hast been faithful over a few things, I will make thee ruler over many things:
> enter thou into the joy of thy lord. (*Matt.* 25:21)

Seeking the open sea, the spiritual sons of Matthew and Joseph, their
thoughts full of 'him,' pass the John of Sunderland making speeches to the
wind. *Joseph, Matthew, Paul, John:* New Time is fast rearriving, the conspiracy to save Him and His born, as of old, in the very shadow of the
Death-dealing Law.

The wizard-enchanter parts belonging to the Magus part of Magwitch
have burned out. There remains only the Magi yearning which, virginal,
commingling with Heaven, brought such requital to desire the very gentiles discerned it in a Star. As 'He' brought forth the Star, so 'he' brings it
forth still, the eyes of history forever turned to the Greatest Story Ever
Told. Before the convict's death, Pip restores to him his long-lost, beloved
child, Estella:

> 'She lived and found powerful friends. She is living now. She is a lady and
> very beautiful. And I love her!' (436)

Again taken by the Law, he bows before the mandate of Death set down by
a higher Law. His story ends as it began, pointing to the life and lessons of
Christ. Pip records:

> Mindful, then, of what we had read together, I thought of the two men who
> went up into the Temple to pray, and I knew there were no better words that I
> could say beside his bed, than 'O Lord, be merciful to him a sinner!' (436)

To return now to the earlier Pip, David Copperfield, *his* early or 'magwitch' era is the superstition-ridden time of his birth. David is born in a
sack or caul, thus attracting gloomy old wives' prophecies that he will be
unlucky in life and see 'ghosts and spirits' (1). How true, but in ways these
prophets of doom never dream. Yes, David *will* be 'unlucky,' i.e., a
stranger to luck, Fortuna, chance; he will inhabit a Providential universe.
Many others, it seems, have no reliance *but* luck. An old lady and a bill
broker, hoping to be 'guaranteed from drowning' (1), vie for David's caul,
proving that David is right to conjecture he was born in an age 'short of

faith' (1). Thus lightly introduced, the theme of faith nevertheless proves a key, *the* key one of the novel. David promptly sides with faith:

> To begin my life with the beginning of my life, I record that I was born (as I have been informed and believe) on a Friday, at twelve o'clock at night. (1)

It is one thing to be duly informed, but another, and the greater, to be informed *'and believe.'*

The old lady in search of magic talismans to 'guarantee her from drowning' (shades of that oldest of old anxieties, the Flood) stubbornly clings to old (Old) ways. No matter that life is unsatisfactory. The old lady will not hear of change, saying: 'Let us have no meandering' (2). In early times, so much for 'the journey.' But the mind of David's father, the first David Copperfield, dared to 'meander,' as Betsey Trotwood recalls:

> 'David Copperfield all over!' cried Miss Betsey. 'David Copperfield from head to foot! Calls a house a rookery when there's not a rook near it, and takes the birds on trust, because he sees the nests!' (6)

Plain-spoken, doggedly literal-minded Betsey, to whom no speck of wonder adheres, holds this business of taking 'on trust' to be pure foolishness. But we see past her harumphing and pooh-poohing to a mythical David, a shadowy spirit behind the present (as such, the closer to *the* David), who believed in wonders invisible, winged glories of the air, the beneficent unseen in the Creation. As another romantic idealist in Dickens, Flora Casby of *Little Dorrit,* says: 'If seeing is believing, not seeing is believing too' (535)—in allegory, a truth doubly true.

No pigeons in the dove-cot of Satis House; no birds at Blunderstone. The Rookery is rook-less; no birds sing. This is just as well. In Dickens, rooks are always raucous, ground-strutting, sly, disputatious birds with a marked clerical air.[16] The OT vision and all worship still formed on it, Dickens implies, soars no higher than rooks, crows, *jackdaws* (recall *Jack Daw*kins, the Artful Dodger, tool of the Jew in *Oliver Twist.*) Blunderstone man blunders in his conception of the Deity; in it too much rook, or black-garbed priestly influence, comes between man and the sky. Yet this is, after all, the first spiritual ground (or sky)-breaking of Western time. The more honor, therefore, to the father of David who boldly struck out in new directions, building 'on trust.'

Dying, David leaves behind a child-wife, Clara, whom he patiently, lovingly taught and formed while he lived. *Clara Copperfield,* a bright 'C'-field first and last. Of course CLARA, Light, brought forth David! In Allegory, the Hebrew David embraces 'Light,' illuminating Judaism with a dream of a Shepherding God of mercies, from which union of David and 'Clara' comes rich harvests of poetic faith. Lead, kindly Light! True, little Clara is not the steadiest or most centered of lights; in the spiritual dawn of

House of David time, vision flickers. But she is coming along quite nicely under David's tutelage, gaining confidence in her lessons in reckoning accounts, even adding a fanciful touch or two of her own, such as a curly tail to numbers. (OT time is great on *Numbers*.) Then David dies, and the Davidic genius, inspired by love of God in its broad spirit, is eclipsed by the retributive might of Law engraved in (Murd)*stone*.

The two identical MURDSTONES which darken the skies over the House of David symbolize the two stone tablets of Mosaic Law, law narrowly conceived in the letter. With David gone, his fond but foolish, easily beguiled widow, guardian of his son, promise in germ of a son of David, falls into Murdstone hands. The tale of a 'Clara' killingly 'loved,' ruled, destroyed by a black Murdstone night is an allegory of how the first visionary hope kindled in a splendid rose-colored dawn of monotheism—hope in a beneficent God Who said, Let there be, not Law, but *Clara,* Light—came to be eclipsed in the rise to dominance in Israel of a passion for the Law, in Dickens always seen in the perspective of the instrument that would kill Christ. Hence 'MURD-stone,' the sinner-stoning decree of death to sons of David, as once to the Son of David, down through time.

Murdstone usurps the father's, even the Father's, place. Now follows the long, wintered, soon orphaned childhood of David Copperfield's discontent. Murdstone rules David as Jaggers, Pip; two orphans losing a Father are afflicted in the Law. In boyhood and after, David falls prey to a whole slew of spiritual maladies which afflicted the Jews of old: for one, idolatry of the imperious Steerforth, from which follows a shameful failure to defend his friend, the Master:-so would the sons of Levi betray 'the Master,' even Christ.

Surviving a bitter 'Hebrew' childhood, schooled by Murdstone in rules, prices, penalties even as the People of David were in the law and the price payable for disobedience to that law, David, who will not take the Murdstone bit in his teeth, is sent into captivity in a city twice termed 'the Modern Babylon,'[17] a symbolic Babylonian Captivity, an exile far from home and life of slave labor, complete down to the lions' den in the form of a public house called 'the Lion' (160). After escaping from Babylon, David resumes Everyman's long, footsore trek in the wilderness of human cruelty and indifference: long is the road through B.C. to A.D., as the following chapters show.

But Hope survives. In such Davids and sons of David the spirit of the Son of David lives on. And as there was Philip Pirrip, there is his son, Philip, or Pip; and *his* spiritual heir, Joe's little Pip. *Phillip Pirrip:* read forward or backward, 'pip' lies within, and a Philip like Philip the disciple, living to magnify Him.

How the latest David and Pip fare on 'the journey' we go on considering next.

# FIVE

## The B.C. Journey of Man:
## The Dark at the Foot of the Stairs

'Mrs. Chillip does go so far as to say,' pursued the meekest of little men, much encouraged, 'that what such people miscall their religion, is a vent for their bad humours and arrogance. And do you know I must say, sir,' he continued, mildly laying his head on one side, 'that I *don't* find authority for Mr. and Miss Murdstone in the New Testament?'
'I never found it either!' said I. (DC, 834)

*In the Beginning was the ward:* Ed*ward* Murdstone recreates that old B.C. condition of helpless dependency, of warder and ward, in young David Copperfield's life. Once alight with the faith of its founder, David's father, the House of David grows dark as the intensely dark-haired, dark-eyed, black-bearded Mr. Murdstone usurps the father's place. Under Murdstone, David's young life is wholly centered on fact, rule, and stiff penalty for the least unwitting infraction of Murdstone law.

*Murdstone,* the sinner-stoning night of Law that lowers over Blunderstone, can inflict captivity and enslavement in a warehouse in 'Babylon' because he embodies the spirit of the *stone*-graved *murder*ous Law that ruled the Hebrews of old, and, Dickens knows, rules Christendom still. From two identical *Murdstones,* symbolizing two tablets of the ark, the old penalties—Flood, Babylonian Captivity, Law, fanatic stress on obedience to the letter, death less hope of resurrection, the whole B.C. fate of mankind in miniature—flow. Murdstone and 'grave,'[1] the Murdstones and captivity, prison, death,[2] are constantly associated. Miss Murdstone's never-opened 'two uncompromising black boxes' (47), the two Murdstones in cunning miniature, are types of sealed graves. *Hard* imagery attaches to both, urging *stone*. Mr. Murdstone's relentless and harsh lessons in numbers which invariably end in: 'Present payment' (55) look to OT Law and the price of payment the defaulter-'debtor' paid. Unable to so 'present,' in a time obviously deaf to: 'Forgive us our debts as we forgive our debtors,' the sons of David are worn in the warehouses of Babylon, now as long ago.

The anti-Christ sentiment in which the Law of Moses served too single-mindedly schooled Israel informs Murdstone governance of the House and son of David. Murdstone's every look, word, posture is at variance with the life and lessons of Christ. The Murdstones dislike children, '(though there *was* a child set in the midst of the Disciples).' Late in the story, David and his old friend, Chillip, bring the Murdstone religious issue into focus:

> 'Does he gloomily profess to be (I am ashamed to use the word in such association) religious still?'
> 'You anticipate, sir,' said Mr. Chillip, his eyelids getting quite red with the unwonted stimulus in which he was indulging, 'one of Mrs. Chillip's most impressive remarks. Mrs. Chillip,' he proceeded, in the calmest and slowest manner, 'quite electrified me, by pointing out that Mr. Murdstone sets up an image of himself, and calls it the Divine Nature.' (834)

'Sets up an image.' That this has strong *graven image* associations for Dickens is seen in *Little Dorrit* in the portrait of the black-garbed widow of the 'wrathful hand' (775) who holds bitter suffering inflicted and borne to be 'the just dispensation of Jehovah' (777), and of whom it is said:

> Yet, gone those more than forty years, and come this Nemesis now looking her in the face, she still abided by her old impiety—and breathed her own breath into a clay image of her Creator. Verily, verily, travellers have seen many monstrous idols in many countries; but no human eyes have ever seen more daring, gross, and shocking images of the Divine nature, than we creatures of the dust make in our own likenesses, of our own bad passions. (LD, 775)

'Forty years' invokes the forty years of Israel in the wilderness, a wandering still not over, Dickens shows, as idolaters like this woman join the reverse Exodus that returns us to Egypt. So impious Murdstone makes the Creator in his own dark image, and tries to make the son of David worship him.

If the Murdstone religion is not authorized in the *New* Testament, as Mr. Chillip and David agree, it is in the Old—as much Law, Captivity, and Babylon imagery attached to Murdstone makes clear. In marked contrast, meek, mild, long-suffering Mr. Chillip, so quick to put, not himself but another, Mrs. Chillip, forward, is a 'Ch' or Child-like, Christ-reflecting soul; from the lips of Chil*lip,* as out of the mouths of babes, Christian truth flows. Attending the birth, Mr. Chillip delivers David. Passing through such hands, David emerges into the world through a 'Ch' portal of one poor in spirit and among the last and least who shall come first, so long awaiting a Saviour.

The two stone-hearted Murdstones are the image of the two-in-one tablets of Hebrew Law. Impassive as death and judgment before the

spectacle of the suffering of the fallen, as merciless as the stony countenance of the Old providence B.C., they lay icy hands—rather, icy instruments—on David's son, recalling the fate of another Son of David at the
hands of the Law.  Law would of course have no ordinary degree of interest
in a son of David.  In their bloodless way, the Murdstones expend much
energy on 'forming,' i.e., breaking him: regularizing, narrowing, setting
strict limits, if they could, to his mind's development, clipping the wings of
wonder, hope, and trust native to his spirit.  The aim of Law is ever to so
rear a David that no Christ will be born of him, or his spirit, to end the
tyranny of the Law; no champion of man to declare, as does Christ: 'The
Sabbath was made for man, and not man for the Sabbath.'

But David Copperfield, his (F)father's son, resists.  Born to outsoar all
OT nights of Law, David survives to fling metaphoric filament after filament into the blue, far beyond the reach and rule of law, into Paul
Dombey's mystic 'farther away!' and dreamt-of land of the Father's more
stately, many mansions, o my soul.  In Dickens, Davidic Judaism lifts up
its eyes unto a God of mercies, a shepherd and Good Shepherd Who shall
feed His flocks.  A carrier of this eternal David spirit, young David is endlessly, brightly curious about so many things:  feeding and stray sheep;
sun-dials which count the steps of the sun to the sweet golden clime;
starfish stranded on sandy Yarmouth shores; a fair Miss Shepherd, in all
such fancies reflecting the David who ennobled Old Scripture with his poetic
praises of God.  Such a heritage and destiny the Murdstones can temporarily darken, but never undo.

David's very mistakes, as for example his costly misinvestment in Steerforth, are precious.  If he errs, it is in generosity of spirit and excess of
idealising love, a Heavenly fault.  The Child is father of the Son of Man.
In time, David comes to the greatest of all reliances, Agnes Wickfield, in so
doing making his own and mankind's way once more to Christ.

Murdstone, force of OT law, bars the forward way.  With oft-raised 'lithe
and limber cane' (56) to which, with malice of forethought, he gives yet
'another poise' (57) before striking, extending the victim's terror, Mr.
Murdstone, pitiless as Law, is the cane-and-Cain-raising image of the
passion (Passion) for punishment at the stone heart of OT Law.  David
wanders hopelessly through impossible Murdstone-devised lessons in
numbers which all stress one grim theme: cost, price, the bill, payment.
To Dickens, its Law was Israel's great stumbling-block or 'Blunder-stone.'
And *blunder* is its theme.  As David records:

> The despairing way in which my mother and I look at each other, as I
> blunder on, is truly melancholy. (54)

One not only blunders, one Falls.  A Murdstone lesson is a journey, and,
mired again and again, David records: 'I tumble down before I get to the

old place' (54). Woe betide backsliders in the Law. Murdstone's lessons in sums stress what is owed, and David, his pile of mistakes growing, soon faces a mountain of 'debts' which become 'an arrear to be worked out when my other tasks are done;' there is 'a pile of these arrears very soon, and it swells' (54). The *debt* metaphor, we think, is Biblical, recalling man's bleak lot before the Lord's Prayer extends the comfort of: 'And forgive us our debts....' (*Matt.* 6:12).

With what 'grave' satisfaction and from what great frigid height Murdstone watches David's helpless stumbles and falls, then delivers the long-threatened blow. Mr. Murdstone is not arbitrarily cruel. No, the Law in its cold, systematic way is more lethal still. The debtor knows in advance, and to the letter, the penalty to be paid for any infraction of the law. Thus the Law can wash its Pilate-like hands of complicity in punishment; the victim bears all blame as well as pain. Dickens deplores that in Christian time the Hebraic 'Murdstone' concept of a Lord God of inexorable penalties, in Whom only formalists of the pharisaical Murdstone (Calvinist, Sabbatarian) school could rejoice, still holds sway.

David and Pip inhabit similar pockets of B.C. Escaping from 'Babylon,' David in flight is still deep in Yahweh country of the spirit as he is mistreated by strangers, or passes 'ships in a muddy river roofed like Noah's arks' (183). He is attacked by a fierce, primitive 'Goroo' man; the cry 'Goroo!' with its hint of 'gore you' or 'gore,' recalling the *Gorming* fate Dan'l Peggotty fears, is like some early, distorted version of 'Gor,' or God.[3] When David finally arrives in Dover, his aunt Betsey, noting he wanders and prowls, in her short-sighted way pronounces the child in such wretched condition 'as like Cain before he was grown up, as he can be' (197). Cain will also haunt Pip's life, for Orlick, the foe who slouches upon the ancient marshes like their evil genius, is, we saw, compared to 'Cain or the Wandering Jew' (105).

Not satisfied with breaking David, Mr. Murdstone needs must turn David's soft-hearted mother to stone. His stony euphemism is *firm*. 'Firmness, my dear!' (45) And: 'Now Clara, be firm with the boy' (53). At first she resists the 'firm' way, protesting: 'I say its's very hard that I should be made so now, and it is—very hard, isn't it?' (45) And again: 'It's very hard that in my own house—' (49) Stressed so, *hard* emerges in the stony sense, a pun. Clara Copperfield, now, alas, Murdstone, timidly pleads for clemency for her son. Her touching: 'Oh, pray, pray' (50), and: 'Pray let us be friends' (51) sent aloft to that immovable stone image is quite as futile as were prayers offered up by victims of the Law in Babylonian dungeons, lions' dens, and fiery furnaces of old. As 'pray' (pun) fails, resistance weakens. 'It is very hard' trails off into the faltering, pathetic plea for approval: 'isn't it?' Such, Dickens shows, is the false image of the Divine Nature the Jews came to set over themselves, as, incredibly, Christians do still.

Deeply loved by David, 'Clara' is all affection and 'pray,' or prayer:-Murdstone, the stone Law that, Othello-like, base Judaean-like, would put out the light, and then put out the Light of the world. Murdstone's ominously prophetic: 'Go you below, my love!' lights her the way to dusty death, the 'below' of the grave. No atom of 'up' in the Murdstones, the way back to Law, crucifixion, and 'to dust shalt thou return,' the time of sad mortality before the birth of hope in the gift of the Resurrection and the Life.

Clara, the light that David beheld, fails. But 'light' she was. *Light* puns attend her. She is a 'weak, light, girlish creature' (114). Her 'bright' (16, 133) curls shine. The Murdstones disapprove her graceful, 'light-hearted' (132) ways. When the 'firm, grave, serious' Murdstone extinguishes the light of her spirit, quenching its hope, her step seems to her son 'not so light as I have seen it' (52). Dark overcomes light in the House of David: dark Murdstone, and the sister 'dark like her brother,' who brings with her those two 'hard black boxes' (47), miniature murdstones, symbolic coffins, and who slams shut cupboards with gleeful hope of having trapped someone inside, as in a dark tomb. All too soon it is out, out, brief candle for the 'light'-hearted, footed, angel-winged young mother of David, the first 'C' field in which the seed of David is sown, the promise in Judaism from its inception that would issue at last in Christ.

How Mr. Murdstone comes to win Clara tells much. Before he appears on the scene, the little ménage at Blunderstone round yon mother, nurse, and child—is doing quite well. If Peggotty's (she is *Clara* too) and little David's favorite fun, fictional fireside bouts of putting sharp timber down hapless crocodile throats, is more antediluvian than Judaeo-Christian, nevertheless a strong mutual affection blesses the house of David. David adores his child-mother, symbol of the first light of Heaven's high intent for him that dawned in man's awakened soul, one destined to behold ever brighter images of light until the brightest should arrive in 'Agnes,' the Light of the world and Palm Sunday at the end of the mind.

Then Murdstone comes, and in little David's hearing, in a way insuring its getting back to her, calls her 'bewitching Mrs. Copperfield' (25). The lady coyly denies it, but clearly the 'bewitching' tribute (?) dazzles her. Wherefore? In allegory, the detail grows especially meaningful. *Bewitching* touches off the old 'witch,' magwitch susceptibility in natural man which lays the groundwork for his mastery by the high priests of the Law, that great witches' sabbath of mummery, rite, and wiglomeration, and for the greatest of all its infamies, the trial and conviction of Christ. David's mother's fate is sealed. Only too pleased to have been found 'bewitching,' she is soon hexed in the Law, the two rigid stone forms devoid of common humanity which come to rule unopposed in a House where once simple faith, hope, and charity, the exalted 'David' heritage, reigned.

Yet not quite unopposed. David's good Peggotty survives. Let Murdstone turn a killing 'darkening face on Peggotty, when he had watched my
mother out' (45) all he pleases, he cannot so easily quench *this* sturdy other
*Clara,* or watch it (pun) 'out.' In this case, the wick is set on a stouter base.
Here is a Clara whose whole devotion is to a mother and child, types of the
Mother and Child, as to her cherished workbox with its sliding lid and
picture of Saint Paul's in rose-hued glory on top. As Miss Murdstone is all
funereally closed black boxes and thinly-disguised death wishes to the son
of David in the form of a triumphant command: 'Master Copperfield's box
there!' (62) when David is sent into exile, how delightful that Peggotty's
Paul-crowned box opens wide—Easters! Further, to comfort David when
he is sent from home, Peggotty secretly slips him 'three bright shillings'
(63) polished up with whitening for his greater delight. *Three* in the
Trinity, polished 'up,' and Saint Paul, almost say all. On the surname as
opposed to the Christian name side, Peggotty of course has her OT tendencies, as have her brother, Ham, David, and the other Israelites of modern
times; the first Christians too were after all Jews. But Clara, the Light in
Judaism that would point the forward way to Christ, prevails, protecting a
small David on his providential way.

David owes his survival in killing Murdstone time to one other agency, a
spiritual legacy from his father. He records:

> My father had left a small collection of books in a little room up-stairs, to
> which I had access (for it adjoined my own) and which nobody else in the
> house ever troubled. From that blessed little room, Roderick Random, Pere-
> grine Pickle, Humphrey Clinker, Tom Jones, the Vicar of Wakefield, Don
> Quixote, Gil Blas, and Robinson Crusoe, came out, a glorious host, to keep
> me company. They kept alive my fancy, and my hope of something beyond
> that time and place. (55)

A lightly but clearly etched religious symbolism unites the *'blessed* room'
upstairs to the *'glorious* host,' *up*-stairs that much closer to Heaven. In a
sanctuary Above, David, reading fictions, communes with his Father
(father and Father mystically fused) through immortal works of the imagination which exercise a child's natural sympathy with the joys, trials,
sorrows and triumphs of all men, without which power to move in spirit
beyond self a Christian is such in name only. David's father's books body
forth to the inner eye another, supra-physical, timeless order of reality that
stirs intimations of other modes of being. Through them David glimpses an
imperishable reality which affords the soul, while yet on earth, the sense of
moving about in worlds not realized. In David's delight in books, so like
the young Charles Dickens's own, is seen man's inborn thirst and hope for
'something beyond...time and place.'

In Dickens, worship of the beneficent Creator awakens in just such
ways:-not in fear and trembling before His Law and wrathful hand, but in

wonder and awe at His goodness, and confidence that He means man's adventures—Tom Jones,' Strap's, Roderick's, Peregrine's—to come to good, the waiting legacy of 'Paradise Hall.' In Dickens, Nature and the soul of man teem with hints of godly design; the world is crowded with finger-posts pointing to wonders yet unbeheld; to risings from us, vanishings, promptings in the Ideal, visions of the unseen world beyond all worlds of 'time and place.'

The rediscovery of A.D. begins with a little child. 'What's money?' Paul Dombey asks his father. 'What's a convict?' Pip, hearing guns boom, asks, and is dratted for his pains. But what indeed? A convict is someone taken, tried, convicted under Law—imprisoned, perhaps doomed. Jesus Christ was a convict. Pip surely asks the right, the only question in the Christmas season. However, to Mrs. Joe and her ilk, the B.C. mind bigoted to Law, no questions remain. She denies mystery. For such as Mrs. Joe and Pecksniff, all has long since been determined, codified, set down in immutable tables of Law, answered; Law is the completion of truth. Happily, Pip has Joe to bring his questions to, as David has both Peggotty and books which let down a ladder for the child's spirit to climb above an ignorant present to the Father. Captive below, in imagination David joins the heavenly fellowship of men who perish, to live again in God. Thus, while Murdstone drills him in the world as manual, not mystery, bent on severing the Davidic artery—the extra-legal, praiseful, inquiring child's spirit—David stays alive, his spirit outward bound on 'the journey.'

Armed with all OT weaponry, MURDSTONE has both the will and power to inflict the Flood. When in the time of courting Mrs. Copperfield Murdstone takes little David aboard a yacht, a crony named Quinion toasts David in the words: 'Confusion to Brooks of Sheffield!' (23) Behind 'Brooks,' a code name for little pitchers with big ears, malicious mockery lies. A seaside invention, BROOKS signifies rising waters. For when David gets home soon after, he finds a new master in residence, a growling dog (a type of him) chained in the yard, and all changed under 'a dull sky threatening rain' (41).

'Brooks' is not forgotten. Shipped off to 'Modern Babylon,' David is again accosted by Quinion in the Murdstone warehouse. 'What! Brooks!' Quinion hails him, evincing the old amused, sinister scorn. Older and wiser now, David stoutly denies it. Whereupon: 'Don't tell me. You are Brooks,' said the gentleman. 'You are Brooks of Sheffield. That's your name' (150). Dickens cannot repeat *Brooks* too often. Why? Because, we think, Murdstone & Co. *would have* 'brooks,' i.e., tributaries of the retributive spirit of the Flood. In neo-OT time boys *had better be* 'Brooks,' if they know what's good for them. *Brooks* are the old drowning punishment on tap, the watery wasting of mankind each taunt of 'Brooks' threatens David with.

Failing to break David, Murdstone first sends him away to Salem House in Blackheath, its headmaster Mr. Creakle. *Creakle!* Here is creak(le) or creek one depth deeper. The sign that Creakle is soon to arrive is the appearance of an ugly man with a wooden leg and overhanging temples carrying 'a mop and a bucket of water' (81). Mr. Creakle himself has 'wet-looking hair' (81) brushed carefully across his temples. (The *temples* pun also points up B.C.) The curious detail of wet hair is not lost. Many years after when David sees his old tormentor again, Creakle is a prison official with 'an office that might have been on the ground-floor of the Tower of Babel' (849). Not only 'Babel,' but the mention of the 'scanty, wet-looking grey hair' (849) still in evidence ties the tyrant to *Genesis* soul-time of Flood. But not only *Genesis*. All-weather symbolism runs the gamut of B.C. Running a prison, Creakle is still happily, waterily and fierily about the Captivity business.

As to flood, Salem House is exceedingly wet. Says David: 'How vividly I call to mind the damp about the house, the green cracked flagstones in the court, the old leaky waterbutt, and the discoloured trunks of the grim trees, which seemed to have dripped more in rain than other trees, and to have blown less in the sun!' (79) Damp creeps in everywhere. When the Master, Mr. Mel, screws his three-piece flute together and tries to play, melodies come 'oozing' (80) out. So fare three-in-one objects and good Masters in this place. Likewise, Mrs. and Miss Creakle are often dissolved in tears, their lives made unbearable by the tyrant Creakle. Perhaps 'Salem' is not only a *dotheboys*-type 'sell 'em' but also a 'Sail 'Em' pun, for David, ruefully reminiscing about his misadventures there, remarks in watery metaphor: 'What a launch in life I think it now' (90).

An anti-Christ spirit rules the place. Here David's son must wear the sign of shame Murdstone has had fixed to his back, a primitive assignment of the Cross. A latter-day son of David bears the agony and public shame of the wooden sign as the Son of David bore the wooden burden of the Cross. At Salem House the good Master, friend of the poor and most compassionate of teachers, is vilified, accused of poverty (!), and tried before a mob of jeering boys in travesty of all justice. Defeated and banished, the Master forgives his persecutors and forgives David for having forsaken him, leaving behind the key to his desk for his successor, even as Christ, the good Master of Masters, the keys of the Kingdom. Brilliant Christian symbolism! It is clear that Murdstone sends David to school in a stronghold of OT law, the old cast of characters again warming up for Calvary.

That Dickens *means* Brooks in a literal sense is dramatically affirmed when David, grown up and preparing for a career in, of all ironic things, the Law, visits the home of Mr. Wickfield's agent, a 'Mr. Waterbrook, in Ely-place, Holborn' (365). WATERBROOK! That is a fathom or two deeper than brooks; the Law is gathering retributive striking might. The old *Brooks* conspiracy launched by Murdstone's two allies, Passnidge and Quinion (*PASS*nidge and quin*ION,* if one wishes, spelling out 'Passion'), is prospering; first Brooks, now *Water*brooks have charge of David's son. Sure enough, at Ely-place OT values—law; ill will towards all but a favored Elect; Flood—rule.  That Dickens is highly conscious of 'waterbrook' in the watery sense is at once made clear:

> When I went to dinner the next day, and, on the street door being opened, plunged into a vapour-bath of haunch of mutton, I divined I was not the only guest.  (371)

'Plunge' and 'vapour-bath' ready the way for imperious Mrs. Waterbrook to come 'sailing in' (371).

Call it A.D., but the Waterbrook soirée is far more like entertainment B.C.  The guests, hugging clannish pride of caste and social station and deep in plots and cabals that insure confusion to many a young Brooks and son of David, symbolize the self-elect Chosen People of modern times.  Not Christ, but YAH commands at Ely-place.  Here David meets an old Creakle boy, a Mr. Yawler, who shortly afterwards gets Tommy Traddles law-copyist work with the Waterbrook firm.  What is this busy legal YAWLER, protégé of Mr. Waterbrook—what but a 'yawl(er)' or vessel setting forth on 'waterbrook' flood tides.  A somewhat tippy Yawler, too, it would seem, what with his nose so far to one side, doubtless the OT side.  In Dickens, many a *Yawler* and *Skiffins* makes 'the journey,' some ships of soul sailing under Yah, some flying the tricolor of the Son and Heir and trusting for safe passage in the dear might of Him Who walked the waves.  It finally dawns on us that there is uncommonly lively Ya(h) activity in Murdstone or Waterbrook precincts:  *y*acht, *y*ard, *y*awl galore, and the anathematising cry 'Ya-a-ah!', we will see.

Now other detail falls into place.  The Waterbrooks live in Ely-place: 'EL*y*' for EL, the Hebrew deity.  Confidence that Dickens was conscious of and used the EL syllable in this way grows as we learn that Dan'l Peggotty's salvation—his surrender of old ways of harsh judgment and his recovery of his beloved little Em'ly—comes about through the fallen woman he once scorned, Martha Endell.  Now as in NT time, MARTHA signifies *ENDELL,* the *END* of *EL* or concept of a punishing, sinner-stoning God of Law, as will shortly be seen.

To return to the Murdstone-inflicted ordeal of David:  after Creakle days, David is exiled to Babylon and there impressed into slave labor in the warehouse of Murdstone and Grinby, wine merchants.  Once, wine flowed in the House of David.  Recalling the era of his birth, David says: 'as to sherry, my poor dear mother's own sherry was in the market then' (1). Now David sees no wine at all in the great wine merchants' establishment, only 'a great many empty bottles...that certain men and boys were employed to examine…against the light, and reject those that were flawed, and to rinse and wash them' (154). Dazzling figural invention. Bottles held *'against* the light' symbolize the Murdstone defiance of the will of Heaven, as in the fate dealt *Clara.* Why only men and boys, *'certain* men and boys' at that? In allegory the odd detail flares into being. This Heaven-defying, soul-wearing labor in the warehouse (*ware* possibly hiding a 'wear' pun) resembles the Hebrew study of the Torah or Law, the Murdstone specialty of the 'wine' in Israel planted as a vineyard, the ancient labor which only males may undertake.

But the bottles we see are empty, as if to say that in Judaism as in Judaic Christianity, preoccupation with the letter eventually drives out the spirit, the way to Christ. The bottles are like the empty casks in the brewery of Satis House, another wilderness void of spirits where once spirits were.

Another, more benign province of 'OT' time in David Copperfield's childhood is Yarmouth, home of Dan'l, doughty boatman-fisherman brother of David's nurse, Peggotty. Dan'l, his orphaned nephew and niece, Ham and Emily, also Mrs. Gummidge, the widow of an old friend, live together here on an ancient beached craft termed 'a black barge, or some other kind of superannuated boat' (29). 'Some other kind' allows for David's inspired fancy that the boat is 'a sort of ark.' As *Ham* lives on the *ark,* the motif kindles. On the walls of the 'ark' hang pictures of…

> Abraham in red going to sacrifice Isaac in blue, and Daniel in yellow cast into a den of green lions. (30)

The Abraham and Daniel scenes spell out the ambiguous, not to say harsh, unmutual terms of man's lot under the Old covenant or contract-bargain with Heaven. We are reminded that, in the old arrangement, good men suffer along with the worst. The very next line in the text reads: 'Over the little mantel-shelf, was a picture of the Sarah Jane lugger, built at Sunderland' (30), which neatly effects a symbolic reunion of one of the first families of *Genesis:* Abraham, Isaac, and *Sarah.* (As to 'Sunderland,' it anticipates 'the John of Sunderland' in *Great Expectations, sunder*land an apt pseudonym for Israel in its prideful apartness from all mankind, scorned as gentiles.) The loud primary colors in the pictures, red, yellow, blue, green, seem suited to the era of man's moral infancy. In the God of trials he celebrates, and in what he himself bears, inflicts, and is, Yarmouth man—Ya(h) man—still extols the Lord Yahweh of hard testings of the faithful and Murd-stoning of sinners; the God Who saved the Noahs and Daniels, but Whose mercy fell short of the entire family of man, Every One.

*Ark* life in 'a great dull waste' (29), a 'waste-place' (321) (*waste* in more senses than one), is vastly unsatisfactory. The drowned fathers of Ham and Em'ly, 'drowndead,' in Peggotty's neat punning splice, lie uneasy in memory 'somewhere in the depths of the sea' (34). Shades of the *drown-dead* numberless of the Flood, which threatens still. Little Em'ly, a mere child, is nevertheless strangely attracted to a watery death. Balancing on a jagged piece of timber high over the water, she has the look of 'springing forward to her destruction (as it appeared to me), with a look that I have never forgotten, directed far out to sea' (36). This memory of 'pretty little Em'ly's dread of death' (444) yet strange attraction to it haunts David. Like an ancient pestilence men strangely long to die of, as Dickens shows in describing guillotine fever that grips men in *A Tale of Two Cities*,[4] the ancient Flood fatalism draws men still, men who long since should have been delivered from loyalty to (pun) 'black,' 'superannuated' arks, forms, and creeds.

The master of the 'ark,' Dan'l Peggotty, is a good man. But ark life has its drawbacks. Mrs. Gummidge, always glooming in corners about 'the old 'un' (40, 140) (who might as soon be *the* 'Old, 'Un,' Old Nick, the Devil himself, as the departed Mr. Gummidge,[5]) spreads her lone-lorn damps. A laconic Ham drops stones in the water; and little Em'ly, spoiled by her doting uncle's too-fierce, unwise love, in her tiny way already coy and cruel, practises by breaking David's baby heart, hiding herself away. An early Estella, she contracts the fatal sickness of wishing to be a 'lady,' as Pip will to be a 'gentleman.' Then there is the 'Gorming' threat that hangs over all. Once, angered at the mention of his charity to Ham and Em'ly, Peggotty smashes the table and swears he will be ' "Gormed" if he didn't cut and run for good, if it was ever mentioned again' (33). What is the meaning of this 'terrible verb passive' (33), TO BE GORMED?? The *Gorming* menace hangs dark and mysterious over Dan'l's brave little sea-girt world which harbors, as if the last straggling survivors of the Flood, a morsel of humanity low in spirits and dwarfed by the wind-scourged, storm-breeding, widow-making, child-unfathering, ever-oncoming, merciless night tides of Yarmouth.

Thus, commuting between Murdstone-blighted Blunderstone and Yarmouth, young David Copperfield, like Pip after him, journeys from pocket to pocket of Old Time, which, like a strong undertow, pulls him back down into B.C.

Yah rules this neo-B.C., as Yah or Yahweh did of old. Arriving uninvited at Blunderstone to welcome a niece, as she confidently expects the unborn child of her deceased nephew will be, Miss Betsey Trotwood, furious at the delay, vents her wrath on Mrs. Copperfield's attending physician, Mr. Chillip, snarling 'Ya-a-ah!' (10) Never did *Yah* of old break out a 'Yah!' more fierce than does this furious old dragon of A.D., her jealousy (it *must* be a girl!) and violence recreating B.C. on the spot. Mr. Chillip, the meek little man who would not hurt a fly, takes the 'Ya-a-ah!' (more terrible in prolongation) and a blow that follows—Miss Betsey sling-shots him with her bonnet held by the strings—to heart, feeling it as 'really calculated to break his spirit' (10). Yahweh also specialized in 'spirit'-crushing blows, the sudden punitive Visitation, like the carrying off of Israel to Babylon, a famous Yah trademark.

The syllable 'Yah' appears only once more in *Copperfield*, and again Betsey Trotwood delivers it. In aftertime recalling her anger at the moment when Mr. Chillip's 'It's a boy!' shattered her fond, selfish schemes of a child made in her own image (so Yah formed man in His), David's aunt erupts a second time in: 'Yah, the imbecility of the whole set of 'em!' (197) '*Whole* set' typified Yah in the way He delivered all mankind, fathers and innocent children alike, to the waiting wrath.

The memorable 'Ya-a-ah!' attack and subsequent Grand Desertion at the dawn of *Copperfield*, a dawn in which Judaeo-Christian history symbolically begins all over again, is executed in serio-comic style, à la Dickens. But it is really not so funny. Miss Trotwood's total abandonment of Clara and her fatherless babe leaves the House of David protectorless and thus wide open to Murdstone infiltration. Nor are Miss Trotwood's fanatic 'No Trespass' spirit and vendettas against strangers and donkeys that stray onto her land very funny. Two mankind-cursing Yah's—'Ya-a-ah!' and 'Yah!'—symbolize the outbreak in a Christian woman of modern times of the ancient parochial YAH spirit of jealousy, wrath, and periodic rejection of its own, as in the Babylonian desert desertion of the beloved, the bride of Yah, Israel. Thus, to all who pose as Christians while Abel is slain, Mr. Chillip Yah'd, David murdstoned, Stephen Stone Lodge'd (*Hard Times*), Charley Hexam Hexed and Headstoned (*Our Mutual Friend*); Sissy, Louisa, and Tom Gradground; Oliver Twisted; Tom Pinched (*Chuzzlewit*); Smike Squeered and lads numberless Dotheboy'd (*Nickleby*), and to all fooled by the smooth, plausible Veneering of social propriety and culture in polite circles, Dickens holds up the glass to reveal a fearsome truth: the fealty of Christendom to Yah, or Jehovah, not Christ.

For all its hardships, David Copperfield's life is far easier than Pip's. The coming of David and Mr. Dick softens Betsey Trotwood's Miss Havisham of a heart anciently bruised by a husband's betrayal and thereafter long shut tight against the world, its youthful softness and sentiment thrust down and buried in a deep grave. Miss Havisham, a later, more tragic Miss Trotwood, is longer in waking. Even when badly shaken by Estella's coldness, she resists the truths Pip discloses to her, refusing to regret having led him on in his tragic hope that she was his secret patron and intended Estella for him. In an interview Pip asks:

> 'Was that kind?'
> 'Who am I,' cried Miss Havisham, striking her stick upon the floor, and flashing into wrath so suddenly that Estella glanced up at her in surprise, 'Who am I, for God's sake, that I should be kind?' (341)

Yes, who is she to be kind 'for God's sake'—*her* God's? The OT deity in whose spiritual realm the passion for retribution bred spirits so fierce they snuffed out the very light of Heaven, the Star set aloft to light the way to Christmas, does not specialize in 'kind' or humankind. That sudden flashing into wrath, stick crashing on the floor, is far more accurate a model of the the punitive, strike-from-above way of Yah Who hastened and chastened His will to make known.

Yet a stricken Miss Havisham finally does acknowledge her fault, and begs Pip's pardon. In so doing she slips from the ideological grasp of the jealous Yah she has served so long and well in her pursuit of vindictive triumph. But the jealous God does not suffer His 'bride' to turn away unpunished:

> In the moment when I was withdrawing my head to go quietly away, I saw a great flaming light spring up. In the same moment, I saw her running at me, shrieking, with a whirl of fire blazing all about her, and soaring at least as many feet above her head as she was high. (380)

How uncannily alive, almost sentient the flaming light seems as it 'spring[s] up;' how the sudden 'whirl of fire blazing about her' seems to pursue the fleeing, doomed woman. The flame that towers above its victim at something like her own height, as if in ironic mockery, that of a height-for-a-height, is surely no naturalistic one, but more like the purposeful, vengeful, flaming tongue of Yah.

Moments before, taking a yellowed 'set of ivory tablets' (376) from her pocket, Miss Havisham piteously implored Pip: 'If you can ever write under my name, "I forgive her," though ever so long after my broken heart is dust—pray do it!' (377) Never before have the words 'pray' or 'forgive' passed those lips, certainly not in the heyday of her passion for revenge when her favorite song was the ballad of the consuming flames, *Old Clem.*

Pip complies, fully and freely forgiving the pleading woman. But OT strictures bind the very cordons of her soul. Miss Havisham cannot believe herself thus easily forgiven; in the OT experience of man there *is* no forgiveness under Heaven without payment of a stiff price. From then until her dying moment, the unexpelled Hebrew self within, so long her master, mumbles ritualistically: 'Take the pencil and write under my name, "I forgive her!"' (382) *'Write'!!* The *written* contract, a likeness of the law graved in stone, the two ivory tablets Miss Havisham carries in her pocket a memorial to the ark or law (why would Dickens be so particular as to mention *two* tablets of ancient appearance, if not to make some vital symbolic point?), forgiveness ratified *in the letter,* in writing, is all the bride of Yah knew or trusted, knows or trusts.

Thus Dickens dramatizes the plight of a People which knew nothing of divine forgiveness without penalty: Flood, the razings of the Temple, the Babylonian Captivity. In the incapacity of the bride to believe herself forgiven (forgiving her, Pip is a surrogate Christ, as in his confrontation with the man among the tombs, who in the NT appears to Christ), the whole tragic History of Israel According to Dickens is retold, as though to say, the Kingdom of the Father was spread bountifully upon the earth, yet they saw it not. And see it not still.

But Old cannot hold off New Time. Asking Pip's pardon, Miss Havisham for the first time enters a Christian Providence; crossing a spiritual boundary, she inherits its Great Expectations. The withered OT self dies. Badly burned and lying swathed in white-cotton wool bandages to the throat, with 'a white sheet loosely overlying that' (381), she is as if newly arrayed for a new bridal in purest white. Yet disbelief, a conviction of being beyond the bounty of forgiveness, haunts her til she dies.

Pip's is a far darker story than David's. For 'Ya-a-ah!' Miss Trotwood comes round in time to live a life useful to herself and others, while Miss Havisham does not. Nor is there in David's life a foe as terrible as Pip's sworn foe, Orlick—not even Uriah Heep.

Orlick, villain and murderer, is constantly associated with the threat of death by fire, child sacrifice in flames, and Hell. A worker at the forge, Orlick gives little Pip to understand 'that the Devil lived in a black corner of the forge, and that he knew the fiend very well: also that it was necessary to make up the fire, once in seven years, with a live boy, and that I might consider myself fuel' (105). 'Once in *seven* years' does special violence to *seven,* sacred cypher of Creation, and to Pip, whose adventures in the little churchyard begin in, he thinks, his 'seventh year' (386). Orlick's threats out-magwitch Magwitch's by far. A terrified Pip sees that Orlick always beats his sparks in his direction, and even makes at him with 'a red-hot bar' (106). (Shades of David Copperfield's red-hot poker murder fantasies in connection with Heep.)

Orlick is and remains the threat of fiery death. Having struck down and effectually killed Mrs. Joe, Orlick some time after lures Pip to an old lime-kiln on the marshes where he means to murder him and destroy the body. Here he taunts Pip with candle flame and: 'Ah! the burnt child dreads the fire! Old Orlick knowed you was burnt' (406). From the very beginning Orlick's identity is in question. Compared to 'Cain or the Wandering Jew,' he clearly has no *Christian* identity, or 'Christian' name: 'He pretended that his Christian name was Dolge—a clear impossibility' (105). 'Old Orlick,' he calls himself, as if an ancient person, as we now find he literally is.

Who or what in allegory is Orlick? Following the bloody trail of death by fire and child-sacrifice (Orlick's 'the burnt child dreads the fire' makes the grown Pip a 'child' again, the child he threatened with sparks and red-hot bar), we come to the roaring ovens of the semitic deity, Moloch. A (M)OLOCH-ORLICK likeness glares. That Dickens knew about Moloch we know through his Christmas story, *The Haunted Man* (1848), in which young Johnny Tetterby tends a fractious baby brother playfully (?)

nicknamed 'Moloch,' both inhabiting 'the Jerusalem Buildings' (CB,340), for the nonce! In a book Dickens had in his Gadshill library, *The Progress of the Intellect, as Exemplified in the Religious Development of the Greeks and Hebrews* (1850), by Robert Mackay, Moloch is described as follows:

> The most usual rivals of the Hebrew Deity are called Baal, "Lord," and Moloch, "King;" the latter being properly called the King of Terrors, the Canaanite Orcus or Erebus, the former the general Nature God, the power of heat, life, and generation. The symbol of Baal was the sun, of Moloch the fire; the former worshipped with licentious rites, the latter with sanguinary ones; both however were ultimately the same Being, and their rites and symbols interchangeable. Human victims were offered to Baal or to idols in general as well as to Moloch, though the latter was more peculiarly the stern aspect to which they were the proper tribute. Thus Jeremiah says, "They built high places to Baal in the valley of the sons of Hinom, in order to consecrate sons and daughters to Moloch." (MI,II,417)

Orlick, Orcus, (M)oloch, all heavy with 'o,' seem one.

Dickens folds Moloch detail into the Orlick portrait. Orlick the outlander becomes gate-keeper of Satis House in its declining days; so did Moloch, alien to Judaism, creep into the Hebrew fold. Pip looks into the little room which is Orlick's dwelling:

> Certain keys were hanging on the wall, to which he now added the gate key; and his patch-work covered bed was in a little inner division or recess. The whole had a slovenly and confined and sleepy look, like a cage for a human dormouse for which it was fitted up—as indeed he was. (220)

'Dormouse' takes on meaning as we learn more about Moloch:

> While the Sun, or God of Heaven, was worshipped on hills or high places, the rites of Moloch were performed in valleys, as that of Hinom, in pits, in watercourses, or in the sombre clefts and caverns of the rocks, for Moloch was a fiery or thirsty power claiming the tribute of blood in cavities emblematic of his own drear habitation, an Orcus, whose sacrifices are called "messengers to hell," and to whom were consecrated the wintry swine and dark-dwelling mouse....(MI,II,421)

Moloch is linked to the 'dark-dwelling mouse;' Orlick to the 'dormouse.' Moloch worship took place in dark caverns; Orlick seeks out the dark, shut-up limekiln, and inhabits a dark cave of a room, sleeping in an inner division of it, a corner of his shadowy corner. Moloch is 'a fiery or thirsty power.' Over and over during Pip's ordeal by fire at Orlick's hands, Orlick gulps 'a fiery drink' (404). The limekiln is an Orcus: 'The sudden exclusion of the night and the substitution of black darkness in its place, warned me that the man had closed a shutter' (401). Moloch-worship infiltrated the Temple itself in OT time. In Dickens, in the waning days of the old House of 'Greek, Latin, Hebrew' associations, Orlick comes to keep the keys, as if of the kingdom of Hell. Struck down by Orlick, Mrs. Joe seeks only to propitiate him, as did crazed, stricken Israel the Deity that devoured its children in flames. Only Pip, the latest spiritual champion of history's forward course to Christian time, makes a stand against Orlick and vanquishes him.

In Mackay, we learn more of Moloch, temptation and bane of the Hebrews, and how he was worshipped:

> The neighbourhood of the altar was as formidable to life as that of the flaming mountain made by the divine presence to ''smoke as a furnace,'' and so converted into a giant Moloch image, which to approach or to touch was death. If superstition may be said to have reached its climax when overcoming the most powerful of human feelings it brought the infatuated parent to kiss the bull-headed instrument of infanticide, it is not astonishing that one despairing Hebrew mother should have ventured to strike the guilty altar with her clipper, saying, 'Wolf! how long wilt thou continue to devour the treasure of Israel's children' (MI,II,429)

Orlick's cry is 'wolf': ' 'Now, wolf,' said he, 'afore I kill you like any other beast—which is wot I mean to do and wot I have tied you up for' (404); and: 'Wolf!' (404); and: 'Wolf, I'll tell you something more' (405), while taunting Pip with a candle and with visions of his fiery death to come. With 'wot,' Orlick's obsessive word, adding a jot of 'ot,' Old Time or Old Testament, the fierce taunt 'Wolf!' glares. Thus into Pip's symbolic OT experience—of Abel, Cain, Noah's ark; the wilderness wandering in the (He)brewery world that cast out Matthew; a far city in which Jews like the kinsman of Habraham Latharuth cower before the Law and vainly beg its intercession in their trials—an Orlick-Moloch enters, still hot to devour the treasure of Israel's children.

As David Copperfield is transported to a life of slavery in 'the Modern Babylon,' so Pip experiences Babylon. London, the city to which he is carried to be a gentleman, is Babylon. In London one finds an abject criminal population kneeling to the great figure of the Law, and especially in terror and awe of his great gold watch with massive chain. Wemmick says of the thief community that 'there's not a man, a woman, or a child, among them, who wouldn't identify the smallest link in that chain, and drop it as if it was red-hot, if inveigled into touching it' (195). As in ancient Babylon the King had erected a huge gold Idol which the Hebrews (sinners, 'criminals' in the eyes of the Law of Yah) were forced to bow to and worship, those refusing cast into fiery furnaces, so in the far City to which Pip travels 'Habraham Latharuth,' of Abraham Lazarus and his tribe, tremble before the gold watch of Jaggers, the touch of which is fiery-furnace 'red-hot.' (King Nebuchad*nezzar* and *Jaggers* of *Gerrard* Street. Is there a NEZZAR-JAGGER-GERRAR likeness, the double medial consonants, 'Z,' 'G,' and 'R' like cruel, jagged transverse slits? In any case....) As Yah used Babylon to punish the Hebrew nation disobedient to His Law, so in modern times in Dickens men are ground in mills of Law. And the all-powerful Lawyer in Court associated with the fearsome gold object is the Nebuchadnezzar of 'the Modern Babylon.'

In the city of doomed men, Pip and his friends live a privileged life, as did certain favored young Israelites of old like Daniel. Yet danger is nigh. A visit to Belinda Pocket and the garden of falling children recycles the Fall. Back home, Trabb's boy's street-corner pantomime, acted for Pip's benefit, though he does not realize it, dramatizes what high and mighty young gentlemen of Pip's stamp who (in Trabb's boy's words) 'don't know yah!' (232), i.e., have forgotten Yahweh and His Law, can expect.

Meanwhile, NT time buds out in the very shadow of Old Time. Once, a pale young gentleman challenged Pip to a fight in the garden of Satis House, a plucky boy who, sparring amateurishly but with great vigor and game show of ferocity, cried: 'Laws of the game!' and 'Regular rules!' (84) Though he upheld them, obviously *laws* and *rules* were foreign to him even then. This is Herbert, a son of Matthew, notably pale from much indoors-keeping, and perpetually inky from overmuch pen-and-ink (or 'pen-and-ink-ubus' (MD,93), in Dickens's inspired pun) scribal chores in the House of the battered bride of Yah. In allegory, in 'Hebrew' time of a house founded on the flood, a young boy dutifully, hebraically practises the manly art of 'smite thine enemy;' hence the ritual battle in the Ruined Garden and stress on '*regular* rules,' *regula* or rule the basis of Law. During the fight, the pale young gentleman announces that his bottle of water and sponge dipped in vinegar is 'available for both' (85). Dubious kindness! The sponge-vinegar detail is comfortless, given:

> And straightway one of them ran, and took a sponge, and filled it with vinegar, and put it on a reed, and gave him to drink. (*Matt.* 27:48)

This, like Estella's 'in Greek, or Latin, or Hebrew,' links the dark world of the bride, its sole theme retribution—justice without mercy—to the crucifixion of Christ.

For a time young Herbert is the boy brought to the House to 'play,' i.e., to provide Estella with a heart to practise breaking. But he does not suit and is sent away, Pip inheriting the honors. In young manhood Pip and Herbert meet again. Arriving in London at Barnard's Inn, Pip awaits the arrival of a roommate who has been identified to him only as 'Mr. Pocket, Junior.' Waiting on the landing, Pip hears footsteps on the stairs:

> Gradually there arose before me the hat, head, neck-cloth, waistcoat, trousers, boots, of a member of society of about my own standing. (164)

How comical (and allegorical) to have Herbert seem to materialize out of

thin air this way.  The vision of 'arising' tells the Gospel truth about this
hopeful, cheerful son of Matthew.

"'By their fruits ye shall know them,' said OUR SAVIOUR.'  As if starting from this text, Dickens labors to make sweet-natured Herbert full of
growing.  Herbert welcomes Pip to sooty Barnard's with nothing less than
a pottle, or half gallon, of strawberries.  When he learns of Pip's love for
Estella, he avers: 'Now, Handel, I am quite free from the flavour of sour
grapes, upon my soul and honour!' (236)  Of course he only means he is not
jealous.  But 'free from...sour grapes' also recalls the OT condition of man
in which: 'The fathers have eaten a sour grape, and the children's teeth
are set on edge' (*Jer.* 31:29).  Herbert is free from all that, too.  Herbert it
is who rechristens Pip 'Handel,' a name crisparkling with Messiah light.
Perhaps *Herb*ert is herbal in putting soothing balm on Pip's painful burns.
And perhaps Dickens had in mind the parable which compares the
Kingdom of Heaven to a mustard-seed...

> Which indeed is the least of all seeds:  but when it is grown, it is the great-
> est among herbs, and becometh a tree, so that the birds of the air come and
> lodge in the branches thereof. (*Matt.* 13:32)

Is Herbert affined to this 'herb' as, joining the Firm of Clarriker, he leaves
home to open 'a small branch-house in the East' (395), *branch* again
looking to tree?

Herbert Pocket is a Christian, a true son of *Matthew.*  Pip's staunch ally
in the effort to save 'him,' Herbert overflows with Great Expectations.  His
ambition:  to be 'A capitalist—an Insurer of Ships in the City' (173).  That
is not all.  'I shall buy up some good Life Assurance shares, and cut into the
Direction' (173).  A flurry of capital letters helps imply that this is the
language of allegory.  Herbert would be a disciple, insuring ships, souls,
on the voyage to Eternity.  'Life Assurance'—note, not ordinary Life
*In*surance—is hope of Life Everlasting; and 'the Direction,' the way, the
truth, and the life.  In Herbert's shining dreams of an Opening up ahead
and the City, something more than ambitions and cities of this world
gleams.  Herbert too would be about his Father's business.

The awaited Opening comes; 'his' fortune secures Herbert a partnership
in the firm of a young merchant just starting out, one Clarriker.  Herbert
also woos and wins little Clara Barley.  *Clar*a and *Clar*riker:  light upon
light!  The newlyweds journey to the East, direction of Sonrise, in behalf of
the House of Clarriker.  Finally Pip joins them.  So long ago the disciples
went forth, two by two, carrying the word and founding many a 'branch-
house' of the tree of the Kingdom in far-off lands.

The 'Clara Barley' tale has much allegorical charm.  Clara's father is old
Bill Barley, an ogre who curses, rants, and roars in his room upstairs,
making the rafters below ring.  While those below dine sparely, huge
feasts of mutton stew are demanded by and sent aloft to old Bill, the

unseen tyrant high above. What sacrifices are gobbled up in that invisible kingdom aloft! In allegory, thunderous BARLEY symbolizes the 'barley' or stuff of the bread of life, spiritually speaking, of Providence B.C., Greek and Hebrew, and most especially the 'Old Bill' of it, i.e., the heavy cost, the price men had to pay to their early gods. Tons of mutton disappearing into the insatiable maw Above recall hecatombs of sheep and cattle sacrificed to gods in ancient times. So much for heaven's blessings in 'old Barley' and 'Old Clem' times. Happily for mankind, One comes who does not snatch up, but multiplies and distributes the *barley* loaves, and no 'bill' attached: Christ, the bread of life.

Yet Clara Barley cheerfully bears all, with kind thoughts for her father, even as Prince bears the burden for old Turveydrop (*Bleak House*). Surely, however, the 'light' and 'prince' in the soul of man, from which the hope of the Son of Man springs, deserves a happier fate, found in the New Testament of Christ.

If the love story of Philip (Pip) and Estella looks back to that of Sir Philip Sidney as recorded in 'Astrophel and Stella,' may not that of Herbert look back to that of George Herbert, Christian poet of 'Easter Wings'? Of course this is pure conjecture.

*Clarriker* prospers. In time the old House is set to be demolished. Brewery and main house, 'LOT 1' and 'LOT 2,' are marked for destruction, LOT in itself recalling Hebrew history—Lot's wife, the casting of lots at the foot of the cross—and heavy with '1*OT*.' With 1 and 2 of the property and stages 1 and 2 of Pip's Expectations over, all is in readiness for the '3' of Christ. In the design of breaking up the House to be sold for building materials, Dickens acknowledges the debt of Christianity to its Greek-Latin-Hebrew past, its foundation. The Old is part of the rising New, which redeems Christ's promise not to destroy but to fulfill.

Pip and Estella too enter A.D. Set free from the witching spell of the past, Estella is the old, disdainful Estella no more. Once she shone on Pip with the frosty, distant light of stars in his childhood, dim lamps that 'twinkled out one by one, without throwing any light on the questions why on earth I was going to play at Miss Havisham's, and what on earth I was expected to play at' (48). Now stars do 'throw light.'

All confused, old 'expected' and expectation at an end, Pip sells all he has and follows Clarriker—his 'I sold all I had...and joined Herbert' (455) echoing: 'If thou will be perfect, go and sell that thou hast...and come and follow me' (*Matt.* 19:21). Returning home after many years abroad, Pip visits the old House site and sees Estella again. Magically, they meet at star-rise:

> A cold silvery mist had veiled the afternoon, and the moon was not yet up to scatter it. But the stars were shining beyond the mist, and the moon was coming, and the evening was not dark. (458)

Gazing on Estella, Pip notes the 'saddened softened light of the once proud eyes' (458); Estella too shines. The loftiness of the old Estella was not spiritual elevation, but hauteur. Estella takes Pip's hand. Like angels bending near the earth, the Star, like the new Heaven revealed by Christ, now inclines towards man.

Pip and Estella speak, and Pip recalls Him from whom Estella sprang:

> The moon began to rise, and I thought of the placid look at the white ceiling, which had passed away. The moon began to rise, and I thought of the pressure on my hand when I had spoken the last words he had heard on earth. (459)

Estella looks around her, the old impassivity gone. 'Poor, poor old place!' (459), she says. And as if Heaven acknowledged her new emotion:

> The silvery mist was touched with the first rays of the moonlight, and the same rays touched the tears that dropped from her eyes. (459)

Estella recalls to Pip words he once spoke to her, which were: 'God bless you, God forgive you!' (460) She wishes his assurance that he means them still, that they are still friends:

> 'We are friends,' said I, rising and bending over her, as she rose from the bench. (460)

Against a spiritual backdrop of 'God,' 'bless,' and 'forgive,' all—moon, mist, stars, two human figures—'rise.'

Now the latest Adam and Eve leave the Ruined Garden, with 'rising' still the theme:

> I took her hand in mine, and we went out of the ruined place; and, as the morning mists had risen long ago when I first left the forge, so, the evening mists were rising now, and in all the broad expanse of tranquil light they showed to me, I saw no shadow of another parting from her. (460)

The long day of man's journey from long-ago 'morning mists' to this tranquil evening moves on; so life pursues its end. The symbolic moment prefigures both a hopeful future, and that Future of futures, Eternity. Beyond the oncoming night, all will rise into light, the Morning to which no night succeeds. Earth's lost Eden fades; the Heavenly Paradise beckons.

Folding allegory within allegory, Dickens in an inspired vision unites the Great Expectations that drew kings and lowly shepherds to a manger; the aspiration that moved Philip, the disciple; Sir Philip Sidney; and the latest disciple, Philip Pirrip, Astrophels of then and now—to fix divinest love and longing on a Star.

The long concealment at an end, the truth is finally known. Emerging from the costly infatuation of supposing he owed all to the (He)brewing fortune, Pip realizes that from the beginning all was really owed to Him, the man of sorrows first glimpsed in suffering Abel; always, through all, 'he' was drawing Pip's life, thought, destiny, to Him. In his 'B.C.' experience, Pip reached for the Chosen Few life of privilege; such seemed the way to the Star. But it only led backwards to Law, Temple, Babylon, and a sense of vanity. Pip finds that it is in renouncing self-seeking to help the wretched man at his door, in whom Christ evermore is, that he gains his own soul.

Before the coming of a Saviour, man's Expectations are doomed to the torment of unfulfilled desire, or are of pain. In *The Life of Our Lord*, Dickens depicts the tormented man among the tombs crying: 'Oh, Son of God, do not torment me!' He expects more punishment. But as Christ does not add to his suffering, but relieves it, it falls to mankind calling itself Christian to do the like. Among the spiritual lessons founded on the life and lessons of Christ that *Great Expectations* redelivers, none is greater than this.

How long Pip cherishes Expectations; how very long man waits and hopes for a Redeemer. In Dickens, as of old:

> And as the people were in expectation, and all men mused in their hearts of John, whether he were the Christ, or not;
> John answered, saying unto *them* all, I indeed baptize you with water; but one mightier than I cometh, the latchet of whose shoes I am not worthy to unloose: He shall baptize you with the Holy Ghost and with fire: (*Luke* 3:15-16)

In *Great Expectations,* to the soul 'in expectation' comes John with fishing-rod and font, and seaworthy Skiff-ins; also there sails in our behalf the John of Sunderland making speeches to the wind. Then, as in the sacred story upon which Dickens founds his own, there follows one greater, Clarriker, the steward of His estates who is not *cleric* only, but, like the Welsh clergyman in 'The Shipwreck,' (via. Chapter II) *clar*-ik, alight with His light. In luminous original symbolism of the kind, Dickens recounts the age-old longing fulfilled at last in the gift, the fortune, the experience of the ultimate vision of what love for mankind means which Christ, its supreme exemplar, carries to mankind from the Father.

In *David Copperfield,* the way to Heaven, the angel, Beatrice, Star in David's life, the mirror of the soul in its perfect bridal with the life and lessons of Christ, is Agnes Wickfield: AGNES, the sacred subject we turn to next.

# SIX

# Agnes Wickfield

'What is it?  What is your secret, Agnes?' (DC, 567)

In time, Murdstone falls away.  The better era of Miss Trotwood, Mr. Dick, Doctor Strong, and the Wickfields arrives.  Rising over several heads at school, David replaces Adams as head boy.  (So an ADAM(s) ceded to a DAVID once before in history, a Chronicle relates.)

A classic *David* adventure ensues, hebraically enough, a battle.  What does young David's fight with the formidable butcher, 'the terror of the youth of Canterbury' (267), recall?  A more terrible, philistinish butcher, in the figurative sense too, is hard to imagine.  Rumor hath it 'that the beef suet with which he anoints his hair gives him unnatural strength' (267).  Shades of the contest of David and Goliath, *and* of Samson, in both hair and unnatural strength.  The Goliath-Samson splice, shading symbolic glare, is the sort of doublet Dickens favors, we know.[1]  Further, 'anoints' quietly antiques the text, its beauty its perfect admissibility on both the literal and biblical-allegorical levels at once.  In *David* country, *anoints* may echo the line of the *Psalm* of David: 'Thou anointest my head with oil.'

Defeated at first, David, ere long newly provoked, will 'go out with the butcher, and gloriously defeat him' (272).  As young David in defeating the Philistines saved his people, so in conquering the butcher, David champions not only himself but the beleaguered 'youth of Canterbury.'

Now appears young love in the form of a tender, fair 'Miss Shepherd.'  A *David-Shepherd* idyll will surely soften the most hardened skeptic of allegory in Dickens, especially in the warm symbolic nest shaped for it.  Trailing rosy cloudlets of glory, the Miss Shepherd era dawns in David's soul:

> But who is this that breaks upon me?  This is Miss Shepherd, whom I love.
> Miss Shepherd is a boarder at the Misses Nettingalls' establishment.  I
> adore Miss Shepherd.  She is a little girl, with a round face and curly flaxen

hair. The Misses Nettingalls' young ladies come to the Cathedral too. I cannot look upon my book, for I must look upon Miss Shepherd. When the choristers chaunt, I hear Miss Shepherd. In the service I mentally insert Miss
Shepherd's name; I put her in among the Royal Family. At home, in my own
room, I am sometimes moved to cry out, 'Oh, Miss Shepherd!' in a transport of love. (265)

The Cathedral setting, worship service, choristers chanting, and prayer
book ('my book,' in the muted Dickens way) set David's rapture in a
context of the divine. Though religious, all is smiling, graceful, light.
Her curly flaxen hair and round face make the darling a bit sheep-like, if we
recall Ham Peggotty's like 'curly light hair that gave him quite a sheepish
look' (29), and the 'spencer' Miss Shepherd wears might just be a sly
'spenser,' i.e., Spenser or allegorical touch. Thus, in ordinary human circumstance arises a small, authentic remembrance and poetic grace of the
'love' story of *Psalms* which flowered in: 'The Lord is my shepherd,' a
vision that also united objects of earth and Heaven.

Only the heir of David could insert 'Shepherd' in the religious service, as
David Copperfield does; and only a David, royal of soul, open and close the
annals of 'the Royal Family'! Once again the day of the *Shepherd* 'breaks
upon' the soul of Western man.

Celebrating the humanistic, poetic strain in Judaism that honored not
only the Law but the God Who transcended Law, Dickens's David like
David of old lifts his eyes from 'the letter' of the prayer book unto the hills
of idealising love that changes the very worship service itself. Note the
faint but unmistakable note of exaltation in diction in the *Miss Shepherd*
passage: in 'breaks upon me,' and in: 'I cannot look *upon*...for I must look
*upon.*' (Look *at* would be more usual.) Language too experiences transport. 'Chaunt,' more antique-seeming than 'chant,' like 'anoints' points
backwards, as if Biblewards, in time. In allegory, a David caught up in the
'Shepherd' vision of David, shepherd of Bethlehem, looks away from
formal worship in the House of God (a typical Dickens one of 'earthy
smell,' 'sunless air,' and 'the sensation of the world being shut out' (265),
as in *Dombey* and *Drood*), and entertains a new emotion, a lover's fancy
which alters the religious service itself, releasing worship to love. In the
'Miss Shepherd' fantasy, at once touching, silly, and sublime, Dickens displays the soul of a David born now as then for rare transport of spirit.

But Time is unripe; soon all flashes away. 'Miss Shepherd comes out of
the morning service, and the Royal Family knows her no more' (266).
'Adoring' Miss Shepherd, as he will idolize Steerforth in the ruinous relationship soon to renew, David wobbles, spiritually speaking. One day he
will find all he sought in lesser loves in the peerless Agnes, who redeems
the promise first quickened in the impulse towards Miss Shepherd. For
the present, however, Agnes is quietly in the background, though David's
unfailing confidante and solace in all. While he recovers from wounds

incurred in the epic battle, Agnes, David reports, 'condoles with me, and reads to me, and makes the time light and happy' (267). Thus does he disport in spiritual infancy, Western man's own, which, for all its awkward moves and flights into absurdity, is touched with intimations of the Above.

David and the terrific adversary fight 'down in a green hollow' (267). Does *green hollow* hie back to the green pastures of the 'Shepherd' *Psalm?* In any event, the Miss Shepherd era is a green time, as green in inexperience as in Nature. The young divinity of David's heart attends the 'Misses Nettingalls'' school. NETTINGALLS! Was ever name more screamingly symbolic? What but the 'school,' in the poetic sense, of 'Nightingales'? Both to sugar and gall, Old Time is equivocal, as 'Net' and 'Gall' in 'Nettingall' imply. David's next heart's idol, Miss Larkins, is more of the playful same—a Lark(ins). What larks! And as Miss Larkins is 'not a chicken' (268), i.e., not young, is she not all the more blithe a lark? In short, in the Dickens way, a great quantity of pun is had by all.

In this era, the unfledged soul of Western man again enters upon Nature worship or pantheism, in which the Creator is still half perceived in the creation. Companioned by a green thought in a green shade, David tumbles blissfully among 'Nightingales,' 'Shepherds,' 'Larks.' Half idolater, half monotheist, he terms the latest goddess of his rioting heart his 'dear divinity,' treasuring up the flower she bestows upon him as a 'sacred pledge' (271). *Divinity* and *sacred* are not wholly figurative. In the time-honored way of a young man's fancy, David, disporting amid sylvan gods and goddesses, flounders at god-making in the age-old way. But he exalts one 'Shepherd,' and therein lies a tale.

How *is* God first sought? How comes man to know he lives to divine ends? After 'hexam-magwitch' time in which religion and witchcraft are one, Nature is set free from spells. Tending his flocks in sight of green hollows, hills, larks winging upward, David the shepherd is stirred. Moved and comforted by what he sees, he comes to intuit a giver of such gifts, the higher Shepherding power they imply. The visible leads awakened curiosity and wonder to make new, visionary connections. In the lamb the shepherd keeps from the wolf, lion, or bear; in still waters that restore a troubled soul, man slowly discerns a life's course as in the keeping of a transcendent guardian spirit far more deeply interfused whose veiled identity and mystery of presence-in-absence is suggested in myriad symbolic ways. The sense of metaphor is born. Natural prospects open spiritual ones into the beyond, drawing the gazing soul to figure to itself, in tracery of the seen, greater wonders unseen: the whispered glories of the life to come. In his unusually strong sense of correspondence, the Psalmist passes from the physical reality of sheep and shepherd to the idea of God as shepherd, and man, the lamb in His care, imagery mystically fulfilled long after in that of the Good Shepherd and Lamb of God. Such are the seeds lying dormant in the innocent little drama of spiritual break of day, the sunrise-sonrise tale of David and Miss Shepherd.

In childhood too David is attuned to Nature and full of wondering interest in all he sees:

> There is nothing half so green that I know anywhere, as the grass of that churchyard [the one at Blunderstone]; nothing half so shady as its trees; nothing half so quiet as its tombstones. The sheep are feeding there, when I kneel up, early in the morning, in my little bed in a closet within my mother's room, to look out at it; and I see the red light shining on the sundial, and think within myself, 'Is the sundial glad, I wonder, that it can tell the time again?' (14)

How all within the budding psalmist soul of this latest David, down to the insentient stone itself, praises the Lord. In eternal present-tense, childish fancies of a sundial 'glad' at sunrise, and of a dark earth welcoming the sun of Heaven, the *anima mundi* dreams futurewards of the Son of God. In David, the Hebrew David and Son of David destinies of man fuse; he houses the Judaeo-Christian intellect in the mystery of passage.

David's watching the sheep (like a shepherd?) is a picturesque motif Dickens strongly intends, for long after, looking back, David will recall 'the rosy mornings when I peeped out of that same little window in my night-clothes, and saw the sheep quietly feeding in the light of the rising sun' (320). One is back in the symbolic sunrise of Judaism, pre-Murdstone time when all is vision and light, and sheep may safely graze; when mankind's way to the high noon of the Messiah lies open beneath blue, cloudless skies.

Walking on the beach at Yarmouth with little Em'ly, David picks up a stranded starfish, and replacing it in the water, wonders (wonder ever a star of David) whether sandy strand or sea is its rightful home. A profound question. Where *does* it belong; and where, half star, that other 'starfish,' the amphibious soul of man which forever swims in two realms, the twin blue radiances of sea and sky, earth and Heaven, Time and Eternity? Musing over one small starfish, thinking it might not have thanked him for placing it back in the sea, David has no deeper thoughts; but somewhere in his nascent curiosity they lie curled like a leaf whose green hour has not yet come. In Dickens, the watery realist man also sails tidal skies, ever a rider to the sea of Eternity. Now, voyager!

Soon after the sheep-sundial time, little David is in church. Remote in mind from the sermon, wool-gathering, he resumes the homely slighted shepherd's trade:

> I look at the sunlight coming in at the open door through the porch, and there I see a stray sheep—I don't mean a sinner, but mutton—half making up his mind to come into the church. I feel that if I looked at him any longer, I might be tempted to say something out loud; and what would become of me then! (15)

The amusing distinction, 'not sinner, but mutton,' is a reminder that in

Dickens the literal/figurative issue is never far off. David's two-fold sense of *sheep* is of course Dickens's own; and, though dismissed, or perhaps *because* dismissed, 'sinner' winks passing by. The ambiguity lingers. A half-entered-in stray sheep, sinner or no, has multiple scriptural relations, Old and New, if ever sheep had. If not some kin, on the Father's side, of the sheep in the parable which the shepherd goes in search of, leaving the ninety and nine, then this undecided, lone lorn fellow seems to be seeking one who says: 'I am not sent but unto the lost sheep of the house of Israel' (*Matt.* 15:24). David is on the verge of making friends, even perhaps, *in loco Parentis,* of asking it in, but fear of stern ecclesiastical authority stops him: no stray sheep welcome here. Regarding churchmen in Dickens, it is ever thus. This charming little scene again proves Dickens the most pleasant and painless of metaphysicians.

In *Copperfield* a small flock is often nearby, figuratively (and otherwise) speaking. David's infant brother who dies is a 'poor lamb' (132); Doctor Strong, 'a very sheep for the shearers' (238). The workers in Mr. Omer's shop are 'so many lambs' (439). Before the wedding, David and friends visit his new home 'in a flock' (629). A lamb-fry with Mrs. Micawber helps pass the time in 'Babylon'; and at the Waterbrook party David plunges into 'a vapour-bath of haunch of mutton' (371). Mr. Micawber with ominous expertise turns ill-cooked mutton into 'a Devil' (413). In his muddled newlywed's life, David wonders 'whether our butcher contracted for all the deformed sheep that came into the world; but I kept my reflections to myself' (642). David and Dora employ a young page who robs them, and then, in miniature comic opera of crime and repentance, leaves to become 'a shepherd of 'up the country' somewhere' (692). (How far, or high, 'up'?) Commonest figures of speech like *lamb* and *flock* live on new terms in a David-Shepherd world. Clearly, the 'flock,' mankind, is in trouble. While much feeding on sheep and turning sheep into Devils proceeds apace, few, it seems, heed the mandate: 'Feed my sheep' (*John* 21:7).

The Miss Shepherd-Miss Larkin era is no exalted one, though in it exaltation first opens its eyes. David still has much 'Hebrew' history to live out. Time marches on: 'A blank, through which the warriors of poetry and history march on in stately hosts that seem to have no end' (268). A whole Old Testament of combatants, and no few Homeric and Roman warriors, might pass through such spacious symbolic portals as those. As B.C. warrior-lover, David smears on 'a great deal of bear's grease' (268). Miss Shepherd, just opening her eyes, proves fickle; her own evolution has hardly begun. OT time cannot hold the lovely 'Clara' or 'Shepherd' dream.

It is a time of Fall. Booking a box seat in the Canterbury coach, David, grandly dressed and proud of cutting a fine figure—in fact, 'glorif[ying] [him]self upon it a good deal' (284) —is nevertheless unceremoniously shoved aside for someone else and forced to ride up behind the coach-box. He states: 'I have always considered this as the first fall I had in life' (284). A *self*-glorifying, dandified David is 'fall' man indeed. The Canterbury stage is en route to the Golden Cross Inn at Charing Cross; but it takes more than Cross on Cross to make a Canterbury pilgrim. Moreover, the Golden Cross, described as 'a mouldy sort of establishment in a close neighbourhood' (285), has itself clearly fallen on hard times. Savouring all that 'Golden Cross' implies, Dickens takes the pulse of Christendom amid its vaunted symbols, finding it mortally low.

It is Fall time in full flower when, as Trotwood, our hero enters upon the study of law in Doctors' Commons. Law, the Murdstone way, is remote from faith, hope, and charity. Not surprisingly, David is predictably wretched in this shut-tight, formalist world of law which, strong for the letter, flagrantly defeats the spirit of justice and truth. For example, take the case of one Thomas Benjamin, which David recounts. Deciding to marry, the gentleman takes out a license in the name of 'Thomas,' suppressing 'Benjamin.' In time, finding wedlock not to his liking, Thomas Benjamin neatly slips the marriage contract by claiming that since he is not 'Thomas' but Thomas *Benjamin,* he was never legally married at all. Intent on nothing but the letter of contractual documents, the Law agrees. The allegorical meaning of the episode is fascinating. A young man tries the 'Thomas,' or Christian-name, Christian way of the 'bridegroom,' turning from 'Benjamin,' the OT faith of his fathers. But like the young man in Scripture who would but cannot bring himself to sell that he has, give to the poor, and come and follow Christ, *Thomas,* finding the way of the cross too hard, falls back on 'Benjamin,' the ways of the tribe of Benjamin, and is 'married' or committed no more.

Law vindicates weasle arrangements of the kind. In it, one glimpses David's future as a member of Doctors' Commons. In this era too David woos and wins lawyer Spenlow's daughter, 'the captivating, girlish, bright-eyed, lovely Dora' (391). The word 'captivating,' like the chapter title 'I Fall Into Captivity,' affirms the Fall-Captivity directions David has taken. The Old hangs on; Dora's companion is none other than the blackest of reactionary strains in the soul of man, Miss Murdstone; no surprise to find her in the precincts of the Law. Studying law, adoring Dora, an ever-distraught David contorts body and soul into alien shapes: is pomaded (bear-greased), 'captivated,' enslaved out of self; and tight-booted and crippled by corns, is put out of commission for 'the journey.'

History, doubling back, repeats itself. As the first David Copperfield to his child-wife Clara, so his son to his own child-wife, Dora. Here is no progress, but retrogression. Loving Dora is a doomed bliss, a brief 'wandering in the garden of Eden' (392). In so charged a symbolic context, even so common a figure of speech takes on new force. Eden cannot last. By divine decree, there is no being struck immortal, no effortless arrival in

Paradise, especially in the shadow of the law.  Nor can a daughter of man
'loved to idolatry' (551) be David's destiny.  Her father, Law *in bono,*
struggles against his partner, 'restraining demon Jorkins' (351), Law *in
malo;* the battle against the Christ-killing, recidivist element in Law is
never won.  For all his frantic bliss, David himself knows something is
amiss.  Casting about, he confesses himself to Agnes 'so unsteady and ir-
resolute in my power of assuring myself, that I know I must want—shall I
call it—reliance, of some kind?'  'Call it so, if you will' (567), is the soft
reply.  Knowing that David is unready to call it what it is, the soul's thirst
for waters that do not flow through Eden, but from the fountain of living
waters, Christ, *Agnes* waits within her Mystery.

OT forces regroup.  The Flood again threatens, and helpless without
Him Who calmed the winds and waves, man is lashed by battering storms
of destiny.  Aware that he is without the power of assuring himself, as his
words to Agnes reveal, David still has not imagined a 'reliance' *beyond*
self, a Saviour.  A ship's salvage case comes up in Admiralty Court; all is
dregs of wreckage—salvage, not salvation.  Beyond *Brooks* and *Waterbrooks,* metaphoric waters continue to rise around David, who, 'steeped in
Dora,' is 'saturated through and through.'  As he puts it: 'Enough love
might have been wrung out of me, metaphorically speaking, to drown anybody in' (474).  Then there is his tippling landlady, Mrs. Crupp, who lives
downstairs 'in a distant chamber, situated at about the level of low-water
mark' (383), and calls David 'Mr. Copperful,' in 'some indistinct
association with a washing-day' (398).  One pictures a huge, steaming
'copper full' of wash water.  Note too, not just 'wash day,' but '*a* washing
day.'  Which??  That of the Flood, Washing-day of days.  (One may recall
that, in *Pickwick,* the magistrate in whose court Pickwick is tried and found
guilty is addressed, not as 'Your worship,' but as 'Your *wash-up*' (347)
—italics mine—in a like strategy.)  Is Copperfield to be a *Copperful?*

Mrs. Crupp in her below-ground chamber, as it seems, exhibits the
C(o)*r*(r)*up*-tion that sets in as man forgets the words:

> Lay not up for yourselves treasures upon earth, where moth and rust doth
> corrupt, and where thieves break through and steal; (*Matt.* 6:19)

I make the Crupp-'corrupt' connection on the strength of Dickens's own
citing of the verse from *Matthew,* as will be seen in Chapter VII.  In OT
time of the novel, 'Copper-field' is treasure in danger of Crupp-tion of
many kinds, and ever threatened by that dire washing-day, the Flood.  As
a squashed Tommy Traddles, visiting the newlyweds, gallantly declares,
while being held at bay by Dora's spaniel, Jip: 'Oceans of room, Copperfield!  I assure you, Oceans' (641).  How true!  As two capital 'O's' insist,
and a 'bay' for good measure, *Oceans* it is.

Uriah Heep is also a source of the old punishment, the Flood.  Grimly and doggedly studying Tidd's Practise, Heep uses the legal knowledge gained to ferret out and exploit Mr. Wickfield's weaknesses. Heep grinds his always-damp palms together 'as if to squeeze them dry and warm' (234), and confides to David he 'always overflowed towards you since the first moment I had the pleasure of beholding you' (381). For once Heep does not lie. 'Overflowed' is picked up minutes later in David's: 'I fathomed the depth of the rascal's whole scheme' (381). Heep boasts that 'it seems to rain blessings on my 'ed' (377); he gives David's reluctant hand a 'damp squeeze' (382) with his 'fish-like hand' (607) of waters.

Dickens keeps it up. One dark night, anxious about Uriah and fresh from stumbling over the clerk's stool (shades of Mrs. Pocket's footstool: see Chapter III), David finds himself...

> dreaming, among other things, that he [Heep] had launched Mr. Peggotty's house on a piratical expedition, with a black flag at the masthead, bearing the inscription 'Tidd's Practise,' under which diabolical ensign he was carrying me and little Em'ly to the Spanish main, to be drowned (236)

So in *Uriah* time of old was the House, or ark, made piratical by its runaway passion for the Law. In such deluge of flood imagery, 'Tidd' of Tidd's Practise begins to look more and more like Tide.

Heep gains; fortune, man's sole reliance, proves fickle; and soon even rich Miss Trotwood is shipwrecked, financially speaking, and found sitting with what is left of her worldly goods, cat, bird, luggage, 'like a female Robinson Crusoe' (497). There is an OT tide in the affairs of Judaco-Christian men which, taken at the Flood, leads back to *Genesis* time of mind, and its jeopardy. In 'My First Dissipation,' David tells of tipsy visions of mist, swimming buildings, and water everywhere. Doctors' Commons is afloat in 'a sea of stationery' (475). And Dora dubs David, lawyer to be, 'Doady, which was a corruption of David' (601), *corruption* in more senses than one, one thinks.

Law and Satan come together. Lo, Uriah Heep is the serpent of Eden, and of ever after. *Now* we comprehend his constant writhings from the waist up, the endless twisting, worming, 'snaky undulations' (378), serpentining, corkscrew and Conger-eel motions of body and soul; and, from popular snake lore, his clammy touch. Heep is the Serpent down to his lashless red eyes. His lowly manner is quite literally that of the 'lowly,' i.e., belly-to-ground, slithering snake! Repelled by Uriah's hideously triumphant writhings over Mr. Wickfield's fall through law—so the Wickfield, symbol of the field of Light of the Father, is darkened by Law—David 'recoils from writing it' (576), *recoils* as from a snake. Calling Heep 'devil' (383) is but one way Dickens prompts recognition of his colossal Satanic theme.

The counterchrist universe of Satan, Law, and Death Everlasting stands against the Christian one. Heep's bony 'skeleton hands' (614), hands of the cadaver constantly reaching for David and Agnes both, intend death. In allegory, Heep stands for Satan who uses the Hebrew-Roman alliance in Law to effect the defeat of Christ. To undo David, in whom a Son of David destiny lies, and Agnes, the way to it, is to insure that none shall rise from the dead, and man shall sink forever into death's dateless night.

Heep flatters David in the same 'humbly' ingratiating, unctuous, wordy way the Serpent took with Eve; the way of Mrs. Coiler in the garden in *Great Expectations* (See Chapter III). He always addresses David as '*Master* Copperfield,' a particularly satanic piece of seductive malice, we said, in the light of: 'Neither be ye called masters: for one is your Master, even Christ' (*Matt.* 23:10). One is back with the fruit of the tree, too, as Heep, his mouth watering for Agnes, says: " 'I suppose,' with a jerk, 'you have sometimes plucked a pear before it was ripe, Master Copperfield?' " and leers 'as if the pear were already ripe, and he were smacking his lips over it' (580). Not the apple, but close enough.

The Heep-death connection is equally tight. When, undone by financial woes, Mr. Micawber becomes confidential clerk to Heep, i.e., cleric to Satan, he takes the name of Mortimer, *Mort* eloquent of his consciousness of the deathward drift of his soul. But at last Micawber, a good if weak man, can bear no more and rises to reject and unmask Heep. Sobbing, struggling, battling an unseen foe, 'like a man fighting with cold water,' floods of it, Micawber in effect says, Get thee behind me, Satan, as he publicly denounces: 'the transcendent and immortal hypocrite and perjurer—HEEP!' (711) A perfect description of Satan, if there ever was one, who would deny.

Heep threatens the friends of the Kingdom of God in still another way. Spreading doubt and discord, he seeks to undo the Strong marriage 'strong' in constant faith and abiding love, earthly love in which is mirrored the heavenly love of bride and Bridegroom, or the soul and God. When Heep-made storms of malicious doubt have subsided, and, thanks to staunch mutual faith, husband and wife been reunited, Annie Strong, kneeling at her husband's feet, cries: 'Oh, take me to your heart, my husband, for my love was founded on a rock, and it endures!' (663) To build on a rock is to found one's life on the word of Christ. In the NT parable:

> And the rain descended, and the floods came, and the winds blew, and beat upon that house; and it fell not: for it was founded upon a rock. (*MATT.* 7:25)

The *Strong* union is thus a type of the love founded upon a rock. Upon such love, constancy, and unshakable faith as it contains, Christ in Dickens builds his church; nor shall Heep prevail against it. When finally David wins Agnes, the NT metaphor rings out again. Taking Agnes to his heart, David sees in her 'the source of every worthy aspiration I had ever had; the centre of myself, the circle of my life, my own, my wife; my love of whom was founded on a rock!' (864)  In a swirl of Christian symbolism—centre, circle, love founded on a rock—the tribute to 'Agnes,' soaring above earth, wings its way into the empyrean.

If *Uriah* in Dickens comes to epitomise all that drew Israel from its assigned destiny in Christ, what of *Heep?*  It is a glaring 'heap,' or burial mound, ash-heap, death pun.  Wherever the word *heap* appears in Dickens, as it not infrequently does, rot, retributive ire, confusion and un-forgiveness, the whole range of OT values, reign.[2]  Uriah Heep thus sums up all evil ranged against the Father, the Son, and man.  As played by Heep, Satan is a Lawyer perfected in insidiously fine argument, the dispu-tatious skill first practised in the Garden (and ever after) to undo Adam and Eve, lose them Paradise, and defeat God.  The Serpent which lost man Eden would lose him it still.

Yet the son of David will not be denied, then or now.  In Dickens as in Dante, and all Christian visions, descent precedes and prepares ascent; Fall precedes rise and 'Rise up!'  Married to Dora, David, though he loves her, is not happy.  The words of Annie Strong about the mistake of ceding to 'the first mistaken impulse of the undisciplined heart' (698) haunt him:

> For I knew now, that my own heart was undisciplined when it first loved Dora; and that if it had been disciplined, it never could have felt, when we were married, what it had felt in its secret experience. (698)

As the dust of the latest domestic crisis settles, David reluctantly faces the fact that the child-wife he yet loves can never be the partner his wakened soul, sentinel of a lulled but unquenchable pilgrim self, desires, as he hopes to go to Heaven.  Haunted by a nameless, missing something, the 'reliance' he groped for words to express to Agnes, David nevertheless avoids all anger, blame, and self-pity.  No shade of impatience or embitter-ment disturbs his relations with Dora.  If his old fault was a tendency towards selfish brooding—for example, he held aloof from fellow captives in the Murdstone warehouse, Mick Walker and Mealy Potatoes, shunning sharing any part of their common lot—David now disciplines his heart and chooses a better way.  He records:

> I had endeavoured to adapt Dora to myself, and had found it impracticable. It remained for me to adapt myself to Dora; to share with her what I could, and be happy; to bear on my own shoulders what I must, and be still happy.  This was the discipline to which I tried to bring my heart, when I began to think.  It made my second year much happier than my first; and, what was better still, made Dora's life all sunshine. (698)

Here is an important moral victory for David.  Putting another before himself, he journeys in spirit in the direction of divine love that takes all sacrifice upon itself:  the love *in imitatio christi*.  Though he does not know it, a new David emerges who is Light years closer to Agnes. To make someone's life 'all sunshine' is to look to the Son.

Dora, 'Blossom' (648) of love's brief Eden, the Garden sprite spied 'sitting on a garden seat under a lilac tree...among the butterflies' (481), proves the sad inconstancy and evanescence of all earthly joys of men. Her age but a day, her untimely death ends David's soul-wasting career in Law. Deeply bereaved and tranced in mourning, he sinks under the insupportable burden of his sorrow, finally seeking relief in travel. None exists. Wandering abroad, David does not mend, but bears an unlifting and 'hopeless consciousness' (813) of loss, never passing out of 'the night that fell on my undisciplined heart' (814). Agnes Wickfield, she alone, ends this night, a symbolic sojourn in the valley of the shadow of death, a drama enacted against the backdrop of the valleys and mountains of Switzerland.

Then a letter arrives from home. David records: 'I opened it, and read the writing of Agnes' (815). Coming to him from afar, the words of Agnes restore his soul; through them he is recalled to life. Agnes commends David to God, speaks of trials that exalt, breathes back into him faith and hope in something beyond the present dark time and place. 'The writing of Agnes': a lofty phrase in which breathes the hope of the NT. Communing with *Agnes,* invisible and as if in a shining Beyond, David is rehearsed in hope. The Christian note sounds in the description of David's restoration as from the dead. 'Try,' Agnes counsels, and:

> I did try. In three months more, a year would have passed since the beginning of my sorrow. I determined to make no resolution until the expiration of those three months, but to try. I lived in that valley, and its neighbourhood, all the time.
>
> The three months gone, I resolved...to resume my pen; to work.
>
> I resorted humbly whither Agnes had commended me;
>
> I worked early and late, patiently and hard. I wrote a Story, with a purpose growing not remotely, out of my experience, and sent it to Traddles....After some rest and change, I fell to work, in my old ardent way, on a new fancy, which took strong possession of me....This was my third work of fiction....
> (816)

*Three* repeatedly rings out: in 'three months more,' 'those three months,' 'three months gone;' and a 'third work of fiction.'

*Three* continues to sound in a context of 'the journey':

> These, with their perplexities and inconsistencies, were the shifting quicksands of my mind, from the time of my departure to the time of my return home, three years afterwards. Three years had elapsed since the sailing of the emigrant ship; when, at the same hour of sunset, and in the same place, I stood on the deck of the packet vessel that brought me home, looking on the rosy water where I had seen the image of that ship reflected.
>
> Three years....(818)

Two matched images of ships heading into rosy, radiant light—the ship on which Peggotty and Em'ly sail to a new life, and the one which carries David home to Agnes—like swans on still Saint Mary's lake float double, swan and shadow. The ship reflected in the water alight with sunset, and blending with a ship floating in memory, suggests the invisible double, another dimension: life as allegory. In David's mind, commuting between present and past, reality melts ideawards. One thinks ahead to the voyage out, the sunset passage of which all earthly sailings are but passing images. With 'Death' behind him, David sails home to Agnes, singing her praises. Three months and three years and works past, the son of David is more than ever a living type of the Son of David who died then rose on the third day.

To return to the labor of those three decisive months: 'I wrote a Story,' David relates. What Story? And why the capital 'S'? What fictions untold are these upon which David, inspired by Agnes, expends 'every energy of my soul' (845)? Not *mind* only, note, but *soul*. Heretofore, Mr. Omer praised David's work as 'compact in three separate and individual wollumes—one, two, three' (734). A three-in-one production, in the Trinity. Allegory alone holds the secret of the 'Story.' David writes no ordinary story, but the David Copperfield-Charles Dickens joint version of The Life of Our Lord, the Story woven into every Dickens story ever told. Writing *Copperfield,* 'D' pens a fiction that holds up the life and lessons of Christ to the world's ever greater wonderment, understanding, and praise.

Home at long last and mindful of Agnes, David begins to 'penetrate the mystery of my own heart, as to know when I began to think I might have set its earliest and brightest hopes on Agnes' (817). As once his mother's love made him feel 'more fit for Heaven than I ever have been since' (109), now Agnes moves to the center of David's Heaven-tending life. The unseen Agnes, so long a treasury of grace in his life, is revealed as the alpha and omega. Finally he understands the meaning of the hand upraised, pointing upward. In *Agnes* shines the holy memory of Christ, ever pointing upward to the Father.

*Agnes Wickfield.* If ever there were a Christ figure on earth, it is she. Two loving Claras shine on David's childhood, and a Miss Shepherd stirs him in passing. But Agnes is above and beyond all the rest.

A new phase of his life begins when in young manhood David enters the Wickfield residence, the manymansioned house with a door knocker that 'twinkled like a star,' and steps 'white as if they had been covered with fair linen;' and corners, carvings, windows, angles (the eye sees 'angels') 'as pure as any snow that ever fell upon the hills' (218). Such intense whiteness, and sense of affinity with the above in star, snow from the sky, hills, raises this above purely naturalistic description.

On first entering, David climbs a 'wonderful old staircase' (222) to a

room in which Agnes, passing through a door in the wall,[3] first appears.
She then leads David and some others up another staircase, an ascent rich
in figural meaning:

> We all went together, she before us.  A glorious old room it was, with more
> oak beams and diamond panes; and the broad balustrade going all the way up
> to it.
>     I cannot call to mind where or when, in my childhood, I had seen a stained
> glass window in a church.  Nor do I recollect its subject.  But I know that when
> I saw her turn round, in the grave light of the old staircase, and wait for us
> above, I thought of that window; and I associated something of its tranquil
> brightness with Agnes Wickfield ever afterward. (223)

Like Beatrice, Agnes plays a divinely ordained role:  to lead man from dark
downness to a wondrous Above.  One has only to see her go before, then
'turn round, in the grave light, and wait for us above,' to grasp her role as
an emblematic Saviour, a perfect reflection of Christ.  Following *Agnes,*
one passes from the Old dispensation and fate, the grave ('*grave* light' a
pun), to glory ('glorious old room'), 'beams' (pun) and diamond panes
suggesting the uncommon radiance and treasure laid up in Heaven.  As
Murdstone is all 'Go you below!' of death everlasting, so Agnes calls the
soul of man to height and points to hope of resurrection.

One notes the fine ambiguity attendant upon the figure in the stained-
glass window with which David then and ever after associates Agnes.  The
non-placement of church and divine subject (we perhaps recall the figure in
the midst of a wondering group in Paul's memory of a picture in a work of
the same era as *Copperfield, Dombey and Son*) makes it the more ethereal.
Thus, from the first, Agnes exists in relation to something more than herself
and to a 'tranquil brightness' from above.  As the church window lets in
light, so Agnes-Christ is the mediator of light from above.  Agnes points
upward in all, as when, joyfully rising to meet her father, she is seen
intently 'listening for his coming up, that she might meet him on the stairs'
(230).  Stairs, like rising and joy, are the way to the Father.

All about and within David changes; Agnes alone is changeless.
Through shift and tumult, fall and rise of human fortune, she remains the
steady center, as David knows:

> The influence for all good, which she came to exercise over me at a later time,
> begins already to descend upon my breast.  I love little Em'ly, and I don't love
> Agnes—no, not at all in that way—but I feel that there are goodness, peace,
> and truth, wherever Agnes is; and that soft light of the coloured window in the
> church, seen long ago, falls on her always, and on me, when I am near her,
> and on everything around. (232)

A high influence 'descends' upon David, as from Above.  'All' and
'always' are *Agnes* words, suggesting her existence from all eternity.  The

love of Agnes has no beginning or end; it is David's long before he comes to know the extent of his for her, and for always. This for Dickens is the unique genius of Christianity: in Christ there are no pledges, covenants in rainbows, made and broken; no castings into Babylon, desertions, or evictions from the Promised Land. Desertion is the wrathful Yah way. *Not* to desert is to Dickens a supreme, distinguishing Christian good.

The constancy of the stained-glass window *Agnes* leitmotif images the constancy of Christ. Once, a passing chariot causes David to look up (ever up) to see what he realizes he has not sought nor seen for too long, but has sorely missed:

> A fair hand was stretched forth to me from the window; and the face I never had seen without a feeling of serenity and happiness, from the moment when it first turned back on the old staircase with the great broad balustrade, and when I associated its softened beauty with the stained glass window in the church, was smiling on me. (509)

This is the third appearance of Agnes in the metaphysical frame of the window. But no, not Agnes. The unnamed one of the fair hand stretched forth is as if bodiless, beyond human bounds. In such ways is Agnes lifted into symbolic heavens on earth, so that she smiles not 'at,' as on a level, but 'on' David, as from above. Again an allusion to the broad staircase of the opening *Agnes* scene. 'Strait is the gate' is not true of Dickensian portals. Following Christ, all may enter in, Every One.

Agnes is more ethereal still. While Dora is all solid little girl of blue ribbons, garden hats, earrings, pups, pens, pouts, Agnes, by contrast, is ever more finely erased as a physical presence—is hardly a being at all. It is her mirror-of-the-soul eyes and their glance that are recalled: her look, spirit, smile, all attributes of an incomparable influence for good shed upon all around her. Agnes is less a self than the embodiment of highest virtue: peace, truth, serenity, patience in adversity, unmurmuring self-sacrifice for her father. She, bright she, is the value-enhancing and discovering, ennobling idea in David's better perceptions of people and reality. In David's thoughts, Canterbury becomes 'the city where she dwelt' (564). Also celebrating a great English Christian tradition, Dickens associates Agnes with the city hallowed by memories of the Canterbury pilgrims, real and Chaucerian, down through time. Agnes and Canterbury, point of arrival, fuse with the idea of homecoming to the City of God. Happy ending, as Agnes welcomes David to her City, and in the *Agnes-David* union A.D. begins anew.

We saw that David connects Agnes with the dome of many-colored glass through which passes the white radiance of Eternity, and with a fabled City. Association is one way of symbolic enlargement, through metaphor the mind outstripping the single, sole, limited object, and always more outward bound. No journey, no passing coach or chariot in Dickens but

points 'c'-wards to 'the journey.' In each connection of Agnes to the
church window, thus to light from above, is recalled the idea of release to
the boundless, infinite, and eternal.

Agnes's realm is the Above. 'Agnes looked up—with such a heavenly
face—and gave me her hand, which I kissed' (567), typifies invention
constantly lifting 'up' and upwards. David thinks Agnes 'superior, in all
respects, to everyone around her' (380); and 'too superior to me in character and purpose...to be long in need of my entreaties' (370). Mr. Micawber
too finds her 'a very superior young lady' (566). A 'heavenly' face hints at
how 'superior' is to be taken, which is, literally. 'Ah, Agnes! You are my
good Angel!' (366) David hails her. She demurs. He insists: 'Yes, Agnes, my good Angel! Always my good Angel!' (367) The motif is developed:

> I felt then, more than ever, that she was my better Angel; and if I thought of
> her sweet face and placid smile, as though they had shone on me from some
> removed being, like an Angel, I hope I thought no harm. (376)

David senses she is a 'removed being' long before he recognizes Whom he
loves in Agnes; to this coming disclosure, 'Angel,' capital 'A,' points the
way. For, like Angels we have heard on high, this Angel echoes still the
joyous strain: Born the King of Angels. Still more Above. When Agnes
weeps for her father, then regains her composure, it is, David says, 'as if a
cloud had passed from a serene sky' (376). A typical Agnes emblem:
'There was a light in the window...and Agnes, pointing to it, bade me good
night' (613). So she points to light as in the midst of troubles she affirms:
'There is God to trust in!' (579)

When Dora dies, David's sole comfort and reliance is Agnes, all else
fading away:

> 'Oh, Agnes! Look, look, here!'
> —That face, so full of pity, and of grief, that rain of tears, that awful mute
> appeal to me, that solemn hand upraised towards Heaven! (768)

The hand upraised blends with the litany of the church window, which now
enlarges as if to suggest David's own slowly but surely enlarging grasp of
the divine significance and purpose of Agnes in his life:

> And now, indeed, I began to think that in my old association of her with the
> stained-glass window of the church, a prophetic foreshadowing of what she
> would be to me, in the calamity that was to happen in the fulness of time, had
> found a way into my mind. In all that sorrow, from the moment, never to be
> forgotten, when she stood before me with her upraised hand, she was like a
> sacred presence in my lonely house. When the Angel of Death alighted there,
> my child-wife fell asleep—they told me so when I could bear to hear it—on her
> bosom, with a smile. From my swoon, I first awoke to a consciousness of her

compassionate tears, her words of hope and peace, her gentle face bending down as from a purer region nearer Heaven, over my undisciplined heart, and softening its pain. (769)

The rapt religious imagery of hand upraised to Heaven and of a figure inclined over David's prostrate form 'as from...nearer Heaven,' and shedding compassionate tears, vividly calls to mind David's earlier remembrance of Christ: 'I have remembered Who wept for a parting between the living and the dead. I have bethought me of all that gracious and compassionate history' (766). Awakening from his swoon, a miniscule death, David sees over him the Heavenly face of Agnes, as if he too had died and gone to Heaven. Agnes restores David; in future time, when he sinks down into a much deeper, darker night of hopelessness and pain, 'the writing of Agnes' will recall him to life.

The novel ends with Dantean words that praise his lady:

> And now, as I close my task, subduing my desire to linger yet, these faces fade away. But one face, shining on me like a Heavenly light by which I see all other objects, is above them and beyond them all. And that remains.
>
> I turn my head, and see it, in its beautiful serenity, beside me. My lamp burns low, and I have written far into the night; but the dear presence, without which I were nothing, bears me company.
>
> Oh Agnes, oh my soul, so may thy face be by me when I close my life indeed; so may I, when realities are melting from me like the shadows which I now dismiss, still find thee near me, pointing upward! (877)

Upon three radiant paragraphs founded on one praiseful idea, a final three-in-one hymn to Agnes, *David Copperfield* ends. The closing of David's task late at night is emblematic, rehearsing the moment of passage to Eternity. The advanced night of the low-burnt lamp, especially in the context of mindfulness of final things, foreshadows the oncoming night of Death. David prays only that Agnes, witness of Christ, will be with him in that final hour, pointing upward. 'Oh Agnes, oh my soul' strongly equates the two, as the face shining on him 'like a Heavenly light' exalts to Heaven. Perhaps too Dickens is conscious of how the number three informs linguistic cadences, as in: 'And that remains.'

In creating Agnes-light occasions Dickens's punning genius is most happily employed. As she rises to meet her father, Agnes's 'bright calm face lighted up with pleasure' (230)—*bright, light,* and *up* mutually reinforcing. Soon to sacrifice herself to Heep for her father's sake (so Christ delivers himself over to Satan and Death for the Father), Agnes tells David: 'I said it would lighten the load of his life—I hope it will!' (370) 'I hope' recurs in: 'She was like Hope embodied, to me' (510). This is no common hope, but (capital 'H' raising it) Hope of Life Eternal. 'Lighten the load' touches the mystery of Christ's sacrifice in which the burden of the cross

'lightens,' or turns to Light. More light! 'It's such a lightening of my
heart, only to look at you!' (510) David says. Communing with Agnes, i.e.,
coming nearer the NT through her, its mirror, David goes away 'with a
lightened heart' (570). Two meanings of *light,* radiance and buoyancy,
merge where Agnes is.

A wick lit at the light of the world, Agnes points to a wick-field of light.
While David mends after his fight, Agnes, his faithful companion, 'makes
the time light and happy' (267). David notes her 'certain bright smile,
which I never saw on any other face' (511) (stress again falls on the unique-
ness of Agnes); her 'beaming smile' (613); her 'mild eyes and radiant
forehead' (511). 'Radiant forehead' is like something seen in emblem
books. In David's vision, Dora and Agnes appear together 'in a bright
perspective' (569). Agnes, the starry fixed point above an inconstant life,
has all David's praise:

> 'Dear Agnes!' said I. 'What should I do without you! You are always my
> good angel. I never think of you in any other light.' (515)

Again, 'always.' So we see that Dickens fills Agnes moments with *light,*
words like 'bright,' 'radiant,' 'beaming,' 'shining' a perpetual halo, the
fixed points of her star.

As with the Constantia wine of the Crisparkles, constancy is Agnes's
glory. OT heavens, we said, are inconstant, divine favor periodically with-
drawn when affronts to the Law excite Heaven's wrath. But even as
Christ, Agnes never forsakes. Not even the mother of Uriah. 'I cannot
always desert Mrs. Heep, you know' (511), she says. In Christ, man
inherits, not forty days and nights of rain, but a holy, compassionate rain of
tears. The Dickens Christ points to a God whose sympathy for sinning,
sorrowing mankind never fails.

Agnes, we suggested, is immaterial, incorporeal, or as nearly so as is
compatible with her being at all. Remembered more often than seen, she
is in that sense too the less real. And when seen, she is still more idea than
actual person. Above all, one recalls her eyes: 'beautiful soft eyes' (369);
'tender eyes' (383); 'mild but earnest eyes' (511); 'beaming eyes' (568);
David responds to her 'cordial eyes turned cheerfully upon me' (840).
(Note the 'c' and 'ch' in *cordial* and *cheerfully*.) In her 'raising her soft
eyes to mine' (569), *raising* points upward. She speaks relatively little, is a
'noiseless presence' (515). Finding his books set in order, David infers
that Agnes has been there. To comfort Mr. Wickfield, who is stricken at
the thought of what Agnes is prepared to bear for his sake, David says: 'I
tried to bring her idea before him in any form' (577). Agnes as 'idea' is
frequently Dickens's theme.

He develops it in various ways. When David's old friends sail to a new
life, David, watching the crowd milling up on deck, thinks he sees...

sitting, by an open port, with one of the Micawber children near her, a figure like Emily's; it first attracted my attention, by another figure parting from it with a kiss; and as it glided calmly away through the disorder, reminding me of—Agnes! But in the rapid motion and confusion, and in the unsettlement of my own thoughts, I lost it again;... (810)

Is it Agnes? We never know. How unearthly the calmly gliding figure, more rarified still as 'it,' seems. Parting from the penitent Emily and from a child with a kiss, it seems to bless the multitude on the verge of sailing into the light. Where souls whose trials have ended depart for a New Life, there the spirit of Agnes is, speeding them on their way.

Dickens weaves a Vita Nuova theme into a glowing symbolic tapestry of this journey:

> We went over the side into our boat, and lay at a little distance to see the ship wafted on her course. It was then calm, radiant sunset. She lay between us and the red light; and every taper line and spar was visible against the glow. A sight at once so beautiful, so mournful, and so hopeful, as the glorious ship, lying still on the flushed water, with all the life on board her at the bulwarks, and there clustering, for a moment, bare-headed and silent, I never saw.
>
> Silent only for a moment. As the sails rose to the wind, and the ship began to move, there broke from all the boats three resounding cheers, which those on board took up, and echoed back, and which were echoed and re-echoed. My heart burst out when I heard the sound, and beheld the waving of the hats and handkerchiefs—and then I saw her!
>
> Then I saw her, at her uncle's side, and trembling on his shoulder. He pointed to us with an eager hand; and she saw us, and waved her last good-bye to me. Aye, Emily, beautiful and drooping, cling to him with the utmost trust of thy bruised heart; for he has clung to thee with all the might of his great love!
>
> Surrounded by the rosy light, and standing high upon the deck, apart together, she clinging to him, and he holding her, they solemnly passed away. The night had fallen on the Kentish hills when we were rowed ashore—and fallen darkly upon me. (811)

As the 'glorious ship' moves into a rose-colored, glowing beyond, all aboard 'solemnly pass[ed] away.' Here is a radiant tableau of the passing away into the mystic rose, Eternity's celestial light. Backs turned to the past and night, all aboard look only to the light as if to the life to come: past sunset to the Son who never sets. In 'passed away,' a death pun; in 'glorious ship,' Glory. One perhaps thinks of pilgrims in the *Purgatorio* who, sailing, sing: 'De Exitu Aegypto Israel.' (If it matters, Dickens knew of Dante.[4]) One also thinks of Paul Dombey, borne down the swift river to the sea of Eternity, the light streaming on him as he goes. Three cheers ring out, *three* wonderfully apt in otherworldly as well as worldly ways.

and echoed in: 'so beautiful, so mournful, and so hopeful.' High on deck (the 'living' are left behind) stand the saved, uncle and niece united in love stronger for trials shared and outlived. A heightened language shapes the long, tiered periodic sentence which begins: 'A sight at once so beautiful,' and ends in three climactic words: 'I never saw.' As in Melville, 'Yes, the world's a ship on its passage out'; but in Dickens, faith in Christ and the Good News of a loving God, and not the pulpit, is its prow.

Agnes comes arrayed for the bridal. Traditional Christian symbolism attends her. Words like 'round,' 'centre,' 'circle' honor the Deity, symbolized in the circle whose center is everywhere, and whose circumference is nowhere. Agnes praises Dora, 'and round the little fairy-figure shed some glimpses of her own pure light, that made it yet more precious and innocent to me!' (519) In the first scene, Agnes turns 'round' and waits above. For David, Agnes is 'the centre of myself, the circle of my life.' Meanwhile, tiny tims of religious puns dot *Agnes* passages. One recalls her 'calm seraphic eyes' (519) and 'angelic expression' (571); with her alone a weary David experiences 'such a blessed sense of rest' (567). Even when under the spell of Steerforth, his 'bad Angel' (367), David is not lost to the appeal of higher things: 'I was never unmindful of Agnes, and she never left that sanctuary in my thoughts—if I may call it so—where I had placed her from the first' (423). Agnes *is* 'from the first.' One marvels at the coincidence by which 'Agnes' and 'all' and 'always,' her words, begin 'in the beginning' with 'A,' as does *anno Domini.*

The Passion of Agnes nears. As Heep (Satan, Law, Death, enmity to all sons of David) looms over the starry Wickfield, Agnes enters upon a long dark night of the soul. Not even her loving father can spare her this. Nor can David, who implores: 'Can I do nothing—*I,* who come to you with *my* poor sorrows?' The reply: 'And make mine so much lighter' (579). What is to come must be borne, and alone. Agnes's soft 'Heaven bless you!' and: 'There is God to trust in!' (579) is her only reply; this and a look, one 'not wondering, not accusing, not regretting' (580), a three-in-one mystery that implies all acceptance and forgiveness. It passes in a flash, replaced by the incomparable smile. At this time, David still has not guessed the secret of Agnes. Glancing at 'the serene face looking upward,' he supposes that 'it was the stars that made it seem so noble' (613). But no. The divinity ennobles the stars, not the stars the divinity.

All life feels the shock of Heep's triumph as, re-enacting the old drama of evil, he nears Agnes. Miss Trotwood is ruined, and Peggotty, losing little Em'ly, undertakes an agonizing, long-unavailing search for his darling, whom all but he think dead. The Strong marriage is shaken; Micawber calls Heep benefactor and friend; Steerforth and his would-be rescuer, Ham, die. In time, Dora's death draws David too into the valley of the shadow of death.

To resume that crucial part of the story: wandering abroad, David at

first seeks to flee his grief.  His first refuge is Nature.  In the Alps are
sights to raise the traveller's eyes:  visions of 'sublimity and wonder' in a
valley above which snow-covered mountain tops soar skywards 'like eternal
clouds' (621).  How striking and metaphysically intriguing  that image is.
As if detached from solid earth and afloat in the blue, snowy crags and pin-
nacles, become clouds, are assumed into the sky.  The landscape turns
symbolic.  As valley to the vast heights of mountains, so earth to Heaven
above:  and so, finally, life to Life Eternal.

In a valley, David hears music native to the soul of David evermore:

> In the quiet air, there was a sound of distant singing—shepherd voices; but,
> as one bright evening cloud floated midway along the mountain's side, I could
> almost have believed it came from there, and was not earthly music. (815)

Bold hint.  It is not only earthly music.  From what distance comes that
'distant singing'?  As from early OT time, 'shepherd voices' float to
David's ear.  Like the rosy pilgrim clouds that float midway on the
mountain side, this music floats somewhere between that of earthly and
heavenly 'Shepherd' choirs, as midway between the times of the Biblical
David and now.  Soon after this, the writing of Agnes reaches David.
*Three* rings out everywhere, the time coffined in grief ends, the Story is
written, and David sails for home.  This crossing, heart alight with Agnes,
symbolizes the final stage of the journey from OT to the always-immanent
Christian time of soul of the House of David.

Home again, David visits his aunt.  Miss Trotwood too has been a
pilgrim, from smiting-deserting 'Ya-a-ah!' to better times.  Now, urged on
by her, David does not remain in London, but seeks out Agnes in Canterbury.  They speak, and he tries to express what he feels:

> 'as you were then, my sister, I have often thought since, you have ever been to
> me.  Ever pointing upward, Agnes, ever leading me to something better; ever
> directing me to higher things!' (843)

'Ever pointing, ever leading, ever directing;' yet another three-in-one
tribute.  David says:  'Until I die, my dearest sister, I shall see you always
before me, pointing upward!' (843)

Vision opens on vision.  Riding home that night, David sees further still.
She is not only a sister; nor is it only *until* death.  Now David knows Agnes
(as) 'pointing to that sky above me, where, in the mystery to come, I might
yet love her with a love unknown on earth, and tell her what the strife had
been within me when I loved her here' (844).

Another veil falls away.  Though deeply aware of his own unworthiness,
David now summons up the courage to declare his love.  Once more, the
Canterbury pilgrim sets out on horseback to offer Agnes his whole soul and
love:  'I went away, dear Agnes, loving you.  I stayed away, loving you.  I

returned home, loving you!' (862) O bright Trinity—'loving you,...loving you,...loving you!'—of praise. Soon, in the presence of cherished friends, they are wed:

> We left them full of joy; and drove away together. Clasped in my embrace, I held the source of every worthy aspiration I had ever had; the centre of my-self, the circle of my life, my own, my wife; my love of whom was founded on a rock!' (864)

In 'love founded on a rock,' the words in *Matthew* sound one final, triumphant time.

And if, long before, Agnes 'played some game at dominoes with me' (232), or was 'quick to divine the truth' (491), retrospective illumination discloses act and attribute as part of her mystery. '*Some* game at dominoes' sets it apart. ('Game *at*,' rather than 'game *of*,' may too.) *Dominoes* looks to Dominus; symbolically, Agnes teaches David, There is God to trust in! An Agnes quick to 'divine' truth, *divine* a pun, is more of the same. The strategy is book-wide. A promise in David's childhood 'redeemed...afterwards' (40) renews *redeem,* a sacred pun. Long lost through careless, loose usage, the idea of redemption, like the pearl in the oyster, is concealed within.

'C' and 'ch' words flock to Agnes in a remarkable way. 'Cheerful' is her special word. 'Her letter was hopeful, earnest, and cheerful. She was always cheerful from that time' (602). Last of three adjectives, *cheerful* is carefully repeated. David says: 'The cheerfulness that belongs to you, Agnes, (and to no one else I have ever seen), is so restored, I have observed today, that I have begun to hope you are happier at home?' (612) Agnes replies: 'I am quite cheerful and light-hearted' (612). (Note again how *hope, always,* and *light* are faithfully by.) Soon after: 'I have brought Agnes from the Canterbury coach, and her cheerful and beautiful face is among us for the second time' (629). And: 'In her beaming smile, and in these last tones of her cheerful voice, I seemed again to see and hear my little Dora in her company. I stood awhile, looking through the porch to the stars' (613). Yet again: '"And what is it?" said Agnes, cheerfully' (567). The cheer of Agnes, like that of the Cheerybles in *Nicholas Nickleby,* is the 'ch' spirit of a Christian soul.

Also note Agnes's 'cordial voice' (491) and 'cordial eyes' (840); her 'sweet composure' (568); 'bright composure' (840); 'sacred confidence' (841); way of 'calmly changing the conversation' (368); and the something in her voice 'that seemed to touch a chord within me, answering to that sound alone' (367). That so many *Agnes* words, like church window, Canterbury coach, chariot, clear, calm, confidence, condole, chord, composure, cordial, charity, care, centre, circle, begin with 'c' must continue to amaze. As in 'sun' and 'son,' the English language seems happily to conspire with the Christian intention of Dickens, 'c' and 'ch' accompanying Agnes until nothing else seems to exist.

David Copperfield is very long in discovering his Christian destiny. In his youth he forsakes the Master, the compassionate teacher of Salem House who, visiting some poor old women, is greeted with 'something that I thought sounded like "My Charley!"' (74). Why the ambiguity, and what 'Ch' name sounds like 'Charley'? It is as if Dickens hints at an undisclosed Ch' identity of the Master, one whose situation (he is accused, tried, vilified by a mob, unjustly condemned, then seen no more) is so close to that of *the* Master, even Christ. Shrinking from the story of Lazarus read to him by his mother and nurse, abandoning the Master to his fate, the young David belongs heart and soul to B.C., and only slowly, with the help of Agnes and others, emerges into NT time of the soul.

One small footnote is due the ancient tale of David and Miss Shepherd. In that far-off time of boyish love, David ponders a mystery: 'Why do I secretly give Miss Shepherd twelve Brazil nuts for a present, I wonder?' (266) Why indeed? It is a most odd, unprecedented gift, and inconvenient, the nuts hard to crack even in doors, as he remarks. We smile. In allegory, in the gift of the 'twelve,' behold a symbol of the twelve disciples, and/or twelve tribes of Israel! What David does, baffling even himself, is, we think, to lay at Miss Shepherd's pretty little feet a whole wishful symbolic New Testament in miniature. Looking light years and theological ages beyond an ignorant present, David intuits in Miss Shepherd a moment of the Agnes to be: Christ, joy of man's desiring. In a diminishing mirror, such as hangs in an inn in *Great Expectations,* behold the twelve disciples, a matched set of rocks perdurably firm. In *Brazil* nuts, maybe Dickens plants the idea of the New world.

It is really not so astounding as it may at first seem, this fusion of Christ and the fruit of the tree. If, as Dickens quotes, ' "By their fruits ye shall know them, said OUR SAVIOUR' (CHE, 411); if Clemency Newcome, her apple tree, and aromatic nutmeg 'wold;' if Pips and rosy pippins like the Toodle brood (*Dombey and Son*), why not twelve nuts? Like the soft seedy biscuits and oranges David also bestows upon Miss Shepherd, the gift implies seed, fruit (oranges like tiny terrestrial suns), and Christ, firstfruits (*1 Cor.* 15:20), and the mysteries of a Testament to come.

The brief Miss Shepherd ecstasy passes, within something just opening its new eyes that David can only fumble adoringly to express, his 'I wonder' anticipating wonders to come. Spiritual history still far off finds one bright, fleeting incarnation in the feeling for Miss Shepherd. Other emotion ripens. In the shifting world of events, Agnes smiles on all David's loves and wars, his comfort and stay in all. Meanwhile, David slowly unfolds towards the Canterbury moment when he will seek what has always been his, recover what was never lost.

'What is your secret, Agnes?' he asks. What but the secret so well kept, and, paradoxically, well disclosed in Dickensian allegory: that of Agnes as a revelation of the life and lessons of Christ.

In the *Dombey* and *Copperfield* era of 1846-48, Dickens's Christmas greetings to his close friend and biographer, John Forster, includes a wish for:

> Many merry Christmases, many happy new years, unbroken friendship, great accumulation of cheerful recollections, affection on earth, and Heaven at last! (FD, II, 31)

The secret of Agnes Wickfield, we think, is man's hope through Christ of 'Heaven at last!'

# SEVEN

# The Book of Daniel

'What they done, is laid up wheer neither moth nor rust doth corrupt, and wheer thieves do not break through nor steal. Mas'r Davy, it'll outlast all the treasure in the wureld.' (DC,728)

In the scriptural treasury of *Copperfield* is found an unabridged Book of Daniel, According to Dickens, an exalted narrative of spiritual search and discovery which, like its OT counterpart, bears witness to the faith of Daniel and the wonders wrought by his God.

The 'Dan'l' plot records the journey of Daniel Peggotty, who, like the Biblical Daniel, is torn from home, undergoes searching trials in far lands, and recounts them in lofty poetry which celebrates the mysterious mercies of God. The scene on the *ark* wall of 'Daniel in yellow cast into a den of green lions' comes all too vividly to life once more. But as the Biblical Daniel survived the lions' dens of Babylon, living to praise the Lord, a Daniel does so again. In Dickens, there still lives a Daniel of glorious faith to look far, far off and affirm in fervent religious accents the existence of a kingdom not of this world that shall stand forever.

On the bleak, wind-scourged Yarmouth flats, our moral fable begins, there dwells a Daniel of uncommon goodness of heart, charity, and strength to endure, who has hewn out a shelter for a small family 'whom God had brought together' (MF,330), a widow and an orphaned niece and nephew, on the edge of the hungrily roaring sea. Whatever the short-comings of 'ark' life or human character (the incurable gloom of Mrs. Gummidge; a capricious streak in little Em'ly that bodes ill; the wildness that seizes Dan'l at the mention of his kindness to the children), Dan'l Peggotty's sterling goodness is beyond all doubt. He makes the best anyone could of a hard existence in the archaic black barge menaced by piercing cold and cutting winds on the Yarmouth wastes by a cruel sea.

In time there appears on the ark the potential destroyer of the good man's peace, hope, and joy, the handsome libertine, Steerforth. In his innocence, David warmly recommends his hero: 'He's as brave as a lion, and you can't think how frank he is, Mr. Peggotty' (142). Killing *double entendre!* How true; you *can't* think how frank he is. Beneath winning shows of candor, Steerforth is duplicity itself. Introduced aboard the ark, Steerforth swiftly charms all, but afterwards, when they are alone, David is shocked to hear his idol mock Ham's 'chuckle-headed' (317) simplicity, and pronounce Dan'l Peggotty a clod because low born. The 'lion' courage boasted by David recalls the time at school when Steerforth led the attack against the good Master, a spectacle of gratuitous patrician cruelty fit for the Roman Colosseum. In time, Steerforth strikes again and steals little Em'ly, with one blow shattering the pieties that bind and hallow Dan'l's brave little world.

A marked Steerforth-lion strategy unfolds. Some time after the 'brave as a lion' introduction, Steerforth invites David on a pleasure outing:

> 'We will go and see the lions for an hour or two—it's something to have a fresh fellow like you to show them to, Copperfield—and then we'll journey out to Highgate by the coach.' (291)

So high-spirited Steerforth commandingly leads off to the lions. His interest in them is oddly keen, almost proprietary. They are obviously his pride; he relishes exhibiting them to a fresh comer, has certainly admired them often before. It is almost as if he enjoys the idea or novelty of delivering gentle, fond David into the presence of so much savage, majestic brute force. This 'showing' them to David has curious, disquieting overtones of a lurking wish to show David *to* the lions, too. Only by slowly re-reading 'a fresh fellow like you *to show them to'* does the reader quiet the uneasy first impression that Steerforth, so great a threat to David in general and the secret seducer stalking the darling of the *ark,* is bent on feeding David, 'fresh' meat, to the lions. It is at best an ambiguous afternoon's sport, one thinks.

A third Steerforth-lion motif is worked as follows. Shortly after the 'go and see the lions' episode, David and Steerforth visit Yarmouth, and before boarding the ark stand together for a moment on the dark, wintry sands:

> 'This is a wild kind of place, Steerforth, is it not?'
> 'Dismal enough in the dark,' he said: 'and the sea roars as if it were hungry for us;' (311)

'Roar' on Steerforth's lips, and his metaphor which makes the sea into a savage beast, for which David's 'wild' sets the stage, again links Steerforth with a wild animal. The 'roaring,' lionish, man-devouring, drowning sea of insatiable appetite for Hebrews in OT time of the Flood, and ever after, comes to seem a 'lion' which Dan'l must contend against in this modern *Dan'l in the lions den* scenario in Dickens. The ruthless predator Steerforth in whom the untamed animal nature is strong recognizes what 'roars' in the dark flood, and gives its existence voice.

The Steerforth-lion theme sounds once more in a confession Steerforth once makes to David aboard the ark:

> 'At odd dull times, nursery tales come up into the memory, unrecognized for what they are. I believe I have been confounding myself with the bad boy who 'didn't care,' and became food for lions—a grander kind of going to the dogs, I suppose.' (322)

Steerforth not as lion, this time, but as 'food for lions' recalls the dark retributive pattern of Old Time, the 'as you do, so shall it be done to you' creed of sin punished in kind. As Steerforth the 'lion' destroys Dan'l's old life, so a terrible drowning fate awaits him in the ever-retributive, lion-roaring sea which, even as he glooms about becoming 'food for lions,' roars impatiently without for prey.

In support of the Steerforth-lion invention, Dickens turns the Steerforth home at Highgate into a veritable pride of lions. Mrs. Steerforth's ungodly 'pride' (673) (surely Dickens intends the pun) is so great that at one point it actually stills her pulse. Her hand is so steady that David, knowing how she must be suffering under the loss of her beloved son, marvels. A visit to the lions followed by a visit to Highgate turn out to be strangely similar events. At Highgate, Rosa Dartle receives Steerforth and guest by turning a naked, 'lynx-like scrutiny' (431) on David. Soon, suddenly enraged at Steerforth and set for one of their frequent savage combats, Rosa readies her attack. Her passions, David says, 'found imperfect utterance in low sounds of her voice, and crouched again when all was still' (435). The growling and animal-like 'crouching' lead to a sudden, violent spring: 'she struck him, and had thrown him off with the fury of a wildcat, and had burst out of the room' (435). 'Wildcat' builds on 'lynx,' as both on lion. Highgate is undeniably the domain of dangerous cats. Feral nature is everywhere: in the 'giant black eyes' of Rosa Dartle with their 'hungry lustre' (431), a searching, 'lurking manner' (430), and way of appearing to 'lie in wait' (430) for the two young men. Once, in one of their savage battles, Steerforth flung a hammer at her, and the scar, which grows livid when she is roused to fury, is visible in 'the nether lip' (452). How sub-human and animalistic 'nether lip' sounds, *the* dehumanizing it the more. Further, animal terms haunt Highgate idiom. Rosa inquires if Dan'l and his kin are not 'really animals and clods, and beings of another order?' (294) Steerforth too attracts animal imagery: calls evening a 'mongrel time' (321), and is 'chicken,' 'ducks' (355), and pet to his slavish admirer, Miss Mowcher, of whom more later.

Rosa Dartle, born as all 'Roses,' Rose Maylie, Rosa Bud, and others, are to grow upwards to light, fragrance, and flower, is all thorn, '*Dart*(le),' and stab of cat claw. Wounded and disfigured by the 'lion,' master of Highgate,

she strikes out and cuts savagely in turn, nursing a great passion for revenge. Yet she clearly loves her tormentor with a passionate, self-
lacerating love embittered by helpless hate. Refusing responsibility,
Steerforth chooses not to know what gnaws at the withered Rosa:

> 'Clever! She brings everything to a grindstone,' said Steerforth, 'and sharp-
> ens it, as she has sharpened her own face and figure these years past. She
> has worn herself away by constant sharpening. She is all edge.' (294)

'Sharp' as a cutting claw, the sharp edge of Rosa comes up again in David's
remarks at a later time: 'I saw her face grow sharper and paler, and the
marks of the old wound lengthen out until it cut through the disfigured lip'
(432). As Gradgrind (*Hard Times*) and the bloody grindstone in *A Tale of
Two Cities* seem to show, man is worn down on stone, symbol of OT law
engraved in stone, wherever the passion for retribution rules his soul.

The ark which Steerforth as lion boards is already crowded with animal
life. As the Yarmouth, Yah-mouth, sea 'roars' like a Babylonian lion,
Noah's ark reappears, erupting as if from unexorcised Hebrew layers of
Judaeo-Christian man's soul. The 'lion' nears, and the beasts break loose
on board. A wildly overheated, gleeful Dan'l cries: 'Gorm the t'other one,
and horroar for it!' (312) The Gorming curse springs from hiding, as does
'horroar!' which compounds *horror* and the lion's *roar*. The OT 'hurrah!'
was, alas, just that, ancient Israel knowing few celebrations under
Yahweh, the Gorming God, free from that ever-overhanging doom. The
Yah Who cast Israel into lions' dens of Babylon for backslidings in the Law
is the spirit behind 'Gorm the t'other one,' with its man-eating finale: 'and
horroar for it!' The curse says: 'Get, Gorm *the other one,* Lord,' which
recalls the widow in *Little Dorrit* whose prayer is: 'Smite thou my debtors,
Lord, wither them, crush them!;' which curse Dickens calls 'the impious
tower of stone she built up to scale Heaven' (LD, 47), this Tower of Babel
image firmly fixing it in OT time of mind. 'Horroar!' sounds again as
Steerforth, lion master of ark revels, gets Peggotty 'to sing, or rather to
roar, "When the stormy winds do blow, do blow"' (316). More *roar*.
Thus an ominous, neo-OT time of lion, hammer, and sword overcomes in
history once more as the 'lion' danger nears and infects the soul of Daniel.

On the night Steerforth steals little Em'ly away, lion-roars fill the ark.
Awaiting the return of his heart's darling, Dan'l is all 'roar of laughter'
(450) and yet 'another roar' (450). He relieves his feelings in animal terms:
'There's a babby for you, in the form of a great Sea Porkypine!' And
again: '*There's* a babby for you,' said Mr. Peggotty, with another roar, 'in
the form of a Sea Porkypine!' And again, as if it cannot be too well heard:

> 'There's a babby for you, in the form of a Sea Porkypine! Right for all that,'
> said Mr. Peggotty, stopping in his roar, and smiting his hands together; 'fur
> here she is!' (450)

Where 'smiting,' 'babby,' and lion 'roar' are, Yah is too, we will see, such insistent repetition part of an incredible punning strategy in its unfolding.

Under the influence of a Dan'l who approves of 'Gorm[ing] the t'other one,' and sits in judgment on the fallen woman, Martha, whom the modern Pharisees drive out of Yarmouth, time veers backwards. Puns detect this. 'Sea *Pork*kpine' adds pork, pig, to porcupine, perhaps the very pig that graces Mrs. Joe's Christmas feast in *Great Expectations*. (vis. Chapter IV) In 'fur here she is!' or: 'It ain't fur off!' (142) (Peggotty says 'for' at times), animal 'fur' flies, an image echoing with his 'ruffling his shaggy hair all over his head' (312); and again: 'Mr. Peggotty ruffled his hair again with both hands' (313). Even before, Ham called David 'Mas'r Davy bor'' (141), and Peggotty hailed Em'ly with: 'A little puss it is!' (141). Peggotty calls Mrs. Gummidge, not 'mother' but 'mawther;' the old mawther is seen 'clapping her hands like a madwoman' (311). In all this shaggy, furry, wild, uncurbed porcupine-pork, 'bor'-boar life on the ark, '*mawther*' too looks to beast life, the 'maw' or gullet, jaws, throat of the wild animal.

There is something frenetic, almost subhuman about such doomed joy. When Peggotty gives Ham a friendly clap on the back, this too overhits the mark: 'Ham staggered, as well he might, under the blow Mr. Peggotty dealt him in his unbounded joy, as a mark of confidence and friendship' (315). Crying 'Yah!' (GE, 38), Mrs. Joe will deliver just such a 'restorative' blow to little Pip the night the convict is captured and stowed aboard the wicked Noah's ark in another extant province of OT time in Christendom. Dickens's point would seem to be that Hebrew ideology, the 'ark,' brewed too-strong spirits, as the hands-smiting, madwoman antics on Dan'l's *ark* show. The God of the fathers of David, Daniel, and Ham regularly favored His people with just such holy assault and battery in token of His jealous love. Imitating Him, *Yah* partisans and those who still dwell in arks do the same, for all that Christ laid the B.C. concept of the deity to rest. So poor Ham staggers under the blow, as did all humanity in the days of his father, Noah.

Dickens's *ark* punning is also spectacular. Peggotty's: 'I'll arks your pardon' (312), boldest of ark puns, staggers *us*. And as a 'roaring' Dan'l goes on and on about 'babby' (*There's* a babby for you!'), while the 'lion' Steerforth is making off with his prey, suddenly one sees what the text strains mightily to deliver: the 'babby'-lion or Babylon pun! It is Babylon and the lions dens all over again, all right, man's unchristian soul terribly attracting the B.C. past. All Hebrew history from Flood and Noah's ark to Babylon, a whirlwind of symbolic debris, flies past. Like the Spirit of the Judaeo-Christian Past, Dickens guides us through visionary scenes of phantom figures which re-enact the grievous errors tippins-turveydrop man fell into all through B.C., the ages without a Saviour.

How many there were and are! Calling little Em'ly 'my little witch!'

(312), idolizing, spoiling, making dangerous much of her, Peggotty in part prepares his own doom.  So 'bewitching Mrs. Copperfield,' Magwitch, and Miss Havisham with 'witch-like eagerness,' we saw, deliver children to evil untold.  Too hot, intemperate, and unfeeling for others ('Gorm the t'other one, and horroar for it!'), both in anger and joy, Peggotty mirrors the spirit of a fierce God whose remedy for transgression against the law was to gorm: Flood, Babylon.  Dan'l recounts that when Em'ly was small, he and she...

> 'made believe as was Turks, and French, and sharks, and every wariety of forinners—bless you, yes; and lions and whales, and I doen't know what all!'  (450)

'Wariety, indeed.  Absorbed in playing anti-Christ (Turk) and shark, Peggotty clearly does not read little Ham and Em'ly *The Life of Our Lord* in any shape or form.  David too while on the ark soaks up its fierce spirit, and in childhood 'only wished that a lion or a serpent, or any ill-disposed monster, would make an attack upon us, that I might destroy him, and cover myself with glory' (148).  A boy's innocent heroics, to be sure.  But, like his and his nurse's pastime of driving timber down crocodile throats, it looks to killing, the *old* glory; as, perhaps, such uses of timber to darker uses still, to cross and cross-guillotine, instruments then as after 'terrible in history' (TTC,2).

In the Dickens account of sacred history replaying itself on the world stage, the lion not only menaces Daniel; it is *in* him, as in the soul of Israel which, lion-like, turned against Christ and His followers, making a Roman Colosseum of the Holy Land in early Christian time.  The Pharisee in Dan'l Peggotty surfaces in his flat rejection of Martha Endell, such harsh judgment reflecting the 'babby'-lion parts of his soul.  When Yarmouth, strong for the stoning law of Yah, makes her life unbearable, Martha comes to her one friend, little Em'ly, for help, pleading: 'Em'ly, Em'ly, for Christ's sake, have a woman's heart towards me' (337).  No casual 'for chrissake' usage here.  Dickens has Martha's words set before us once again:

> 'For the matter o' that, Mas'r Davy,' replied Ham, 'all's told a'most in words, "Em'ly, Em'ly, for Christ's sake, have a woman's heart towards me.  I was once like you!"  She wanted to speak to Em'ly.  Em'ly couldn't speak to her theer, for her loving uncle was come home, and he wouldn't—no, Mas'r Davy,' said Ham with great earnestness, 'he couldn't, kind-natur'd, tenderhearted as he is, see them two together, side by side, for all the treasures that's wrecked in the sea.'  (337)

Images of treasure lost at sea are most apt.  Rejecting Martha, keeping Em'ly's charity from the fallen woman, Peggotty betrays his innermost heart's allegiance to the God of the Flood who cast so much treasure of humanity into the drowndeadly deep.

When David and Em'ly were small, Dan'l and the others watched them playing together with 'something of the sort of pleasure in us, I suppose, that they might have had in a pretty toy, or a pocket model of the Colosseum' (37). Stupendous hint! Why, of all odd things, *a pocket model of the Colosseum,* except in the service of Christian allegory? (And 'pocket,' Pocket-anticipating, to boot?) The point is that a Martha making an appeal for compassion 'for Christ's sake' is a NT Martha, and the 'ark' dwellers and Yah-ites of Yarmouth with Hebraeo-Roman souls, turn her, and thus Christianity, down.

But Em'ly does help Martha, in secret, and Martha flees Yarmouth. Soon after, Steerforth lures Emily herself away. With fierce immediacy, a stricken Dan'l Peggotty leaves his ark home, undertaking a journey to find Em'ly which changes him wholly and forever. His 'witch,' 'roar,' 'babby'-lion, ark, judgmental B.C. soul dies, and he is reunited with his little Em'ly at last. In the mystery of Providence, it turns out that the agent both of this profound change of heart and of the recovery of Emily is none other than the fallen woman, Martha Endell.

Dan'l's journey takes him to far places, as if to the ends of the earth. One night, while prowling the London streets, Martha happens to seek shelter from the cold in the doorway of an inn called the Golden Cross. Here she overhears Peggotty, home from abroad, telling David about his unavailing search. The great scheme to recover little Em'ly born this night has its origins at the sign of the 'Cross.'

Martha well remembers the gentle girl who pitied and helped her 'for Christ's sake,' and vows to help find her. She does—how, we will shortly trace in detail. All ends in the recovery and raising up of the lost, fallen Emily, a miraculous restoration which Dan'l relates in fervent religious language in this climactic passage of the 'Book of Daniel':

> 'Mas'r Davy!' said he, gripping my hand in that strong hand of his, 'it was you as first made mention of her to me. I thankee, sir! She was arnest. She had know'd of her bitter knowledge wheer to watch and what to do. She had done it. And the Lord was above all! She come, white and hurried, upon Em'ly in her sleep. She says to her, 'Rise up from worse than death, and come with me!' Them belonging to the house would have stopped her, but they might as soon have stopped the sea. 'Stand away from me,' she says, 'I am a ghost that calls her from beside her open grave!' She told Em'ly she had seen me, and know'd I loved her, and forgive her. She wrapped her, hasty, in her clothes. She took her, faint and trembling, on her arm. She heeded no more what they said, than if she had no ears. She walked among 'em with my child, minding only her; and brought her safe out, in the dead of night, from that black pit of ruin!' (729)

The Martha who finds the fallen woman in her lost life and summons her forth with the words: 'Rise up!' is surely related in spirit to the NT Martha who witnessed the raising of Lazarus from the dead, as 'Rise up!' first rang out in history. The Martha who affirmed: 'Yea, Lord: I believe that thou art the Christ, the Son of God' (*John* 11:27) again points to Christ as the miracle of 'resurrection' re-enters history. In raising upon raising (Dickens wholly caught up in, magnifying his mighty theme), Em'ly 'rises': from 'worse than death,' prostitution; from death's second self, sleep; 'from beside her open grave;' from the 'black pit,' as of Hell, the second death; all in the 'dead of night,' *dead* darkening night the more.

Em'ly 'rises' from the dead in other ways, too. As a child, she walked on timber jutting out over the sea, as if 'springing forward to her destruction' (36); in childhood, she was tranced in death, her father's and her own. Then too, the girl sought in vain 'in the dead of night' (674) has long been as if dead to all but her uncle. His faith alone has staved off 'death': 'My niece, Em'ly is alive, sir! I doen't know wheer it comes from, or how 'tis, but I am told as she's alive!' (675) (Dan'l is 'told,' we imagine, by whatever force told the Biblical Daniel there was hope beyond Babylon.) So when Em'ly is found by Martha, she is recovered from symbolic death upon death, as from the literal danger of dying of disease and want. Best of all, she can now live, 'rising up' a coy, capricious, easily-swayed little girl no more. The faith of Daniel and the Christian vision of Martha unite to defeat death. Again in history the words Christ spoke to Lazarus ring out old Time, and ring in the Christ that is to be.

High poetry accompanies a high theme. In the perfect iambic pentameter rhythms of:

' 'Rise up from worse than death, and come with me!'' Dickens accents the upstroke. In a triumphant march of syllables, all is ˘ ′: 'Rĭse ÚP!' Further, accent on *three,* the number of resurrection in Christ who rose on the third day, in: 'She was arnest;' 'She wrapped her;' 'She took her,' affirms: 'And the Lord was above all!'

We note that Martha is not directly heard. The way her words are quoted in grandeur in a solemn religious narration lends them added scriptural life. In the same way, one does not hear the words of Martha in the NT except in the reverent narration of the evangelist.

The subsequent reunion of Peggotty and Em'ly has a strong NT character of its own. To quote again from the religious narrative of Daniel:

> 'It was hours before she knowed me right; and when she did, she kneeled down at my feet, and kinder said to me, as if it was her prayers, how it all came to be. You may believe me, when I heerd her voice, as I had heerd it at home so playful—and see her humbled, as it might be in the dust our Saviour wrote in with His blessed hand—I felt a wownd go to my 'art, in the midst of all its thankfulness.' (725)

The allusion to 'the dust our Saviour wrote in with His blessed hand' recalls how in *Bleak House,* Esther Summerson reads 'from St. John, how our Saviour stooped down, writing with his finger in the dust, when they brought the sinful woman to him' (19). Dan'l's words identify Emily with the fallen woman whom Christ saves from those who would stone her in the name of the Law; the shadowy 'they' and 'them' whom Martha opposed to rescue Em'ly might be the Pharisees of old. The Daniel who can feel a 'wownd,' as if Christ's own, is very different from that other, lion-shaggy, roaring-horroaring Peggotty of *ark* times. *Never once* back then did he ever allude to the NT. In Old Time, he looked on outsiders as 'forinners,' and cast out the fallen woman who appealed for pity 'for Christ's sake.'

The great change in Dan'l's life begins after Steerforth and Em'ly run away. 'Struck of a heap' by the news and frantic to be gone in search of her, Dan'l is comforted by Mrs. Gummidge. This in itself is amazing change. The old woman who til then never spared a thought for any troubles but her own suddenly leaves off lamentation and murmurs: 'My lone lorn Dan'l' (349). Putting her head on his shoulder and recalling to him his charity to two orphan children, Mrs. Gummidge reminds Dan'l of the words of Christ: "As you have done it unto one of the least of these, you have done it unto me" (454). In this tremendous moment, a NT sentiment crosses her lips *for the very first time.*

Soon Daniel leaves the ark. He and Ham will sail no more from Gravesend (pun?), and live no more in the yawning Yarmouth lion's mouth. Looking back, we realize with David that only Dan'l's extraordinary humanity made the ark habitable at all; otherwise, it was a cramped old boat in which lobsters and crawfish pinched churlishly in dank corners, and an old lady gloomed about Old Nick. About to depart, Dan'l speaks of his old home:

> 'My station, Mas'r Davy,' he returned, 'ain't there no longer, and if ever a boat foundered, since there was darkness on the face of the deep, that one's gone down. But no, sir, no; I doen't mean as it should be deserted. Fur from that.' (456)

A reference to 'darkness on the face of the deep,' and perhaps 'fur,' looks back to *Genesis* time. However, Dan'l's loyal determination not to desert the ark looks forward to the Daniel-to-be in Martha or NT time. Thus Dickens celebrates the tragic loyalty of Jews like Daniel to their God and His way of salvation, the ark that failed.

Before he begins his journey, Dan'l visits Steerforth's mother at Highgate. They are counterparts in tragedy: he has lost a niece-daughter, she a son. He comes to win the mother's consent to the marriage of Steerforth and Emily. But, in an ironic way, as Peggotty once shunned Martha, so Mrs. Steerforth shuns the fisherman's daughter as too low-born for her beloved son. 'Raise her up!' (468) Peggotty cries. (It is 'Rise up!' to come in small, the book long readying the way of its all-ruling theme.) But the time is not ripe, and he appeals in vain. At Highgate, enclave of OT time where pride, judgment, retributive passion, and 'lion' hold sway, Mrs. Steerforth will acknowledge no common bond of humanity and shared sorrow with a common boatman. Like Miss Trotwood, Miss Havisham, or Mrs. Clennam, she is the symbol of the stiff-necked people of Yah suffering in prideful aloneness a beloved son's desertion, and refusing to forgive. (So Israel viewed Christ's 'desertion' of the Law, and would not forgive.) Ironically, the high-born lady and the lowly fisherman share the same narrow provincialism of mind, despising the fallen woman. In the domain of OT time, High is the gate of Highgate, and none may enter in.

Peggotty tries valiantly to move Mrs. Steerforth. He vows that if Highgate will accept Emily as its son and heir's wife, he will give her up forever:

> 'We'll be content to let her be; and we'll be content to think of her, far off, as if she was underneath another sun and sky; we'll be content to trust her to her husband,—to her little children, p'raps—and bide the time when all of us shall be alike in quality afore our God!' (468)

The unselfish words ring with a faith that looks past death. Beyond the earthly 'far off' to which Dan'l's thoughts, seeking Emily, will ever tend, lies the world to come. It is the genius of *Daniel* to look past the kingdoms of the world, as the Biblical Daniel saw past the Assyrian, Persian, and Macedonian, to the kingdom of God:

> And in the days of these kings shall the God of heaven set up a kingdom, which shall never be destroyed; and the kingdom shall not be left to other people, but it shall break in pieces and consume all these kingdoms, and it shall stand forever. (*Dan.* 2:44)

As shall the kingdom in which, in Dan'l's words, 'all...shall be alike in quality afore our God!'

Peggotty and Mrs. Steerforth inscribe profoundly contrasting profiles in Eternity. Though wounded by Em'ly's flight, he does not think of himself. 'My unchanged love is with my darling child, and I forgive her!' (473) But Mrs. Steerforth thinks only of herself, and puts a high price, the old Yah price, on her pardon: her son will have to beg it on bended knees. He goes far seeking his child; she remains stonily fixed at Highgate, walling out the world. Such is the symbolic relation of each to 'the journey.'

Beginning his pilgrimage, Dan'l shoulders a heavy cross. Meanwhile, within his hard, lonely present a future blessing readies. Time, perhaps ages, passes. One bitter cold night, David, married and hurrying home to Dora through St. Martin's lane, sees Martha Endell again. Soon after, he meets Peggotty, and the two turn into the Golden Cross where Martha, huddled in the doorway, overhears the tale of the unavailing search for Emily. Yet Dan'l's narrative is not gloomy. On the contrary, it is filled with his discoveries. In his wanderings he met good people: '...and many a woman, Mas'r Davy, as has a daughter of about Em'ly's age, I found a-waiting for me, at Our Saviour's Cross outside the village, fur to do me sim'lar kindnesses' (584). These are 'forinners,' gentiles, no more, but friends to the weary traveller who says: 'I'm very thankful to you! God bless you!' (585) The soul of Peggotty visibly expands, its Yarmouth narrowness passing from it forever. When he leaves the Golden Cross, *Cross* echoing 'Our Saviour's Cross,' David thinks that the night itself is 'hushed in reverence for him, as he resumed his solitary journey through the snow' (589).

Some time later, David seeks out his old friend. 'Often and often, now, had I seen him in the dead of night passing along the streets, searching... for what he dreaded to find' (674). His faith holds: 'No! Em'ly's alive!' (675) When David asks him what Ham might do if he ever saw Steerforth again, Peggotty replies: 'I doen't know, sir. I have thowt of it oftentimes, and I can't arrize myself of it, no matters' (676). NT time nears in those words, too. Like Matthew Pocket who cannot lift himself up by the hair, or David groping for a 'reliance' he cannot name, Peggotty discovers that man cannot 'arrize himself,' which is the beginning of the realization of the need for a Saviour. Though the pull of death ('dead of night') remains strong, and he puzzles over Ham's unknown state of mind 'a mort o' times' (677), *mort* a jot of Yarmouth dialect heavy with death, change readies.

Peggotty agrees with David that they cannot find Em'ly alone, and must seek Martha's help. Now the new spirit of Dan'l, witness of a Pilgrim's Progress, shines forth:

> 'The time was, Mas'r Davy,' he said, as we came down-stairs, 'when I thowt this girl, Martha, a'most like the dirt underneath my Em'ly's feet. God forgive me, there's a difference now!' (676)

Two 'Hebrews' in passage to NT time, David and Daniel set out together to find Martha, portal to Christ. David records: 'We had come, through Temple Bar, into the city' (677). The words seem wonderfully symbolic. In allegory, 'Temple' and 'Bar,' in both senses, of Law have been outdistanced, and two pilgrims enter the City.

Suddenly they spy Martha. Not quite Martha; rather, 'a solitary female figure flitting along' (677). The unnamed figure is all the closer to the Martha of Scripture. 'We crossed the road' (677), David says, *crossed* surely a part of the fine-meshed, subliminal symbolic scheme. The figure heads for a dilapidated neighborhood down by the river, a *Murdstone and Grinby* sort of world of old, rotting warehouses down low-lying streets, decayed walls plastered with handbills offering rewards for drowned men, the river here all slime and stagnant tides. Utterly distraught, crushed, and plainly suicidal, Martha gazes into the dark waters. In her fallen life, she has obviously discovered what Nancy, Sike's girl, in *Oliver Twist* knows about how Christians treat her kind.

The two men approach her.  She raves about deserving to die (the Pharisees of Yarmouth and London have done their work well), and sinking
down on the stones and hiding her face among them, seems to wish and
inflict upon herself the old stoning-of-sinners decree.  David says:

> Knowing this state must pass before we could speak to her with any hope, I
> ventured to restrain him [Peggotty] when he would have raised her, and we
> stood by in silence until she became more tranquil.
>     'Martha,' said I then, leaning down, and helping her to rise—she seemed
> to want to rise as if with the intention of going away, but she was weak, and
> leaned against a boat... (681)

'Raise' and 'rise' are prominent in the scene.  In 'helping her to rise—she
seemed to want to rise,' rise follows rise.  David asks her: 'Are you
composed enough to speak on the subject which so interested you—I hope
Heaven may remember it!—that snowy night?' (682)  Martha would reply,
but the old agony of mind distracts her: 'Sinking on the stones, she took
some in each hand, and clenched them up, as if she would have ground
them' (683).  Stones so 'clenched' in fists and hurled invoke OT law.
Martha wants to die as passionately as partisans of the law could ever have
wished.  Like Em'ly when found, Martha is past her own help.  One hopes
with David that 'Heaven may remember' the night of the Cross (one thinks
of Christ crucified as well as of Daniel) when Martha's haggard face
appeared in the doorway and her folded hands 'Begged me—prayed
me—not to cast it forth' (585).  A stand-in for the Son of David, David
answers Martha's piteous prayer, accepting, not rejecting her, and the era
of NT miracles is reborn.

Grown calmer, Martha speaks of her old affection for Em'ly, entreating
Peggotty to believe her sincere.  The old Dan'l would have bridled at
Martha's daring to speak familiarly of Emily.  But the new Peggotty
does not:

> He looked upon her, while she made this supplication, in a wild distracted
> manner; and, when she was silent, gently raised her.
>     'Martha,' said Mr. Peggotty, 'God forbid as I should judge you.  Forbid as
> I, of all men, should do that, my girl!  You doen't know half the change that's
> come in course of time, upon me, when you think it likely!' (684)

Pegotty accepts Martha, i.e., NT revelation.  The fall-would rise-fall-RISE!
strategy of this finely wrought 'resurrection' scene climaxes in the three
final words: 'gently raised her.'  'My girl!' reveals a profound change of
heart.  Once, only Em'ly mattered.  Now Peggotty extends his protection
to the sinful woman, even as Christ.  His having asked Mrs. Steerforth to
raise Emily up while the Marthas of the world were dirt under his feet was
the flaw in his great love.  The change reflected in 'God forbid as I should

judge you!' almost says all.

Now Peggotty turns to Martha with: 'Help us all you can to find her, and may Heaven reward you!' To her: 'Will you trust me?' he replies: 'Full and free!' (685) Now Martha leaves off writhing and twisting convulsively and clenching stones in merciless, satanic self-judgment: 'She lifted up her eyes, and solemnly declared she would devote herself to this task, fervently and faithfully....If she were not true to it, then might all help, human and Divine, renounce her evermore!' (685) Her lifting up her eyes, like *rise* and *raise,* points upward.

But old habits die hard. Suddenly Martha's new-found confidence wavers, and she turns again towards the river. Now it is David who comes strongly and religiously to the fore:

> 'In the name of the great Judge,' said I, 'before whom you and all of us must stand at His dread time, dismiss that terrible idea! We can all do some good, if we will.' (686)

'If we will' recalls that man's will counts. Even back in ark time, Dan'l frequented a public house called The Willing Mind; to will good and be willing are passports to 'the journey.'[1] Martha rallies. The blessing born in Em'ly's response for Christ's sake, and nurtured one snowy night at the Golden Cross where, in a Little Dorrit of a doorway, Martha prayed a son of David not to drive her away, now widens still more. Believed in (as Martha testifies to belief in Christ, so again Martha is the focus of belief), Martha takes up the saving task that leads her to summon forth one sunk in 'worse than death' with the words spoken to Lazarus: 'Rise up!'

After Martha is raised from the stones, her shawl remains on the ground. Peggotty lifts it up, gently placing it around her shoulders. Nothing finally remains unraised under Dickensian heavens.

Dickens's Martha is MARTHA ENDELL, her surname like her Christian one signifying ENDELL, the END of EL, the Hebrew God. Why does Dickens make much of the snowy night of the Golden Cross, when 'it snew so hard' (676), and again, 'the night when it snew so hard' (684)? It SNEW?? The pun leaps up: 'It *S NEW*'! The *New* Testament arrives anew with 'Martha,' as with Clemency Newcome, newness symbolized in the pure white snowfall that covers old, as Old, tracks of pilgrim man. Perhaps a soupcon of New hides as well in Dan'l's praise of Martha, who, 'trew to her promise' (729), saved Emily. Not true, but tr*ew,* the 'ew' too as if in inmost sympathy with n*ew.*

Martha leads both Dan'l and David into NT time. In childhood, David shrinks from the story of the raising of Lazarus, and must experience the raising force of faith, forgiveness, and trust in his own life before he understands and believes. Typically, Dickens recreates the NT story, not through Lazarus, the principal, but through a bystander, the sister of Lazarus, a humble witness of highest truth.

In Dickens, two fallen women, Martha and Emily, point to the lessons of Christ. Emily in her own right is a brilliant gloss of a NT text. In one of Rosa Dartle's tirades against her there gleams a small figurative jewel that reveals what Em'ly, beloved of so many, symbolises and is:

> 'The devil whom you made an angel of, I mean this low girl whom he picked out of the tide mud,' with her black eyes full upon me, and her passionate finger up, 'may be alive,—for I believe some common things are hard to die. If she is, you will desire to have a pearl of such price found and taken care of. We desire that, too; that he may not by any chance be made her prey again...' (672)

Like gold on ground, 'pearl of such price' looks to the NT parable which reads:

> Again, the kingdom of heaven is like unto a merchantman, seeking goodly pearls:
> Who, when he had found one pearl of great price, went and sold all that he had, and bought it. (*Matt.* 13:45)

Little Em'ly is a type of 'the pearl.' No wonder, then, that so many— David, Dan'l, Ham, Steerforth—yearn towards her. Or that, losing her, Dan'l, leaving behind all ease and worldly possessions to recover her, paying 'such price,' should find his way leading from station to station of the Cross: Our Saviour's Cross, the Golden Cross, thence to Martha and 'Rise up!' Losing 'the pearl,' symbol of the Kingdom of Heaven, Dan'l, like the merchantman in the parable, sells all he has to buy it.

Interwoven NT mysteries and miracles shine in Emily, mirror of 'the pearl.' After she leaves Steerforth, she wanders among simple folk in a far country by the sea. For a time she is lost and bewildered. Slowly she mends. She learns their language, and one day, thanks to a child, her confusion of mind ends. In the Book of Daniel we read:

> 'And of a sudden this child held out her hand, and said, what would be in English, 'Fisherman's daughter, here's a shell!''—for you are to unnerstand that they used at first to call her 'pretty lady,' as the general way in that country is, and that she had taught 'em to call her 'Fisherman's daughter' instead. The child says of a sudden, 'Fisherman's daughter, here's a shell!' Then Em'ly unnerstands her; and she answers, bursting out crying; and it all come back!' (727)

'Fisherman's daughter' reminds us that Dan'l and Ham are simple fishermen, like the ones who leave their nets to follow Christ, Who makes them fishers of men. As Christ is the Fisherman, the Fisherman's daughter, 'the pearl,' is His own, a gift from the sea of Eternity. We never learn the

name of the far country where people speak the unknown, or unidentified, language, and hail the Fisherman's daughter.  Erasing earthly addresses, Dickens, dusting his parable with stardust of ambiguity, wraps 'the pearl' in the ethereal and eternal.  The far-off place might be Heaven.  Until found, the pearl lies on the strand like the starfish David and Em'ly once found in their wanderings by the sea.  The child holds out a shell, which perhaps reminds the Fisherman's daughter of her first, Heavenly home.
    Peggotty continues his lofty narrative:

> 'She had a little money, but it was less than little as they would take for all they done.  I'm a'most glad on it, though they was so poor.  What they done, is laid up wheer neither moth nor rust doth corrupt, and wheer thieves do not break through nor steal.  Mas'r Davy, it'll outlast all the treasure in the wureld. (728)

Here Peggotty quotes from the Gospel of *Matthew* 6:19-21.  Course after shining NT course is set before us at this Convivio of Christian themes.  Once, Ham linked Peggotty to treasure lost in the sea.  Now Peggotty's theme is treasure that can never be lost and outlasts world and time, 'the pearl.'  Losing the whole world, he gains his immortal soul.
    His long narrative to David ends.  The last echoes of 'Rise up!' die away:

> He ceased to speak, and his hand upon the table rested there in perfect repose, with a resolution in it that might have conquered lions. (729)

*'Might have* conquered lions.'  But the 'Daniel and the lions' era is over, the roaring seas, babby-lions and lons stilled.  Like his Biblical predecessor, Dan'l has glimpsed the kingdom of God which shall stand forever, and through a life renewed in faith, hope, and charity, won hope of possessing the treasure laid up in Heaven, the pearl.
    A moment before, Heaven stopped the mouth of the last lion menacing Daniel.  Before Martha's note brings him to Em'ly's side, Rosa Dartle finds the girl.  Hot to tear her limb from limb, she curses and vilifies her.  David witnesses the meeting:  'I saw the flashing black eyes, and the passion-wasted figure; and I saw the scar, with its white track cutting through her lips, quivering and throbbing as she spoke' (718).  Again, how like a jungle track through dense underbrush that 'track' of scar sounds as the wildcat with 'cruel eyes' and 'curled lip' (719) nears her prey.  Hands clasped as if in prayer, Em'ly can raise only one defense:  'I believed him, trusted him, loved him!' (720), a three-in-one pledge, its soul and core faith and love, which in Dickens is the whole way of Christ and the way to the kingdom.  All the lions of Babylon and Rome cannot prevail against it.  Footsteps are heard on the stairs; in one great rush, Dan'l gains the summit of the Beautiful Mountain.  Entering, he catches up the fainting Em'ly and covers her face, now a 'veiled face' (723).  (Is it the Hebrew, or

racial memory, in Daniel that instinctively veils the Holy of Holies from profane eyes?) Then:

> 'Mas'r Davy,' he said, in a low tremulous voice, when it was covered, 'I thank my Heav'nly Father as my dream's come true! I thank Him hearty for having guided of me, in His own ways, to my darling!' (723)

In Dickens, as in Tennyson, men may rise on stepping-stones of their dead selves to higher things, *In Memoriam Christi.*

But how comes the angelic little Em'ly first to fall? How did ark man lose his divine vision of 'the pearl,' the kingdom? Certainly he loved it and fain would have clasped it to his heart forever, even as David, in childhood fancy, 'raised up something round that blue-eyed mite of a child, which etherealized, and made a very angel of her' (37). Like Estella, Rosa, Christiana, Ada Clare, angelic Emily was made by her Creator to love and be loved, to fill hearts with faith, hope, and charity, guiding them the starry way to Heaven. Indeed, little Em'ly's childish thoughts follow her own lost father to Heaven, Peggotty tenderly wondering if 'maybe she believed—or hoped—he had drifted to them parts, wheer the flowers is always a-blowing, and the country bright' (583). 'Believed' and 'hoped' point to faith, flower-fresh in little Em'ly's pure heart.

But she is loved unwisely and too well—fiercely, idolatrously. In the Dickens parable, Judaism corrupts its own first sky-blue vision, 'bewitches' its *Clara* in the Law. The 'my little witch!' (312) love of Dan'l spoils Em'ly. A 'capricious coyness' (306) which gives David's baby heart many a pang, takes hold. Like some early Estella, Em'ly practises breaking hearts as with teasing laughter she runs off and hides herself away. (So did Israel hide *its* soul, the ark, away in a Holy of Holies.) The Chosen People infection sets in. Em'ly begins to dream: 'If I was ever to be a lady' (35). Dan'l idolizes her, and she makes him into an Idol, thinking that if she could, she would deck him out in a 'sky-blue coat with diamond buttons, nankeen trousers, a red velvet waistcoat, a cocked hat, a large gold watch, a silver pipe, and a box of money' (35). What heaps of treasure laid up on earth to load onto Peggotty! Fatal vision! So, with gold and jewels, Miss Havisham and Magwitch make two living children into Idols and worship them. As to the box of money, Heaven forbid: it is the undoing of Barkis. Though only a child, David has wisest doubts about the wisdom of the cocked hat. In Dickens, only stern dispensers of the barren lawful charity like Mr. Bumble the Beadle wear cocked hats.

In the ironic 'glorious vision' of little Em'ly, Dan'l sounds not a little like the symbolic figure in the dream of King Nebuchadnezzar of Babylon, one with head of gold, breast and arms of silver, belly and thighs of brass, which, interpreted by Daniel, stands for the heathen kingdoms destined to be consumed when the God of Heaven establishes His kingdom which will stand forever. Israel sets up an Idol, its Law, and worships it; the Law and its stern judgment without mercy is deep in Dan'l's pre-journey soul.  The graven image motif arises again in connection with Emily: a shining sail makes 'such a pretty little image of itself, at the moment, in her bright eye' (34).  The hebraic-souled Christians on the ark repeat old mistakes as they suffer little Em'ly to slip idol-wards: to punish, rule, dream ruinous dreams, all in her 'own little tormenting way' (317).  The original vision of OT time is 'sky-blue,' but Judaism cannot secure it.  Idolizing its Law, Israel becomes like the heathen kingdoms which surround her; stoning sinners, her soul houses the lions' dens and fiery furnaces of the lands of her foes.  Such, we think, is Dickens's version of Hebrew history, the ironic situation on which he builds.  But what OT man cannot keep safe, NT time recovers, the lost, fallen Em'ly rising anew as 'the pearl.'

One wonders if the sister-women, Martha and Em'ly, M-artha and M-ly, are types of the Biblical Martha and Mary: Martha at her raising work in the world, Em'ly behind the 'veil,' and working wonders in an unseen beyond.  In any case, Dickens in *Copperfield* pays tribute to Judaism in which were spun the first golden visionary threads which mankind followed out of labyrinths of error, which gold shines in the golden hair of Em'ly, Lucie Manette, and Ada Clare.

Ham Peggotty also loves little Em'ly, and through this love finds his way—a way apart—to the Kingdom.  The morning after Em'ly's disappearance, David sees Dan'l and Ham on the beach.  Dan'l, though stricken, speaks; Ham says not one word, but is seen 'looking out to sea upon the distant light' (457).  And again, looks far off, his eye 'still directed to the distant light' (457).  'One may even then think of little Paul's sighting a shore 'farther away—farther away!' (vis. Chapter III).  In aftertime, Dan'l tells David how Ham, whom he has not seen since, is faring under the blow of his great loss:

> 'He ain't no care, Mas'r Davy,' said Mr. Peggotty in a solemn whisper—
> 'kinder no care no-how for his life.  When a man's wanted for rough sarvice in rough weather, he's theer.  When theer's hard duty to be done with danger in it, he steps for'ard afore all his mates.  And yet he's as gentle as any child.  Theer ain't a child in Yarmouth that doesn't know him.' (588)

The connection with children, like his eyes upon a distant light, tells of a great Christian moment readying in Ham's life, 'the child' ever a central figure in Christian mystery in Dickens.[2]

Deep suffering ennobles Ham.  If Peggotty cannot 'arrize' himself of what Ham might do if he found Steerforth, we begin to think we can.  For there is in Ham's new feelings about Em'ly a sublimity:

> ' 'Tan't that I forgive her.  'Tant that so much.  'Tis more as I beg of her to forgive me, for having pressed my affections upon her...' (737)

'Forgive' is the Clemency Newcome passport to NT time.  Ham asks David to tell Emily 'anything as might bring her to believe as I was not tired of my life, and yet was hoping fur to see her without blame, wheer the wicked cease from troubling and the weary are at rest—anything as would ease her and her sorrowful mind' (738). One sees that Ham's inner eye too is on the distant light, now perceived as an emblem of the life to come. Having lost hope of the kingdom of this world, Ham fixes his heart on Heaven. He dies shortly after this, his death, suffered in the effort to save another, one *in imitatio Christi.*

Dickens signs it with the cross. At their final meeting, David awaits Ham 'at a retired part of the sands, which I knew he would cross, and turned back with him' (737). Ham speaks of Emily, and the two men say farewell:

> With a slight wave of his hand, as though to explain to me that he could not enter the old place, he turned away. As I looked after his figure, crossing the waste in the moonlight, I saw him turn his face towards a strip of silvery light upon the sea, and pass on, looking at it, until he was a shadow in the distance. (738)

One sees in this 'passing on,' as in the pilgrims on the ship's deck who 'solemnly pass[ed] away,' the beginning of the journey to death, but death which cherishes hope of Heaven. Here 'cross' shows to advantage in 'knew he would cross,' and 'crossing the waste.' Also, 'strip of *s*ilvery light upon the *s*ea,' alliterative poetry rich in silvery, sibilant 's' sound, whispers of Eternity. Ham turns from the 'old place,' the ark. Noah's son has found a new way of salvation in the new Noah, Christ.

Looking back (always, from New perspectives, the Old becoming more clear), we realize the latent Christian promise in Ham from the start. Quiet, gentle Ham with 'simpering boy's face and curly light hair that gave him quite a sheepish look' (29), belongs to the flock. Dickens insists on *sheep* with Ham 'smiling sheepishly over the shell-fish' (103). From early times of his 'lazily dropping stones in water' (40), the old *ark* life in which all plummets down into the flood, the 'stones' time of Murdstone and Blunderstone, Ham in his mild, dreamy life is the sheep awaiting the Shepherd. He beguiles slow time by telling fortunes with a pack of dirty cards. But for all his involvement in the luck-Fortuna game B.C., at the same time he is 'printing off fishy impressions of his thumbs on all cards he turned' (32). No wonder he comes to love the Fisherman's daughter. Allegory smiles sheepishly. 'Fishy impressions': the sign of the fish, of Christ.

Ham is even back then a carrier of New Time. It is he who, quite literally, carries little David on his broad back on his first visit, transporting the child 'past gas-works, rope-walks, boat-builders' yards, shipwrights' yards, shipbreakers' yards, caulkers' yards, riggers' lofts, smiths' forges, and a great litter of such places, until we came out upon the dull waste I had already seen at a distance; when Ham said, 'Yon's our house, Mas'r

Davy!'' (29) In Yarmouth, where Yah ways overcome Christian ways in men's souls, Ham, a Saint Christopher figure, carries the son of David *past* yard after yard after yard (Dickens does not break stride), i.e., past ya(h) after ya(h) after ya(h), in the seaport symbolic of the soul's place of embarkation with, not Christ at the helm, but Yah. But in those times, Ham can only deliver David's son 'Yon,' to the ark. The son of Noah, like all men, has two testamentary promises in him: that of Noah, and that of Christ. It is not the way of his father, but of the Father he chooses in the end.

In the Dickens version of the parable which compares the kingdom of heaven to treasure hid in a field (*Matt.* 13:44), *Copperfield,* all men love, yearn after, seek 'the pearl.' One who loves her seeks and recovers his treasure in this life, 'passing away' with it held close as into the life to come. Another, losing the beloved, hopes to behold her again in Eternity. This, Ham's, is the very pattern in the later work, *A Tale of Two Cities.* Like Peggotty, Charles Darnay wins Lucie in this life; like Ham, Sydney Carton, dying in the transfiguring Light ('Lucie') of a self-sacrificing love, looks to the far, far better rest to come, his eyes, like Ham's, upon a distant light. Both Ham and Carton 'cross' the waste; both die for others, repeating the death upon the Cross. '*Ch*uckle-headed,' simple, loving Ham, son of Noah, has the Son of Noah in his heart from always.

Like Dan'l and David, Emily and Martha, and almost everyone else in *Copperfield,* Ham journeys from OT to NT time before his journey is done. He starts out 'a very dragon at his catechism' (10), which in Dickens means he has had all his native instincts and divine fancies gradground out of him by religious instruction at an early age. In this time he is not Ham, but 'Am,' a young chip off the block of YAH:

'Here's my Am!' screamed Peggotty, 'growed out of knowledge!' (29)

In 'Am,' Peggotty, a self-styled Yarmouth Bloater, or watery loyalist of old ways, tickles the famous *Yah* definition: 'I Am That I *AM*'! Happily, however, children grow up. 'Growed out of knowledge' is the very expression Mr. Chillip uses on another occasion to applaud David's happy progress:

'Dear me!' says Mr. Chillip, meekly smiling, with something shining in his eye. 'Our little friends grow up around us. They grow out of our knowledge, ma'am?'
This to Miss Murdstone, who makes no reply. (130)

That twinkling little smile implies much. 'Grow out of our knowledge,' like 'grow out of knowledge,' first of all means, grow up, grow tall, grow into full people. But it also means (and this is what the 'something shining' in Mr. Chillip's eye portends) that children 'grow out of,' i.e., outgrow, the knowledge of their fathers, old, 'our,' knowledge! The meek, mild 'Ch' friend of the son of David, Mr. Chillip, quietly rejoices that David has moved beyond Murdstone knowledge, that of stern Law. Whatever good Peggotty means by *her* 'growed out of knowledge,' the same potential double meaning lies in her words about Ham. Yes, Ham starts out a very 'dragon,' but like St. George, a truly Christian inner life will slay the dragon of the Catechism. Thus checked, Miss Murdstone can only retreat into silence, unable to muster a single 'letter.'

We have explored the *Daniel* significance of the name 'Daniel Peggotty.' What of PEGGOTTY? In Dickens, Christian names have one (and Christian) life, surnames—Twist, Pinch, Blackpool, Magwitch, Hexam, Carstone, et al.—often another. While Clara, Dan'l, and Ham seek the light, PEGGOTTY, as natural man, belongs to Yarmouth and Old Time. First noting the 'ot' dead center, we search out Dickens's sense of PEG. The infamous Creakle school has 'pegs for hats and slates' (77); and when 'struck of a heap,' Peggotty cannot pull his coat down from 'its peg in a corner' (453). So, *peg* simply means nail or hook. Elsewhere, 'peg' functions as a verb, too, with gorming effect. In *The Old Curiosity Shop,* a grandfather and grandson 'peg away at each other with mutual wiolence' (19). (Dick Swiveller dislikes the spectacle, and in time Swivel(ler)s to better ones.) In *Chuzzlewit,* the murderous Jonas Chuzzlewit orders poor, gentle Mr. Chuffey to 'peg away at his bread' (MC, 180). In *Our Mutual Friend,* wicked Silas Wegg, devoted to the Decline and Fall, à la Rome and à la Roman-souled Wopsle in *Great Expectations,* threatens our friend Nicodemus Boffin, and is seen 'shaking his fist at Mr. Boffin and pegging his motto into the floor with his wooden leg, in a threatening and alarming manner' (657). This *pegging* is bad, but worse is to come: 'Wegg, who was all for clinching the nail he had so strongly driven home, announced that Boffin should see it [a document] without an hour's delay' (657). This intense flurry of 'pegging,' hammering, driving in of nails, wooden-legged-peg business in the hands of an afficionado of Rome, the purpose of which is to dominate *Nicodemus,* has darkest Christ-killing implications in a work centering on the fortunes of a *Nicodemus* and a *John,* if we recall how Nicodemus is born again in the Gospel of *John.* Figurative as well as literal 'pegging' can nail Christ, now as then, to the cross.

Thus, deep within PEGGOTTY is the potential of 'peg,' hook or nail, the weapon of the enemies of Christ.

Now we better understand what pulls a good Dan'l towards Gorming, 'babby'-lion, roars, and harsh judgment of the fallen woman. The spirit of religious persecution that claims Christ as a victim is born in 'Peggotty' time. Even little David is, symbolically speaking, 'crucified' on the ark, where he first comes across Foxe's Book of Martyrs. He relates:

> I was chiefly edified, I am afraid, by the pictures, which were numerous, and
> represented all kinds of dismal horrors; but the Martyrs and Peggotty's house
> have been inseparable in my mind ever since, and are now. (148)

Interesting that Dickens should make a special point of the connection, and
stress, or portray, David's unconscious reaction to the 'dismal horrors': 'I
kneeled on a chair, opened the casket where this gem was enshrined,
spread my arms over the desk, and fell to devouring the book afresh' (148).
The spread arms half suggest crucifixion; the kneeling posture, worship.
On the ark, there are 'hooks in the beams of the ceiling, the use of which I
did not divine then' (34).    If pegs and hooks are for hanging coats and
hammocks, what else may they be for?    In many ways, Dickens hints that
the potential of the Cross dwells in Judaism almost from the start.

   Clara Peggotty, David's nurse, also has a B.C. side.   As she and David
read the beloved 'Crorkindills' book, a Foxe's Book of Crocodile Martyrs,
as it were, Peggotty is 'thoughtfully sticking her needle into various parts
of her face and arms all the time' (17).   This, like the wood driven down
crocodile maws, may imply the needle-in, nail-in act of crucifying.   Or it
may recall tortures of later Christian time.   For example, in 'Mr. Pickwick's Tale' in *Master Humphrey's Clock,* we learn a fascinating set of
facts about torture in the time of King James the First of England:

> You know very well that in those times there flourished divers evil old
> women who, under the name of Witches, spread great disorder through the
> land, and inflicted various dismal tortures upon Christian men; sticking pins
> and needles into them when they least expected it, and causing them to walk
> in the air with their feet upward, to the great terror of their wives and fam-
> ilies... (58)

A droll touch or two does not erase the evil portrayed.   As if this primitive
Witch reflex lodged somewhere in a substratum of mind, good Peggotty
'pegs away' at herself with a needle.   The unregenerate, unchristianized
part of man's soul is excited by violent tales, barbaric uses of timber (no
crocodile so benighted that it is not a 'c' creature, with all rights and priv-
ileges thereof, in a beneficent Creator's scheme); and at home in the
spongy, soppy Bloater's life of Yarmouth by the sea.   David's Peggotty will
not hear one word of criticism of Yarmouth.   In response to David's timid
one, she stoutly insists that 'we must take things as we found them' (28), in
which sentiment she resembles the old lady of Chapter I of *Copperfield*
whose anti-change motto is: 'Let us have no meandering.'   Like the like-
minded lords of the state preserves of loaves and fishes who rule in the
opening era of *A Tale of Two Cities,* Peggotty supports the Yarmouth-Yah
position that things in general are settled forever.   Then along comes the
latest son of David to unsettle them.

   Happily, though, in her Clara or Christian name self and soul, Peggotty is all Saint Paul; three bright shillings; the good and faithful servant; faith, hope, and charity; and boundless love for the son of David.

We have seen how Dan'l Peggotty loses and recovers the pearl, hope of the Kingdom of Heaven, and, holding it close, sails into the radiance of Eternity. Even when he returns to visit, his thoughts are on that far place beyond the rosy light: that unseen 't'other wureld' (588), earthly symbol of *the* Other World. On one visit home, before setting out on the return journey, he stoops down and gathers earth and grass from Ham's grave to carry back to Emily, explaining: 'I promised, Mas'r Davy!' (873) Always in his Homing thoughts, and the centre to which they tend, is 'the pearl;' as in her heart, her request shows, is cherished eternally the memory of him (Him) who died the Christ-imitating death, and dreamed of Heaven. Though we have said it before, it bears repeating. In Dickens, as in many Christian poets, the high way to the kingdom is through the Fisherman's daughters of the world, for love of whom men plunge into the deep, deep-calling-unto-deep pearl fisheries of Time and Eternity. First stirred by woman's beauty and virtue to idealising, ennobling love, man slowly awakens to the love which outstrips the finite objects towards which it is directed, seeking the infinite object of man's desiring which is God.

In interpreting the dream of a king, the Biblical Daniel foresaw the kingdom of God which would replace it, and all others, and stand forever. So in Dickens a Daniel survives bitter times in 'Babby-lon' with its lions, and with all his soul seeks the kingdom of Heaven. Finding his way at last, he speaks a final prayer of thanksgiving: 'I thank my Heav'nly Father as my dream's come true!' (522) Here is Biblical dream for 'dream,' one which we, as students of both Books of Daniel, are called upon to interpret anew. So the story of Daniel is woven into David Copperfield's exalted Story, and a wondering world applauds.

From the stories of Dan'l and Ham we turn now to that of another man who sees, desires, and wins 'the pearl,' the Heaven-storming Steerforth. What it means when sons of David mistake their way and 'Steer forth' by *Steerforth* lights, we now more closely explore.

# EIGHT
## Steerforth

> Here, among pillows for six, I soon fell asleep in a blissful condition, and
> dreamed of ancient Rome, Steerforth, and friendship until the early morning
> coaches, rumbling out of the archway underneath, made me dream of thunder
> and the gods. (DC, 289)

How very naive and untried is 'young Copperfield,' as Steerforth calls him,
in the 'Rome, thunder and the gods' age of false gods and friends.

The name 'STEERFORTH' is like a boast that here is Steering Forth
worthy of 'the journey.' In Dickens, one does well to be wary of what
flaunts and professes so. Like David's, our first impression of him is
derived from viewing his handiwork on an old door at school:

> There was one boy—a certain J. Steerforth—who cut his name very deep
> and very often, who, I conceived, would read it in a rather strong voice, and
> afterwards pull my hair. (79)

David's intuition is just. Steerforth's is indeed the deep-'cutting' mode of
friendship. But the David-'J' relationship has another side, and perhaps
glances at the Biblical one of David and Jonathon, David surviving, as of
old, to mourn the beloved in the spirit of David's lament for Jonathon:
'How are the mighty fallen.' [1]

Once, by mistake, Dan'l Peggotty calls the dashing newcomer to the ark
'Rudderford,' explaining: 'Well! And ye steer with a rudder, don't ye? It
ain't fur off' (142). Intensifying the symbolism, *Rudderford* neatly points
'Steerforth' towards the idea of life as a journey by sea. In Steerforth's
case, a failed one, as his greeting: 'Why, Daisy, old boy, dumb-foundered!' (424) boldly hints, *foundered* a dark forecast of his drowning end to
come.

As J. Steerforth sails, recklessly, relentlessly buffeting the night tides
off Yarmouth, so he lives. Lives a life exemplifying the futility of the
journey without guide, destination, or Heavenly star to steer by. In

Dickens, to Steer Forth, however boldly, is not enough.  The too 'self-possessed' (290), like Steerforth, centered solely on resources of self and world, must, as temporal seafaring looks to eternal, founder.  Squandering superior gifts, high spirits, fervent energies, Steerforth, like head-on, bully Stryver in *A Tale of Two Cities,* misses that other 'striving' and 'steering forth' which, by nautical ways of faith, hope, and charity, and regard for others before self, finds out safe passage to Eternity, as the swift river bears us to the ocean.  Steerforth's love of the sea and expertise in matters of ships, rigging, and the like, is thus deeply ironic.  In vain his pilot's prowess in Yarmouth, or Yah, waters in which, outbraving the stormy elements, he pitches and tosses whole moonlit nights.  For what do such brilliant maneuvers lead to but to still more mighty, oncoming tides of night, and finally the night of death.  Here is a stark emblem of the *Steerforth* life, a dazzling, pointless contest with Nature that no man wins in the end.

Dickens plays up the idea of sea as religious metaphor.  Consulted by a deferential David, Steerforth confidently describes Doctors' Commons as a place where disputes about ecclesiastical law, wills, marriages and ships are settled.  The church-ship connection startles David.  'Nonsense, Steerforth!' he says.  'You don't mean to say that there is any affinity between nautical matters and ecclesiastical matters?' (343)  Dickens, of course, means to imply just that.  Throughout Dickens, we know, seafaring is a metaphor of the soul's voyage to Eternity.  The beached, superannuated ark lying on Yarmouth sands symbolizes the stranded dead end of the OT quest for salvation; whereas the return of Paul's ship, the *Son and Heir,* a return as if in answer to the prayers of those who faithfully watched and waited, says that Christ, the Son and Heir, will come again. (vis. Chapter III)  The sea-journey symbolism is implied again as a salvage case comes up in Admiralty Court which the lawyers cannot resolve.  The judge must 'entreat[ed] two old Trinity Masters, for charity's sake, to come and help him out' (396).  So, in allegory, *Trinity* and *charity* save the day.  But as long as Doctors and law dominate human affairs, mankind must settle for 'Salvage' (396), losing salvation.

Steerforth's name is very ironic.  Appearing as he does to stride on an unswerving forward way, he is actually always heading back in time from A.D. to B.C.  As 'lions,' he menaces Dan'l, the latest Daniel in babby-lon. As 'J,' Jehovah-like he looses lions against the faithful.  As pagan and heathen, Greece, Rome, oriental East in one, Steerforth, a multi-faceted self, is a whirlwind (and whirlwind-sowing) tour of all Time B.C.  Constantly changing temper and face, anarchic Steerforth is a composite of all anti- and counterChrist forces latent in ancient time that threatened, and threaten still, the emergence in man of a fully evolved, i.e., Christian, soul: all energy in the unregenerate self—pull of pagan, anarch, Jew, gentile— to Time's end.  *Steering Forth* in his wake, David Copperfield is long backwatered in B.C., and in livest danger of being lost to his destiny:  the emergence in the most recent House of David of the genius of the Father and the Son of David.

One Steerforth self is pure Greek. Steerforth sneers at 'Ixions of these days' (324) bound to wheels of work; he despises all means that imply serious ends. David he calls, and wills, a 'Sybarite' (424). Sponsoring David's first dissipation, he hails his handiwork as 'my Bacchanal' (424), the 'my' as dangerous to David as Peggotty's 'my girl!' to Martha is good. No sooner does Steerforth say 'Bacchanal' than he is 'jovially' (425), i.e., à la Jove, pouring himself out a glass of wine. The Ixion-Sybarite-Bacchanal-'jovial' imagery is matched in the Byronic Apollo look of the handsome Steerforth, whose physical charm, love of strenuous contest, and strength, as seen in hammer-throwing and bouts with the waves, strongly suggest the classic Greek statue of the athlete or god.

He also comes on a Turk, an Eastern despot who turns young David into 'the Sultana Scheherazade' (93) of a thousand-and-one-nights of enforced story-telling to entertain a restless, wakeful prince. At a later time, Steerforth imperiously imports his own 'Turkey-carpeted' (290) splendor into his apartment at the Golden Cross, where his word is law. Allegory grows vivid as 'Turk,' or Saracen, anti-Christ, overcomes at the *Cross*. David, his votary, says: 'I could not enough admire the change he had wrought in the Golden Cross' (290). A.D. falls back again.

J. Steerforth v. the *Cross* retells an old Hebrew-Roman tale. Like a muttering king magnificent moving among hinds, Steerforth captivates the souls on Dan'l's ark, also his mother and Rosa Dartle. Then, when they could not love and revere him more, this anti-Christ and false saviour makes off with the universal hope and joy, 'the pearl,' hope of the Kingdom of Heaven.

The 'J' god of David's early heavens rules him and all even as 'J' ruled the people of David in ancient time. The ascendancy of this J marks the return of the smiting, hammer-throwing, harsh Spirit that loosed the Assyro-Babylonian Empire with all its lions, fiery furnaces, and idols, against His own in retributive punishment for sin. David's 'bad Angel,' Steerforth, also sums up all within B.C. resistant to the coming into being of the idea of an immortal soul and of the responsibility of the moral life as defined in Christian terms. David must choose between his 'bad Angel' and 'good Angel,' Agnes, as history between Old Testament light and New.

Deep in the 'J' nature of J. Steerforth is the Hebraeo-Roman seed of the anti-Christ. At school, Steerforth launches the trial and persecution of the Master, a Christ figure, for which infamy he is not only not condemned, but 'exalted to the skies' (101). Like Jehovah, 'J' holds the deep allegiance of David. He commandeers David's mother's gift to him of seven shillings, to buy a feast of food and wine. *Seven* is stressed. 'What money have you got, Copperfield?' 'I told him seven shillings' (84). The 'whole seven shillings' worth' (85) is spent. The gift of *Clara, seven,* is offered up; 'J' plunders the very cypher of Creation. David further surrenders sovereignty over his own in begging Steerforth to do him the honor of presiding over the 'royal spread' (85), one 'royal' enough for a King David. Plundering the 'copperfield,' J passes off David's riches as his own. In the Dickens view of OT time, the old Providence accepts man's humble sacrifices and thanks for what man himself bestows on Heaven! At the feast, David sits 'on his [Steerforth's] left hand' (85); whereas Christ sets the righteous on the *right* hand of the Father.

David also sacrifices to Steerforth Peggotty's loving gift of cake, oranges, and wine. 'This treasure, as in duty bound, I laid at the feet of Steerforth' (93). The imagery of idolater and Idol charts the sad lot of David in thrall to his god.

The Hebrew 'J' in Steerforth leaps out memorably in one dramatic scene. Steerforth and Rosa Dartle, always at odds, quarrel over a cast of the dice, and suddenly the scar on her lip of a hammer wound Steerforth gave her long before grows livid, starting forth 'like the old writing on the wall' (295). The image instantly conjures up the scene of Belshazzar's feast in Babylon at which, the Book of Daniel relates, a man's hand appears and writes on the wall: MENE, MENE, TEKEL, UPHARSIN, which means: 'God hath numbered thy kingdom, and finished it' (*Dan.* 5:25). Now the Daniel-lions-Steerforth ties grow stronger still. Further, backgammon, the game Steerforth and Rosa are playing when the 'old writing on the wall' erupts, is an old Babylonian game. [2]

Alas, Babylon! J. Steerforth has another old J habit, hammering the beloved. In the OT we read: 'Is not my word like as a fire? saith the LORD; and like a hammer that breaketh the rock in pieces?' (*Jer.* 23:29). All 'J' history of woe, it seems—roaring lions, babbylons, hammer scars, the writing that appeared in Babylon, the enmity to Christ—J. Steerforth again visits on the sons of Noah, Daniel, and David, as if they had not had enough of it in Old Time. Or rather, men visit it on themselves.

Steering forth after Steerforth, his idol and god, David symbolically re-enters Greek, Roman, and Hebrew camps pitched in the ongoing B.C. of mankind's moral minority, in exiting from which, slowly and painfully, man recapitulates the soul's journey from *agon* to Agnes. Why does David adore Steerforth? Perhaps because he beholds in him some image, however imperfect, of the Most High. Steerforth previews the God Yet To Be Known, is the image of terror and allure which questing B.C. man lighted (darkened) on, on the rock of whose love was built a strong, unquestioning trust until all came crashing down in betrayal in the end. The punishing Jehovah was all man knew until Christ. And like Jehovah, the latest 'J' sets himself against the closing down of the Old dispensation through the coming of the New. J Steerforth, lions loosed against Daniel, foe of the Master, Turk taking over the Cross, crowns his anti-A.D. campaign by making off with 'the pearl,' Christ's word made flesh, the promise of Heaven, in so doing leaving the sons of men bereft of Hope.

Steerforth is the light of the world B.C.. Coming as light, he does all with 'an incredible lightness' (310), passing from subject to subject 'with a carelessness and lightness that were his own' (291). His gifts are 'more and more brightly exhibited as the hours went on' in a 'brilliant game' of charming Dan'l and his tribe. One sees his 'gay light manner' (104), and how 'lightly and easily he carried on,' drawing listeners into 'irresistible sympathy with what was so pleasant and light-hearted' (316). David avoids praising Steerforth's generosity, when he himself made 'so light of it' (324). (*What* generosity? Ironically, David attributes to Steerforth his own.) Steerforth has 'a light way' (344) of discussing Doctors Commons, and dismisses the subject of virtue 'with a light nod, and smile' (424). So on and on he bewitches, charms, appears to fill a world of despondent souls with 'light.'

He comes to the ark like its Saviour. As the Son of man entered poor men's dwellings and shared their joys and sorrows (David recalls a Christ 'Who wept...'), so this other only-begotten son enters a poor fisherman's dwelling and brings joy and light, rousing even Mrs. Gummidge from thoughts of the Old 'Un. Spending nights on the waters, 'afloat, wrapped in fisherman's clothes, whole moonlight nights' (319), he is the lion in Fisherman's clothing. Christ offers men the pearl of great price. His anti-type, Steerforth, steals it away. In Dickens, woman is man's awakening to intimations of immortality, initiating his quest for higher things, beckoning him to joys undreamed of, enlarging the aspiring soul within. Thus, to draw a young girl from the paths of honor and virtue, as Steerforth does Emily, is indeed to rob men of the way to Heaven. In OT time that Steer-forth re-establishes on earth, the 'light,' or highest wisdom, proves at odds with all good and godly things: the Master, the Cross, the 'pearl.'

To see that He is never born in the greatly expectant souls of men! This is Steerforth's aim. Corrupting David, he would make an anti-Christ of the son of David! After schooldays end, David and Steerforth chance to meet again at the Golden Cross at Charing Cross: Cross upon Cross. Steer-forth rules at the Cross. Finding that David has been given 'a little loft over a stable' (288), he angrily commands that he be moved into more lux-urious quarters. No lowly mangers for David's son, if David's mighty pro-tector has his way! And he does. In comes Turkey-carpeted Eastern opulence, and David is wholly entranced by the effect. Next morning, a glorified (reduced) David is seen forlornly...

peeping out of window at King Charles on horseback, surrounded by a maze of hackney-coaches, and looking anything but regal in a drizzling rain and a dark-brown fog, until I was admonished by the waiter that the gentleman was waiting for me. (290)

The royal figure standing forlorn out in rain and fog may remind us of Pip's convict, exiled from Christmas Day. In so highly charged a Christian context, King Charles, the Royal martyr led to the scaffold and slain, recalls another 'Ch' King, the King of Kings: First in a noble 'Ch' line in which Charles the First stands. No room for Him at the inn, the Cross. Deeply under the spell of Steerforth, young David Copperfield spares the King but a glance before a summons from 'the gentleman' (ominous title!) compels him to hurry away.

The stupendous irony of the exile of a Christ-recalling figure from the Cross is a perennial Dickens theme. In Dickens, churches boast beadles in Babylonian collars, funeral trappings on display even at christenings, ranting Boanerges Boilers that discourage the half-entered-in sheep. As in Tennyson:

> There is none that does his work, not one;
> But the churchmen fain would kill their church,
> As the churches have kill'd their Christ.

In another component of a complex being, Steerforth is man becalmed in Nature. Coming into a sick room 'like healthy weather' (310), like weather he resists the imposition in his life of human, spiritual values and so comes to share the evanescence and volatility of all life rooted in Nature alone. Strong in 'animal spirits' (104), he wills himself a lion's less than fully human soul. Nothing lasts for him. He refuses continuity: chooses no profession or course, shuns preferences, lets nothing take root in him. A fleeting whim, passion, fancy, mood, human bauble seizes and attracts him for one burning moment, then is gone. Dickens stresses the dominance in him of 'nature': his 'natural gift of adapting himself to whomsoever he pleased' (310) (ominous versatility); his winning manner 'so graceful, so natural, and agreeable' (310); his insistence that David stay on the ark where he 'naturally' (310) belongs. Anchorless in one fixed self or character, Steerforth can produce himself 'sentimental or comical' (303) on demand; 'could become anything he liked at any moment' (342), in the mercurial, endlessly changing way of Nature. Rosa Dartle, the rose garden withered, made all thorn, by him, despite herself succumbs to his 'delightful art—delightful nature I thought it then' (434). And on. So much *natural* and *naturally* seems not by chance, and lends Steerforth the rich, unselective profusion and vitality of Nature before objects in Nature, seed, fruit, branch, vine, pearl, enter the granaries of Judaeo-Christian metaphor which OT and NT prophets press into the service of Eternity, finding in them means to express the nature and mysteries of God.

A stumbling-block in the son-of-David destiny of David, Steerforth would draw his young acolyte back into the brief life lived in Nature. He dubs him 'Daisy,' for: 'The daisy of the field, at sunrise, is not fresher than you are' (288). A richly ambiguous compliment. For, for all its sunrise (and

Sonrise) charm, the daisy is soon gone. A twinkling, white-gold pledge of summer, its action no stronger than a flower, it is idly plucked, then lightly tossed away. For too long David *is* Steerforth's Daisy, the amusement of idle moments, the disciple whose abject worship Steerforth carelessly accepts, but cannot prize. To do him justice, Steerforth, so little in earnest and so uncommitted in all, does experience David's ardor and constancy as something of value. And yet, when the two meet again in post-Creakle time, Steerforth, like Mr. Micawber after 'Babylon,' has quite forgotten David.

Many, including David, Emily, Rosa, his mother, the boys at school, adore, serve, suffer for Steerforth, who returns no like notice, pang of requital, love or lasting care. In this too he is Nature's own son. His strivings, exertions, overspillings of physical energy are purposeless because directionless. One could speak of his pursuit of wine, woman, and song, except that it is not even so marked a thing as a pursuit. Losing himself (and his soul) in sailing, boxing, riding, adventure, Steerforth exemplifies the incapacity of 'B.C.' man to emerge from the state of Nature; even as the early gods, made in man's own fallen image,[3] from a proclivity for violence, the hammering that shatters the rock. Steerforth symbolizes the dogmatic refusal of the idea of which Christianity is born: that of life as a moral search, testing of souls, a heading somewhere, a spiritual progress with a reckoning to come, a striving after the Kingdom of Heaven. Refusing all reliances as he does a supreme Reliance, Steerforth is the emptiness of self possession, the barren and unpropertied possession of the self without ties to God.

Steerforth is both ironic light and height. Much is made of his high spirits, 'spirits' (pun) a mockery where no spiritual life is. He toys with people 'for the employment of high spirits, in the thoughtless love of superiority' (310) (*high* and *superior* one invention). He has 'high spirits' (426) belonging to him alone (even as Agnes a cheerfulness which is hers alone), spirits to which David appeals in vain; and a 'high spirit' (296); 'great spirits' (302); a 'spirited good humour' (310); 'potent spirits' (426). He possesses all but the Spirit which giveth life. He is purposely, relentlessly flip on grave occasions. Growing serious for a moment, he quickly dismisses it in jest. This willed stopping short in Nature and display of 'spirits' vacant of spiritual life—in ceaseless dashing about, the diversion of the moment, the here and now—is his choice, and tragedy.

David is long the 'Daisy' Steerforth elects him, a young fellow going to the lions (and dogs) and growing tipsy on wine. He is only Daisy, the season's brief pledge, until the trust placed in his god, an innocent, daisy-petaled 'He loves me!', turns to the cold, wintry morn of realization that 'He loved me not.'

The J. Steerforth plight is metaphysical, as he himself at moments knows. His genuinely anguished: 'David, I wish to God I had had a judicious father these last twenty years!', and: 'I wish with all my soul I had been better guided! I wish with all my soul I could guide myself better!' (322) really *means* 'God' and 'soul,' as the repetition of 'with all my soul' shows. It is to David, note, not Daisy that Steerforth speaks these solemn words: to David such utterance belongs. But this too passes; Steerforth's regret lasts no longer than anything else. Renewing the dashing from distraction to distraction, Steerforth never stands still long enough—he dare not—to ask why the race of life is run. Conceiving of no other, he devours the goods of this world with a frantic appetite which the world, in Dickens, never satisfies, then plunders fitfully on.

In his 'gentle Daisy' (324), as he is moved to call him, Steerforth, we were saying, finds a rare delicacy, idealism, selflessness in friendship, generosity of spirit, constancy, and gift of taking things much to heart, of cherishing and remembering long, that haunts him, stirring in him a nostalgia for the unlived life of the soul. Few in Dickens not arrant villains of the Squeers-Pecksniff sort remain wholly untouched by aspiration, even if they betray it in the end. In the Dickens Christian universe, man is born to be saved. The godless-God conflict deep within Steerforth which the 'I wish to God' speech betrays, the outcry for the father implying the soul's cry for the Father, too, is a conflict at the very heart of the matter. One also sees in Steerforth a Christ-killing and Christ-seeking struggle, one rife in Bible times as in all personal divine history ever after.

Israel worshipped 'J' as David does 'J,' in strange, passionate self-deception converting the punishing, exploiter god of his youth into a noble benefactor-protector. To Mrs. Steerforth David holds forth on her son's honor, generosity, nobility. Gratified but not at all surprised, she accepts this version of the character of her son. That David is actually Steerforth's slave and plaything, and that there is no true confidence or mutuality between them (so in B.C. in a condition of Unmutual Friendship, all service went from man to God), is a fact that David accepts, glorifying the yoke he wears, symbol of man's servitude to and sadly mean expectations of his first gods.

To follow Steerforth in his nautical/theological plunges into Flood tides of Yarmouth, maw of Yah, and oblivious Nature, as David does, is to journey back into pre-Christian time of mind when crass casualty, the great Chancery of chance, salvage, and law were all, and man the sport of his gods and fate. Like the Pied Piper, Steerforth leads back into Time long behind us (alas, not long enough) when the multitudes, unfed by the loaves and fishes, were cowed into giving thanks for thin gruel, celestially speaking: back into realms the religious imagination devised before the soul felt its worth. In Steerforth time of the journey, man, like Pip in the hands of Wopsle, subsists on intellectual crumbs, and Crummles (*Nickleby*), of Rome; on the old Bill Barley bread of life thunderously advertised Above, but not forthcoming. Little Oliver Twist's timid, unprecedented: 'Please, sir, I want some more' put before the astonished master stationed at the copper launches a New era of expectation, a day finally dawning in Western consciousness when the Old arrangement, symbolized in the full copper and empty bowl; the unSatisfying Satis House dole flung down onto the brewery-yard stones, is patently *not* Enough any more.

The religious significance of Steerforth is in part revealed in a semi-ironic religious diction that trails after him. For example, David thinks 'how blest I was in having such a friend as Steerforth' (321); and Steerforth's adoring mother pleasures to recall how Creakle, 'remorseless Idol' of Salem House which drove out the Master, prostrated himself at her son's feet:

> 'My son's high spirit made it desirable that he should be placed with some man who felt its superiority, and would be content to bow himself before it; and we found such a man there.'
>
> I knew that, knowing the fellow. And yet I did not despise him the more for it, but thought it a redeeming quality in him, if he could be allowed any grace for not resisting one so irresistible as Steerforth. (296)

The words *blest, spirits, redeem, grace,* in such concentration, are tinged with second, literal meaning. One sees how little the David of this era knows of the true meaning of blessing, redemption, or grace.

Yet all is and must be what it was. David's exalting Steerforth in this fashion shows how man's soul in all times hungers for what Emerson calls the 'all-sufficient, all-abstaining, all-aspiring' love. Blunderstone man, a blundering beginner, settles for 'high spirits' which attain only the height of haughty removal from man abased in dust below. Only with Christ's coming, Dickens shows, does *high* come to mean spiritually lofty; He stands at so heavenly a height that He can stoop in pity for the fallen woman, writing in the dust, that NT moment recast in *Copperfield* and *Bleak House.* Young David's eagerness to take the J way of Steering Forth to Eternity, one which entails acceptance of bondage and other barren self-denial, recalls a (to Dickens) like-unsatisfactory Jehovah worship in the House of David many Judaeo-Christian centuries before.

'J' becomes the sole Star of David. Having driven out the Master and been exalted to the skies (literally so), Steerforth, even after they part, commands David's heavens. When David runs away from Murdstone in 'Babylon' and sleeps out of doors, he suddenly awakens 'sitting upright, with Steerforth's name upon my lips, looking wildly at the stars that were glistening and glimmering above me' (182). Once, on the ark, David asks Steerforth: 'Have I called you down from the stars?' (321) Of course he only means, were you day-dreaming? Do I intrude? But *stars* has one reflex more in allegory. And when David becomes his mentor's Bacchanal, he murmurs tipsily: 'Steerforth, you'retheguidingstarofmyexistence' (360).

There is a marked upsurge of the pagan in David's life after his idol sweeps away manger and man of sorrows at the Golden Cross. On the very night he and Steerforth meet again, David has been to the theatre and seen 'Julius Caesar and the new Pantomime' (286). As with the Dead March in Saul in *Dombey and Son,* and the John of Sunderland in *Great Expectations* (vis. Chapter III), no trace of title-making punctuation touches Caesar. For Time careens backwards, and it is, symbolically speaking, as much the time of Rome's Caesar himself as of Shakespeare's 'Julius Caesar.' The David Copperfield located squarely in nineteenth century England also lives, spiritually speaking, in ages past. For Dickens the Christian, no later reality supercedes Bible time, or those ages implicated in Christian history. The Caesar David sees is at once Shakespearean and pre-Shakespearean. Allegory doubles vision, which, set free from the binding, single-frame illusion of time, shuttles at the speed of the light of the world between Time and Eternity.

On the Caesar occasion, the 'new Pantomime' is also shown. Soon after, Steerforth leads forth to the lions, then to 'a Panorama and some other sights,' including 'a walk through the Museum, where I could not help observing how much Steerforth knew' (291). Of course Steerforth is an expert on Museums: he *is* a walking Museum full of exhibits of ancient time, Greek, Roman, and Hebrew. In context, Pantomime and Panorama, capital 'P' insistent, catch the pagan light reflected from surrounding Greek-Roman surfaces, and suddenly PAN, the Greek god, and maybe even the PANtheon in Rome, glares. Much Graeco-Roman atmosphere fills David's experience in this time. As Bacchanal, David assures a friend of Steerforth's that none need fear insult under his roof 'where the Lares were sacred' (361). And the morning after, David, suffering from a hang-over, feels 'as if a body of Titans had...pushed the day before yesterday some months back' (366). The Titans *are* pushing time back into B.C. as Steerforth presents his friend, Miss Mowcher the dwarf, as 'one of the seven wonders of the world' (327). In his pagan period, David is all 'headache, sickness, and repentance' (365), especially when he thinks of Agnes. He need not suffer on that score, at least. If *J* punishes and exploits, Agnes, even as Christ, always understands David's lapses and freely forgives.

The 'J' passion is Law. J. Steerforth would of course be strong for David's entering upon the study of law. 'On the whole, I would recommend you take to Doctors' Commons kindly, David' (343); and: 'Daisy, my advice is that you take kindly to Doctors' Commons' (344). With his Chosen People, elitist mentality, Steerforth instinctively approves the tight, exclusive society apart lawyers erect and jealously guard with legalistic mumbo-jumbo by which the laity is walled out. While studying law, David lives in 'the Adelphi' (355), which is linked to his time in 'Babylon' as he recalls 'the old days when I used to roam about its subterranean arches' (355).  The Adelphi is Greek.  Law draws Rome into prominence too: 'There was an old Roman bath in those days at the bottom of one of the streets out of the Strand—it may be there still—in which I have had many a cold plunge' (506).  Again: 'I began the next day with another dive into the Roman bath, and then started for Highgate' (521).  The Roman bath-Highgate proximity makes sense.  Highgate, where the Steerforths live, is 'lion,' i.e., Roman Colosseum, country.  Thus new Pantomimes and Pans, and Romans noble and ignoble materialize out of thin air as Jehovah and Jove reclaim the skies of man from Christ.

The anti-Christ in Steerforth also shows in his attitude towards Martha Endell.  Christ loves Martha, raising Lazarus her brother from the dead.  By contrast, Steerforth repudiates her.  Seeing her shadow flit by as, despised by all but Emily, she flees Yarmouth, Steerforth is startled, then says: 'Where the Devil did it come from, I wonder!'  Then, in relief; 'It's gone.  And ill go with it.  And now for our dinner!' (326)  Steerforth wishes at the Devil what Christ compassionately raises up.  We note that *devil* is often on Steerforth's lips.  At the Golden Cross: ''And what the devil do you mean,' retorted Steerforth, 'by putting Mr. Copperfield into a little loft over a stable?'' (288)  They bring David down, in more ways than one.  And: 'You're a devilish amiable-looking fellow, Copperfield!' (287), he says.

In Dickens, as we said, no man easily forgets God.  The God-Devil conflict within Steerforth, as within Judaism as pro and anti-Christ forces clashed in early NT time, is strong.  One dark night (dark indeed), David returning to the ark finds Steerforth there alone.  Suddenly Steerforth is 'wishing to God' things were different, an outburst betraying the stifled conscience churning within.  Moodily he glances about the little room, as if picturing what the loss of its dearest treasure, little Em'ly, will mean.  He is torn by 'passionate dejection':

> 'It would be better to be this poor Peggotty, or his lout of a nephew,' he said, getting up and leaning moodily against the chimney-piece, with his face towards the fire, 'than to be myself, twenty times richer and twenty times wiser, and be the torment to myself that I have been, in this Devil's bark of a boat, within this last half-hour!' (322)

Like Milton's Satan, he all but states: 'I myself am Hell.'  Concerted infernal symbolism—'Devil's bark,' mention of torment, the speaker's face turned to the fire, a thought arising in mind to 'cross him so unusually' (322)—drives home the point.

A minute before, David, coming upon Steerforth, asked if he called him down from the stars.  The ''No,' he answered.  'No'' (321), as if he felt the irony of being connected with anything as sublime as stars, suggests he has not 'come *down*' from anywhere, but, on the contrary, *up* from—the Other place.  Clearly, though for one intense moment he struggles against it, the Devil has him in thrall; he is on the verge of stealing off with 'the pearl.' The thwarted soul within hates and abjures what grips it, would yet build a Heaven in Hell's despite. Then, an instant later, the holy ghost of conscience is routed, and the 'J' spirits are again 'at their usual flow' (323), *flow* reconnecting him with the God of the Flood.

This very night when the shadow passes and one hears 'a third voice aloud—Martha's' (388), Steerforth consigns it, and the *three* of 'Rise up!' ('third') along with it, to Hell.

Littimer, Steerforth's servant, is one force pulling straight down to Hell. Littimer and the Devil are on close terms. Seeking his master, Littimer comes upon David and the Micawbers who are concocting a dish of mutton called 'a Devil' (413). Mr. Micawber, clerk to Heep, is especially warm for a Devil. In allegory, sheep-converted-to-Devil fairly sizzles with the message: to Hell with the Lamb. Suddenly, unsummoned and unheard, like an evil spirit that does not enter through human portals, Littimer appears, David 'aware of a strange presence in the room' (414). Littimer takes over at the gridiron (hot!) and amid much pepper (hotter still), conjures up a perfect Devil. David's miscarried feast also features a 'delusive' (413) pigeon-pie. As in the empty dove-cot behind Satis House, there is no Holy Spirit in residence in this quarter of Christendom where (He)brewing and Devil hold sway.

Littimer's appearance utterly confounds David:

> As for me, I was a mere infant at the head of my own table; and hardly ventured to glance at the respectable phenomenon, who had come from Heaven knows where, to put my establishment to rights. (414)

Heaven knows where, all right: as the splutter and blaze hints, up from Hell.

The Littimer-Hell association is stronger still. Steerforth to David: 'Did I tell you Littimer had come down?' And: 'Oh, yes! came down this morning' (324). And again: 'Yes. He is come down, that man of mine' (325). Nothing about 'come down' justifies such harping on it except, we think, its usefulness in allegory. 'Down,' a pun, recalls Shakespeare's use of it in 'Richard II' in which Richard, summoned to the base court, in bitterness of spirit puns both on *base* ('base court, where kings grow base/To come at traitors' call and do them grace') and on *down:* 'Down, down I come, like glist'ring Phaethon.' Impassive as death, Littimer has neither feeling nor conscience, and pulls his master down without a flicker of interest or remorse.

In all ways, Littimer points to the Old dispensation. He is 'as respectable a mystery as any pyramid in Egypt' (342). He condemns Emily, NT revelation, in Hebrew terms: 'She had no more gratitude, no more feeling, no more patience, no more reason in her, than a stock or a stone' (669). Miss Havisham too speaks of, and shrinks from, the stock and stone, or graven idol, she has made. Another 'Hebrew' touch is Littimer's having 'rather a stiff neck' (299); the Jews are the incorrigibly 'stiffnecked people' (*Ex.* 32:9), and are condemned by OT and NT prophets for being 'stiffnecked and uncircumcised in heart and ears' (*Acts* 7:51). *Egypt, stock* and *stone, stiff neck,* echo with moral danger to and within Israel in Bible time.

Littimer is the high priest of other ancient Mystery. When David asks the time, Littimer takes out his hunting-watch, and, opening it a crack, 'looked in at the face as if he were consulting an oracular oyster, and shut it up again, and said, if I pleased, it was half-past eight' (300). *Oracular* touches oracle. In Old Time, the priest jealously guards the mysteries of time (the shut-up watch) and eternity (the oyster: 'the pearl'), dispensing them to man. By contrast, in NT time, man, guided by the life and lessons of Christ, may seek his own salvation, finding not the 'oyster,' but 'the pearl.'

The Littimer-priest symbolism is made explicit when he is termed, in no complimentary way, the 'reverend nature of respectability in the abstract' (299), *reverend* a pun. Perfect enabler of the Devil and servant of the anti-Christ, Littimer is everything Dickens cordially detests and deems satanic in 'reverend' gentlemen of the Littimer school of service to the Master, in whose official, cold, dispassionate, impeccably 'respectable' keeping Christ and His flock languish. The clergy who fail to turn the compassionate, crisparkling, Kingdom-offering face of the Welsh clergyman ('The Shipwreck') (vis. Chapter II) to the needy and fallen, as to all, *in imitatio Christi.* Like the use of 'decent' in Joyce's 'Araby' in *Dubliners,* 'respectable' is a euphemism for frigid, remote, incapable of common humanity, of unbending in sympathetic laughter and tears. As to 'respectability in the abstract,' no quality *in the abstract* attracts Dickens. In *Chuzzlewit,* Pecksniff names his two daughters Mercy and Charity, which are as sounding brass because no mercy or charity abide therein.

Thus, as Littimer to the false saviour, his master, so all too many Right, Very, and Most Reverend gentlemen to the Master, Christ. Littimer symbolizes the Christian functionary who performs his sacred duties only to the letter; no going beyond to the spirit. The name 'Littimer' tells this tale. LITTimer, we think, looks to the Latin LITTera, or letter: the litterati learned in letter and word, the intelligentsia and doctors of the law who proudly affix 'Litt.D.' to their names. Like many a self-proud, floridly rhetorical clergyman in Dickens, a figure in black coming between man and the sky. Not permitting David to consult the shut-tight oracular oyster himself, Littimer is like the high priest that keeps from the petitioner the means of his salvation. In the essay 'The Begging-Letter Writer,' Dickens stresses that men must be partners in the Mystery, pointing out...

That the crowning miracle of all the miracles summed up in the New Testament, after the miracle of the blind seeing, and the lame walking, and the restoration of the dead to life, was the miracle that the poor had the Gospel preached to them.  That while the poor were unnaturally and unnecessarily cut off by the thousand, in the prematurity of their age, or in the rottenness of their youth—for of flower and blossom such youth has none—the Gospel was NOT preached to them, save in hollow and unmeaning voices.  That of all wrongs, this was the first mighty wrong the Pestilence warned us to set right. (RP, 385)

David's relationship to Littimer, which so reduces him, is a model of Old relations of priests and men, one non-mutual and hierarchic, which Christ replaces with the injunction to the disciples that 'ye love one another as I have loved you.'  In the essay 'Two Views of a Cheap Theatre,' Dickens first criticizes a preacher for a certain too-theatrical manner, then adds:

> But, in respect of the large Christianity of his general tone; of his renuncia-tion of all priestly authority; of his earnest and reiterated assurance to the people that the commonest among them could work out their own salvation if they would, by simply, lovingly, and dutifully following Our Saviour, and that they needed the mediation of no erring man; in these particulars, this gentleman deserved all praise. (UT, 37)

To all who confuse 'respectable' with genuinely Christian lives, Dickens holds up the portrait of Littimer, symbol of 'hollow and unmeaning' service in the Master's name.  Beware, letter-proud Doctors of the academy, mediators of the word to the unlettered, before whom the sons and daughters of David retreat in timid confusion, cowed by so much holier-than-thou!  For 'God is a Spirit:  and they that worship him must worship him in spirit and in truth' (*John* 4:24).  Presiding at the gridiron, Littimer produces a perfect Devil.  Thus does Dickens consign to Hell all social snobbery and professorial, priestly aloofness from mankind.

How deftly the Littimer vignette pinpoints the imposture by which the servants of Hell pass for those of Heaven.  Looking at the watch, Littimer 'said, *if I pleased,* it was half-past eight.'  He is all 'beg your pardon, sir' (414), and:  'If you'll excuse me, sir' (415), a Uriah Heep showcase of polite forms that conceal the spiritual void within.  Actually, what David 'pleases' does not enter into it at all.  Such *pro forma* show of consulting him only nullifies David the more.  Like Heep's unflagging 'humility,' used to lash David, it mocks the value it counterfeits.  Littimer is in some ways worse than Steerforth.  He, at least, feels, regrets, can 'wish to God.'  Miss Mowcher senses the difference when, after the elopement, she cries: 'May the Father of all Evil confound him [Steerforth], and ten times more confound that wicked servant' (463).  *Ten* times, perhaps, because ten is the cypher of the law, in the letter of which, the '*Litt*imer,' OT man lost and still loses the spirit.

Meanwhile, as a young lawyer, David labors in the service of Doctor

Strong and the Dictionary, another province of the 'letter.' This work has its dangers, too. Buried in the search for Greek roots (as he is always looking down at the ground as he cogitates, David supposes this digging for *roots* 'a botanical furor on the Doctor's part' (237)), Doctor Strong, never looking up, forgets the love founded on a rock. Dickens, we have noted, is always ambivalent about doctoral knowledge, fearing the inroads a 'pen-and-ink-ubus' passion makes into lives.[4]

Although Steerforth strains mightily against A.D., he is haunted by the unlived life of the soul. We see this in his fervent 'wish to God,' and in the toast he proposes to David:

> 'We'll drink the daisies of the field, in compliment to you: and the lilies of the valley that toil not, neither do they spin, in compliment to me—the more shame for me!' (295)

which closely echoes:

> And why take ye thought for raiment? Consider the lilies of the field, how they grow; they toil not, neither do they spin:
> And yet I say unto you, That even Solomon in all his glory was not arrayed like one of these. (*Matt.* 6:28-9)

Steerforth also jests about being a 'prodigal son' (427). But the words remind us that every man who returns to the Father is the Prodigal. The son in every man cries out, yea, for the living God.

'J' of J. Steerforth, we suggested, has multiple religious meanings, Jove-Jehovah and possibly ironic Jesus ones, J symbolizing the many ways man's soul Steers Forth from Greek, Roman, and Hebrew times on. Remarkably, the initial J has one startlingly consistent history in *David Copperfield*. Sinister, blighting 'J' characters fill the novel, AND NO OTHER KIND! J always looks B.C.-wards to ark, law, and Yah. Consider the formidable J retinue: Jane Murdstone, whose sins against mother and child cry to Heaven; Joram, inseparable in mind from the RAT-tat-tat of the grave; 'demon Jorkins,' reactionary law partner in the firm of *Spenlow and Jorkins;* Jack Maldon, ne'er-do-well whose illicit pursuit of Annie Strong threatens the love founded on a rock; Jip, Dora's tyrannical spaniel and David's serio-comic peculiar torment and trial; Jack Ketch, the hangman mentioned by Heep. (Heep and J are of course old bedfellows in Death.)

There is also Julia Mills, Dora's other companion, termed, Hebraically enough, a 'little patriarch' (486). *Patriarch* she is, warning David and Dora of lovers stranded in 'the desert of Sahara' (485), where quite a number of patriarchs wound up in the wilderness wandering, one imagines; and exhibiting 'a dreadful luxury in our afflictions' (555). 'J,' or Jehovah, pursued the same themes: stranding Israelites in deserts of old, and luxuriating in their afflictions.  Julia Mills winds up 'steeped in money to her throat' (875), having laid up for herself such treasure of earth as 'a golden salver, and a copper-coloured woman in linen' (875) to serve her. (The bronze-skinned servant sounds a bit Middle Eastern.)  In Julia, no rising above gold-copper fields to Marigold ones of Heaven.  MILLS too, with 'Gradgrind,' 'Millers,' and law grinding all 'in a mill,' looks to Law. (vis. Chapter III)

The 'Ya-a-ah!' spirit, Miss Trotwood, is highly partial to 'J.'  There is her servant, *Janet*; her dogged insistence that Peggotty be called *Jackson*; because it is 'much more easy to be born a Jackson' (502); and her conversion of the name 'Chillip' into *Jellips* (197).  Can *so* much 'J' activity in a 'Yah!' vicinity—Janet, Jackson, Jellips—be called coincidence?  She is right: it *is* easier to be born, and to stay, a Jackson, never rising above the 'J' components of violence, judgment, and unforgiveness.  *Jellips* adds theological insult to injury.  Having first 'Ya-a-ah!'-d and struck Mr. Chillip, in a way meant to crush his spirit, Miss Trotwood proceeds to unchristen him, 'Ch' undone in 'J.'  Clearly, *J* sticks like grim death to this short-tempered, combative, inflexible, intransigent old battleax of a Betsey who, in J style, deserts (pun) mother and child and makes war on stray children and donkeys.

The Miss Trotwood-Janet relationship, mostly a partnership in war, is quite as grim.  Janet, recall, is 'one of a series of protégées whom my aunt had taken into her service expressly to educate in a renouncement of mankind, and who had generally completed their abjuration of mankind by marrying the baker' (194).  Here, promptly diverted into comedy, is a first sketch of the tragic Miss Havisham-Estella relationship of the work of twelve years later, *Great Expectations*.  Janet is an Estella who gets away. But not before Miss Trotwood uses her in many a property-jealous assault on luckless passers-by who chance to stray onto her sacred green, the lady instantly dispatching Janet to the magistrate, the law, for redress of grievances.  All is NO TRESPASS, and no: 'Forgive us our trespasses,' literal or figurative, in Betsey Trotwood time.  In short, there is a marked unchristian, in fact resoundingly Hebrew, pre-Lord's Prayer spirit and side to this Christian dame of modern time.

As to Jack Maldon, nemesis of the marriage of Annie and Doctor Strong, MALDON tells that the MAL(L) is DON(E), i.e., the green growing time at an end.  Comes 'J,' and the wilderness reappears; man is back in *Genesis* time, and looking out on the 'maldon,' lost, ruined Eden.  Sure enough, in the story Jack is off roaming the burning deserts, and making deserts at home by stealing Annie's cherry-colored ribbon.  With her sharp *Yah* eye and tongue, Miss Trotwood calls Mrs. Markleham, Annie's mother who keeps insinuating Jack into Annie's life, 'the old Animal' (663).  How true! A m*ARK*leham with 'J' bias can house a whole zoo; and markleHAM to boot.  In allegory, Markleham-J forces would sunder the letter, the Doctor with his knowledge of the word, from the spirit, the constant faith and abiding love of Annie Strong. The plot finally fails, and the Strong union, shining mirror of NT faith, the love founded on a rock, survives. In an Annie of faith, *annie Domini*[5] emerges Stronger than ever before.

'J' depths also lie in *J. Steerforth*. The two cronies who join him in getting David drunk are Grainger and Markham: J is flanked by gRAINger and mARKham; indeed, markHAM. Dickens could have spelled it 'Granger,' but in *Grainger*' he can recall the forty days and nights of rain that launched Noah's ark. On the night of his first dissipation, David, accompanied by Steerforth, Grainger, and Markham, is tipsily aware of much 'indistinct talk of its being wet;' and of the Opera, like a mass launched on the flood, looking 'as if it were learning to swim' (362). The trio would draw David backwards into Hebrew (rain-ark) and Greek (Bacchanal) time, sundering him from Agnes and his new life. The 'J' life always brings back the Flood. Late in the story, when David leaves Mrs. Steerforth and Rosa Dartle still bitter and unsoftened by grief over Steerforth's death, still blaming little Em'ly and refusing to forgive, he sees that 'a mist was rising like a sea, which, mingling with the darkness, made it seem as if the gathering waters would encompass them. I have reason to remember this, and think of it with awe; for before I looked upon these two again, a stormy sea had risen to their feet' (673). Graphic representation of the Flood, manifestation of the retributive spirit at its worst in hearts unwon to Christ.

J. Steerforth comes with Littimer on one side, and on the other, Miss Mowcher the dwarf, one of the 'seven wonders of the world.' She too mans a post in B.C. See her waddle in, tiny sack crammed with remedies for time-ravaged complexions, restoratives of the glow of youth in aging swains when youth is irrevocably flown, cosmetics for corpses, as it were: rouge, sponges, combs, wigs, artifices numberless to curl, primp, tease, counterfeit the lost bloom of youth in the Daisy that has blown. Nature is her realm. 'Face like a peach!' she hails David, and: 'Quite tempting! I'm very fond of peaches' (329). Steerforth, her favorite, is greeted: 'What! My flower!' (328) All ripens as for her hand. Steerforth is 'my chicken' (335), 'my pet' (329), a duck and 'downy fellow' (328). Her admiring: 'Did he sip every flower!' (333), applauding his fickle ways, casts him as humming-bird or bee. Her clucking refrain: 'Now, ducky, ducky, ducky, come to Mrs. Bond and be killed' (331) is a reminder that all 'bonded' to Nature, 'Mrs. *Bond,*' must eventually come and get killed. Behind all Miss Mowcher's lively, light, incessant chatter, one hears the old tune: RAT-tat-tat.

'Ain't I volatile?' (333) she trills. *Volatile,* yes. The word, from the Latin *volare*-to fly, means lively; but also transitory, readily vaporizable, that which melts away into thin air. Of a client of hers, Mithers, Miss Mowcher says: *'There's* a man. How *he* wears!' Mithers and Lady

Mithers 'wear,' all right. Behind the wearing, or lasting, quality she admires, is the (pun) sure 'wearing' out and fading, for all that. There is no profit, finally, in opposing Time. The ripest peach cheek, most fragrant, delicate Blossom like Dora, and whole summers of daisy-starred fields of earth, Time's nether heavens, fade, wither-mither, pass away. All hourly moves on to the night in which beauty, summer's honey breath, and Time's best jewel in Time's chest too soon lie hid, the night of Death.

Take for example one Mowcher client, Charley Pyegrave. Even he, poor old fool, once had a face like a peach. But time passed, and when the 'PYE(grave)' is opened, Charley my darling is discovered to have one foot in the 'Pye*grave.*' Within the gaudy, dyed 'Pyegrave'—maggots, worms, RAT-tat-tat. Pink, paint, prop, elixir, gammon, humbug the blown fruits of earth and Pyegraves into the semblance of first freshness, preserve the jellies of Jellyby (*Bleak House*) gardens howsoe'er she may, Miss Mowcher cannot halt mortality, nor wield strong hand to hold his swift foot back. The fruitful time for man in Nature passes, and man is no more than chicken, duck, thrall to Nature if he tends only the flesh, the physical life in Nature, world, and time.

Not taken in by her own sweet deceits, impish Miss Mowcher, wonder of the ancient world (she babbles about a 'Griffin' (332) as if on familiar terms with it), yet caters to and profits from those many infatuated ones who are: who live only to recapture by artifice, black magic, if need be, the rosy glow of youth. Who, like Steerforth, live to ogle, dazzle, dart killing glances, sip every flower, break hearts—to lightly do such damage as Steerforth does to one fragrant 'flower' (315), little Emily, and not pay. Thanks to Miss Mowcher, they may. In Nature, man neither finds nor develops a conscience or soul. Under the dwarf's preternaturally green thumb, sunken cheeks know a brief afterbloom and spring; ancient dandies and crones of the Turvey-drop (*Bleak House*) and Mrs. Skewton (*Dombey and Son*) variety enjoy one last dizzy waltz around Vanity Fair. Meantime, none tend the fruits of the spirit grown of the seed which is the word of God, gardens that lie beyond earth's passing Edens and the killing frosts of Time.

I venture to guess that the name MOWCHER, built on MOW, identifies Mowcher with one that by and by 'mows' all gardens down, the Grim Reaper. Nature in soulless profusion raises, then kills her own; behold 'summer's green all girded up in sheaves/Borne on the bier with white and bristly beard.' The killing power in Miss Mowcher shows when, capturing Littimer, she holds onto him 'like grim Death' (856). Trimming, clipping, snipping her sure way along the Mithers-Pyegrave rows of griffins, monstrous painted ones, even as Wemmick along his Newgate rows of (Dickens's metaphor) doomed plants, she mows, weeds, and waters. She even saves distinguished clients' nail-parings, her little gunny sack filled with ancient winnowings. The mowing proceeds apace. There is fooling the world. But there is no fooling the Reaper, the Mower of Gardens, who follows after, and who, alas, will know the dyed moustachios of a Charley Pyegrave (or Charley Dickens) for all their aggressively juvenile black or auburn hue.

'Vain man, in his little brief authority' (CB, 56), muses the omniscient narrator in A Christmas Carol. Such is the saving perspective on human life *sub specie aeternitatis* easily lost sight of in the hurry-scurry of life, and reacquired only in the celestial company of Three Spirits.

Not only vain man, but foolish man, relying on Nature when Nature can blunder so, producing a deformed creature like a dwarf. Sad little pseudo-Mother Nature, Miss Mowcher, who dyes that men may dream they will never die! Sitting on a footstool before the fire, 'making a kind of arbour of the dining-table, which spread its mahogany shelter above her head' (328). But it is not a lasting shelter. The tree was felled; all in Nature dies. In the Mowcher cameo, Dickens records the consequences of man's refusal to accept the God-ordained, rightful passage of all through Nature to Eternity, in which grows the evergreen to which man may cling forever, Christ.

At the start, Miss Mowcher is a prop of B.C. Delighting in Steerforth's amorality and 'scapegrace' (334) ways (yes, he does just fall short of grace), she curries him—not that he needs it—for upcoming conquest. But when news of his treachery reaches her, Miss Mowcher greatly rues her part in such wrong, vowing: 'If ever I can do anything to serve the poor betrayed girl, I will do it faithfully, please Heaven!' (465) Heaven pleases. In time, Miss Mowcher spots Littimer through his disguise (she is good at what lies behind disguises), and brings him to justice. Thus ends the career of the bad and faithless servant of the false Master. In that act, Miss Mowcher's 'three foot nothing' (464) height proves as tall and pointing-upward a *three* as ever graced Christendom.

Once upon a time, her vanity-of-vanities instruments 'tumbled into a heap upon the chair' (329), she coaxed besotted fools to bloom one false season more: to be peach, pet, ducky, barnyard creatures without immortal souls. Then, though planted a natural body, Nature herself in the person of Miss Mowcher is raised a spiritual body as she develops a soul in the time of 'the pearl.' Off with the 'heap' of instruments. Battling Littimer for Em'ly's sake, Miss Mowcher is very like Miss Pross at the end of A Tale of Two Cities as she does battle with Madame Defarge for Lucie's sweet sake. Each woman is hurt in the struggle, each feels (as Dan'l calls it) the 'wownd,' or wound, suffered in defense of Heaven: *Lucie*, Light, and the pearl.

No wonder Steerforth likes Miss Mowcher. The divine decree that life in Nature swiftly passes is precisely what he so adamantly resists. Once, he brings David a letter from Peggotty containing the sad news that Barkis is dying:

While I deciphered it, Steerforth continued to eat and drink.

'It's a bad job,' he said, when I had done; 'but the sun sets every day, and people die every minute, and we musn't be scared by the common lot. If we failed to hold our own, because that equal foot at all men's doors was heard knocking somewhere, every object in this world would slip from us. No! Ride on! Rough-shod if need be, smooth-shod if that will do, but ride on! Ride on over all obstacles, and win the race.'

'And win what race?' said I. (426)

'Ride on,' the Steerforth passion, is an ironic version of 'the journey.' David's final question quietly strikes home. Yes, *what* race? To 'hold our own' in *'this* world' is all in all to Steerforth. While Barkis's imminent death calls the whole toiling, temporizing, time-squandering world to account, Steerforth, who *will* eat and drink as usual, will not heed. (Once before, too, Steerforth's: 'Now for our dinner!' (326) denied Martha, thus NT time.) Perverse man, dining in the very teeth of the proof that the appetitive life must grind to a halt one day.

'Ride on!' sums up the anti-'journey' dogma of the Steer Forth life. To what end its brilliant athleticism and contest? No man halts the tides of Nature; there are no olympics of Immortality. Steerforth recalls King Canute the Dane whose life is sketched by Dickens in *A Child's History of England*. Canute commands the sea not to wet the edge of his robe, insisting: 'Thus far shalt thou go, and no farther!' But: 'The great command goes forth to all the kings upon the earth, and went to Canute in the year one thousand and thirty-five, and stretched him dead upon his bed' (CHE,162).

Steerforth's 'Ride on!' figure shows that he has a figurative sense of life, is no dry literalist of a Littimer. How tragic! With his 'lillies of the valley' so close to Christ's 'lilies of the field,' and his race to the idea of 'the journey,' the speaker falls short. Pagan that he is, he eats, drinks, speaks of setting suns, disclosing the limits of his apperceptive field, his enslavement (ironic in one who seems so free!) to Nature, world, and time. In the Steerforth physics is no metaphysics. His 'rough-shod, smooth-shod' formula strikes the old exploitive, pragmatic, expedient note. No moral sense in it of spiritual No Thoroughfares like little Em'ly. Snatching back thought from Barkis's death and trying to force David to do the same, Steerforth re-enters the lists in ever more determined pursuit of—what? David parts from him still a disciple, but inwardly wishing, for the first time, 'he had some worthy race to run.' (427).

*The race* is not 'the journey.' The guerdon of the Dickens heaven is not, like steeplechases of the world, to the swift, the world-beater, the one rider of all with spurs sharp enough to prick the sides of his intent. Nor is it at all a question, as Steerforth thinks, of being *'scared* by the common lot.' Sobered, rather: made thoughtful. Every object in this world must one day slip from us, clutch though we may. As doggedly as Steerforth pits himself against such an idea, so strongly do David and Dickens stand behind it.

With his idol Steerforth gone, never to return, the God-seeker in David emerges with new force:

> Yes, Steerforth, long removed from the scenes of this poor history! My sorrow may bear involuntary witness against you at the Judgment Throne; but my angry thoughts or my reproaches never will, I know! (455)

Now for Dan'l and David, separately and together, 'the journey' really begins. Ark, Yarmouth, babby-lion, and judgment are left behind. Time passes. Eternity nears. How quickly the snow covers the 'late footprints' (589) of the two men on the night of the Golden Cross, *late* looking to death as to time as the new track too begins to 'die away (it snowed so fast) as I looked back over my shoulder' (589). So soon is Orpheus man's past and finally his whole life left behind. Now and then, for a moment, the 'human tide rolling westward' (DS,34) slows down; there is 'a temporary lull in the eternal tread of feet upon the pavement' (473). But never for long. In Dickens, all hums with the Great Change to come, and sights 'the shore where all forgotten things will reappear' (131). Though dashing madly from Highgate to Blackheath to Yarmouth to London to Europe, before turning homeward in the end, Steerforth cannot escape the mortal condition or the certainty of the reckoning to come before 'the Judgment Throne.'

Not that Dickens is a stern moralist on the subject, or fails to smile indulgently on the oblivious, green-gold days of youth. Nothing young David cares or should care in the heedless, lamb-white days of tuneful turning in Nature, or splendor and glory in grass and flower, that love's wanderings in Eden with Dora must end. Nor, looking back, does the mature David ever disown that former self. Wistfully he muses: 'What an idle time! What an insubstantial, happy, foolish time!' (400) The exclamation mark approves. Yet always in Dickens, 'gather ye rosebuds' is softly trailed by the echoing sigh: 'while ye may.' Like echoing footsteps in *A Tale of Two Cities,* the time comes slowly but surely when fled is that earthly music, and for the soul it is urgently a question of wake or sleep.

Like Macbeth, the Steerforth who stifles the Christ and God within kills a King. Once, aboard the ark, the 'Devil's bark of a boat,' he is visited by the holy ghost of conscience, as Macbeth by Banquo's ghost. He is badly shaken for a moment. Then, as always, the mood breaks:

> 'So much for that!' he said, making as if he tossed something light into the air, with his hand.
> " 'Why, being gone, I am a man again,'
> like Macbeth. And now for dinner! If I have not, Macbeth-like, broken up the feast with most admired disorder, Daisy.' (323)

How often in Dickens as in Shakespeare the great theme is: to kill a king, with its implication of the killing of Christ the King.  In bringing on the Ghosts in *A Christmas Carol,* Dickens tips his hat to Shakespeare; he does so again in *Copperfield* when Mr. Chillip, a 'Ch' figure, enters the story 'walk'[ing] as softly as the Ghost in Hamlet' (9).[6]  Driving off the Ghost, Steerforth shares Macbeth's delusion that with it gone, he is 'a man again.' As if man *were* fully man without the *geist,* or ghost, spirit, the voice of the imperative of moral accountability behind the world that summons Macbeth, Scrooge, and Steerforth in the accents of the Judgment to come. Whatever others make of Shakespeare, clearly to Dickens he is a Christian poet, ever mindful of the Ghostly Father's great mandate to the Son.

Steerforth's Christian name is James, one overshadowed by 'J.'  James was a brother of Christ.  Is Dickens at all mindful of this as he models the son of David-James relationship almost of brothers:  does it rest on the Son of David-James one?  If so, that would explain the Saviour role he plays for a time in David's life.  James has other NT significance, too.  In 'City of London Churches,' Dickens mentions the Boanerges, James and John, the disciples.  *Boanerges* refers to their loud voices; and Steerforth first impresses David as one who will speak 'in a rather strong voice.'

Fond of permuting names, as if to bring forward new facets of meaning, Dickens has Miss Mowcher call Steerforth *Jemmy,* which is perhaps a *gem* pun recalling the Steerforth who once vowed he would not drive Em'ly away from her place by Dan'l's fireside 'for the wealth of the Indies!' (316), only to wind up stealing away 'the pearl,' the teardrop of Eternity with sparkling eyes 'like jewels' (143).  If *Jemmy* is a gem pun, it is an ironic one.  For, seizing David's seven shillings, Steerforth cannot value the devotion and idealism in David's love for him that outshines all monetary and metal-rich copperfields of earth; mindful of gold and silver 'wealth of the Indies,' cannot prize the heavenly love, constancy, and trust which are his for the prizing in the heart of 'the pearl.'  Dickens symbolically tells us that in Israel, 'J' had a loving, trusting, God-seeking people, but the fierce Jehovah nature of hammer and lion did endless harm to His own, His David and son of David; His rose; His pearl.  So modern 'J'-cast man, made in His image, though having all that Heaven allows, and more, *J. Steerforths* the OT 'J' way to bankruptcy and doom from which mankind is saved only with the coming of Christ.

In Steerforth is memorialized all the hazardous Rudder-fording of the flood man knew before Christ, pilot of the Galilean lake, calmed the wind and waves.  And what ocean-littering, wreck-strewing, *Sarah Jane*-sinking, Salvage-making, lion-roaring seas mankind sailed to Eternity in before a Star rose in the east.  Why a Christian A.D. dissolves back into such rags of B.C., of reliance on a *Littimer* body of servants of the Master, of failure to defend the Master and to cherish the poor and fallen in His name, Dickens will never know.  For 'J,' God of Israel, is better than all that in His heart. One glimpses in the latest J to cloud and brighten man's heavens something of the power and majesty which drew forth the burning love of the nation of David. In a rare moment of accord with Rosa, who is playing her harp, Steerforth greets David with: 'Here is Daisy, too, loves music from his soul' (435). The moment in time fades. One thinks of David, harpist, psalmist of Israel, who also loved music 'from his soul.' Another David and J, Jonathon, are grouped in memory, in their midst a harp.

In retrospect, we see that a mighty 'J' Providence sought to keep David from the way, the truth, and the life; and yet, paradoxically, set him on the path to the way, the truth, and the life. 'J' both retarded and sped David on his mighty forward way. This deep ambiguity would seem to flash in 'Daisy,' the sun-centered flower with star-ray petal corona of white ablaze in terrestrial heavens, and sun-like, pointing to the Son. Nor are Steerforth's 'daisies of the field' and 'lillies of the valley' far afield from Christ's 'lilies of the field.' Moreover, if the J Deity of man's early heavens was harsh and inconstant, this too had its use. It was the gap He left in the hearts of the sons of David, Daniel, Ham, Levi that led them to seek and expect a New version of the Founder of Heaven and earth, which Testament is forthcoming with Christ. J had to exist, reign, and fall for the glory of *Agnes* to be revealed.

Undoing the Master, the Cross, the pearl, J. Steerforth costs David dear. And yet, and yet. In his last farewell to David, 'God bless you, Daisy, and good-night!' (436), it is as if the Old dispensation, Sleep nigh, releases the New and blesses it on its way. The power of the J who carved his initial deep in an old door ends: the 'old door' itself, shut tight on debtors and gentiles, is replaced by Christ and His order hospitable to all men: 'I am the door: by me if any man enter in, he shall be saved, and shall go in and out, and find pasture' (*John* 10:9). The star of J sets, the Star of Agnes, the brightest Star of David, rises in David's soul.

If Dan'l's ark is a 'Devil's bark of a boat,' many another bark sails in *Copperfield* as well. Of one such journeying Bark, Barkis the carrier, we now speak.

# NINE
## Barkis

> The carrier had a way of keeping his head down, like his horse, and of drooping sleepily forward as he drove, with one of his arms on each of his knees. I say "drove," but it struck me that the cart would have gone to Yarmouth quite as well without him, for the horse did that; and as to conversation, he had no idea of it but whistling. (DC,28)

Perhaps the funny-saddest, most touching journey of all journeying souls in *Copperfield* is that of Barkis the carrier. Un-steerforthing it on the slow Blunderstone-to-Yarmouth road all his born and far from livelong days, Barkis ventures just so far and no farther, the body setting the pace for the soul.

He comes early upon the scene as a man of well-untravelled thought:

> After we had jogged on for some little time, I asked the carrier if he was going all the way?
> 'All the way where?' inquired the carrier.
> 'There,' I said.
> 'Where's there?' inquired the carrier. (64)

Is there life Beyond Yarmouth? Not one jot of speculation about such matters exists in the Barkis nature:

> 'Are you only going to Yarmouth, then?' I asked.
> 'That's about it,' said the carrier. 'And there I shall take you to the stage-cutch, and the stage-cutch that'll take you to—wherever it is.' (64)

So much for eternal settings-forth and destinations, too.

Barkis is a Bark(is), or ship of soul, one of many in the great Dickensian fiction-wide metaphor of life as a journey by sea. A bark made of the heavy Old Incuriosity-shop lumber, and Yarmouth-Yah country is its port. There he carries, marries, falls ill and dies. Almost without warning, David's old friend the carrier, husband of C.P. Barkis and rabid miser, is ailing; then, with shocking suddenness, 'the carrier was making his last journey rather fast' (425). At journey's end, the epitaph is solemnly writ in water: 'And, it being low-water, he went out with the tide' (445).

Do *low* and *out* hint at something that overshadows his hope of 'entering in'? Perhaps not. But what shall we make of Barkis's box, the coffer crammed with money and other treasure which he always carries in his cart; then, in invalid time, hides jealously under his bed? Barkis claims he is only holding it for a mysterious, never-seen Mr. Blackboy. BLACKBOY: fearful name! If Mr. Blackboy is only a miser's dodge, Barkis yet invents better than he knows.

Let the Recording Angel record: 'Barkis is willin'.' Back in In the Beginning time of our story, there dawns in a carrier's humdrum life of short shuttle the wondrous possibility that the Yarmouth circuit may not be the whole story of his life—the 'about it,' B.C. terminus, journey's end— after all. For Barkis too inhabits a Providential universe in which a sturdy, centered *Clara,* a shining Christian light and conductress to grace, swims into his ken. In honor of which event, stolid, phlegmatic, head-down Barkis sits up straight, begins to show unmistakable signs of life, and puts the world (or one vital speck of it, David) on notice that 'Barkis is willin'' (65). Divine opportunity knocks, and Barkis answers. Cautious, slow, un- stirring, but definitely kindled to interest—*willing!* And in just the right direction, too, as Heaven lies.

Yet willing as a Barkis, who weighs a moral ton, is willing. First he must test every inch of ground. Doubting Barkis warily circles the possibly- beloved in his close-keeping, incommunicative way, and at a safe distance. He notifies David that he is willing: David, not the lady herself. First, however, Mr. Barkis carefully inventories the housewifely gifts of the intended, noting with special interest her 'apple parsties' (65). This is no impulsive investor, but a country carrier not to be carried away. As to some warmer shade of pursuit or more direct approach to the object of regard, no. Entrusting all to the infinite credential of being 'willing,' Barkis sits back (he always sits until bed-ridden, then lies), awaiting a favorable reply.

To what? He never says, 'Will you be mine?' or words to that effect. This putting Peggotty on notice in a three-word message entrusted to a go- between not nine years old is as far as Barkis goes. 'That's about it.' It never dawns on him that this might not do. In Barkis's mind, all is decided, it seems, when the lady's qualifications pass muster: in the fact that *she,* and her parstics, suit *him.* An hilarious piece of wooing— Peggotty laughs heartily at it all—but with serious implications for allegory. No contradiction here. In Dickens, as we have noted before, comedy and allegory work together, man being eternal in all facets of his natural life, and humor the outlook of the Happy Ending.

Clara Peggotty, the bride-to-be, points to the love that outlasts death, as the scene of Mrs. Copperfield's funeral shows:

> We stand around the grave. The day seems different to me from every
> other day, and the light not of the same colour—of a sadder colour. Now there
> is a solemn hush, which we have brought from home with what is resting in
> mould; and while we stand bare-headed, I hear the voice of the clergyman,
> sounding remote in the open air, and yet distinct and plain, saying: 'I am the
> Resurrection and the Life, saith the Lord!' Then I hear sobs; and, standing
> apart among the lookers-on, I see that good and faithful servant, whom of all
> people upon earth I love the best, and unto whom my childish heart is certain
> that the Lord will one day say: 'Well done.' (130)

David's voice grows Biblical here; his idiom blends Hebrew and Christian
destinies of the House of David, which meet in peace. 'The day seems
different to me from every other day' seems faintly to echo the Passover
question: 'Why is this night different from all other nights?' Then,
bathed in the light of 'the Resurrection and the Life,' the words 'good and
faithful servant,' and 'Well done,' look to the joyful climax of the NT
parable, which reads: 'Well done, thou good and faithful servant: thou
hast been faithful over a few things: enter thou into the joy of thy Lord'
(*Matt.* 25:21).

Clara Peggotty is attuned to Christian values in other ways, too. In an
earlier chapter we noted her three shillings and box with the view of St.
Paul's Cathedral on its sliding lid. Now we note how Dickens develops the
theme. After Barkis dies and Peggotty returns home, St. Paul does too:
'She had fallen back, already, on the society of the work-box with Saint
Paul's upon the lid, the yard-measure in the cottage, and the bit of wax-
candle' (448). Soon after, David and she, ever close friends, enjoy an
excursion to London and a climb to the top of St. Paul's Cathedral:

> All these wonders afforded Peggotty as much pleasure as she was able to
> enjoy, under existing circumstances: except, I think, St. Paul's, which, from
> her long attachment to her work-box, became a rival of the picture on the lid,
> and was, in some particulars, vanquished, she considered, by that work of
> art. (475)

Peggotty's constancy, and preference for the ideal over the real, the
symbolic over the seen, is the point. And in the very last chapter, there
she is, still surrounded by yard-measure, candle, and the pink-domed
'work-box with a picture of St. Paul's upon the lid' (874). Seen in rosy light
of sunrise or sunset, 'Paul's Church,' as John Browdie in *Nicholas Nickleby*
calls it, is all the closer to the sun and Son of Heaven, taking its place
beside Martha and other NT symbols which testify to faith in the Resurrection and the Life.[1]

Her Christian soul is revealed in other ways as well. There is her work-
roughened forefinger which guides David's first baby steps, 'like a pocket

nutmeg-grater' (13); and 'cheeks and arms so hard and red that I wondered that birds didn't peck her in preference to apples' (13), also genius for apple parsties. Nutmeg-grater and apples surely recall that other goodly, Godly dame, Clemency Newcome, and *her* nutmeg-grater inscribed: 'Do as you wold be done by,' and apple-tree. It is interesting to note that 'The Battle of Life' (1846) and *David Copperfield* (1849-50) are but a few years apart. In this nutmeg-apples-Christian cluster, Dickens once again seems to have in mind: '"By their fruits ye shall know them," said OUR SAVIOUR' (CHE, 411).

Doing nothing by halves (and all by Doubledick doubles, we believe), Dickens enlarges apple-ripe Peggotty into a whole tree or grove. Does she have so massy and indeterminate a shape—'no shape at all, and eyes so dark that they seemed to darken the whole neighbourhood in her face' (13—to suggest a great, leafy tree? In her frequent, affectionate squeezes of David, the buttons of her gown go flying in all directions. In *Great Expectations*, 'buttons' retain the old meaning of 'buds':

> 'Why, what do you make out that they done with their buttons then, Jack?' asked the landlord, vacillating weakly.
> 'Done with their buttons?' returned the Jack. 'Chucked 'em overboard. Swallered 'em. Sowed 'em, to come up small salad. Done with their buttons!' (418)

Perhaps Peggotty's many bursting buttons are, symbolically speaking, buds, spores seeding the Creation with her faith, hope, and charity Clara loves the son of David, in which love her Christian nature shines especially bright.

Well, then, no wonder that in beholding Peggotty, Barkis should actually perk up and even grow solemn with unwonted emotion. Travelling in Barkis's cart, David offers the carrier a cake which She made. '"Ah!" said Mr. Barkis. 'Her."' (64), a tribute which avoids profaning the revered name. No sooner does 'Clara,' Light, enter his life than Barkis begins to 'reflect' (pun) Light:

> 'So she makes,' said Mr. Barkis, after a long interval of reflection, 'all the apple parsties, and does all the cooking, do she?' (65)

He gets *pastries* backwards in 'parsties,' putting the lazy horse before the cart, so to speak. But otherwise, he is moving ahead. Told by David: 'Her christian name is Clara,' Barkis, much taken by the intelligence, again lights up:

> 'Is it though?' said Mr. Barkis.
> He seemed to find an immense fund of reflection in this circumstance, and sat pondering and inwardly whistling for some time. (108)

When David asks him if Peggotty knows he expects an answer:

> 'No—no,' growled Mr. Barkis, reflecting about it. (108)

The dark, planetary soul of Barkis has found its Star.  Add to 'reflection' upon reflection Barkis's 'attempts to be particularly lucid' (138) as he speaks of Peggotty, *lucid* more light punning on 'light,' and there is suddenly a whole windfall of light.  Yet even as Barkis tries to be lucid, his B.C., Miss Havisham of a face remains 'the face of a clock that has stopped' (138).

However, to his Eternal credit, 'Barkis is willin'.'  Yet what a study in passivity withal!  He woos Peggotty only *after* she accepts him, thus guaranteeing himself against loss and damages.  Moreover, in courting her he still barely stirs or lifts a finger:-in short, is as usual.  He may be willing, but by God, that's *all* he is.  To borrow his own words: 'That's about it.'

Barkis and Peggotty are wed.  It seems no sooner does she say, 'Clara is willing' than the miser latent in Barkis leaps from hiding.  He keeps 'a heap of money in a box under his bed, which he pretended was only full of coats and trousers' (150).  HEAP of money, a Devilish sign.  Treasure laid up on earth, *literally* on earth, too, as the box is on the floor, slowly becomes Barkis's consuming passion and delight.  A 'little near' to begin with, Barkis constantly grows 'a little nearer' (309).  Choice ambiguity! 'Near' first of all means tight-fisted, miserly.  But as 'near' and 'nearer' resound, the second and eternal sense emerges.  How ironic that all the while he hoards, Barkis is 'near' all he or any man needs to make himself eternal, the shining example of a good, selfless Christian wife.  How sad to keep getting 'nearer,' in the penny-pinching, Heaven-defeating sense, when Time's moving on is bringing man ever 'nearer' to the hour of his death—in Barkis's case, untimely death.  And when 'near' understood aright portends: 'Nearer my God to Thee.'

Barkis's health soon begins to fail.  No man is long for this world, and some are shorter.  Yet he continues to fib brazenly about the box being filled with old clothes, to hide away his Heepish heap and count his coins even as failing health warns of a nearing end.  Barkis the Willing is not unlike the man in the Gospels who is told that to win Life Eternal he must sell all he has and follow Christ.  Like Barkis, the man is willing, but just not able, for, again like Barkis, 'he had great possessions' (*Matt.* 19:21).

Mere nearness to Light assures nothing, we see.  It is not enough to fall in love with *Lucie* Manette, Ada *Clare,* or *Clara* Barley (or Clara Peggotty); one must also strive upwards towards the Light.  At great personal risk and self-sacrifice, Charles Darnay returns to France to try to save an old family servant, Gabelle; and Herbert Pocket rescues Clara, befriends Handel and 'Him,' and in Clarriker's behalf goes forth to found a branch-house in the

East.  By contrast, Richard Carstone, obsessed with futile hope of the Law, does not win the new life his for the willing in the love of Ada Clare; law-zealous *Carstone,* imitating OT man in his blindness to the 'Clare' of Christ, is journeying man in the *car* turned to *stone.*  Like Captain John Bunsby aboard the *Cautious Clara* in *Dombey and Son,* man can be too circumspect and cautious, and lose the Light.  And if he does not watch his step, a Barkis can become (in Steerforth's words) a Devil's bark(is) of a boat.

Enter Mr. Scratch, the Devil, by the time-honored way of galloping avarice and lies:

> For years and years, Mr. Barkis had carried this box, on all his journeys, every day.  That it might the better escape notice, he had invented a fiction that it belonged to 'Mr. Blackboy,' and was 'to be left with Barkis till called for;' a fable he had elaborately written on the lid, in characters now scarcely legible. (446)

Who is Mr. Blackboy, owner-to-be of all that Barkis hoards behind a smokescreen of lies, who but the Father of Lies, the Blackest *Black-boy* of them all, Old Nick.  In the classic way, Barkis sells his soul to the Devil for worldly wealth.  He imagines, in self-delusion, that he invents the *Blackboy* fiction.  But truer lies were never spoken.  How only too true that 'Mr. Blackboy' will one day come for the box, as for Barkis's heavily mort-gaged soul.  Indeed, the box *becomes* Barkis's soul: 'For where your treasure is, there will be your heart also' (*Matt.* 6:21).  As Mr. Blackboy slips aboard Israel's lion-roaring ark, the '*black* barge;' as he looks from the black-eyed Mr. Murdstone; and from Salem House in *Black*heath, which sees the spiritual scourging of the Master; and from the works of Mr. Micawber's favorite jurist in his era of serving Heep, Justice *Black*stone (and black*stone*), so he steals into the fold of Barkis, turning him into something perilously like a Devil's Bark(is) of a boat.  The characters on the fatal box may be faded and scarcely legible, but when he comes, Mr. Blackboy will know his own.

Peggotty's slide-open St. Paul's box has Heavenly reference.  But Barkis's box held in trust for Mr. Blackboy tells a tale of Paradise Lost.  This we discover after the carrier's passing when David examines the con-tents, unseen til then, and reports: 'He had hoarded, all these years, I found, to good purpose.  His property in money amounted to nearly three thousand pounds' (447).  Nearly *three,* three, like 'near,' once again, tolling in mournful irony.  Barkis falls short of 'three,' i.e., Christian arrival.  What does David mean saying that Barkis hoarded to *good* purpose?  The irony of his own words escapes him, probably because he is now a lawyer.  In a Steerforth era of false directions, David is fatuous, priggish, and blind:

> I felt myself quite a proctor when I read this document aloud with all pos-
> sible ceremony, and set forth its provisions, any number of times, to those
> whom they concerned. I began to think there was more in the Commons than
> I had supposed. I examined the will with the deepest attention, pronounced it
> perfectly formal in all respects, made a pencil-mark or so in the margin, and
> thought it rather extraordinary that I knew so much. (447)

This light but pointed satire at David's expense takes the measure of all
fussy, futile legalism of mind indifferent to anything beyond the narrow
limits of the 'perfectly formal.'

The Blackboy temptation dogs David, too. Knocking at Dora Spenlow's
door, soon after, he panics and has 'some flurried thought of asking if that
were Mr. Blackboy's (in imitation of poor Barkis), begging pardon, and
retreating' (487). In a way, the lawyer's residence in which demon Jorkins
and Jane Murdstone come and go *is* Mr. Blackboy's. One half wishes
David *would* cut and run. There are signs that courting Dora is a mistake.
For example, David once rides so close to her carriage that his horse grazes
a foreleg against the wheel, which "took the bark off,' as his owner told
me, 'to the tune of three pun' sivin'—which I paid, and thought extremely
cheap for so much joy' (488), David says. *Three* and *seven* and 'tree'
(horse) stripped of 'bark' seem a heavy loss, a blow to 'the journey,' whatever David in his love delirium thinks, as 'pun'' alerts to double meaning.

Aside from 'nearly three thousand pounds' (no embezzled Heavens in
Dickens), the box holds other objects amassed in a hoarding lifetime. One,
an oyster-shell, gives pause:

> From the circumstance of the latter article having been much polished, and
> displaying prismatic colours on the inside, I conclude that Mr. Barkis had
> some general ideas about pearls, which never resolved themselves into any-
> thing definite. (447)

What 'general ideas about pearls' entered that slow mollusk of a mind
whilst Barkis lived? Perhaps only schemes of wealth, of dredging up
pearls in coral seas. Ah, but perhaps something quite different The lingering description, the suggestive haze of language ('*some* general ideas about
pearls,' so oddly teasing), plus the fact that Barkis saves, not a pearl but
only the single empty shell, may imply that, like the merchantman of the
parable, Barkis in *Clara* time felt within stirrings of desire for 'the pearl,'
the Kingdom of Heaven. We picture him sitting, slowly polishing the shell
to high lustre. Suddenly poor Barkis seems no Blackboy's disciple, but a
Dante manqué, the journeying bark of the soul come within inches and els of
its salvation, but, like a Barkis in the night, passing it by.

Barkis's Blackboy box also holds a piece of camphor. Foolish man, wag-
ing losing battles against ravaging Time, laying up treasure in earthly beds
'where moth and rust do corrupt.' Camphor is no match for moths in the

end. The Dickens fiction teems with Midas-like souls like Barkis; Scrooge; Mr. Dombey; old Nickleby; Nicodemus Boffin, the Golden Dustman; Julia Mills, up to her ears in gold; Mr. Dorrit, in debtors' prison exacting paupers' 'tributes;' and teems with villains like the fortune-hunter, Jingle (*Pickwick*), deafened to higher calls by 'the jingle of little worldly things' (LD,546). But God is not bought or mocked; there is no reaching after Heaven with a tight fist. In Dickens as in Scripture, it is only in renouncing wealth and losing the whole world, as Pip finally does, that man gains the Kingdom of his soul. Money is well used when Cheerybly, charitably used to raise up the fallen, as Emily does Martha, 'for Christ's sake.' Barkis's heavy misinvestment and its possible eternal cost are matters much on Dickens's mind.

The box contains still other mute, touching tokens of dreams of 'the journey.' A horseshoe: for luck? for the road?; an imitation lemon filled with tiny cups and saucers, which David intuits Barkis bought for him as a child, but could not bring himself to part with. If 'By their fruits ye shall know them,' the hoarded lemon is sour enough. Also the gold watch Barkis wore on his wedding day, and never again. He hid it away, and with it, man's best reminder of the ticking on of time to eternity, and of the need to watch, lest coming suddenly He find him sleeping.

How bright Hope shone upon Barkis's wedding day! Barkis *is* willing, which is where all journeys to Heaven begin. That day, all looks up. At night, Barkis drives the wedding party while David, his faithful intercessor with the bride, recall, holds forth on 'the subject of stars' (147). And, no doubt, the Star of David. If anyone can get droopy, slouch-forward Barkis to raise his eyes, the son of David can. David says of the stars: 'I was their chief exponent, and opened Mr. Barkis's mind to an amazing extent' (147). To pry open that closed bivalve of a mind—awesome oyster-knife work and accomplishment! Barkis is twice blessed, flanked by David and Clara. In his appreciation, he dubs David 'a young Roeshus' (147), or Roscius, the famous Roman actor of ancient time. O comic blunder, assigning the Christ-prefiguring genius of 'David' to, of all antipathetic strains, Rome!

If Barkis is willin' and *nihil obstat,* then what impedes? How does Blackboy first get a foothold in his life? It must be the B*ark*is at the core, the deep-dyed B.C. mentality that never gets beyond some general ideas about oysters to the heart of the matter, the pearl. Barkis is weighed down by his box even as Judaism by its like jealously hidden-away Holy of Holies, the *ark*. Hence the fixity in Blunderstone-Yarmouth *blunder-Yah* stages of the journey, and minimal interest in what lies beyond. Like ancient Israel stolidified around its ark of the covenant, the law, Barkis is living (more dead than alive, but to be charitable) proof of what an ark instead of a heart at the core does to man.

The ark in bARKis glares as he proves a punisher of the worthy, specifically the Christian. Once, Peggotty, who has been walking near her

mistress's new grave, gets into Barkis's cart weeping, her handkerchief at
her eyes. While she weeps, Barkis 'gave no sign of life whatever,' but 'sat
in his usual place and attitude, like a great stuffed figure' (137). Slowly
Peggotty regains her composure:

> 'Peggotty is quite comfortable now, Mr. Barkis,' I remarked, for his satis-
> faction.
> 'Is she, though?' said Mr. Barkis.
> After reflecting about it, with a sagacious air, Mr. Barkis eyed her, and
> said:
> '*Are* you pretty comfortable?'
> Peggotty laughed, and answered in the affirmative.
> 'But really and truly, you know. Are you?' growled Mr. Barkis, sliding
> nearer to her on the seat, and nudging her with his elbow. 'Are you? Really
> and truly, pretty comfortable? Are you? Eh?' At each of these inquiries Mr.
> Barkis shuffled nearer to her, and gave her another nudge; so that at last we
> were all crowded together in the left-hand corner of the cart, and I was so
> squeezed that I could hardly bear it. (137)

Providence intervenes. 'Peggotty calling attention to my sufferings, Mr.
Barkis gave me a little more room at once, and got away by degrees' (137).
Soon, though, he is bearing down again as hard as ever, still inquiring in
his obtuse way: 'Are you pretty comfortable, though?' (137) So did Israel
journey on with its *ark,* feeling the crushing mercy and 'comfort' of Yah's
ambiguous 'love.' Barkis reacts not at all to Peggotty's tears. By contrast, one recalls Agnes's holy rain of tears, recalling Christ Who wept for a
parting between the living and the dead.

So Barkis, with that central ton in him, cannot go all the way. In emblematic form, the problem is expressed as follows:

> 'It's a beautiful day, Mr. Barkis!' I said, as an act of politeness.
> 'It ain't bad,' said Mr. Barkis, who generally qualified his speech, and
> rarely committed himself. (137)

Ah, but the way, the truth, and the life require a (pun) commitment, a rare
one, too.

Where the ark is, Yah and El are not far behind. Sure enough, the
message 'Barkis is willin'' is delivered to David in the old 'comforting'
way, 'with a nudge of his elbow that gave me quite a stitch in my side'
(108). Likewise, Barkis inquires after Peggotty's comfort, in that celebrated way, while 'nudging her with his elbow' (137), and with yet
'another nudge' (138). He swallows a cake Peggotty made for David in one
huge gulp, 'like an elephant' (64). The elbow-elephant activity in Barkis
(and Omer) (vis. Chapter X) precincts is truly remarkable. To wit.:

> As this was a great deal for the carrier (whose name was Mr. Barkis) to

say—he being, as I observed in a former chapter, of a phlegmatic temperament, and not at all conversational—I offered him a cake as a mark of attention, which he ate at one gulp, exactly like an elephant, and which made no
more impression on his big face than it would have done on an elephant's. (64)

If Dickens did indeed build EL, the Hebrew God, into his 'Waterbrooks of
Ely-place' theme, (vis. Chapter V) then very possibly he lit on *el* of *el*bow
and *el*ephant (note: both are carefully repeated more than twice) with
delight. Like EL, Ancient of Days, Barkis, heavily intending to make those
in his keeping comfortable, knows not what (H)e does to the sons of David
and Light.

The name 'Barkis' hides meaning within meaning, like a nest of Chinese
boxes, in the Markham-Markleham way. Besides ark, there is *bark*, both
of ship and tree. If Barkis is indeed the 'bark,' or unliving outer husk of
the living tree, that would explain his unusual, acquisitive interest in apple
cheeks, arms, and parsties. Bloomless Barkis aspires to bloom:

> 'You look very well, Mr. Barkis,' I said, thinking he would like to know it.
> Mr. Barkis rubbed his cheek with his cuff, and then looked at his cuff as if
> he expected to find some of the bloom upon it; but made no other acknowledg-
> ment of the compliment. (107)

On his wedding day, Barkis *does* bloom!:

> Peggotty was dressed as usual, in her neat and quiet mourning; but Mr.
> Barkis bloomed in a new blue coat....His bright buttons, too, were of the
> largest size. (145)

If 'buttons,' as we suggested before, are also buds, then what a riot of
bloom is this. A bark weighed down by a stone ark cannot make much
headway; the bark of the tree of the Kingdom cannot bloom. But by
Heaven's light, all is possible.

Alas, Barkis's blooming time is short. Soon an ailing Barkis, his carrier
days over, removes the box from the cart and hides it under his invalid's
bed. Watched by a compassionate but helpless Peggotty, he now pursues
a grotesque career of twisting pain-wracked rheumatic limbs to get at the
box; endures 'a martyrdom' (309) in his Blackboy devotion to the box
concealed from all eyes. A league Nearer my God to Thee every hour, but
so little ready. The NT says: 'No man, when he hath lighted a candle,
covereth it with a vessel, or putteth it under a bed; but setteth it on a
candlestick, that they which enter in may see the light' (*Luke* 8:16). But
that is just what Barkis does do, bed, box, and shining CLARA, or candle.

The wonder is that, even so, *Barkis is willin'!* Even as he clings to lies
and to the box (increasingly a symbolic coffin), he clings as tenaciously to
memories of the old days on the road, David, and the happy time he was

first willing.  Visiting his old friend, David finds him too stiff in the joints even to shake hands.  But he speaks, and in what he says flashes the Dark (*Black*boy) and Light ('Clara') dispositions of his Old way-New way soul:

> When I sat down by the side of the bed, he said that it did him a world of good to feel as if he was driving me on the Blunderstone road again.  As he lay in bed, face upward, and so covered, with that exception, that he seemed to be nothing but a face—like a conventional cherubim—he looked the queerest object I ever beheld.
>
>   'What name was it as I wrote up in the cart, sir?' said Mr. Barkis, with a slow rheumatic smile.
>   'Ah!  Mr. Barkis, we had some grave talks about that matter, hadn't we?'
>   'I was willin' a long time, sir?' said Mr. Barkis.
>   'A long time,' said I.
>   'And I don't regret it,' said Mr. Barkis.  'Do you remember what you told me once, about making all the apple parsties and doing all the cooking?'
>   'Yes, very well,' I returned.
>   'It was as true,' said Mr. Barkis, 'as turnips is.  It was as true,' said Mr. Barkis, nodding his nightcap, which was his only means of emphasis, 'as taxes is.  And nothing's truer than them.'
>   Mr. Barkis turned his eyes upon me, as if for my assent to this result of his reflections in bed; and I gave it.
>   'Nothing's truer than them,' repeated Mr. Barkis; 'a man as poor as I am, finds out that in his mind when he's laid up.  I'm a very poor man, sir!'
>   'I am sorry to hear it, Mr. Barkis.'
>   'A very poor man, indeed I am,' said Mr. Barkis. (308)

Yes, Barkis is poor, for all his nearly three thousand pounds; how poor he will never know.  Never having forsaken treasure of earth and become a Poor Traveller, he is poor.  Too rich and pontifical to boot, he is also not poor enough.  His sententious proclamation of turnips and taxes as the truest truths shows that 'reflections in bed' reflect everything but Light.  The lying in bed, lying face upward unable to move, burial in bedclothes and nightcap all suggest the corpse to be.  Yet how unready the spirit to meet its Maker.  Though he praises Peggotty, it is as a Lady Bountiful of apple parsties more than anything else; to him she is more substance and source of comfort than spirit.  His very way of alluding to her, 'C.P. Barkis,' is heavy on the Barkis, light on the Clara, or light.  Poor Barkis, indeed.  And yet, for one moment he is back on the road and offering up to his confessor, the son of David, an eager: 'I was willin' a long time, sir?' which receives the absolution of: 'A long time.'

'Poor' Barkis recalls Dickens's *The Poor Relation's Story* in which the hero leaves the house of his heartless Uncle Chill and weds his beloved Christiana, a shining allegory of man's turning from bleak, comfortless (*Chill*) OT expectations to a new (NT) life of joy untold with *Christiana,* even Christ.  He loses former Expectations of Uncle Chill: 'But, having

Christiana's love, I wanted nothing upon earth' (CS,33). So man comes to look past this world ('wanted nothing upon earth') to Heaven, in which journey of hope his helpmeet is Christ. The story has a happy ending. 'My Castle is in the Air!' (39), capital letters helping celebrate arrival in Heaven. But one must be a 'poor relation,' willing to forsake Blackboy-Chill inheritances of earth. And Barkis is not.

Then comes that equal foot at all men's doors: Death arrives betimes for Barkis. Delayed by Steerforth (how true, vis à vis eternal appointments too), David arrives in Yarmouth to see Barkis a last time. Waiting before the kitchen-fire, David feels the solemn hush of death around him. Then Peggotty enters, embraces and blesses him for coming:

> She then entreated me to come up-stairs, sobbing that Mr. Barkis had always liked me and admired me; that he had often talked of me, before he fell into a stupor; and that she believed, in case of his coming to himself again, he would brighten up at sight of me, if he could brighten up at any earthly thing. (444)

We hold our breath. *Will* Barkis come to himself again, that better self, and 'brighten up' at last, as bright looks to Christian Light?

David climbs the stairs, and finds Barkis:

> The probability of his ever doing so [brightening up], appeared to me, when I saw him, to be very small. He was lying with his head and shoulders out of bed, in an uncomfortable attitude, half resting on the box which had cost him so much pain and trouble. I learned that, when he was past creeping out of bed to open it, and past assuring himself of its safety by means of the divining rod I had seen him use, he had required to have it placed on the chair at the bedside, where he had ever since embraced it, night and day. His arm lay on it now. Time and the world were slipping from beneath him, but the box was there: and the last words he had uttered were (in an explanatory tone) 'Old clothes!' (444)

One recalls an earlier conversation between David and Barkis:

> 'Old clothes,' said Mr. Barkis.
> 'Oh!' said I.
> 'I wish it was Money, sir,' said Mr. Barkis.
> 'I wish it was, indeed,' said I.
> 'But it AIN'T,' said Mr. Barkis, opening both his eyes as wide as he possibly could. (309)

*Old clothes,* in Biblical as in Carlylean metaphor, symbolizes the B.C. garment of the soul. In *Dombey and Son,* a novel of the *Copperfield* era, the metaphor, as we saw in Chapter III, appears:

> The old, old fashion! The fashion that came in with our first garments, and will last unchanged until our race has run its course, and the wide

firmament is rolled up like a scroll.  The old, old fashion—Death!

In the same breath, Dickens looks away from Death to hope of Heaven:

> Oh thank GOD, all who see it, for that older fashion yet, of Immortality!
> And look upon us, angels of young children, with regards not quite estranged,
> when the swift river bears us to the ocean! (226)

As Barkis, in great pain, fishes for his box with a divining rod, one thinks
that 'divining' (pun) is no route to the divine.  Barkis the Diviner embraces
the box 'night and day.'  One perhaps thinks of Dickens's advice to his two
sons, Edward and Henry, about saying a Christian prayer night and
morning. (vis. Chapter II)  Time and the world are slipping from him, yet
Barkis repeats the bald-faced, infernal lie: 'Old clothes!'  Only it is no lie.
His heap has shaped the garment of his soul: 'the old, old fashion, Death.'
   Why does Barkis fail when a Christian Providence smiles so broadly on
his life?  For although 'Barkis is willin'' is possibly the least lover-like
proposal on record, Peggotty understands and accepts him.  At first Barkis
thinks no answer will come.  Told this, little David is astonished:

> 'There was an answer expected, was there, Mr. Barkis?' said I, opening my
> eyes.  For this was a new light to me. (107)

Man 'expects;' the era of great Expectations is born, 'a new light.'  The
brightness increases.  In the disclosure: 'Her christian name is Clara,'
Barkis seems to find 'an immense fund of reflection' (108).  Soon we learn
that Barkis's expectations are requited.  'It didn't come to an end there'
(138), Barkis confides to David.  Nor, in a Christian universe, does it end
with Death.  Clara Peggotty knows Barkis's shortcomings (Heaven knows
man's failings), but with infinite charity sees through all to the 'good, plain
creatur'' (139) beneath.  How sad that soon the 'immense fund' of spiritual
treasure, Heaven's grace won for the mere 'willing,' should be lost in a
passionate lust for worldly wealth.
   In other quarters of *Copperfield, willing* is accompanied by *able*.  Dan'l
Peggotty, who possesses even as he visits 'The Willing Mind,' adds to it a
readiness to leave all he has and travel to the ends of the earth seeking 'the
pearl.'  As David affirms:

> His was not a lazy trustfulness that hoped and did no more.  He had been a
> man of sturdy action all his life, and he knew that in all things wherein he
> wanted help he must do his own part faithfully, and help himself. (714)

Nor is 'lazy trustfulness' David Copperfield's way:

> My meaning is, that whatever I have tried to do in life, I hav tried with all my
> heart to do well; that whatever I have devoted myself to, I have devoted

myself to completely; that in great aims and in small, I have always been thoroughly in earnest. I have never believed it possible that any natural or improved ability can claim immunity from the companionship of the steady, plain, hard-working qualities, and hope to gain its end. There is no such thing as fulfillment on this earth. Such happy talent, and some fortunate opportunity, may form the two sides of the ladder on which some men may mount, but the rounds of that ladder must be made of stuff to stand wear and tear; and there is no substitute for thorough-going, ardent, and sincere earnestness. Never to put one hand to anything on which I could throw my whole self; and never to affect depreciation of my work, whatever it was; I find now, to have been my golden rules. (606)

From such 'golden rules,' it is not far to the Golden Rule. Barkis never journeys this way. How sad and ironic that with both a son of David *and* a Clara at his beck and call, surely all that Heaven allows, and then some, Barkis falls behind.

Dickens lights on some sad-funny sumbols of his plight, that of a man who comes to the very brink, then stops short. For example: 'He made up his mouth as if to whistle, but he didn't whistle' (64). His very horse obeys a summons to look alive: ''Then, come up,' said the carrier to the lazy horse; who came up accordingly' (63). But Barkis does not.

If an *ark* nature perplexes and retards, *Yah* forces also drag him down. Early in our story, Barkis, under orders from Mr. Murdstone, carries David and his box (!) into the inn-yard in Yarmouth:

> The coach was in the yard, shining very much all over, but without any horses to it as yet; and it looked in that state as if nothing was more unlikely than its ever going to London. I was thinking this, and wondering what would ultimately become of my box, which Mr. Barkis had put down on the yard-pavement by the pole (he having driven-up the yard to turn his cart), and also what would ultimately become of me, when a lady looked out of a bow-window where some fowls and joints of meat were hanging up, and said:
> 'Is that the little gentleman from Blunderstone?' (65)

*Yar*d is everywhere, in 'yard' and 'yard-pavement;' Dickens cannot cite it enough. It is Yah country for fair, with its hanging joints and the waiter in the Inn, who, under pretext of serving him, sees to David's comfort (he seems a malign version of Barkis in this) by robbing him of his dinner of chops, batter-pudding, and ale. He also tempts David's appetite by telling the story of Topsawyer's fall. So are man and boy served, batter-pudding'd, and toppled in Old Time.

Barkis is no sooner willing than he is handed Heaven on a silver platter, or half-shell. Shortly thereafter his carting days are over, and he is Barkis the carrier no more. Still, Dickens calls him 'the carrier,' prompting realization that every man is really a 'carrier,' carrying the seed of immortality within. Once upon a time, Barkis values what he carries, 'writing up,

inside the tilt of the cart, 'Clara Peggotty'—apparently as a private mem-
orandum' (108). With *Clara* inscribed in the upward or Heavenly slope,
how can he forget? (One thinks of the gold watch inscribed D.N.F., Do Not
Forget, the hero's legacy from his father in *Little Dorrit,* a watch like the
one in Barkis's box.) Yet, in privileged midsts of spiritual plenty, Barkis,
un-elephant-like, forgets. Ah, Barkis! Ah, humanity!

   In a long bed-ridden time, Barkis has ample time to think things over, to
reflect on where all signs say he is heading, and turn from the coffer-
coffin of Mr. Blackboy whilst this machine is to him Barkis. Yet his final
hour finds him making one last excruciating effort to embrace, not wife or
friend, but the box. The penultimate moment comes. 'Old clothes,' he
says, then, slipping away, becomes 'as mute and senseless as the box'
(445). But more is to come:

> We remained there, watching him, a long time—hours. What mysterious
> influence my presence had upon him in that state of his senses, I shall not pre-
> tend to say; but when he at last began to wander feebly, it is certain he was
> muttering about driving me to school.
>    'He's coming to himself,' said Peggotty.
>    Mr. Peggotty touched me, and whispered with much awe and reverence,
> 'They are both a-going out fast.'
>    'Barkis, my dear!' said Peggotty.
>    'C.P. Barkis,' he cried faintly. 'No better woman anywhere!'
>    'Look! Here's Master Davy!' said Peggotty. For he now opened his eyes.
>    I was on the point of asking him if he knew me, when he tried to stretch out
> his arms, and said to me, distinctly, with a pleasant smile:
>    'Barkis is willin'!'
>    And, it being low water, he went out with the tide. (445)

The 'mysterious influence' David has on the dying man, the power to turn
his wandering thoughts again to 'the journey,' is surely born of deep
spiritual ties to the Son of David. Suddenly Barkis is back 'on the road' in
the time he first beheld the Light in the good and faithful servant and
entrusted his Expectations to David's son. Smiling, he stretches out his
hand as if to grasp the vision of that happy time, pre-Blackboy time, when
he carried a little child to the starting-point to 'wherever it is.' Once more
he is the smiled-upon, favored Mr. Barkis of great expectations.

   Finally, where does Barkis stand vis à vis Eternity? Since Dickens does
not, one presumes to say. In Dickens, judgment is Heaven's part;[2] our
part, to look with Mr. Peggotty's own awe and reverence upon the mystery
of death, and with Dickens's own wide, smiling charity upon the carrier,
charity the more golden because it never looks away from truth. Ambiguity holds to the end. On the one hand, 'Barkis is willin',' falling short
by a final 'g' (for God?), is too easy a final self-absolution, it may be, considering all that remains unregretted and unchanged. Ark man could not

comprehend the glory sprung upon his sight, not Clara nor the Clar of all Claras and Clarrikers, Christ. Opening his eyes very wide, and never wider than when fibbing about 'Old clothes,' Barkis hardly sees a thing worth seeing. In B.C., hope of the Kingdom bloomed, but only briefly, feebly, proving more Bark than bloom. When Martha Endell's courage fails and she considers suicide, David opposes her aim:

> 'In the name of the great Judge,' said I, 'before whom you and all of us must stand at His dread time, dismiss that terrible idea! We can all do some good, if we will.'

'Will' and 'willing' imply directed action on behalf of the good. What then shall we think of Barkis who confronts with such simple, smiling serenity and perilous innocence, in his last hour, what other men confront with such mingled hope, dread, and awe?

On the other hand, much is owed Barkis, type of ark man, the B.C. consciousness which, for all its stolidity, groped towards the Light, and played carrier to that which was greater than itself.

Mercifully, we are spared the sight of Mr. Blackboy arriving to claim his own. Perhaps he never does. On the hopeful note of 'willing,' the Barkis story ends. Who could frown upon so perfect a child-like faith as Barkis's in an infinity of renewable beginnings? If, knowing full well how 'comfortable' she is likely to be, Peggotty even so takes Barkis for her own, then perhaps the Recording Angel, standing on the far shore, will take that outstretched hand, and suppressing a sigh, charitably allow that 'Heaven is willin',' too.

# TEN
# Mr. Omer

'And by that sort of thing we very often lose a little mint of money,' said Mr. Omer. 'But fashions are like human beings. They come in, nobody knows when, why, or how; and they go out, nobody knows when, why, or how. Everything is like life, in my opinion, if you look at it in that point of view.' (DC,125)

'OMER, DRAPER, TAILOR, HABERDASHER, FUNERAL FURNISHER, & C.' (125), reads the sign on Mr. Omer's shop in Yarmouth by the sea. Doubtless other work is done there too, but all we see is trade in coffins and mourning clothes: Barkis's 'old clothes' for the old, old fashion in mortal dress, the contents of the old box, Death.

Behold Mr. Omer, the shop's proprietor, merry as a grig and presiding over all. The vivid contrast between mirthful man and mournful métier intrigues us, as it is surely meant to do. The name 'Omer' is intriguing also. Like *Joram,* a most odd name for a true-born Englishman. But there is nothing unaccountable about either *Omer* or *Joram* in allegory in which the great secret of OMER explodes in gleeful laughter as irrepressible as Mr. Omer's own.

To recall a minor figure like Mr. Omer at all is to remember the point constantly made about his failing wind. He comes upon the scene 'a fat, short-winded, merry-looking, little old man in black, with rusty little bunches of ribbons at the knees of his breeches, black stockings, and a broad-brimmed hat' (124). 'Short-winded' is promptly verified as Omer comes 'puffing up to the coach-window' (124), out of breath. On David's next visit, Omer is visibly 'more short-winded than of yore' (303). Wind—breath, the peril of losing it, its being in short supply—emerges as the great Omeric theme:

'I'm not more self-interested, I hope, than another man,' said Mr. Omer. 'Look at me! My wind may fail me at any moment, and it ain't likely that, to my own knowledge, I'd be self-interested under such circumstances. I say it

ain't likely, in a man who knows his wind will go, when it *does* go, as if a pair
of bellows was cut open: and that man a grandfather,' said Mr. Omer. (439)

How simple, naive, and child-like Mr. Omer is. 'Look at me!' frankly and
cheerily invites inspection, and looking, one sees at a glance pretty much
all there is to see. Losing wind at a great rate, Omer apparently regards
himself offhandedly as not much more complicated than 'a pair of bellows,'
a wind-making machine. True, he is not 'self-interested,' as he twice
states. Indeed, Mr. Omer seems only marginally aware that he *is* a human
self, regarding himself more as an apparatus, a pair of lungs.

Gamely recovering, enduring bout after bout in an 'ineffectual struggle'
(305) to recapture an elusive, unrecapturable wind, expiring steadily, he
blandly foresees the end up ahead: a sudden 'cut open,' then curtains.
This fate he contemplates with perfect directness and equanimity from our
first glimpse of him to the last. A dismal prospect, one would think, yet
Mr. Omer never bats an eye. He even puns gaily, à la Dickens, about his
shortness of breath and fast-failing wind: 'And so, young gentlemen, that
you may not consider me long-winded as well as short-breathed....' (306)

Omer wages an epic battle for his never-for-long-recapturable wind. He
is spied 'recruit[ing] his wind by the aid of his pipe' (439); and 'very much
out of breath, gasping at his pipe as if it contained a supply of that necessary, without which he must perish' (438). He is on the wrong track there;
his sense of cures is pretty primitive, we see. The most remarkable thing
about the dying wind is Omer's perfect imperturbability about it all. He
must know from past experience that jokes bring on laughter, and
laughter, wheezing, gasping, more shortness of breath. Yet he goes on
enjoying his innocent little pleasantries, which are hardly as funny as he
obviously finds them, paying dearly for every one with such fits of panting
as almost topple him behind the counter. Yet a moment later he is as
usual; no one would guess that a near death-throe lay minutes behind.

Emotional evenness—one bluff, changeless mien—is the key to the good
old soul's King Cole temperament. Mr. Omer is nothing if not a stoic:

'Oh! nothing to grumble at, you know,' said Mr. Omer. 'I find my breath
gets short, but it seldom gets longer as a man gets older. I take it as it comes,
and make the most of it. That's the best way, ain't it?' (304)

Pleased as a boy to be attended to and understood—as if anything he said
was at all hard to grasp!—Mr. Omer exults: 'I believe my breath will get
long next, my memory's getting so much so' (305). Grand optimism
indeed in the face of the grave matter of a fast-failing wind.

Who is this plucky, bubbling little old man in rusty ribbons in a 'close
and stifling little shop' (125) in a narrow street, one dressed like some
antiquated ('rusty') country gentleman in Fielding or Smollett and bounc-
ing undaunted from breathtaking adventure to adventure—who but a

Child's History version of Homer?  Mr. (H)*omer* is a brightly colored, poster-size portrait of Homer; and the insoluble problem of a failing wind, the old Aeolus dilemma—Agamemnon faced it, Odysseus faced it—the ancient Greek perplexity born of a total dependency on Nature.  Like Homeric, Omeric man is wholly at the mercy of inconstant winds, seas, fate.

This Omer knows perfectly well and accepts.  There never was such a comfortable fatalist on the subject of life and death as Mr. Omer, except, perhaps, Mr. Homer.  In his seaside armchair life full of teapot-size rough and tumble centering on a 'wind,' Omer is the liveliest of onlookers at and gossipy chroniclers of events in Yarmouth, that provincial seaport where many old echoes and ideas linger so long it might be a preserve of B.C.  Here, overseeing the bustling Funeral Furnishing business, Omer remains preoccupied with an unruly wind, the same obstacle to safe homecoming it was in *Odyssey* times of the world's soul.

Mr. Omer thus symbolizes man immersed in and wholly subject to physical forces in Nature beyond his control.  Yet while in this unenviable position, he never complains.  It is as if he had never once even entertained the idea that man has a destiny not only *in* but beyond Nature:  has the 'breath,' divine afflatus, spirit within that leaves lungs and global winds and seas behind, an immortal soul to outsoar our mortal night and be exhaled skyward again.

This philosophical gap belongs to the Homeric Greek world too.  Omer's flat, incurious, unnuanced: 'I take it as it comes' sounds very like Odysseus's: 'Our lives are as the days are, dark or bright.'  No excess of speculation here; no exaltation or 'aspiration,' in either sense of the word, in this practical, easy-going, genial and simplistic view.  With sturdy-minded Omer we are instantly back in the clear, sunny Greek morning of Western man when mankind's biggest problem was external Nature, and life far closer to physics than metaphysics, the very gods only projections of the forces of Nature and weighted to earth with human attributes.  Not the later Greek age of Steerforth, more self-conscious, polished, inclining to decadence, but the earlier and, to Dickens, clearly more wholesome, hearty, epic time of that indomitable voice of courage in the face of adversity, of swift recovery from disaster, and the energizing, ceaseless battle of life, Homer.

While Mr. Omer is a most attractive figure, his scope is decidedly small.  In his quaint little shop and life, he reflects the limitations a Christian like Dickens could not but see in the ancient Greek world view, especially a pervasive lack of interest in, an incapacity for serious, sustained consideration of the great, burning questions of existence, the mystery of Being.  Omer has no tragic muse!  In the always busy, prosperous, crowded, intensely physical domain of *Omer and Joram*, i.e., early Greek and Hebrew time, all is rush, bustle, light-hearted palaver over shrouds and coffins, with no one paying the least attention to the 'old tune' playing out back, the sombre 'RAT-tat-tat' that, in David's words, never *does* leave off. OMER & C. bundles bodies off to Eternity with nary an afterthought or care. In the Omeric world there are no memories or echoes, except of physical fact. After a quick shake and shrug, it is up and off again on the next adventure.

At *Omer and Joram's* no one is exactly unkind. It's just that no one notices or sees. Not a soul running around the shop tries to comfort a small child, David, sitting grief-stricken and alone, waiting to be measured for mourning. Here is glimpsed the essential failing, as Dickens saw it, in an otherwise not unattractive cosmic view—it remained unaware of the higher and lower reaches and destinies of the soul, it steered past mystery. Whatever its Mysteries were, it lacked the symbolic second sight which registers objects in Nature like wind as emblems of the eternal.

In short, it is without the concept of a transcendent God. This idea dawns on the reader on the sad occasion of David's first visit to the shop as a not unkind but yet wonderfully oblivious Mr. Omer appears and takes charge:

> I preceded Mr. Omer, in compliance with his request; and after showing me a roll of cloth which he said was extra super, and too good mourning for anything short of parents, he took my various dimensions, and put them down in a book. While he was recording them he called my attention to his stock and trade, and to certain fashions which he said had 'just come up,' and to certain other fashions which he said had 'just gone out.'
>
> 'And by that sort of thing we very often lose a little mint of money,' said Mr. Omer. 'But fashions are like human beings. They come in, nobody knows when, why, or how; and they go out, nobody knows when, why, or how. Everything is like life, in my opinion, if you look at it in that point of view.' (125)

But no! By Dickensian lights Omer is wholly wrong. Human life does *not* drift in and out like fashions and tides in an essentially blind, mechanical, ultimately meaningless way. Mr. Omer's is clearly a universe without a benign overarching Providence and scheme of salvation; whereas the Dickens Christian universe, if the reader will forgive its being said one more time, stands solidly upon the faith in one human 'fashion' that never goes out of style, 'that older fashion yet, of Immortality!' (DS,226) If Barkis clings to the rags of 'old clothes' and Omer to a nihilism of 'fashions,' it is because each dwells morally as physically in Yarmouth, realm of B.C. and Death Eternal.

Mr. Omer's speech shows him to be short-sighted in other ways as well. Assigning grades to mourning attire, the 'best' only for parents, Omer is not unlike Camilla Pocket in *Great Expectations* in her priggish insistence that children in mourning for a mother wear proper ceremonial frills, the deepest of trimming, a formalism that drives Matthew Pocket wild with despair. Not that kindly Mr. Omer is in any way the creature of law, punctilio and orthodoxy that Camilla is. Yet, as such detail implies, both Hebrew and Greek stress clan or tribe, founding societies on the divisions among men. A 'close and stifling' little shop and world outlook, too. Further, note the reifying force of Mr. Omer's words about mourning wear too good 'for anything short of parents.' *'Thing,'* not 'one.' It hardly matters, and yet the human is faintly slighted, submerged. The dimensions Omer is good at are physical ones; he never goes beyond what is measurable in inches, feet and yards.

The Omeric eye sees no further than the Heraclitan flux governing all. Its unawed sense of death, of men coming and going, 'nobody knows when, why, or how,' may well recall the monotonous leaf-fall of souls in pagan underworlds in the *Odyssey* and the *Aeneid*. The words reflect the weariness of generation and undifferentiation in death, the 'Tithonus' quality of: 'Man comes and tills the soil and lies beneath' that filled ancient time. In Dante's *Inferno* too, the anonymus fall into oblivion of the damned is stressed, and more tragic still because this is not pagan but Christian time, and souls undergoing a B.C.-like extinction in the second death need not have perished at all, but could have clung evergreen to the Christological tree for all Eternity.

No Christian speaks Omer's speech about the planless, arbitrary nature of life and death. *For Omer* life is this procession in and out: a brief straying impassioned in the littering leaves, as the poet says, a 'com[ing] up' like the sun and dropping back below the verge into darkness, both rising and sinking signifying nothing. Entering *Omer and Joram's,* one re-enters Homer's world and OT time; one might be literally doing just that, for all that there is anything post-B.C., Christian, person-distinguishing in the place. Here it is always business as usual, quite as if the shop and everyone in it busily snipping, chatting, hammering away inside were not situated in the shadow of the always dimly rumbling volcano, Death. All are, yet not one hearkens to the sound, or, looking up, notices a warning wisp of smoke.

Whenever David leaves Mr. Omer's shop, he returns to the very different though neighboring world of Judaeo-Christian time. He has only to step across to Peggotty's or her brother's houses to be instantly caught up in worlds of powerful emotion, shattering loss and recovery, soul-stirring, transfiguring spiritual adventure, and a sense of the enormity of arrival and departure temporal and eternal that fills all, even so small a moment as:

> 'Peggotty!' I cried to her.
> She cried, 'My darling boy!' and we both burst into tears, and were locked in one another's arms. (307)

In 'Hebrew' parts of Yarmouth, death is mighty and awful: is 'that great Visitor, before whose presence all the living must give place' (438); 'that dread surprise' before which 'all other changes and surprises dwindle into nothing' (442). In 'Greek' time, however, only the physical facts of death exist. And such is the stolid, complacent, amiable indifferentism in Omer's realm that not even the ceaseless traffic in death, reminder perpetual that to this end all must come, makes the least dent.

Mr. Omer's 'Everything is like life, in my opinion' means that the old sage has a taste for philosophy, a simple one, as the rudimentary simile shows. But, ironically, he never nears the purpose of all philosophy: the examination of the great questions of Being. The point is made again in Omer's 'if you look at it in that point of view.' *In*, not 'from,' for here is more inlook than outlook. Immersed *in* matter, physical reality, Mr. Omer cannot think outside of world, death, and time.

Famous Homeric and other Greek motifs flash in and out as Dickens cartoons along. For one, in the little back-parlour of the shop (back, back in space and time, too) amid smells of warm black crepe sit 'three young women at work on a quantity of black materials, which were heaped upon the table' (125). And again: 'The three young women, who appeared to be very industrious and comfortable, raised their heads to look at me, and then went on with their work. Stitch, Stitch, Stitch' (125). Nameless, faceless, heads raised as one, the three Stitchers have an uncanny, mythic air. With the capital 'S' so relentlessly repeated, they seem types of the Three Fates, joiners and cutters of the thread of life. Here is the three-in-one Trinity of death of Time B.C., all of *three* man has without hope of the Resurrection and the Life. Black garments and filled coffins flowing in a steady stream from *Omer and Joram's*, black piles 'heaped' adding one more jot of death, signify the triumph of the old, old fashion, oblivious Death.

Greek myth also looks up as Mr. Omer and his daughter discuss the ostracism of little Em'ly in Yarmouth:

'Em'ly's her name,' said Mr. Omer, 'and she's little too. But if you'll believe me, she has such a face of her own that half the women in this town are mad against her.'

'Nonsense, father!' cried Minnie.

'My dear,' said Mr. Omer, 'I don't say it's the case with you,' winking at me, 'but I say that half the women in Yarmouth, ah! and in five mile round, are mad against that girl.'

'Then she should have kept to her own station in life, father,' said Minnie, 'and not given them any hold to talk about her, and then they couldn't have done it!

'Couldn't have done it, my dear!' retorted Mr. Omer. 'Couldn't have done it! Is that *your* knowledge of life? What is there that any woman couldn't do, that she shouldn't do—especially on the subject of another woman's good looks?' (305)

Women raging 'mad' against another woman, disclosing unsounded depths of fury in the female breast, is a subject about which Omer, innocent as he seems, appears to know a thing or two.  Warming to it, he is so overwhelmed that he collapses coughing, and the ensuing struggle to recover his wind is monumental in scope.  It is as if he explodes from the effort to suppress a vast fund of knowledge on the subject of the world-shaking consequences of a woman's beauty.

What knocks the wind out of Omer?  Is it not the vestigial Homeric Greek rivers of experience of passion surging within, still so mighty that they promptly launch an impromptu Aeolus adventure, sending Omer off in search of his 'wind'?  Omer is perhaps thinking of the beauty of Helen, the raging madness of the Bacchae, Phaedre, Medea, the whole realm of raw passion so far beyond brittle categories of 'couldn't' and 'shouldn't.'  As Omer disdainfully asks:  'Couldn't have done it?  Is that *your* knowledge of life?'  Implying that under the rusty ribbons and mellowness of age is a knowledge of the range of human experience that puts such tame notions to shame.

In Yarmouth by the sea two ancient cultures live on, stronger than the Christian present around them.  In the Hebrew, the flight of 'J' Steerforth with the treasure of the ark is a Judaeo-Christian adventure of 'the pearl.'  But in the Greek, (and Steerforth, recall, is Ixions-Sybarite-Bacchanal), the illicit flight with the beauty becomes a type of the flight of Paris with another unhappy beauty, Helen.

Besides much attention to 'wind,' the endless, salty Omeric chatter turns on the subject of 'passages.'  'Passages' brings on gales of laughter which, again, Omer barely weathers:

> 'Will you take something?  A glass of srub and water, now?  I smoke on srub and water, myself,' said Mr. Omer, taking up his glass, 'because it's considered softening to the passages, by which this troublesome breath of mine gets into action.  But, Lord bless you,' said Mr. Omer, huskily, 'it ain't the passages that's out of order!  'Give me breath enough,' says I to my daughter Minnie, 'and *I'll* find passages enough, my dear.'
>
> He really had no breath to spare, and it was very alarming to see him laugh. (439)

Why on earth such laughter?  It is in allegory and only there that the answer lies.  Mr. Omer's solid confidence that, given wind enough, he'll find passages aplenty secretly applauds the indisputable fact that Homer did in truth have little trouble in finding epic 'passages' of both the poetic and watery kind!  Like *wind, passage*s is a huge pun.  With a good wind in the sails, there are poetic and nautical Homeric passages or seaways enough stored up in Omer, genial host to realms of mortality and tireless chronicler of life in a small provincial world beside the surging sea.  For him, armchair sailor, the great thing is to 'get into action.'  (As to a partiality to 'srub and water,' is the missing 'h' of *shrub* a tiny hint of the missing 'H' of *Homer?*)

Elsewhere, Dickens calls the Christ story 'the most solemn passage which our minds can ever approach' (OL, 8). One wonders if, stressing 'passages,' he is mindful of the missing Christian dimension in 'passage' in Omeric dilations upon the theme.

Like Homer, Omer looks to the sea, and to poetry. At heart an old salt, Omer has a marked sea-chantey taste in verse. With gusto, he reels off a line to illustrate what he means by saying that little Em'ly, visibly drooping, lacks 'heart': "'A long pull and a strong pull, and a pull altogether, my hearties, hurrah!'" (440) Mr. Omer hasn't the faintest idea of the meaning of 'heart' in its richer sense: the heart that loves, feels compassion, can be broken. Such heart pulses exist only on the Judaeo-Christian side of town. Omer's cure for all ills is pluck and strenuous doing. Says he: 'What I wish is, that parties was brought up stronger-minded' (439). *Parties*, like *thing*, is more of the unindividuating idiom of anonymity favored by Omer which reveals the pallor of his sense of clients, 'parties,' as people, individuals, souls.

The 'long pull, strong pull' poetry Mr. Omer quotes or spins might come straight from A Child's History of the *Odyssey*. Its broad flat rhythms recall those of: 'They come in, nobody knows when, why, or how; and they go out, nobody knows when, why, or how.' The cadences in both mime the simple ebb-flow cycles of Nature. The unshaded Omeric line is like the straight line of waves coming in and going out on a long beach; in it one hears the monotonous, soothing rhythms of the gainless cycles of Nature. Coordination and parallelism, the primal construction innocent of subordination or other syntactic nuance, match the eventless, repetitive horizontal of existence and the soul B.C. Hearing 'long, strong pull,' one can picture the faceless, identityless men that line the rowing benches in Greek epic and smite the sounding furrows on long-strong-pulling voyages until claimed by usually sudden, calamitous death. What endless Vallombrosan autumnal worlds of human wanwood leafmeal-lying now as then in parts of Christendom still more in fealty to Zeus or Jehovah than to Christ! Regarding the Omeric poetic, Dickens's imitation of Homer may not be the most fair or flattering ever devised; still, we know what he means.

At the mercy of fast-deteriorating lungs and limbs, Mr. Omer is in slightly worse shape on each of David's later visits. But only his physical condition changes. Otherwise he remains Omer, as dependably affable and full of chatter as he is short of height and depth. He clearly feels no jolts nor belated stirrings of soul as he nears his journey's end. Soul! The very word is out of place—dark, Hebraic, as from another world. Omeric man has enough to worry about with his wind, let alone the soul. He seems fine without one, toiling, gossiping, stating elementary conclusions about life with boyish glee, his chief concern the hardware of death: the trade of shipping bodies off to (to borrow Barkis's phrase) wherever it is. Dickens subtly implies that man did not inherit a soul, in the full sense of the word, until the time of the one God deepened his acquaintance with grief. Needing a reliance in the battle for a wind, Mr. Omer looks no farther than his pipe.

'A porpoise' (125), Minnie Omer calls her father. Just so—a simple, benign sea creature living half submerged in and not yet fully separated from brute Nature. It was not in the Greek genius of Homeric time to seek a rock to cling to in the midst of life's buffeting seas. Ruled by arbitrary gods like Aeolus and Poseidon, with only a thankless trip down to the shades as his reward in the end, Homeric man accepted good and bad with equal thanks, endured, and died. So does the Omeric hero down through time.

Omer and Joram become partners, and Joram marries Minnie. The partnership signifies that Greek (Omer) and Hebrew (Joram) shared and share one realm of death without a Redeemer. The two metaphysics are alike in other ways. Homer and the writers of the Old Testament tell a similar tale of bloody battle below and smitings of hapless man from Above, of raids on foes, live sacrifices to the deity to propitiate the always-overhanging divine wrath, whether of one god or many. 'Funeral Furnishing' is the common Greek-Hebrew theme. What piling up of bodies in all pre-Christian time! Both Zeus and Yahweh whet man's natural aggression; Poseidon is as vindictive a lord of the waves as is the Lord God of the drowning Flood.

The name 'OMER' has a Hebrew dimension too. By an amazing coincidence, as Omer looks to Homer, *omer* is also a Hebrew unit of measure. No wonder, then, that Mr. Omer is so devoted to measurements, and facts about inches and yards are so much in the forefront of his prosaic mind, as we see in the scene of David's first visit to the shop:

> 'I have been acquainted with you,' said Mr. Omer, after watching me for some minutes, during which I had not made much impression on the breakfast, for the black things destroyed my appetite, 'I have been acquainted with you a long time, my young friend.'
>
> 'Have you, sir?'
>
> 'All your life,' said Mr. Omer. 'I may say before it. I knew your father before you. He was five foot nine and a half, and he lays in five and twen-ty foot of ground.'
>
> 'RAT-tat-tat, RAT-tat-tat, RAT-tat-tat,' across the yard.
>
> 'He lays in five and twen-ty foot of ground, if he lays in a fraction,' said Mr. Omer, pleasantly. 'It was either his request or her direction, I forget which.'
>
> 'Do you know how my little brother is, sir?' I inquired.
>
> Mr. Omer shook his head.
>
> 'RAT—tat-tat, RAT—tat-tat, RAT—tat-tat.'
>
> 'He is in his mother's arms,' said he.

'Oh, poor little fellow!  Is he dead?'
'Don't mind it more than you can help,' said Mr. Omer.  'Yes.  The baby's dead.'
My wounds broke out afresh at this intelligence.  I left the scarcely tasted breakfast, and went and rested my head on another table in a corner of the little room, which Minnie hastily cleared, lest I should spot the mourning that was lying there with my tears. (126)

The contrast between Omer's and David's natures is marked.  Omer, to whom 'knowing' seems limited to measuring with a ruler, is tight shut to certain colors in the spiritual and emotional spectrums.  His telling David how his father lies in the grave—in what length of ground—and doing so 'pleasantly' is mildly shocking.  'Don't mind it more than you can help,' he advises.  The Omeric soul bears no wounds, if it can help it.  In the presence of Omer and Minnie, David is as good as alone with his grief.

As *Omer* spans two ancient realms, Greek and Hebrew, no wonder he gets a 'Jewish' son-in-law, Joram, and maintains such a lively interest in the 'Hebrews,' David, Barkis, and little Em'ly.  As he speaks, the ominous RAT-of graves tattoo, 'RAT—tat-tat' punctuates his words.  Nodding 'retrospectively' (304), Mr. Omer is literally nodding backwards at Time B.C. when man in death as in life wears 'the muddy vesture of our clay,' as Dickens in the now-familiar clothes metaphor elsewhere says. [1]

Not to disparage Mr. Omer—Dickens never does—he is and remains a worthy, sunny, even-tempered, bright-side character all his busy days of readying 'parties' for their last resting place in earth.  *Days* is just the word for it; there are no long dark nights of the (H)omeric soul.  Omer is not unkind; it just never occurs to him to comfort little David, any more than to seek comfort himself.  With all good intentions, his: 'My dear, would you like to see your—' (127), meaning 'your mother's coffin,' is shocking.  Minnie halts him in mid-line; cool as she generally is, even she senses this is going too far.  Not understanding, Omer acquiesces, explaining: 'I thought it might be agreeable, my dear.  But perhaps you're right' (127). *Agreeable?!*

He is as obtuse about little Em'ly, chatting about her woes with all the interest of a natural teller of tales.  It is hardly surprising that he cannot see far into the mystery of 'the pearl,' and can only pronounce Em'ly 'a little down and a little fluttered' (441).  Perhaps Dickens repeats 'a little' so we may fully savour the irony.  Em'ly is wildly distraught.  Not seeing this, Mr. Omer attributes Em'ly's troubled look to lack of heart, by which he means never-say-die gusto.  A grand vitality, optimism, pluck, and ready sympathy of sorts flow from Mr. Omer.  But with no tragic muse, he is, as fabled, blind.

'Minnie' Omer also has a part in the allegory.  Sharper than Omer, she has not half so good a heart as her father.  Minnie's haste to clear away the garments on the table lest David spot them with his tears (a nice irony: mourning finery too fine for tears) reveals her emotional limitations. Riding with Minnie and Joram in the van that holds his mother's coffin, David feels 'cast away among creatures with whom I had no community of nature' (128); their love-making and hilarity shock him. ('Cast away': the old seafaring leads to shipwreck on desert isles, or in desert Babylons of desertion.) After Em'ly's elopement Minnie judges her harshly. 'A deceitful, bad-hearted girl,' said Mrs. Joram. 'There was no good in her ever!' (459) That is the 'J' of 'Mrs. Joram' talking, the Hebrew bent for judgment. Minnie's 'if she hadn't, then they wouldn't' takes her measure; Omer, recall, challenges her narrow formula which falls so short of life.

Not that Minnie is bad. But there is a hardness in her not found in her father. Indeed, Omer dare not express sympathy for Martha Endell in front of Minnie for fear of a harsh retort. No, the ungenerous streak in Minnie is not inherited from the Omer of universal good will. There is no bent for judgment in *Omer,* the Greek way.

Where does it come from, then? From the 'Minnie' or Minerva, the Roman, side. We read: 'Minnie laughed, and stroked her banded hair upon her temples' (304). *Temples,* a pun, is everywhere in Dickensian neo-OT time—in Hebraic Temple Bar and in Mr. Creakle's 'overhanging temples'—and has a Roman meaning too. The banded hair on Minnie's temples gives her away; it is a staple of Greek and Roman statues of women and goddesses. In allegory, *Omer* fathers *Minnie:* the Greek gives rise to Roman culture. The Greek is genial and open to many currents. Though born of the Greek, the Roman is harder, more confined in spirit, with a bent for law ('hadn't,' 'wouldn't' formulas) and judgment which disposes it to the fatal alliance with Hebrew Law.

That alliance looms again in Dickens. In Minnie and Joram's union Rome and Israel marry again, posing the old threat to emerging Christian time. Mrs. Joram sits in judgment on the fallen woman who pitied another 'for Christ's sake.' She is and remains hostile to the mysteries of sin, suffering, and redemption embodied in 'the pearl,' lost in Omer-Joram time, and only in Christian experience recovered and secured.

As Omer's health declines, Minnie and Joram come more to the fore. Joram takes over the Funeral Furnishing trade in a time that Furnished Funerals aplenty beside the widow-making, child-unfathering deep, Yarmouth a symbol of the Yah-mouth of the Flood open wide to devour seafarers still adrift in B.C. The Greek (Omer) fades; the Roman-Hebrew (Minnie-Joram) inherits the business of Death. History records what Rome and Israel together made of their Father's business. And make still as heartless condemnation of the fallen—Minnie's of Martha and Em'ly—and the sound of 'RAT—tat-tat' of nails being driven into wood, echo of crucifixion, return to the world stage, no Christian sentiment or sound overcoming.

But Mr. Omer is no part of this. In Dickens as in history, the broad Greek spirit smiles on the nascent Christian and speeds it on its way. Mr. Omer is concerned about Em'ly, apprenticed to him for 'three years' (306), *three* never long out of sight of 'the pearl.' Omer is not one to hold her to the letter of a contract-bargain and releases her. 'Now, don't consider Em'ly nailed down in point of time' (441), he says. No 'nailing down,' i.e., bent for crucifixion, any more than for law, in the Greek spirit. Dickens honors the breath of sincere well-wishing that blew from failing Aeolian winds of the Greek towards the Christian. Moreover, from some Homeric authorial esprit de corps, it must be, Mr. Omer later applauds David's creative achievement, in Omer's words 'compact in three separate and indiwidual wollumes—one, two, three;' (734). Admiring the three-in-one work of a son of David, Omer hails coming Christian time. It is his pleasure to 'lay that book upon the table, and look at it outside' (734). The pagan spirit never gets *into* it, but the sympathy and good will are there.

Mr. Omer is never more a Greek than in his outlook on death, about which he holds forth in his way:

'Dear me!' said Mr. Omer, 'when a man is drawing on to a time of life, where the two ends of life meet; when he finds himself, however hearty he is, being wheeled about for the second time, in a speeches of go-cart; he should be over-rejoiced to do a kindness if he can. He wants plenty. And I don't speak of myself particular,' said Mr. Omer, 'because, sir, the way I look at it is, that we are all drawing on to the bottom of the hill, whatever age we are, on account of time never standing still for a single moment. So let us always do a kindness, and be over-rejoiced! To be sure!' (735)

Here in a nutshell is the Greek ontology:-life seen as a journey 'to the bottom of the hill,' a descent to the shades, a pale wandering in the underworld. No hope or expectation—in fact, no concept—of ascent. Greek aspiration is not Heavenly; it is wind. The symbol of pagan time is the circle, as seen in Omer's view of old age as a second childhood, a meeting of 'the two ends of life.' In Christian time Christ breaks the circle, the weary cycle of generation and decay, sending the soul on a course straight for Heaven. Greek man goes down, down; Christian man climbs, following *Agnes.*

Omer's 'two childhoods' view of man's life misses in its own way. If in old age man is reduced to a state of physical helplessness reminiscent of early childhood, surely morally and spiritually he has come a long way. While it is hoped he retains certain qualities of the child, its innocence, bright fancy, sympathy, in that sense 'become as a little child,' still the man fathered by the child is more: has been a pilgrim, felt the 'wound,' as Dan'l says; kept watch o'er man's mortality. Mr. Omer is closed to such experience. His *'speeches* of go-cart' is pre-Christian 'speeches' *and* species, down to the view that we do a kindness because we need one.

('Do unto others *because you need them to do unto you'* is not quite on target.)  But the decency and abundant energy ('*over*-rejoiced') never fail, and one likes Mr. Omer even while staring in the face the perceptual limits of the pagan mind at work on the world.

Says Omer: 'You'd be surprised at the number of people that looks in of a day to have a chat.  You really would!' (733) Does Dickens add 'You really would!' off in its own emphatic line complete with exclamation point because we really, but *really* would?  I suspect so.  Yes, to be sure, we would be surprised; tens of thousands, maybe more, 'look in of a day' on Omeric Homer as on Homeric Omer, relishing the yarns about winds, passages, long-and-strong-pulls, and the colorful rest.  David Copperfield, in his long trek through pre-christian to Christian time, occasionally looks in on the realms of gold that deep-browed Homer ruled as his demesne, where 'mingle[s] Grecian grandeur with the rude/Wasting of Old Time,' as Keats almost for Dickens says.[2]  Looks in as Dickens himself did many a time.  Dickens owned the *Iliad* and *Odyssey* in the Cowper blank verse translation (1802), and a *Greek Tragic Theatre* (1809) of Aeschylus, Sophocles, and Euripides.[3]

Dickens must have brushed up on Greek-Roman culture to make the 'pagan' parts of *Dombey and Son* as convincing as they are.  Much allusion to Titus, Domitian, Nero, Tiberius, Caligula, Heliogabalus (158); to Cicero 'in his retirement at Tusculum' (147), and the like, implies recent research.  Dickens not only owned, he read the *Odyssey,* one *Dombey* interlude shows.  In the Greek-Roman school little Paul attends there is a pupil named Briggs, a 'stony boy' (155), turned to stone by so much immersion in pagan waters; Briggs surely looks to the 'brig' or ship turned to stone in the *Odyssey.*  Briggs goes the Greek route, enduring the old punishment Poseidon in his wrath inflicted on the charitable Phaecians; but young Johnson, force-fed Roman history, refuses to swallow it.  Where souls are ships, Paul the *Son and Heir,* a 'stony' Briggs motif in 'greek' waters cannot very easily be by chance.

Rather, the 'Paul-Greek/Roman' plot of *Dombey and Son* (1848) and the 'Omer-Greek' one of *Copperfield* (1850) seem allied to one inspiration. Both show what life, death, and 'heart' were before Christian time:  before Paul, David's son, Martha and others appeared on the human scene and man dared dream of death as a journey *up from* the 'bottom of the hill.'

How much Greek myth glances in Omer's wise sayings is hard to tell, though his habit of self-quotation ('says I to my daughter Minnie' (439)) and fondness for saws hoary with age seem in the Homeric vein.  When he states: 'The proverb says, 'You can't make a silk purse out of a sow's ear.' Well, I don't know about that.  I rather think you may, if you begin early in life' (440), is he half thinking of that 'early in life,' the life of Western man, when Circe turned Odysseus's men to swine?  IF one believes *Omer* is *Homer,* these little innuendos tease the mind.  In a 'Greek' atmosphere, even the saw that 'a man must take the fat with the lean' (733) could, if one were so minded, conjure up whole Boetias and Asia Minors of hecatombs of sheep and cattle coming to the sacrifice. And when 'Mr. Omer' 'shut[s] up one eye as a caution' (442), it is hard not to think of the Cyclops or of blind Homer.

In his last appearance, Mr. Omer, now confined to a wheel-chair, is being wildly whizzed around the ground-floor room of his house by his grand-daughter, the 'little elephant,' as he delightedly calls her. No surprise here. Sow Rome (Minnie) with Israel-Judah (Joram) and reap the whirlwind, an *el*-ephant, or miniature EL. At first somewhere upstairs and unseen, only heard, the 'elephant' plays the invisible ancient Deity, El, à la Bill Barley in *Great Expectations*. Preceded by her voice, whirl-winding down from Above, curls flying, the elephant, a charge of irresistible energy, butts her grandfather's chair with her head from behind, upon Omer's over-rejoiced: 'Once, elephant. Twice. Three times!' (736). (Pe*ll* me*ll*, that is.) Happily, Old Time is on the wane, so the descent of 'el' is not too dire. On 'Three!' the elephant delivers its party more or less safely (the danger of head-cracking on the door-post safely past) to 'wherever it is.' Working as he likes best in comic miniature, Dickens depicts the latent man-spilling might in any 'el,' great or small.

Like all Homeric heroes, Omer is too deep in the adventure of the moment to dwell on his physical condition, which is grim. His limbs have given out; it is the wheel-chair *and* ground-floor, i.e., the flats, the top-of-bottom of the hill, from now on. No more exhilarating dives after his wind now. Yet he has his reward. Just before 'Greek' time drops away forever once more, Omer, in his words, gets into action, the 'el' finding passages aplenty between parlor scyllas and charybdises through which to dash and fling him along an incalculable course.

Like David, D.C., Dickens, C.D., must have been a rapt 'onlooker' at many such Homeric performances when he dropped in on Homer now and then for an easing of the nerves, a glimpse of a simpler, unshadowed world, a bracing whiff of sea air, and the ring of 'my hearties, hurrah!' No lionish 'horroor' in *that* 'hurrah!' The Greek gods in their rivalries and descendings among mortals could be dire. But they did not carry off to Babylon, feed to lions, or crucify as the Hebrews and Romans did in the name of their gods. Free of malice, Dickens shows, the Omeric spirit is Homerically spacious and large, like the swing of Omer's open vowels sounding in consonance, or the synchronized dipping of oars into sparkling blue Homeric seas.

Behold Omer, plunging into a peril-strewn unknown like Odysseus or some other Homeric hero recalled to life. Is he afraid? Not at all: he is in his Element. Before disappearing from sight, he casts a look back over his shoulder at David which implies that here is no trial, but rather 'the triumphant issue of his life's exertions' (736). Such is the Greek way sung by Homer. Man, plaything of Nature and the gods, those untamable

elephantal-elemental forces (Dickens puns them into one[4]), driven from
trial to trial, knows that disaster is only inches away. Omer can have no il-
lusions on that score, any more than on the subject of his failing wind. Indeed, every word he utters mirrors his unadorned perception of the
unalterable framework of human life. Yet he is as free from 'self-interest'
as from complaint. In the staunch Omeric life, a moment-to-moment
course of lose-win-lose, knowledge of imminent disaster in no way intrudes
on things.

The situation of an old salt ('A long pull…!') shoving off on still another
adventure, possibly the last, weakened in body but spiritually undaunted,
rings a bell. The art of one Victorian Christian poet echoes that of another.
Is this not the dramatic finale of Tennyson's 'Ulysses' to the life? Dickens,
we know, greatly admired Tennyson; he owned the *Collected Poems,*
second edition (1843); also *Poems* (1862), and an *Idylls of the King.* The
cataloguer of books in Dickens's Gadshill library remarks: 'The numerous
pencil marks made by Dickens against various poems in these volumes
show how attentively he read them.'[5] An even more eloquent testimonial
to Dickens's regard for Tennyson is the fact that he named a son Alfred
Tennyson Dickens. Watching the heroic, never-say-die 'Mr. Omer' go out
in a blaze of glory, we think of Ulysses who, despite age and bodily in-
firmity, also affirms:

> Though much is taken, much abides; and though
> We are not now that strength which in old days
> Moved earth and heaven, that which we are, we are—
> One equal temper of heroic hearts,
> Made weak by time and fate, but strong in will
> To strive, to seek, to find, and not to yield.

Thus Tennyson joins Sir Philip Sidney and Doctor Johnson in the well-
travelled allegory of Dickens, its cargo the whole spiritual history of mankind.

David Copperfield's relationship to Omer and the Homeric world he
restores is akin to that of Hamlet and Horatio; or, in Dostoevsky, of Raskolnikov to Razumihin. The deep, complex, self-divided, thought-tormented
Hamlet and Raskolnikov, laden with moral mandate, racial memory, a
highly developed consciousness and conscience, are quite understandably
drawn to young men like Horatio and Razumihin who inhabit the sunny,
clear-morning realms of life. Sturdy Horatio of the classical name and
soul! In a like way, Huck Finn, destined for rare moral adventure, admires
Tom Sawyer, whom Huck thinks a master adventurer—lordly, silly,
shallow Tom, so insistent on precedent, so full of pat answers. We understand the attraction. Yet it is not from Omer, Horatio, Razumihin, or
pseudo-adventurer Tom Sawyer that Judaeo-Christian history flows,
though it encompasses these; but rather from the sons of David, the
Hamlets, Hucks afflicted with ideas, thrashing around in painful wakeful-

ness, constantly roused from comfort and certainty, forced to outgrow, to dare damnation.

A wild Huckleberry ripens on the long river journey—in Western literature always 'the journey.' Sweetest of huckleberry ripenings, to come to set another, nigger Jim, before oneself. The bookish heroics of Tom are pale by comparison; as, compared to David's journey of mind, Omer's battle for wind—the struggle of the physical life—is.

Dickens honors Homeric courage and stoic cheer, the broad spirit that took and takes both prosperity and overthrow as in the way of things, Greek man's rancourless content in such unsupported conditions of life and death as it seems impossible he could have sanely endured. What with jealous Poseidon, Yah and El, and the cry-havoc Roman dogs of war, the survival of B.C. man is a wonder. For all the constant mad-dash physical action, there are adventures of the spirit he never knows. Omer's life is spiritually static. A good life. But beyond the good in Dickens is the holy, and this is beyond the Omeric scope. Visiting the little shop of *Omer and Joram,* David pays his respects to the realm of perpetual moral childhood, then resumes his pilgrimage.

(H)omer lives before Christ furnishes Funeral Furnishing man with something better than death. In Omer's small world it is as if mankind were back in the 'no help for it,' now dark, now bright epochs of man's tempest-tossed absorption in the elements before he sought and followed a Saviour, before there were disciples like Herbert Pocket, son of Matthew, aspiring to be an 'Insurer of ships in the City' (GE, 173) and 'cut into the Direction' (173). Blown about by winds, Omer has no leisure to discover a Direction, or even dream of one. In Dickens, the Greek genius is simply unequal to the higher wonder. It was first to spin yarns of home-seeking and the journey; but its maritime figures—of wind, passage—were not quite bold enough.

And so, ascentless on his ground-floor mediterranean, doughty old Omer stages a last gala Homeric-Tennysonian performance, happily wearing out until the sudden spill to the bottom of the hill. Heading out into the great unknown, he seems the very same hearty Omer he was at the start. Others, like David, Dan'l, Martha, Em'ly, Ham, fall, suffer, rise again. Not so Omer, who is one unevolving self and adds nothing to what he amply, attractively already is. It lies upon the gods' great knees whether he will survive this latest descending of 'el.' No matter. No conserving, fretting, regretting in Mr. Omer, any more than soul for wonder.

Where is he heading on the last voyage out? Perhaps for the Happy Isles where spirits gat them home; the Elysian Fields of eternal fair weather and unfailing winds. Or for the ongoing sunny Greek morning of man's spiritual childhood under cloudless skies from which many a traveller has never returned, preferring mindless contest, or azure calm and lotus fruit—the mixed allurements and hazards of Old fortune—to the Bread and Wine.

The Omeric enterprise of struggle in Nature, adventure, and death harbors that within which will journey on when its own day is done, its sun set.  In:  'OMER, DRAPER, TAILOR, HABERDASHER, FUNERAL FURNISHER, & C.,' the '& C.' is, of course, for 'And Co.,' or 'Et Cetera.' But 'C.,' never an indifferent letter in Dickens, recalls Omer's always sympathetic interest in David and his friends, carriers of New Time.  As Homer shaped a poetic fiction that first established the metaphor of 'the journey' on which Christianity would build, and in the Greek language in which the NT would first appear, perhaps that final '& C.' also implies the 'And Christ' to come.  It is '& C.' that, funerals left behind, finally carries man, long battered as becalmed at sea, 'all the way' Home.

From the Greek time of *Copperfield* we turn back to a great formative force in David's Judaeo-Christian life, the 'Ya-a-ah! lady, Miss Betsey Trotwood.

# ELEVEN
## Betsey Trotwood

'She couldn't even have a baby like anybody else,' said my aunt. 'Where was this child's sister, Betsey Trotwood? Not forthcoming. Don't tell me!'

Mr. Dick seemed quite frightened.

'That little man of a doctor, with his head on one side,' said my aunt. 'Jellips, or whatever his name was, what was *he* all about? All he could do was say to me, like a robin redbreast—as he *is*—'It's a boy.' A boy! Yah, the imbecility of the whole set of 'em!' (DC, 197)

With 'Ya-a-ah!' (10) and a grand swoop down on gentle Mr. Chillip for the high offense of ushering a son of David into the world, the formidable Betsey Trotwood crowns her universally disquieting visit to Blunderstone Rookery in the dawn of Time D.C., soon after vanishes, and never comes back again. The 'Ya-a-ah!' and retributive anger mean she comes much as Yahweh came in another dawn of Time to the House of David: YAH, equivocal Providence of Old Time, Israel's scourge and stay alike, both fiery and darkly fond. In the dogmatic, hard-soft Miss Trotwood's nurture of David and a certain Mr. Dick is retold the story that has no end. Heavens to Betsey, what a stormy story that was, and is!

The testy, touchy great-aunt of David (she is his dead father's aunt) arrives on the Blunderstone scene one bright, windy March afternoon; the evening wind is rising in the elms, and the wintry twilight is 'shading down into darkness' (6). Looking up, David's recently widowed young mother-to-be, who has been softly weeping, beholds 'a strange lady coming up the garden' (3). So Yah first appeared in a garden long before.

An ancient drama recommences on the spot:

My mother had a sure foreboding at this second glance, that it was Miss Betsey. The setting sun was glowing on the strange lady, over the garden-fence, and she came walking up to the door with a fell rigidity and composure of countenance that could have belonged to nobody else. (3)

This is the being of legend who, in a mythic past, broke with David over his

choice of 'Clara' for a wife. David is gone. Sunset falls on the House of
David. Light thickens, crows make wing to the rooky wood of the Rookery.
One sees no rooks, however, only weather-beaten, empty, 'ragged old
rooks'-nests' high in the ancient elms at the bottom of the garden that
swing in the groaning upper branches 'like wrecks upon a stormy sea' (5).
The whole symbolic scene—rooks; elms all the more the gloomy children of
El for their look, as David fancies it, of sharing 'wicked' confidences and
falling into a 'violent flurry' (5), not at the top, but at *the bottom* of the
garden; empty nests, suggesting the Holy Spirit flown; imagery of wrecks
upon a stormy sea, or flood—foreshadows the fast-renewing ascendancy of
OT time of mind in the land of the sons of David. Whilst night's black
agents, two Murdstones, to their prey do rouse.

At this moment, Time teeters between the two spiritual possibilities ever
latent within, retrogressive and progressive. With David gone, what will
happen to Clara, the Light he blew into bright promise of being, in the
ordeal that lies ahead? Will 'Light' survive in the nation of David; will
mankind, taking David's visionary way to a loving God, outleap vast
deserts of Law lying between B.C. and A.D., delivering itself to its true
Messiah, Christ? Avoiding the Murdstones, the letter, make straight for
the Spirit?

'Ya-a-ah!', a powerful potential defender of David's interests, will not
help. Her old resentment still rankles, in the slow-to-forgive Yah way.
Moreover, deep is her scorn for the legacy of faith to which the name of the
House bears witness:

> 'David Copperfield all over!' cried Miss Betsey. 'David Copperfield from
> head to foot! Calls a house a rookery when there's not a rook near it, and
> takes the birds on trust, because he sees the nests!' (6)

The issue is taking 'on trust.' YAH does not; David does. David may not
have seen as far or high into the heavens as man, enlightened by the Son of
David, would one day see, as both *Blunderstone* and *Rookery* show,[1] but all
honor is due his stalwart faith in the existence of wonders of air unseen.
By contrast, Miss Trotwood takes up arms against faith. Confidently
expecting the wonderful child yet unborn (what Expectation attends it!) to
be a girl, Miss Trotwood means to have her god-daughter 'guarded from
reposing any foolish confidences where they are not deserved' (7).

YAH means: 'I Am That I Am.' In that consummately assured fullness
of divine being, Yah makes man in His own image. The imperious 'Ya-a-
ah!' figure also demands that the child about to be born to the House of
David be an exact replica of Herself: be made in *her* own image. Impious
demand! In the rejection of the very idea of *a son* of David is perhaps
mirrored the ancient hostility to that other much-awaited blessed event,
the birth of the Son of David.

The ancient YAH nature sticks out all over this 'Ya-a-ah!' dame. I suspect that 'the twitch of Miss Betsey's head' (7) after her tirade against taking on trust shows there churns within some of David's mother's own fatal fascination with being 'bewitching Mrs. Copperfield;' the *twitch-mag witch-Hex*am-*hex*-traordinary weakness in the B.C. soul which darkens the first religious fabric of the mind. Also, Miss Trotwood is given to 'stopping her ears with jewellers' cotton,' keeping no less than 'a magazine of jewellers' cotton in her pocket' (9). YAH would not, 'Ya-a-ah!' will not hear the Good News that unto us a Child is born, a Son given. In B.C., the ears of the deaf are not unstopped. Self-deafened (and with *jew*ellers' cotton at that), 'magazine' pointing up the warrior within, the terrible Betsey pulls out the cotton 'like a cork' (10), corking and uncorking the vintage of the grapes of wrath, the jealously guarded wine. [2]

Like another self-deafened, rejected bride who will not hear the voice of Matthew (*Great Expectations*), the aunt who rejected David and rejects his unborn son is long deaf to the voices of New Time. It still rankles that, long before, her favorite, David, lost his heart to 'Clara,' Light; it suits as ill that of this union, as of old, should be born, not 'Ya-a-ah!' II, but a son.

The aunt asks Mrs. Copperfield's attending physician, Mr. Chillip, how things stand. 'Well, ma'am, we are—we are progressing slowly, ma'am' (10), the timid reply, draws down on him the punitive blow and 'Ya-a-ah!' he long remembers as 'really calculated to break his spirit' (10), *spirit* very much to the point. Miss Trotwood will not surrender her long-settled expectations B.C., *Before Copperfield-Before Clara*, which might be summed up as. 'I AM That I Am Unchanged Forever.' Refusing David, Clara, Chillip and child, she is like the people of Yah that would not look up and see a great Light.

Worse is to follow:

> 'The baby,' said my aunt. 'How is she?'
> 'Ma'am,' returned Mr. Chillip. 'I apprehended you had known. It's a boy.'
> My aunt never said a word, but took her bonnet by the strings, in the man ner of a sling, aimed a blow at Mr. Chillip's head with it, put it on bent, walked out, and never came back. (12)

Not only walked out, but, Yah-like, disappeared into thin air: 'She vanished like a discontented fairy: or like one of those supernatural beings whom it was popularly supposed I was entitled to see: and never came back any more' (12). 'Vanished' and 'supernatural,' passing for mere figures of speech, wink at allegory. So does the fatal sling, which, recalling David's weapon against Goliath, must look up uncommonly in the House of David ever after.

The 'Ya-a-ah!' ire at and warfare on Chillip marks a new anti-Christ dawn in Judaeo-Christendom. In Dickens, there are mighty and awful holy Spirits, like the Three in *A Christmas Carol;* but a humble, meek and mild

Chillip, a poor traveller, is no less important a carrier of New Time and 'ch' portal for the sons of David.

Ages thence, recalling the moment she first heard of the birth of a son, Miss Trotwood will kindle back into wrath: 'Yah, the imbecility of the whole set of 'em!' (197). Another YAH reflex twitches. Yah too had a bent for wholesale ('whole set of 'em') indictment, and for 'visiting the iniquity of the fathers upon the children unto the third and fourth generation of them that hate me' (*Exodus* 20:5). So a 'Yah!' of jealousy and wrath looms over the *genesis* era of a David's life, repeating the old rupture with the father with the son.

We note the highly significant fact that Dickens uses 'Yah!' only twice in the novel, and the same speaker speaks it both times.

To return to that first, dark Visitation. Arriving at Blunderstone, the legendary Miss Betsey who, her nephew said, 'seldom conducted herself like any ordinary Christian' (4) (how right he was there is no end of saying), does not knock or ring the bell, but peers in the window instead:

> My mother had left her chair in her agitation, and gone behind it in the corner. Miss Betsey, looking round the room, slowly and inquiringly, began on the other side, and carried her eyes on, like a Saracen's Head in a Dutch clock, until they reached my mother. Then she made a frown and a gesture to my mother, like one who was accustomed to be obeyed, to come and open the door. My mother went. (4)

The Hebrew underplot thickens as *Saracen's Head* recalls the spectacular *Sarah's Son's Head* punning that insinuates the old peril of Sarah's son, Isaac, into a Saracenish, sacrifice-of-sons *Dotheboys* era of *Nicholas Nickleby*.[3] *Saracen,* the 'Sarah' pun aside, also looks to the anti-Christ. Moreover, Saracen-Sarah's Son symbolism fuses. The old danger to the sons of Sarah and of Mary are one, in that Isaac is an OT type of Christ. 'Ya-a-ah!'-'Yah!' plays the old Yahweh role with Ham Peggotty, too:

> Ham Peggotty, who went to the national school, and was a very dragon at his catechism, and who therefore may be regarded as a credible witness, reported next day, that happening to peep in at the parlour-door an hour after this, he was instantly descried by Miss Betsey, then walking to and fro in a state of agitation, and pounced upon before he could make his escape. That there were now occasional sounds of feet and voices overhead which he inferred the cotton did not exclude, from the circumstance of his evidently being clutched by the lady as a victim on whom to expend her superabundant agitation when the sounds were loudest. That marching him constantly up and down by the collar (as if he had been taking too much laudanum), she, at those times, shook him, rumpled his hair, made light of his linen, stopped *his* ears as if she confounded them with her own, and otherwise touzled and maltreated him. This was in part confirmed by his aunt, who saw him at half-

past twelve o'clock, soon after his release, and affirmed that he was then as
red as I was. (10)

The dame whom David afterwards refers to as the 'Dragon of that night'
(835), pounces on a smaller 'dragon,' or YAH-'AM', Ham. If he *is* 'a very
dragon at his catechism,' i.e., has had all a child's natural wonder and Heaven-seeking fancy gradground out of him, so much the worse for Christendom.
'Overhaul the Catechism!' rings out in *Dombey and Son*. Dragons prowl as in
the time when Yahweh threatened 'to make the cities of Judah desolate,
and a den of dragons' (10:22). Again the Yah tempest brews, and no Saint
George has yet appeared to strike the Christian heroic hour.

Yah marches poor Ham up and down, enforcing a miniature, modern
wilderness wandering and captivity. So lived and ever live the sons of
Noah in the hands of the angry Lord God the children of Israel will not
surrender despite nineteen Christian centuries. Meanwhile, high overhead, as if in an Above, disembodied voices foretell the birth of a son of
David; and Yah *will not* hear, nor permit a son of Noah to hearken to the
glad sound, lest word come of a Son through whom man's view of the
Father will change forever.

But Yahweh was more than the jealous, wrathful God, and the 'Ya-a-ah!'
Providence in David's life proves the same. Two souls are in her: one
strong to drat, one to bless. Moved in spite of herself at the sight of her
nephew's widow's youth and beauty, she says: 'Bless the baby!' (6) True,
the unregenerate, short-sighted, reclusive, deserting, faith-scorning, Yah-
recalling nature long estranges a better self. But in time, Miss Trotwood
will prove David's staunch ally and firm reliance in the world, as he hers.
So, as of old, a child born in defiance of the wishes of Yah is destined to
change the Yah nature itself through love. Pretty emblem of the Christian
mystery!

Old and New hotly contend in Miss Trotwood, even as Christ-denying
and Christ-nurturing tendencies in the Yah soul and nation of old. A
conflict of unforgiving and forgiving, warlike and conciliatory, selfish and
generous, judgmental and merciful, deserting and faithful impulses in her
reveal the ongoing tension between Old and New testamentary tendencies
within man and history down through time, one which sparks her extraordinary double life. Even as the sling-shot blow aimed at Mr. Chillip recalls
holy war,[4] Miss Trotwood touches David's mother's curls 'with no
ungentle hand' (5). (Comes the echo long after in David's long-cherishing
memory: 'with no ungentle hand' (176).) For ages, this harsh, stiff-
necked, 'Ha!' (8), 'Ba-a-ah!' (10), and 'Ya-a-ah!'-loosing relation of
David's is like the miller who lived by the Zuyder Zee and sang the Yah
Defiance: 'I care for nobody, no, not I; and nobody cares for me.' Then, at
some unspecified time, she rescues Mr. Dick from an asylum-place; then
David, too. In these acts we discern the image of moral majesty of the first

Yah Who abandoned a nation to, then rescued it from Babylon. This is Yah in His higher nature, not that indistinguishable in time from *Murdstone,* the sinner-stoning spirit of retribution of Mosaic Law, which came to dominate in OT time.

Miss Trotwood also reproduces opposed facets of the double Yah nature in holding pro and anti-law sentiment. On a visit to Mr. Wickfield's office, her suspicion of the Law is glimpsed:

> 'Well, Miss Trotwood,' said Mr. Wickfield; for I soon found that it was he, and that he was a lawyer, and a steward of the estates of a rich gentleman of the county; 'what wind blows you here? Not an ill wind, I hope?'
> 'No,' replied my aunt, 'I have not come for any law.'
> 'That's right, ma'am,' said Mr. Wickfield. 'You had better come for anything else.' (220)

Not evil in itself, Law proves a fertile field for Satan, or Heep. No work of pen-and-ink in 'the letter' in Dickens that does not have its latent 'pen-and-*ink-ubus*' (MD, 93) incubus attached. And yet, Miss Trotwood finances David's career in Law. Then, after David breaks with law and begins to write a Story, his aunt urges him on to Agnes in Canterbury. But when David asks her to accompany him there...

> 'No!' said my aunt, in her short abrupt way. 'I mean to stay where I am.' (836)

Like Barkis quite 'near' by then, she chooses not to go all the way.

After two early Yah! volleys aimed at the discomfort of mankind, a thaw sets in. In time, David grows accustomed to change: to 'the general rapidity of my aunt's evolutions' (217). She softens towards the son of David. Yet the bride scarred by a faithless husband's betrayal of her youthful love never fully recovers from those ancient wounds. Dickens adopts the 'bride' metaphor from the OT. So did Israel, the 'bride' of Yah who offered Him the love of her espousals, suffer casting off and desertion in deserts of Captivity. Ironically, the battered bride takes on the Yah nature, becoming 'Yah!' to the life: like the Striker, striking; like Him, demanding retribution; undoing others as she was undone. Finally, a Yah-imitating Israel strikes down what its priests of Law have made it see as the foe instead of the fulfillment of the Law, Christ.

The Christ-killing germ is deep in Miss Trotwood too. Her 'fell rigidity of figure' (4) implies 'fell,' or deadly, intent in the House of David. Her attack on Mr. Chillip, the 'Ch' figure, speaks symbolic volumes for itself. And yet, it is the *Yah!* arrival that sets the wheels of sacred history in motion once more. David records: 'She gave my mother such a turn, that I have always been convinced I am indebted to Miss Betsey for having been born on a Friday' (4). Fantastic ambiguity! 'Indebted' recalls the whole debtor relation of OT man under Law to his God, the weary view of man as transgressor that would last until Christ paid the debt to Heaven once and for all, Every One. *Yah* precipitates the birth of a son of David on Friday. Thus the child that might have stayed safe in the womb til Easter Sunday arrives betimes, inheriting the whole Good Friday experience of the Son of man. But could there be the former without the latter?

The name BETSEY TROTWOOD in all four syllables bursts with meaning for the allegory. First, Dickens actively uses the 'Bet' of Betsey in two ways. For example, when the Murdstones come to remand David to custody after David has thrown himself on his aunt's mercy, they sternly warn her against 'abetting him in this appeal' (210). *Bet*sey is NOT to 'a*bet*':

> 'You may possibly have some idea, Miss Trotwood, of abetting him in his running away, and in his complaints to you. Your manner, which I must say does not seem intended to propitiate, induces me to think it possible. Now I must caution you that if you abet him once, you abet him for good and all;' (211)

That makes four *abetting-abet*'s in a row. But Aunt BETsey *does* aBET David for good and all; and very good it is. What she failed to do in the time of the Father, she does in the time of the Son.

The word 'abet' appears in Betsey connection one more time. As the story opens, Miss Trotwood, the abandoned bride, is no friend to brides-to-be, who doubtless remind her of the hopeful, trustful bride she herself once was. She rejected her nephew's intended, sweet, yielding little Clara, calling her 'a wax doll' (3). (Of course. What else? A *Clara*, or a wax candle, melts. It is not stone, or Murdstone; such gives off no light.) Then over the years Miss Trotwood trains servant girls to be as unconfiding and untrusting as she: to abjure marriage, and live and die unwed. Such is the Betsey of 'Ya-a-ah!' time. Then comes David. She makes great spiritual strides, and late in the story, actually forwards the wedding plans of her old 'J' comrade-in-arms in raids on children and donkeys, Janet...

> ...aiding and abetting the bride, and crowning the marriage-ceremony with her presence. (836)

Happy 'abetting'! An *abetting Betsey* helps usher in a new time of bride and Bridegroom, symbol of the coming of the soul to its true Master, and rejects *Clara*, Light and grace, no more.

Another *bet* exists in the Betsey Trotwood life, Dickens shows, which reflects sudden reversal, overturn, Fortune's fickle wheel in its dizzy spinning, the roll of the dice: life as, a best, a *bet*. Things go well for a time. Then Heaven's countenance darkens, the Yah wrath ignites, and suddenly it is farewell to the Promised Land and off to Babylon. Once, Miss Trotwood and Mr. Dick, her protégé, are playing backgammon (the game Steerforth and Rosa play), and tender-hearted Dick, knowing David will soon go away to school and they must part, becomes 'so low-spirited at the prospect of our separation, and played so ill in consequence, that my aunt, after giving him several admonitory raps on the knuckles with her dice-box, shut up the board, and declined to play with him any more' (217). Here is the old Yah-*peculiar treasure* (Israel) relationship at a glance. Like Barkis, Betsey knows nothing of how Mr. Dick feels. Rules of the game and law, not emotion, are her forte. First comes a painful admonition, a Prophetic rap on the knuckles with the dice-box; then the Grand Desertion ('declined to play with him any more'). Yah punishes and deserts. But Christ never deserts. We note, parenthetically, that wherever game, gammon, backgammon, Gamfield (*Oliver Twist*), Gammonrife,[5] or dice or Jarn*dyce* (*Bleak House*) appear, Old Time and its values hold sway.[6]

Women named Bet, Betsy, and Betsey pop up often in Dickens, always where old (OT) echoes linger. In *Oliver Twist,* the girl Bet is one of the Jew's tools. In *The Old Curiosity Shop,* Betsy Quilp is wife to the evil, roaring Daniel (much Daniel-lions imagery in tow). In *The Poor Relation's Story,* snappish Betsy Snap is servant to Uncle Chill; a cold-'Snap,' and things are Chill, winter freezing man's toes and soul until the return of the Son. In *Martin Chuzzlewit,* priggish Betsey Prig is the most snappish, chill Betsey of them all. Betsey *Prig* is the prig bigoted to rule, form, the literal and seen; the prig exalts law and unseats Mystery. Sure enough, Betsey Prig holds tenaciously to the seen, known, and edible, and will NOT believe in the great reliance of Sarah Gamp's life, the unseen Mrs. Harris, sneering: 'I don't believe there's no sich person!' (756) '*I don't believe*'! Not for the Prig or Betsey Prig thereof is faith in wonders longed for or unseen, in which is reflected man's age-old hope of a Reliance. Selfish, crotchety, and queer as Sarah Gamp is, there is hope for her once she and Betsey Prig part.

*Is* there a Mrs. Harris? Elsewhere, Dickens himself speaks up for *Mr.* Harris and the wish for wonders yet unseen he excites in the hearts of uncommercial travellers.[7]

Another interesting Betsy sails in Dickens. In *Great Expectations,* the boat carrying Pip, Herbert, and Provis passes...

> ...the John of Sunderland making a speech to the winds (as is done by many Johns), and the Betsy of Yarmouth with a firm formality of bosom and her knobby eyes starting two inches out of her head. (414)

In Chapter III we spoke of the John of Sunderland, but not of the Betsy, who, boasting such 'firm formality of bosom,' sounds not unlike two earlier Betsys, Trotwood and Prig. *Betsey* Trotwood snarling '*Ya-a-ah!*' returns in spirit in the *Betsy* of *Ya*rmouth, as the Miss Trotwood-young girl theme in the Miss Havisham-Estella one. Note, it is not 'the *Betsy* of Yarmouth,' a ship but, bold as brass, Betsy, still holding her firm, formal own despite all the Johns in Christendom.

We see that each *Bet* female in Dickens has some crotchet, moral deformity, or myopic limitation that puts her beyond the reach and healing power of NT time.

TROTWOOD too has multiple meaning for allegory. Miss Trotwood renames David *Trotwood,* or *Trot,* and the second, or mounted-on-horseback stage of his journey begins. First, the footsore trek from Babylon, then 'Trot,' from which it is nothing to the canter of Canterbury. The pilgrim's life begins. Regarding Miss Trotwood herself, she is and remains a traveller of the Old school, when driving sitting high and stiff as a state coachman, commanding her grey pony in a 'masterly manner,... keeping a steady eye upon him wherever he went, and making a point of not letting him have his own way in any respect' (217). Mr. Dick fares little better, kept on short rations of his favorite treat, gingerbread. So the first Yah reigned over and reined in a nation, keeping Israel off the Highway to Christ.

'Trotwood' as a surname or, as Barkis puts it, 'nat'ral name,' is one thing. When it becomes a first or Christian name, *Trotwood* is worn with a difference, a Christian one. Like Trotty Veck, pilgrim from 'Veck,' or Vecchio, Old, to New Time [8] (*The Chimes*); and Esther Summerson, alias Dame Trot (*Bleak House*), Trotwood Copperfield in *Agnes* time sets out upon the long, winding Canterbury trail. One reads:

> 'Riding to-day, Trot?' said my aunt, putting her head in at the door.
> 'Yes,' said I, 'I am going over to Canterbury. It is a good day for a ride.'
> (858)

The 'wood' of *Trotwood* signifies too. Wood looks to the cross, to Dante's dark wood (of crosses), as to all pilgrims' rude awakenings in dark woods ever after. As *wood* looks darkly to crucifixion, it also looks to the redemptive power of the cross: to 'the blessed later covenant of peace and hope that changed the crown of thorns into a glory' (LD, 793).[9] Like branches of the tree of the Kingdom are the good physician, Allan Woodcourt (*Bleak House*) and Mortimer Lightwood (*Our Mutual Friend*), ally of the hero, John Harmon. By contrast, no 'wooden-faced' (161) Wemmick saying 'Yah!' (246) and indifferent to the victims of the law (*Great Expectations*); no heartless wood-sawyer like Samson working his guillotine, a species of cross (*A Tale of Two Cities*); no wooden-legged servant of the Judge who presides over the trial and Passion of the Master (*David Copperfield*); or wooden-legged Silas Wegg (wooden-legged = *Wegg?*) pegging away at and nailing down Nicodemus in the old Roman style as he ladles out huge doses of Decline and Fall (*Our Mutual Friend*);- no wood of the kind in Dickens but has blatant connection with the wood, or tree, of the Cross.

Preparing for a career in the Law, Trotwood gets lost in the proverbial dark wood, the shining Agnes way of ascent temporarily lost. Courting a lawyer's daughter, he becomes a wood-sawyer:

> What I had to do, was, to take my woodman's axe in my hand, and clear my own way through the forest of difficulty, by cutting down the trees until I came to Dora. (520)

He agonizes over 'how I could best make my way with a guitar-case through the forest of difficulty, until I used to fancy that my head was turning quite grey' (544). Studying shorthand to prepare to sit among the gammonrife Parliamentarians who make the magwitch-crushing laws of the land, David, struggling with legal hieroglyphs, enters an 'Egyptian Temple' (545). The dark wood image returns: 'Every scratch in the scheme was a gnarled oak in the forest of difficulty, and I went on cutting them down, one after another' (545). So in OT time Mosaic Law felled the trees from which came the wood for the cross.

Miss Trot*wood* has in her a streak of the spirit that was strong for crucifying Christ. This shows in her persecution of the innocent child and patient beast:

> Janet had gone away to get the bath ready, when my aunt, to my great alarm, became in one moment rigid with indignation, and had hardly voice to cry out, 'Janet! Donkeys!'
> Upon which, Janet came running up the stairs as if the house were in flames, darted out on a little piece of green in front, and warned off two saddle-donkeys, lady-ridden, that had presumed to set hoof upon it; while my aunt, rushing out of the house, seized the bridle of a third animal with a bestriding child, turned him, led him forth from those sacred precincts, and boxed the ears of the unlucky urchin who had dared to profane that hallowed ground. (194)

'Ya-a-ah!' guards her bit of English ground as jealously as ever Yah His altar and prerogatives of old. The figurative expressions '*sacred* green' and '*profane* that *hallowed* ground' address the religious issue head on. Yah glares in this reception of the child; it reeks of Herod. The imagery of a woman journeying and a 'bestriding child' on a donkey turns up its eternal side, glancing as far off as the flight of Mary into Egypt, or Mary mounted on a donkey entering Bethlehem; or even to the entrance of Christ into Jerusalem on an ass. That the child rides a *third* animal focuses the Christian issue the more.

Miss Trotwood, like Yah, stands on Law, and dubious ground it proves:

> To this hour I don't know whether my aunt had any lawful right of way over that patch of green; but she had settled it in her own mind that she had and it was all the same to her. (195)

In the living Bible age of Dickens's Christian imagination, the sacred pattern repeats itself. In Dickens, what is done to the meek and defenseless, Chillip, child, and donkey, is done unto Him.  In *Oliver Twist,* Mr. Gamfield, at the old Gam, beats boy apprentices and donkeys to death.  In such company do those at enmity with child and donkey move.  The reversion of a Christian woman of modern time to old Yah ways illustrates what Dickens elsewhere calls the great retrogressive principle at work in Christendom which impiously reverses 'the appointed order of the Creator.'

The wars of Miss Trotwood, the slaughter of the innocents, do not end even with the coming of David and Dick into her life.  She may soften towards children, but donkeys she hates to the bitter end.  Even when she leaves her cottage for London, she sits in the coach 'exulting in the coming discomfiture of vagrant donkeys, with Janet at her side' (355).  David soon returns to Dover to check on the property:

> I found everything in a satisfactory state at the cottage; and was enabled to gratify my aunt exceedingly by reporting that the tenant inherited her feud, and waged incessant war against donkeys. (563)

By Canterbury time she has actually relented about horses that stray onto the 'forbidden ground' (858) (how like the unapproachable altar of Yah that sounds; and how like His high priest exceedingly wroth against any who dare approach it, she).  But as to donkeys, those patient beasts of burden that carried Mary and Christ, never.  Truly, she does not go all the way.

As *Copperfield* opens, the Yah Providence that reappears after Heaven known how long, comes, tyrannizes over all, and disappears.  When, years later, David, arriving in Dover, finally beholds the fearsome apparition of Blunderstone Tales, the mythic aunt of his father, what does he see?  A figure in a garden (again, as long before, in a garden), who, crying: 'Go away!' and 'making a distant chop in the air with her knife' (191), extends the ancient greeting of Yahweh to the wilderness-wandering sons of David: 'Go along! No boys here!' (191)  So in *Bleak House* the Law, in the person of a police constable, orders Jo, the waif of Tom-all-Alone's, to 'move on' (267).  (What 'Jo' is this the Law persecutes: Joses, the brother of Jesus?  A new Joseph?)  'Move on!' begins the Wilderness Wandering again in England's green and pleasant land.

Marching soldier-style to a corner of the garden, the Yah personage stoops 'to dig up some little root there' (191), another 'uprooting' gesture symbolizing the exile from the Garden, as from the Promised Land.  Strong for multiple analogy, as if to educate the reader in analogy, bedrock of allegory, Dickens tucks symbol within symbol.  Yah, in shut-away pocket, sunderland garden, retreats still further in her narrow world, crouching in a corner of that corner, inscribing seclusion within seclusion.  Fresh from 'Babylon,' David relives the return of Israel from the Captivity and its restoration to the favor of Yah.

Now little David identifies himself.  'Oh, Lord!' (191) says his aunt, and sits down flat in the garden path.  Her reaction to the tale of abuse, suffering, and woe that bursts from David is strictly a Yah one:

> My aunt, with every sort of expression but wonder discharged from her
> countenance, sat on the gravel, staring at me, until I began to cry: when she
> got up in a great hurry, collared me, and took me into the parlour. (191)

'Every expression but wonder.' In Yah is plenty of 'collaring,' or Captivity reflex, and dosing with non-restorative restoratives, as David discovers by and by; but of faith or wonder, not a drop:-no sense of the
marvelous and unseen, or capacity to imagine invisible worlds and joys yet
unbeheld til time and world to nothingness do sink. Over and over,
Dickens shows it is Heaven-seeking curiosity and a sense of a God beheld
in mystery rather than in 'walk-in-the-same' paths of Catechism and rote
obedience to tenets of law that sets OT and NT worship apart.

   The look 'discharged' from the 'Ya-a-ah!' countenance foretells war. Indeed, minutes later Miss Trotwood retreats behind a fan and 'ejaculate[s]
at intervals, 'Mercy on us!' letting those exclamations off like minute guns'
(191). Between the mercy of Yah and the rifles' rapid rattle ('minute
guns'), one thinks, there is little to choose. (One recalls Mrs. Joe's like-
comfortless 'Lord-a-mussy-me!', *its* mercy also indistinguishable from
'mussy'). The guns also recall the magazine of jewellers' cotton of her first
appearance, and the menace of that distant knife chop in air. Yah-ites
through the ages are arsenals of ill will towards men. Under Yah, Israel is
almost never literally or figuratively at peace. Either she is making war on
a neighboring tribe, or Yah has collared an Assyrian or other heathen
nation to come down on her like a wolf on the fold to smite her for trans-
gressions of the Law.

   The latest scion of the House of David, little David Copperfield, experiences that equivocal, jealous Yah love and rescue from that first
moment on. That night, he is delivered to a hot bath in manner 'kindly,'
but even so 'in some sort like a prisoner, my aunt in front, and Janet
bringing up the rear' (198); and afterwards locked in for the night. The
Yah instinct demands hot immersions and lock-ups like the fiery furnaces
and dungeons of Babylon. While Dickens turns it to dark fun, he keeps the
Captivity motif alive, as for example when the Murdstones come for
David:

> 'Shall I go away, aunt?' I asked, trembling.
> 'No, sir,' said my aunt. 'Certainly not!' With which she pushed me into a
> corner near her, and fenced me in with a chair, as if it were a prison or a bar of
> justice. (208)

In the protective custody of Yahweh, OT man never knew the joys of
freedom and the equality of Mutual Friendship with his God.
   Where Yah is, the Flood soon threatens anew. David's first night in

'captivity' passes, he relates:

> On going down in the morning, I found my aunt musing so profoundly over
> the breakfast table, with her elbow on the tray, that the contents of the urn
> had overflowed the teapot and were laying the whole tablecloth under water,
> when my entrance put her meditations to flight. (200)

Happily, the arrival of David from upstairs, as from Above, saves mankind
from a second Deluge. But Yah *will* work watery and other destruction on
journeying children and donkeys:

> In whatever occupation she was engaged, however interesting to her the con-
> versation in which she was taking part, a donkey turned the current of her
> ideas in a moment, and she was upon him straight. Jugs of water, and
> watering-pots, were kept in secret places ready to be discharged on the of-
> fending boys; sticks were laid in ambush behind the door; sallies were made
> at all hours; and incessant war prevailed. (195)

In jug of water, a 'current' of ideas, and *el*bow on tray, the old, old catastrophe lurks, a Flood in a teapot, in the ingenious Dickens way.

Miss Trotwood pulls backward too in pressing David's natural gifts, as if
to keep him rooted in Nature, as we see when David expresses the wish to
visit his old nurse in Yarmouth:

> 'Well,' said my aunt, 'that's lucky, for I should like it too. But it's natural and
> rational that you should like it. And I am very well persuaded that whatever
> you do, Trot, will always be natural and rational.' (274)

She adds: 'Your sister, Betsey Trotwood, would have been as natural and
rational a girl as ever breathed' (274). Her 'that's lucky' recalls her dice-
box. Heavy on the natural and rational, or law, Yah says nothing of the
*super* natural, transcendent, mystical destiny of the son of David, the in-
estimable treasure in her keeping. She cannot. Retreating behind a large
green fan to scatter-gun 'Mercy!' on all from behind the veil, like the
unseen Yah, she symbolically retreats into Nature, the 'green' screen. She
habitually works 'with the green fan between her and the light' (201). So
captives in the Murdstone warehouse held bottles up 'against the light.'
For Dickens, the whole OT enterprise is one against the Light of the world,
its relations to the supernatural marred by a fatal over-emphasis on the
manifest and demonstrable, the Law, which led to a confounding of the
Divine Nature with that single aspect of it evidenced in the law for holy
living in this world. Dickens emphasizes that too great an absorption in
Nature, reason, theology, the Talmudic enterprise, can come between man
and the higher glory that eye hath not seen, nor ear heard, awaiting him in
the life to come.

On that first visit compared to a 'discontented fairy' (12) that vanishes like a supernatural being, David's aunt is very like the fairy godmother of so many tales who appears at the christening of the little prince and wishes him all manner of sturdy virtues to see him safely through the world: that he be (in Betsey's words) 'a good, sensible, and a happy man' (346), strong-willed, natural, and rational, with her own dry brand of intelligence which is proof against faith, ambiguity, and mystery. This fairy, feeling slighted, withdraws her favor and angrily flies away. Thank Heaven that another, gentler fairy, watching from behind the curtain all the while, tiptoes out when she is gone, and, touching the sleeping babe with a starry wand, whispers: 'Ah, but this wonderful son of David will have *super*natural gifts and *un*-worldly expectations and honors, too.'

Miss Trotwood is equally strong for self-reliance, urging David to 'begin, in a small way, to have a reliance upon yourself, and to act for yourself' (275). She holds that the study of law 'would make me firm and self-reliant, which was all I wanted' (354). She persists: 'Trot, have you got to be firm and self-reliant?' (498); and rejoices when he proves 'persevering, self-reliant, self-denying!' (776). Whatever the virtues of a Yah upbringing, it does not ready man for a Saviour. Self-reliance is *not* all David wants. While it is all well and good, a Christian sooner or later acknowledges the limitations of self, and the need for a rock or reliance higher than self. In Agnes's words: 'There is God to trust in!' Miss Trotwood is just what Mr. Dick admiringly calls her: 'the most wonderful woman in the world' (275). Though the acme of worldly wonderfulness, she is a stranger to the wonder that seeks out still other worlds and seas; that, seeing an eddy in the tide, instantly thinks metaphorically, as both Little Nell and Sydney Carton do, of how it flows like mortal life to meet Eternity. In Dickens, wisdom begins with Matthew Pocket's discovery that one can't lift oneself by the hair, or Daniel Peggotty's discovery: 'I can't arrize myself of it.'

The deepest of mysteries to sound the life to come is allegory. Naturally, Miss Trotwood knows nothing of it personally. But the subject arises as Mr. Dick, despite her best efforts to head it off, keeps confounding the sorrows of his own most un-self-reliant self with those of a long-dead, martyred King. Miss Trotwood discusses Dick's curious dilemma with David:

> 'Did he say anything to you about King Charles the First, child?'
> 'Yes, aunt.'
> 'Ah!' said my aunt, rubbing her nose as if she were a little vexed. 'That's his allegorical way of expressing it. He connects his illness with great disturbance and agitation, naturally, and that's the figure, or the simile, or whatever it's called, which he chooses to use. And why shouldn't he, if he thinks proper?'
> I said: 'Certainly, aunt.'
> 'It's not a business-like way of speaking,' said my aunt, 'nor a worldly way.

I am aware of that; and that's the reason why I insist upon it, that there shan't
be a word about it in the Memorial.' (205)

Miss Trotwood may insist all she pleases, but the 'Ch' King whose suffering and death echo with the suffering and death of Christ *will* slip into what
many an allegorical Dick and Dickens write. 'There shan't be a word about
it in the Memorial,' or official manuscript she sets Dick to. Perhaps not.
But there *will* be a symbol, the head of King Charles, which a troubled Mr.
Dick, why he probably could not say, sketches on page after page he
writes, taking a self-invented, unique, lone 'allegorical way.'

How Miss Trotwood dispatches Dick's mystery is (to borrow her own
words) Yah from head to foot. In this speech bristling with 'naturally' and
'the reason why,' natural-rational Betsey attacks the wholly foreign subject
of allegory, fumbling with unfamiliar terms—'the figure, or the simile, or
whatever it's called.' It is all stuff and nonsense to her, her dismissive
'whatever it's called' implies. As Mr. Podsnap in *Our Mutual Friend*
waves away all things unfamiliar with a lordly: 'Not English!', so one
imagines Miss Trotwood on her high horse of common sense confronting
the subject of allegory and stating: 'Not natural! Not rational!' She
handles Dick's mystery by removing it from the realm of metaphysics,
where it belongs and makes sense, and shifting it to comfortable, prosaic
ground of rights where she grants a free-born Englishman the right to
muddle around with any tomfoolery he 'chooses' to, and thinks 'proper.'
Little does she dream that Mr. Dick's dilemma involving kings and kites is
not for one minute a matter of propriety or rights, reason or will. With
Dick, all happens many psychic and spiritual light universes away from
sense, mind, and choice, as will shortly be seen. For Dick *must* have his
'allegorical way of expressing it.'

Miss Trotwood's resolute, uncompromising mind is as tidy, close-
clipped, and trimly formal as her garden walk, and immaculate house and
servant. But the mind of child-like Dick, its opposite, is full of twilights
and misty inter-penetration of sorrows of time long past and present in
which the agony and death of a great King is an unforgotten, unforgettable
theme within his own well-remembered pain, with distinction of heart and
mind, then and now, tragic figure of sorrows and self, world and sky, well
lost. Within the soul of Mr. Dick, this strange power to sorrow over
grievances foregone and fore-bemoaned moan, both gift and affliction,
leads skywards, like his kite, to blue skies of poetry, allegory, and Heaven.

Miss Trotwood is right in one respect: there *is* something in Dick's un-
business-like, kite-flying ways for which it is hard to find the right word,
the 'whatever it's called.' Her confident 'He connects...naturally' is
wrong. Mr. Dick tends, not naturally but supernaturally to the memory of
the man of sorrows, King Charles. Being fond of Dick, Miss Trotwood,
who sees only as far as she sees (she is like the Betsy of Yarmouth with

knobby eyes starting two inches out of her head, yet seeing nothing), trims him to size—Yah-size. Seizing on his common sense, actually the least of his virtues, she magnifies and warmly praises it. So did Yah I, rescuing a wan, dusty tribe from desert-wandering and captivity, come to harbor within Yah spiritual precincts precocious dreamers, poets, high-flyers like David and Dick, souls born for New, allegorical ways: born, in effect, to overhaul the Catechism. Dickens's tale of how a Yah-ite nurtures, without really understanding them, two children destined for adventure in allegory and glory, a wonderful son of David and a grey-haired, eternal child, Mr. Dick, represents the age-old relation of Old to New mystery in which the latter is always born a wise simpleton, a stranger, and a child.

Miss Trotwood, weak on allegory, is strong on law and precedent, as is seen in her nightly preparation for bed in one unvarying way:

> I then made her, according to certain established regulations from which no deviation, however slight, could ever be permitted, a glass of hot white wine and water, and a slice of toast cut into long thin strips. (346)

The voice may be that of a living, breathing Trotwood, but the hand is the hand of Yah. In her is a narrow-constructionist bent for law in all. Such was the nightcap another ill-used 'bride,' the chosen one of Yahweh, took on a long night's journey to the infamy of the crucifixion.

Yah glares from Miss Trotwood in other ways. She tends to harsh judgment. After Em'ly's flight, David's pitying: 'Poor Em'ly!' draws from his aunt a cool, censorious: 'Oh, don't talk to me about poor. She should have thought of that, before she caused so much misery!' (503) Not in Yah ways of heaven and earth is to be found, Blessed are the poor in spirit: for theirs is the kingdom of heaven. In Dickens Yah annals, there is little divine poverty of purse or spirit, the 'poor' of humility. That, 'Oh, don't talk to me about poor' speaks symbolic volumes.

Happily, Miss Trotwood evolves out of the old B.C. self. With the collapse of her fortunes, an experience of 'poor,' all vaunted self-reliance ends. Her reliances become David and Mr. Dick, and the journey that does not quite end in Canterbury begins.

The flight-furthering fall of this lady midway in *David Copperfield* is like the equally sudden, spiritually significant 'drop' (208), as Joe calls it, of Mr. Wopsle midway in *Great Expectations,* one that ends his Roman child-and-convict-mauling church career of punishing Amens. We digress briefly to consider it, supposing it closely related to the 'allegorical way' of Mr. Dick and his mystery centering on a King.

After Pip leaves home for a faraway city of pleading Jews (Habraham Latharuth) and doomed men, he loses sight of old friends. Then one day Joe pays him a visit, and, among other things, reports that Wopsle has had a fall, and 'left the church and went into the playacting' (208). Once hot for amateur blood-and-thunder spectacles, Wopsle is now a professional, ''the celebrated Provincial Amateur of Roscian renown, whose unique performance in the highest tragic walk of our National Bard has lately occasioned so great a sensation in local dramatic circles.'' (208) Wopsle may model himself on Roscius, the Roman actor (recall Barkis's tribute to David as a 'young Roeshus'), but he now wears his Rome with a difference, playing on the Christian, not the lions side.

Pip and Herbert go to see Wopsle, now Waldengarver, in *Hamlet.* The play begins normally enough in Denmark, with the Queen, Ophelia, and specimens of Danish nobility in attendance. The royal Ghost enters. Now the tragic actor himself appears, a pure and blameless young Prince whose sufferings of flesh and spirit are jeered by a pitiless, debased mob (the audience). At the height of his lonely agony, the Actor, performing in 'the highest tragic walk' of the Drama, comes to a place of skulls. Now a black box appears, a coffin, but—behold!—no body inside, this discovery occasioning the outbreak of 'a general joy' (241). The Prince, an unnamed 'individual obnoxious to identification' (241), has come a long way of ignominy from a 'primeval forest' (240) sort of place, a dark wood, to the graveyard.

What tragic Actor upon the world stage, reviled, forsaken, slain in the rotten kingdom of the world, does this figure of sublime utterance and high tragic assignment recall? Never called Hamlet, the nameless one moves along his dark, appointed way. If he is Hamlet, a still greater Prince and Son awesomely burdened by a royal Father looks through his eyes and suffers his Passion. As we watch, *Hamlet* turns transparent. All grows misty, placeless, echoic. Passing through a series of sliding scenes and moments cleverly dovetailed, foreshortened, and superimposed, we arrive in still another corrupt kingdom of Judaeo-Christian time which put to death its Son and Heir to Heaven's throne in a drama which *Hamlet,* in the Dickens interpretation, but re-enacts. Here is discovered or uncovered the lost Ur-*Hamlet,* the story of the King's son forced to carry out the will of the Father, to suffer rejection and death for his Father's sake; and whom flights of Angels sing to his rest. Through words the Prince speaks to a skull (significantly, the name Yorick never appears), one suddenly sees piercingly through to the first, most terrible Place of Skulls, Golgotha, as to Calvary and the Cross. Christ too spoke an immortal soliloquy *in extremis,* and was hooted by a vile auditory such as 'Waldengarver' faces, a rabble which knew not what it did.

Beginning casually enough in something like Shakespeare's Denmark (the blur instantly created by bad acting a distancing device fully exploited by Dickens), Wopsle's Hamlet ends in the dominion of the blood and sepulchre. The Shakespearean focus slips; the Tragedy unfolds in an artful jumble of selected moments designed to bring major Christ-Hamlet similarities to the fore. The Prince undergoes his greatest trials in a

primeval forest, even as Christ in the prime-evil (my pun) 'forest,' or
dark wood, of crosses. Whereupon, enter 'an empty black box with the
lid tumbling open' (240), symbolizing the empty tomb. *He is risen!!*
As the audience jeers 'Wai-ter!', it is only playing its appointed role;
there is indeed a 'waiter,' linen in hand, at the tomb, faithfully awaiting Him. With the recognition of the long-suffering Wopsle, there is
an outburst of joy. On one level wholly sardonic, mere derision, on another, the eternal, it looks to the real joy to follow ignominy in Time. Once
again, sacred history uses all—a Roman player 'murdering' the Prince;
the provincial setting: a barbaric mob hot for the sublime hero's defeat
and death; fumbled props and human follies in which *Hamlet* as *Hamlet* is brilliantly lost, and found; a tragedian who does not begin to be
Hamlet, and yet becomes something uncannily more—to its own marvelous ends.

Unbeknownst to himself, Mr. Wopsle, who once dreamed of a church
'thrown open' so he could make his mark on it, achieves his ambition to
revive the Drama, and does so in ways undreamed of in his philosophy.
The rabid 'Roman' Wopsle who helped the soldiers track 'Him' now plays
on the other side of the cross. He becomes *Waldengarver* in truth, one
g(c)*arved* in the *walden,* or forest, darkwood, of the cross: nailed to the
tree, c(g)arved as a dish fit for the gods. Playing the royal Father, Son,
and holy Ghost, he is torn in the grim machinery of the world which
murders its Son and Heir evermore.

Even as he dismisses this preposterous show (if Macbeth doth murder
sleep, Wopsle doth murder Hamlet), Pip is oddly moved. He finds himself
allied to the actor, and 'feeling keenly for him.' He explains:

> I laughed in spite of myself all the time, the whole thing was so droll; and yet I
> had a latent impression that there was something decidedly fine in Mr.
> Wopsle's elocution—not for old associations' sake, I am afraid, but because it
> was very slow, very dreary, very up-hill and down-hill, and very unlike any
> way in which any man in any natural circumstance of life or death ever ex-
> pressed himself about anything. When the tragedy was over, and he had
> been called for and hooted, I said to Herbert, 'Let us go at once, or perhaps
> we shall meet him.' (241)

But they do not go, and do meet him, as, soon after, 'Him.'

In describing the performance in just that way, as 'very slow, very
dreary, very up-hill and down-hill,' Pip strikes on eternal truth, the something in it 'decidedly fine.' True, the trek of the man of sorrows to Calvary
*is* very slow, dreary, up-hill and down-hill. In such figurative usage, Pip
unconsciously falls into Christian 'journey' idiom: his words trace the way
of the Cross. In truth, these are not '*any* natural circumstances of life or
death;' or any 'natural' ones, either. Nor '*any* way in which *any* man...
ever expressed himself about *any*thing.' He is not '*any* man,' or, for that

matter, any *man*, but a stand-in in the role of the Son of man in The Greatest Tragedy and Divine Comedy Ever Told. To play Hamlet, especially in the indescribable, incredible, nigh unearthly way Waldengarver does, is to play Christ. In Dickens, once again, all the world's a stage for the Mystery play within the play, and play of plays, the Passion, Death, and Resurrection of Christ. As it does with all, Providence, enjoying a little joke, makes the once-Roman Wopsle its instrument; and by Heaven's grace, in his staggering unworthiness (in this, a type of us all), he is worthy.

The provincial audience, relishing and adding to his agony, might be the very one that spat on a tragic Actor on the way to the Cross, so visibly dull of soul is it. No 'provincial amateur of Roscian renown' in the original *amo, amus, amat 'amat*cur' days of Rome ever had a harder nut to crack than this one has, at the mercy of such a crowd. This English province might be a province of the Roman Empire, the one called Judea. Yet, when the mob breaks into wild applause as the empty box arrives (a fumbled prop on this stage, it is a luminous resurrection symbol one stage higher), it provides exactly the right response, as Eternity's script goes. In Dickens, *Hamlet* is finally revealed as the history of a type of the Saviour charged with braving a killing cursed spite to set right a world out of joint. So is Waldengarver's folly, together with all folly and evil in history, transmuted into Heaven's sense.

In early time of *Great Expectations,* Mr. Wopsle, Mrs. Joe's guest, 'reviewed the sermon with some severity, and intimated in the usual hypothetical case of the Church being 'thrown open'—what kind of sermon *he* would have given them' (23). Wopsle finally has his chance, and thanks to him, albeit as much in spite as because of him, Pip's soul, if not the Church, is thrown open a bit more to its divine Master.

We *know* Dickens is staging a Passion play within a play, working a Christ scenario, when after the performance—rather, 'the tragedy'—Pip and Herbert go backstage and witness a second staging of the Passion that night. Waldengarver's dresser turns out to be 'a Jewish man with an unnaturally heavy smear of eyebrow' (241). ('Unnaturally,' for, again, these are not any *natural* circumstances.) The tragic Actor is discovered in a hot little packing-case of a room, in a 'frightful perspiration' (242) as he struggles to put off his princely sables. Noting his master's agony, the Jew moves in to help: 'With that, he went upon his knees, and began to flay his victim' (242). *Flay!* What an inordinately forceful figure of speech, one thinks. In allegory, of course, it strikes literal truth, or near. All the while held rigidly upright and helpless (the space is cruelly small), the Prince, thus painfully uncostumed, is 'being ground against the wall' (242) by the Jew, who, seemingly the servant, is really the master, and who glibly holds forth on the subject of his relations with ever so many Hamlets he has known:

> 'But I'll tell you one thing, Mr. Waldengarver,' said the man who was on knees, 'in which you're out in your reading. Now mind! I don't care who says contrairy; I tell you so. You're out in your reading of Hamlet when you get your legs in profile. The last Hamlet as I dressed, made the same mistake in his reading at rehearsal, till I got him to put a large red wafer on each of his shins, and then at that rehearsal (which was the last) I went in front, sir, to the back of the pit, and whenever his reading brought him into profile, I called out, 'I don't see no wafers!' And at night his reading was lovely. (242)

Sacred history, bent on awakening men's souls, restages the Passion play with the Jew cast in his traditional role of anti-Christ. His is a story electrifying in its implications, of how a Jew readied a Prince for the tragic stage. As he speaks, there comes into focus the darkest chapter in the spiritual unconscious of Western man. Who was that shadowy, obedient 'last Hamlet' the Jew directed, then with deep satisfaction watched deliver a memorable performance of one crawling between heaven and earth? It is perhaps the parenthesis, '(which was the last),' that first drops a hint of mortality, *last* echoing as in 'My Last Duchess.' The Jew delights to tell how he corrected the Prince, as the Prince of Peace was 'corrected' in *His* 'reading' of the Testament and the Law. As the Jew directed a Hamlet; as his last Hamlet did as he was told, as Waldengarver is flayed by the Jew, so Christ hung on the Cross before the Jews.

The two red wafers (*wafer,* implying communion, an added irony) scream Crucifixion. Who has not seen Christ in the familiar half-profile pose in paintings of the Passion, red circles marking the bleeding spots where the nails were driven in? All is made ready. It is night; the Jew watches from 'the back of the pit,' as of Hell. Still dripping piety, the Jew is again on his knees before his Master, Waldengarver, in ironic posture of worship. So is 'the Master' crucified; so do His foes, Jew and Christian alike, like Hebrew and Roman of old, receive Him today.

The *Hamlet* chapter of *Great Expectations* suggests that, whatever others make of Shakespeare, Dickens finds in the creator of morally earnest Ghosts that do not let men's consciences sleep, and of a Son who dies for the sake of the Father, a kindred spirit and guide in a Christian life's work. Mr. Chillip enters like the Ghost of Hamlet (*Copperfield*), and Marley's ghost triggers mention of Hamlet's Ghost (*A Christmas Carol*), as if it had something to do with Dickens's own world-overturning Christian Spirits to come. Dickens communes deeply with Shakespeare in other ways, too. In *The Life of Charles Dickens,* Forster relates that while living in Genoa in 1844, Dickens was having difficulty finding a title for a new work, and keeping Forster in touch by mail. Forster records:

> Only two days later, however, came a letter in which not a syllable was written but 'We have heard THE CHIMES at midnight, Master Shallow!' and I knew he had discovered what he wanted. (FD, II, 118)

The title *The Chimes* is born as Dickens recalls a line from a play by Shakespeare in which he once played Justice Shallow. To Dickens, the Shakespeare who shaped Staffs Fals(e) and true to guide pilgrims' feet on Gadshill, was a Christian poet. Coming to live at Gadshill, how Dickens must have relished being literally, as figuratively, on Shakespearean (not to mention Gads, or God's) ground, and (Gads *hill*) rising ground at that.

Thus we see that Mr. Wopsle's immortal Hamlet is worthier still of immortality. Dickens shows that nothing men do can keep the Christ myth at the heart of *Hamlet,* and history, from returning to the kingdom of the living. Then it ends. Waldengarver goes back to being plain Wopsle, full of chatter about himself and his future plans:

> I forget in detail what they were, but I have a general recollection that he
> was to begin with reviving the Drama, and to end with crushing it; inasmuch
> as his decease would leave it utterly bereft and without a chance or hope. (243)

So Waldengarver is not Christ after all. For, far from leaving man 'utterly bereft,' the death of Christ is the source of his every chance and hope of Life Eternal.

In Dickens, as in NT *Acts,* the play's the thing. After her own drop, Miss Trotwood forges on. 'We must learn to act the play out' (499), she says.

Nothing changes overnight. The Yah past clings. She maintains 'a continuous state of guerrilla warfare' (514) with David's landlady, Mrs. Crupp: it is Yah v. C(o)r(r)up-tion, in the old foe-crushing way. But now we learn that Miss Trotwood never Yah'd her faithless husband; rather, she supported and protected him from the Law. He appears, astonished at such clemency from one he treated so ill: 'And why don't you abandon me to my deserts?' (687) he asks. Why? Because Miss Trotwood has in her more than Yah 'justice' of sandy deserts and desertions, those dire just deserts.

Late in the story, when her husband dies, Miss Trotwood, who never reposed trust or confidence in anyone before, opens her heart to David. She tells how, when her husband deserted her, she abandoned love and faith, 'put all that sort of sentiment, once and for ever, in a grave, and fill[ed] it up, and flatten[ed] it down' (688). Thanks to the son of David and to Mr. Dick, she rises from that 'grave' and death. Relating her sad story, Miss Trotwood does not dwell on her husband's sins against her; she is no longer full of claims of Self, as on that fateful visit to Blunderstone ages before. David and she attend the funeral, and afterwards she speaks of the past once again:

> 'Six-and-thirty years ago, this day, my dear,' said my aunt, as we walked
> back to the chariot, 'I was married. God forgive us all!'

> We took our seats in silence; and so she sat beside me for a long time, hold-
> ing my hand. At length she suddenly burst into tears, and said:
>
> 'He was a fine-looking man when I married him, Trot—and he was sadly
> changed!'
>
> It did not last long. After the relief of tears, she soon became composed,
> and even cheerful. Her nerves were a little shaken, she said, or she would not
> have given way to it. God forgive us all!' (782)

In this moment, the Old and New Betsey Trotwood meet. The brusque
pulling back from sentiment, a giving way to tears, looks backward. But
there is a new, generous, humble spirit in: 'God forgive us all!' A 'composed, and even cheerful' lady, touched with 'c' and 'ch,' is the ally of
Agnes and Canterbury. Then, growing shy of emotion, she draws back.
Perhaps David's words that ruefully echo her own, 'God forgive us all!',
sigh for all human inconstancy of the kind.

In the end, the once-'Ya-a-ah!' dragon sings the praises of Agnes:

> 'You will find her,' pursued my aunt, 'as good, as beautiful, as earnest, as
> disinterested, as she has always been. If I knew higher praise, Trot, I would
> bestow it on her.' (837)

Higher praise does exist for Agnes, as high as Heaven. Why does good
Miss Trotwood not know it? For the same reason she cannot bring herself
to relent towards donkeys. The stiff-necked Chosen People of Yah could
not accept as their Messiah one so poor in spirit and lowly of heart that,
although King of the Jews, He was born in a manger, moved among commoners, outcasts, and criminals, and rode on an ass. Though suffering two
little children to come unto her, David and Dick, Miss Trotwood drives off
donkeys and the bestriding woman and child. Even when she praises
Agnes, she will not accompany David to Canterbury. She is like Virgil in
Dante, the light of wise worldly governance and reason that illumines the
path of Christian time to be, but itself remains behind for the last stage of
the journey to Paradise. Dante and David, epic Christian heroes, are
guided out of their dark waldens by Virgil and the virgilian Miss Trotwood,
geniuses both of earlier moral/spiritual time who themselves remain
behind.

Miss Trotwood's story begins when David's father ups and chooses a
Clara for his bride. One can just picture Aunt Betsey hearing of the betrothal of her favorite, and, storming around in Yah-style, muttering:
''*Clara*'?! Why could he not have picked some nice Jewish girl—a Littera,
Verba, Regula, or a 'J' like that sensible Jane Murdstone, or Judy Smallweed? Or Sarah Gamp, always guzzling Old Tipper, and converting everything to 'J' on the spot, denouncing a 'topjy turjey' (MC, 812) world, some
'perfeejus wretch!' (758), or declaring life to be a 'Piljian's Projiss of a
mortal wale' (404)?!' But no, David loves Clara, light which signals the
dawn of the Light of the world.

Had she stayed away from Blunderstone, we said, mankind might have bypassed the whole weary Good Friday time of law and crucifixion and shot straight up into the Sonrise of Easter morn. But Providence sacred and Dickensian wills it otherwise. Descent must precede ascent. Moreover, in Dickens, reason for regret so often shades into reason for rejoicing, and what hurt David at one moment in retrospect so often proves to have helped—tempered, deepened him—that judgment throws up its OT hands and withdraws. The Yah lady who 'seldom conducted herself like any ordinary Christian' in time proves, truly, no ordinary, but a most extraordinary one. It seems that history must always come in like Yah and the lions of Babylon for pilgrim Time to go out with the Lamb.

'She couldn't even have a baby like anybody else,' Miss Trotwood once complains of Clara Copperfield. In time, she thanks her lucky Stars that David's mother was not like anybody else, nor her baby like any baby else. When finally Agnes and David wed, the A.D. so rejoined does not destroy, it fulfills fondest Yah hopes, for of that union a little Betsey Trotwood is born at last. The story opens one blustery March day with 'Ya-a-ah!' bursting in like a wintry blast to chill all souls. But if March come, can April with her sweet showers and tender Christian crops in the word, the sunny Chaucerian-Dickensian season of the unburying year which Recalls to Life, be far behind? In Dickens, as in Scripture, all things slowly but surely work together for them that love the Lord.

No portrait of Miss Trotwood would be complete without its companion-piece, that of Mr. Dick. United in mutual admiration are the worldly lady who sweeps all before her, and unworldly, retiring Dick. Miss Trotwood holds that: 'It's in vain, Trot, to recall the past, unless it works some influence upon the present' (347). But Mr. Dick succumbs to memories of time past despite all he can do. Policing, praising, prompting Dick, publishing a Trotwood version of his common sense high and low, even so Miss Trotwood never manages to channel his wandering thoughts of King Charles or to yoke his kite-flying ways to her chariot of reason. How droll to watch *yah* trying to foist her own shrewd, hard, cynical views of Mrs. Crupp on Dick, so wholly incapable of objectivity, much less blame, in a campaign to bring his innocence into line with her sharp-eyed experience. Mr. Dick will probably never know anything the world deems worth knowing. Nor, in Dickens, is it intellect alone that saves.

Like figures in profile on a Biblical bas-relief, Miss Trotwood and Mr. Dick move forward: busy lady carrying shawls and pillows, on her way to the ailing little Dora's bedside; and Mr. Dick, who 'would not have relinquished his post as candle bearer to any one alive' (700), gladly bringing up the rear. Holding his bright candle, and, as if that were not enough light, coming to live over a chandler's shop, Mr. Dick (in Miss Trotwood's words) 'sets us all right' (193) as only a vision of 'Mr. Dick'-ensian allegory finally brings to light.

We now fall in behind the procession, the better to sound the mystery of the author and friend to David's son, Dickens's Mr. Dick, as well as that of yet another author and friend to the sons of David, Mr. Dickens.

# TWELVE
# Mr. Dick

'You'll consider yourself guardian, jointly with me, of this child, Mr. Dick,'
said my aunt.

'I shall be delighted,' said Mr. Dick, 'to be the guardian of David's son.'

'Very good,' returned my aunt, '*that's* settled. I have been thinking, do
you know, Mr. Dick, that I might call him Trotwood?'

'Certainly, certainly. Call him Trotwood, certainly,' said Mr. Dick. 'David's son Trotwood.'

'Trotwood Copperfield,' you mean,' returned my aunt.

'Yes, to be sure. Yes. Trotwood Copperfield,' said Mr. Dick, a little
abashed. (DC, 214)

In a quiet corner of *David Copperfield,* one of those small last-shall-come-
first Dickensian nooks of inconspicuous consequence, lives gentle, retiring,
oft-troubled, and perhaps slightly mad Mr. Dick. While his decidedly un-
retiring patroness, Miss Trotwood, volubly rules all—'Trotwood Copperfield, you mean,' she commands—Dick, when allowed, stays in the background. Though interested in everything and wonderfully sympathetic,
Mr Dick says little, but expresses much, an original symbolic vocabulary
of squints, winks, nods, significant coughs, liftings of eyebrows, flutters of
confusions, sudden onsets of boyish delight, revealing what he has too few
words or perhaps too little confidence in life left to say.

Worldly Miss Trotwood and unworldly Mr. Dick: truly 'a curious couple
of guardians' (215) for, as Dick *will* call him, David's son. Between 'Ya-a-
ah!' and Dick, who is a fugitive from ancient woe involving betrayal by
close kin, the latest son of David is well raised, he and Dick, in spite of a
great difference in age, soon becoming, like Pip and Joe Gargery, 'the best
of friends' (216).

When on that memorable day a footsore, ragged David arrives in Dover
and stands before his aunt's cottage, the first person he sees is not the
lady herself, but a distinctly odd, young-old, entirely original person he will
shortly thereafter know as Mr. Dick:

> The unbroken stillness of the parlour-window leading me to infer, after a while, that she was not there, I lifted up my eyes to the window above it, where I saw a florid, pleasant-looking gentleman, with a grey head, who shut up one eye in a grotesque manner, nodded his head at me several times, shook it at me as often, laughed, and went away. (190)

What mysterious message does the not-yet Mr. Dick overflow with and energetically try to communicate in secret symbols and laughter to David? Why, thereafter, does he speak 'with infinite secrecy, and always in a whisper' (249); and impart his innocent confidences 'with an air of mystery' (249)?

Soon after the incident of the upper window, Miss Trotwood, unaware that Dick and David have, in a manner of speaking, already met, summons Dick down to inspect the newly-arrived child. As Dick enters, David recognizes 'the gentleman who had squinted at me from the upper window' (192), and who is still, or again, laughing to himself at Heaven only knows what. (And it does.) Impatiently, Miss Trotwood orders Dick not to be a fool. Whereupon:

> The gentleman was serious immediately, and looked at me, I thought, as if he would entreat me to say nothing about the window. (192)

So an unspoken understanding is born between David and Dick. Dick is subdued. 'Yah'd' out of laughter, brought down by Miss Trotwood, in more ways than one, how submissive, absent-minded, and lost Mr. Dick suddenly seems. Sober and abashed, he now gazes 'vacantly' (193) at David (his 'vacant manner' (194) and bowed grey head will often be noted), and seems to be trying to collect his wandering wits and rise to Miss Trotwood's rapid-fire queries about what to do with David. Demanding instant, practical, common-sense advice from Dick, chiding what she insists is his 'pretending to be wool-gathering' (193), she brings him down to solid earth, for better and worse, with a thud.

Presenting David to Mr. Dick, she asks: 'What shall I do with him?':

> 'What shall you do with him?' said Mr. Dick, feebly, scratching his head. 'Oh! do with him?'
> 'Yes,' said my aunt, with a grave look, and her forefinger held up. 'Come! I want some very sound advice.'
> 'Why, if I was you,' said Mr. Dick, considering, and looking vacantly at me, 'I should—'The contemplation of me seemed to inspire him with a sudden idea, and he added, briskly, 'I should wash him!'
> 'Janet,' said my aunt, turning round with a quiet triumph, which I did not then understand, 'Mr. Dick sets us all right. Heat the bath!' (193)

At the sight of the son of David, despondency and vacancy vanish. Lost but a moment before, Mr. Dick is suddenly restored, recalled to life. With

David, now as in OT time, dawns 'the idea.'

Who is this slightly adrift, abstracted Mr. Dick, this uncertain, grey-haired, eternal child-man often laboring away in an upstairs room where he launches hopeful, ambitious start after start on a literary-historical Memorial amid confused bundles of manuscripts, pens, and half-gallon jars of ink?  What driving, incommunicable passion of authorship possesses him despite unending bog-down and woe?  One wonders what gentle Mr. Dick makes of Miss Trotwood's incessant wars, rages at law, and plans 'to appeal for redress to the laws of her country and to bring action for trespass against the whole donkey proprietorship of Dover' (198); or of her ruling that his soft, distracted, bewildered self is nothing of the sort, but 'sharp as a surgeon's lancet' (193).  Whatever Dick thinks, we slowly come to suspect that there is something uniquely wonderful in him that *Yah,* though full of admiration for his common sense, does not know the half of.

Technically speaking, *Mr. Dick* is really Richard Babley, whom a brother years before had committed to 'some private asylum-place' (204), a terrible incarceration far from home.  Babley dooms Mr. Dick to a kind of Babley-lon, as it were, an exile and captivity.  This ordeal inflicted by kin is never forgotten, and in aftertime, how we never know, merges in Mr. Dick's affected mind with a not unsimilar betrayal to agony untold, the ordeal of King Charles the First.  After Mr. Dick's rescue, the lost head of Charles, a misty symbol of his own 'lost head' or deranged, stolen, lost mental faculties and hope, keeps finding its way into his manuscripts despite all Miss Trotwood, and he himself, can do to keep it out.  The plight of the royal martyr seems vividly present to Dick.  He cannot believe that centuries separate him from the slain King: 'Because, if it was so long ago, how could the people about him have made the mistake of putting some of the trouble out of *his* head, after it was taken off, into *mine?*'

Usual remedies for such distress—time passing, the *Yah* formula of living misfortune down—prove inapplicable to the curiously wounded soul of shy Mr. Dick, which all the will-stiffening moral poultices and shibboleths of worldly wisdom cannot cure.  Like Barkis's rumbling cart, these cannot go all the way.  Rather, Dick's salvation lies in a unique 'allegorical way' of dealing with ancient, unbanishable agitation of mind, the King's and his own, one 'not a business-like way of speaking, nor a worldly way' (205), in Miss Trotwood's words.  The way which is a wool-gathering in the Lamb.

It is as simple as it is inspired.  Mr. Dick takes a kite, which 'must have been as much as seven feet high' (203), and covers it with leaves from the unwieldy Story he has been working on for ages, leaves 'closely and laboriously written' (203), remnants of many attempts to chronicle the history of 'the Lord Chancellor, or the Lord Somebody or other' (205).  ('Somebody or other' leaves the identity of the 'Lord' wide open.)  Laden with portions of the life of the Lord, also the tragic history of the King and Mr. Dick in symbolic form (the severed head), the kite is launched and rises up, up into the heavens to sail peacefully among the larks. Thus Mr. Dick the author comes to repose the weary weight of all this unintelligible world, the burthen of the mystery, in God. A kite *seven* feet high, the very kite for sacred journeys of allegory, carries a symbolic history of man back up to the Creator.

Its chief theme is woe. Captivity in the modern Babylon lies in David's recent past; Babley-lon in Mr. Dick's. The latter's vacant looks, lost wits, and oft-bowed grey head mutely testify better than words could to sufferings past and a still-unhealed spirit. The searing Murdstone age is not far behind David. The piteous, unavailing: 'Oh, pray!' of Clara Copperfield lies murdstoned in the grave. Ruled by law as stony as that of the Jews, Christendom has lost touch with faith and prayer. The ambiguous *Yah* Providence that both doomed David to and rescued him from 'Babylon' mistakes him for Cain; like Cain, he wanders and prowls. It is against this dark background that Mr. Dick emerges, and, in the greatness of his need for comfort, rediscovers a glorious, forgotten pathway to the Above, which, to borrow Miss Trotwood's words, 'sets us all right.'

Mr. Dick's mystery looks to the sky:

> 'There's plenty of string,' said Mr. Dick, 'and when it flies high, it takes the facts a long way. That's my manner of diffusing 'em. I don't know where they may come down. It's according to circumstances, and the wind, and so forth; but I take my chance of that.' (203)

Like Mr. Dickens, Mr. Dick discovers 'the allegorical way of expressing it' (205), the sky-journey that carries literal fact, the letter, a long way. As the kite rises into the blue with the history of the Lord, a slain 'Ch' King, and Mr. Dick aboard, in symbolic form, a magical change takes place in Dick himself; as David, ever sympathetic and observant, relates:

> It was quite an affecting sight, I used to think, to see him with the kite when it was up to a great height in the air. What he had told me, in his room, about belief in its disseminating the statements pasted on it, which were nothing but old leaves of aborted Memorials, might have been a fancy with him sometimes; but not when he was out, looking up at the kite in the sky, and feeling it pull and tug at his hand. He never looked so serene as he did then. I used to fancy, as I sat by him of an evening, on a green slope, and saw him watch the kite high in the quiet air, that it lifted his mind out of its confusion, and bore it (such was my boyish thought) into the skies. As he wound the string in, and it came lower and lower out of the beautiful light, until it fluttered to the ground, and lay there like a dead thing, he seemed to wake gradually out of a dream; and I remember to have seen him take it up, and look about him in a lost way, as if they had both come down together, so that I pitied him with all my heart. (216)

As Dick 'rises' into the heavens, the passage itself rises like an allegory or a prayer. With intuitive sympathy following Dick's flight, David shapes graceful sentences in which to house the sky-blue theme. See the written line, like the string of the kite, unwind phrase by phrase, from: 'I used to fancy,' the first between-commas loop, to the farthest reach, several linguistic line-lengths on, of the triplet: 'into the skies;' then, from azure height of 'skies,' begin a slow descent, down, down to the perfect quietude of the final triplet phrase: 'come down together.' So Mr. Dick experiences rise and fall. Behold a perfect attunement of subject and form, its glory 'three.'

Mr. Dick is not conscious of what it all means. He only knows that in flying alone he finds blessed relief and peace, the way, if only for a moment, to the realm of 'the beautiful light.' The idea that Mr. Dick rises in spirit with the kite is born in David's fertile fancy. The parenthesis, '(such was my boyish thought),' is tentative, half apologetic, almost, reminding us that as an author, David is still shy of his figural gifts, which, like Mr. Dick's allegorical way, are reflected nowhere around him in realms of common sense. David is still a novice in the fancying, wondering ways of the New curiosity. Agnes has just come upon the scene; David's Canterbury Tale has just begun. As to Dick, he has no words. The wordy burden he entrusts to the sky, and wordlessly ascends in spirit. But only for a while. There is no staying aloft in this life, as David elsewhere remarks; too soon, all comes fluttering palely down. Yet Dick is proof that something in man seeks its Heavenly home.

Mr. Dick, the dear, hale-hearty old gentleman who even as a child melts with delight at a word of praise, loves gingerbread and games, is defenseless when hurt but easily made glad again, is man become as a little child. He is one of a small band which includes David, Mr. Chillip, Clara Peggotty, the Master, people whose histories of Yah-J harassment and woe reveal the need for a new covenant and for a Saviour. When they play backgammon, the *Yah* patroness rewards Mr. Dick with a rap on the knuckles. But Dick never complains. A natural Christian, though neither he nor David throws around such terms, Dick instantly forgives and forgets without even knowing he does, or channeling such thoughts through the rational mind.

Dickens hints at the religious significance of Dick and his allegorical way. As he speaks of his kite, Dick's pleasant face has 'something so reverend in it, though it was hale and hearty' (203), that David, not understanding, concludes he is jesting with him. Laughing, the two friends part. Though he hardly knows it, David strikes the very word. In Mr. Dick is the 'reverend' spirit Dickens loves; far from it the Very, Right, and other Reverend gentlemen of the cloth Dickens finds so lamentably full of religious cant, and short of Christian spirit. (vis. Chapter II) New orders of imagination abide in Mr. Dick, as we find on his visits to David at school:

> He was an universal favourite, and his ingenuity in little things was trans-
> cendent.  He could cut oranges into such devices as none of us had any idea
> of.  He could make a boat out of anything, from a skewer upwards.  He could
> turn crampbones into chessmen; fashion Roman chariots from old court cards;
> make spoked wheels out of cotton reels, and birdcages of old wire.  But he was
> greatest of all, perhaps, in the articles of string and straw; with which we were
> all persuaded he could do anything that could be done by hands. (251)

Like the kite, his 'transcendent' ingenuity points upward.  From the first
glimpse of him flashing signs and symbols in the upper-story window, Mr.
Dick is affined to the Above.  Urging on childish imaginings, creating and
launching tiny tims of barks on 'the journey,' Dick brings into being what
before him no one, literally or figuratively speaking, 'had an idea of.'  Shy
of the letter, Mr. Dick redelivers the long-lost idea.[1]  Turning 'a face of
unutterable interest' (251) upon the boys at play (*unutterable,* in truth:  his
language is symbolic), Dick affirms the value of joyful play and imagination, in the handiwork of which man rediscovers the marvels of the
Creation, and learns to praise.

Like Agnes, but in a very small, modest way, Mr. Dick points upward.
When watching the boys at play, Dick stands 'mounted on a little knoll,
cheering the whole field on to action, and waving his hat above his grey
head, oblivious of King Charles the Martyr's head, and all belonging to it!'
(251) 'Mounted' on his little nell of a knoll, Dick, cheering the whole field,
Every One, sits as high in the saddle as any pilgrim to Canterbury under
the sun.

Faith, grateful love, and service are Dick's whole way.  His service is,
again, more symbolic than otherwise.  Making toys that invite wonder and
dreams of wonders unseen, bearing his candle, or carrying his small
earnings, coins 'arranged in the form of a heart upon a waiter, with tears of
joy and pride in his eyes' (529) to Miss Trotwood (the heart, again,
symbolic), he gives the little that is much.  Faith is his forte:  'his faith in
the wisest and most wonderful of women, and his unbounded reliance on
my [David's] intellectual resources' (501).  Mr. Dick is the holy fool, like
the Fool in *King Lear,* Don Quixote, Dostoevsky's saintly Idiot, Barnaby
Rudge, and Melville's Pip, the cabin-boy in *Moby Dick;* unknown conduits
from unseen worlds empty into each and all.  Dick the tireless scribbler
pens for Dickens another shining chapter in the allegory of the Genius of
Christianity entitled 'In Praise of Folly,' and in praise of humble reverence,
transcendent imagination, self-giving, and the undying memory of a great,
sorrowful King.

Like many others in this Book of David, Mr. Dick starts out in OT time in
a symbolic Bableylon-Babylon.  (Incidentally, the 'Bab' syllable is
especially prominent in early ages of *Copperfield.*)[2]  Returning from
captivity a dazed, broken man, Dick is set to write a history of the Lord in
Yah realms where an unallegorical common sense prevails.  But writing is

not the answer. Real relief comes only with the feel of a tug on the string as an unseen breath, the winds of heaven, lifts the kite bearing the multi-layered story of human woe into the sky.

Christianity discovers its lost self in Mr. Dick, both its wound and hope. Of course everyone ignores or mistakes him, thinking him a fool. Even David supposes Dick's story of a strange man who follows Miss Trotwood a 'delusion' (250), but it is true. In Dick, Dickens confronts the problem of coming to terms with evil and injustice in a divinely ordered universe, and of human suffering from the times of the Captivity to the Crucifixion. Sensitized by his own experience of betrayal, Mr. Dick remembers the trials of King Charles only too well. The secret would seem to be to strike a balance between the world's callous indifference (one recalls the statue of King Charles standing forgotten in brown drizzle outside the Golden Cross), and Mr. Dick's own too-acute, nigh-paralysing remembrance. As in *The Battle of Life* Benjamin Britain becomes mired in eroding cynicism, so in *Copperfield* Mr. Dick for a time succumbs to memory and despair, risking dissolution in the tears of things.

Miss Trotwood's friendship and David's too do much for Dick. So does kite-flying. But more is needed.

The answer is active doing in the world: service to the Strongs, in behalf of the love founded on the rock. Venerating the Doctor and his great work, the Dictionary, Mr. Dick, Boswell-like, pays tribute to high knowledge he never acquired, or that woe drove out of his head in those 'lost head' years of unmerited confinement:

> This veneration Mr. Dick extended to the Doctor, whom he thought the most subtle and accomplished philosopher of any age. It was long before Mr. Dick ever spoke to him otherwise than bareheaded; and even when he and the Doctor had struck up quite a friendship, and would walk together by the hour, on that side of the court-yard which was known among us as The Doctor's Walk, Mr. Dick would pull off his hat at intervals to show his respect for wisdom and knowledge. How it ever came about that the Doctor began to read out scraps of the famous Dictionary, in these walks, I never knew; perhaps he felt it all the same, at first, as reading to himself. However, it passed into a custom too; and Mr. Dick, listening with a face shining with pride and pleasure, in his heart of hearts, believed the Dictionary to be the most delightful book in the world. (252)

Here one walks on allegorical ground from the start. Dickens's Doctor, Dictionary, and the humble penman who venerates both, Dick, constitute a living memorial to Doctor Johnson and the Dictionary if ever there was one. Someone even mentions Doctor Johnson, Dickens ever prompting actively along the way.[3] Dick does not know, he 'believe[s]'. The learned Doctor is 'the letter,' and worshipful, ignorant Dick is 'the spirit' which completes it. Faith, reverencing love, the blind-but-sighted leap of the soul towards the ideal object, the finite earthly beauty in which is glimpsed the infinite virtue and beauty of the Eternal, abides in symbolic-allegorical Mr. Dick.

Entering the troubled Strong world, soon Mr. Dick does more than admire and listen. Like a bashful knight, he silently offers his loving service to Annie Strong, so sore beset by foes: Heep, Mrs. Markleham, and Jack Maldon. The rational mind of Dick, struck a near-mortal blow in Babley days, remains clouded. But into (in David's words) the 'mind of the heart, if I may call it so, in Mr. Dick, some bright ray of the truth shot straight' (623). He becomes Mrs. Strong's faithful companion in her garden, helping her trim flowers and weed beds; and loved by both, becomes a link between the Strongs. David says:

> When I think of him, with his impenetrably wise face, walking up and down with the Doctor, delighted to be battered by the hard words in the Dictionary; when I think of him carrying huge watering-pots after Annie; kneeling down in very paws of gloves, at patient microscopic work among the little leaves; expressing as no philosopher ever could have expressed, in everything he did, a delicate desire to be her friend; showering sympathy, trustfulness, and affection, out of every hole in the watering-pot; when I think of him never wandering in that better mind of his to which unhappiness addressed itself, never wandering in his grateful service, never diverted from his knowledge that there was something wrong, or from his wish to set it right—I really feel almost ashamed of having known that he was not quite in his wits, taking account of the utmost I have done with mine.
>
> 'Nobody but myself, Trot, knows what that man is!' my aunt would proudly remark, when we conversed about it. 'Dick will distinguish himself yet!' (623)

As Dante mends the soul-body breach in loving Beatrice both as a living being and a celestial spirit, so, in his 'mind of the heart,' Mr. Dick reconciles two principles too often opposed, mind and heart, with *mind* subordinate to right feeling, *heart*. As soon he cannot sort out the King's sorrows from his own, so there is no telling heart and mind apart. In Mr. Dick, opposites are reconciled, and, like past and present and letter and spirit, live at peace.

Mr. Dick finds another symbolic way of serving Doctor Strong and the love founded on a rock:

> 'I have sent his name up, on a scrap of paper, to the kite, along the string, when it has been in the sky, among the larks. The kite has been glad to receive it, sir, and the sky has been brighter with it.' (652)

Again, what a sentence for unwinding, length on length, until with it, fully unfurled, one is high and serene 'among the larks.' Like a great word-winged bird, the kite, a symbol of the soul, carries the name of Doctor Strong aloft in prayer. In allegory, Dick prays for his friend! Not even

David guesses what Dick is up to.  Misreading altogether, he concludes, ironically, that Dick has 'settled into his original foundation, like a building; and I must confess that my faith in his ever moving, was not much greater than if he had been a building' (651).  O ye of little faith!

Ever and always, the Mr. Dick mode of expression is symbolic.  His hat swept off signifies reverence for learning.  As the idea of sending the Doctor's name up dawns, up shoot Dick's eyebrows, 'lifted up as high as he could possibly lift them' (653).  He always illustrates points in images. Once, he is disconsolate; he speaks of making his will and leaving every-thing (he has nothing) to Miss Trotwood.  The woeful thought finds appropriate symbolic action to complete it:

> Mr. Dick took out his pocket-handkerchief, and wiped his eyes.  He then folded it up with great care, pressed it smooth between his two hands, put it in his pocket, and seemed to put my aunt away with it. (652)

It is a symbolic burial in a 'pocket,' or grave.  But not for long.  When the idea of the kite breaks, with an excited: "Then I have got it, boy!' Dick takes out the pocket-handkerchief 'as if it did represent my aunt' (653). She is risen!  Not only that, but Dick leaps to his feet, too.  Not catching on, David can only think that Mr. Dick is 'farther out of his wits than ever' (653).  Yet David is right, for all that.  *Wits* and chuzzlewits, i.e., mind, knowledge, reason, common sense, have no part in Dick's mystery.  Dick *is* ever farther out of his wits all the time.  When David pronounces Dick in 'a flighty and unsettled state of his mind' (654), he is again both wrong and right.  Dick *is* 'flighty,' as the kite flies, as men's hopes fly up to Heaven. Hat swept off, pocket-handkerchief dug out, eyebrows raised as high as possible, signals in upstairs windows, the leaping up, and more, show that, like Martha Endell, Mr. Dick's genius turns on: 'Rise up!'  It also turns on the unique discovery, allegory, that returns a forgotten King of sorrows, and all he recalls, to living history.

'Dick's nobody!  Whoo!' (654) cries Mr. Dick, in merry self-disparage-ment, reflecting that of the world, symbolically blowing himself away. Well does he know that nobody minds him.  But it is this very anonymity and, in effect, invisibility that permits him to work his wonders.

The Strong marriage is sore beset.  Every hour sees Mrs. Markleham at her deadly work of putting asunder what God has joined together.  One evening, when David and his aunt stroll over to the Strong cottage, they find the Doctor in his study making his last will and testament.  Convinced by his foes that he stands in young Annie's way, he means to remove himself from her life.

The family and David and Miss Trotwood gather in the study.  Annie enters on Mr. Dick's arm.  Dropping on one knee before her defeated husband, with hands prayerfully raised, she lifts a look of supplication to him.  The Doctor is deeply moved.  'Rise, Annie, pray!' he pleads.  'But she did not rise' (657). The 'rising' moment has not yet come. Looking only to the Doctor, speaking, as she says, 'before him, and before God afterwards' (658), Annie begs him to believe in her faithfulness to her marriage vows. Annie and the Doctor, symbolizing faith and the word, the spirit and the letter, are reunited.

Now Annie rises. 'Mr. Dick softly raised her; and she stood, when she began to speak, leaning on him, and looking down upon her husband—-from whom she never turned her eyes' (658). Soon after, she kneels to him again and avows:

> 'I can lift my eyes to this dear face, revered as a father's, loved as a husband's, sacred to me in my childhood as a friend's, and solemnly declare that in my lightest thought I had never wronged you; never wavered in the love and fidelity I owe you!' (662)

Father, husband, friend: three-in-one. Now Mr. Dick again raises Annie, who cries: 'Oh, take me to your heart, my husband, for my love was founded on a rock, and it endures!' (663) Her words, like the *raise up-rise* theme, the chime of the Trinity, the love of the bride and bridegroom, point to the NT and these words of Christ:

> Therefore whosoever heareth these sayings of mine, and doeth them, I will liken him unto a wise man, which built his house upon a rock;
>
> And the rain descended, and the floods came, and the winds blew, and beat upon that house; and it fell not: for it was founded upon a rock. (*Matt.* 7:24-25)

Mr. Dick plays a vital part in preserving the love founded on a rock. Here is a worthy life's work for many a flyer of word-kites and master builder in the kingdom of the Master like Mr. Dick, or Mr. Dickens.

In such endeavour Mr. Dick slowly works free of old woe. If Miss Trotwood lives misfortune down, Mr. Dick, by God, lives it up: quite literally, as figuratively, the *up* of kites, knolls, and the happy adventure of coming to live over a chandler's shop, its smallness not for an instant dimming for Dick 'the glory of lodging over this structure' (500). Glory be! And more *up*. Making Micawber's acquaintance, Mr. Dick says: 'You must keep up your spirits!' (709) That is useful advice in the era in which Micawber serves Heep, calls himself Mortimer, and reads the works of Justice Blackstone, surely first cousin to Mr. Blackboy. Returning the compliment, Mr. Micawber rechristens Dick 'Dixon,' a name which so delights Dick...

> ...that he shook hands with him[Micawber] again, and laughed rather childishly.
>
> 'Dick,' said my aunt, 'attention!' (744)

*Dixon,* with an 'x,' or sign of the cross in the middle, is *Dick's son.* Serving the 'Strong' cause, Mr. Dick points to the *Son*. *Yah,* on guard against the child, and 'childish' laughter in her dependents, calls a halt to Dick's joy.

Mr. Dick and symbolism go together. When Miss Trotwood's fortune is lost, Dick stands on a street-corner 'with his great kite at his back, a very monument of human misery' (502). He also thinks in symbols, as is seen when he and David discuss the Strongs:

> I delighted him by saying, most heartily, that the Doctor was deserving of our best respect and highest esteem.
> 'And his beautiful wife is a star,' said Mr. Dick. 'A shining star. I have seen her shine, sir. But,' bringing his chair nearer, and laying one hand upon my knee—'clouds, sir,—clouds.'
> I answered the solicitude which his face expressed, by conveying the same expression into my own, and shaking my head.
> 'What clouds?' said Mr. Dick.
> He looked so wistfully into my face, and was so anxious to understand, that I took great pains to answer him slowly and distinctly, as I might have entered on an explanation to a child. (653)

'Shining star' and 'clouds' are the heavenly height from which Mr. Dick must be helped down. Happily, the son of David is there to translate the language of sky into that of earth, in the way of the Son of David.

In his turn, Mr. Dick, a walking symbolic primer, teaches David from the start. In his very first appearance in the upper window, he causes David to look up! In Dickens, the fool says, there *is* a God. In flying his kite, in cheering Mr. Micawber, serving the Strongs, and holding fast to his faith in the wonderfulness of 'the most wonderful woman in the world,' Mr. Dick proves the truth of what an admiring Tommy Traddles says about him: 'There's Mr. Dick, too, has been doing wonders!' (774) Many are the wonders the truly 'reverend,' disinterested, 'transcendent' spirit can perform in the service of the love founded on a rock, which is faith in Christ's revelation of the will of God.

Mr. Dick gently, humbly points new directions. For example, Mrs. Crupp, David's landlady, dourly observes that Dick's little room over the chandler's shop is not big enough to swing a cat in. Really? That is fine with Dick, who confides:

> 'You know, Trotwood, I don't want to swing a cat. I never do swing a cat. Therefore, what does that signify to *me!*' (500)

Weighing a creaky old figure of speech by the moral facts of his own life and finding it wanting, Mr. Dick quietly blows it away.

At the end of the novel, Mr. Dick is an old man. One finds him still making and flying giant kites, surrounded by the sons of David and Agnes. Flying kites...

> ...and gazing at them in the air, with a delight for which there are no words.

> He greets me rapturously, and whispers, with many nods and winks, 'Trotwood, you will be glad to hear that I shall finish the Memorial when I have nothing else to do, and that your aunt's the most extraordinary woman in the world, sir!' (874)

Good Doctor Strong will polish words and fix their denotations all his worthy days. But Mr. Dick, or Dixon, will gladly surrender those heavy words to the sky, finding in this act a blessed release, and perhaps a glimpse of the coming time when all souls, like the kite freighted with histories of weal and woe, will fly up to immortal destinations. To express the wonders his great kite armada in its upward journey implies, truly 'there are no words.'

The reader has probably guessed by now what I am about to suggest, which is that Mr. Dick is a whimsical, sentimental self-portrait by Mr. Dickens, one of a number which include that of Dick the blackbird in *Nicholas Nickleby,* Dick Swiveller in *The Old Curiosity Shop,* and Richard Doubledick in *The Seven Poor Travellers.* How alike are Mr. Dick and Mr. Dickens, two harried authors in upstairs rooms knee-deep in pens, ink-pots, and piles of manuscripts, mementos of many attempts to write a great Memorial to the Lord that never gets properly written. Dick and Dickens, both caught up in the 'un-business-like,' 'allegorical' way; both beset by dark, painful memory; both lighting on a unique, allegorical solution which releases great word-and-symbol-covered birds of Paradise which hallow the memory of a man of sorrows and King, to the whims and winds of Heaven. Valued-undervalued, often overlooked 'Mr. Dick' is, we think, the Dickens whose whole devotion was to the advancement of Christianity, the love founded on a rock.

Dickens too lived with the: 'Dick's nobody! Whoo!' popular myth that he was an amiable, sentimental old fellow with a good heart, but more than a little weak in the head. One recalls Trollope's satiric portrait of Dickens in *The Warden* in which he appears as 'Mr. Popular Sentiment,' a novelist-reformer of namby-pamby whose 'good poor people are so very good, his hard rich people so very hard, and the genuinely honest so very honest:' and whose 'immaculate manufacturing hero may talk as much twaddle as one of Mrs. Ratcliffe's heroines and still be listened to.' [4] Dickens chafed under many a scoffing, condescending bit of raillery of the kind, we know. [5] But he held firm. Criticized by an American friend, Professor Felton, for a certain unspecified *Chuzzlewit* matter, possibly the harshness of his anti-American satire, Dickens staunchly predicts that one fine day Felton and other critics will stop short, turn around and say: ' "My dear Dickens, you were right, though rough, and did a world of good, though you got most thoroughly hated for it." ' (SL, 94). Like Mr. Dick with his 'Dick's nobody, Whoo!', Dickens remains light-hearted and free of rancour on the subject of his public image. Why not? It serves him well. Dismissed by the learned, serious, and wise, 'Mr. Dick,' the inspired simpleton working wonders, is all the more free to serve the STRONG interest in the exiling, exalting work of allegory.

Dickens *is* 'Dick,' as a letter to a friend reveals:

> God bless you and yours. If I look like some weather-beaten pilot when we meet, don't be surprised. Any mahogany-faced stranger who holds out his hand to you will probably turn out, on inspection, to be the old original Dick. (LLS, II, 258)

One senses that Dickens relishes the idea of passing for a sunburnt, salty old sea-captain like his own character, Captain Cuttle, the old sage in *Dombey and Son* who, Dickens-like, teaches dispirited multitudes to keep a bright lookout forward for the return of the *Son and Heir,* even as the Son and Heir, Christ. The old original Dick does in a very real sense go incognito through the world, passing for 'good old Dickens,' a sentimentalist with a large store of good will and common sense. Meanwhile, no one sees through to his spectacular un-common sense, the kite-flying work of Christian allegory. Like Mr. Dick, Dickens sends ten thousand thousand laboriously hand-written leaves Heavenwards to sail far over our heads, in more ways than one. Also like Dick, Dickens takes many a rap on the knuckles and slight which a *Yah* world, the natural, rational, sensible, implacably literal-minded, more than a little unchristian, if generous, public Providence bestows. Dickens renders unto Caesar, as he must. But when no one is looking, surely, just like Dick, Dickens lets a donkey and child stray unharmed onto the sacred green.

In allegory, the 'lost head of Charles' motif and symbol makes luminous sense. Mr. Dick, robbed of his higher faculties, hope, and confidence by a kinsman's betrayal, 'loses his head.' That is, he comes back from that terrible, enforced confinement dazed in his wits. Like King Charles, he 'loses his head.' The (King) Charles-Dick connection has intimate relevance to the Charles-Dick(ens) one. As the lost head of *Charles* haunts Mr. *Dick,* so the lost head of *Charles* Dickens—all that little Charles, deprived of schooling when forced into a drudge's life at the age of nine, never learned—never ceases to haunt Mr. *Dickens.* The deep suffering of 'Charles'—King Charles, Charles Dickens, and, first and foremost, the 'Ch' figure of the King, Christ, to which all suffering of the wronged and forsaken looks—comes to symbolize for Mr. Dick his own inexpressible sense of having been wronged. Thus 'Mr. Dick,' the grey-haired child-man, the child grown old and hopeless long before his time, whom Charles Dickens became in childhood, and carried around with him inside all his life.

The circumstances of Dickens's youthful trauma are these. In Forster's *The Life of Charles Dickens,* we learn that young David Copperfield's captivity in menial labor in the Murdstone warehouse, a period of agony of body and spirit, near starvation, and abandonment, is the young Charles Dickens's own story in every detail. As Forster points out, the David Copperfield-Charles Dickens, D.C.-C.D. identities are one. Dickens tells a part of his story in both David and Dick. Like Dick, David is cast into Babylon. Not strangers, but family betray both Mr. Dick and Mr. Dickens (and David) to sufferings neither ever can forget. The young Charles Dickens, at the slave-labor of pasting labels on blacking bottles, and the young David slaving among empty bottles in a cellar; and the ever young-old Mr. Dick being confined in an asylum-place, never located or identified, are one and the same terrible memory haunting Dickens.

John Forster, the close friend and biographer to whom alone Dickens confided the painful facts, relates that in Dickens's childhood, James Lamert, a sort of cousin, introduced him into the blacking trade. Instead of being sent to school like his older sister Fanny, Dickens, when hardly ten years old, is sent to labor from morn to night in a rat-infested, tumble-down old tenement. Dickens's own most painful memory of this turns, not on the hunger and loneliness that ensued, which were terrible, but rather on the realization, never come to terms with, that his parents were willing and even eager to surrender him to this drudge's life. In a moving disclosure Dickens states:

> It is wonderful to me that I could have been so easily cast away at such an age. It is wonderful to me, that, even after my descent into the poor little drudge I had been since we came to London, no one had compassion enough on me—a child of singular abilities, quick, eager, delicate, and soon hurt, bodily and mentally—to suggest that something might have been spared, as certainly it might have been, to place me at any common school. Our friends, I take it, were tired out. No one made any sign. My mother and father were quite satisfied. They could hardly have been more so, if I had been twenty years of age, distinguished at a grammar-school, and going to Cambridge. (FD,1,31)

Forster adds:

> His sister Fanny was at about this time elected as a pupil to the royal academy of music; and he has told me what a stab to his heart it was, thinking of his own disregarded condition, to see her go away to begin her education, amid the tearful good wishes of everybody in the house. (FD, I, 19)

An even more terrible psychological blow awaits Dickens. Hope of release dawns. Dickens's improvident father, John Dickens, quarrels with his son's sponsor in the blacking warehouse, and Charles is dismissed and sent home. Dickens himself records what happens next:

> My mother set herself to accommodate the quarrel and did so next day. She brought home a request for me to return next morning, and a high

character of me, which I am very sure I deserved. My father said, I should go back no more, and should go to school. I do not write resentfully or angrily: for I know how all these things have worked together to make me what I am: but I never afterwards forgot, I never shall forget, I never can forget, that my mother was warm for my being sent back.

From that hour until this at which I write, no word of that part of my child-hood which I have now gladly brought to a close, has passed my lips to any human being. I have no idea how long it lasted; whether for a year, or much more, or less. From that hour, until this, my father and my mother have been stricken dumb upon it. I have never heard the least allusion to it, however far off and remote, from either of them. I have never, until I now impart it to this paper, in any burst of confidence with any one, my own wife not excepted, raised the curtain I then dropped, thank God.

Until the old Hungerford-market was pulled down, until old Hungerford-stairs were destroyed, and the very nature of the ground changed, I never had the courage to go back to the place where my servitude began. I never saw it. For many years, when I came near to Robert Warren's in the Strand, I crossed over to the opposite side of the way, to avoid a certain smell of the cement they put upon the blacking-corks, which reminded me of what I was once. It was a very long time before I liked to go up Chandos-street. My old way home by the borough made me cry, after my eldest child could speak.

In my walks at night I have walked there often, since then, and by degrees I have come to write this. It does not seem a tithe of what I might have written, or of what I meant to write. (FD, I, 49-50)

With this dramatic disclosure, deeply moving, the Mr. Dick-Mr. Dickens, alias Dick, resemblance grows. Mr. Dick also has ties to Hungerford-market, where he comes to live:

The chandler's shop being in Hungerford Market, and Hungerford Market being a very different place in those days, there was a low wooden colonnade before the door (not very unlike that before the house where the little man and woman used to live, in the old weather glass), which pleased Mr. Dick mightily. (500)

Mr. Dick comes to live *over* the chandler's shop in Hungerford Market, glorying in his new abode, as Dickens eventually 'rises above' terrible memories of Hungerford-market days. For both men, the hunger-haunted Hungerford time is transmuted into a 'chandler's shop' of candles, or light. The Dick-Dickens story begins in tragedy, and ends in triumph.

It is interesting, and perhaps relevant, that both Dick and Dickens suffer a brother's betrayal. Dick's brother has him committed: and Dickens's brother, Augustus, causes him much grief. Dropping the Babley name, Mr. Dick never speaks of his brother again. Dickens too, after the break with Augustus Dickens, refuses to speak of the matter between them ever again.[6]

After his rescue by Miss Trotwood, a *Yah* Providence, Mr. Dick buries the past. The old anguish, thus suppressed, emerges only in well-distanced, symbolic form, as the wandering head of Charles which Dick draws on manuscript pages. The lost head of Charles haunts Mr. Dick; the lost head of little Charles Dickens, cruelly deprived of schooling in the days of captivity in the blacking house, haunts Mr. Dickens. All that Mr. Dick is—child-like, thumb-sucking, eager, easily wounded, clouded, needy, bearing the signs of some unspeakably painful old wound to his spirit—speaks of what little 'Dick' was in the days his own parents willingly, even eagerly, saw him sold into captivity: Mr. Dick is the part of Dickens that grew grey-haired, old, hopeless when not yet ten years old. I would guess that the child, little Dick, the touching little waif who dies young in *Oliver Twist,* is an earlier memorial to the part of Charles Dickens that died to hope in this bleak childhood time.

But early time passes. Like Mr. Dick, Dickens is rescued and supported by an exacting but generous, supremely rational, common-sensical patron, his Yah-ish sponsor, the world. 'Mr. Dick' is warmly praised for his common sense, and for how he 'sets us all right.' Dick smiles, laughs that secret laugh of his, struggles with his official writing stints, and, when nobody is watching, goes on with his inspired Child's play. So was Dickens feted for the least of what he deserved praise for, and forever grateful to the sharp-tongued, short-sighted Providence that supported him and made it possible for him to 'do wonders.'

As David advances from Murdstone-Babylon to *Agnes* time, Mr. Dick advances from Babley to Dixon time. Aswirl in strains of allegory, Dick, we said, plays Boswell to the Doctor, author of a Dictionary: to a type of Doctor *Johnson,* the son of John who works with the word, thus readying the way of a higher glory to which word and letter point. Mr. Dick, in Dickens's own way, helps mend the disastrous breach between the word, the Doctor, and the spirit and faith, Annie, without which knowledge were nothing.

At Annie Strong's side, Mr. Dick humbly works in the garden, helping bring to flower the seed which is the word of God. Dick does not water the garden. Rather, one finds him 'showering sympathy, trustfulness, and affection out of every hole in the watering-pot.' The 'Dick' who gardens and co-guardians a son of David pens a Christ child's Garden of NT verses. See Mr. Dick, or Dickens, weeding among new (NT) shoots, tending garden, and story, plots, ever at his 'patient microscopic work among the little leaves': *leaves* of green plants, and leaves of books to be sent, leaf on leaf, into the blue where, high above the optic line, words and letters fade, and 'the letter' at last cedes wholly to the spirit, the image, the sky. Thanks to Mr. Dick's busy, unsung telegraphy of names sent up along the string, the written 'line,' there is a new natural-supernatural husbandry of

Heaven, the candles are all relit at the light of the world, and, though it does not quite know it or know how, the world reaps benefits untold. Farming many a NT verse, Mr. Dick makes a vineyard of the curse; makes sunflowers glad of time. Florid-faced Dick and his tropological garden bloom eternally in the sweet golden clime of the Son.

Thanks to Mr. Dick, the world inherits a history of the Lord, not the one Yah set him to, to be sure, but one recording human grandeur and woe, a Memorial which celebrates a great King and Doctor of letters of everlasting fame, yet in its sweep does not overlook the humblest Boz of a Boswell, or most vacillating and swiveling of Dick Swivellers. Mankind has only to look up, skywards, to behold the handiwork of 'Dick,' and so remember, in the words of Dan'l Peggotty, 'the Lord was above all!'

In Dickens, *Dick* plots prove autobiographical and allegorical. For example, in *Nicholas Nickleby*, Dick the blackbird is a Dickensian Gospel in small. Tim Linkinwater, the hero's friend, tells how he acquired poor Dick...

> How, compassionating his starved and suffering condition, he had purchased him with a view of humanely terminating his wretched life; how he determined to wait three days and see whether the bird revived: how, before half the time was out, the bird did revive; and how he went on reviving and picking up his appetite and good looks until he gradually became what—'what you see him now, sir,' Tim would say, glancing proudly at the cage. And with that, Tim would utter a melodious chirrup, and cry 'Dick': and Dick, who for any sign of life he had previously given, might have been a wooden or stuffed representation of a blackbird indifferently executed, would come to the side of the cage in three small jumps, and, thrusting his bill between the bars, turn his sightless head towards his old master; and that moment it would be very difficult to determine which of the two was happier—the bird or Tim Linkinwater. (470)

In this charming Christian fabliau a half-dead Dick is rescued by a merciful master, and within three days, before the third day, rises from the 'dead'! In allegory, Tim, i.e., Timothy, a voice of the NT, *in loco Christi,* recalls Dick the blackbird, as small and starved as little 'Dick,' Charles Dickens, in his *black*ing warehouse days, when he must have crept back to his lonely attic smeared with blacking all over, to life. Christian symbolism abounds: in the three days; in 'three small jumps' which are Dick's joyful response to his Master's voice; in the 'melodious chirrup,' all 'ch' in Christ, of Tim; and also in the world of the Cheeryble brothers, Charles and Ned, Tim's employers in a firm whose whole reason for being seems to be to be about their Father's business of faith, hope, and charity. In allegory, Tim, a disciple of this 'Ch' Firm, calls, and man's soul, in the cage of the flesh, the world, and mortal blindness, is roused to hope of something beyond its present place.

Tim Linkinwater praises Nicholas, and, excited by the happy clamor of voices, Dick the blackbird utters a feeble croak. So Dickens humorously represents his life's work, a humble, feeble 'croaking' in his Master's praise. In the Cheeryble counting-house, men count on a Redeemer. Thanks to young Nicholas, Tim, and John Browdie, a J.B. or John Baptist figure, the *Saracen-Sarah's Son* 'Dotheboys' danger to Christendom, set to turn the clock back, is undone.

In *The Old Curiosity Shop,* Dick Swiveller is another Dick recalled to life. Forster records that Swiveller is close to Dicken's heart:

> He had very early himself become greatly taken with it. 'I am very glad indeed,' he wrote to me after the first half-dozen chapters, 'that you think so well of the *Curiosity Shop,* and especially that what may be got out of Dick strikes you. I *mean* to make much of him. I feel the story extremely myself, which I take to be a good sign; and am already warmly interested in it.' (FD, I, 180)

Mentioning Dickens's interest in another character, Sampson Brass, Forster adds: 'Undoubtedly, however, Dick was his favourite' (FD, I, 180). Amazingly, young Dick Swiveller looks like young 'Dick' Dickens, as a writer for the *Morning Chronicle,* visiting Dickens, reports:

> In the most crowded part of Holborn, within a door or two of the Bull-and-mouth inn, we pulled up at the entrance of a large building used for lawyers' chambers. I followed by a long flight of stairs to an upper storey, and was ushered into an uncarpeted and bleak-looking room, with a deal table, two or three chairs and a few books, a small boy and Mr. Dickens, for the contents. I was only struck at first with one thing (and I made a memorandum of it that evening as the strongest instance I had seen of English obsequiousness to employers), the degree to which the poor author was overpowered with the honour of his publisher's visit! I remember saying to myself, as I sat down on a ricketty chair, 'My good fellow, if you were in America with that fine face and your ready quill, you would have no need to be condescended to by a publisher.' Dickens was dressed very much as he has since described Dick Swiveller, *minus* the swell look. His hair was cropped close to his head, his clothes scant, though jauntily cut, and after changing a ragged office-coat for a shabby blue, he stood by the door, collarless and buttoned up, the very personification, I thought, of a 'close sailer to the wind.' (FD, I, 86)

In Dick Swiveller, the *Dick the blackbird* and *Mr. Dick* pattern is seen again. Swiveller, a young man who hangs around in the law circles of Daniel Quilp and his lawyer cronies, Sarah and Sampson Brass, much as young Dickens in his days of law reporting in Parliament, falls ill. He lies, 'Dead, all but,' for 'Three weeks to-morrow' (476). *Dead* echoes. 'You have been ill?' asks Abel Garland, a friend. 'Very,' replied Dick. 'Nearly

dead' (487). Again, a 'Dick' passing a time in 'death;' again, the conspic-
uous use of *three,* the time Christ lay in the bonds of Death.

Like Dick the blackbird and Mr. Dick, Dick Swiveller rises from the dead
a new man. Once, he sought that inconstant earthly solace, the alcoholic
drink, 'purl.' Then, Dick Whittington-like, Dick Swiveller Swivel(ler)s or
turns from lesser treasure to the *Abel Garland* flowering world of *N*ell
*Tre*nt and *Christopher* Nubbles which, flowing like the River Trent and like
mortal life to meet Eternity, points past purl to 'the pearl.'

The 'Dick' pattern holds throughout Dickens. In *The Seven Poor Travellers,* a young Richard Doubledick, sunk into a life of dissipation, is rescued
from it by his superior officer, Major Taunton. Taunton dies. Visiting his
mother, Dick Doubledick avows: 'He saved me from ruin, made me a
human creature, won me from infamy and shame. O, God for ever bless
him! As He will, He will!' (CS, 84) Another *Dick*ens *double, Doubledick,*
finds a saviour, by God's grace. In *Oliver Twist,* an abandoned little Dick,
who dreams of 'Heaven, and Angels, and kind faces that I never see when I
am awake' (49), dies. So, we think, did 'little Dick,' nine years old
Dickens, when abandoned by parents and all in the blacking warehouse
time, die to childhood and to hope.

In young manhood, at nineteen or so, a semi-directionless Dickens, alias
Dick Swiveller, drifts into law, becoming an attorney's clerk and then a
reporter in the greatest, deadest citadel of Law in the land, the House of
Commons. Then something happens, to which all the 'Dick' portraits cited
above bear witness. The aimless, vacillating, swivel-around life ends; how
and why is not clear, but at some point a Christian literary life's work
dawns. A Dickens dedicated to exposing social evil and righting wrongs
comes forth. 'Dick' snatches back his quill from Quilp service to the law
and the windy, ineffectual lawmakers he has observed first-hand in the
Gallery, like Mr. *Gregsbury* of *Nickleby,* who will *bury* the *greg,* or flock, and
begins to employ it in the service of the love founded on a rock.

I strongly suspect that Dick Datchery, who shows up late in the
unfinished *The Mystery of Edwin Drood,* a grey-haired, energetic Dick
who, like Mr. Dick, rattles his money in his pockets, is yet another Dick
who will help the beleaguered *Crisparkle* forces in the end.

Returning to Mr. Dick of *David Copperfield,* something deep in him
says, Go fly a kite, and he does. In the midst of trouble, contempt, or
careless praise, the Christian abides. In suffering unmerited, such
suffering as neither Dick nor Dickens can bear to speak of afterwards, he is
privileged to know more than most do of the experience of his Saviour on
earth. In time, Dickens comes to understand and accept 'how all these
things have worked together to make me what I am:' and perhaps to understand, in the burden of his father's debts he, Dickens, carried all his days,
more of the mystery of the Father and the Son. It is an ample fame. In
small 'Dick' plots, folded into larger allegories, Dickens celebrates and

commemorates over and over the divine hand of Providence that took pity on a little Dick, the blacking-bird, and recalled him to life.  Forsaken by his earthly father, Dickens finds his Father in Heaven.  The Babley-Swiveller-cage time past, Dickens recovers hope and forgets the past in the work of making Christendom, beset by foes within and without, STRONG again. Heep, Satan, would put asunder the letter and the spirit; but Mr. Dick, a surrogate Dickens, comes along and 'raises' the spirit again.  Like Mr. Dick, Mr. Dickens 'never waver[s] in his grateful service' to the Strong cause; and is never 'diverted from his knowledge that there was something wrong, or from his wish to set it right.'

How Mr. Dick loves the son of David.  And how Dickens loves the sons of David for the Son of David's sake.  Signaling from the upstairs window, Mr. Dick calls to mind Agnes and the stained-glass window.  If Agnes looks to heaven's light, Dick in his small way does too.  The signs and symbols Dick flashes, we note, are for David's eyes only.  Moments later, Dick wordlessly implores David not to give him away.  He knows only too well what the Yah world, bent on common sense and literal truth, does to its allegorical fools.  Mr. Dick communicates in secret language only with those he trusts.  Thus anyone foolhardy enough to give him away to the Trotwoodmen (their name is legion), the stalwarts of no-nonsense common sense, while hoping for the best, may expect the worst.

'You are a very remarkable man, Dick! and never pretend to be anything else, for I know better!' (663) Miss Trotwood says.  Such is the generous, just, yet maddeningly short-of-the-mark praise Dickens lived with all his days.  Mr. Dick only smiles.  His kingdom is not praise or fame, but wonders.  By the end of the story, he has filled the skies with word-winged giant kites which carry the saga of mankind a long way, kites that will sail overhead as long as men gaze skywards into the heavens of Dickensian fiction.  A fiction like Mr. Dick himself, at once child-like and simple, and touched with mystery.  Up go the seven-foot kites into the seventh heaven of Agnes Wickfield, the beams of the kite making the sign of the cross.

In summation, the Mr. Dick story tells how Dickens, after sorrow and strange calamity, came to dwell over the chandler's shop in Hungerford-market, i.e., rose above hunger-haunted blacking warehouse days of anonymity in pain, to dwell in the House of Light forever.  One smiles at the modest self-portrait with its touches of innocent vanity, as 'Mr. Dick' becomes a doer of wonders which the mighty cannot do, and wouldn't if they could.  See Dick clapping his worsted-gloved hands to cheer on the whole field of boys, a very St. Francis of a good old fellow, freezing and praising.  And see Dickens, signaling many a secret 'Cheer up! He is coming soon!' message carried by many a Christiana, Christopher, Crisparkle, Clara, Clare, Clemency, Cheeryble, chirruping cricket on the hearth, Cratchit, Copperfield, Chillip, chick and child, world without end.

Anguish passes.  The blessed later covenant of peace and hope changes the crown of thorns into a glory. 'Mr. Dick,' long deeply wounded in spirit, makes a comeback. Possibly, Dickens even came to accept the incredible non-recognition of his greatest achievement, allegory, as a divinely ordained chapter in its destiny. One thinks of the moment in *Barnaby Rudge* when Gabriel, asked whether Mary and her son still live, makes this memorable, Angelic reply:

> 'God knows,' rejoined the locksmith, 'many that I knew above it five years ago, have their beds under the grass now. It's a hopeless attempt, sir, believe me. We must leave the discovery of this mystery, like all others, to time, accident, and Heaven's pleasure.' (BR, 319)

So *Gabriel,* like the angel of old, musing on the mystery of *Mary* and child, points to Heaven, and to all that will be disclosed at the appointed hour. In Dickens, the telling of the story of The Life of Our Lord has no ending. *'God knows.'* Like Gabriel, who opens many doors, and Mr. Dick, Dickens humbly rests his case on the sky.

We leave Mr. Dick blissfully gazing up at his kites, flying them to the very end, and beyond, in the delight 'for which there are no words;' the wordless symbolic stance which implies: there shall be no end.

# THIRTEEN

## Tommy Traddles

> Poor Traddles! In a tight sky-blue suit that made his arms and legs like German sausages, or roly-poly puddings, he was the merriest and most miserable of all the boys. He was always being caned—...and was always going to write to his uncle about it, and never did. After laying his head on the desk for a little while, he would cheer up somehow, begin to laugh again, and draw skeletons all over his slate, before his eyes were dry....(DC, 91)

Sky-blue-clad Traddles, dressed to perfection in 'that older fashion yet, of Immortality,' calls to mind what the so-Emersonian Mr. Emerson of E.M. Forster's *A Room with a View* affirms: 'that there is only one perfect view—the view of the sky straight over our heads, and that all these views on earth are but bungled copies of it.'[1] Cheerful, good-hearted Tommy, who follows the proof and argument way of the law, as did another, a doubting Thomas, and who weds Sophy Crewler, thereby inheriting the care of ten sisters, is surely a one for allegory.

'Poor Traddles!' David sighs. And again: 'Poor Traddles—I never think of that boy but with a strange disposition to laugh, and with tears in my eyes' (94). Tommy is not only poor in being caned unjustly, persecuted for righteousness' sake, as when he alone of all the boys stands up for the Master, but is poor in spirit, as the Seven Poor Travellers and the Poor Relation who weds Christiana are poor: humble, unassuming, expectant; and therein lies a Christian tale.

In Dickens, the poor-in-spirit, like Mr. Dick, Mr. Chillip, and Tommy Traddles, do wonders. In Tommy's case, it is what he accomplishes with ten Crewler sisters. To win Sophy, i.e., Wisdom, he must take on ten sisters, *ten,* cypher of OT law, an unruly crew of Crewlers which he tames, civilizes and softens, turning them to new tractable, hopeful ways.

'Dear Mr. Traddles and dear Trotwood' (776), Agnes Wickfield addresses David and his close friend and best man, Traddles, who, by divergent yet united ways of law and faith, spirit and letter, merit her trust and love.  Standing up for David, in more ways than one, in sterling style, Tommy becomes the worldly channel through which, in its author's absence, the wondrous Story finds its way past copyright laws and other impediments to a waiting world, Tommy gladly shining by reflected light and glorying in the son of David's 'rising fame and fortune' (848).  So, in the Author's absence, does a disciple transmit the word; so do the sons of Thomas publish Him abroad forever.

Traddles enters David's life in Creakle school days.  In those benighted times, all the boys except Tommy are participants or onlookers in the infamous trial, persecution, and banishment of the Master, a figure who, in his charity to the poor and infirm, his moral superiority to base accusers, and noble forgiveness of those who revile and banish (slay) him, is clearly a type of Christ.  In this neo-B.C. episode, only one voice protests the vile proceedings: 'Shame, J. Steerforth! Too bad!' (97)  When even David, the Master's friend, is silent, Traddles speaks out.  As 'J' Steers Forth, mankind in his wake, to a replay of the crucifixion, and for his act is exalted to the skies, Tommy alone proves a Christian worthy of the name.

Murdstone law, lying in wait for a son of David now as long ago, enforces the ignominy of a sign tied to David's back, a type of cross.  By just being himself, Tommy comes to the rescue:

> It was a happy circumstance for me that Traddles came back first.  He enjoyed my placard so much, that he saved me from the embarrassment of either disclosure or concealment, by presenting me to every other boy who came back, great or small, immediately on his arrival, in this form of introduction, 'Look here! Here's a game!' (84)

Tommy's saving work in David's behalf, which will span a lifetime, begins. But no one saves Tommy himself.  Soon after the incident of the Master, the aftermath of which is a caning for Tommy for being discovered in tears, the boys enjoy a smuggled feast of shellfish.  All get off scot free, all except Tommy, 'the most unfortunate boy in the world' (91).

> But Traddles couldn't get happily out of it.  He was too unfortunate even to come through a supper like anybody else.  He was taken ill in the night— quite prostrate he was—in consequence of Crab; and after being drugged with black draughts and blue pills, to an extent which Demple (whose father was a doctor) said was enough to undermine a horse's constitution, received a caning and six chapters of Greek Testament for refusing to confess. (105)

What an inquisition!  There is something sinister and magwitch-y about those black draughts, even as a slight oddity in phrasing and the capital 'C' in 'in consequence of Crab' lends Tommy's digestive woes something of a dark astrological air.  As the Master is driven out, and all is retributive ire, Temple-Demple, and black magic, Christianity suffers.  Tommy and a few others aside, one looks in vain for faith, hope, and charity.

Mourning the Master, Tommy, soon lifting his head from his desk, 'reliev[es] himself as usual with a burst of skeletons' (100). Skeletons, symbols of death, a *relief??* Perhaps they are, in offering the ironic *sic transit* consolation that this too shall pass—in Death. Grim B.C. comfort for a child of A.D., queer relief from a sense of the futility of it all. Throughout Dickens, fits of despondency, hopelessness, and an unlifting weight of mortality afflict the young. In *Dombey and Son,* young Toots, trapped in Greek-Roman schooling, glooms about 'the silent tomb' (781). In *Our Mutual Friend,* Jenny Wren, so often dragged down and misguided, can imagine no release but death, and cries: 'Come up and be dead!' (282) In the same work, two young lawyers, Lightwood and Wrayburn, lounge disspiritedly about the Temple in offices that look out over a burial-ground, or the silent tomb. Locked into law and death, Lightwood slips into the cynical posture of: 'Everything is ridiculous' (166). In *anno Dombei* precincts, no one teaches the message of the Resurrection and the Life, or translates the Greek Testament, used punitively by masters in both *Dombey* and *Copperfield,* into a living, breathing, inspiring *The Life of Our Lord.*

More trouble follows. When Steerforth laughs in church, the Beadle accuses and removes, not the worshipped 'J,' but the innocent Tommy, whose nobility and despondency are again seen:

> He never said who was the real offender, though he smarted for it next day, and was imprisoned so many hours that he came forth with a whole church-yard of skeletons swarming all over his Latin Dictionary. (91)

This is no Lazarus-like coming forth, but a sad parody of it in a Danse Macabre of Death.

An imprisoned Tommy expresses a profound sense of the inevitability of captivity, companion to a sense of doom, by constructing 'models of elephants' dens in writing-paper to put flies in' (402), a B.C. Captivity montage if ever there was one. In the *el*ephants' dens (El again), flies, like captives of old, languish. Writing-paper walls add pen-and-ink-ubus, the letter, the law, which kept and keep mankind captive in Old Time.

In *Copperfield,* Tommy is quite alone. But in *Dombey and Son,* Paul and Florence Dombey, in Greek-Roman schooldays, have each other:

> Oh, Saturdays! Oh, happy Saturdays, when Florence always came at noon, and never would, in any weather, stay away though Mrs. Pipchin snarled and growled, and worried her bitterly. Those Saturdays were Sabbaths for at least two little Christians among all the Jews, and did the holy Sabbath work of strengthening and knitting up a brother's and a sister's love. (DS, 163)

Dickens means 'Christians' among 'Jews.' What with beadles in Babylonian collars and the Dead March in Saul, and much more, *Dombey* is a
hotbed of unchristian time and values. To exalt Roman cruelty, and use
the Greek Testament in place of the strap, as Paul's schoolmasters do, is,
in Dickens's view, to feed young Christians to the lions of Babylon and
Rome.

Schooldays end, and Traddles in the sky-blue suit that constricts his
growing limbs, as the old theology the new-fledged soul, drops from
David's Steerforth-ruled skies. As young men, the two meet again at the
Waterbrook soiree at Ely-place, a stronghold of Chosen Few pride of
caste, snobbery, law, and the Flood. Traddles, now 'a sober, steady-
looking young man of retiring manners, with a comic head of hair, and eyes
that were rather wide open' (372), recognizes David and greets him
warmly. David sees 'the old unfortunate Tommy' (372) standing before
him. How true. *Unfortunate*, yes. Like 'poor,' unfortunate has a second
and Christian meaning, singling out one who does not belong to the whirl-
ing, inconstant universe of luck, chance, dice-box and bet; who is, rather,
as Beatrice says of Dante: 'My friend, not Fortune's friend.'

The Waterbrook crowd of course despises Tommy on sight. Damning
with faint praise, Mr. Waterbrook declares him 'quite a good fellow—
nobody's enemy but his own;' and 'one of those men who stand in their
own light' (373). For that matter, Waterbrook circles could use somebody
who *is*, literally speaking, nobody's enemy but his own; here everyone is
everybody else's sworn enemy, conversation seething with cabal, plot, cold
malice, and 'mysterious dialogue across the table for our defeat and overthrow' (375). With David, we marvel at how sunny Traddles seems to have
forgotten the canings he suffered in old Creakle days, and recalls only the
boyish fellowship shared. Good-hearted fellow, there was precious little of
that! However, in the Tommys and Joe Gargerys in Dickens, charity is not
strained. Christians do not fester, Elephant-like, with retributive ire that
never forgives or forgets. A Clemency Newcome of a soul, Tommy
registers none of the open or covert hostility trained on him now, either, in
the Waterbrook camp of Flood. In the very shadow of Ely-place, Tommy
does indeed stand in his, and His, own light.

But what finds him in such company, *and,* sad to say, 'reading for the
bar' (373)? One is relieved to learn that he was invited only at the last
minute when Henry Spiker's brother was suddenly called away. (Spiker
frère doubtless had to re-Spike(r) a debtors prison wall, or the like.) Somehow, as way leads on to way, Traddles is washed on from brooks and
Creakle shallows into flood-tides of Waterbrooks; and like David, and many
others shaped by the legalistic-literalist spirit of the age, turns to the law.
Call it English and Christian, but in a neo-Roman-Hebraic time of justice
without mercy and judgment without clemency, it is not Christian but
*Waterbrook*, i.e., primitive Flood justice men inherit, wholesale cruelty

that must recall the old destruction of mankind.

An old Creakle boy, Mr. Yawler, recommends Traddles to law-copyist work. In allegory, this legal 'Yawler, with his nose on one side' (404) and free access to Waterbrook channels, is self-evidently, and comically, a *Yawl*-er, i.e., a Ya(h) vessel like the Murdstone yacht or Yarmouth ark. A tippy, unsafe yawl too, it would seem, leaning to one side. But as the old saying goes, any yawl in a storm. With the Master lost and no *Son and Heir* in sight, Tommy boards the Yawler life at law and inherits the dubious honor of pleading before 'Your Wash-up,' as the magistrate is called in *Pickwick,* the 'your worship' of intensely cold, wet OT time of mind once again covering the earth: '*Koeldwethout,*' as we read in *Nickleby.*

*Waterbrook* time it is. Forty drenching days and nights of retributive 'justice' descend on mankind. On the Waterbrook night, as Flood waters and Captivity symbols (Spiker) gather to rally strength, Uriah Heep of the 'damp cold hand' confides to David that 'it seems to rain blessings on my ed' (377), which, if true, means curses on everybody else's. Working David's reluctant hand up and down 'like a pump handle' (517), Uriah is out for water, a copper-full. In his personal life, David, 'steeped' in Dora, we saw, 'saturated through and through,' overflows with love of the lawyer's daughter, enough 'to drown anybody in.' Ominous portent. It is water, waterbrook everywhere. Ships' salvage cases come up in Doctors' Commons. David is thoroughly laundressed by his landlady, Mrs. Crupp, who lives way down at low-water mark and calls him 'Copperful...in some indistinct association with a washing-day' (398). More watery disaster. The *Little Em'ly* is swamped off Yarmouth; and 'a ribald Turncock attached to the waterworks' (412), having all power in waterproud times like these, turns off the Micawber family's water. Meanwhile, liabilities Mr. Micawber contracted with a view to 'immediate liquidation' remain (one is tempted to add, happily) unliquidated. The chapter title 'A Little Cold Water' sums up troubles in the honeymoon cottage, where Tommy Traddles, kept 'at bay' by Dora's barking spaniel and crowded into corners, nevertheless cheerfully asseverates: 'Oceans of room, Copperfield! I assure you, Oceans!' (641) A 'dumb-foundered' Steerforth, and a Micawber who goes under in the battle to stay afloat and declares himself 'a foundered Bark' (701), not to mention a ruined Betsey Trotwood, sitting on her luggage, a very few pieces pulled from the wreckage, like a female Robinson Crusoe on the shore of brackish seas, all make clear a universal backwards slide of mankind into B.C. conditions of body and soul.

How wonderfully hopeful, therefore, that Traddles should carry 'a plain old silver watch; the very watch he once took a wheel out of, at school, to make a water-mill' (629). So we see that even back in dripping-wet Creakle days, Tommy's mind was on flood control.

In time, Tommy falls in love with dear Sophy Crewler. Her family strongly objects. But Tommy never loses hope. Looking forward to the time when they can wed, Tommy purchases 'a little round table with a marble top...an admirable piece of workmanship—firm as a rock!' (405) Again the NT symbolism of the rock, as in the Strong love and the love of David for Agnes, both 'founded on a rock.' In allegory, Tommy, an *anima naturaliter Christiana,* chooses 'Sophy,' or Wisdom, and with her at his side embarks on the journey of life. He asserts: 'We have put to sea in a cockboat, but we are prepared to rough it!' (825) With Sophy's nine sisters, a sort of dowry in reverse, along, there are ten Crewlers aboard, a *Crew*(ler) to keep a Criscraft ship-shape on its true course for Eternity.

It is in the *Thomas* nature to found belief on theology, evidence, proof. Thus, law. Traddles, the latest Tommy, or Thomas, to grace A.D., stand up for the Master, even Christ, and seek to make Wisdom his own, inherits 'the ten,' as in the Ten Commandments: *ten,* the cypher of OT law. What an inheritance! The nine would tax the patience of a saint. Alas, this is the price doctors of law and divinity such as Mr. Thomas Traddles of the Inner Temple must pay for 'Sophy,' wisdom won only through endless, laborious, grinding study which can so easily lead to the somber, prideful, petty expertise in matters of the letter, and away from faith, hope, and charity.

Tommy is a Christian Christian name. What of *Traddles?* Dickens loads it with meaning. When Mrs. Crupp recommends skittle-playing to David as a nice, healthful pastime, he suddenly remembers Traddles, struck by 'a certain similarity in the sound of the word skittles and Traddles' (400). *Skittles-Traddles:* poor Tommy! Throughout Dickens, *skittles* has strong, dark Old dispensation ties. It goes with imprisonment. In *Copperfield,* Mr. Micawber, in prison, and down but a minute before, picks up to play 'a lively game of skittles, before noon' (165). In *Little Dorrit,* the debtors' prison-skittles connection is stressed. The Marshalsea, a debtors prison, the one in which Charles Dickens's own father was confined, has a skittle ground, as the opening description of the Dorrit family and its sad place of confinement makes clear:

> It was an oblong pile of barrack building, partitioned into squalid houses standing back to back, so that there were no back rooms; environed by a narrow paved yard, hemmed in by high walls duly spiked at the top. Itself a close and confined prison for debtors, it contained within it a much closer and more confined jail for smugglers. Offenders against the revenue laws, and defaulters to excise or customs, who had incurred fines which they were unable to pay, were supposed to be incarcerated behind an iron-plated door, closing up a second prison, consisting of a strong cell or two, and a blind alley some yard and a half wide, which formed the mysterious termination of the very limited skittle-ground in which the Marshalsea debtors bowled down their troubles. (57)

A grim series of lock-ups, one narrower than the last, we see, has its terminus in a skittle-ground. Thanks to the turnkey, we finally understand what this *prison-skittles* connection is all about. A debtor asks about his wife bringing the children:

> 'The children?' said the turnkey. 'And the rules? Why, lord set you up like a corner pin, we've a reg'lar playground o' children here. Children? Why, we swarm with 'em. How many a you got?' (58)

'Lord set you up like a corner pin!' almost says all. It puts the whole Jehovah-debtor relationship of OT time in a nutshell. In B.C. time of Fall, of merciless punishment of 'debtors,' or sinners, before Christ teaches men to pray: 'Forgive us our debts as we forgive our debtors,' man is 'set up' only to be swiftly bowled down again like a skittle. In the still-extant Hebrew moral economy Dickens sees operant all around him, in which the mills of retributive justice grind sinners to dust as if Christ had never appeared on earth teaching the better way of mercy and compassion, the 'raise up' born of 'Rise up!', mankind is in the position of young Tip Dorrit, little Dorrit's brother who is constantly in and out of Debtors' Prison. *Tip,* Fall man without a Saviour, *tip*s, teeters, tumbles, topples on and on in helpless obedience to the moral/spiritual law of gravity, the gravity of the grave, set in motion by Adam's Fall. To Dickens, such imprisonment of debtors, who rot away behind walls, is infamous, unconscionable. With such Captivity inflicted on debtors and their innocent families, B.C. returns with a vengeance. B.C. also glares in the *very limited* skittle-ground; and in the arrangement wherein the sins of the fathers are visited upon the children.

*Skittles* appear prominently in the doctoral province of Doctor Strong in *Copperfield*. Again, the context is dark:

> Next morning, after breakfast, I entered on school life again. I went, ac-companied by Mr. Wickfield, to the scene of my future studies—a grave building in a courtyard, with a learned air about it that seemed very well suited to the stray rooks and jackdaws who came down from the Cathedral towers to walk with a clerkly bearing on the grass lot—and was introduced to my new master, Doctor Strong.
>
> Doctor Strong looked almost as rusty, to my thinking, as the tall iron rails and gates outside the house; and almost as stiff and heavy as the great stone urns that flanked them, and were set up, on the top of the red-brick wall, at regular distances all round the court, like sublimated skittles, for Time to play at. He was in his library (I mean Doctor Strong was), with his clothes not par-ticularly well brushed, and his hair not particularly well combed; his knee-smalls unbraced; his long black gaiters unbuttoned; and his shoes yawning like two caverns on the hearth rug. Turning upon me a lustreless eye, that re-minded me of a long-forgotten horse who used to crop the grass, and tumble over the graves, in Blunderstone churchyard, he said he was glad to see me; and then he gave me his hand; which I didn't know what to do with, as it did nothing for itself. (226)

This first sketch of Doctor Strong, linked to rooks, graveyard, a decrepit horse, and skittles, is not prepossessing. The Doctor shows David and Mr. Wickfield around, and 'jogged on before us, at a queer, uneven pace' (228). Dickens never forgets that it was learned doctors of law, bigoted to 'the letter,' who sealed the fate of Christ.

Enter *skittles*. Like Mr. Micawber or any other debtor behind walls, Time plays at skittles on the red-brick wall. In *Copperfield*, Time only slowly comes of age. When David and Em'ly are children roaming the sandy shores of Yarmouth: 'The days sported by us, as if Time had not grown up himself yet, but were a child too, and always at play' (37). Then Time is captive, as is mankind, in the B.C., *Babylonian Captivity*, debtor-sinner, bowled-down world hemmed in by the Fall. The adjective 'sub-limated' applied to skittles adds a fine irony; there is no true elevation or sublimity in those on-high stone urns, like burial urns, or in that high, en-closing wall. The slight ambiguity released in: 'He was in his library (I mean Doctor Strong)' is useful, too. For a moment it seems, as Dickens intends, that Time were in *his* library, the doctoral stronghold of Judaic Law, where man first equates virtue with learnedness in minutiae of law; worship with knowledge; and service to God with fanatic zeal for the word. By contrast, in Dickens one sees that 'a man is not justified by the works of the law, but by the faith of Jesus Christ' (*Gal.* 2:16). We know that Dickens thinks the pocket library of Clemency Necome, which consists of a thimble and a nutmeg-grater inscribed 'For-get and for-give,' and 'Do as you-wold-be-done-by,' is all the divine wisdom man needs to be saved.

Doctor Strong is a good man. But in his preoccupation with roots of words (a *roots* pun looks to gardens), he forgets the flower grown of the seed which is the word of God, which is not the letter but the spirit. As the Mr. Dick story shows, it is not knowledge alone, an owlish 'professional profundity' (*OMF*, 92), that saves man, but faith in a love and care so strong it raised one from the dead. Christ-imitating compassion and trust in the Father powers the Celestial Omnibus. The letter carries man only so far. High up, words melt ideawards; in the kingdom of sky where letter is soon indistinguishable from letter, all is released to spirit. Involving secrets, mystery, astonishing revelation in his works, Dickens seems to say, we have *not* got it all down in words, nor can it all be set down! Heaven's purposes and wonders are not, as Old law implied, reducible to statute, ritual, and text. Only the faith of Annie, unshakable as the rock of Christ's testament to the Father, saves Doctor Strong. Faith, hope, and charity keep root, letter, and word 'Strong.' Faith, not law; Mr. Dick's loving 'mind of the heart,' not mind, shall purify the sons of Levi.

Dickens goes further. Too often, he shows, information-ful, fact-ful are the opposite of wonder-and-praiseful. Thanks to Murdstone-Headstone schooling, epidemic in Christendom, young craniums become leaden caskets, and no Lazarus activity in sight. Thus, thrice welcome Captain Cuttle, with his: 'Overhaul the Catechism!' and 'air of downright good faith that spoke volumes' (DS, 210). It is those volumes humanity needs. Dickens would see minds move freely among the wonders of Creation, by causeways of metaphor drawn ever farther away to build castles in air, until one fine day there dawns the idea of Christiana and *the* Castle in Air, a vision to dwarf all knowledge yet garnered in the theologies of men: that of the life to come.

Thus, with *skittles* in OT (debtor) connection, *Traddles* takes its place beside surnames in Dickens which mirror the natural, inherited, old, pre-Christian condition of man. Barring the forward, Christian-name way of JOHN is *Westlock;* of TOM, *Pinch* (*Chuzzlewit*); of OLIVER, *Twist*; of PAUL, *Dombey;* of SUSAN, *Nipper* (*Dombey and Son*); of STEPHEN, *Blackpool* (*Hard Times*); of JESSE, *Hexam* (*Our Mutual Friend*); of ABEL, *Magwitch* (*Great Expectations*), et al.

Skittles evoking in David thoughts of Traddles, he looks up Tommy and finds him living near a veterinary school, his decayed, refuse-ridden street 'principally tenanted...by gentleman students, who bought live donkeys, and made experiments on those quadrupeds in their private apartments' (401). Shades of donkey-beating Mr. Gamfield (*Oliver Twist*), and donkey-hating Miss Trotwood. The medical students are clearly *Sawyer, late Nockemorf* Sawbones in the making. (vis. Chapter III) The unchristian character of their world is glimpsed in its resemblance to the debtors' prison world of Babylon:

> The general air of the place reminded me forcibly of the days when I lived with Mr. and Mrs. Micawber. An indescribable character of faded gentility that attached to the house I sought, and made it unlike all the other houses in the street—though they were all built on one monotonous pattern, and looked like the early copies of a blundering boy who was learning to make houses, and had not yet got out of his cramped brick-and-mortar pothooks—reminded me still more of Mr. and Mrs. Micawber. Happening to arrive at the door as it was opened to the afternoon milkman, I was reminded of Mr. and Mrs. Micawber more forcibly yet.
>
> 'Now,' said the milkman to the very youthful servant girl. 'Has that there little bill of mine been heard on?' (400)

'Forcibly' and 'more forcibly,' puns, the repetition leads one to suspect, press the memory of David's captivity in 'the Modern Babylon.' So does the tradesman who presents a bill, and, fixing the young servant by the chin, holds her captive, as it were. Moving on, the bill collector utters a 'vindictive shriek' (401), reminiscent of the 'Goroo!' cry that terrified David in his wilderness wandering after his flight from Babylon. In *Murdstone* or Old Law time, all is 'blundering boy' or Blunderstone, bills and Present payment!

Tommy Traddles lives in this depressing 'B.C.' domain. Nevertheless, 'Tommy' life has no part in it, though the dull *Traddles* perplexes and

retards. Like a Christian colossus, Traddles straddles Old and New time. [2]
He goes into law, but with a difference. He tells David: 'Three others and
myself unite to have a set of chambers—to look business-like' (402). He, no
more than Mr. Dick, is really business-like, except as each is about his
Father's business. The 'three...unite' hints at the three-in-one sympathies
of his soul.

Tommy falls in love with 'a curate's daughter, one of ten, down in Devonshire' (405). The symbolic fun begins when Sophy's family objects to
the match. Sophy is far too useful at home, all agree, to be spared to bliss.
In time, the Crewlers become reconciled to Tommy, all but Sarah Crewler,
Sophy's sister, who exploits the distinction of having a mysterious,
privilege-making 'something the matter with her spine' (592). Learning of
the betrothal, Sarah shuts her eyes, turns grey and 'perfectly stiff' (593),
rigid as a post, all over, and *will not have it!*

What larks. Allegory beams. The unidentified 'something' the matter
with Sarah's spine is obviously and palpably the 'something' that never
ceased to plague the tribe of *Sarah,* the Jews:-the moral rigidity and stiff-
necked pride bred in the bone by the Law. In allegorical terms, SARAH will
not relinquish SOPHY into new (NT), Thomist, hands, as the Hebrews would
not relinquish 'the bride,' Israel, the soul, to her new and chosen Master,
Christ. Ah, but *Sophy,* knowing where true happiness lies, longs for *Tommy,* apostle of a new spirit. Always wonderfully charitable, Tommy puts the
kindest possible construction on Sarah's selfishness, assuring David that
she is 'a very charming girl, but she has a great deal of feeling' (593).

To digress briefly, *Sarah Crewler* is one of a sizable band of jealous,
crabbed, reactionary, wizened, primitive-souled *Sarahs* in Dickens. It is
highly supportive of our theory of religious allegory that one finds these
particular Sarahs in Dickens, AND NO OTHER KIND. As we saw, a dark
Saracen's Head-Sarah's Son's Head plot restages the near-sacrifice of
Sarah's son, Isaac, in the *Dotheboys* do-the-boys world of *Nicholas Nickleby.* In *The Old Curiosity Shop,* Daniel Quilp, lionish, roaring foe of all
good, consorts with Sarah and Sampson Brass, lawyers, in an 'as sounding
Brass' world utterly devoid of faith, hope, and charity, and bent on the
destruction of *Nell* Trent. The most famous and infamous of Dickensian
Sarahs is surely Sarah (Sairey) Gamp of *Martin Chuzzlewit,* the garrulous,
self-serving nurse who thumps helpless patients, sups shamelessly at their
expense, dithers and raves, tipples Old Tipper, glooms about *Jonadge's
belly* and *wales,* like any orthodox denizen of B.C., and in general makes a
mockery of her vocation as ministering angel of mercy. Sarah Gamp,
friend of Mould the undertaker, sweetly declares she would gladly lay out
all her friends for nothing, sich is the love she bears 'em. We believe her.
Sarah and *Mould,* dust of the silent tomb, are old bedfellows in Dickens.

In *Bleak House,* a Sarah pops up in the sermon of Reverend Chadband, a
hateful harangue in which, in Hebrew idiom, the clergyman brands Jo,

street waif of Tom-all-Alone's, a heathen, gentile, and wanderer on the
earth. To sample it:

> 'Or, my juvenile friend,' says Chadband, descending to the level of their
> comprehension, with a very obtrusive demonstration, in his greasily meek
> smile, of coming a long way downstairs for the purpose, 'if the master of this
> house was to go forth into the city and there see an eel, and was to come back,
> and was to call untoe him the mistress of this house, and was to say, "Sarah,
> rejoice with me, for I have seen an elephant!" would *that* be Terewth?'
> Mrs. Snagsby in tears. (360)

Is this *Sarah* Chadband's disciple, Mrs. Snagsby, law-stationer's wife? In
any case, linked to heartless religious rant, e*el* and *el*ephant, and law,
*Sarah* is at home. In *Great Expectations,* Sarah Pocket, Pip's jealous foe,
follows the classic OT *Sarah* pattern in her enmity to a boy child not of her
own flesh, recalling the Biblical Sarah who drove Hagar and Ishmael, her
son, into the desert. In Dickens, Sarah after Sarah is part of a moribund
old order and dead set against the emergence of a New.

Choosing Sophy, flower of the ten, Tommy Traddles inherits all ten,
Sarah too. His struggle to tame ten Crewlers (Crewler and Crueller) is a
merry symbolic operetta in which the hero, the Deity's Disciple, embarks
on the goodly, Godly work of converting a crowd of Hebrew-Roman priva-
teers to Christian service. Tommy lovingly vs. *the ten,* his mighty labors to
shape ten *Crew*lers into a *Crew* fit for a cockboat, symbolizes the New v.
the Old spirit of the Law, which Christ does not destroy, but fulfills.

Law is Christianity's inheritance from OT time, and a prickly inheritance
it is. But Tommy prevails. A Kinder converts a Crewler. In time, Tommy
turns the whole quarrelsome, domineering, exacting set of sisters into a
nest of singing birds, a bower of roses. Thanks to the patient work of faith,
hope, and charity, peace and joy come to reign among the ten. For His
yoke is easy and His burthen light. *This* is what Tommy teaches, not in
words, but by the example of his own steady, cheerful, Crisparkling
nature. In his professional life, he is Traddles of the Inner Temple, with all
that implies. But the newlyweds' domestic arrangements, he confides to
David, are 'quite unprofessional altogether' (285), which means: *no law
here!* Instead,:

> 'Yes,' said Traddles. 'Now the whole set—I mean the chambers—is only
> three rooms; but Sophy arranges for the girls in the most wonderful way, and
> they sleep as comfortably as possible. Three in that room,' said Traddles,
> pointing. 'Two in that.' (825)

*Three* thrives: three rooms, three in a room. *Ten* softens: as in the divine
numerology of Dante, *three* proves the root of nine. The girls sleep 'as
comfortably as possible,' implying, perhaps, that the law is never wholly
comfortable. Meanwhile, Tommy and Sophy have a little room in the roof,

with a fine view. High up, Tommy lives and labors to keep the household afloat. For behold, he that keepeth Israel ('Watch ye therefore!') shall neither slumber nor sleep.

No sooner wed to Sophy, his heart's delight, than saddled, or sTRAD-DLEd, with the ten, Tommy cheerfully shoulders the load. In Dickens, 'Let nothing you dismay!' is the watchword of merry Christian gentlemen, who, with cheery names like *Cheeryble, Gay, Harmon,* and *Sweedlepipe* (Paul, or Poll, Sweedlepipe *sweedly pipes* a Song of Paul in the 'Paul' part of *Martin Chuzzlewit*), and in patience and hope, faithfully await the return of the Son and Heir. With the shining exception of Sophy, the off-spring of the Reverend Crewler are just so much excess baggage. But as there is no having Sophy without the rest, all come along; and soon even Sarah is 'immensely better!' (825) The old, abrasive, commandeering 'Reverend Crewler' or priestly quality of law, the ten, fades as, under Tommy's tutelage, emphasis shifts from: 'Thou shalt not,' to the Christian commandment that 'ye love one another as I have loved you.' Thus sweetly does Dickens fantasize the conversion of the Jews.

When David first calls on Dora Spenlow's two aunts to seek permission to court her, he wisely brings Tommy along. David's inspired babblings about love move the stern ladies not at all. Only when Traddles is produced does David win favor in their eyes:

> 'The light—for I call them, in comparison with sentiments, the light—inclinations of very young people,' pursued Miss Lavinia, 'are dust, com-pared to rocks. It is owing to the difficulty of knowing whether they are likely to endure or have any real foundation, that my sister Clarissa and myself have been very undecided how to act, Mr. Copperfield, and Mr.—'
>
> 'Traddles,' said my friend, finding himself looked at.
>
> 'I beg pardon. Of the Inner Temple, I believe?' said Miss Clarissa, again glancing at my letter.
>
> Traddles said 'Exactly so,' and became pretty red in the face. (397)

*Inner Temple* instantly lends David credence, as does the word that Traddles is engaged to 'one of ten, down in Devonshire' (598). *Temple, ten,* and maybe even *down* open the door to respect in the lawyer's home where Jane Murdstone and Julia Mills reside.

Inner Temple service leaves its mark on Tommy. As he and Traddles enter the Spenlow home, David finds himself wishing his friend 'had never contracted the habit of brushing his hair so very upright' (591), 'contracted' a legal pun in the exhibition of a head of hair with the requisite institutional stiffening. The priggish, 'so very upright' comic hair is seen again on the day Sophy arrives: 'Traddles presents her to us with great pride; and rubs his hands for ten minutes by the clock, with every individ-ual hair upon his head standing on tip-toe, when I congratulate him in a corner on his choice' (629). Again, *ten.* This is not quite the spiky, dangerous prison-wall head of hair of Jerry Cruncher, odd-jobman of

Temple Bar in *A Tale of Two Cities*. But stiff it is. The moral: choose, not Clara, Christiana, Clemency, Magdalen, or Agnes, but 'Sophy,' and one walks, not on air, but on earth.

However, because she *is* Wisdom, SOPHY steps clear of Reverend Horace and Sarah and cleaves to Tommy, whose unfailing good cheer reflects a spirit born, not for Death, but for Life. Though born in Greek-Roman and Hebrew time of *sophos, Horace,* and *Sarah,* the Lady Wisdom finds her true home in Christian truth. Sophy aside, however, the nine, an inheritance that must come along, is a rugged one.

How Tommy and Sophy go about taming the sisters tells all. It is done, not in the old, lawful, hasten-chasten Yah way of punishment, penalty, and price, but in a new spirit. If a girl breaks down in her knitting, Sophy instantly 'put[s] the defaulter in the right direction' (829). 'Defaulter,' a bit heavy, even as arch figures of speech go, meets the legal-theological issue head on, speaking directly to the contract-bargain arrangement man held with Heaven under Mosaic Law (very much *under*.) Viewed from the top of Mount Sinai, Fall man shrinks in stature to eternal ower, defaulter, debtor always (in Murdstone era idiom) in 'arrears.' With *the ten* comes the problem of the Fall. 'Somebody's hair fell down, and nobody but Sophy could put it up' (829). With no punitive time in Babylon intervening, the 'sinner' is promptly, lovingly restored to grace.

The conversion of the Crewler sisters is, of course, slow work. Rome was not unbuilt in a day. So imperious, spoiled, and demanding are their charges that Tommy and Sophy must 'squeeze themselves into upper rooms, reserving the best bedrooms for the Beauty and the girls' (877). All things work together for them that love the Lord. Leaving the ever-quarrelsome articles of Law, the nine-of-ten, below, bride and bride-groom fly to those high chambers with the view, nearer my God to Thee.

London's Doctors' Commons and Inner Temple remain for Dickens the gloomy, precedent-bound, unenlightened precincts of law, and very much the Temple of B.C. Though he throws himself into improving 'the ten,' as did the first disciples of NT time, Traddles cannot change the system. Taking, not the way of faith, but of wisdom and law, man incurs a certain jeopardy. Law in Dickens never quite outdistances its OT origins, or its guilt in the betrayal of Christ to Rome. The signs of its origins remain, as one of Tommy's anecdotes of life with Sophy makes clear:

> 'When it's fine, and we go out for a walk in the evening, the streets abound in enjoyment for us. We look into the glittering windows of the jewellers' shops; and I show Sophy which of the diamond-eyed serpents, coiled up on white satin rising grounds, I would give her if I could afford it; and Sophy shows me which of the gold watches that are capped and jewelled and engine-turned, and possessed of the horizontal lever-escape-movement, and all sorts of things, she would buy for me if *she* could afford it.'

The jewelled (*jew*elled) serpents ever hissing of man's first disobedience, in the Heep, Mrs. *Coiler* way (vis. Chapter III), remind us that knowledge, gateway to wisdom, is among the most equivocal of man's blessings. Full of study and self, forgetful of humility and trust in a higher Power no scrutiny of texts, however minute, can reveal, men who set up as guardians of His word and law run the risk of missing...

> ...the character of the Redeemer, and the great scheme of His religion, where, in its broad spirit made so plain—and not in this or that disputed letter—we all put our trust. (PPM, 488)

Walking in the City, Tommy and Sophy bypass the serpents on white satin rising grounds (ascent ever in the offing), and the watch-machinery, which, cumbersome and 'horizontal,' recalls the Old machinery of man's salvation. Such temptations behind them, they delight to buy half-price theatre tickets to see a play, 'which Sophy believes every word of, and so do I' (847), Tommy confides. With 'believes,' and such riches of belief, we re-enter NT time. Past heaps of treasure laid up on earth, the Serpent glittering in its midst, pilgrim man, 'Sophy' at his side, takes his way Home.

This walk recalls the one Florence Dombey and Walter Gay take on their bridal morning in the work preceding *Copperfield, Dombey and Son,* another pretty symbolic miniature of the journey of life:

> They take the streets that are the quietest, and do not go near that in which her old home stands. It is a fair, warm summer morning, and the sun shines on them as they walk towards the darkening mist that overspreads the City. Riches are uncovering in the shops; jewels, gold, and silver flash in the goldsmith's sunny windows; and great houses cast a stately shade upon them as they pass. But through the light, and through the shade, they go on lovingly together, lost to everything around; thinking of no other riches, and no prouder home, than they have now in one another. (806)

We know that Dickens is thinking metaphorically and religiously as memories of little Paul, the ethereal child of 'that older fashion yet, of Immortality,' mingle in the lovers' thoughts which build a kingdom beyond time and place, in the *anno Domini* that leaves dark *anno Dombei* behind:

> 'As I hear the sea,' says Florence, 'and sit watching it, it brings so many days into my mind. It makes me think so much—'
> 'Of Paul, my love. I know it does.'
> Of Paul and Walter. And the voices in the waves are always whispering to Florence, in their ceaseless murmuring, of love—of love, eternal and illimitable, not bounded by the confines of this world, or by the end of time, but ranging still, beyond the sea, beyone the sky, to the invisible country far away! (DS,811)

To return to the journey of David Copperfield, after Dora dies, David stays abroad for three years. Thanks to Agnes, the three of death-in-life passes; a time in death past, he rises as from the dead. Now a new *Tommy* chapter begins. Back in England again, David looks for his old comrade in Gray's Inn, and learns that Traddles, a young aspirant to pre-eminence in Law circles, has not done very well, by official measure:

> 'Do you know where Mr. Traddles lives in the Inn?' I asked the waiter, as I warmed myself by the coffee-room fire.
> 'Holborn Court, sir. Number two.'
> 'Mr. Traddles has a rising reputation among the lawyers, I believe?' said I.
> 'Well, sir,' returned the waiter, 'probably he has, sir; but I am not aware of it myself.'
> The waiter, who was middle-aged and spare, looked for help to a waiter of more authority—a stout, potential old man, with a double chin, in black breeches and stockings, who came out of a place like a churchwarden's pew, at the end of the coffee-room, where he kept company with a cash-box, a Directory, a Law-list, and other books and papers.
> 'Mr. Traddles,' said the spare waiter. 'Number two in the Court.'
> The potential waiter waved him away, and turned, gravely, to me.
> 'I was inquiring,' said I, 'whether Mr. Traddles, at number two in the Court, has not a rising reputation among the lawyers?'
> 'Never heard his name,' said the waiter, in a rich husky voice.
> I felt quite apologetic for Traddles.
> 'He's a young man, sure?' said the portentous waiter, fixing his eyes severely on me. 'How long has he been in the Inn?'
> 'Not above three years,' said I.
> The waiter, who I supposed had lived in his churchwarden's pew for forty years, could not pursue such an insignificant subject. He asked me what I would have for dinner?
> I felt I was in England again, and really was quite cast down on Traddles's account. There seemed to be no hope for him. I meekly ordered a bit of fish and a steak, and stood before the fire musing on his obscurity. (820)

The 'churchwarden's pew' simile and severity of manner of the priestly figure in black, also the mention of his having waited 'forty years' in this wilderness of the Temple, implicitly tie this cheerless place of law to the Hebrew dispensation. Three years in the valley of the shadow of Death, and David, through the writing of Agnes, rises. Three years in Law, but for Traddles no 'rising' ('rising reputation' is carefully repeated twice) in sight. Traddles has indeed chosen 'an arduous place to rise in' (821). There is 'no hope for him.' David gives Tommy up 'for lost' (822), *lost* echoing in this grave place, a monument to man's hopeless condition vis à vis Eternity before Christ, one in which, like the mild waiter, he is reduced to helpless, hopeless 'waiting.'

Discovering that Traddles occupies chambers on the top story of number

two, David ascends the stairs. Where Law dominates, the way up proves
hazardous:

> A crazy old staircase I found it to be, feebly lighted on each landing by a club-
> headed little oil wick, dying away in a little dungeon of dirty glass. (822)

In this typical Dickensian serio-comic miniature, the dying wick in its
solitary dungeon captivity (so Jews languished in Babylon, one learns in
*Our Mutual Friend*[3]) doth an Old tale repeat. As in Satis House, light but
faintly troubles an encompassing darkness. Whereas to follow Agnes
Wickfield up the great staircase to the glorious room ablaze with light
above is to inherit a whole shining wickfield of Light.

David pursues the arduous journey upward:

> In the course of my stumbling up-stairs, I fancied I heard a pleasant sound
> of laughter; and not the laughter of an attorney's clerk or barrister's clerk, but
> of two or three merry girls. Happening, however, as I stopped to listen, to
> put my foot in a hole where the Honourable Society of Gray's Inn had left a
> plank deficient, I fell down with some noise, and when I recovered my footing,
> all was silent. (822)

On man's pilgrimage to Heaven B. C., under Law, the wick dies and man
Falls and gropes, very much on his own, for, as David words it, 'the rest of
the journey' (822).

Arriving at the top, David, after a brief delay, is at last admitted to a
cubicle...

> ...and next into a little sitting room; where I came into the presence of my old
> friend (also out of breath), seated at a table, and bending over papers.
> 'Good God!' cried Traddles, looking up. 'It's Copperfield!' and rushed into
> my arms, where I held him tight.
> 'All well, my dear Traddles?'
> 'All well, my dear, dear Copperfield, and nothing but good news!'
> We cried with pleasure, both of us. (823)

O, bliss! Dickens mounts a happy vision of arrival, on earth as it shall be in
Heaven. Might it not *be* Heaven, as one feared lost proves found, saved?
'Good God!' rings out. *Good* God, indeed, to keep bringing sons of David
into the world to cause men, buried in the head-down labors of law, to look
up. Good God, and 'good news,' a gospelful in small. Always in Dickens,
words work free from dulling indifferent usage to regain the lost, original
celestial height. It is the Good News of Christ, as Tommy reports the great
success of the Story, the David-Dickens-Mr. Dick allegory of a journey from
Old to New Testament time, which must read very like *David Copperfield*.

With: 'All well?' and the graceful antiphon, 'All well...good news!' we
rise still higher into choric Heavens of praise:

'My dear fellow!' said Traddles. 'And grown so famous! My glorious
Copperfield! Good gracious me, *when* did you come, *where* have you come
from, *what* have you been doing? (823)

With puns in 'glorious' and 'gracious' like a rose-petal carpet strewing the
way, the 'when, where, what' triplets, a Trinity of pearls, shine the more.
All is joy. The girls, Tommy, and his clerk have been romping; all are out
of breath, as men will be, literally and figuratively, when they arrive in
Heaven. The arrival of a son of David fills hearts with light.

Like other betwixt-and-between law and faith Toms in Dickens, including Tom Grig in *The Lamplighter* and Tom Pinch in *Martin Chuzzlewit,*[4] Tommy Traddles begins in *Traddles,* i.e., skittles, bowled-over, Fall,
captivity, 'debtor' time, recalling the B.C. condition of man, and ends in
the 'Tommy' time of Christian law, which, shedding severity and harshness, gives 'the ten' a New home in faith, hope, and charity. Traddles
takes the 'number two,' or law, way to rise, a hard one. But in his upper-
story chambers, he leaves the coffee-coffin house of grave figures,
precedents, and law-directory, of church-wardens and wigs, below. High
up, all is glory, grace, and joy.

In Dickens, the Good News is joyful, stressing that man was not meant
for Death, but for Life Eternal. All religious instruction that does not
magnify this central truth is out of touch with the life and lessons of Christ.
Dickens is saying: let doctrine, law, theology, the codified and canonized
insights into the nature of the Deity which, in first blush, were pure poetry,
rapture, intuition unconfined, the heart's loving leap towards the Creator,
return to their original state: decondense, deliquesce; and rising like
vapour or incense, be exhaled back into pure spirit:-to become what all was
before it congealed into priestly rule, patter, form. In Dickens, as in
Emerson, time turns to shining aether the solid angularity of facts. The
pity is that a Thomas Gradgrind, Dickens's Thomas of law, grinds minds
down on the stone of law, so that men forget that God is a spirit, a joyful
mystery whose message is not Damnation, but, because He *so loved* the
world, *Recalled to Life!*

After the 'reunion Above' scene which reunites Tommy and a son of
David, Tommy explains that he and 'the girls' were making merry when,
hearing someone coming, they ran away to hide:

'I am sorry,' said I, laughing afresh, 'to have occasioned such a dispersion.' (824)

Happy new dispersion, or Diaspora. The ten are fast learning to unbend,
and smile. But law takes its toll. Mr. Traddles of the Inner Temple grows
bald, his scant remaining hair 'made more rebellious than ever by the
constant friction of his lawyer's wig' (876). Or does the straight-up

standing hair bespeak, not priggery of uprightness in law, but rebellion against wig and wiglomeration of law, and leap upward?

Close to the end of the story, David and Tommy meet again on a most happy occasion:

> It is Sophy's birthday; and, on our road, Traddles discourses to me of the good fortune he has enjoyed.
>
> 'I really have been able, my dear Copperfield, to do all that I had most at heart. There's the Reverend Horace promoted to that living at four hundred and fifty pounds a year; there are our two boys receiving the very best education, and distinguishing themselves as steady scholars; there are three of the girls married very comfortably; there are three more living with us; there are three more keeping house for the Reverend Horace since Mrs. Crewler's decease; and all of them happy.' (876)

Tommy's new good news is alight with the Trinity. 'There are three; there are three more; there are three more;' thus, three three's united in: 'and all of them happy.' The *ten* of law have become a blessing to mankind at last. The three who return home to keep house for their Father show a welcome change of heart: they were happy enough to leave him, once. On Sophy's birthday, all celebrate an influx of new Wisdom, indeed.

'The girls' are waiting to welcome Tommy home:

> Here, when we go in, is a crowd of them, running down to the door, and hand-ing Traddles about to be kissed, until he is out of breath. Here, established in perpetuity, is the poor Beauty, a widow with a little girl; here, at dinner on Sophy's birthday, are the three married girls with their three husbands, and one of the husband's brothers, and another husband's cousin, and another husband's sister, who appears to me to be engaged to the cousin. Traddles, exactly the same simple, unaffected fellow as he ever was, sits at the foot of the large table like a Patriarch, and Sophy beams upon him, from the head, across a cheerful space that is certainly not glittering with Britannia metal. (877)

In a living present tense, as if all this is ongoing and eternal, *three* shines everywhere. Dickens really could, and might more conveniently and naturally have said: 'three married girls *and their husbands.*' That he insists: 'three married girls *with their three husbands,*' suggests that he can never resist a 'three.' It seems that Tommy and Sophy have their dreamed-of silver spoons at last. Or *is* it silver? One looks again across that 'cheerful space that is certainly not glittering with Britannia metal?' No name is given to whatever it is that glows. It may be no treasure laid up on earth; but what lies past copper, silver, and goldfields of earth, the divine treasure of light garnered in the Christian life. Thanks to Tommy and Sophy, *the ten,* once so destructive, have become a blessing to mankind. 'Three' fast multiplies, attracting fiancés and cousins that are reckoned by the dozens, in three, until it seems nothing else is.

Dickens's tale of Tommy and the ten is a Christian parable of how Judaic-Roman law outgrows its old ways: rabbinic rituals, stress on consequences of disobedience to the Law, the clean-unclean preoccupation found in OT Books of the Law, and binding formalism. Disburdened of such materialism, moving away from such pharisaical, bludgeoning obsession with outward cleanliness as is seen in Mrs. Joe and Mrs. Macstinger (*Dombey and Son*), in Christian time law shifts emphasis to inward and spiritual states of being: the quality of mercy, as to a hopeful, cheerfully, because Christful, trust in God.

There is nothing Traddles likes so much as oysters, David reminds Dora. And, as the parable of Christopher and three dozen oysters in *The Old Curiosity Shop* shows, there is nothing in Dickens that points more truly than oysters point to 'the pearl.'[5] When Dora does her best and serves oysters, something is terribly wrong with them. She is distressed. Tommy, however, contemplates them with characteristic good-humor and equanimity:

> 'Do you know, Copperfield,' said Traddles, cheerfully examining the dish.
> 'I think it is in consequence—they are capital oysters, but I *think* it is in
> consequence—of their never having been opened.' (642)

Yes, one must open the oyster to get at the pearl! The time is not ripe. But, as Tommy's 'two feet ten in circumference' (405) little round table with the marble top, firm as a rock; and as 'number two,' and two sons, all imply, the world is getting closer to *three* all the time. '*Cheerfully*,' knowing his Redeemer lives, Tommy waits and hopes.

As the Doctor-Dictionary plot in *Copperfield* has clear Doctor Johnson overtones; and the Philip (Pip)-Estella one in *Great Expectations,* clear Sir Philip Sidney 'Astrophel and Stella' ones, the Tommy-Sophy story may well echo the Tom-Sophia one of Henry Fielding's *Tom Jones.* Dickens names a son Henry Fielding Dickens. More to the point, perhaps, is his reference to *Tom Jones* in *David Copperfield.* David numbers Tom Jones among the 'glorious host' of works which, in the Murdstone era, 'kept alive my fancy, and my hope of something beyond that place and time' (56), in which hope is prefigured man's hope of the Beyond more blessed still. He adds: 'I have been Tom Jones (a child's Tom Jones, a harmless creature) for a week together' (56). 'Glorious host,' looking to Angels, is true. A Tom who wins the fair Sophia—Sophia, Wisdom, wisely loves the music of Handel more than any other—and who, after a long pilgrimage inherits Paradise Hall, is surely a figure in Christian allegory.[6] Like David, Dickens owed much to books that kept alive his fancy and hope in the blacking warehouse, 'Babylon' time. As he celebrates the idealistic love and passion for knowledge with which Sir Philip Sidney and Doctor Johnson inspired him, so in *Copperfield,* we think, he pays tribute to the outline of

Christian allegory found, or fancied, in Fielding.  Making of Tom Jones the 'child's Tom Jones, a harmless creature' that David in childhood imagines him to be, Dickens reunites 'Tommy' with 'Sophy,' and once again sends him on his way to that shining Paradise Hall of Halls, Heaven.  Such is the secret blessing and *bon voyage* one wishes an infant son one names 'Henry Fielding Dickens.'

Thus the Tommy Traddles tale.  Not the exalted Story of David which a whole world would praise.  But it is humble, faithful Tommy who delivers that Story of the son of David to the world.  And it is no small thing to have subdued 'the ten,' and for his pains, won Sophy: to be beamed on by Wisdom all his livelong days.  Wisdom comes dear.  Ah, but Tommy does not think in old ways of price, payment, 'present payment.'  In the Christian Tommy is a new spirit of self-giving and priceless forgiving, by which Star man sails to Eternity.

When, after three years, Tommy and David are reunited in that top-storey set of chambers, their joy knows no bounds.  So, when life ends, Tommy and the son of David will meet high above all earthly inns of court in the Court in which, temporal addresses having long since melted into eternal ones, Traddles will again look up, and, with 'Good God!' on his lips, praise his 'glorious Copperfield,' and speak in the tongue of angels what on earth sounded to the ears of men as:

> Hosanna to the Son of David;
> Blessed is he that cometh
> in the name of the Lord;
> Hosanna in the highest. (*Matt.* 21:9)

# FOURTEEN
## Mr. and Mrs. Micawber

'Under the impression,' said Mr. Micawber, 'that your peregrinations in this metropolis have not as yet been extensive, and that you might have some difficulty in penetrating the arcana of the Modern Babylon in the direction of the City Road—in short,' said Mr. Micawber, in another burst of confidence, 'that you might lose yourself—I shall be happy to call this evening, and instal you in the knowledge of the nearest way.'

I thanked him with all my heart, for it was friendly in him to offer to take that trouble. (DC, 156)

A thankless task, to subject to analysis those great originals, Mr. and Mrs. Micawber:- originals, although, we know, close copies of Dickens's own parents, John and Elizabeth Dickens. But analysis has this poor excuse and recompense: the Micawbers prove as astonishing in allegory as, in the words of Mr. Micawber, 'in statu quo.' We see that Dickens has very mixed feelings, fond and pained, about the shabby-genteel, grandiloquent, benign, wonderfully oblivious, self-absorbed debtor father who shares a never-to-be-forgotten childhood captivity in 'Babylon;' then, one fine day, in a triumphant burst of hope and amid spangled flights of words, bids little David, or little Charles Dickens, a fond farewell and merrily drives away.

In his up-down-up debtor's life of endless hapless plunges from high hope to blackest despair, then up again, Mr. Micawber, ever insolvent and in the shadow of debtor's prison, is a replica not only of John Dickens, but of OT man in the precarious condition of the life of 'debt,' the state of arrears B.C. man never outdistanced. Imprisoned in London, the Modern Babylon, under a law as stringent and cruel as the one that decreed the first Babylonian Captivity, Mr. Micawber might be an ancient Jew, both when in prison and when newly released from 'captivity' (259). Babylon behind him, Mr. Micawber promptly sets out for Canterbury, 'on account of the great probability of something turning up in a cathedral town' (261). Through all adventure of collapse and fall, our Canterbury pilgrim never ceases to hope and dream of a great spring forward, the moment when 'certain expected events should turn up' (407). Through Micawber's betwixt-and-between B.C. and A.D. predicament, exploited mainly for comedy, Dickens creates a memorable portrait of Fall man which confirms the view of George Meredith that the cause of Comedy and of Truth is the same.

In Forster's *The Life of Charles Dickens,* we learn that John Dickens is the original of Mr. Micawber; also, I imagine, of other improvident, self-centered, highly 'eloquent' fathers in Dickens's works such as Mr. Turveydrop and Harold Skimpole (*Bleak House*), and Mr. Dorrit (*Little Dorrit*). These, and the well-meaning but ineffectual, not father but father figure who befriends David, in his fashion, in Babylon; the patronizing, flowery, remote Mr. Micawber, are types of John Dickens, who calmly suffered his frail, often unwell, quick, eager nine year old son Charles, sensitive and easily hurt in body and soul, to sink into a life of slavery and heartbreaking loneliness in the blacking warehouse time.

Picking up the story begun in the chapter entitled *Mr. Dick,* we focus in more closely on Dickens's father's role in the affair, again quoting Dickens's words:

> My rescue from this kind of existence I considered quite hopeless, and abandoned as such, altogether; though I am solemnly convinced that I never, for one hour, was reconciled to it, or was otherwise than miserably unhappy. I felt keenly, however, the being so cut off from my parents, my brothers, and sisters; and, when my day's work was done, going home to such a miserable blank; and *that,* I thought, might be corrected. One Sunday night I remonstrated with my father on this head, so pathetically and with so many tears, that his kind nature gave way. He began to think that it was not quite right. I do not believe that he had ever thought so before, or thought about it. It was the first remonstrance I had ever made about my lot, and perhaps it opened up a little more than I intended. A back-attic was found for me at the house of an insolvent court-agent, who lived in Lant-street in the borough, where Bob Sawyer lodged many years afterwards. A bed and bedding were sent over for me, and made up on the floor. The little window had a pleasant prospect of a timber-yard; and when I took possession of my new abode, I thought it was a Paradise. (FD, I, 39)

Poor little 'Dick' Dickens, grateful for a pitifully small change in his distressed condition, and in his lonely back-attic, thinking himself in Paradise. Is not this incredibly passive, trouble-distracted, remote, yet—and this is possibly more painful and incredible still—not unkind, basically good-natured father who, when prodded, belatedly sees a bit further, the very soul of Mr. Micawber? 'He began to think...!' '*Had never thought about it before*'! How the mature Dickens, remembering his childish plight and profound gratitude for the boon of a back-attic, a slightly cleaner, more airy solitude, must have pitied the innocent he was back in the sad, sad days when, only because *he* undertook to speak of it, he was finally taken notice of by his own father.

Something of this unconscious, colossal selfishness and tendency to see his son exploited carries over into the portrait of Mr. Micawber. Like little Charles, little David Copperfield, though a mere child, must bear not only his own poverty in a life of drudgery and exile from home, but the Micawbers' troubles too:

> Mr. Micawber's difficulties were an addition to the distressed state of my mind. In my forlorn state I became attached to the family, and used to walk about, busy with Mrs. Micawber's calculations of ways and means, and heavy with the weight of Mr. Micawber's debts. On a Saturday night, which was my grand treat,—partly because it was a great thing to walk home with the six or seven shillings in my pocket, looking into shops and thinking what such a sum would buy, and partly because I went home early,—Mrs. Micawber would make the most heart-rending confidences to me; also on a Sunday morning, when I mixed the portion of tea or coffee I had bought over-night, in a little shaving-pot, and sat late at my breakfast. (162)

'Heavy with the weight of Mr. Micawber's debts,' as Charles Dickens with his father's, as Christ with mankind's, David Copperfield, a son of David figure, might be living in the B.C. in which the sins of the fathers were visited upon the children. Too full of themselves and their troubles to see David as the child he really is, the Micawbers, husband and wife both, un-thinkingly burden the waif who pays dearly for their friendship. In casting his father in the role of a grandly remote, even when near, friendly stranger (one's father a pleasant stranger!), Dickens, with marvelous charity, forbearance, and tolerance, quietly and poignantly says close to all.

A freshly orphaned David Copperfield, the D.C. who is C.D., is thus absorbed into the slightly stale, endlessly repetitious melodrama of a large, indigent family's battle for survival, Dickens's family's own. David is the quick, cast-adrift child no member of a fast-growing family has the time, presence of mind, or generosity of spirit to really see. This fact pierces us over and over in Mr. and Mrs. Micawber's conversations—rather, solilo-quizing discourses—with David. For example, in the farewell scene between the Micawbers and David when the Micawbers, newly sprung from prison, leave Babylon:

> 'Master Copperfield,' said Mrs. Micawber, 'God bless you! I never can for-get all that, you know, and I never would if I could.'
> 'Copperfield,' said Mr. Micawber, 'farewell! Every happiness and pros-perity! If, in the progress of revolving years, I could persuade myself that my blighted destiny had been a warning to you, I should feel that I had not occu-pied another man's place in existence altogether in vain. In case of anything

turning up (of which I am rather confident), I shall be extremely happy if it should be in my power to improve your prospects.'

I think, as Mrs. Micawber sat at the back of the coach, with the children, and I stood in the road looking wistfully at them, a mist cleared from her eyes, and she saw what a little creature I really was. I think so, because she beckoned me to climb up, with quite a new and motherly expression in her face, and put her arm around my neck, and gave me just such a kiss as she might have given to her own boy. I had barely time to get down again before the coach started, and I could hardly see the family for the handkerchiefs they waved. It was gone in a minute. The Orfling and I stood looking vacantly at each other in the middle of the road, and then shook hands and said good-bye; she going back, I suppose, to St. Luke's workhouse, as I went to begin my weary day at Murdstone and Grinby's. (175)

And so, with momentarily heartfelt, richly strewn flourishes, blessings, and good wishes, with much ceremonial, highly visible waving of handkerchiefs, the Micawber entourage, like a splendid circus, or the Crummles provincial touring company in *Nickleby,* moves off in a cloud of dust to its next bravura engagement. No blame attaches to them, exactly; the Micawbers have too many mouths of their own to feed to be expected to worry about two orphans, David and Orfling, their servant, who, left behind, stand watching in the road as the last echoes of the brave bass and quavering soprano duet of Farewell slowly die away.

And yet, how sad. The Orfling (Orphan) flung the Micawbers' way is now abandoned, dropped back into the workhouse; David is abandoned too. Mr. Micawber calls him 'Copperfield;' his wife, 'Master Copperfield.' Such mode of address insures immunity from vision and guilt. For so addressed, David is not a small child, but a contemporary and equal, and the fantasy in which the Micawbers feel no responsibility for him can sail smoothly on. It is a moral convenience to Mr. and Mrs. Micawber alas, no doubt it was to John and Elizabeth Dickens—to suppose the child they load with their troubles and send to pawn their spoons older than he really is. To be less than one's parents' own child! And further, to have to realize, as Dickens came to, that these parents were by no means monsters, but in their way lovely, charming people. One wonders if such blindness is not worse than deliberate cruelty. We begin to grasp the situation that so staggered Dickens, one that pained him so deeply that, except for the disclosure in later life to Forster, brought as swiftly as possible to a close, he could never bring himself to speak of it to a living soul.

Before the Micawbers depart, for one brief moment Mrs. Micawber sees, not a fictitious Master Copperfield, but a lone, lorn, pathetic little child. Still she does not come down. She beckons David to climb up, then kisses him with 'just such a kiss as she might have given to her own boy.'

Breathtaking 'as if.' But little Charles *was* Elizabeth Dickens's own boy. Then how can one explain her eagerness to see the quarrel made up and Charles returned to the warehouse life? We note that David pays for that belated motherly kiss, for the coach starts abruptly and he must hastily clamber down or be thrown to the ground. Why do the Micawbers not consider taking David with them? (Why did the Dickenses cut their small son off from the brood?) Off they go, amid airy, futile clouds of sentiment and well-wishing: 'Copperfield, farewell! Every happiness and prosperity!' Which amounts to splendidly waving him away.

The Micawbers are not unkind. It just never occurs to them that, all through the time of their acquaintance, David is close to starving; and with their removal will be totally alone. No wonder that in so many works, Dickens dramatizes the plight of the little pauper, the abandoned child; or that Mrs. Nicodemus Boffin, waking from a dream about a lost boy, sobs: 'Don't you see the poor child's face? O shelter the poor child!' (OMF, 91) No wonder, too, that Dickens reverences above all else the Saviour Who set a child in the midst of the Disciples, making it the way of ways to the Kingdom.

There is a distinctly seamy side to Mr. Micawber, for all that David in his great need is so touchingly grateful to his 'rescuer' in Babylon. Micawber borrows a shilling for porter from David, who earns but a miserable few shillings a week and often goes hungry. We know the debt will never be thought of again, much less repaid. Micawber sees nothing. Established as 'middle-aged' (175), he is so addled by cares and pretensions that when he and David meet again, he hails him as the companion of his youth. His *what??* And what of David's youth, which really was one—or, rather, a missed childhood? Micawber effusively calls him: 'Our old and tried friend, Copperfield' (412). 'Tried,' yes, sorely and often, one thinks: more truth than poetry here, as Micawber does not begin to see.

So the picture is brilliantly mixed. All due honor to open, affable, malice-free, genial and comfortable Mr. Micawber, and to his flustered, intensely loyal (to him), confiding wife, Nature's own fount, always knee-deep in children. But, parting the frothy curtain of Micawber rhetoric, emotionalism, and high intentions, Dickens steadily eyes these foster parents of David's sad youth, and in sympathy and truth reveals them in all their sober and comic better and worse, and better-worse.

Again, there *is* a worse. The third time they meet, Mr. Micawber does not even recognize David; has quite forgotten him. Then memory dawns: 'And what are you doing, Copperfield? Still in the wine trade?' (257) he asks. More *Copperfield,* as to a contemporary; more blithe non-recognition. 'The wine trade' prettifies the old, soul-deadening labor among empty bottles; Micawber simply chooses not to know how it really was for the boy. Not only does Micawber fail to recognize David, but he does not 'recognize' him, either, as we see when he confides to Heep (dark forecast of the fatal relationship to come!) that, in his view, David 'has a mind capable of getting up the classics, to any extent' (258). The classics indeed. We smile at a slight of such breathtaking proportions, especially as sighted from the watchtower of allegory. Doubtless Mr. Micawber would have formed a like opinion of the intellectual gifts of another Son of David. Indeed, as men are to David, they are to the Son of David.

However, Mr. Micawber begins to be impressed with David's rise in life. He says to his wife: 'My dear, allow me to introduce to you a pupil of Doctor Strong's' (259). Dickens shows the impression that his growing name made on the father who, in the way of Micawber with David, distantly and occasionally glanced in on his life, and dealt with him, as with all, in one and the same uncapturably smiling, unruffled, and, smiling or frowning, amiably impersonal way. In Dickens's memory, his parents were the Micawbers who, befriending him in that self-involved, oblivious way of theirs, with no trace of redeeming emotion or lasting memory of the event, in effect said goodbye and drove away.

The vacuum, blank, and silence into which Dickens's haunting childhood misery, never acknowledged by his otherwise endlessly voluble parent, fell, seems to me as painful a fact as the helpless, mute, suffering time itself. In after time, Dickens's parents never offered even the token gesture of recognition that their abandonment of their son was as terrible as it was, much less apologized. Perhaps this is why asking forgiveness and being forgiven are themes that loom large in Dickens, and why Dickens highlights Christ's forgiveness of sin. How solemnly splendid are moments when Alice Marwood (*Dombey and Son*) and Miss Havisham (*Great Expectations*) ask forgiveness of those they have wronged.

We smile at and sympathize with the debt-harried, basically decent Micawbers, but can never quite read them sentimentally. Little David carries too much of their burden along with his own. His lonely agony, unnoticed by the Micawbers, is great. All the while he is taking to heart their tales of woe, pawning their spoons, suffering their daily alarms, falls, and exhausting momentary recoveries, David is laboring from Monday through Saturday night, with 'no advice, no counsel, no encouragement, no consolation, no assistance, no support, of any kind, from any one, that I can call to mind, as I hope to go to Heaven!' (159) Lonely, prowling, enduring an unlifting 'sense of unmerited degradation' (166), David in his total aloneness clings to the Micawbers. In time, he is 'relieved of much of the weight of Mr. and Mrs. Micawber's cares; for some relatives or friends had engaged to help them at their present pass, and they lived more comfortably in the prison than they had lived for a long while out of it' (DC, 166). But still David pays court to them, visiting them in prison, walking up and down the parade ground with Mr. Micawber, playing casino with

Mrs. Micawber, listening to her Belinda Pocket-like reminiscences of her dear papa and mamma, things little Charles Dickens did when visiting his father in the Marshalsea. [1]

No Miss Havisham, Dickens eventually forgets and forgives—at least, forgives. His sense of a Providence governing his life grows. He accepts that his parents could neither see nor save him, caught up as they were in the banal hysteria of the day to day. Dickens presents 'the Micawbers' fairly, even generously, but, again, they are not lovable. How perfect both are at the language of distraught feeling, yet how little truly distraught. David's tears flow often for them, never theirs for him: the relationship is almost a one-way street. It would probably have been easier for Dickens if his parents had been outright villains, not merely the thrashing-about, fantasizing, weak, inconsistent, wonderfully unreflective duo they were. Dickens never solves the painful mystery of why his sister Fanny was sent to school, and he was not: why he was reserved for 'beheading,' like another unlucky Charles, for the 'crucifixion' and 'death' of that dark time.

Childhood passes. Dickens lives past such bafflement, hurt, and silent dismay. He comes to see his father in a favorable light, as this reminiscence preserved in Forster records:

It is proper to preface them [passages from letters of Dickens depicting his father] by saying that no one could know the elder Dickens without secretly liking him the better for those flourishes of speech, which adapted themselves so readily to his gloom as well as to his cheerfulness, that it was difficult not to fancy they had helped him considerably in both, and had rendered more tolerable to him, if also more possible, the shade and sunshine of his checquered life. 'If you should have an opportunity *pendente lite,* as my father would observe—indeed did on some memorable ancient occasions when he informed me that the ban-dogs would shortly have him at bay'—Dickens wrote in December 1847. 'I have a letter from my father' (May 1841) 'lamenting the fine weather, invoking congenial tempests, and informing me that it will not be possible for him to stay more than another year in Devonshire, as he must then proceed to Paris to consolidate Augustus's French.' 'There has arrived,' he writes from the Peschiere in September 1844, 'a characteristic letter for Kate from my father. He dates it Manchester, and says he has reason to believe that he will be in town with the pheasants, on or about the first of October. He has been with Fanny in the Isle of Man for nearly two months: finding there, as he goes on the observe, troops of friends, and every description of continental luxury at a cheap rate.' Describing in the same year the departure from Genoa of an English physician and acquaintance, he adds: 'We are very sorry to lose the benefit of his advice—or, as my father would say, to be deprived, to a certain extent, of the concomitant advantages, whatever they may be, resulting from his medical skill, such as it is, and his professional attendance, in so far as it may be so considered.'

On and on, through many a memorable Micawberesque sentence, to

Forster's closing remark:

> Nobody likes Micawber less for his follies; and Dickens liked his father more,
> the more he recalled his whimsical qualities. 'The longer I live, the better
> man I think him,' he exclaimed afterwards. The fact and the fancy had united
> whatever was most grateful to him in both. (FD, III, 11)

Yet somewhere in this eventual accommodation remains an unbanishable
('I never afterwards forgot, I never shall forget, I never can forget') dismay
that his own father and mother could so lightly have cast him away. Depicting himself in *Copperfield* as an orphan with living parents, Dickens
makes as touching, eloquent, and profound a symbolic comment on his
childhood as anyone ever made.

Mr. Micawber, half amiable fellow, half humbug, with harried wife and
ever-increasing tribe of children, declares that the 'God of day' (165) has
gone down in his life. In the 'B.C.,' debtor stage of the journey, no God of
both day *and* night exists for him. But Micawber does not chafe at his fate.
So accustomed is he to crisis, to every small rise being promptly followed
by fall, that he never imagines a Providence in whose keeping one is not
periodically shipwrecked, or, as he words it, 'forever floored' (175). (Allit-
erating 'f's' are some comfort, anyway.) In debtors' prison, Mr. Micawber
energetically sets about framing a petition 'praying for an alteration in the
Law of imprisonment for debt' (168). 'Praying,' intentional or not, helps,
and shortly thereafter the Babylonian Captivity once again ends.

But the long inactivity of the debtor's life leaves its mark. Like a character actor too long in one role, Mr. Micawber loses touch with reality. The
edge of tragedy blunts. By the hundredth performance, the player, too
fluent in lines of grief and despair, but struts and frets, a plate of shrimp in
one hand, the ornamental eye-glass in the other. Reinspirited by his
own noble speeches on sacred themes, such as friendship and woman,
Mr. Micawber somehow each time regains the will to live, the cue for
passion recovered somewhere between the hot kidney pudding ordered for
breakfast and a brisk game of skittles before noon. Inevitably, Micawber
drifts into matinee self-idolatry, a vast moral indolence underlying a stagey
emotionalism. His over-rehearsed, routinized expressive flights, the
flowery diction of 'canker,' 'shipwreck,' and 'devouring element,' disguise
hard facts, so that all real sense of his situation, let alone David's, is lost.
On occasions that hardly call for Cicero, Micawber is Cicero. However, as
George Meredith says, there are some matters too serious for metaphor.
Mr. Micawber never finds them.

In prison and with no chance for solid accomplishment at hand, Mr. Micawber settles into being the too-communicative grand master of 'ostenta-
tious resignation' (534), inactivity, the short cut, and the ruinous habit of
borrowing without repaying. Giving Traddles his I.O.U., Micawber clearly
considers he has repaid the debt. (So in *Great Expectations* Pip and
Herbert, in days of vanity and debt, tally accounts and bask in the illusory

relief of having left unpaid bills behind.) Helping himself to liberal serv-
ings of the only commodity plentiful in a debtor's cramped life, shabby-
elegant Mr. Micawber becomes a purveyor of bombast and verbal display:
words, words, words. But he relates to what he utters only in the letter.
The spirit escapes him, as we see when, only minutes after a speech about
his shattered state, filled with darkest innuendo, he is discovered in
excellent spirits, humming a hornpipe and preparing to dine.

Dickens's deepest sympathies lies with multitudes of debtors like
Micawber, ghost of his own father, literally rotting away behind high
spiked walls of debtors' prisons. One finds them movingly portrayed in
*Pickwick, Copperfield,* and *Little Dorrit.* It is no Christian society that fails
to look with Christ's own compassion on the fallen, whether felon, debtor,
pauper, or orphan, and does not square its laws and concept of charity
with: 'Forgive us our debts.' In the fifth and sixth chapters of his *The Life
of Our Lord,* Dickens makes much of the mercy of Christ towards sinners
and His lessons on leniency towards debtors.[2] If the Lords of the Court of
Chancery in Dickens read the NT, they could not deliver transgressors of
the Law to 'Babylon' as did the first Lord of Chancery and chance,
Jehovah, the Jews, His debtors, of old.

In depicting 'the Modern Babylon,' as Micawber calls it, Dickens
presses ancient Babylon-Modern Babylon parallels. In Fall time, Mrs. Micawber drinks 'flip' (171); as David celebrates a lonely birthday with 'a
glass of the Genuine Stunning' (161), and is flipped, Stunned. In
'Babylon,' David enters a public house called 'the Lion' (160); one cannot
have a Babylon without, if not a whole den, at least one Lion. Tipp the
carman works with David at Murdstone and Grinby's; just as Tip Dorrit
appears in debtors' prison in *Little Dorrit. Tipp* and *Tip,* like Lady Tippins
in *Our Mutual Friend,* are symbolic shorthand for Fall man, ever 'tipping'
over and falling in a B.C.-like world unwon to Christ. More pre-Christian
time forms. A terrifying man, positioned 'near the Obelisk, in the Black-
friars Road' (177), pounces on little David, stealing his box and then,
adding insult to injury, turning on David as if he himself, not David, were
the injured party:

> 'Wot!' said the young man, seizing me by my jacket collar, with a frightful
> grin. 'This is a pollis case, is it? You're a-going to bolt, are you? Come to
> the pollis, you young warmin, come to the pollis!' (178)

And still more rant of 'pollis': 'Come to the pollis! You shall prove it
yourn to the pollis' (178). First, *obelisk,* pointing to that other place of
captivity for Israel, Egypt. Then, a pun Dickens revels in, tossing up and
catching half a dozen times in sheer delight, *pollis,* or police, in which
'polis,' or Greek city-state, sports. Also, a lone David wanders under
shadowy arches of the Adelphi. Greek-Roman time piles up again.

The vicious 'wot' man ('Wot job?' 'Wot box?' (178)) drags David against the donkey, then rattles away in his cart, stealing David's box.  A nightmare ensues:

> I ran after him as fast as I could, but I had no breath to call out with, and should not have dared to call out, if I had.  I narrowly escaped being run over, twenty times at least, in half a mile.  Now I lost him, now I saw him, now shouted at, now down in the mud, now up again, now running into some-body's arms, how running headlong at a post...(179)

A 'Wot!' menace, the wot heavy with OT, inflicts an ancient ordeal on donkeys and a son of David.  David being run headlong at a post, the very connection of a son of David and a post, flashes crucifixion.  A City so barren of pity for dumb beast and child is so far behind A.D. that it might well be ancient Babylon.

Mr. Micawber knows nothing of this, or of David's other ordeals.  Ask no such knowing or caring of him, and he is a likable fellow with laudable ambitions.  Long-winded as he is, he can and does now and then suddenly break off a flossy speech, and, in a burst of confidence, with a timely 'in short,' come directly to the point.  His room in prison is 'top story but one' (165), and so in a sense is he.  He has plans to secure the upper part of a house in which, 'by throwing out a bow window, or carrying up the roof another story,' he can 'live comfortably, and reputably, for a few years' (422).  But he never makes top story, or carries the roof up.  Why?  It has something to do with contracting the debtor's mentality of shift, drift, and the substitution of dreams for deeds.  He develops a dangerous toleration, even fondness, for prison life.

Another downfall is words.  The inflated verbal style of Micawber, always on display, effectively blinds him to the shabby truth of his condition.  Lulled by the siren song of his own music, he hardly knows or cares what he means.  He stops seeing.  All the while he goes on about Canterbury, David, the real authentic thing, is right there before him.  In short, Mr. Micawber would not know the Son of God if he fell over Him.

Dickens can take just so much John Dickens-Wilkins Micawber bombast, and then must stop the story abruptly, step out in front of the footlights, and with rare vehemence, deliver a long frontal attack on the dangers of in-fatuation with mere words, the: " 'To wit, in manner following, that is to say' (753) of Micawber, which reaches epidemic proportion in the era of Micawber's going to the Devil and becoming confidential clerk to Uriah Heep.[3]  Dickens does not relent.  Mr. Micawber's windy reference to arrangements which 'should be concluded as between man and man' elicits from a usually patient David: 'I don't know that Mr. Micawber attached any meaning to this last phrase; I don't know that anybody ever does; but he appeared to relish it uncommonly, and repeated, with an impressive cough, 'as between man and man.'  Both the continual 'formal piling up of words' (753) by Micawber and his absolute passion for letter-writing—'I believe he dreams in letters!' (774), Miss Trotwood says—point to a captivity in 'the letter,' bulwark of OT law. Micawber does indeed know his way around 'the arcana of the Modern Babylon;' and there is more than a little *ark* in any *arc*ana he, whose choice of words it is, has to do with.

Taken all in all, Mr. Micawber is a walking Captivity symbol, with his high wall of a collar and ornamental, or fake, eyeglass he never looks through, and could not see through if he did. While a victim of unchristian times and a victim of Fall, Micawber carries B.C. and Fall around inside him, too.

Exploitive, ineffectual, grandiloquent father figures in Dickens, surely John Dickens again and again, reappear. Mr. Dickens's peculiarity of speech, recorded by Forster in:

> 'Pray, Mr. Dickens, where was your son educated?'
> 'Why, indeed, Sir—ha! ha!—he may be said to have educated himself!'
> (FD, I, 68)

echoes in Micawber's little cough, and in Mr. Dorrit's: 'I—ha!—I can't think what it's owing to' (226), and: 'Who am I that you—ha—separate me from other gentlemen?' (LD, 459) Like Dickens's father, Mr. Dorrit settles into debtors' prison and is shamelessly dependent on others, exploiting other debtors and his own children, and hardly noticing that his son, Tip, is going to ruin under his very eyes. Then there is Mr. Turveydrop of *Bleak House,* unregenerate Fall man still hurtling downwards in the Topsy-*TURVEY drop*—the pride, vanity, selfishness that places terrible burdens on the son—ended only with the coming of Christ, that highest Model of Deportment in the ways of self-sacrifice and love for others.

Mr. Turveydrop seems Mr. Micawber taken a bit farther. Like Micawber, Turveydrop is an aging dandy, showily dressed, and given to waxing oratorical on all occasions. Micawber-Turveydrop parallels are marked. Each grandly holds court, attended by vast retinues of words, slaves the owner is in turn enslaved to. Mr. Micawber eulogizes: 'Woman, in the lofty character of Wife' (413), but in Heep time wounds Mrs. Micawber by adopting a manner distant, cutting, and cold. Likewise, while Mr. Turveydrop with fluting tongue expatiates upon the theme of 'Wooman, lovely Wooman' (BH, 194), the unadorned truth is that he worked his poor wife to death, and will his gentle son, if he can. Micawber 'borrows' from son figures, David and Traddles; Turveydrop lives off Prince, his son. Both are endlessly patronizing. Mr. Turveydrop pulls it all off as if he were not the taker, but were conferring estates. A topsy-Turveydrop state of affairs, indeed: morally speaking, all upside down. Both Micawber and Turveydrop overflow with perfumed sentiment: with 'My dear child!' and 'my son,' 'bless you!' or 'my own!' But theirs is the grasp of such sentiment only in the letter. Looking like the flower, florid enough to be one, many a fine talker in Dickens like Skimpole, Micawber,

Turveydrop, Bounderby, and Honeythunder, is the Serpent under it, the one that entered history at the dawn of language in the Garden.

In the case of each of the above, the relation of the father to the son has profound religious implications. The father mirrors the Father; the son, the Son. Bearing the whole burden of his father, young Prince Turveydrop of *Newman* Street looks both to the Prince of Peace and the 'New man': like *New*man Noggs (*Nickleby*) and Clemency *New*come (*The Battle of Life*) (see Ch. III), he shines with New, or NT, ideals. Another son who bore the burden of a father, Charles Dickens, we think, came to grasp his life's purpose as being in some obscure yet glorious, Providential relation to the Son, the 'Ch' to whom his Christian name, *Ch*arles, pointed. In *Copperfield*, Dickens casts himself as a son of David, i.e., a son of the Son of David, whom the 'D' of his surname holds aloft. In multiple ways, C.D., even as D.C., magnifies the life and lessons of Christ.

How Mr. Micawber goes to the Devil—in his wife's words, '[sells] himself to the D.' (703)—is a tale from Shakespeare, as is first hinted in much real-and-pseudo Shakespearean ornamentation he affects. His poor man's tragic theatre of: 'Take him for all in all, we ne'er shall—' (174) makes King Hamlet of Mrs. Micawber's dear, departed papa. And in: 'If any drop of gloom were wanting in the overflowing cup which is now 'commended' (in the language of an immortal Writer) to the lips of the undersigned' (428), Mr. Micawber plays Macbeth. There are also bardic lustres, as: 'if I may so Shakespearingly express myself, to dwindle, peak, and pine' (751); and: 'This was bad enough; but, as the philosophic Dane observes, with that universal applicability which distinguishes the illustrious ornament of the Elizabethan era, worse remains behind!' (752)

Garbed in Shakespeareana, Micawber steps straight from the pages of Shakespeare. Who is this 'tragic' hero of gifts of nature and language, Canterbury affinities, and theatrical mien, who, through a fatal flaw, and with the help of an intensely loyal but misguided wife, incurs a fatal ambition to rise, and goes straight to the Devil? Brace yourself, reader: Micawber is a poor player's Macbeth; and Lady Micawber, his helpmeet, Lady Macbeth. Detail first gives it away. While Micawber, who has journeyed to Canterbury in high hopes that something good will turn up there, warms to his Canterbury theme, he...

> ...is sensible of sounds in the next room, as of Mrs. Micawber washing her hands, and hurriedly opening and shutting drawers that were uneasy in their action. (407)

Micawber has Canterbury, i.e., Christian, impulses, however weak; but his Lady, washing her hands and distracting him, the multitudinous seas incarnadines. Not too long afterwards, Mr. Micawber is declaring 'that there are few comestibles better, in their way, than a Devil' (413), and full of enthusiasm for Devil, Heep, and Justice Blackstone.

Mic-awber: Mic-beth? The fallen Thane of *Caw*dor: Mi-*caw*-ber? In
*Macbeth,* whilst night's black agents to their prey do rouse, crows make
wing to the rooky wood. In Dickens, crow, rook, and jackdaw always
gather where priestcraft blots out the sun and light of the Son of God. Perhaps the *caw* syllable in Micawber, symbolising the rook's raw, disputatious cry, looks to his fatal weakness for letter, form, and the word.

Consider some striking Micawber-Macbeth parallels. Macbeth the
Scotsman contracts a fatal ambition and sells himself to the Devil. Quoting
Robert Burns and going on, Scotswise, about Auld Lang Syne and 'a right
gude willie waught,' Micawber, energetically preparing and serving 'a
Devil,' and serving the Devil, Heep, allies himself with forces that would
destroy the love founded on a rock. Macbeth kills a King. Affecting the
courtly manner' (257) of a king, Micawber, set to deliver Agnes Wickfield
into Heep's hands, symbolically nears the killing of the King of Kings.

The hands-washing motif in the portrait of Mrs. Micawber tells a truth.
As Lady Macbeth urges Macbeth on in evil when he hesitates and would
stop, so Mrs. Micawber, under her own family's influence, unwittingly
embroils her husband in evil:-urges him 'to raise a certain sum of
money—on a bill' (419), which gets him deeper in debt. Taking her advice,
Micawber heads into the Money Market, which way Heep lies. In Dickens,
'a bill,' bills, and debt (*debt* taken in both temporal and eternal ways)
signify a resurgence of the moral economy of B.C.. This is made clear
when Micawber speaks of: 'Bills—a convenience to the mercantile world,
for which, I believe, we are originally indebted to the Jews, who appear to
me to have had a devilish deal too much to do with them ever since' (771).
The *Jews-indebted-devilish-bills* symbolic cluster, which appears in *Oliver
Twist,*[4] locks the *bill* mentality into OT time. Like empty words, 'Bills'
sink Micawber, keeping him in the psychological and spiritual 'debtor'
prison of the B.C. frame of mind; and it is his loving wife who first suggests
them.

Mrs. Micawber does not stop there. Goading her husband on, admiring
his fatal flow of language, she cozzens him in moral indolence in the very
act of airing such opinions as:

> 'And here is Mr. Micawber without any suitable position or employment.
> Where does the responsibility rest? Clearly on society.' (419)

She fairly glitters with desire for Micawber to rise in that darkest of all
callings in Dickens, the Law:

> 'What I particularly request Mr. Micawber to be careful of, is,' said Mrs.
> Micawber, 'that he does not, my dear Mr. Copperfield, in applying himself to
> this subordinate branch of law, place it out of his power to rise, ultimately, to
> the top of the tree. I am convinced that Mr. Micawber, giving his mind to a
> profession so adapted to his fertile resources, and his flow of language, *must*

distinguish himself. Now, for example, Mr. Traddles,' said Mrs. Micawber, assuming a profound air, 'a Judge, or even say a Chancellor....' (532)

Every word of Mrs. Micawber's, every cadence, even, alarms. Her newly-acquired 'profound air' is especially disquieting. The once famously natural, confiding, weeping, loving, simple and domestic Mrs. Micawber, who, like Lady Macbeth, gave suck and knew what 'twas to love the babe that milked her, here sounds Like Mr. Micawber at his worst: that is, like a lawyer. Such a turgid, tendentious prose and involuted, painfully formal style! Suddenly, Mrs. Micawber is quoting her papa on the 'judicial mind' (533), and picturing Micawber at 'the top of the tree.' *Tree* in connection with law and judiciary hints darly of the Cross. Clearly, Mrs. Micawber, in this new role, will not rest until Micawber is Up There with the stern lords of law, one of the Sanhedrin of England, trying and dooming luckless wretches like Abel Magwitch, the face of His suffering face.

Rising in the Law, Micawber will in time resemble doctors of law like 'the Reverend Temple Pharisee' in the 'extensive rectory of Camel-cum-Needle's-eye,' as Dickens bitterly terms the descendants of the old Christ-destroying breed.[5] Mrs. Micawber is sure that her husband was 'reserved to wear a wig' (534), like lawyers of the Inner Temple. If so, the ladder to the top of the tree will be that quenchless, formal, Flooding 'flow of language,' tributary of the force in 'the letter' that respects only its own narrow decrees, and makes its power its shores.

The play within the play, Dickens's 'Almost Tragedy of Micawber,' d'après *Macbeth*, would be nothing without the witches. Behold Mr. Micawber, gleefully presiding over the preparation of a bowl of steaming spirits, 'a 'Brew' of the agreeable beverage for which he was famous' (530). Double, double, toil and trouble! On the very occasion of his preparing a mutton dish called a Devil, Micawber stations himself at a steaming cauldron to concoct his *Brew:*

> His recent despondency, not to say despair, was gone in a moment. I never saw a man so thoroughly enjoy himself amid the fragrance of lemon peel and sugar, the odour of burning rum, and the steam of boiling water, as Mr. Micawber did that afternoon. It was wonderful to see his face shining at us out of a thin cloud of these delicate fumes, as he stirred, and mixed, and tasted, and looked as if he were making, instead of punch, a fortune for his family down to the latest posterity. (412)

The face suspended in the swirling cloud of steam, the fumes of a rare brew, seems as if risen from it, not quite of earth. Like Mrs. Micawber washing her hands, it tickles a famous moment in *Macbeth*. Dickens loosely scatters *Macbeth* motifs like symbolic confetti. Perhaps the allusion at the end to 'latest posterity,' not in itself, but in this context, glances at the prophecy made to Banquo that his sons shall be king.

With Devil and witches' Brew, we re-enter the He-Brewing B.C. with its devilishly strong spirits, spirits in the Hebrew breast which Satan employed in his Law-sprung campaign to kill Christ. To Dickens, the witchery afoot in the foggy, Sonless dawn-of-B.C. magwitchian demon worship, and the three witches that appear to Macbeth long after in another foggy dawn of evil in *Macbeth,* spring from one eternal source. Indeed, Macbeth-Micawber *might be* Magwitch; and Magwitch, Macbeth-Micawber. In *Great Expectations,* when Pip glimpses Magwitch's estranged wife, the mother of Estella, he makes the connection with lightning speed:

> I cannot say whether any diseased affection of the heart caused her lips to be parted as if she were panting, and her face to bear a curious expression of suddenness and flutter; but I know that I had been to see Macbeth at the theatre, a night or two before, and that her face looked to me as if it were all disturbed by fiery air, like the faces I had seen rise out of the Witches' caldron. (201)

Seen under the single aspect of the demonic, Macbeth, Micawber, and Magwitch, the latter, we showed, recalling the man among the tombs tormented by devils (vis. Chapter IV), might be one. It is the incomparable genius of Dickens that detects likeness of the kind, and shows that, in all ages, the devil-witch temptation lays the same snares for the soul of man. And Lady Micawber actually *wants* Micawber in Brewing!

Unlike Macbeth, Micawber says, 'Get thee behind me, Satan!' in time. When 'Mortimer,' the name he adopts in the Heep era, can bear no more *Mort* in his soul, and no more law or blackboyish Justice *Black*stone, he denounces Heep. His higher nature—inspiration of his praying for a release of debtors; his exuberant plans to lift the roof; his setting out for Canterbury—prevails, and indolent, weak-willed Micawber finally takes a stand. Before a crowd of people, and like one 'swimming under superhuman difficulties,' 'fighting with cold water' (711), i.e., breasting the Old dispensation, the Flood, Micawber, in words for once free from all exaggeration, mightily denounces the 'transcendent and immortal hypocrite and perjurer—HEEP!' (711) Heep, later termed a 'HEEP of infamy' (751); very possibly, the undying HEEP-ocrite, too.[6] A snarled, 'The Devil take you!' (750), Heep's response to his former clerk, could not be more à propos. But it is too late. Micawber has been there, and come back.

The soul of Mr. Micawber is a wonderful comic mystery from the start, and wonderfully equivocal. In one episode, in the depths of some fresh despair, Mr. Micawber solemnly shakes hands with David and says: 'Copperfield, you are a true friend; but when the worst comes to the worst, no man is without a friend who is possessed of shaving materials' (261). Thinking he means to slit his throat, a wildly weeping Mrs. Micawber throws herself into his arms. But is that really what is on Micawber's mind? Consider what shaving means elsewhere in Dickens. In *Martin Chuzzlewit,* Paul Sweedlepipe, alias Poll, a barber, shaves young Bailey.

While Bailey, a lad in the peach fuzz stage of whiskerdom, is hardly in need of a barber, accommodating Paul, understanding the delicate issue of manly pride involved, 'wouldn't have ventured to deny on affadavit that he [Bailey] had the beard of a Jewish rabbi' (460). In allegory, Paul *Sweedle-pipe,* bird-fancier and *sweet piper* of the new tune of 'Paul,' shaves off a beard and thus nips a Jewish rabbi's career in the bud. To put it another way, he keeps young Bailey from winding up an Old Bailey, or OT man. Thus, alluding to shaving materials, maybe Mr. Micawber only means one can always shave off the beard, i.e., turn away from the Babylonian Captivity of the debtor's life of bills, debtors' prison, and law. Or, if Mr. Micawber does not yet know what what he says means, Dickens knows it for him.

Mrs. Micawber is equally distressed when Micawber announces he has 'sold himself to the D' (703). Latent in 'D' is not only Devil or Deuce, but Dominus and Deity. He commits other dramatic acts which his good, if not too clear-headed, wife also interprets as calamitous, but which, looked at from another angle, seem anything but, and which forecast the eventual rescue and redemption of Micawber. For example, Mrs. Micawber reports:

'Last night, on being childishly solicited for twopence, to buy "lemon-stunners"—a local sweetmeat—he presented an oyster-knife at the twins!' (703)

The oyster-knife, which terrifies Mrs. Micawber, need not terrify us. Perhaps the oyster-knife signifies something far sweeter than lemon-stunners: namely, the stunning idea of 'the pearl.'

Mr. Micawber is full of Fall, and promise of rise. He prides himself on his Devil, but is also delighted with Mr. Dick, renaming him 'Mr. Dixon' on the spot. He calls Agnes the only starry spot on his horizon, a sign of superior taste. It is when he associates himself with bills and Heep that everything falls apart. Whereupon, like Macbeth, for whom the savour of life is lost after the murder of the saintly King, Micawber sees his life as fallen into the sere, the yellow leaf. He then outdoes himself—Macbeth, too—in great soliloquies on the futility of it all. The Micawbers' home life dissolves. Once upon a time, his wife's fervent: 'I will never desert Mr. Micawber!' brought the tearful avowal: 'Emma, my angel!' and: 'My life! I am perfectly aware of it!' (172) In Heep time, Micawber's ardor cools, and Mrs. Micawber's pledge elicits only the dry: 'My dear, I am not conscious that you are expected to do anything of the sort' (531).

He is dead wrong. Deserting is just what 'the Modern Babylon' matron, imitating the Power that deports Israel to Babylon, *is* supposed to do. The God of desertions, deporting a people to Assyro-Babylonian sandy deserts and merciless just deserts, is the original Model of *Deport*ment. When

Mr. Micawber ceases to value the spirit in 'I will never desert,' he is indeed 'pledged and contracted' (531) to Heep, the Devil's own in the last outposts of body and soul.

To thank Mr. Micawber for helping recover her fortune from Heep, Miss Trotwood finances the Micawbers' ocean journey to the new world.  Here perhaps is the long-awaited 'Spring of no common magnitude' (771).  Congratulating the family, David says he hopes Mrs. Micawber will write from her new home:

> 'Please Heaven, there will be many such opportunities,' said Mr. Micawber.  'The ocean, in these times, is a perfect fleet of ships; and we can hardly fail to encounter many, in running over.  It is merely crossing,' said Mr. Micawber, trifling with his eye-glass, 'merely crossing.  The distance is quite imaginary.' (806)

Lingering on 'crossing,' as earlier on the Canterbury theme, Mr. Micawber again almost arrives.  Done with bills and brewing, Heep and law, he stands at the brink of a new life.  Sensing that distance and space are imaginary, as he does, it is as if he perceives with the vision of eternal things.  But he does not.  Trifling with the ornamental eye-glass, he trifles with 'crossing' as well.  It *is* a matter of crossing, but there is no 'merely' about it, just as there is no being delivered or consigned to a New Life just by crossing earthly seas.

The Micawber way with Shakespeare turns poetry to parody.  Micawber inflates every sentiment so:  what then is left for Lear?  Full of rant and gesture, Micawber's *Macbeth* is melodrama.  Forster records that Dickens sat through abominably bad performances of Shakespeare.[7]  Reviewing a performance of *King Lear,* Dickens records that in his day, Nahum Tate, an adapter, 'omitted the grandest thing, the *Fool.*'  Happily, such ignorant defacement of Shakespeare ends.  In Dickens's article, 'The Restoration of Shakespeare's "Lear" To The Stage,' in *The Examiner,* Dickens delights in the return of the Fool, and makes clear that he believes there are no better examples of 'the higher objects and uses of the drama,' no more profound explorations of the battle of good and evil in men's souls, than are found in Shakespearean tragedy.[8]

The Drama is in trouble in Dickens's day, and he knows it.  In *Nicholas Nickleby,* the Crummles theatrical touring company plays only blood-and-thunder melodrama.  While in the company, poor Smike calls himself Digby, surely for the sense of mortality his starvling roles give him: *Digby,* like Pecksniff's Dust Shovel, denotes *dig,* dust and earth, the grave.  In *Great Expectations,* Mr. Wopsle turns *Hamlet,* the Christ myth reborn, to hash.  The coarse spectators pelt Wopsle with nuts.  Weak actors interacting with a debased audience, coarsened in part by long subjection to just such empty, poll-parrot, strut-and-fret actors more intent on showy costume and stance, in Micawber and Model of Deportment style, than on meaning, reduce the sublime moral parables of Shakespeare to vanity. Mr. Micawber's great personal dilemma, the drift of a man of noble instincts and high gifts into blackest evil, is mined from Shakespeare's own quarry. But, as Micawber plays it, who would know it?

To many, Dickens knows, Shakespeare is what Mr. Micawber makes of him, a strew of high-flown cadences, flossy metaphors, and bathetic fits, indulgence in emotionalism too facile in its dips from high to low. Micawberian acting turns Shakespeare itself to bilgewater, the kind the Duke and Dolphin serve up for goodly sums to gawking provincials in *Huckleberry Finn*. Dickens knows that the shallow bardolatry of his day is not only aesthetically but morally perilous. For, far from a grab-bag of quotable tags, Shakespeare to Dickens is the sublime, serious moralist who sends forth holy Ghosts to cry out against the killing of men and kings. The armed head that rises to break up the feast with most admired disorder in *Macbeth*, and again in *Copperfield*, insists upon the existence of an eternal order, an invisible reality bent on justice, behind the world. Accompanied by the Ghost of King Hamlet, specifically mentioned in connection with each one, Dickens's great ghosts and figures—the ghost of Banquo which haunts Steerforth; and Mr. Chillip, spokesman for NT truth—come to reclaim souls and point out to men the lost perspective of Eternity. One can see why Dickens so often invokes Shakespeare, and why he would feel so strong a spiritual kinship with him, openly as well as allegorically displayed.

Like Micawber, actors of Dickens's time 'Shakespearingly' deliver great lines, literally Shake*spearing*, or stabbing him to death. As Mr. Micawber shows, phrase-mongering does a brisk business. Stick a sprig of *Hamlet* in your hatband, and the banal may be passed off as the elevated. So trivialized, Shakespeare is a poison poured in the porches of the ear, a leprous distilment to kill a King. By contrast, Dickens himself makes deep commitments to Shakespeare. In Dickens, Shakespeare never sleeps, as the surprise appearance of a new relation of King Claudius, and clearly his moral kin, 'Hamlet's aunt' in *Copperfield*, makes clear. Lines of Shakespeare run through the mind of Dickens. As Forster records, the timely remembering of: 'We have heard THE CHIMES at midnight, Master Shallow!' gives Dickens the title that has for some days escaped him, *The Chimes*. This is one of many links forged by Dickens between his own and Shakespeare's timeless purposes, hailed by him time and again.

In short, for Dickens, the Christian energies at work in Shakespeare work still. Or could, with the rise of better producers than Tate. If living Micawbers could see Macbeth well played, they might have a good deal less appetite for the Devil. A Shakespeare whittled down to the ornamental moment of the 'dwindle, peak, and pine' kind is lost as a source of enlightenment and edification.

To return to Mr. Micawber *in statu quo*, thanks to David, Mr. Dick, and others, he throws off Heep and sets sail for a New Life. One sees him

'solemnly pass away' into the rosy glory of a sacramental sunset palpi-
tating with Glory.  Does Mr. Micawber finally see the Light?  Some time
after, David reads a clipping from the Port Middlebay Times, published in
the far-off land across the sea, describing a testimonial dinner tendered the
highly popular 'Wilkins Micawber, ESQUIRE, Port Middlebay District
Magistrate' (870), and lauding 'the smoothly-flowing periods of his
polished and highly ornate address' (871).  Oh dear:  same old playbill, we
see.  As a Middlebayer, Micawber is still in Mid-ocean between B.C. and
A.D.  Once it was *Med*way Coal:  now, *Mid*dlebay.  As a magistrate, Mr.
Micawber is where Mrs. Micawber wanted him to be, hugger-mugger with
the law.  David's old friend, the Master, now Doctor Mell, is also in 'Bush'
(869) country in the new world.  With words, 'Doctor,' and law so
prominent, it might be original Burning Bush and wilderness wandering
country.  Mankind begins all over again under the spell of letter and law.
    'Flowing periods' have no part in the authentic spiritual life.  This we
see again when David undertakes to apologize to Agnes for a drunken
appearance before her:

> I must have written half a dozen answers at least.  I began one, 'How can I
> ever hope, my dear Agnes, to efface from your remembrance the disgusting
> impression'—there I didn't like it and tore it up.  I began another, 'Shake-
> speare has observed, my dear Agnes, how strange it is that a man should put
> an enemy in his mouth'—that reminded me of Markham, and I got no farther.
> I even tried poetry.  I began one note, in a six-syllable line, 'Oh, do not re-
> member'—but that associated itself with the fifth of November, and became
> an absurdity.  After many attempts, I wrote, 'My dear Agnes.  Your letter is
> like you, and what could I say of it that would be higher praise than that?  I
> will come at four o'clock.  Affectionately and sorrowfully, T.C.' (365)

Abandoning the Micawberesque conceit of 'Shakespeare has observed,'
with its too-tuneful 'My dear Agnes' in mid-line, David writes what he
feels in simple words.  An almost boastful self-criticism is finally
compressed into one word:  'sorrowfully.'  The finished note looks to
Agnes:  its theme, not David and his faults, but her praise.  So much for a
tinsel 'Shakespeare has observed' relation to Shakespeare.
    In 'Babylon' days, the Micawbers never saw David for the pathetic waif
he was.  When he is a world-famous author, do they recognize him at last?
It seems not.  Micawber's letter to David, published in the Port Middlebay
*Times* for all the world to see, tells the tale.  Its ostensible subject is
David's meteoric rise to fame, but its true subject, as usual, is Mr. Micawber himself.  Ever on parade, Micawber never changes.  Dickens had to
accept that, whatever he became for others, he remained forever invisible
to his father:  accept, understand, smile, and walk away.
    Mr. Micawber's adulatory letter hails the 'intellectual feasts' (872)
David has spread before the world.  In so characterizing these works, he is

no farther from the mark, really, than the rest of mankind. We know that David, for Dickens, invites to more than intellectual nourishment; rather, to a convivio of the New Testament, a fifth Gospel. The D.C.-C.D. life's work is Christian allegory. Like another promising young Charles D., Charles Darnay of *A Tale of Two Cities,* Dickens escapes an Old Regime existence deathly with law; falls in love with *'Lucie* Manette,' as MANette, little man, in the prison of OT time and his days with the Light of the Son of Man. In Dickens, there sound again the thrilling words that raised man from the dead, as they do Doctor Manette from years of burial in a dark, grave-like cell: RECALLED TO LIFE. 'Charles D.' loves LUCIE, the Light of the world shining in one pure, human soul: Lucie, Heaven's gift to Manette, as to mankind. In all works, Charles Dickens retells the wonder of his rescue and coming to Christ, that men may glimpse in stories that praise God and adjure us to faith, hope, and charity, the Kingdom eye hath not seen nor tongue uttered, one ever in the world as forward of it.

'Mr. Micawber,' or John Dickens, had a great gift for words and an ear for the music in language, one largely devoted to vanity, given to the winds. Inheriting the gift, his son employs it to worthy ends. If Dickens satirizes his father, he also dwells on his excellent qualities and leanings: indomitable hope; enthusiasm for 'Mr. Dixon,' Agnes, and Canterbury; and the basic decency which eventually can tolerate no more of Heep. We have noted that in what Micawber says carelessly or obliviously, truth often lies, as the 'shaving materials' and oyster-knife moments show. The last words Micawber ever writes hold such truth:

> 'Among the eyes elevated towards you from this portion of the globe, will ever be found, while it has light and life,
>
> The
> Eye
> Appertaining to
> WILKINS MICAWBER,
> Magistrate.' (872)

How true that man will not always have 'light and life.' Life is brief, Eternity—as Jacob Marley discovers—long. If only Mr. Micawber saw beyond the alliterative tune in 'light and life' to the truth therein. In WILKINS is something 'aKIN' to WILL, but not will or The Willing Mind itself. Mr. Micawber cherishes and never loses a complacent faith that crossing the ocean will 'consign us to a perfectly new existence' (535). As if one were 'consigned' to salvation, and by a change of location struck immortal! Even after denouncing the Devil, man has an arduous pilgrimage to make to scale the heights of God. One imagines that Mr. Micawber never does; but you never know.

Then farewell to Mr. and Mrs. Micawber, may their tribe increase. As it surely will. Their little son sings 'Non Nobis,' or: 'Not to us, Lord, but to

Thee be praise,' and father and mother bask in the reflected glory. Nobly and wisely, David never reproaches Mr. Micawber, the remote-even-when-near father figure who cannot save him in their shared Babylon. The sounding board for all Mr. Micawber's tales of woe, and of plans for future success, David in all the years he knows him never jostles a single Micawber fantasy; and never asks for that anciently borrowed shilling back. *In loco Dickensis,* David Copperfield accepts a remarkable destiny in which he is never to know the love, protection, and recognition of an earthly father; but in which, with Mr. Dick, he finds all in offering up all to his Father in Heaven, coming by way of sky-blue allegory to the deliverance and happiness 'for which there are no words.'

# Afterword

My Dear Children,
I am very anxious that you should know
something about the History of Jesus Christ.
For everybody ought to know about Him. . . . (LL, ii)

So ends this study of *David Copperfield*, one of Dickens's Lamb's Tales from Shakespeare, as from everywhere else under the Son.

*Copperfield* is a version of the parable which begins: 'Again, the kingdom of heaven is like unto treasure in a field' (*Matt.* 13:44). Man's first treasure is laid up on earth; like copper, a semi-precious ore, in ancient times a source of wealth, the early visionary treasure vouchsafed the monotheist at the dawn of Judaeo-Christian time is only that, first riches, a beginning. But in the Copper or 'C'-field of 'Clara,' or Light, sown by David, there shines *in potentia* the Light of the world to come, the Son of David. In Dickens as in Biblical history, the light in the House of David is destined to grow brighter, in time's fullness emerging in the radiance past compare of 'Agnes Wickfield,' mirror of Christ, shining center ('wick') and field of endless Light, and soul of David's soul.

*David Copperfield* opens with this memorable line:

Whether I shall turn out to be the hero of my own life, or whether that station will be held by anybody else, these pages must show. (1)

Allegory dawns in the suggestive ambiguity of these words. When all is said and done, who *is* the hero of this far-echoing life of David? Behind a living, modern David whose heart in hiding stirs for a 'Shepherd,' who blunders into stone law in Blunderstone-Murdstone ages, and suffers a 'Babylonian' captivity in exile, followed by barren apprenticeship in the Law, stands the shadowy figure of that other David, shepherd of Bethlehem and psalmist of the Shepherd, in whose soul lies the promise of the Good Shepherd.

Mining the Dickens parable, one brings many wonders to light. Forster relates that Dickens did not immediately decide to name his hero David Copperfield. The surprising tentative first choice was:

*'Mag's Diversions.*

'Being the personal history of
'MR. THOMAS MAG THE YOUNGER,
'Of Blunderstone House.' (FD, II, 432)

Dickens tries it out on Forster, who records:

> This was hardly satisfactory, I thought; and it soon became apparent that he thought so too, although within the next three days I had it in three other forms. *'Mag's Diversions,* being the Personal History, Adventures, Experiences and Observations of Mr. David Mag the Younger, of Copperfield House.' The third made nearer approach to what the destinies were leading him to, and transformed Mr. David Mag into Mr. David Copperfield the Younger and his great-aunt Margaret; retaining still as his leading title, *Mag's Diversions.* (432)

Why, of all the queer, supremely uneuphonious names under the sun, MAG? What hold had *mag,* 'Thomas Mag,' then 'David Mag,' on Dickens's interest? At last we dare venture a guess. In Hebrew, *David Mag* has great meaning. The Star of David, or David's shield, is called the *magen David.* In *magen David,* David and mag form a sacred bond. As was shown in Chapter III of this study, *Mag* is the root of Magus, Magian, Magi, magic; *mag* stands at the confluence of the religious consciousness of East and West in earliest Judaeo-Christian time. In the Zoroastrian, extra-Judaic portion of sacred history, the Magi, the Wise Men of the gentile East who would one day follow the Star, Stellar companion of the *magen David,* lie curled up like embryo plants in seed awaiting the destined moment of germination when the world's wintered soul would feel shining full upon it the Life Eternal-giving sun of the Son of God. So, through the Magi, ancient astrologers who cross the divide into Christian time, and through the *magen David, mag* points to Christ, Day-star of stars.

Missing the starry message, we resemble good Mr. Grewgious in *Drood,* whose . . .

> gaze wandered from the windows to the stars, as if he would have read in them something that was hidden from him. Many of us would, if we could; but none of us so much as know our letters in the stars yet—or seem likely to do it, in this state of existence—and few languages can be read until their alphabets are mastered. (205)

Such is our dilemma in relation to another celestial mystery, the language of allegory.

The *'Mag's Diversions'* passage in Forster with its repeated mention of 'three days,' 'three other forms,' and 'the third,' shows Dickens's mind in this creative time magnetized by *three*. On the third try and occasion, as Christ on the third day, *David Copperfield* rises to life! By degrees, *Mag* falls away. The idea is unripe; in 'David Mag' its symbolism glares. Twelve years must pass before it will flow comfortably in Dickens's Christian imagination, emerging fully evolved at last in *Great Expectations* in 'Magwitch,' the figure who so powerfully mirrors multiple NT mysteries, and from whom springs the celestial Beauty created by Heaven to lift men's hearts and draw them on to higher things: Estella, the Star.

So Thomas Mag and David Mag become David Copperfield, and *Thomas*, perhaps, becomes Tommy Traddles of *Copperfield*. In Forster's word, the 'destinies' are indeed at work. Forster it is who makes a discovery about the choice of 'David Copperfield':

> It is singular that it should never have occurred to him, while the name was thus strangely bringing itself together, that the initials were but his own reversed; but he was much startled when I pointed this out, and protested it was just in keeping with the fates and chances which were always befalling him. 'Why else,' he said, 'should I have so obstinately kept that name when once it turned up?'' (FD, II, 433)

So, by accident or plan human or divine, 'C.D.' and 'D.C.,' Charles Dickens and David Copperfield, fuse destinies; and *Mag*, twice tried and dropped, slips back in among (in David's words) 'the possibilities of hidden things,' awaiting its hour, that of the Christ-prefiguring slain, sacrificed *Abel*. Meanwhile, David Mag, christened Copperfield, begins the long journey from Blunder-'bewitching'-murdstoning Law eras of the soul to the starry epoch of fulfillment, hope, and joy, Agnes. In this and all works, Dickens shows how long mankind, from its 'in the beginnings' on, waits and hopes, stumbles and falls, conjures and brews, cherishes expectations, its soul running wishfully on magic release, an Opening up ahead, Life assurance, a requital to messianic desire, the Recall fo Life which comes only with the arrival of a Saviour.

'C.D.' the author joins bright multitudes of his own creating on the unending journey to Canterbury. He comes, we said, in many symbolic guises:-as Dick the blackbird, which in three small, joyful hops answers the summons of his Master's voice (*Nickleby*); as 'Doubledick' (*The Seven Poor Travellers*); as young Dick Swiveller (*The Old Curiosity Shop*); as Mr. Dick, and all crossroads, betwixt-between Dick figures in his fiction. I strongly suspect that Dickens also appears as many a Charles and Charley: for example, Charley Bates, the young thief saved in the nick of time in *Oliver Twist*; and Charley, the overburdened child that tends a brood of little brothers and sisters in *Bleak House;* or young Charley Hexam, the light of his spirit snuffed out in *Our Mutual Friend*. Something of Dickens's own history is told in each Charley's life. Nor, as was suggested earlier, is it likely that one promising 'Charles D.,' Charles Dickens, would create another promising 'Charles D.,' Charles Darnay (*A Tale of Two Cities*), unconscious of what he did. Quietly slipping in among the crowding phantasms of his works, Dickens is a reality half melted into unreality, as if to dramatize the more that in this life, man is but momentary smoke, a passing dream. For what are Chaucer's and Dickens's Chaucerian pilgrims on roads leading to 'Agnes' in Canterbury but invisibilities, by fiction eternalized, prefiguring the coming entrance into Eternity?

How richly destined yet tremulous and humble Dickens at his 'D' or Dominus-magnifying life's work must have felt; urged on by 'the fates and chances,' how amazed and awed at every new unfolding of his (His) powers. How astounded at the nigh-incredible coincidence that a *John* Forster should celebrate a Christian *Ch*arles, as *John* of old, *Ch*rist. Sooner or later, we imagine, he saw in his own name—in both the 'Charles,' the Christian, and the 'nat'ral' one—an epitome of men's destiny, and worked vigorously with it. As in the works many an Oliver, Stephen, Charley, Abel, Tom, and John must work free of the *Twist, Blackpool, Hexam, Magwitch, Pinch, Westlock* or Old Dispensation destiny, so Charles Dickens had to escape from the 'Dickens,' devil or deuce. In childhood abandoned to the life of a street urchin, prowling low streets, he ran the risk of all half-starved, unprotected children in the Fagin's dens of London, or Babylon. Recalling that black time, Dickens states:

> I know that, but for the mercy of God, I might easily have been, for any care that was taken of me, a little robber or a little vagabond. (FD, I, 37)

As we saw, Dick after Dick in Dickens shares both that plight and mercy. Writing to Forster about young Dick Swiveller, so like himself in his vacillating, law-circle days, Dickens says: 'I cannot yet discover that his aunt has any belief in him, or is in the least degree likely to send him a remittance, so that he will probably continue to be the sport of destiny' (FD. I 180). But no Dick in Dickens stays the sport of destiny, because 'the old original Dick,' Dickens himself, did not. Born to a father with a fatal Micawber-like tendency to go to the Devil, Charles Dickens, bearing too many of the family's burdens in childhood and deprived of home and education, nevertheless fought his way clear of this heritage, and finding New uses for his pen, withdrawing it from service to the law, was caught between 'D' and 'D,' the Devil and the deep blue sea of Eternity, no more. 'Boz,' the famous Dickens pseudonym, is, he relates . . .

> the nickname of a pet child, a younger brother, whom I had dubbed Moses, in honour of the Vicar of Wakefield; which, being facetiously pronounced

through the nose, became Boses, and, being shortened, became Boz. (SB,xxi)

Consciously or unconsciously lighted on at the start of his career, Boz proves an amazing choice. For Dickens in truth becomes *Boz,* a type of Moses, who would lead the children, wilderness-wandering mankind, into the Promised Land of a true A.D., after so long.

Dickens, we saw, also seems aware that, as commonly pronounced, BOZ sounds like 'Bos' in Boswell. Mr. Dick, the earnest scribbler humbly trailing after a learned Doctor with Dictionary in hand, is surely a bright type of Boswell. So is the original Mr. Dick, Dickens, a *Boz*-well who, pen in hand, reverently and devotedly chronicles the life and lessons of yet another Doctor Strong, the Strong of Strongs, the love founded on a rock: chronicles and celebrates an immortal 'Johnson,' as it were, THE *son* of *John,* Christ. Though lightly spun, in the Dickens way, how deep is that most unassuming of nicknames, Boz.

From the very beginning, Dickens's passion is religious truth, as this statement in the Preface to *The Pickwick Papers* shows:

> Lest there be any well-intentioned persons who do not perceive the difference . . . between religion and the cant of religion, piety and the pretense of piety, a humble reverence for the great truths of Scripture and an audacious and offensive obtrusion of its letter and not its spirit in the commonest dissensions and meanest affairs of life, to the extraordinary confusion of ignorant minds, let them understand that it is always the latter, and never the former, which is satirized here. . . . It may appear unnecessary to offer a word of observation on so plain a head. But it is never out of season to protest against that coarse familiarity with sacred things which is busy on the lip, and idle in the heart; or against the confounding of Christianity with any class of persons who, in the words of Swift, have just enough religion to make them hate, and not enough to make them love, one another. (PP, xiii)

But Dickens does not often rail *against;* he prefers to redeliver the happy message of the angels, as Polly Toodle does in *Dombey and Son* as she seeks to comfort a child grieving for her dead mother:

> 'Once upon a time,' said Richards, 'there was a lady—a very good lady, and her little daughter dearly loved her.'
> 'A very good lady and her little daughter dearly loved her,' repeated the child.
> 'Who, when God thought it right that it should be so, was taken ill and died.'
> The child shuddered.
> 'Died, never to be seen again by any one on earth, and was buried in the ground where the trees grow.'
> 'The cold ground?' said the child, shuddering again.
> 'No! The warm ground,' returned Polly, seizing her advantage, 'where the ugly little seeds turn into beautiful flowers, and into grass, and corn, and I don't know what all besides. Where good people turn into bright angels, and

fly away to Heaven!'
    The child, who had drooped her head, raised it again . . . (24)

So in Dickens's Book of Paul, as we called it in Chapter III, another of St. Paul's lessons in Christ, which Paul delivers in the very metaphor of Christ, shines: that of the seed, man: 'sown a natural body, raised a spiritual body' (*1 Cor.* 15:44). Hearing this wonderful story, little Florence—*flor* for flower—flower-like raises her drooping head, in token of 'Rise up!' The sister of Paul suddenly sees beyond 'that old, old fashion, Death' to hope of 'that older fashion yet, of Immortality!' In *Chuzzlewit,* Paul Sweedlepipe is called Poll; which prompts realization that in *Dombey,* Polly Toodle, the good Christian lady who rescues Florence, is a *Poll*-y or *Paul*-y spirit, a 'toodle' or note in a choric rendering of the 'Messiah.'

    And always that tiny intimation of Mystery, the Glory yet furled to human eyes: 'and I don't know what all besides.'

    Nearing the close of his great labors on *Copperfield,* Dickens in exalted mood writes this to his faithful confidant in all:

> I am (21 of October) within three pages of the shore; and am strangely divided, as usual in such cases, between sorrow and joy. Oh, my dear Forster, if I were to say half of what *Copperfield* makes me feel tonight, how strangely even to you, I should be turned inside out! I seem to be sending some part of myself into the Shadowy World. (FD, II, 462)

Speaking here once again in familiar sea journey metaphor, Dickens half veils, half discloses the secret of the book, hinted in 'within three pages of the shore.' As it will in climactic final moments of *A Tale of Two Cities* (see Ch. III), the number *three* throbs amid visions of Departure and Arrival. In this regard, consider something Dickens writes to an American friend, Jonathon Chapman, on June 2, 1842:

> I write God bless you, once more, as if that were a satisfaction. Who that has ever reflected on the enormous and vast amount of leave-taking there is in this Life, can ever have doubted the existence of another! (DL, III, 249)

Once, after the Murdstones have blighted his world, David on a sad visit home finds that his old neighbors, the Graypers, are gone. Rain has seeped through the roof of their empty house. The Graypers, like the grapes, the wine, are found no more in the Law-blighted land. *Copperfield* tells how it happens again and again in all ages: how, losing the first visionary gleam, as in the first OT time, mankind must blunder upon, then work free of ruinous fixation on law, dogma, and doctrines of exclusive election; emerging at long last, thanks to the teachings of Christ, into the fruitful era of the Son and the wine.

    Like Dickens—rather, as Dickens—David Copperfield also comes within sight of the shore. In the last pages of the story, a host of old friends, a 'fleeting crowd' (874), gathers one final time, among them David's old nurse of the apple cheeks and unwavering devotion to him and the workbox crowned by St. Paul's, Peggotty; also Mr. Dick; Mrs. Steerforth and Rosa Dartle; Julia Mills; and the Strongs of the love founded on a rock. And, if not Thomas Mag the Younger, then what probably became of him, Tommy Traddles the ever Younger at heart, his charges, the once-unruly *ten*, converted into pleasant, loving, ever-enlarging clusters of *three*.

Twelve months before his death in 1870, Dickens writes these solemn words:

> I direct that my name be inscribed in plain English letters on my tomb. . . . I conjure my friends on no account to make me the subject of any monument, memorial, or testimonial whatever. I rest my claim to the remembrance of my country on my published works, and to the remembrance of my friends upon their experience of me in addition thereto. I commit my soul to the mercy of God, through our Lord and Saviour Jesus Christ; and I exhort my dear children humbly to try to guide themselves by the teaching of the New Testament in its broad spirit, and to put no faith in any man's narrow construction of its letter here or there. (FD, II, 38)

So, here as elsewhere, Dickens looks away from the letter graved in stone, from marble and the gilded monuments of princes, as if from all that would suggest man's kingdom is finally of this world.

As Dickens's last testament looks past memorials of this world to hope through Christ of Heaven, so David Copperfield's does too. The son of David, King Solomon, for all the earthly riches of his copper mines, never beheld shining 'copperfield' to compare with the treasure New Time brought forth: the Son of all sons of David, a King's Ransom, Christ. *Copperfield* closes on three passages founded upon one sacred theme: a final, luminous three-in-one hymn of tribute to *Agnes*. Ending his story, the latest David, with his unfailingly symbolic imagination, sees in this two-fold end—of story, of day—the image of life's approaching end, and his last words rehearse a faith that looks past death to hope of Heaven, which hope rests in Christ. Thus:

> And now, as I close my task, subduing my desire to linger yet, these faces fade away. But one face, shining on me like a Heavenly light by which I see all other objects, is above them all and beyond them all. And that remains.
>
> I turn my head, and see it, in its beautiful serenity, beside me. My lamp burns low, and I have written far into the night; and the dear presence without which I were nothing, bears me company.
>
> Oh Agnes, oh my soul, so may thy face be by me when I close my life indeed; so may I, when realities are melting from me like the shadows which I now dismiss, still find thee near me, pointing upward!

# Notes

*Chapter I*

1. Chapters titled 'The Beginning of a long Journey' and 'The Beginning of a longer Journey' help set the stage for the great final event, David Copperfield's journey on horseback to Canterbury and Agnes. One at last realizes this joyful 'Canterbury pilgrimage' for the wondrous metaphoric venture it is. 'The journey' is long in the making. In Chapter I David muses upon his arrival in the world in 'journey' imagery:

> I lay in my basket, and my mother lay in her bed; but Betsey Trotwood Copperfield was for ever in the land of dreams and shadows, the tremendous region whence I had so lately travelled; and the light upon the window of our room shone out upon the earthly bourne of all such travellers, and the mound above the ashes and the dust that once was he, without whom I had never been. (12)

If striking one's mortal being into bounds is 'travell[ing],' remembering is 'tread[ing] the old ground' (169). David speaks of his 'progress to seventeen' (272), and, narrating on, resumes 'the journey of my story' (633). Phantom memories move by 'in dim procession' (626); and David, lost in love as in a dark wood, pictures himself a woodman, axe in hand, 'cutting down trees until I came to Dora' (520); or taking up a hammer 'to beat a path to Dora out of granite' (520). Dan'l Peggotty must make a long, arduous journey before he journeys, spiritually speaking, from the darkness of harsh judgment to the light of forgiveness.

2. In *Nicholas Nickleby,* 'Cheeryble' shouts 'cheery' loud enough to unstop the ears of the deaf; and perhaps the 'Ch' of Cheeryble is more eloquent still of the nature of these two charitable Christian gentlemen overflowing with faith, hope, and charity. Besides what so frankly meets the eye, there is the more-than-meets-the-eye. For example, it is readily apparent that flowers, fruits, trees, and weeds in human form grow in Dickensian gardens: a 'green' Oliver Twist and Rose Maylie (OT); Abel Garland and Jem Groves (OCS); Esther Summerson, Lawrence Boythorn, Joshua Smallweed, Mr. Weevle (BH); Florence, Berry Pipchin, and Withers (DS); Miss Peecher (OMF); Rosa Bud (MD). But if, as Dickens quotes in *A Child's History of England,* '"By their fruits ye shall know them," said OUR SAVIOUR' (411), who knows but that all such Smallweeds and Chickweeds, Sowerberrys, Roses, Pips and Pipchins, thorns and flowers, fruits of jellies and Jellybys, souls sprung of good seed and bad, as in Biblical metaphor, grow in a (Christ)-Child's Garden of NT verse.

3. Eternity is a constant theme in Dickens. Recalling his mother's funeral with its

strongly Christian cast (the clergyman intoning: 'I am the Resurrection and the Life, saith the Lord,' and Peggotty termed 'that good and faithful servant'), David states: 'All this, I say, is yesterday's event. Events of later date have floated from me to the shore where all forgotten things will reappear, but this stands like a high rock in the ocean' (131). In a providential universe, nothing is lost; 'all...will reappear.' Chapter I of *Little Dorrit* closes with 'so deep a hush...on the sea, that it scarcely whispered of the time when it shall give up its dead' (14). But the sea *will* give up its dead. In the vision of Saint John in *Revelation:* 'And the sea gave up the dead which were in it;' (20:13). Likewise in *Oliver Twist* mad Monks touches on the theme. Throwing proof of Oliver's identity into the swirling waters, he exults: 'If the sea ever gives up its dead, as books say it will, it will keep its gold and silver to itself, and that trash with it' (285). But if, as David Copperfield knows, he and Steerforth will stand together 'at the Judgment Throne' (455), then so will evil Monks. In *Pictures from Italy* Dickens also sights Eternity, seeing in ancient Italian ruins evidence 'that the wheel of Time is rolling for an end, and that the world is, in all great essentials, better, gentler, more forebearing, and more hopeful, as it rolls!' (PI, 433)

Man is meant for Heaven. Recalling his young mother's sweet embrace, David, stung by the memory, says: 'I wish I had died. I wish I had died then, with that feeling in my heart! I should have been more fit for Heaven than I ever have been since' (109). In *Little Dorrit,* Frederick Dorrit is plagued by 'the little peevish perplexities of this ignorant life, mists which the morning without a night only can clear away' (639). The two Dorrit brothers die. Behold in death the solemn spectacle of 'two figures, equally still and impassive, equally removed by an untraversable distance from the teeming earth, though soon to lie in it.' And: 'The two brothers were before their Father; far beyond the twilight judgments of this world; high above its mists and obscurities' (652). In *The Seven Poor Travellers,* the Christian meaning of which is discussed in Chapter III, the narrator says: "Our whole life, Travellers, is a story more or less intelligible, generally less; but we shall read it by a clearer light when it is ended"' (CS, 77).

So throughout Dickens. In *Little Dorrit,* Arthur, the hero, watches flower petals float away in the river, the narrator intoning: 'and thus do greater things that once were in our breasts, and near our hearts, flow from us to the eternal seas' (338). In *Dombey and Son,* the narrator passes quickly beyond the event of little Paul's death to a fervent celebration of hope of resurrection: 'Oh, thank GOD, all who see it, for that older fashion yet, of Immortality!' and the prayer that 'angels of small children' will look upon us with regards not quite estranged, 'when the swift river bears us to the ocean!' (226) In 'Capital Punishment,' an essay, Dickens sets judge and prisoner in the context of Eternity, stating: 'and when the judge's faltering voice delivers sentence, how awfully the prisoner and he confront each other; two mere men, destined one day, however far removed from one another in time, to stand alike as suppliants at the bar of God' (143).

The 'ocean of Eternity' metaphor recurs in *A Tale of Two Cities.* In prison, the doomed await their fate: 'Fifty-two were to roll that afternoon on the lifetide of the city to the boundless everlasting sea' (329). And in *The Mystery of Edwin Drood* Dickens does not say that someone has died. Instead: 'But he, too, went the silent road into which all earthly pilgrimages merge, some sooner and some later' (80). 4. On the first visit, Joram's steady 'RAT-tat-tat, RAT-tat-tat, RAT-tat-tat' is 'a kind of tune' (125). Time passes. On David's next visit, 'The glass door of the parlour was not open; but in the workshop across the yard I could faintly hear the old tune playing, as if it had never left off' (303). David and Mr. Omer discuss little Em'ly's troubles. And: 'The tune across the yard that seemed as if it never had left off—alas! it was the tune that never *does* leave off—was beating, softly, all the while' (306). When Barkis is dying, David again visits the Funeral Furnishing shop. Says David: 'I had my apprehensions, too, when I went in, of hearing the old tune' (438). 'Old *t*une,' I think, deftly recalls all that awaited man, the coffin and sad mortality, before Christian time, and all that overcomes as man loses sight of Christian hope and truth.

5. In *Martin Chuzzlewit,* murderous Jonas Chuzzlewit, while in bogus show of mourning for a father he meant to do in, consumes 'sundry jorums of hot punch' (319). As Seth Pecksniff the hypocrite serves these *jorums, Seth* very literally a son of Adam as he 'falls' down a flight of stairs (see Preface), the OT atmosphere is all the thicker. In a world of sharpsters like *Jonas, Seth, Elijah* Pogram and *Zephaniah* Scadder ('Elijah' and 'Zephaniah' who sell men a bill of goods about a wilderness settlement called Eden surely meant to recall the Hebrew prophets: the fiery *Elijah* in his fierce chauvinism a whole Prophetic establishment in himself, a dealer in oratorical violence, an Elijah *Pogram* become a Pogrom or OT Program to lure men's thoughts backwards to Old modes of being and the old earthly Paradise, when man's hope lies in his moving forward more and more deeply into NT time of mind), in such as these, or *Sarah* Gamp, selfish and self-seeking with her patients, OT time of mind lives again. The word *jorum* is at home in this 'B.C.' realm.

In *The Old Curiosity Shop,* behold another portable B.C. that boasts an evil Daniel Quilp, his legal cronies Sarah and Sampson Brass, an Isaac List, et al. *Daniel, Sarah, Sampson,* and *Isaac* are like Hebrew stations of the Cross. Along this peril-strewn way the heroine little Nell and her grandfather, pilgrims from an old (Old) to a new (New) life must come. We see Daniel Quilp's wife drinking with him, 'taking deep draughts from a jorum of her own' (366).

In *Great Expectations,* stiff-spined Miss Skiffins, as stiff-necked as ever the children of Israel and as much in need of a John as ever they were of the ministry of John the Baptist, brews a 'jorum of tea'. Then the bridegroom *John* comes, an event with great Christian significance (see Chapter III), and she brews her jorums and OT tempers no more.

*Chapter II*

1. Dickens describes his experience in church as follows:

> Not that I have any curiosity to hear the powerful preachers. Time was, when I was dragged by the hair of my head, as one may say, to hear too many. On summer evenings, when every flower, and tree, and bird, might have better addressed my soft young heart, I have in my day been caught in the palm of a female hand by the crown, have been violently scrubbed from the neck to the roots of the hair as a purification for the Temple, and have then been carried off highly charged with saponaceous electricity, to be stamed like a potato in the unventilated breath of the powerful Boanerges Boiler and his congregation, until what small mind I had, was quite steamed out of me. In which

pitiable plight I have been haled out of the place of meeting, at the conclusion of the exercises, and catechised respecting Boanerges Boiler, his fifthly, his sixthly, and his seventhly, until I have regarded that reverend person in the light of a most dismal and oppressive Charade. (UT, 83)

How the young Charles Dickens is harshly scrubbed 'as a purification for the Temple' (it *is* more a Hebrew Temple than a Christian church; *Temple* is less figurative than otherwise) recalls how young Pip Pirrip is readied for presentation at Satis House in *Great Expectations:*

> With that, she pounced upon me, like an eagle on a lamb, and my face was squeezed into wooden bowls in sinks, and my head was put under taps of waterbutts, and I was soaped, and kneaded, and towelled, and thumped, and harrowed, and rasped, until I really was quite beside myself. (I may here remark that I suppose myself to be better acquainted than any living authority with the ridgy effect of a wedding-ring, passed unsympathetically over the human countenance.)
>
> When my ablutions were completed, I was put into clean linen of the stiffest character, like a young penitent into sackcloth, and was trussed up in my tightest and fearfullest suit. I was then delivered over to Mr. Pumblechook, who formally received me as if he were the Sheriff, and who let off upon me the speech that I knew he had been dying to make all along: 'Boy, be for ever grateful to all friends, but especially unto them which brought you up by hand!' (GE, 48)

Pumblechook with his scripture-sounding 'unto' is not unlike a preacher. In Chapter IV we try to show that Pip, purified for presentation at the great House, like a penitent in sackcloth, is in effect delivered to a Temple, or Hebrew time past, as this is the dark House which rejected the counsel of clemency and conciliation of *Matthew,* i.e., the Gospel of *Matthew.*

2. Among the books in the Gadshill library, as listed in the *Catalogue of the Library of Charles Dickens,* edited by J. H. Stonehouse, London: Picadilly Fountain Press, 1935, are:

| | |
|---|---|
| Austin Layard | *A Popular Account of the Discoveries at Nineveh,* 1851. |
| Robert William Mackay | *The Progress of the Intellect as Exemplified in the Religious Development of the Greeks and Hebrews,* 1850. |
| Charles Rollin | *The Ancient History of the Egyptians, Carthaginians, Assyrians, Babylonians, Medes and Persians, Grecians, and Macedonians,* 1828. |
| Richard Thomson | *London—and Londoners, or a Second Judgment of 'Babylon the Great': Manners and Customs of London,* 2 vols., 1836. |

3. In 'The Sunday Screw,' Dickens calls sabbatarian crusades 'outrageous to the spirit of Christianity, irreconcilable with the health, the rational enjoyments, and the true religious feeling, of the community' (226). Quoting: ' "The Sabbath was made for man, and not man for the Sabbath," ' Dickens declares that 'the declared authority of the Christian dispensation over the letter of the Jewish Law, particularly in this especial instance, cannot be petitioned, resolved, read, or committee'd away' (227). When two hundred merchants and bankers in Liverpool form a committee to effect the closing of the post-office on Sunday, Dickens is outraged:

> In the name of all the Pharisees of Jerusalem, could not the two hundred merchants and bankers form themselves into a committee to write or read no business-letters themselves on a Sunday—and let the Post-Office alone? (230)

The Hebrew-Christian contrast is strongly fixed in Dickens's mind, and Christ's challenge to the rigid Hebrew attitude towards the Law a staple of his thought.

*Chapter III*

1. In an enclave of Law lives Tulkinghorn; law and a passion for retribution share his whole nature between them. On his painted ceiling:

> Allegory, in Roman helmet and celestial linen, sprawls among balustrades and pillars, flowers, clouds, and big-legged boys, and makes the head ache—as would seem to be Allegory's object always, more or less . . . (130)

And again:

> Here, beneath the painted ceiling, with foreshortened Allegory staring down at his intrusion as if it meant to swoop upon him, and he cutting it dead, Mr. Tulkinghorn has at once his house and office. (131)

Again, Dickens eyes the scene overhead:

> From the ceiling, foreshortened Allegory, in the person of one impossible Roman upside down, points with the arm of Samson (out of joint, and an odd one) obtrusively toward the window. Why should Mr. Tulkinghorn, for such no reason, look out of window? Is the hand not always pointing there? So he does not look out of window. (222)

So much for Allegory, capital 'A,' clumsy, 'foreshortened' in perspective, and 'upside down,' in more ways than one. Hebrew-Roman in cast (*Samson* plus *Roman*), it never teaches anything, pointing heavily in that dull, too-didactic way. This 'Above,' no sky but only a painted Heaven, does not lift eyes or hearts; one can hardly make out what it all means. Tulkinghorn never looks or knows. 'Much too heavy, Neville; *much* too heavy' (MD, 156), says Mr. Crisparkle to his young pupil, Neville Landless, speaking of a walking-stick the lad has chosen for his journey. The same could be said for this drearily instructional Allegory, so little Christian, and no help at all to pilgrims pursuing 'the journey.' To point too long and hard is to lose one's audience, we see.

The Dickens lesson always is, keep it Light. In Dickens, old-style Allegory throws off the old bulk, heavy symbolism, and didacticism, and becomes, little Nell-like, 'allegory,' small 'a.'

*Chapter IV*

1. When Pip tells the convict that a man like himself is prowling the marshes, one with a badly bruised face, the reaction is swift: ' "Not here?" exclaimed the man, striking his left cheek mercilessly with the flat of his hand.' "Yes, there!" (32) Pip replies. Later on, the 'old bruised left side of his face' (32) is mentioned again. Especially as *left,* the 'sinister' side, is stressed, the evil 'C' figure who takes the life of Abel bears something very like the mark of Cain.

2. Pip's last words about the convict are:

> Mindful, then, of what we had read together, I thought of the two men who went up into the Temple to pray, and I knew that there were no better words that I could say beside his bed, than, 'O Lord, be merciful to him a sinner!' (436)

The reference to the two who go up into the Temple to pray, Peter and John (*Acts* 3:1), gives NT coloration to the undisclosed 'what we had read together.'

3. This is pure conjecture, but I wonder if 'Georgiana, wife of the Above' pays tribute to Dickens's beloved sister-in-law, Georgina, a member of his household until his death, his stay and confidante, and a devoted friend to his children: no *man's* wife, but wife of the Above.

4. In "Notes to *Great Expectations*" by T. W. Hill in an issue of *The Dickensian,* Volume Fifty-Three, 1957, p. 124, we learn that *mooncalf* refers to an ancient superstition that a mooncalf, or idiot, is brought about by the malign influence of the moon.

5. In the essay 'City of London Churches,' Dickens tells how in boyhood he was seized and scrubbed unmercifully by a harsh female, 'as a purification for the Temple' (UT, 83). Mrs. MacStinger in *Dombey and Son* and Mrs. Joe in *Great Expectations,* comfortless females of the same order, also clean with wrathful, Temple-offering zeal. One wonders if Dickens was dramatizing the warning:

> Woe unto you, scribes and Pharisees, hypocrites! for ye make clean the outside of the cup and of the platter, but within they are full of extortion and excess. (*Matt.* 23:25)

6. See Chapter II, Note 1.

7. In *The Dickensian,* Volume Forty-Three, 1947, p. 61, a note on *Great Expectations* reads: 'It is interesting to note that Dickens's original name for Joe Gargery was George Thunder, the correction being made some time after the book was commenced.' In a later issue, Volume Fifty-Three, 1957, in 'Notes to *Great Expectations*' by T. W. Hill, we read:

7. JOE GARGERY. 'Dickens's original name for the blacksmith was George Thunder, and, as shewn by the MS. at Wisbech, Joe Gargery was not substituted until the narrative had been for some time under way.' (120) See *The Dickensian*, 1947, page 61.

8. 'George Thunder,' or Joe, seems to have been originally conceived as a Greek god, or force of Nature personified. A powerful blacksmith, he recalls Hephaistos, or Vulcan. He is termed 'a sort of Hercules in strength, and also in weakness' (6). He is associated with fire (he constantly tends and replenishes the fire in early scenes; and there is also the forge fire), sun, sky, and clouds. I think Dickens intends a blue sky-white clouds scheme in his having 'eyes of such a very undecided blue that they seemed to have somehow gotten mixed with their own whites' (6); like suns, his eyes roll 'round and round the flowered pattern of my [Pip's] dressing gown' (208). Visiting Pip in sooty, sunless London, Joe seems to bring all Nature with him. His eyes shine on the flowery meads of Pip's gown. He carries a hat 'like a bird's-nest with eggs in it' (208); even gropes in it, as for an egg. His: 'Pip, how AIR you, Pip?' (208), AIR a pun, carries welcome fresh 'air' with it. In the Greek camp once again, there is the reference to Hercules, also his pronunciation of the word 'architectural': he 'would have prolonged this word...into a perfect Chorus, but for his attention being providentially attracted by his hat, which was toppling' (210). So Joe does not go the 'Chorus' way. His is not the Greek Chorus, or tragic genius. On the contrary. When Pip comes to him with a moral question about lies, Joe promptly takes the case 'out of the region of metaphysics, and by that means vanquished it' (65).

   Black-eyed, black-tempered Mrs. Joe long eclipses fair-haired, blue-eyed Joe. When she dies, he marries Biddy, the little (chicka)*biddy* who comes to the forge with her 'speckled box' (115) so like a speckled bird's egg. Like Joe, Biddy is full of Nature's own nurture and simple wisdom. One sees her 'plucking a black-currant leaf' (141). After Pip falls ill, Joe tends him, and sunshine floods the scenes of recovery in which Joe and the mending Pip are together.

   Dickens, I think, builds a Christian *Joseph* figure on a Greek 'George Thunder' base. Greek and Roman, perhaps, too: I think of how in his immature age of idolising Steerforth, David Copperfield dreams of 'ancient Rome, Steerforth,...thunder and the gods.' *Thunder* and the pagan gods run together in Dickens's mind.

9. Recalling a time with Estella, Pip says: 'We walked round the ruined garden twice or thrice more, and it was all in bloom for me. If the green and yellow growth of weed in the chinks of the old wall had been the most precious flowers that ever blew, it could not have been more cherished in my remembrance' (225). Sarah Pocket, 'green' with jealousy of Pip's advancement, as she supposes, in Satis House, becomes 'constitutionally green and yellow by reason of me' (221); she is referred to as 'my green and yellow friend' (228). At dinner, Jaggers 'took a dry delight in making Sarah Pocket greener and yellower, by often referring in conversation with me to my expectations' (228). Why does Dickens paint the weeds in the ruined garden and Sarah Pocket the same yellow and green? For the same reason he makes Miss Havisham a withered flower decked in yellowed- withered bridal flowers, and ties her to a garden chair and earthy paper hem: to tie inner and outer ruined gardens together, and both to OT values sown and reaped.

10. Referring to Camilla Pocket, Joe says:

'Mrs.—what's the name of them wild beasts with the humps, old chap?'

'Camels?' said I, wondering why he could possibly want to know.

Joe nodded. 'Mrs. Camels,' by which I presently understood he meant Camilla... (441)

11. In *Pickwick Papers,* Peter Magnus, a priggish, proud fellow, points out the 'P.M.—post meridian' (300) significance of the initials of his name. For this reason I suspect Dickens would not have been unaware of the significance of the initials 'A.M.' in Abel Magwitch, which so uncannily hit yet another symbolic mark.

12. Pip states: 'We had left Barnard's Inn more than a year, and lived in the Temple' (298). Again: 'Alterations have been made in that part of the Temple since that time, and it has not now so lonely a character as it had then, nor is it so exposed to the river' (298).

13. Before Christ comes again, 'ye shall hear of wars and rumors of wars' (*Matt.* 24:6); there will be 'famines, and pestilences, and earthquakes, in divers places' (24:7). Also tribulation, and the sun will grow dark. He will come from the east:

For as the lightning cometh out of the east, and shineth even unto the west; so shall also the coming of the Son of man be. (*Matt.* 24:27)

In the novel, 'His' second coming is also heralded by catastrophe, and extraordinary upheaval in Nature. As in the Bible, stress is laid upon the east:

It was wretched weather; stormy and wet, stormy and wet; mud, mud, mud, deep in all the streets. Day after day, a vast veil had been driving over London from the East, and it drove still, as if in the East there were an eternity of cloud and wind. So furious had been the gusts, that high buildings in town had had the lead stripped off their roofs; and in the country trees had been torn up, and sails of windmills carried away; and gloomy accounts had come in from the coast, of shipwreck and death... (298)

Nature and world reverberate, as if 'his' return were an event of preternatural consequence in the universe.

14. In the parable, certain laborers complain when others, hired later than themselves, at the eleventh hour, receive the same wage. But the householder who hired them says:

Is it not lawful for me to do what I will with my own? Is thine eye evil because I am good?

So the last shall be first, and the first last: for many be called, but few chosen. (*Matt.* 20:15-16)

Pip, we know, comes late to a spiritually purposeful life. Long mired in vanity, ingratitude, indifference to his fellow man (he walks through Newgate Prison without a flicker of pity for rows of doomed men), Pip awakens at this 'eleven o'clock' hour as Saint Paul's strikes: the eleventh hour of the parable. Though a latecomer to the vineyard, he may hope to be saved.

15. In Dickens, waiters are not nondescripts in the background, but often actors in

dramas. In the Inn to which Pip takes Estella to rest between stages of her journey, a waiter, carrying in 'Moses in the bulrushes typified by a soft bit of butter in a quantity of parsley,' staggers, 'expressing in his countenance burden and suffering' (GE, 254). While this is droll, it adds its bit to the allegorical B.C. drama unfolding in the purblind time before Pip recognizes and accepts 'Him,' through whom A.D. re-enters history.

The waiter staggering under the burden of (among other things) Moses recalls those 'waiters' for salvation of the wilderness wandering; and those who patiently watched and 'waited' for deliverance, Jehovah's witnesses manning the Watch-towers in Assyrian deserts, on the look-out for a Messiah. Glooming, imploring, despondent waiters in Dickens in the Temple (*Copperfield*) and elsewhere have a small but significant part in allegory.

In 'A Christmas Tree,' the Waits play.

16. In Dickens, rooks congregate where Law and 'letter' rule. In *Copperfield*, stray rooks and jackdaws 'came down from the Cathedral towers to walk with a clerkly bearing on the grass-plot' (226), like priests strutting about 'with their heads cocked slyly, as if they knew how much more knowing they were in worldly affairs than he [Doctor Strong]' (238). (More about the rooks-Church connection anon.)

In *The Old Curiosity Shop,* little Nell on her journey hears 'the cawing of the rooks who had built their nests among branches of some tall old trees, and were calling to one another high up in the air. First one sleek bird, hovering near his ragged house...uttered his hoarse cry....Another answered, and he called again, but louder than before; and each time the first, aggravated by contradiction, insisted on his case more strongly' (OCS, 128). Note the legal touch in 'case.' Rooks are linked to Church and to law.

In *Bleak House,* Joshua Smallweed, 'weed' indeed, a usurer in a black skull-cap, is 'an ugly old bird of the crow species' (369). The black skull-cap implies the orthodox Jew, as the Shylock calling, usury, and name Joshua also do. In the same work, in the Dedlock world of 'NOAbody' (see Chapter III), rooks are again pictured 'all breaking out again in violent debate, incited by one obstinate and drowsy bird, who will persist in putting in a last contradictory croak' (156). The black rooks again are like black-robed doctors of the law.

In *Oliver Twist,* Dickens works energetically on a rook-crow-jackdaw-Jew allegorical scheme. The rooks and jackdaws that will appear in *Copperfield* (recall Blunderstone Rookery, too) first appear here. Behold Jack Dawkins, 'jackdaw'-kins, as it were, the Jew's 'peculiar pet and protégé' (54). Jack Dawkins, the Artful Dodger, is what A.D. was before the coming of Christ when Judaism perverted the spirit in the letter of theological law. Like the *jackdaw,* a glossy, black, crow-like bird, *Jackdawkins* is a bird. He calls Oliver 'my covey' (52), and calls magistrates 'Beaks,' explaining: 'a beak's a madgst'rate' (53). To express being fundless, he says he has only 'one bob and magpie' (53). He has a 'rather flighty and dissolute mode of conversing' (55). The *beaks, covey, magpie, flighty* invention hits us in the eye. The jackdaw-Jew connection is what is implied in all *rook* invention in Dickens through which Dickens condemns the Pharisaical, priestly passion for law that infects Christianity still.

In *The Mystery of Edwin Drood,* Dickens makes the rook-church law connection one last satiric time:

> Whosoever has observed that sedate and clerical bird, the rook, may per-
> haps have noticed that when he wings his way homeward towards nightfall, in
> a sedate clerical company, two rooks will suddenly detach themselves from the
> rest, will retrace their flight for some distance, and will poise and linger; con-
> veying to mere men the fancy that it is of some occult importance to the body
> politic that his artful couple should pretend to have renounced connection
> with it. (5)

So much for clerics and sects ('renounced connection'), the high priesthood of
Christendom, so formal, ceremonious, and 'occult,' which flies backwards ('retrace
their flight'); the 'sedate clerical company' that scorns 'mere men.' Dickens condemns the talmudists of the Christian church whose disputes always turn on the
obscure letter of some Old Testament text. The *'artful* couple' may recall the *Artful*
Dodger, another rook.

The 'blackbird,' or churchman in glossy black, is a holdover from B.C. priest-
hoods, and in his doctoral pride, mocks the life and lessons of Christ.

Perhaps Dickens is also not unmindful that, as a verb, to *rook* means to cheat,
defraud. One is tempted to say, no 'perhaps' about it.

17. First encountering David in the *Murdstone and Grinby* office, Mr. Micawber
kindly offers to direct him, supposing he 'might have some difficulty in penetrating
the arcana of the Modern Babylon' (156). And in one of his letters, Micawber
speaks of 'bidding adieu to the Modern Babylon' (530). Dickens presses the old
cliche, London as Babylon, into the service of allegory in a secretly lateral way.

*Chapter V*

1. Mr. Murdstone has 'a grave smile that belonged to him' (46); he walks David to
his room to be caned 'slowly and gravely' (57); has a 'graver manner' (24), and a
way of inquiring 'gravely' (57). That *grave* thus insistently repeated has a burial-
chamber, tomb meaning is suggested in the way he always points downward, as to
the grave. His ominous: 'Go you below, my love' to Mrs. Copperfield; and:
'David and I will come down together' (45); also: 'David, go to bed!' (51) looks to
the *down* and *below* and *bed* of the grave. Miss Murdstone is also linked to burial,
as she slams shut a door in hopes of having trapped someone in the dark cupboard
inside, and in her tight-shut black boxes. Duties 'undertaken' (49) by her are *undertaken* (pun) in the undertaker way.

2. Miss Murdstone has a 'jail of a bag' (47) on a heavy chain; also 'two uncompromising hard black boxes never seen open or known to be left unlocked' (48).
The chain implies captivity, as does 'jail.' Two Murdstones; two black boxes: two
Murd-*stone* tablets of Mosaic Law. Miss Murdstone has a 'jail-delivery' (50) way
of raising her pocket-handkerchief to her eyes, *pocket* an added grave touch, a la
Pocket symbolism in *The Battle of Life* and *Great Expectations*. She displays 'little
steel fetters and rivets' (48) of personal adornment. Such Captivity symbolism of
high density anticipates David's banishment to *Babylon,* as it equates captivity
and law.

3. 'Goroo!' and 'Gorm,' both curses, seem to look to B.C. ways of the deity and His
law. GOD and LAW sound in the 'Gaw,' or Gor sounds of GORoo and GORm. In
*Great Expectations,* Mrs. Joe, a fanatic partisan of punishment under law, cries:

'Lor-a-mussy me!', and her LOR seems a similar conflation of LORd and LAW.  As 'drowndead' shows, Dickens likes such a splice.

4.  In *A Tale of Two Cities,* Dickens observes: 'In seasons of pestilence, some of us will have a secret attraction to the disease—a terrible passing inclination to die of it.  And all of us have like wonders hidden in our breasts, only needing circumstances to evoke them' (268).  The disease, or 'species of fervour or intoxication' referred to, is the passion to die by the guillotine.  So Emily is attracted to a drowning death, the very death Noah's ark dwellers were surrounded by as all mankind sank in the Flood.  In *Little Dorrit,* the disease of soul is a life lived as one long, self-inflicted penitential performance in sackcloth and ashes, which Mrs. Clennam passionately embraces as exemplifying 'the just dispensation of Jehovah.'

5.  In *A Tale of Two Cities,* Jerry Cruncher points out revolutionists in a tavern drinking the health of 'the Old Un's' (275).  Who is that? asks Miss Pross.  'Old Nick's' (275), is the reply.  Thus our suspicion that Mrs. Gummidge's 'old 'un' may not be the deceased Mr. Gummidge, but Old Nick, the Devil.  This 'Old 'Un' would be right at home on a *'black* barge' like the ark, as Chapter VII will show.

Or maybe Mr. Gummidge *was* Old Nick!

*Chapter VI*

1.  'Drowndead' (33), combining *drowned* and *dead,* is like Steerforth's greeting to David: 'Why, Daisy, old boy, dumb-foundered!' (424).  Steerforth means he is 'dumb*founded*' to see his friend after such a long time.  Dumb-*foundered,* however, is brilliantly to the point, anticipating Steerforth's drowning, 'foundering' death to come.  Dickens is a punning virtuoso, we have seen.

2.  *Heap* signifies ruin.  Finding Emily gone, Peggotty tries to pull his coat from its peg.  'Bear a hand with this!' he cries.  'I'm struck of a heap, and can't do it!' (453)  Mourning his lost niece, his treasure, he says: 'All the heaps of riches in the wureld would be nowt to me...to buy her back!' (468)  David's efforts to learn Murdstone lessons pile up only 'a heap of failures' (57), for which Murdstone comes down on David the way Yah did on the ancient Jews.  Madly jealous of Em'ly, Rosa Dartle consigns her to 'doorways and dust-heaps' (722).  In the Heep era, Mr. Micawber, Heep's clerk, is surrounded by documents full of falsification, 'a heap of books and papers' (773).  The tempest in which Steerforth and Ham drown is heralded by ominous clouds 'tossed up into the most remarkable heaps' (786).  Perhaps Dickens has a Biblical sense of *heap,* as in the Jehovah warning to Israel: 'And I will make Jerusalem heaps, and a den of dragons' (*Jer.* 9:11).  (The portrait of *Jeremiah* Flintwinch who frequents the *Jerusalem* Coffee Shop in *Little Dorrit* indicates that Dickens knew the Book of Jeremiah.)

In *Pickwick Papers,* fiery old Lobbs, a miser, has 'heaps of money' (229).  In a tale told in *Nicholas Nickleby,* an evil monk (this monk, and wicked Monks in *Oliver Twist* reveal Dickens's strong anti-Catholic feeling, as do letters) tells young maidens to turn from happiness and memories of joyful years: 'Bury them, heap penance and mortification on their heads, keep them down, and let the convent be their grave' (599).  In the same novel, Squeers, vicious master of Dotheboys, is struck down at last and lies 'all of a heap' (435) on the floor.  In *The Old Curiosity Shop,* the evil Daniel Quilp's wharf is crowded with rotting, rusting objects, including 'two or three heaps of old sheet copper, crumpled, cracked, and battered' (29).

(Ever curious about Dickens's sense of *copper,* heart of *Copperfield,* we linger here.)  In *Bleak House,* Krook's ancient shop, standing in the shadow of the Law courts, has in its dark interior 'heaps of old crackled parchment scrolls' (50); clearly Old Time broods here.  In *Little Dorrit,* the widow devoted to Jehovah and ruled by Jeremiah calls her servant Affery 'a heap of confusion' (767).  Affery replies that if this is so, her mistress and Jeremiah have made it so.  In *Our Mutual Friend,* evil Riderhood offers Headstone, slayer of young minds and spirits, 'a heap of thanks' (795).

Where 'heaps' are, old values in decay are; and their adherents put up the same bitter resistance to new values as did adherents of old Law in the time of Christ.
3.  Coming through a door in a wall, Agnes points to *John* 10:9: 'I am the door:  by me if any man enter in, he shall be saved, and shall go in and out, and find pasture.'  By adding the wall, Dickens makes clear that Christ is the way out of many debtors' prisons of world, the flesh, and time.  The 'door' metaphor is further dramatized in *Little Dorrit.*  As was suggested in the Preface, she symbolizes the *Do(o)rit* to NT time of mind.  Going in and out of Debtors' Prison on errands of mercy for others, Little Dorrit is the word of *John* made flesh, in all pointing to Him, as in:  'Be guided only by the healer of the sick, the raiser of the dead, the friend of all who were afflicted and forlorn, the patient Master who shed tears of compassion for our infirmities.  We cannot but be right if we put all the rest away, and do everything in remembrance of Him' (792).  Minutes later, she and Mrs. Clennam, staunch partisan of the stern, wrathful creed of Jehovah, leave the prison and enter a world that seems transfigured—released to Christian time—through her words:

> As they crossed the bridge, the clear steeples of the many churches looked as if they had advanced out of the murk that usually enshrouded them and come much nearer....The beauties of the sunset had not faded from the long light films of cloud that lay at peace in the horizon.  From a radiant centre over the whole length and breadth of the tranquil firmament, great shoots of light streamed among the early stars, like signs of the blessed later covenant of peace that changed the crown of thorns into a glory. (793)

4.  In the Italian journey section of *Little Dorrit,* the shallow young Mr. Sparkler (no Cris-sparkler, he) knows Dante only as 'an eccentric man in the nature of an Old File, who used to put leaves round his head, and sit upon a stool for some unaccountable purpose, outside the cathedral at Florence' (499).  Clearly, Dickens has a different view of Dante.  (He knew Dante, owning an English translation of the *New Life,* the Catalogue of books in his Gadshill library states, p. 26)

*Chapter VII*

1.  When Steerforth is searching his pockets for a note for David, he comes across a paper that reads:  ' "J. Steerforth, Esquire, debtor, to The Willing Mind." ' (425)  'That's not it,' he says, tossing it aside.  What Steerforth owes he apparently does not bother to pay.

In the NT we read:

> For if there be first a willing mind, *it is* accepted according to that a man hath, *and* not according to that he hath not. (*2 Cor.* 8:12)

If Steerforth slights The Willing Mind, others do not.  Dan'l Peggotty visits The Willing Mind.  And there is Barkis, the 'willing' carrier of: 'Barkis is willin'.'

In OT time, man's will is often exerted in wrong ways, as in the case of the schoolmaster who persecutes, tries, and banishes the Master, Creakle:

> 'When I say I'll do a thing, I do it,' said Mr. Creakle; 'and when I say I will have a thing done, I will have it done.'
> '—Will have a thing done.  I will have it done,' repeated the man with the wooden leg. (82)

The killing enmity of the schoolmaster to the Master, so strong in Christ-crucifying implications, brings to mind the enmity of other schoolmasters in Dickens like Headstone and Gradgrind to children, the spirit, and the NT.  (See Chapter III.) One reads Death in their very names.  Perhaps in each shoolmaster v. Christianity motif, Dickens is mindful of the verses in *Galatians* 3:24-25:

> Wherefore the law was our schoolmaster *to bring us* unto Christ, that we might be justified by faith.
> But after that faith is come, we are no longer under a schoolmaster.

2.  In Dickens, many a Christopher figure carries a little child, symbol of the Christ child and the child Christ sets in the midst of the disciples.  In *The Old Curiosity Shop,* Christopher Nubbles carries his little brother, Jacob, on his back.  Happy *figura: Christopher,* or NT time, carries *Jacob,* or Israel, to New Time.  In *A Tale of Two Cities,* a child figures in Sydney Carton's symbolic adventures on the night he steps out of darkness and into the glorious sacramental sunrise in the Son of God (See Chapter III.)  Crossing the Seine for lighter streets (so he 'crosses' towards the light), he leaves the darkest part of the night, and his long-nighted soul, behind:

> At one of the theatre doors, there was a little girl with a mother, looking for a way across the street through the mud.  He carried the child over, and before the timid arm was loosed from his neck asked her for a kiss.
> 'I am the resurrection and the life, saith the Lord:  he that believeth in me, though he were dead, yet shall he live:  and whosoever liveth and believeth in me, shall never die.' (299)

So a 'ch' figure, a child, looks to Carton for aid, and in becoming a Christopher he moves that much closer to the Christ-imitating decision to die for another—many others, as we see.  The kiss of the child seems to bring on the words of Christ, which sound, we suppose, in Carton's mind.  But really, we do not know how or where they are heard:  they simply are, omnipresent and triumphant.

*Chapter VIII*

1.  David's lament for Jonathon, with its refrain: 'The beauty of Israel is slain upon thy high places:  how are the mighty fallen!' (*2 Sam.* 1:19-27) is high religious poetry.  In Dickens, David again mourns a lost 'J' in lofty poetry: 'Never more, oh God forgive you, Steerforth, to touch that passive hand in love and friendship. Never, never more!' (437)

In the same sorrowing strain: 'My sorrow may bear involuntary witness against you at the Judgment Throne: but my angry thoughts of my reproaches never will, I know!' (455)

2. The game backgammon dates back to the heydays of Ur and Babylon. In a *lions, Daniel, 'old writing on the wall'* context in Dickens, backgammon pulls time backwards to Babylon all the more. If Dickens did not know that backgammon was a Babylonian game, perhaps he uses it because the word suggests the past (*back*) and the game (*gammon*) of chance, complete with cast of the dice, which symbolically sums up what life was for B.C. man in the hands of a punishing, angry God.

3. We have quoted before the lines in *Little Dorrit* about the widow devoted to Jehovah who 'still abided by her old impiety—still reversed the order of Creation, and breathed her own breath into a clay image of her Creator.' (775)

4. *Doctor* is no title of comfort in Dickens. In *Great Expectations*, as Pip and Estella climb the stairs in Satis House, 'the Temple,' they meet 'a gentleman groping his way down' in darkness, a man exceedingly dark in complexion who informs Pip that boys are a bad lot and he had better behave:

> With those words, he released me—which I was glad of, for his hand smelt of scented soap—and went his way down-stairs. I wondered whether he could be a doctor; but no, I thought; he couldn't be a doctor, or he would have a quieter and more persuasive manner. (77)

But Pip's hunch is just. He just does not have the right 'doctor' in mind. For Jaggers, a lawyer who like Pontius Pilate washes his hands of the infamous work of the Law, is what the NT terms 'a doctor of the law' (*Acts* 5:34). Such doctors of law eventually put the law above Christ, delivering Him over to Rome. In the hostility the dark, downward-groping 'doctor' shows the child, Pip, in this stronghold of brewing-Hebrewing spirits, the soul of the place the passion for retribution, we see the Law-v.-Christ child theme.

Dickens tells of Christ and the doctors in his *The Life of Our Lord*:

> They found Him, sitting in the Temple, talking about the goodness of God, and how we should all pray to Him, with some learned men who were called doctors. They were not what you understand by the word "doctors" now; they did did not attend sick people; they were scholars and clever men. And Jesus Christ showed such knowledge in what He said to them, and in the questions He asked them, that they were all astonished. (LL, 21)

We note parenthetically that heroes in Dickens are never 'scholars and clever men.'

In Dickens, healers are 'physicians,' not doctors. In *Bleak House*, Esther Summerson's love, the noble Allan Woodcourt, is a 'surgeon,' and a 'young practitioner' (238). In *Little Dorrit*, the Christ-like Physician, compared to 'the Divine Master of all healing' (702), is never called doctor. Dickens uses the term for men learned in the letter and the law like the scholar and maker of a Dictionary, Doctor Strong.

5. In *A Tale of Two Cities*, Jerry Cruncher, who bullies his wife for 'flopping against him,' i.e., getting down on her knees and praying, thinks that 'anno Domini' has reference to a female named Anna Dominoes, known for playing the game of that name. That's how much Cruncher knows of 'A.D.' In *Dombey and*

*Son, anno Domini* is contrasted with its dark anti-type imposed by Mr. Dombey, *anno Dombei*. We see that Dickens makes virtuoso symbolic use of *anno Domini*, and is well aware of the 'Anna' possibilities within. It is therefore possible that the Annie-Anno connection occurred to him, and in an 'Annie' *Strong* in faith he meant to symbolize the soul of *anno Domini*.

6. *A Christmas Carol* opens with strong assurances that Marley is dead:

> If we were not perfectly convinced that Hamlet's Father died before the play began, there would be nothing more remarkable in his taking a stroll at night, in an easterly wind, upon his own ramparts, than there would be in any other middle-aged gentleman rashly turning out after dark in a breezy spot—say Saint Paul's Churchyard for instance—literally to astonish his son's weak mind. (CB, 7)

Dickens's comic genius makes the point lightly. But made it is. The Ghost of Marley and the Ghost of King Hamlet are in some wise compared. As the Ghost of Hamlet comes from Eternity bearing a moral mandate for his son, so the Ghost of Marley and Three Spirits come to charge Scrooge to mend his ways lest he pay the price Marley must pay in chains for all eternity.

In *Copperfield,* Mr. Chillip 'walked as softly as the Ghost in Hamlet, and more slowly' (9). Again the comic detail through which serious meaning shines. Hamlet's Ghost, the Father, comes to charge his son with the great, tragic task of righting grievous wrongs in a world out of joint. Dickens, we think, sees this drama as a type of the Christ story of the Father and the Son, an argument we make in the *Wopsle's Hamlet* section of Chapter XI. Like the Ghost, Mr. Chillip carries the 'Ch' message that there is *no* authority for the Murdstones in the NT!

*Chapter IX*

1. St. Paul's is also worked into the Martha plot of *Copperfield*. One night, Dan'l and David, partners in saving Martha, part:

> It was midnight when I arrived at home. I had reached my own gate, and was standing listening for the deep bell of Saint Paul's, the sound of which I thought had been borne towards me among the multitude of striking clocks, when I was rather surprised to see that the door of my aunt's cottage was open, and that a faint light in the entry was shining out across the road. (687)

As in *Great Expectations,* the sound of the deep bell of St. Paul's ushers in Christian adventure. Having just left Martha, David now learns that for years, his aunt has protected the husband who betrayed her youthful love and trust. The 'Ya-a-ah!' nature, which in early time she reflects in her desertion of her own, is gone. In her fidelity to her husband, a new (NT) character shines.

2. Judgment belongs to Old Time. When little David, grieving for his mother, rides in the van with the coffin, he is shocked at the lovemaking and hilarity of Joram and Minnie, riding with him. David stays in a corner, 'almost wondering that no judgment came upon them for their hardness of heart' (128). It is the OT nature in man that expects a judgment.

*Chapter X*

1. In Forster's *Life of Dickens,* volume III, is recorded Dickens's description of a visit to Niagara Falls in 1868. After telling of the struggle to get above the river in an open carriage, he tells of watching the rush of green-white waters, standing with his back to the sun and facing the Falls:

> The majestic valley below the Falls, so seen through the vast cloud of spray, was made of rainbow. Nothing in Turner's finest water-colour drawings, done in his greatest day, is so ethereal, so imaginative, so gorgeous in colour, as what I then beheld. I seemed to be lifted from the earth and to be looking into Heaven. What I once said to you, as I witnessed the scene five and twenty years ago, all came back at this most affecting and sublime sight. The "muddy vesture of our clay" falls from us as we look.... (FD, III, 398)

The phrase 'muddy vesture of our clay' may recall *Claypole* and 'mask of clay' imagery in *Oliver Twist.*
2. The Keats sonnet quoted here begins: 'Much have I travelled in the realms of gold.'
3. In *Catalogues of the Libraries of Charles Dickens and William Makepeace Thackeray,* p. 52.
4. The 'el' syllable appears throughout *Copperfield,* we saw, in 'Ely-place' and Martha Endell, to name but two instances. Mr. Micawber in describing his thralldom to Heep terms himself 'a straw upon the surface of the deep...tossed in all directions by the elephants—I beg your pardon; I should have said the elements' (708). Heep informs Micawber that without his (Heep's) patronage he would be 'a mountebank about the country, swallowing a sword-blade, and eating the devouring element' (710). So many 'el' *el*ements like 'the devouring element,' fire, beset man. The elbow-elephant activity in Barkis environs works to the same end, we think.
5. See *Catalogues of the Libraries of Charles Dickens and William Makepeace Thackeray,* p 14

*Chapter XI*

1. Disputatious, artful rooks in glossy black in Dickens symbolize the clergy that come between man and the sky. *Rook* also means a cheat; to rook means to swindle. In the O.E.D., an 1824 usage in *Hist. Gaming* 50, one reads: 'We scarcely know whether yet to class him with the rooks or the pigeons.' One thinks of Mr. *Gulpidge* in *David Copperfield,* with 'gull' and 'pigeon' parts.
    Blunderstone Rookery, in *Blunderstone,* looks to the *blunder* it was to fix on the *stone* law, and in *Rookery,* to the black-garbed doctors of divinity that swarmed over religion, the talmudists and their successors in Time A.D., the priests that rooked and rook mankind still.
2. One reads in the Book of *Jeremiah:*

> For thus saith the LORD GOD of Israel unto me: Take the winecup of this fury at my hand, and cause all the nations, to whom I send thee, to drink it.

And they shall drink, and be moved, and be mad, because of the sword that
I will send among them. (25:15-16)

3. In *Nicholas Nickleby,* the hero's friend, John Browdie, one of Dickens's 'many
Johns,' a J.B. complete with booming voice and boundless admiration for 'Paul's
Church' (501), as he calls St. Paul's Cathedral, arrives in London, and asks the
hackney-coach driver to 'gang to the Sarah's Head, mun.' The man does not
understand:

'To the *vere?'* cried the coachman.
'Lawk, Mr. Browdie!' interrupted Miss Squeers. 'The idea! Saracen's
Head.'
'Surely,' said John. 'I know'd it was something about Sarah's Son's Head.
Dost thou know thot?'
'Oh, ah! I know that,' replied the coachman gruffly, as he banged the
door. (502)

*Saracen's Head-Sarah's Son's Head* is one of Dickens's most spectacular religious
puns. The 'vere,' or truth, about the Saracen's Head Inn is that *Sarah's son,* Isaac,
is again being led to be sacrificed in England. It takes canny John Browdie to see
it. In the novel, a cruelly smitten, smashed, smothered, smifligated young lad
named Smike—'smifligation and bloodshed...in the main one and the same thing'
(349)—is Sarah's son Isaac symbolically come back to life. A *smi*fligated Isaac, Ike,
is a *Sm-ike!* Dickens's point is that in A.D., children are being sacrificed just as in
Hebrew times of Abraham and of Moloch. In *Dotheboys* England, 'Hebrews,'
'Saracens,' and 'Romans' *do-the-boys.*

In first OT time, Isaac is bound, and wood gathered for the sacrificial altar. In
Dickensian OT time of *Nickleby,* Squeers of Dotheboys Hall catches and binds poor
Smike: 'The news that Smike had been caught and brought back in triumph, ran
like wild-fire through the hungry community' (152). *Wild-fire,* a metaphor,
substitutes for the real fire.

Judaism cannot exorcise the devil of a passion for child-sacrifice in ancient time.
Nor can Christendom conquer it, or the Saracen, until men take to heart the life and
lessons of Christ.

4. The 'Third Quarter' of *The Chimes,* 'Third' significant, opens the a vision of
Resurrection:

Black are the brooding clouds and troubled the deep waters, when the Sea of
Thought, first heaving from a calm, gives up its Dead. Monsters uncouth and
wild, arise in premature, imperfect resurrection; the several parts and shapes
of different things are joined and mixed by chance; and when, and how, and by
what wonderful degrees, each separates from each, and every sense and object
or the mind resumes its usual form and lives again, no man—though every
man is every day the casket of this type of the Great Mystery—can tell.
(CB, 120)

The Great Mystery is the resurrection of Christ. Dickens sees its pattern everywhere. The passage tells us that what will emerge triumphant at last sometimes

has a crude, imperfect tryout on the stage of history. Dickens weaves in a verse from the Book of *Revelation:* 'And the sea gave up the dead which were in it' (20:13)

A passage celebrating resurrection is well situated at the portal to Part III, the Third Quarter of *The Chimes.*

5. In the essay 'A Few Conventionalities' in *Old Lamps for New Ones,* Dickens satirizes the bullies and blowhards in Parliament, terming one sort 'my Honourable friend, the Member for Gammonrife' (OL, 238); for *gammon,* or humbug and law, is *rife* in the land! the old *gam,* or game, and penalty for losing.

6. Two backgammon games in *Copperfield,* both laced with violence, look to the 'gammon' of B.C., which gammoned mankind. In *Bleak House,* poor Miss Flite, driven mad by a futile waiting upon the Law like the Jews of old, never knows 'flight.' As if she knew the fate of all souls so imprisoned in law, she keeps caged birds, named: 'Hope, Joy, Youth, Peace, Rest, Life, Dust, Ashes, Waste, Want, Ruin, Despair, Madness, Death, Cunning, Folly, Words, Wigs, Rags, Sheepskin, Plunder, Precedent, Jargon, Gammon, and Spinach' (200). Note that in this list, objects of desire shade into terms of law: law consumes all. Gammon and spinach I take to be gammon and spinnage.

Returning to gammon, John Jarndyce teaches Esther Summerson to play backgammon. The 'dice' in Jarndyce here tells. In his John, or Christian Christian name life, he ushers in New Time. But in Jarndyce we look back, *Jarn* a crude, primitive first attempt at John, it may be, according to Dickens's own idea of how truth must struggle upward and ideas 'arise in premature, imperfect resurrection.' That is, *Jarn,* not yet John, and *dyce,* like backgammon, look to OT time.

The old gammon or game is played in *The Old Curiosity Shop,* too. Old Luke winds up 'plucked, pigeoned, and cleaned out completely' (221) in a game of dice with Isaac List. The Isaac, or OT spirit, wins; Luke Withers shows how the Gospel of *Luke* withers in an atmosphere so hostile to Christian truth.

7. Why Mrs. Harris? On the trail of what Dickens intended by 'Harris,' we come across this interesting passage in 'To Rome by Pisa and Siena' in *Pictures from Italy:*

> The moon was shining when we approached Pisa, and for a long time we could see, behind the wall, the leaning Tower, all awry in the uncertain light: the shadowy original of the old pictures in school-books, setting forth "The Wonders of the World." Like most things connected in their first associations with school-books and school-times, it was too small. I felt it keenly. It was nothing like so high above the wall as I had hoped. It was another of the many deceptions practised by Mr. Harris, Bookseller, at the corner of St. Paul's Churchyard, London. *His* Tower was a fiction, but this was a reality— and, by comparison, a short reality. Still, it looked very well, and very strange, and was quite as much out of the perpendicular as Harris had represented it to be. The quiet air of Pisa too; the big guard-house at the gate, with only two little soldiers in it; the streets with scarcely any show of people in them; and the Arno, flowing quaintly through the center of the town; were excellent. So, I bore no malice in my heart against Mr. Harris (remembering his good intentions), but forgave him before dinner, and went out, full of confidence, to see the Tower next morning. (PI, 357)

Mr. Harris leads people to imagine wonders that prove not so wonderful when seen. To believe in Mr. Harris, therefore, is to be led astray. But there is no malice or intention to defraud in him. And some of the Harris wonders *are* quite wonderful.

In *Martin Chuzzlewit,* Sarah Gamp believes implicitly in Mrs. Harris. The unseen Mrs. Harris is the great Reliance of her life. *We* see very little in this oracle, Heaven knows. But Dickens gives Sarah Gamp credit for the tenacity and fervor of her faith, however misplaced: and as to that, it is not certain it *is* misplaced altogether. In any case, it bespeaks a capacity for Faith.

A blind belief in Mrs. Harris may not be *the* way, the truth, and the life. But the Betsey Prig Priggery that denies Mrs. Harris entirely, all scorn and denial, that credits no Wonder unseen, is far worse.

The point seems to be that in *Sarah* (and Jonas, Seth, Elijah, Zephaniah) time of *Chuzzlewit,* man *has* no Reliance. Not until young Martin Chuzzlewit marries his true love, Mary, is Christian time reborn.

8. The inspired idea that the name *Veck* may come from *Vecchio,* Italian for old, comes from Professor John B. Harcourt. Subsequent to our conversation, I discovered that Dickens was living in Italy when he wrote *The Chimes,* which increases the odds that he was thinking in Italian terms when he named its hero, Trotty Veck.

9. In *Our Mutual Friend,* young Mortimer Lightwood is caught between MORTimer, or deathly world of law and Temple (his law-office looks out over a burying ground), and LIGHTWOOD, an association with young John Rokesmith, finally revealed as the long-lost John Harmon. In Dickens, stick with John, and you are on the way to Christ.

In the same work, Betty Higden helps reveal the meaning of 'tree.' Though a good and charitable woman, caring for a child named Johnny, she begins in the Betty, or Bet time of 'the letter.' Nicodemus Boffin, like *Nicodemus* in the Gospel of John a carrier of New Time, gently unfixes her simple mind from the concept of *the letter,* as the following exchange reveals:

> The letter was written, and read to her, and given to her.
> 'Now, how do you feel?' said Mr. Boffin. 'Do you like it?'
> 'The letter, sir?' said Betty. 'Aye, it's a beautiful letter!'
> 'No, no, no, not the letter,' said Mr. Boffin. 'The idea. Are you sure you're strong enough to carry out the idea?' (300)

Betty Higden grasps 'the idea.' Now she begins a long journey of rescue. She is not strong. The body fails, but her spirit glows. As her life draws to an end, she sees with the double vision of allegory, grasping the idea of this life as a foreshadow or forelight of the life to come:

> 'Water-meadows, or such like,' she had sometimes murmured, on the day's pilgrimage, when she had raised her head and taken any note of the real objects about her. There now arose in the darkness a great building full of lighted windows. Smoke was issuing from a high chimney in the rear of it, and there was the sound of a water-wheel at the side. Between her and the building lay a piece of water, in which the lighted windows were reflected, and on its

nearest margin was a plantation of trees. 'I humbly thanks the Power and the Glory,' said Betty Higden, holding up her withered hands, 'that I have come to my journey's end.'

She crept among the trees to the trunk of a tree whence she could see, beyond some intervening trees and branches, the lighted windows, both in their reality and their reflection in the water. She placed her orderly little basket at her side, and sank upon the ground, supporting herself against the tree. It brought to her mind the foot of the Cross, and she committed herself to Him who died upon it. Her strength held out to enable her to arrange the letter in her breast, so as that it could be seen that she had a paper there. It had held out for this, and it departed when this was done.

'I am safe here,' was her last benumbed thought. 'When I am found dead at the foot of the Cross, it will be by some of my own sort; some of the working people who work among the lights yonder. I cannot see the lighted windows now, but they are there. I am thankful for all!' (511)

The lighted windows in the great dark building, 'both in their reality and their reflection,' point to light in this life and in the life to come. One sees the lights, one sees their reflection in water. As her earthly vision fails, Betty's Heavenly one strengthens. She perceives a tree as the Cross; lying at the foot of the tree, she is like Mary or Mary Magdalene, at the foot of the Cross. She can no longer see the shining windows, but she knows they are there! 'If seeing is believing, not seeing is believing too.' (*Little Dorrit*.)

*Our Mutual Friend* is about how NT time is reborn. How mankind moves from 'Hexam' time of superstition to the times of *Nicodemus* and *John*, once more.

*Chapter XII*

1. In *Our Mutual Friend*, when Betty Higden, mistaking his point, admires a letter, Nicodemus Boffin cries: 'No, no, no; not the letter. The idea!' (390) Betty learns to see through to the idea. Dying at the foot of a tree, she sees it figuratively as the Cross. In *Great Expectations*, the Pockets, formalists strong for 'the letter,' insist on the propriety of highly formal mourning garb for little children. Matthew Pocket objects. For this Matthew who looks to *Matthew*, it is sentiment, spirit that counts. Camilla Pocket, recalling his indifference to rule and form, cries: 'Was there ever such a fancy! The i-*de*-a!' (76) I suspect that she stresses the 'd' syllable for the same reason little Pip copies at home a large old English D which he takes to be a design for a buckle, and which is never explained. This is 'D,' or Deuteronomy time of law; rule and precedent overcome 'the idea.'

2. The husband of Miss Trotwood, David records, was 'a Baboon; but I think it must have been a Baboo—or a Begum' (3). Miss Trotwood calls Mrs. Copperfield 'a very Baby!' (5) and exclaims: 'Bless the Baby!' (6) The capital 'B' raising 'Bab' to prominence, in an era of Dan'l's roars, horroars, and incessant chatter of 'babby,' sets BAB in lions' den country in no casual way. Add 'Babley,' and Babylon stands once again.

3. Hard at work undermining Doctor Strong's faith in himself and in his wife's love for him, Mrs. Markleham, in the guise of praising it, sneers at his work, the Dictionary, saying: 'Without Doctor Johnson, or somebody of that sort, we might have

been at this present moment calling an Italian-iron a bedstead.  But we can't expect
a Dictionary—especially when it's making—to interest Annie, can we?' (650)
4. The quotation is from Chapter 15 of *The Warden* by Anthony Trollope.
5. Dickens opens a defense of his own work, in 'Curious Misprint in The Edinburg
Review' (*The Works of Charles Dickens,* XIX, 440-445) with this statement:

> The Edinburgh Review, in an article in its last number, on "The License of
> Modern Novelists," is angry with MR. DICKENS and other modern novelists,
> for not confining themselves to the mere amusement of their readers, and for
> testifying in their works that they seriously feel the interest of true Englishmen
> in the welfare and honour of their country. (440)

Holding firm against the attitude of moral laissez-faire in those who attack him,
Dickens, in light ironic mood, records the charges made against him:

> Mr. Dickens's libel on the wonderfully exact and vigorous English govern-
> ment, which is always ready for any emergency, and which, as everybody
> knows, has never shown itself to be at all feeble at a pinch within the memory
> of men, is License in a novelist. (440)

To Dickens, real license and offense lies in one reviewer's outrageous libel on *Little
Dorrit,* which claims:

> Even the catastrophe in 'Little Dorrit' is evidently borrowed from the recent
> fall of houses in Tottenham Court Road, which happens to have appeared in
> the newspapers at a convenient period. (441)

Dickens warmly denies this, and insists that Circumlocution Office parts of the
novel give a true account of the muddle in English government.
6. I am grateful to my friend, Florence Atkin Granowitter, for sending me an article
entitled 'A Christmas Story About the Dickens Brothers,' which appeared in a *New
York Post* article of December 22, 1967.  It is an account of the rift that developed
between Dickens and his favorite brother, Augustus, who married the daughter of a
high-ranking British officer, then either divorced or deserted her, and came to
America with another wife, settling near Cairo, Illinois.  Failing at farming, he
drifted from job to job, becoming a heavy drinker and dying in 1866 at the age of
forty.
   A year later, when Dickens came to America on a second reading tour, a Chicago
reporter covering a performance in Philadelphia broached the subject of his brother
to Dickens, who, the reporter notes, "looked straight at his accoster and said
nothing."
   The *Post* article exonerates Dickens of the charge of hard-heartedness in his
persisted-in refusal to help his brother.  Certainly it looked like cruelty when some
of Augustus Dickens's fellow railroad employees wrote to his famous brother about
his desperate plight, and received no reply.  We learn why Dickens rejected the
appeal:

> In a letter to a friend, Charles Dickens told why he had not gone to Chicago

to help out his brother's second wife. Dickens said he already was supporting the genuine Mrs. Augustus Dickens, who lived in England.

The 'Augustus' story reappears in Dickens's American novel, *Martin Chuzzlewit*. In it, Augustus Moddle in cowardly fashion jilts his fiancée, Mercy Pecksniff, and runs away. If that were not enough, Augustus covers his tracks in a shameful, self-exonerating letter in which he invokes the authority of the Talmud (!) to justify his breach of faith:

> But it was written—in the Talmud—that you should involve yourself in the inscrutable and gloomy Fate which it is my mission to accomplish, and which wreathes itself—e'en now—about my temples. I will not reproach, for I have wronged you. May the Furniture make some amends! (836)

An Augustus who falls back on the Talmud is morally at home in a book in which Jonas, Sarah, Elijah, Zephaniah, and 'The Lord No Zoo,' i.e., the Lord of NOah's ZOO, the ark, send Time careening back into a purblind B.C.

*Chapter XIII*

1. E. M. Forster, *A Room with a View*, Chapter XV.
2. My thanks to James R. Travis for this beguiling idea that Traddles-straddles work well together.
3. In *Our Mutual Friend*, Riah the Jew sits wearily down 'on the raw dark staircase, as many of his ancestors had probably sat down in dungeons, taking what befell him as it might befall' (421). In the Jew's resignation in time present and past, Dickens sees the effects of long centuries of Babylons, and like punishment for disobedience to the Law. I think that in the image of the wick in its solitary prison on a dark stairs, found in *Copperfield*, a wick, moreover, 'imprisoned' in the Temple of Law, Dickens makes symbolic reference to man's fate in the Old dispensation. The captive wick and the mild, forlorn waiter in the Inn of Court below seem a matched pair.
4. In 'The Lamplighter,' Tom Grig is another promising 'Tom' who mistakes his way. The story begins with Tom:

> 'If you talk of Murphy and Francis Moore, gentlemen,' said the lamplighter who was in the chair, 'I mean to say that neither of 'em ever had any more to do with the stars than Tom Grig had.' (UT, 603)

Tom the lamplighter, merry as a grig—'always merry, was Tom, and such a singer' (606)—has a natural affinity for light, the heavenly bodies, and song. Then a wizard seduces him into the scientific world of astrology and sums, the calculations and charts of which change celestial objects of wonder into matter, clay, law.

In *Martin Chuzzlewit*, sweet-natured Tom Pinch invests all the faithful trust of his heart in the charlatan, Pecksniff. But Tom, like Tommy Traddles, has that within which suggests he will find worthier objects, in time. Like young David Copperfield, Tom Pinch delights in imaginary figures, Robinson Crusoe, Cassim Baba, and other fictions:

> Which matchless wonders, coming fast on Mr. Pinch's mind, did so rub up and
> chafe that wonderful lamp within him, that when he turned his face towards
> the busy street, a crowd of phantoms waited on his pleasure, and he lived
> again, with new delight, the happy days before the Pecksniff era. (71)

The Pecksniff era, with its Seth, Jonas, Sarah, Elijah, Zephaniah contingent of OT
characters, is a dose of B.C. all over again. Allied to none of it, Tom Pinch, like
Mr. Crisparkle of *Edwin Drood,* loves music, and, playing the church organ, fills
the quiet chapel with tones that 'find an echo...in the deep mystery of his own
heart' (72), and awaken hope and expectation of beauty yet unknown. Many a
Christian is, like Tom Pinch, caught in the Pinch of a society Dickens shows to be in
the grip of the Pharisees.

Toms Grig, Pinch, and Traddles all have a native bent for wonder and the starry
sky. Each is, literally or figuratively, a lamplighter, lighting the lamps of Heaven
in inclining towards simple faith, mystery, wonder, the ideal. Science and law are
the temptation or weakness of *Tom* in Dickens, giving into which a Tom goes the
way of Thomas Gradgrind in *Hard Times* who credits nothing that is not subject to
solid, factual definition and description, and bears a high-sounding Latin name.
5. One day, Christopher Nubbles walks boldly into an oyster-shop and orders the
waiter 'to bring three dozen of his largest-sized oysters, and to look sharp about it!'
The waiter does, and Christopher and friends fall to upon the supper in delight.
All enjoy the feast...

> But the greatest miracle of the night was little Jacob, who ate oysters as if he
> had been born and bred to the business—sprinkled the pepper and the vinegar
> with a discretion beyond his years—and afterwards built a grotto on the table
> with the shells. (295)

In the allegory, *Christopher* brings his little brother, *Jacob,* i.e., Israel, to oysters in
the number of *three,* thus symbolically to the idea of 'the pearl.'
6. In *Tom Jones,* Squire Western is what 'Western' man was before the birth of
Sophia, or Wisdom—specifically, Christian wisdom with its tender heart, forgiving-
ness, and capacity for spiritual idealism. Consider the relation of father and
daughter to music:

> It was Mr. Western's custom every afternoon, as soon as he was drunk, to
> hear his daughter play on the harpsicord, for he was a great lover of music, and
> perhaps, had he lived in town, might have passed for a connossieur, for he
> always excepted against the finest compositions of Mr. Handel. He never
> relished any music but what was light and airy, and indeed his most favorite
> tunes were Old Sir Simon the King, St. George was for England, Bobbing
> Joan, and some others.
> His daughter, though she was a perfect mistress of music, and would never
> willingly have played any but Handel's, was so devoted to her father's pleas-
> ure that she learnt all those tunes to oblige him. However, she would now
> and then endeavour to lead him into her own taste; and when he required the
> repetition of his ballads, would answer with a "Nay, dear sir," and would
> often beg him to suffer her to play something else. (Book IV, Chapter V, p. 161)

*Sophia,* Wisdom, holds the sacred music of Handel above all. But, being Wise, knows better than to force 'Western' man, and instead gradually leads him towards the light, the sublime strains of Handel.

So in the creation of Tommy and Sophy in *Copperfield,* which I fancy is a glance backwards at *Tom Jones,* as in the creation of a Pip rechristened Handel, and a Mr. Crisparkle whose delight is Handel, Dickens celebrates anew the 'Creation' and the 'Messiah.'

*Chapter XIV*

1. In Chapter I of Forster's *The Life of Charles Dickens,* Dickens describes a visit to his own father in debtors' prison. Details of this visit, including the borrowing of another debtor's knife and fork and the errand to pawn items for the family, reappear in *Copperfield* when David visits Mr. Micawber in debtors' prison.
2. In Chapter the Fifth of his *The Life of Our Lord,* Dickens writes:

> One of the Pharisees begged Our Saviour to go into his house, and eat with him. And while Our Saviour sat eating at the table, there crept into the room a woman of that city who had led a bad and sinful life, and was ashamed that the Son of God should see her; and yet she trusted so much to His goodness and His compassion for all who, having done wrong were truly sorry for it in their hearts, that, by little and little, she went behind the seat on which He had sat, and dropped down at His feet, and wetted them, and dried them on her long hair, and rubbed them with some sweet-smelling ointment she had brought with her in a box. Her name was Mary Magdalene.
>
> When the Pharisee saw that Jesus permitted this woman to touch Him, he said within himself that Jesus did not know how wicked she had been. But Jesus Christ, who knew his thoughts, said to him, "Simon"—for that was his name—"if a man had debtors, one of whom owed him five hundred pence, and one of whom owed him only fifty pence, and he forgave them, both, their debts, which one of the two debtors do you think would love him the most?" Simon answered, "I suppose the one whom he forgave most." Jesus told him he was right, and said, "As God forgives this woman so much sin, she will love Him, I hope, the more." And He said to her, "God forgive you!" The company who were present wondered that Jesus Christ had power to forgive sins, but God had given it to Him. And the woman, thanking Him for all His mercy, went away.
>
> We learn from this that we must always forgive those who have done us any harm, when they come to us and say they are truly sorry for it. Even if they do not come and say so, we must still forgive them, and never hate them or be unkind to them, if we would hope that God will forgive us. (LL, 47-49)

At the end of this chapter, Dickens again stresses the role of Christ in winning forgiveness for sin:

> But He said to them that on the third day after He was dead, He would rise from the grave, and ascend to Heaven, where He would sit at the right hand of God, beseeching God's pardon to sinners. (LL, 53)

In Chapter the Sixth, Dickens returns to the theme:

And He told His Disciples this story: He said, "There was once a servant who owed his master a great deal of money, and could not pay it, at which the master, being very angry, was going to have this servant sold for a slave. But the servant kneeling down and begging his master's pardon with great sorrow, the master forgave him. Now this same servant had a fellow-servant who owed him a hundred pence, and instead of being kind and forgiving to this poor man, as his master had been to him, he put him in prison for the debt. His master, hearing of it, went to him, and said, 'O wicked servant, I forgave you. Why do you not forgive your fellow servant?' And because he had not done so, his master turned him away with great misery. So," said Our Saviour, "how can you expect God to forgive you, if you do not forgive others?" This is the meaning of that part of the Lord's Prayer, where we say "Forgive us our trespasses"—that word means faults—"as we forgive them that trespass against us." (LL, 59)

3. Dickens is strongly critical of Mr. Micawber's passion for legal jargon and words. In the scene in which Micawber exposes Heep, we read:

"'Second. HEEP has, on several occasions, to the best of my knowledge, information, and belief, systematically forged, to various entries, books, and documents, the signature of Mr. W; and has distinctly done so in one instance, capable of proof by me. To wit, in manner following, that is to say:"
Again, Mr. Micawber had a relish in this formal piling up of words, which, however ludicrously displayed in his case, was, I must say, not at all peculiar to him. I have observed it, in the course of my life, in numbers of men. It seems to me to be a general rule. In the taking of legal oaths, for instance, deponents seem to enjoy themselves mightily when they come to several good words in succession for the expression of one idea; as, that they utterly detest, abominate, and abjure, or so forth; and the old anathemas were made relishing on the same principle. We talk about the tyranny of words, but we like to tyrannise over them too; we are fond of having a large superfluous establishment of words to wait upon us on great occasions; we think it looks important, and sounds well. As we are not particular about the meaning of our liveries on state occasions, if they be but fine and numerous enough, so the meaning or necessity of our words is a secondary consideration, if there be but a great parade of them. And as individuals get into trouble by making too great a show of their liveries, or as slaves when they are too numerous rise against their masters, so I think I could mention a nation that has got into many great difficulties, and will get into many greater, from maintaining too large a retinue of words.
Mr. Micawber read on, almost smacking his lips:
"'To wit, in manner following, that is to say....'" (753)

4. In the allegory of *Oliver Twist,* The Jew and 'Bill,' Bill Sikes, are a pair.
5. Doctor Temple Pharisee, symbol of OT law which still rules England, appears in 'The Great Baby' in *Household Words* of August 4, 1855, pp. 356-361.

6. Thanks to Professor Robert M. Durling for the idea that Heep and Heep-ocrite sound alike.

7. Dickens writes to Forster:

> At the theatre last night I saw *Hamlet,* and should have done better to "sit at home and mope" like the idle workmen. In the last scene, Laertes on being asked how it was with him replied (verbatim) "Why, like a woodcock—on account of my treachery." (29th Jan.)

8. The review of the new *King Lear* opens:

> What we ventured to anticipate when Mr. Macready assumed the manage- ment of Covent Garden Theatre, has been every way realised. But the last of his well-directed efforts to vindicate the higher objects and uses of the drama has proved the most brilliant and the most successful. He has restored to the stage Shakespeare's true *Lear,* banished from it, by impudent ignorance, for upwards of a hundred and fifty years. (WCD, XVIII, 417)

Commenting on the omission of 'the grandest thing, the *Fool*', Dickens says:

> The *Fool* in the tragedy of *Lear* is one of the most wonderful creations of Shakespeare's genius. The picture of his quick and pregnant sarcasm, of his long devotion, of his acute sensibility, of his despairing mirth, of his heart- broken silence—contrasted with the rigid sublimity of Lear's suffering, with the desolation of Lear's sorrow, with the vast and outraged image of Lear's madness—is the noblest thought that ever entered into the heart and mind of man. (418)

Dickens thinks that Shakespeare 'would have as soon consented to the banishment of *Lear* from the tragedy as to the banishment of his Fool.' He says:

> We may fancy him, while planning his immortal work, feeling suddenly with an instinct of divinest genius, that its gigantic sorrows could never be present- ed on the stage without a suffering too frightful, a sublimity too remote, a grandeur too terrible—unless relieved by quiet pathos, and in some way brought home to the apprehension of the audience by homely and familiar illustration. At such a moment the Fool rose to his mind, and not till then could he have contemplated his marvelous work in the greatness and beauty of its final completion.

Like Shakespeare, we think, Dickens seeks to give a sublimity otherwise possibly too remote to 'homely and familiar illustration.' Many are the humble characters, the Fool-like Barnaby, Mr. Chillip, Mr. Dick, Mr. Pancks, Poll Sweedlepipe, amid a host of 'little' Nells, Tims, Dorrits, crickets on the hearth, who help bring home to the apprehension of the audience Dickens's divine themes. As the Son makes the remote sublimity of the Father comprehensible to human minds, so Dickens too, knowing one cannot stare straight at the sun (or Son), with his own 'instinct of Divinest genius,' gives to Heavenly truth and all it comprises a local habitation and a name.

# Index